OXFORD STUDIES
IN
MODERN LEGAL HISTORY

GENERAL EDITOR

A. W. Brian Simpson
Professor of Law, University of Michigan

OXFORD STUDIES
IN
MODERN LEGAL HISTORY

The series aims to publish monographs of high quality and originality on legal history covering the period from 1750 onwards.

The Origins of Adversary Criminal Trial

JOHN H. LANGBEIN

OXFORD

UNIVERSITY PRESS

OXFORD

UNIVERSITY PRESS

Great Clarendon Street, Oxford OX2 6DP

Oxford University Press is a department of the University of Oxford.
It furthers the University's objective of excellence in research, scholarship,
and education by publishing worldwide in

Oxford New York

Auckland Bangkok Buenos Aires Cape Town Chennai
Dar es Salaam Delhi Hong Kong Istanbul Karachi Kolkata
Kuala Lumpur Madrid Melbourne Mexico City Mumbai Nairobi
São Paulo Shanghai Taipei Tokyo Toronto

Oxford is a registered trade mark of Oxford University Press
in the UK and in certain other countries

Published in the United States
by Oxford University Press Inc., New York

British Library Cataloguing in Publication Data

Data available

Library of Congress Cataloging in Publication Data
Langbein, John H.
The origins of adversary criminal trial/John H. Langbein.
p. cm.—(Oxford studies in modern legal history)
Includes index
1. Criminal procedure—Great Britain—History—18th century. 2. Defense (Criminal
procedure)—Great Britain—History—18th century. 3. Prosecution—Great
Britain—History—18th century. 4. Evidence, Criminal—Great Britain—History—18th
century. 5. Trials—Great Britain—History—18th century. 6. Adversary system
(Law)—Great Britain—History—18th century. I. Title. II. Series.
KD8220.L36 2002
345.41'05—dc21   2002035562
ISBN 0–19–925888–0

1 3 5 7 9 10 8 6 4 2

Typeset in Palatino by
Cambrian Typesetters, Frimley, Surrey
Printed in Great Britain
on acid-free paper by
T.J. International Ltd, Padstow, Cornwall

General Editor's Preface

What counts as a crime, or at least as a serious crime, is not very different in London or New York from in Rome or Paris; the stories told by Georges Simenon adopt more or less the same conception of criminality as do those of Arthur Conan Doyle. But the arrangements under which criminal trials are conducted are radically different. In continental Europe, and in countries which have adopted the civil law system, what is known, perhaps not very happily, as the inquisitorial system, is in force, under which the judge plays a dominant part in the management and control of the trial. The conception of the judicial function requires the presiding professional to play an active role in the pursuit of truth and justice. In the common law world, where the adversary system prevails, it is for the lawyers on both sides to dominate the proceedings. The judicial function is reduced to something more like that of a referee in a football game. The judge is not expected to take positive steps to ensure that truth and justice prevail, but rather to see that the conflict between prosecution and defence is fairly conducted, and that the accused's lawyer has a real opportunity to test the prosecution case. To this end the proceedings have come to be governed by elaborate rules, which include the arcane rules of criminal evidence, which exclude from consideration much information which, in common sense, possesses obvious probative value. These rules have no counterpart in continental procedure.

It has long been understood that a criminal trial in, say, Elizabethan England, was very different from what it had become by the end of the eighteenth century, by when the adversary system of today was well on the way to being established. But when it all came about, and why, was either not explained at all, or not very convincingly explained; in particular the relationship between procedural developments and the evolution of doctrines intimately associated with the adversary trial was simply not understood. A basic reason for this was that historians of the subject had largely confined their attention to the collection of trial accounts published as the *State Trials*. Such state trials were by no means typical, and reliance on this source gave a distorted picture of the typical run-of-the-mill criminal trial.

John Langbein's work has entirely transformed our knowledge of what happened, when it happened, and why. For he was the first scholar to make effective use of a rich source of information on the criminal trial, the *Old Bailey Sessions Papers*, whose importance no other scholar had grasped. Making use both of this historical gold mine, and of course of other primary materials, he set about the task of rewriting the legal history of the English criminal trial. Some of his findings have already been published in periodicals, but much of what appears in this book is quite new. More importantly, publication in book form has provided him with an opportunity to assemble the various pieces of the jigsaw into a whole, and construct a general account of the dramatic changes in the nature of the criminal trial which took place between the seventeenth and nineteenth centuries.

John Langbein is a comparative lawyer as well as a historian of the common law, and is very familiar with the radically different conception of the criminal trial which evolved in continental Europe, and with its history. It is his belief that the common law took a wrong turn when it followed a different path. In this book he not only seeks to explain why the English were unable to learn from the continental European tradition, but to convince his readers that his evaluation is correct. In consequence this book is concerned not only with the past but with the present. It is a real pleasure to welcome it into this series.

A. W. Brian Simpson

Preface and Acknowledgments

Under the adversary system of criminal trial, lawyers for prosecution and defense gather and present evidence, examining and cross-examining witnesses before a relatively passive court. Although this lawyer-dominated mode of trial has become one of the defining institutions of the Anglo-American legal tradition, it took shape relatively late in English legal history, without plan or direction, across the century or so from the 1690s. In this book I undertake to explain how and why this remarkable recasting of common law criminal procedure occurred. The book also supplies an account of the formation of the law of criminal evidence, a development of the eighteenth century that was deeply intertwined with the forces that gave rise to adversary criminal trial.

The Sessions Papers. The research that underlies this book is based heavily upon a set of sources, the *Old Bailey Sessions Papers*, that have come to the attention of legal historians only in recent years. The scholars who shaped our initial understanding of the history of early modern English criminal procedure (Stephen, Wigmore, Holdsworth, Radzinowicz) did not know them. The *Sessions Papers* were contemporaneously published pamphlet accounts of the trials at the Old Bailey. As the court with jurisdiction over cases of serious crime in metropolitan London, the Old Bailey was the most important criminal court in the Anglo-American world throughout the eighteenth century. The *Sessions Papers* commenced in a trickle in the 1670s and were continuously published for almost two and a half centuries, until the eve of World War I. They underwent many changes in format and function, which are sketched in Chapter 4 of this book.

I remember vividly my first chance encounter with the *Sessions Papers*, in the spring of 1977 in the Bodleian Law Library, where I had gone looking for other materials. It became clear that the *Sessions Papers* could provide an incomparable window on what actually transpired in criminal trials, allowing the historian to overcome some of the limitations of conventional legal materials. I called attention to the *Sessions Papers* in a pair of law review articles, and the discussion of the *Sessions Papers* in Chapter 4 of this book draws upon those papers: *The Criminal Trial before the Lawyers*, 45 Univ. Chicago L. Rev. 263 (1978); and *Shaping the Eighteenth-Century Criminal Trial: A View from the Ryder Sources*, 50 Univ.

Chicago L. Rev. 1 (1983). Across the years I have returned to the *Sessions Papers* as prime sources in a series of articles about various facets of the history of the trial. This book draws upon some of that work in various places. Chapter 3 revises and expands material that, although written for this book, was prepublished as *The Prosecutorial Origins of Defence Counsel in the Eighteenth Century: The Appearance of Solicitors,* 58 Cambridge L. J. 314 (1999). Section E of Chapter 1, treating what I call the "accused speaks" mode of trial, derives from *The Historical Origins of the Privilege Against Self-Incrimination at Common Law,* 92 Michigan L. Rev. 1047 (1994), as does some of the discussion of the privilege in Chapter 5.

Editorial conventions. I adhere in this book to conventions that I have followed in prior work when quoting manuscript and antiquarian sources. Words abbreviated or rendered partially in superscript in the originals have been written out, missing punctuation has been supplied, and obvious misspellings have been corrected, all without disclosure. Spellings have been modernized and Americanized, but not in the titles of books or pamphlets. Punctuation is overwhelmingly original, but modernized when required for clarity; accordingly, I have sometimes supplied a comma, an apostrophe, or a set of quotation marks in accord with modern usage. I have also altered some terminal punctuation, supplying a period where the original ends a sentence with a colon, a semicolon, a dash, or nothing at all. I do not preserve italic typeface when the original source uses italics merely as a typeface convention (for example, putting all the proper names or place names in italics). When the original uses italic typeface to show indirect discourse, I delete it and supply quotation marks and adjusted capitalization and punctuation. Capitalization in quotations is otherwise original, except that in rendering the titles of works I follow modern standards of initial capitalization. Where the sources supply varying spellings of a proper name, I have followed when possible the usage preferred in the *Dictionary of National Biography.* I intend these adaptations to make the book easier to read while remaining faithful to the sources.

Acknowledgements. I wish to express my thanks for the support and encouragement that this research has enjoyed from the Yale Law School and its deans, Guido Calabresi and Anthony Kronman. I am grateful to the Law Faculty of Cambridge University, whose invitation to serve as the Arthur Goodhart Professor in Legal Science for 1997–1998 allowed me to return to archives and collections in the United Kingdom; and to the master and fellows of my Cambridge college, Trinity Hall, for welcoming me as a fellow for that year.

I have benefitted from the resourcefulness of many library and archive staff. I wish particularly to record my debt to Gene Coakley, Harvey Hull, and Fred Shapiro at the Yale Law Library; to Judith Wright, the University of Chicago Law Librarian, and David Warrington, Curator of Special Collections at the Harvard Law Library, who have helped me across the years to work with the rich holdings of *Sessions Papers* in their collections; and to Jeremy Smith of the Guildhall Library for guidance on the illustrations reproduced in this book.

Across the years several able student assistants from Yale College and Yale Law School have helped me locate sources and check citations: Stuart Chinn, Marie DeFalco, Robert James, Cary Berkeley Kaye, and Simon Stern. I presented a forerunner of Chapter 3 of the book as the Iredell Lecture in Law and History for 1998 at the University of Lancaster, and I presented what is now Chapter 2 as the Fulton Lecture in Legal History for 1999 at the University of Chicago Law School. I am grateful for suggestions from those learned audiences. I wish also to acknowledge suggestions on earlier drafts of some or all of these chapters from Mirjan Damaska, Simon Devereaux, Richard Friedman, Thomas Gallanis, Henry Horwitz, Allyson May, James Oldham, Michael Prichard, and Alexander Shapiro. I owe a special debt to John Beattie of the University of Toronto, the master historian of crime in early modern England, who has for so many years shared with me his unrivalled knowledge of the sources and the issues, and who made many suggestions on a prepublication draft.

Permissions. The illustrations are reproduced with the permission of the copyright holders, for which I express my gratitude: "Justice Hall at the Old Bailey," reproduced in Chapter 1, and "The Manner of Execution at Tyburn," from *A Book of Punishments* (London c. 1680, shelfmark AN.18.3.25), in Chapter 5, are used by permission of the Guildhall Library, Corporation of London. In Chapter 2 the depiction of the Popish Plot is from *The Plot in a Dream* (London 1681, shelfmark *EC65.A100.681p12, facing 115), and that of Titus Oates in the pillory is from *The Doctor Degraded* (London 1685, shelfmark p*EB65.A100.685d3), both used by permission of the Houghton Library, Harvard University. The execution of Mary Blandy, from *The Secret History of Miss Blandy* (London 1752), in Chapter 3 is used by permission of the Harvard Law School Library Special Collections. The cartoon of "Dick Swift, Thieftaker, Teaching His Son the Commandments," in Chapter 3, is used by permission of the Beinecke Library, Yale University; another version, dated 1765, appears in J.A. Sharpe, *Crime and the Law in English Satirical Prints 1600-1832*, at 155 (1986). The rendering of "Mrs. Margaret Caroline Rudd on her Trial" used in Chapter 4 is from *The Malefactor's Register* (London 1779, shelfmark 1485.p.8, facing 181) and is reproduced with the permission of the

Trustees of the British Library. The depiction of the Old Bailey in Chapter 4 and of the Bow Street Office in Chapter 5, are from Rudolph Ackermann, *Microcosm of London* (London 1808–10). They are reproduced by permission of the Yale Center for British Art, Yale University, Paul Mellon Collection, as is Thomas Rowlandson's cartoon of "Being Nervous and Cross-examined by Mr. Garrow" from the series "Miseries of Human Life" (1808). "The Old Bailey Advocate Bringing Off a Thief," *c.* 1789, reproduced in Chapter 5, is used by permission of the British Museum.

John H. Langbein
New Haven, Connecticut
May 2002

Summary Table of Contents

Contents

List of Illustrations

List of Abbreviations

1696 Act	Treason Trials Act of 1696 (An Act for Regulating of Trials in Cases of Treason and Misprision of Treason), 7 Wil. 3., c. 3 (1696)
1836 Report	*Second Report from Her Majesty's Commissioners on Criminal Law* (Parliamentary Papers vol. 36) (London 1836)
Beattie, *Crime*	John M. Beattie, *Crime and the Courts in England 1660–1800* (1986)
Beattie, *Policing*	John M. Beattie, *Policing and Punishment in London, 1660–1750: Urban Crime and the Limits of Terror* (2001)
Beattie, "Scales"	John M. Beattie, "Scales of Justice: Defense Counsel and the English Criminal Trial in the Eighteenth and Nineteenth Centuries," 9 *Law and History Rev.* 221 (1991)
BL	British Library
Blackstone, *Commentaries*	William Blackstone, *Commentaries on the Law of England* (Oxford 1765–9) (4 vols.)
Burn, *JP*	Richard Burn, *The Justice of the Peace and Parish Officer* (3rd edn. London 1756)
Cairns, *Advocacy*	David J. A. Cairns, *Advocacy and the Making of the Adversarial Criminal Trial 1800–1865* (1998)
Cockburn, "Introduction"	J. S. Cockburn, "Introduction", *Calendar of Assize Records: Home Circuit Indictments Elizabeth I and James I* (1985)
Coke, *Third Institute*	Edward Coke, *The Third Part of the Institutes of the Laws of England: Concerning High Treason, and Other Pleas of the Crown, and Criminal Causes* (London 1644) (posthumous publication, written *c.*1620s–1630s)
Cottu, *Administration*	Charles Cottu, *On the Administration of Criminal Justice in England* (London 1822), trans. of *De l'administration de la justice in criminelle en Angleterre* (Paris 1820).

East, *PC*   Edward Hyde East, *A Treatise of the Pleas of the Crown* (London 1801) (2 vols.)

Exact Account   *An Exact Account of the Trials of the Several Persons Arraigned at the Sessions-House in the Old Bailey for London & Middlesex: Beginning on Wednesday, Decemb[er] 11, 1678, and Ending the 12th of the Same Month* (London 1678)

Fielding, *Enquiry*   Henry Fielding, *An Enquiry into the Causes of the Late Increase of Robbers* (1st edn. 1751), in Henry Fielding, *An Enquiry into the Causes of the Late Increase of Robbers and Related Writings* 63 (Malvin R. Zirker ed.) (1988)

Foster, *Crown Law*   [Michael Foster], *A Report of Some Proceedings . . . for the Trial of the Rebels in the Year 1746 . . . To Which Are Added Discourses upon a Few Branches of the Crown Law* (Oxford 1762)

Foster, Hale MS   Michael Foster, handwritten marginalia c.1755 to Matthew Hale, *Pleas of the Crown: Or, a Methodical Summary of the Principal Matters Relating to That Subject* (London 1716 edn.) (1st edn. 1678) (transcript by James Oldham)

Gilbert, *Evidence*   [Geoffrey Gilbert], *The Law of Evidence* (Dublin 1754) (posthumous publication, written before 1726)

Green, *Verdict*   Thomas A. Green, *Verdict According to Conscience* (1985)

Hale, *HPC*   Matthew Hale, *The History of the Pleas of the Crown* (S. Emlyn ed.) (London 1736) (2 vols.) (posthumous publication, written before 1676)

Hawkins, *PC*   William Hawkins, *A Treatise of the Pleas of the Crown* (London 1716, 1721) (2 vols.)

Hawles, *Remarks*   *John Hawles, Remarks upon the Tryals of Edward Fitzharris [et al.]* (London 1689)

Hay and Snyder   *Policing and Prosecution in Britain: 1750–1850* (Douglas Hay and Francis Snyder eds.) (1989)

Holdsworth, *HEL*   William Holdsworth, *A History of English Law* (1922–66) (16 vols.)

King, *Crime*   Peter King, *Crime, Justice, and Discretion in England: 1740–1820* (2000)

Langbein, "CTBL"   John H. Langbein, "The Criminal Trial before the Lawyers," 45 *Univ. Chicago L. Rev.* 263 (1978)

Langbein, "Evidence"   John H. Langbein, "The Historical Foundations of the Law of Evidence: A View from the Ryder Sources," 96 *Columbia L. Rev.* 1168 (1996)

Langbein, *PCR*   John H. Langbein, *Prosecuting Crime in the Renaissance: England, Germany, France* (1974)

Langbein, "Ryder"   John H. Langbein, "Shaping the Eighteenth Century Criminal Trial: A View from the Ryder Sources," 50 *Univ. Chicago L. Rev.* 1 (1983)

Maitland, *HEL*   Frederick Pollock and Frederic W. Maitland, *The History of English Law* (2nd edn. 1898) (2 vols.)

May, Thesis   Allyson N. May, "The Old Bailey Bar, 1783–1834" (unpub. Ph.D. thesis, University of Toronto, 1997)

OBSP   *Old Bailey Sessions Papers* (titles vary, *e.g., The Proceedings on the King's Commissions of the Peace, Oyer and Terminer, and Gaol Delivery . . . in the Old-Bailey, on [certain dates])* (c.1670–1913) (cited by month and year)

Oldham, *Mansfield*   James Oldham, The Mansfield Manuscripts and the Growth of English Law in the Eighteenth Century (1992) (2 vols.)

Padoa Schioppa, *Trial Jury* *The Trial Jury in England, France, Germany: 1700–1900* (Antonio Padoa Schioppa ed.) (Comparative Studies in Continental and Anglo-American Legal History) (1987)

Philips, "Engine"   David Philips, " 'A New Engine of Power and Authority': The Institutionalisation of Law-Enforcement in England 1780–1830," in *Crime and the Law: The Social History of Crime in Western Europe since 1500*, at 155 (V. A. C. Gatrell, Bruce Lenman and Geoffrey Parker eds.) (1980)

PRO   Public Record Office

Radzinowicz, *History*   Leon Radzinowicz, *A History of English Criminal Law and Its Administration from 1750* (1948–68) (4 vols.)

Ryder, "Assize Diary"	"Legal Notebook of Sir Dudley Ryder, 1754/55," doc. no. 19(f), Harrowby Manuscripts, Sandon Hall) (typescript transcript, copies on deposit at Lincoln's Inn Library and University of Chicago Law Library)
Ryder, "Judge's Notes"	"Law Notes of Sir Dudley Ryder" (1754–56), doc. Nos. 12–17, Harrowby Manuscripts, Sandon Hall (typscript transcript, copies on deposit at Lincoln's Inn Library and University of Chicago Law Library)
SAP	Surrey Assize Papers (The Proceedings at the Assizes ... for the County of Surrey ... on [certain dates]) (1688–1774) (cited by month and year)
Select Trials	Select Trials at the Sessions-House in the Old Bailey (London 1742 edn.) (4 vols.) (1st edn. 1735)
Smith, De Republica	Thomas Smith, De Republica Anglorum (Mary Dewar ed.) (1982) (1st edn. 1583, written c.1565)
Stephen, General View	James Fitzjames Stephen, A General View of the Criminal Law of England (London 1863)
Stephen, History	James Fitzjames Stephen, A History of the Criminal Law of England (London 1883) (3 vols.)
St. Tr.	T. B. Howell, A Complete Collection of State Trials and Proceedings for High Treason and Other Crimes and Misdemeanors (London 1809–26) (33 vols.) (1st edn. London 1719)
Thayer, Evidence	A Preliminary Treatise on Evidence at the Common Law (1898)
Wigmore, Evidence	John H. Wigmore, A Treatise on the Anglo-American System of Evidence in Trials at Common Law (3rd edn. 1940) (10 vols.)

Introduction

The lawyer-conducted criminal trial, our so-called adversary system, is the defining feature of criminal justice in England and in countries like the United States that are founded on the English common law. What distinguishes criminal adjudication in the Anglo-American world from the European and European-derived systems is not simply that our system allows lawyers for prosecution and defense. The European procedure does too. The striking peculiarity of the Anglo-American trial is that we remit to the lawyer–partisans the responsibility for gathering, selecting, presenting, and probing the evidence. Our trial court, traditionally a jury sitting under the supervision of the judge, conducts no investigation of its own. The court renders a verdict of guilt or innocence by picking between or among the evidence that the contesting lawyers have presented to it.

In the European systems, by contrast, evidence is gathered by judges or judge-like investigators, public officers who operate under a duty to seek the truth. Criminal investigation is understood to be a public rather than a private function. At trial, the presiding judge examines the witnesses. The lawyers for the prosecution and defense play subordinate roles, mostly recommending lines of inquiry, sometimes supplementing the court's questioning of witnesses.

This difference in the organization of criminal investigation and trial is hugely consequential, because most of what a criminal trial is about is deciding matters of past fact. As Blackstone remarked, "experience will abundantly show, that above a hundred of our lawsuits arise from disputed facts, for one where the law is doubted of."[1] Was the traffic light red or green? Was it the accused or someone else who fired the shot or took the diamonds? Find the facts and the law is usually easy.

Adversary criminal procedure exhibits two striking defects, to which I shall refer in several contexts in this book: the *combat effect* and the *wealth effect*. By the combat effect, I refer to the truth-impairing incentives of the adversary system. In an Anglo-American trial, the job of each adversary is to win the courtroom struggle. Winning often entails tactics that distort or suppress the truth, for example, concealing relevant witnesses, withholding information that would help the other side, preparing witnesses to affect their testimony at trial (coaching), and engaging in abusive cross-examination. By the wealth effect, I refer to the enormous advantage that adversary

---

[1] 3 William Blackstone, *Commentaries on the Laws of England* 330 (Oxford 1765–69) (4 vols.) [hereafter Blackstone, *Commentaries*]. Blackstone was speaking of civil disputes; the point is at least as true of criminal cases.

procedure bestows upon persons who can afford to hire skilled trial counsel, and to pay for party-conducted factual investigation. Because most
persons accused of serious crimes are indigent or near indigent, the wealth
effect is a profound structural flaw in adversary criminal procedure.

This book inquires into the historical origins of this system of adversary criminal trial. The lawyer-conducted criminal trial appeared late in
English legal history, and quite rapidly. Into the 1690s defense counsel
was still forbidden in all cases of serious crime, both treason and felony.
Prosecution counsel was permitted, but apart from cases of treason in
which the crown was always represented, prosecution counsel was virtually never employed. A century later, by the 1790s, the main characteristics of adversary criminal trial were in place for cases of serious crime.

A. Overview

Our starting point for studying the movement from lawyer-free to
lawyer-dominated criminal trial is the later sixteenth and the seventeenth
centuries, the so-called early modern period, in which the historical
sources first allow us a reasonable understanding of the trial procedures
that had emerged at the end of the Middle Ages. Chapter 1 explains that
the criminal trial transpired in a relatively unstructured "altercation"
between accusers and accused. The main purpose of the trial was to give
the accused the opportunity to speak in person to the charges and the
evidence adduced against him. I call this style of proceeding the "accused
speaks" trial. In this conception of the function of the trial, there was no
room for defense counsel to intermediate between the accused and the
court. Indeed, defense counsel was forbidden in matters of fact. The logic
of that rule was to pressure the accused to speak in his own defense. Part
of what motivated the rule against defense counsel was the fear (fully
justified in hindsight) that defense counsel would interfere with the
court's ability to have the accused serve as an informational resource.

Not only did sixteenth- and seventeenth-century criminal procedure
operate without lawyers, it also functioned without police or public prosecutors. Public authority, did however, reinforce private prosecution
through the so-called Marian procedure of investigation, conducted by
lay justices of the peace (JPs). Chapter 1 explains how the Marian pretrial
procedure undergirded the lawyer-free criminal trial and reinforced the
pressures on the accused to speak in his own defense.

Into the eighteenth century it was confidently asserted that denying
defense counsel benefited the accused. If falsely charged, the accused
would clear himself through "the Simplicity and Innocence" of his
responses, whereas the responses of guilty defendants would "help to

disclose the Truth, which probably would not so well be discovered from the artificial Defense of others speaking for them."[2]

The belief that denying defense counsel promoted truthful outcomes was shaken in the celebrated treason trials that occurred under the later Stuarts, especially the Popish Plot (1678–80), the Rye House Plot (1683), and the Bloody Assizes (1685). Chapter 2 reviews these venomous prosecutions, in which perjured evidence resulted in the conviction and execution of innocent persons, including political notables. Revulsion at these failures of justice led in the aftermath of the Glorious Revolution of 1688–9 to the Treason Trials Act of 1696, which introduced a package of reforms, whose centerpiece was allowing treason defendants to have trial (and pretrial) counsel. Chapter 2 probes the main provisions of the Act, with particular attention to the question of why the reformers of 1696 limited the nascent adversary procedure to the rare and otherwise atypical offense of high treason. The framers of the Act believed that treason prosecutions were uniquely problematic. Unlike trials for ordinary crime, in which the interest of the crown was slight, and in which prosecution counsel virtually never appeared, in treason cases the crown conducted the prosecution with partisan vigor and always through counsel. Furthermore, the bench, which still served at the pleasure of the crown, had not behaved impartially to treason defendants. The solution worked out in the 1696 Act was to allow treason defendants to engage partisan helpers of their own, defense counsel.

Adversary criminal trial was initially devised, therefore, as a special-purpose procedure for cases of treason, meant to even up for the particular hazards that such prosecutions were thought to pose for defendants. The new mode of proceeding was introduced to serve wealthy grandees accused of treasonable intrigues (mostly offenses touching dynastic succession or religious establishment). For such persons, paying for lawyers was the least of their troubles. Only later and in circumstances that were quite unforeseen was this adversary procedure extended to common felony. A style of proceeding devised to help aristocrats fend off trumped-up charges of treason would be transposed to the world of paupers accused of stealing sheep or shop goods. In the 1730s, in circumstances explored in Chapter 3, the judges retreated from the rule forbidding felony defense counsel. They began to allow the defendant to have the assistance of counsel for the purpose of examining and cross-examining witnesses. Defense counsel was the bearer of adversary criminal procedure. Slowly at first, then ever more visibly in the later eighteenth century, the lawyers came to dominate the felony trial.

---

[2] 2 William Hawkins, *A Treatise of the Pleas of the Crown* 400 (London 1716, 1721) (2 vols.) [hereafter Hawkins, *PC*].

A central thesis of this book is that the judges' decision to allow trial counsel to assist the felony defendant was a response to complex changes in prosecutorial practice, especially in London and its environs. Chapter 3 points to three main strands: (1) the growing use of lawyers in the conduct of prosecutions, especially the use of solicitors to investigate and manage certain types of criminal prosecutions, but also the use of prosecution counsel at trial; (2) the reward system, which offered huge bounties to encourage the prosecution of certain serious property crimes, at the risk of inducing false witnesses; and (3) the crown witness system for obtaining accomplice evidence in gang crimes, a prosecutorial technique that created further risks of perjured testimony.

By the 1730s experience with these new prosecutorial techniques caused the bench to conclude that many criminal trials were ceasing to resemble the ancient altercation of unaided victim and accused. Especially in London, prosecution was becoming ever more the province of lawyers and of a questionable corps of reward-seeking thieftakers. These determined operators were employing means that increased the danger that the accusing evidence coming before the courts could be unreliable. By allowing defense counsel to cross-examine prosecution witnesses, the judges attempted to correct for the imbalance that had opened between the unaided accused and the professionals and quasi-professionals who were increasingly shaping the most troubling prosecution cases.

The judges of the 1730s fell back upon defense counsel to even up the scales, as Parliament had done in the Treason Trials Act of 1696. Defense counsel would be allowed at trial to help the defendant probe accusing evidence and expose potential perjury, especially by cross-examining prosecution witnesses.

The institutions and the resources that were devoted to investigating crime in England were chronically inadequate. The English perpetuated a system of private prosecution (reinforced by amateur justices of the peace and amateur village constables) into the urban industrial age. Chapter 3 emphasizes how the shortcomings of this primitive pretrial system came to weigh ever more heavily on the trial. The judges found themselves adapting their trial procedure for the purpose of repairing defects of the pretrial. The decision to admit defense counsel, the bearer of the adversary system, was one such effort at repair; another was the development of the law of criminal evidence, whose formation is traced in Chapter 4. Although this is a book about the transformation of the trial, the nexus between trial and pretrial will be an ever-present theme. The pretrial shaped the trial. Had English governments faced the need to devote thought and resources to the problems of criminal investigation and prosecution in the pretrial phase, the lawyers would not have had their opening into the eighteenth-century criminal trial. Adversary trial was the judges' response at the trial level to the dangers of the pretrial process.

Although the judges admitted defense counsel to the felony trial in the 1730s, they continued to forbid him to "address the jury." This restriction prevented defense counsel from making opening and closing statements, and thus from replying directly to the charges and the evidence against the accused. The purpose of this restriction was to maintain the pressure on the accused to speak about the events in question, hence to continue to serve as an informational resource for the court.

In addition to allowing felony defendants to have the assistance of counsel, the judges undertook a further effort to provide safeguard at the trial level against the mounting dangers of the pretrial process for gathering accusing evidence. They created the law of criminal evidence. Chapter 4 traces the origins and development of this new body of law in the eighteenth century. The two most important rules, the corroboration rule for accomplice testimony and the confession rule excluding suspect pretrial confessions, were designed in part to counteract the same dangers inherent in the new prosecutorial practices that had motivated the judges to allow defense counsel. Although the law of criminal evidence was a judicial creation, it played into the hands of the lawyers, by opening to oversight and demand of counsel matters of trial conduct that had previously been the exclusive preserve of judge and jury.

My account of the development of adversary criminal trial and the formation of the rules of evidence is based heavily upon the *Old Bailey Sessions Papers*, as well as other pamphlet sources of the eighteenth century. The *Sessions Papers* give us a remarkable but still impaired view of the events that transpired in the trial courts. In Chapter 4, I discuss the strengths and weaknesses of these sources, which have become known to legal historians only in recent years.

How did adversary trial come to displace the old altercation trial, and to do it so rapidly? The judges who initiated the process by admitting defense counsel into the felony trial had no intention of working such a revolution. The judges allowed defense counsel for the limited purpose of helping the accused examine and especially cross-examine witnesses. The judges thought that by continuing to forbid defense counsel from stating the defendant's case or interpreting the evidence to the jury, counsel would merely supplement the accused's conduct of his own defense. Thus, the judges thought that they could admit defense counsel and still preserve the "accused speaks" trial. Chapter 5 shows why they failed. Defense counsel worked a structural change in the criminal trial, breaking up the two roles, defending and speaking to the merits, that had previously been concentrated in the hands of the accused. By articulating and enforcing the prosecutorial burdens of production and proof, counsel largely silenced the accused. This development led to the privilege against self-incrimination and the beyond-reasonable-doubt standard of proof. I emphasize that the adversary dynamic changed the very theory of the criminal trial. Whereas the old altercation trial had been understood as an opportunity for the accused to speak in person to the charges and the evidence against him, adversary criminal trial became an opportunity for defense counsel to test the prosecution case.

As lawyers took increasing command of the conduct of the trial, they diminished the courtroom roles of both the accused and the trial judge. A French observer, Cottu, remarked in 1820 that during the examination and cross-examination of witnesses, the English judge "remains almost a stranger to what is going on . . . ." As for the accused, he does so little in his own defense that "his hat stuck on a pole might without inconvenience be his substitute at the trial."[3] Chapter 5 points to the way in which the long-entrenched but impoverished conception of the judicial function in England facilitated the advance of adversary procedure. The job of an English trial judge was to process cases to juries. The judges had always taken the evidence as outsiders delivered it. English judges had never been responsible for fact-gathering; they lacked the resources, the authority, and the mission to investigate what they were deciding. Because the judges were administrators rather than adjudicators responsible for the accuracy of the cases they processed, they found it easy enough to accommodate to the role of administering the truth-impairing norms of the evolving adversary combat.

Chapter 5 also develops the view that the growing aversion to capital punishment in the second half of the eighteenth century played an important role in causing the suspect premises of adversary criminal trial to go unchallenged. By that time the understanding was widespread that English criminal law over-prescribed capital punishment, hence that a main function of the criminal trial was to winnow down the number of persons actually executed from the much larger cohort of culprits whom the "Bloody Code" threatened with death. If we are to understand why the authorities were not more troubled about the truth-defeating dimensions of adversary criminal trial, it helps to understand that this form of proceeding became entrenched at a period in which too much truth meant too much death. Subsequently, in the middle decades of the nineteenth century, the English confronted their excessive reliance on capital punishment directly and eliminated the death penalty from all but a few offenses. The Bloody Code was repealed, but its legacy endured in a criminal procedural system that subordinated truth.

---

[3] Charles Cottu, *On the Administration of Criminal Justice in England* 88, 105 (London 1822), translation *De l'administration de la justice in criminelle en Angleterre* (Paris 1820) [hereafter Cottu, *Administration*].

I conclude this book with a glance at the path not taken, explaining why the English viewed with disdain the truth-seeking procedures of European criminal procedure.

B. Criminal and Civil Justice

The lawyer-free world of English criminal procedure in the sixteenth and seventeenth centuries contrasts strongly not only with the adversary criminal procedure that developed in the eighteenth century, but also with the lawyer-suffused world of English civil procedure. To some extent, the development of adversary criminal procedure can be depicted as the absorption into criminal procedure of a model already operating in the civil trial. Thereafter, the English legal system came to exhibit a broadly similar adversary system for both civil and criminal cases.

The primacy of the civil side of the English legal system was such that the administration of criminal justice was barely more than an appendage to civil jurisdiction. Neither a specialist criminal bench nor specialized criminal courts developed in England until recent times. The trial judges who presided at provincial assize courts and at the Old Bailey in London were seconded from the three central courts of civil jurisdiction for a few weeks a year.

The hundreds of volumes of nominate law reports published from the sixteenth to the nineteenth centuries, which are mostly devoted to civil cases, underscore the dominance of civil jurisdiction. Yet despite the mounds of reported cases, we know relatively little about the conduct of civil trials before the nineteenth century. The law reports tell us about pleading, about decisions on issues of law, and about the post-verdict review of trial outcomes, but they do not tell us much about how civil trials actually transpired.

There is good reason for thinking that, despite the centrality of civil jurisdiction in England, the influence of civil procedure on the development of the adversary criminal trial may have been limited. Whereas criminal justice was *trial-centered*, in the sense that the legal system sought to resolve most criminal business at trial, English civil jurisdiction was *trial-avoiding*. The central function of the common law courts on the civil side was the pleading process, which sorted cases into those that the judges could resolve without trial on issues of law, and those that the judges forwarded to jury trial for decision on an issue of fact. Even when a civil case went to trial, that trial was characteristically more restricted in scope than a criminal trial. The civil pleading process strained to narrow the issue that went to the jury, leaving in some circumstances only a single question of fact, isolated from the larger transaction, with proofs that were correspondingly narrowed.

Another attribute of civil practice that radically diminished the scope and efficacy of civil jury trial was the exclusion of the testimony of the parties. The parties were disqualified on account of interest, that is, they were treated as not competent to testify about the transaction in controversy—ostensibly in order that they not be tempted to the sin of perjury, and also to spare the courts from receiving perjured testimony. The testimonial disqualification of civil parties reinforced the centuries-long effort of English private law to encourage transacting parties to conduct important business by means of written instruments, preferably authoritative writings such as those concluded under seal or confessed on court records.[4] The conclusive effect afforded to such documents would usually prevent or resolve disputes without litigation.

Although the principle of disqualification for interest applied nominally in criminal procedure, it had little consequence on the criminal side,[5] because the crown rather than the prosecutor was treated as the plaintiff. The victim testified on oath, and the criminal defendant was heard unsworn. In the trial of civil cases, by contrast, disqualification of the parties to litigation silenced the most valuable potential witnesses, limiting their participation to the averments of their counsel.

Accordingly, while much of the detail of the relationship between civil and criminal procedure in the development of the adversary system eludes us, the basics are not in doubt. The adversary model came from the civil side, where the parties routinely engaged counsel to shape the course of litigation to partisan advantage, but the significance of the adversary system expanded greatly when transposed to crime. The proofs in the typical criminal trial (which pitted victim against accused) were richer than in most civil trials, in which the pleading process and the preference for authoritative written evidence limited the scope for ventilating issues of fact, and in which the most likely fact witnesses, the parties, had been suppressed.

The development of adversary criminal trial raised an acute theoretical challenge, which has never been satisfactorily resolved in the Anglo-American tradition: how to justify the truth-impairing tendencies of a procedure that remits to partisans the work of gathering and presenting the evidence upon which accurate adjudication depends. Civil litigation arises from private interests, which is why the law encourages the parties

---

[4] I have discussed these matters in John H. Langbein, "Historical Foundations of the Law of Evidence: A View from the Ryder Sources," 96 *Columbia L. Rev.* 1168 (1996) [hereafter Langbein, "Evidence"].

[5] For the detail, see 2 Hawkins, *PC* 433–4, discussed *infra* Ch. 1, n. 139.

to settle their case without regard to any public interest. The purposes of the criminal law, by contrast, are prevailingly those of the public interest, which is why in the European legal tradition the work of investigating and adjudicating cases of serious crime is treated as a public responsibility assigned to neutral professionals who bring the resources of the state to bear both for and against the accused. The saga of the emergence of adversary criminal trial in England is a topic of legal history much more than of legal theory, because it is the story of how we came to live under a criminal procedure for which we have no adequate theory.

1

The Lawyer-Free Criminal Trial

English criminal procedure was for centuries organized on the principle that a person accused of having committed a serious crime should not be represented by counsel at trial. In the sixteenth and seventeenth centuries, when the surviving sources first allow us to see something of how criminal trials transpired,[1] we see the judges resolutely enforcing this prohibi-

---

[1] 'The report of the trial of Throckmorton is the earliest which is full enough to throw much real light on the procedure which then prevailed." 1 James Fitzjames Stephen, *A History of the Criminal Law of England* 325 (London 1883) (3 vols.) [hereafter Stephen, *History*], citing *R. v. Nicholas Throckmorton*, 1 *State Trials* 869 (1554) [hereafter *St. Tr.*]. Regarding the reliability of that report, and of the *State Trials* series in general, see *infra* nn. 24, 216, 218; Ch. 2, n. 49.

tion on defense counsel, despite persistent complaint from defendants.[2] The juristic literature of the early modern period is equally emphatic. Staunford (1554),[3] Pulton (1609),[4] Coke (c.1630),[5] and Hawkins (1721)[6] all expound the prohibition as a rule of law.[7]

The notion that criminal defense was a suitable do-it-yourself activity developed at a time when the whole of the criminal trial was expected to transpire as a lawyer-free contest of amateurs. In cases of felony (that is, serious crime other than treason), the prosecution was also not represented by counsel. The victim of the crime commonly served as the prosecutor. (In homicide cases, either the victim's kin prosecuted, or the local coroner stood in.[8]) As Blackstone would later say, "indictments . . . are preferred in the name of the King, but at the suit of any private prosecutor . . . ."[9] Reinforcing this system of private prosecution was the Marian pretrial procedure, which lent official support to the prosecuting victim but which also narrowed his autonomy in ways that are discussed later in this chapter. Three centuries later the French observer Cottu, who visited England to study the criminal procedure in 1820, was astonished to find this ancient system still in place. He marvelled that "the business of prosecution, instead of being performed on the behalf of the public by an officer appointed expressly for the purpose, is committed entirely to the

[2] For instances of criminal defendants complaining about being denied counsel, see, e.g., *R. v. John Udall*, 1 *St. Tr.* 1271, 1277 (Croydon Assizes 1590); *R. v. John Lilburn*, 4 *St. Tr.* 1269, 1294–6, 1317 (1649), discussed *infra* Ch. 5, n. 89; *R. v. Christopher Love*, 5 *St. Tr.* 43, 52–5, 61 (High Court 1651); *R. v. John Twyn*, 6 *St. Tr.* 513, 516–17 (O.B. 1663); *R. v. Edward Coleman*, 7 *St. Tr.* 1, 13–14 (K.B. 1678); *R. v. Stephen College*, 8 *St. Tr.* 549, 570, 579–80 (Oxford Assizes 1681); *R. v. Richard Noble et al.*, 15 *St. Tr.* 731, 747 (Surrey Assizes 1713). Chief Justice Edward Coke defended the rule in *R. v. Walter Thomas*, 2 Bulstrode 147, 80 *Eng. Rep.* 1022 (K.B. 1613).
[3] William Staunford, *Les Plees del Coron* 151ᵛ (London 1557 edn.) (1st edn. 1554) [hereafter Staunford, *PC*].
[4] Ferdinando Pulton, *De Pace Regis et Regni* 193 (London 1609) [hereafter Pulton, *De Pace*].
[5] Edward Coke, *The Third Part of the Institutes of the Laws of England: Concerning High Treason, and Other Pleas of the Crown, and Criminal Causes* 137 (London 1644) (posthumous publication, written c.1620s–1630s) [hereafter Coke, *Third Institute*].
[6] 2 Hawkins, *PC* 400–2.
[7] Protests also appear in the tract literature. An Elizabethan writer pointed out that even in cases in which the prosecution is represented by counsel, "no Man is suffered to defend, instruct, or speak for the accused: which is the greatest injustice that can be devised; and no doubt but infinite innocent Blood is shed by this means, and lyeth upon the heads of our Judges [and] Juries . . . ." "A Memorial of the Reformation of England" (1596), published as *The Jesuit's Memorial, for the Intended Reformation of England* 250 (London 1690) [hereafter Parsons, *Memorial*]. To the same effect, see William Sheppard, *England's Balme: Or, Proposals . . . Toward the Regulation of the Law* 197 (London 1657) [hereafter, Sheppard, *Balme*]. Further examples of critical tract literature are cited *infra*, nn. 142–3.
[8] See generally R. F. Hunnisett, "Eighteenth-Century Coroners and Their Clerks," 76 *Wiltshire Archaeological and Natural History Mag.* 123 (1982).
[9] 4 Blackstone, *Commentaries* 300; accord, Staunford, who wrote: "To give evidence, anyone will be admitted for the King," Staunford, *PC, supra* n. 3, at 163.

hands of the injured party, who, by this means, becomes the arbiter of the culprit's fate . . . ."[10]

The English system of privatized criminal investigation and prosecution was not seriously defended in the contemporary juristic literature. There was no positive theory of private prosecution, no body of thought explaining or justifying it. No one tried to make the case that it was a desirable practice to have an avenger in charge of gathering prosecution evidence. Indeed, it was widely understood that the system did not provide adequate incentives to prosecute. In the second half of the eighteenth century that concern led Parliament to enact a series of statutes providing subsidies for prosecution costs under various circumstances.[11] Private prosecution was a default system, accepted because devising an effective alternative would have required the political community to confront a nest of divisive issues about financing and controlling a public prosecutorial corps.[12] Comparable concerns prevented the development of the uniformed police until the second quarter of the nineteenth century.[13]

The rule against defense counsel had no counterpart on the prosecution side. Yet even though the prosecutor was permitted to engage counsel, in cases of felony he virtually never did, until the changes in eighteenth-century practice discussed in Chapters 3 and 5 of this book. In cases of treason, by contrast, prosecuting counsel invariably appeared.[14] Treason was the crime of taking or plotting against the life of the

---

[10] Cottu, *Administration* 38.

[11] The statutes, beginning with 25 Geo. 2, c. 36 (1752), are collected in 2 Leon Radzinowicz, *A History of English Criminal Law and Its Administration from 1750*, at 76–8 (1948–68) (4 vols.) [hereafter Radzinowicz, *History*]. The statutes of 1752 and 1754 gave "the courts power to award expenses to *poor* prosecutors and witnesses in felony cases where there was a conviction; a 1778 Act extended this to *all* prosecutors and witnesses even if there was no conviction; an 1818 Act . . . empowered the courts to award an allowance for time and trouble to all prosecutors and witnesses in felony cases." David Philips, " 'A New Engine of Power and Authority': The Institutionalisation of Law-Enforcement in England 1780–1830," in *Crime and the Law: The Social History of Crime in Western Europe since 1500*, at 155, 179 (emphasis original) (V. A. C. Gatrell, Bruce Lenman, and Geoffrey Parker eds.) (1980) [hereafter Philips, "Engine"]. Peter King reports evidence of growing levels of subsidy for prosecutors in Essex assize and quarter sessions cases in the second half of the eighteenth century. His data indicates that by 1790 half the prosecutors of property crime received some expense money. Peter King, *Crime, Justice, and Discretion in England: 1740–1820*, at 47–52 and fig. 3.1 (2000) [hereafter, King, *Crime*].

[12] Those issues remained divisive and unresolved throughout the nineteenth century and beyond. See Philip B. Kurland and D. W. M. Waters, "Public Prosecutions in England, 1854–79: An Essay in English Legislative History," 1959 *Duke L.J.* 493.

[13] Philips, "Engine" 171–89.

[14] "[T]he King's Counsel are the only prosecutors in the King's case, for he cannot prosecute in person" in his own court. "Orders for the Trial of the Regicides," *Kelyng* 7, 8, 84 *Eng. Rep.* 1056, 1057 (1660).

monarch, or raising armed rebellion.[15] Such cases occurred quite rarely, but because treason was a crime of state, high officers of state took charge of prosecuting it. Usually the law officers of the crown (the Attorney General and the Solicitor General) conducted the pretrial investigation, often with the active participation of members of the executive (the Privy Council).[16] At trial, the law officers and other crown counsel conducted the prosecution, making opening and closing addresses to the jury, and examining and cross-examining witnesses.

A. The Altercation

Our enduring image of the criminal trial as a lawyer-free contest between citizen accusers and citizen accused comes from the notable Elizabethan tract, Sir Thomas Smith's *De Republica Anglorum*, written about the year 1565.[17] Smith's account is the earliest window we have on the early modern trial. He depicts a hypothetical felony trial held at a provincial assize court. The victim and accusing witnesses engage the defendant in a confrontational dialogue about the circumstances of the alleged offense. The victim–prosecutor (Smith calls him the "partie pursuivaunt," the pursuing party) testifies on oath, saying "thou robbest me in such a place, thou beatest me, thou tookest my horse from me, and my purse, thou hadst then such a coat and such a man in thy company." Other accusing witnesses—"all those who were at the apprehension of the prisoner, or who can give any *indices* or tokens which we call in our language evidence against the malefactor"—also testify on oath. The defendant, speaking unsworn, replies to the accusing testimony: "the thief will say no, and so they stand a while in altercation . . . ."[18]

Smith's depiction of accused and accuser "in altercation" about the evidence underscores the lawyer-free character of the trial. The accused's merged roles as defender and witness were inextricable. In order to resist

---

[15] See, e.g., 1 Hawkins, *PC* 33–46; [Michael Foster], *A Report of Some Proceedings . . . for the Trial of the Rebels in the Year 1746 . . . To Which Are Added Discourses upon a Few Branches of the Crown Law* 183, 193–207 (compassing the King's death), 208–20 (levying war and adhering to the King's enemies) (Oxford 1762) [hereafter Foster, *Crown Law*].

[16] Prosecutorial practice in the treason trials of the later Stuarts is discussed in Ch. 2 *infra*.

[17] The modern scholarly edition is Thomas Smith, *De Republica Anglorum* (Mary Dewar ed.) (1982) (1st edn. 1583, written *c.*1565) [hereafter, Smith, *De Republica*]. Smith was a prominent figure, particularly respected for his knowledge of mid-sixteenth-century governance. See Mary Dewar, "Introduction," ibid. at 2; see generally Mary Dewar, *Sir Thomas Smith: A Tudor Intellectual in Office* (1964). Trained as a civil lawyer, that is, in the Roman-canon law, Smith was the first holder of the Regius professorship of civil law at Cambridge. He wrote *De Republica* while serving as ambassador to France under Elizabeth. He had seen service as a JP and an MP and "as Principal Secretary to Edward VI and ministerial confidante to Protector Somerset" during the regency. Dewar, "Introduction," in Smith, *De Republica* 2.

[18] Smith, *De Republica* 114.

or probe the evidence of the accusers, the accused found himself constantly speaking about his role in the events. Because the accused was forbidden to testify on oath (a disqualification that was not removed in England until 1898[19]), he was not conceived to be a witness. Although he spoke unsworn, he performed what was in function a testimonial role, by speaking to his knowledge of the events.

Once the altercation of accusers and accused had run its course, the trial judge left the jurors to decide the case based on what they had learned from the exchange, usually with little instruction. Smith's judge merely tells the jurors that "ye have heard what these men say against the prisoner, you have also heard what the prisoner can say for himself . . . ."[20] The question for the jury to decide, the issue of the trial, was whether the accused had adequately explained away the evidence adduced against him. Acquittal rates from the later sixteenth century and beyond indicate that the defendant succeeded in a third or more of felony cases.[21] In treason prosecutions, by contrast, acquittals occurred quite rarely.[22]

Because the historical sources tell us very little about the trial of cases of ordinary felony[23] until the late seventeenth century and beyond, most of what is known about trial procedure in the sixteenth and seventeenth centuries comes from a relative handful of celebrated treason trials. These trials were chronicled in contemporary pamphlets or manuscripts that were not prepared as law reports, but retrospectively compiled in the eighteenth century in the series known as the *State Trials*.[24] (The trials are

---

[19] Criminal Evidence Act, 61 & 62 Vict., c. 6 (1898), see *infra* text at n. 206.

[20] Smith, *De Republica* 114.

[21] "Approximately 40 percent of all those arraigned at Home Circuit assizes between 1558 and 1625 were acquitted by the trial jury." J. S. Cockburn, "Introduction," *Calendar of Assize Records: Home Circuit Indictments Elizabeth I and James I*, at 113–14 (discussing table 10) (1985) [hereafter Cockburn, "Introduction"]. "[O]ne in three of those [tried] on charges of theft or robbery or burglary were found not guilty" in Surrey between 1660 and 1800. John M. Beattie, *Crime and the Courts in England 1660–1800*, at 412 (1986) [hereafter Beattie, *Crime*], discussing table 8.3, ibid. at 411.

[22] Instances of acquittal: *R. v. Nicholas Throckmorton*, 1 *St. Tr.* 869 (1554); *R. v. John Lilburn*, 4 *St. Tr.* 1269 (1649). Among the factors that explain the higher conviction rate in treason trials are better selection and preparation of cases, better courtroom prosecution, more timid judicial behavior, and overawed juries. Treason trials are discussed in Ch. 2 *infra*.

[23] "Sources for trial process in the 16th and 17th centuries . . . are limited to Smith's account, some precious manuscript fragments, ambiguous references to trial procedure in sensational pamphlets, and a few court records." Cockburn, "Introduction," 88. For earlier times the situation is worse. "The only matters routinely recorded in criminal trials were the indictment . . . , the defendant's appearance and plea, the selection and swearing in of the trial jurors, their verdict, and the sentence." Edward Powell, "Jury Trial at Gaol Delivery in the Late Middle Ages: The Midland Circuit, 1400–1429" [hereafter, Powell, "Jury Trial"], in *Twelve Good Men and True: The Criminal Trial Jury in England, 1200–1800*, at 78, 81 (J. S. Cockburn and Thomas A. Green eds.) (1988) [hereafter Cockburn and Green].

[24] The definitive edition is T. B. Howell, *A Complete Collection of State Trials and Proceedings for High Treason and Other Crimes and Misdemeanors* (London 1809–26) (33 vols.) (1st edn. London 1719). Regarding the compilation of the series and the several editions, see J. G.

themselves commonly called "State Trials" after the name of the series.) The major treason trials preserved in the *State Trials* differed from ordinary criminal trials in various respects,[25] especially in having prosecution counsel, but they share the dynamic of Sir Thomas Smith's altercation-style trial. In the earliest well-reported trial, of Sir Nicholas Throckmorton, who was tried for treason in 1554,[26] we see the defendant responding piecemeal to each new item of accusing evidence, and to the questioning of the prosecutors and the bench.

Without counsel to order the proofs and to examine and cross-examine witnesses and accused, the responsibility for directing felony trials fell to the judge. "The admission and presentation of evidence in court was organized by the trial judge, who examined witnesses and the prisoner and commented upon their testimony as it was being given."[27] In some circumstances the clerk of assize appears to have supplemented the judge in the work of calling and questioning witnesses.[28] In conducting the trial, the judge worked from the indictment, that is, the formal criminal charge. To assist the judge in this work it was "usual for [the] clerk of assize to prepare for the judge an abstract of the indictments as soon as [the grand jury] found [them]."[29] Sometimes the judge would also have consulted the pretrial examinations of witnesses and accused, commonly called depositions, which the committing magistrate had prepared and filed with the court. (The Marian pretrial process that generated these documents is discussed below.) From these materials the judge could

---

Muddiman, *State Trials: The Need for a New and Revised Edition* (1930). Regarding the shortcomings of the *State Trials*, see John H. Langbein, "The Criminal Trial before the Lawyers," 45 *Univ. Chicago L. Rev.* 263, 264–7 (1978) [hereafter Langbein, "CTBL"].

[25] Discussed in Ch. 2, *infra*, text at nn. 167–82.

[26] *R. v. Nicholas Throckmorton*, 1 *St. Tr.* 869 (1554); regarding the reliability of the report, see *infra* nn. 216, 218.

[27] Cockburn, "Introduction" 109; accord, Beattie, *Crime* 342 (in the eighteenth century the "common practice clearly was for the judge to take [the prosecutor and the witnesses] through their testimony line by line, acting as both examiner and cross-examiner . . ."). For a particularly detailed example of a trial judge conducting what must have been an exceptionally careful and well-planned examination-in-chief of prosecution witnesses, see the trial of a defendant for perjury arising from an earlier false prosecution for reward, Bartholomew Harnet, *OBSP* (Dec. 1732, #84), at 24–7. The case is further discussed in Ch. 3 *infra*, text at nn. 232–4.

[28] Sir Dudley Ryder, newly appointed Chief Justice of King's Bench, riding his first circuit as an assize judge in August 1754, recorded in a diary various tips on the conduct of trials from his colleague on the Home Circuit Sir Michael Foster. Foster was then an experienced trial judge, who would shortly publish his *Crown Law* (1762). Foster told Ryder that "the clerk of assizes takes on him[self] sometimes [to act] as prosecutor for the King to examine witnesses, but [Foster] has sometimes stopped him. Though note, it don't seem to me improper for him to do it." "Legal Notebook of Sir Dudley Ryder, 1754/55," at 15, doc. no. 19(f), Harrowby Manuscripts, Sandon Hall [hereafter Ryder, "Assize Diary"] (typescript transcript; copies on deposit at Lincoln's Inn and University of Chicago Law Library).

[29] Dudley Ryder's account of the practice as of 1754. He noted further: "I think I should read the indictments themselves to see there is no mistake." Ryder, "Assize Diary" 15.

"prompt" the prosecutor,[30] "helping [him] to tell his story as clearly and succinctly as possible, asking the questions that would produce the clearest evidence of the prisoner's guilt."[31]

The judge's supervision of the conduct of the trial included oversight of the altercation. He would on occasion intervene to keep the exchange relevant or to prevent abusive questioning.[32] By the early eighteenth century at the latest, the trial judge was intermediating the accused's questioning (cross-examination) of prosecution witnesses. In the trial of Arthur Gray for burglary in 1721, the judge told the accused: "If you have any Question to ask, you ought to direct it to the Court, and the Court, if the Question is proper, will require an Answer from the Witness."[33]

The judge was also expected to assist the accused, indeed, in the phrase of the day, to serve as counsel for the accused. We shall see that the extent and limits of this responsibility were intertwined in a complex way with the rule against defense counsel.[34]

B. The Rapidity of Trial

The altercation trial was an abrupt affair. At provincial assize courts in the Elizabethan-Jacobean period (1558–1625) the average duration of a trial, including time for jury deliberations, has been reckoned at between fifteen and twenty minutes.[35] These were cases of felony, which still in Elizabethan times routinely resulted in death sentences upon convic-

---

[30] Thomas A. Green, *Verdict According to Conscience* 135 (1985) [hereafter Green, *Verdict*].

[31] John M. Beattie, "The Criminal Trial in England," in *The Age of William III* 89, 90 (P. Maccubbin ed.) (1989).

[32] For example, in the case of Thomas Bambridge, tried for theft in 1729, the accused asked a prosecution witness: "What money have you received, and how long have you been maintained to be an Evidence against me?" The judge immediately intervened, saying, "That's not a proper Question. If you can prove any such Thing as you insinuate, you may." 3 *Select Trials at the Sessions-House in the Old Bailey* 158, 161 (London 1742 edn.) (4 vols.) (1st ed. 1735) [hereafter *Select Trials*]. The reason the judge thought the question was improper was that answering it would have obliged the witness to incriminate himself, contrary to the witness-privilege branch of the nascent privilege against self-incrimination, discussed *infra* Ch. 5, text at nn. 138–50.

[33] 1 *Select Trials* 98. Using nearly identical language, the trial judge told the so-called "thieftaker general," Jonathan Wild, at his trial in 1725: "You must not propose your Question to the Witness, but to the Court; and, if your Question is proper, the Court will require the Witness to answer it." 2 ibid. 212, 226.

[34] *Infra*, text at nn. 90–116.

[35] Cockburn, "Introduction" 110. Working from the records of the gaol delivery on the Midland Circuit in the first three decades of the fifteenth century, Powell concludes in a similar vein that "trials can rarely have taken as much as an hour, and they frequently must have taken much less time than this." Powell, "Jury Trial," *supra* n. 23, at 99.

tion.[36] In the eighteenth century the use of capital punishment declined precipitously, as the alternative sanctions of transportation and imprisonment took hold.[37] By the mid-eighteenth century the average trial time at assizes may have lengthened slightly, to about half an hour per trial.[38]

The Old Bailey was the London-area equivalent of the provincial assize court. Because of the greater caseload of the metropolis, the Old Bailey sat eight times a year whereas assizes sat twice a year.[39] In the later seventeenth and early eighteenth centuries the Old Bailey, which was the felony trial court for London and the surrounding county of Middlesex, processed between twelve and twenty jury trials per day through a single courtroom.[40] So characteristic was the brevity of trial that when an exceptional criminal trial lasted for some hours, its duration became a subject

[36] Stephen suggests that executions were running at around 800 per year in Elizabeth's last years. 1 Stephen, *History* 468. Cockburn's data indicates that there were about 22 executions per year in the county of Devonshire for a 28-year sample across the period 1598–1639. James S. Cockburn, *A History of English Assizes 1558–1714*, at 94–6 (table 1) (1972) [hereafter Cockburn, *Assizes*].

[37] The "penal death rate" declined to 12.3 per year for the entire country in the period 1800–10. 1 Radzinowicz, *History* 141–2. (The phrase is from 3 J.C. Jeaffreson, *Middlesex County Records* xvii–xviii (1986–92).) See also Beattie, *Crime* 451–6, 500–19 (displacement of capital punishment by transportation in the eighteenth century, Surrey data); accord, King, *Crime* 261 (Essex figures, later eighteenth–early nineteenth centuries).

[38] Beattie, *Crime* 377–8 (trial times at Surrey Assizes, summer 1751). A few years later Dudley Ryder recorded handling an assize calendar of eleven trials in a day and a half. Langbein, "Ryder" 120. For the claim of an experienced early nineteenth-century criminal attorney that the average duration of an Old Bailey trial for felony was by his day eight and a half minutes, see *infra*, Ch. 5, text at n. 319 (discussing the memoir of Thomas Wontner).

[39] The sittings for the year 1755 are shown in a tabular calendar in Langbein, "Ryder" 12.

[40] Langbein, "CTBL" 277–8. Accord, John M. Beattie, *Policing and Punishment in London, 1660–1750: Urban Crime and the Limits of Terror* 260 (2001) [hereafter Beattie, *Policing*] ("average of fifteen to twenty cases a day was entirely typical at the Old Bailey in the late seventeenth and early eighteenth centuries, and of the trial of felonies at the county assizes in the same period").

Using the same sources (the *Sessions Paper* reports, which I discuss in detail in Ch. 4 *infra*, text at nn. 7–52), Feeley and Lester find much lower figures for the Old Bailey in the eighteenth and nineteenth centuries (three to five cases per day). They express their results as "Trials per Judge per Day." Malcolm Feeley and Charles Lester, "Legal Complexity and the Transformation of the Criminal Process," in *Subjektivierung des justiziellen Beweisverfahrens: Beiträge zum Zeugenbeweis in Europa und den USA (18.–20. Jahrhundert)* 337, 352–3 and fig. 5 (André Gouron *et al.* eds.) (1994) [hereafter Feeley and Lester]. The authors do not explain the construction of this data, but I suspect from the title of their figure 5 that they have divided the reported number of cases for an Old Bailey sessions by the number of judges listed in the trial commission, and then by the number of days that the court was in session. The resulting number is not, however, meaningful, because the Old Bailey did not sit in parallel sessions. That is, in the eighteenth century all trials occurred in a single courtroom, with one or more of the named judges sitting. Furthermore, not all session days were used for trials. For discussion of staffing patterns at the Old Bailey and on assizes, see Langbein, "Ryder" 31–6, 115–23. See also ibid. at 34, reprinting in full an entry from the diary of Dudley Ryder, which includes Ryder's observation "that at the [Old Bailey] sessions in September [1754] seldom any [of the scheduled] judges attended." Ryder, "Assize Diary" 18. Only one judge, the recorder of London, attended with regularity throughout an Old Bailey sessions.

of remark.[41] Still in the early nineteenth century Cottu was struck to find that ten or twelve trials "may be dispatched in a morning . . . [to] one single jury,"[42] whose deliberations typically lasted two or three minutes.[43] The conveyor belt at the Old Bailey ran so monotonously that on one occasion a trial went its course before anybody realized that the court had just tried the wrong man: One John Smith was indicted and tried for stealing nine pounds of raisins. Put to his defense after the prosecution evidence, Smith replied, "I am not the person. I know nothing of this matter. I was committed upon suspicion of forgery." The astonished prosecutor, "looking at the prisoner," acknowledged that "[t]he man at the bar is not the person."[44]

Many factors bear on the rapidity of the altercation trial, including the absence of lawyers. In modern circumstances jury trial has become a relatively exceptional proceeding, reserved for the handful of difficult cases that resist "diversion" into such channels as plea bargaining. By contrast, in the age of Sir Thomas Smith and for centuries after, jury trial was the routine dispositive procedure for all cases of serious crime, including the many cases that were not seriously contested. Persons who had been caught in the act, or in flight, or with the stolen goods, or who had confessed, were sent to full jury trial. In such cases the Marian pretrial examination (described below) would often have provided the trial court with a confession or other cogent incriminating evidence. Thus, the average trial times reflect a mix of perfunctory trials in hopeless cases that took only a few minutes, together with seriously contested cases that might run longer.

1. No Plea Bargaining

Just as the want of plea bargaining helps explain the rapidity of the trial times, the rapidity of trial helps explain why there was so little use of guilty pleas. Modern plea bargaining entails the surrender of the defendant's right to trial in exchange for a lesser sanction. A plea-bargaining defendant effectively trades back to the state his right to put the criminal

---

[41] Reporting on the trial of Captain Turton at Oxford Assizes, who was acquitted of having murdered a chimney sweep, the *Gloucester Journal* noted that "after a Trial of Seven Hours, 13 Witnesses being heard against the Defendant, and 17 in Favor of him, the Jury in Seven Minutes' Time brought in their verdict, 'Not Guilty.' " "Select Occurrences," *Gloucester Journal*, 22 July 1755, at 3. Another example: the *Gentleman's Magazine* noted that the trial of Mary Blandy, 18 *St. Tr.* 1118 (Oxford Assizes, 1752), for the murder of her father lasted twelve hours. 22 *Gentleman's Magazine* 109 (1752) (the case is discussed in Chapter 3, *infra*).

[42] Cottu, *Administration* 75.

[43] Ibid. at 99.

[44] John Smith, *OBSP* (Feb. 1772, #308), at 142, 143.

justice system to a time-and-resource-consuming trial. But when trials were short and rapid, the crown had no particular incentive to engage in the exchange, and thus the defendant had no bargaining chips. In fact, quite the opposite tendency can be observed in the sources. Trial judges actively discouraged criminal defendants from tendering guilty pleas.[45] Matthew Hale, in his posthumously published treatise written sometime before 1676, explained that when a defendant attempts to plead guilty, "it is usual for the court . . . to advise the party to plead and put himself upon his trial, and not presently to record his confession . . . ."[46] Thus, in a trial held in Gloucester in 1772 and reported in a pamphlet account, we are told that "[t]he prisoner at first said he was guilty; but being apprised by the Judge of the ill consequences of pleading guilty, and being called upon to plead, he pleaded not guilty . . . ."[47] Occasionally we see some hopeless defendant insist on pleading guilty—for example, Thomas Nevil, charged at the Old Bailey in 1680 with burglary, horse theft, and jail-breaking, "pleaded Guilty, nor could he be persuaded to do otherwise. His reason was because he knew it would be proved against him, and that he had no hopes of life."[48] Apart from an occasional despondent figure such as Nevil, however, "[v]irtually every prisoner charged with a felony insisted on taking his trial, with the obvious support and encouragement of the court. There was no plea bargaining in felony cases in the eighteenth century"[49] or before. Although the potential was ever present to deal with caseload pressure by encouraging guilty pleas,[50] so long as

[45] For example, in the trial of Robert Flaman, *OBSP* (July 1748, #448), at 271, prosecuted for highway robbery, "[t]he prisoner said he would not give the court any trouble and would plead guilty to the indictment, but was advised to take his trial."

[46] 2 Matthew Hale, *The History of the Pleas of the Crown* 225 (S. Emlyn ed.) (London 1736) (2 vols.) [hereafter Hale, *HPC*] (posthumous publication, Hale died in 1676). As late as 1820 the French observer Cottu noticed a similar bent in the practice of the assize courts. When an accused would plead guilty to a capital offense, the judge, joined by "the clerk, the gaoler, almost all the counsel, even the prosecutor's, persuade him to take the chance of an acquittal . . . ." Cottu, *Administration* 73.

[47] *The Trial of William Morgan for the Murder of Miss Mary Jones . . . at the Assizes Held at Glo[u]cester, On [11 Mar. 1772]*, at 3 ([Gloucester 1772]) (BL, shelfmark 115.h.32) [hereafter *Morgan Trial*].

[48] Thomas Nevil, *OBSP* (Apr. 1680), at 3 (BL, shelfmark 1480. c.25.8). Further examples are noticed in Langbein, CTBL 278–9.

[49] Beattie, *Crime* 336–7 and n. 52 (discussing a large sample of cases from the county of Surrey for the years 1663–1802). See also Feeley and Lester, *supra* n. 40, at 345–6 (1994) (finding few guilty pleas in the Old Bailey until 1835).

[50] Cockburn has documented some plea bargaining on the Home Circuit for a period of three decades beginning in 1587. Cockburn, "Introduction" 65–70, 105. In the Bloody Assizes of 1685, discussed in Ch. 2 *infra*, Chief Justice Jeffreys lightened his heavy trial calendar by allowing some of the captured rebels to plead guilty and be transported rather than go to trial. G. W. Keeton, *Lord Chancellor Jeffreys and the Stuart Cause* 321, 329 (1965) [hereafter Keeton, *Jeffreys*]; H. Montgomery Hyde, *Judge Jeffreys* 217 (1948 edn.).

Outside the sphere of serious crime, it appears that a defendant might commonly negotiate a guilty plea resulting in a small fine in response to an indictment for a misdemeanor, as

jury trial remained rapid and lawyer-free, there was usually no disposi-
tion to do it.[51]

The trial court's role in sentencing and clemency, discussed later in this
chapter, also militated strongly against guilty pleas, even in cases in
which conviction was certain.[52] Unless he pleaded not guilty, the accused
would lose all opportunity for the court to consider evidence of mitigating factors. Thus, at the trial of Stephen Wright, caught robbing a surgeon
at gunpoint in 1743, the accused initially told the Old Bailey that he
wanted to admit his guilt, in order to spare the court trouble. The trial
judge "informed him, if there were any favorable Circumstances in his
Case, if he pleaded guilty, the Court could not take any Notice of them;
and that the Jury cannot report any favorable Circumstances, because the
Circumstances do not appear to them: Upon which he agreed to take his
Trial."[53]

2. The Accused as an Informational Resource

Because the accused conducted his own defense at trial, he necessarily
made himself an informational resource for the court. Below in this chapter I canvass the variety of ways in which the trial procedure put pressure
on the accused to speak in person about the charges and the evidence
adduced against him. The present point is that having the accused speak

part of an agreement to compensate the victim. See the important article by Norma Landau,
"Indictment for Fun and Profit: A Prosecutor's Reward at Eighteenth-Century Quarter
Sessions," 17 *Law and History Rev.* 507 (1999) [hereafter Landau, "Indictment"]; see also
Beattie, *Crime* 457–8. These practices manipulated criminal procedure to do the work of tort.
On the reasons why tort was unable to do the work of tort, see Langbein, "Evidence" 1178–9.
For more evidence of concessionary criminal procedures in the sphere of lesser crimes, see
Neil H. Cogan, "Entering Judgment on a Plea of Nolo Contendere," 17 *Arizona L. Rev.* 992,
1003–16 (1975) (nolo contendere-type plea, called *ponit se in gratiam*, in misdemeanor practice); George Fisher, "The Birth of the Prison Retold," 104 Yale L. J. 1235, 1275–6 and table 10
(1995) (increasing use of guilty pleas in Manchester quarter sessions in the last two decades
of the eighteenth century).

    [51] See generally Albert W. Alschuler, "Plea Bargaining and its History," 79 *Columbia L.
Rev.* 1 (1979); John H. Langbein, "Understanding the Short History of Plea Bargaining," 13
Law and Society Rev. 261 (1979). Another characteristic channel of "diversion" away from jury
trial in American practice, so-called bench trial, which entails encouraging the accused to
waive trial by jury and to have the trial judge adjudicate alone in return for a reduced sanction if convicted, was unknown in English practice. See Susan C. Towne, "The Historical
Origins of Bench Trial for Serious Crime," 26 *American J. Legal History* 123 (1982).

    [52] Even persons who confessed at trial pleaded not guilty. For example, in the trial of John
Morphew and Nathanael Jackson for highway robbery, *OBSP* (July 1722), at 3, it was
reported: "Before the Prosecutor had finished his deposition [that is, his testimony], the prisoners confessed they were guilty of the Fact."

    [53] Stephen Wright, *OBSP* (Feb. 1743), at 115, discussed in Langbein, "CTBL" 278. If the
jury that convicted a defendant reported favorable circumstances, the court would bring
that information to the attention of the monarch in the routine clemency review proceedings
discussed later in this chapter.

about the events was a factor that contributed importantly to the rapidity of early modern trials. The accused is virtually always the most efficient potential witness at a criminal trial. Even when he has a solid defense, the accused has usually been close to the events in question, close enough to get himself prosecuted.

3. The Pace of Jury Deliberations

Another aspect of the procedure that contributed to the rapidity of jury trial was the compression of jury deliberations. In Sir Thomas Smith's day the practice was to try several unrelated cases to one jury, then send that jury out to deliberate while a second jury heard further cases.[54] In the early decades of the eighteenth century individual verdicts began to be taken at the conclusion of each trial.[55] When the Old Bailey switched to this system in 1738,[56] the jurors' seats in the courtroom had to be rearranged. Previously the jurors sat divided, on both sides of the court-room.[57] As part of the switch to taking the verdict after each trial, the court placed the jurors' seats so "that they might consult one another and give in their Verdict immediately . . . ."[58] Even under the old system of batch verdicts, the jurors sometimes decided "without coming from the Bar"[59]—that is, they huddled and agreed with such dispatch that they did not need to retire from the courtroom.

---

[54] Smith says that sometimes when a jury had been charged with two or three cases, the jurors would say, "my Lord, we pray you charge us with no more, it is enough for our memory." Smith, *De Republica* 114. A clerical manual explains that as the trials progressed the clerk of assizes would prepare a schedule of the names and offenses of the persons tried, "and when the Jury is ready to go from the Bar, he delivereth it unto them for their better direction and help of their memory to know who they have in charge." *The Office of the Clerk of Assize* 48 (London 1682) [hereafter *Office of Clerk of Assize*]. In order to prevent mistakes in administering this batch verdict system, the practice developed that when the jury returned with its verdicts, the clerk would read out the name of each defendant "and bid him hold up his hand," before asking the jury's foreman to deliver the verdict upon that defendant. Ibid. at 49.

[55] Beattie, Crime 395–6.

[56] It fell to the Lord Mayor of London, a ceremonial member of the court, to announce the rationale for the change. He spoke of "the Inconvenience in the usual Method of trying Prisoners, in which the Jurors sat . . . commonly to give Verdicts on 12 or more Trials together, depending on their Memories, or Assistance of Notes . . . ." Henceforth, the jurors would be seated together so "that they might consult one another and give in their Verdict immediately, or in case of any Difficulty, withdraw for Consideration." 8 *Gentleman's Magazine* 659 (Dec. 1738) (entry for 6 Dec. 1738). See also Beattie, *Crime* 396 (*London Evening Post* report of the Lord Mayor's announcement).

[57] *Office of Clerk of Assize*, supra n. 54, at 45.

[58] The language of the Lord Mayor's announcement, *supra* n. 56.

[59] The case of John Baltee, reported in *An Exact Account of the Trials of the Several Persons Arraigned at the Sessions-House in the Old Bailey for London & Middlesex: Beginning on Wednesday, December[er] 11, 1678, and Ending the 12th of the Same Month* (London 1678), at 5, 6 [hereafter *Exact Account*]. This source, discussed in Langbein, "CTBL" 279–81, is a pamphlet

This practice of rendering verdicts without withdrawing for deliberation[60] became the norm under the system of individual verdicts. Deep into the nineteenth century foreign writers were astonished at how swiftly the trial jury reached its verdict at the conclusion of an ordinary trial. The French observer Cottu recorded that the jurors "gather round their foreman, and in about two or three minutes, return their verdict . . ."[61] The German scholar Gneist marvelled that "[a]mong a hundred criminal cases only roughly three to five remain on the average in which it is necessary [for the jury] to go into the deliberation room."[62]

Among the reasons that the jury could formulate its verdict so rapidly is that the relations of judge and jury were more informal and much less time-consuming than we now expect. The early modern trial was unhindered by the exclusionary rules of the modern law of evidence, whose administration is so cumbersome, and whose origins in the eighteenth and nineteenth centuries is the subject of Chapter 4 of this book. Judicial instruction of jurors was mostly perfunctory.[63] The practice of trying several cases at a time, while it lasted, was not conducive to giving detailed instructions at the conclusion of each case. Since there was no effort to divert open-and-shut cases from jury trial, a high proportion of the cases tried were exceedingly simple. Even contested cases for the most part raised only simple issues of law and law-applying. The patterns of jury selection varied, but it was common for juries to contain persons who had served before, veterans who needed less instructing.[64] The standard

that recounts in exceptional detail for the period all the trials at a single sessions of the Old Bailey. It was a forerunner of the series later known as the *Old Bailey Sessions Papers*, discussed in Ch. 4, *infra*, text at nn. 7–52. Beattie suggests that the reason "why the trials were reported at such unusual length [in this pamphlet] and why the recorder's speeches to the prisoners as he sentenced them are printed verbatim" is that "this was Sir George Jeffreys' first session as recorder . . . ." Beattie, *Policing* 260 n. 2. Jeffreys "had been elected recorder at Charles II's urging . . . to control unrest in the City at the height of the Popish Plot . . . . [Publishing the detail of the trials and the text of] Jeffreys' speeches, which naturally emphasized the duty of obedience to lawful authority, [was] presumably part of that campaign." Ibid. Regarding Jeffreys and the Popish Plot trials of the period 1678–80, see *infra* Ch. 2.

[60] For example, at the conclusion of a well-reported murder trial held at Gloucester Assizes in 1772: "The Jury turned round for a very few minutes only, and then found the prisoner Guilty." *Morgan Trial, supra* n. 47, at 14.

[61] Cottu, *Administration* 99.

[62] R. Gneist, *Vier Fragen zur deutschen Strafprocessordnung mit einem Schlusswort über die Schöffengerichte* 150–1 (Berlin 1874).

[63] Recall that in Smith's account the judge left the jury to decide the case with no guidance. "[Y]e have heard what these men say against the prisoner, you have also heard what the prisoner can say for himself . . . ." Smith, *De Republica* 114.

[64] For discussion of this phenomenon at the Old Bailey in the 1720s, see Langbein, "CTBL" 276–7, concluding that "in early modern times most juries were full of jurors who were 'old hands' at the job, and . . . those who were not experienced at the start of a sessions were veterans by the end." Ibid. at 277. Accord, Beattie, *Policing* 266–7, 270. For Surrey, Beattie found that "some members of every trial jury in the eighteenth century had served

of proof, a main component of the modern jury instruction, was as yet inchoate; the beyond-reasonable-doubt standard was not formulated until the end of the eighteenth century.[65] We shall see in Chapter 5 that a variety of factors (including the lawyerization of the trial in the later eighteenth century) broke up the older informal working relationship of judge and jury, leading to new and much more time-consuming techniques of jury control.

Even in early modern times a handful of criminal trials entailed more complex facts than those that typified the world of twenty- or thirty-minute trials. Sometimes one of these cases of complexity bumped up against the rule that no criminal trial could be adjourned. Once the presentation of evidence to the jury commenced, trial had to be completed and the jury charged[66] with the case in a continuous proceeding, no matter how long or how late the court had to sit. If necessary, the members of the jury were to "be kept without Meat, Drink, Fire or Candle, till they agree."[67] Indeed, in 1588 a jury was fined when members were detected "having Figs and Pippins in their Pockets, though they did not eat them."[68] (The rule against adjournment was limited to criminal trials; there was no objection to a civil trial enduring many days.[69]) These rules preventing jurors from separating for meals or lodging had as their ostensible rationale that they protected against tampering by outsiders, but the effect was also to hasten deliberation.[70] The rule against adjournment

---

before." Beattie, *Crime* 385. "[A] third or more of every trial jury consisted of experienced men . . . ." Ibid. at 386. The phenomenon is further documented in P. G. Lawson, "Lawless Juries? The Composition and Behavior of Hertfordshire Juries; 1573–1624," in Cockburn and Green, *supra* n. 23, at 117, 144–6; and in Douglas Hay, The Class Composition of the Palladium of Liberty: Trial Jurors in the Eighteenth Century," in Cockburn and Green, *supra* n. 23, at 305, 344–5. King reports for Essex that about 10% of jurors were repeaters in the 1770s and 1780s, but that after changes in recruitment in 1784 "most jurors had both previous experience of jury work and a previous acquaintance with their fellow jurors." King, *Crime* 245. But see Cockburn, "Introduction" 61–3 (repeat service less pronounced for Home Circuit assizes *c.*1558–1625).

[65] Discussed below in this chapter, text at nn. 17–18; and especially *infra* Ch. 5, text at nn. 35–63.

[66] Unless the judge withdrew the case from the jury before verdict, a rarely employed technique of jury control discussed *infra* Ch. 5, text at nn. 353–6.

[67] William Nelson, *The Office and Authority of a Justice of the Peace* 386 (6th edn. London 1718) (1st edn. 1704). Baker writes: "These precautions were necessary to prevent the treating of jurors by or on behalf of the parties . . . . There was also the not unimportant element of compulsion: if the jurors' plight were made too comfortable they might never agree, and if one or two of the jurors were able to eat and drink they might resist the others." J. H. Baker, "Introduction," 2 *The Reports of Sir John Spelman* 112 (1978) (Selden Society vol. 94).

[68] Ibid., citing *Mounson v. West*, 1 *Leonard* 132–3, 74 *Eng. Rep.* 123 (C.P. 1588).

[69] E.g., *Annesley v. Anglesea* (*Craig v. Anglesea*), 17 *St. Tr.* 1139 (Exchequer Ireland 1743), discussed by Geoffrey C. Hazard Jr., "An Historical Perspective on the Attorney–Client Privilege," 66 *California L. Rev.* 1061, 1074ff (1978). The trial lasted fifteen days.

[70] Describing late medieval practice as glimpsed in yearbook cases, Seipp says: "The original motivation for the rule forbidding food and drink to jurors was not merely to prevent

meant that a jury once assembled would not be allowed to leave the supervision of the court or its officers until the jury returned its verdict. When the rule against adjournment was abrogated in the trial of Thomas Hardy in 1794 (under pressure from the noted defense counsel Thomas Erskine), the court spoke of the difficulty of arranging to sequester jurors.[71] In that case, the sheriff arranged for beds and mattresses to be brought to the court.[72]

Whatever its rationale, the rule against adjournment obviously risked undue haste and compression in the proofs, as well as diminished attentiveness in the triers.[73] The rule bespoke a certain callousness toward the conduct of criminal business. Haste was programmed into the assize calendars, which sent royal judges from the central courts into the counties to try civil and criminal cases pending there. The schedule for these twice-yearly circuits (in spring and late summer) was established and publicized well in advance, to allow litigants, witnesses, jurors, and court officers to assemble at each assize town on the judges' circuit.[74] Once promulgated; the assize calendar was inflexible. All criminal cases pending at an assize venue had to be tried in the time allotted. Clearing the jails of persons in pretrial detention took priority over civil cases, which could be postponed to the next assizes if time ran short. If the caseload at a particular assize venue proved large or complex, the trial days would have to run long,[75] even though cases tried late in the day might come

petty bribery, not merely to keep them sober and awake, but rather to force them to agree on a verdict." David J. Seipp, "Jurors, Evidences, and the Tempest of 1499," in *"The Dearest Birthright of the People of England": The Jury in the History of the Common Law* 75, 88 (John W. Cairns and Grant McLeod eds.) (2002).

[71] *R. v. Thomas Hardy*, 24 *St. Tr.* 199, 414 (1794), for discussion of the rule against adjournment and nourishment.

[72] Ibid. at 418.

[73] Stephen noticed the pressure that the rule exerted in the celebrated murder trial of Spencer Cowper, a barrister (and later a royal judge) who was prosecuted by the kin of a young woman who had probably committed suicide when he declined her affections. Stephen remarked that "the rule which prevailed then and long afterwards of finishing all criminal trials in one day must often have produced cruel injustice." 1 Stephen, *History* 422, discussing *R. v. Spencer Cowper* (1699), 13 *St. Tr.* 1105 (1699). Macaulay supplies a succinct account of the circumstances surrounding the case. 6 T. B. Macaulay, *The History of England from the Accession of James II*, at 2935–8 (C. H. Firth ed.) (1915) (1st edn. 1849–61).

[74] Regarding the calendars for the six assize circuits, see Cockburn, *Assizes*, supra n. 36, at 23–7; the sheriff's work in summoning the participants in advance is noticed, ibid. at 61–2. The sequence of steps at a particular assize sitting in 1754 is described in Langbein, "Ryder" 115–23.

[75] Cockburn notices instances of assize sittings beginning at 7 a.m. and running as late as 11 p.m. Cockburn, *Assizes*, supra n. 36, at 111. William Ballantine, a barrister who had a significant practice at the Old Bailey and on assize in the middle third of the nineteenth century, recalled the Old Bailey schedule of his day in a memoir: "The sittings of the court commenced at nine o'clock in the morning, and continued until nine at night. There were relays of judges. Two luxurious dinners were provided, one at three o'clock, the other at five. The Ordinary of Newgate dined at both. The scenes in the evening may be imagined, the actors in them having generally dined at the first dinner. There was much genial hospitality exercised

before jurors who were exhausted or worse.[76] The Old Bailey also featured marathon trials, for example, a trial in 1787 for conspiracy that "began at a quarter past five in the afternoon, and lasted till half past seven the next morning."[77]

These calendar pressures exemplify rather than explain or justify the sense of haste about English criminal trials. Beneath the surface of judicial administration there was an element of callousness or disdain toward criminal business. Criminal trials were the travail of the lower orders, a necessary evil that could be hurried along, unlike civil business, which deserved care. (I shall have more to say about the plight of the criminal defendant at the end of this chapter.) The unseemliness of these packed trial calendars inspired at least some contemporary unease,[78] captured in Pope's verse from 1714:

> Mean while declining from the Noon of day,
> The Sun obliquely shoots his burning Ray;
> The hungry Judges soon the Sentence sign,
> And Wretches hang that Jurymen may Dine.[79]

To summarize: The administration of criminal justice in early modern England presupposed that large numbers of felony defendants, many of them transparently guilty, would be processed rapidly in jury trials that would have the character of Sir Thomas Smith's lawyer-free altercation of accusers and accused.

towards the bar, . . . but one cannot but look back with a feeling of disgust to the mode in which eating and drinking, transporting and hanging, were shuffled together." 1 William Ballantine, *Some Experiences of a Barrister's Life* 80 (London 1882) (2 vols.).

[76] The Revd Martin Madan, writing in 1785, complained of drunkenness, disorder, and inattention among jurors. "Another cause of much evil is, the trying [of] prisoners after dinner; when, from the morning's adjournment, all parties have retired to a hearty meal; which, at assize-time, is commonly attended, among the middling and lower ranks of people, at least, with a good deal of drink. The symptoms of this vulgar species of festivity are usually too apparent, when the court assembles in the afternoon—the noise, crowd, and confusion, which these occasion, seldom cost the Judge less than about an hour, before the court can be brought into any kind of order; and when this is done, drunkenness is too frequently apparent, where it ought of all things to be avoided, I mean, in jurymen and witnesses. The heat of the court, joined to the fumes of the liquor, has laid many an honest juryman into a calm and profound sleep, and sometimes it has been no small trouble for his fellows to jog him into the verdict—even where a wretch's life has depended on the event!— This I myself have seen—as also witnesses, by no means in a proper situation to give their evidence." [Martin Madan], *Thoughts on Executive Justice, with Respect to Our Criminal Laws, Particularly on the Circuits* 142–4 (1st edn. London 1785).

[77] William Priddle *et al.*, OBSP (Apr. 1787, #448), at 580, 623 (conspiracy, in wrongfully prosecuting George Crossley for perjury).

[78] The Jesuit Robert Parsons complained that the accused's fate "is shuffled up in haste, put upon the verdict, malice [or] ignorance . . . of twelve silly Men who presently also are forced to give verdict without time, or means, to inform themselves further, than that which they have heard there at Bar . . . ." Parsons, *Memorial, supra* n. 7, at 250.

[79] Alexander Pope, *The Rape of the Lock* 20 (London 1714) (canto 3, lines 19–22).

C. The Rule against Defense Counsel

The rule against defense counsel in felony trials applied to matters of fact as opposed to law. In theory, a criminal defendant was allowed to engage counsel to make submissions of law, particularly at the arraignment or pleading phase,[80] which occurred in advance of trial, sometimes in a separate proceeding, but usually as a preliminary stage of the trial proceeding. The vast preponderance of criminal defendants raised no issues of law on arraignment, but simply pleaded not guilty. Pleading was about law, trial was overwhelmingly about fact.

Sir Edward Coke emphasized the law-fact distinction when explaining the rule against defense counsel: Only after the accused had pleaded not guilty and entered the trial phase of the proceeding, "which goeth to the fact best known to the [accused] . . . shall [he] have no counsel to give in evidence, or allege any matter for him . . . ."[81] We see in this passage the idea that animated the rule against defense counsel: As experts in law, lawyers have nothing to contribute to the fact-finding work of the court. The lawyerization of the criminal trial that occurred in the eighteenth century, and which is the focus of this book, would require the abandonment of this idea that counsel should have no role in presenting or ventilating evidence of fact.

The rule against defense counsel did not, therefore, purport to apply to questions of law. When "some Point of Law arise[s], proper to be debated,"[82] the accused was entitled to have defense counsel to argue it, even in a case of treason or felony.[83] Such cases of acknowledged legal complexity were, however, infrequent.[84] The standard as Foster expressed

[80] Most objections to law were raised in response to the indictment, hence on arraignment, but some were raised on legal points that surfaced during the trial. For example, in the pamphlet report of a murder trial held at Kingston (Surrey) Assizes in 1713, the co-defendants were allowed counsel during the trial to argue a legal objection connected with their arrest. The court overruled the objection and continued with the trial. *A Full Account of the Case of John Sayer, Esq., from the Time of His Unhappy Marriage with His wife to His Death, Including the Whole Intrigue between Mrs. Sayer and Mr. Noble* 34–5 (2nd edn. London 1713) (Lambeth Palace Libr., shelfmark OB 55 2.14) [hereafter *Sayer–Noble Trial*].

[81] Coke, *Third Institute* 137.   [82] 2 Hawkins, *PC* 400.

[83] For example, in a murder case tried at Surrey Assizes in 1713, the defendants were allowed counsel to argue that they had been wrongfully arrested, "upon which Points they moved for a Special Verdict, intending thereby to have judgment respited." *Sayer–Noble Trial, supra* n. 80, at 35. The court overruled the motion, took the jury's verdict that the slayer was guilty, and ordered him executed. Jonathan Wild, tried in 1725 for receiving stolen goods, was represented by two counsel, see n. 87 *infra*. They attempted to get the trial postponed, they challenged the indictment, and they "attended to speak to any Point that should arise . . . ." 2 *Select Trials* 212, 223.

[84] But not unknown: Seipp has identified several dozen yearbook cases for the fourteenth and fifteenth centuries in which counsel act for criminal defendants at this stage. David J. Seipp, "Crime in the Year Books," in *Law Reporting in England* 15, 22 (Chantal Stebbings ed.) (1995).

it in a handwritten note made in the margin of his copy of Hale's *Pleas of the Crown* was: "At common law no counsel was allowed in capital cases except in questions of law, and then only in doubtful, not in plain cases."[85] Furthermore, the burden was on the defendant to show that his was an appropriate case, for "in no case" wrote Coke, can the defendant "pray counsel learned generally, but must show some cause."[86] Such cause commonly took the form of an objection to the sufficiency of the indictment, usually upon arraignment, hence in advance of trial, although usually as part of a continuous session.[87] The practice of refusing to allow the accused to have a copy of the indictment made such a challenge diffi- cult to mount;[88] the precise terms of the indictment were disclosed to the

[85] Michael Foster, a King's Bench judge from 1746 to 1763, was the author of Foster's *Crown Law* (1762), see *supra* nn. 15, 28. The work cited in text is a copy of Matthew Hale, *Pleas of the Crown: Or, a Methodical Summary of the Principal Matters Relating to That Subject* (London 1716 edn.) (1st edn. 1678) (posthumous publication, Hale died in 1676) (this work is differ- ent from Hale's treatise, the two-volume *History of the Pleas of the Crown*, which I cite as Hale, *HPC* in this book). Foster signed the flyleaf of his copy in December 1755 and made hand- written notes in the margins. I quote from a transcript of those notes prepared by James Oldham from a photocopy of the original, which is owned by Anthony Taussig, London. I hereafter cite Oldham's transcript as Foster, Hale MS, using Hale's page numbers. The passage quoted above in text appears at Hale p. viii. (I acknowledge the kindness of Professor Oldham in bringing this source to my notice and permitting me to use the tran- script, and of Mr. Taussig for allowing this use.)

[86] Coke, *Third Institute* 137.

[87] But not always; some objections arose at trial, in light of the evidence presented there. For example, at the trial of Jonathan Wild, it was reported: "When they had heard what the Witnesses had said, the Counsel for the Prisoner, which were Mr. Serjeant Bains and Mr. Kettleby, urged that the Prisoner was not nor could not be Guilty of the Indictment as set forth, so that [i.e., because] it did not appear that he, the Prisoner, was present when the Robbery was committed, but that was again Opposed by Mr. Attorney General," who reviewed the language of the statute against receiving stolen property. "The Whole Proceedings of the Tryal of Jonathan Wild" 1ʳ (London 1725) (BL, shelfmark 1851 c. 10). This account does not disclose the detail of the judge's instruction on the issue. It says only that "[t]he Judge delivered the charge very Carefully to the Jury," which found Wild "Guilty of the Indictments" after deliberating for half an hour. Ibid.

Another example, discussed *infra* Ch. 3 n. 254, occurred in a case at Worcester Assizes in 1708, when defense counsel was allowed to argue (unsuccessfully) that the testimony of a crown witness should be disqualified for interest. Counsel's role in blurring the fact–law line in the eighteenth century is discussed *infra*, Ch. 5, text at nn. 239–73.

[88] Practice on the point in the Old Bailey was stated at the Restoration and reaffirmed in 1739. See *OBSP* (May 1739), at 87, republishing "Orders and Directions to be Observed by the Justices of the Peace, and Others, at the Sessions in the Old Bailey . . . Made 16 Car. [1660]," a decree issued by several common law judges including the chief justices of King's Bench and Common Pleas. Section 7 provides "[t]hat no Copies of any Indictment for Felony be given, without special Order, upon Motion made in open Court . . . . For the late Frequency of Actions against Prosecutors (which cannot be without Copies of the Indictments) deterreth People from Prosecuting for the King upon Just Occasions." Ibid. at 87–8; see also Orders and Directions . . . at the Sessions in the Old Bailey, *Kelyng* 3, 84 *Eng. Rep.* 1056 (O.B. 1660). Regarding the trial judge's discretion to decide whether an acquitted defendant should be allowed to sue the prosecutor in tort for malicious prosecution, Chief Justice Holt declared that "if A. be indicted of felony, and acquitted, and he has a mind to bring an action, the Judge will not permit him to have a copy of the record, if there was probable

accused only at the arraignment, when the clerk orally translated the indictment from the Latin original. Moreover, most criminal defendants were paupers who could not afford to hire counsel to make such motions.

Even when counsel was allowed on a law point, that counsel had no right of audience with respect to the rest of the trial. Thus, Edward Fitzharris, tried for treason in 1681, was allowed counsel for a jurisdictional challenge, which the court rejected. At the trial phase, Chief Justice Pemberton told him, "now we are come to a matter of fact only, and we cannot by the rules of law allow you counsel."[89]

1. Court as Counsel

Because so few defendants engaged counsel to raise objections of law, the procedural system left it to the trial judge to spot legal flaws in criminal prosecutions *sua sponte* (that is, without prompting from counsel). The court, it was said, would be counsel for the accused. Sitting on a felony trial in King's Bench in 1613, Coke observed that the trial judge was expected "to look unto the indictment, and to see that the same be sound, and good in point of law. The Judge ought to be for the King, and also for the party indifferent."[90] Would it not be better for the accused to have counsel of his own? Not according to Coke, who said that "it is far better for a prisoner to have a Judge's opinion for him, than many counsellors at the Bar. The Judges . . . have a special care of the indictment and to see that the same be good in all respects; and that justice be done to the party."[91] Thus, in Coke's formulation there was as yet no recognition that the job of advancing the interests of the accused might not be congruent with the court's mission to obtain the just outcome.

Presiding judges appear to have taken seriously their responsibility to

cause of the indictment, and he cannot have a copy without leave." *Groenvelt v. Burrell*, 1 *Ld. Raym.* 253, 91 *Eng. Rep.* 1065 (K.B. 1697). When, however, the trial judge was persuaded that the prosecution had been malicious, he would grant the acquitted defendant a copy of the indictment. For example, at the trial of George Hunt for theft in 1678 at the Old Bailey, it was reported that "it appeared upon the Evidence [to be] a Prosecution out of Malice, because of an [earlier] Action of slander, by the Prisoner commenced against the Prosecutor. And there being no color for the Accusation, the Court directed the Jury to find the prisoner not Guilty . . . . And the Court, taking notice of the malicious prosecution, gave him leave to take a Copy of the Indictment." *Exact Account* 24–5. See generally Douglas Hay, "Prosecution and Power: Malicious Prosecution in the English Courts, 1750–1850," at 343, 352 n. 31, 383 n. 132 [hereafter Hay, "Malicious Prosecution"], in *Policing and Prosecution in Britain: 1750–1850* (Douglas Hay and Francis Snyder eds.) (1989) [hereafter Hay and Snyder].

[89] 8 *St. Tr.* 243, 330 (K.B. 1681). The point came up in connection with Fitzharris' request that he be allowed to consult with his solicitor. Pemberton was explaining that Fitzharris had earlier been allowed a solicitor in order to instruct counsel on the law point, but since counsel was not to be allowed at trial, he had no need of a solicitor either.

[90] *R. v. Walter Thomas*, 2 *Bulstrode* 147, 80 *Eng. Rep.* 1022 (K.B. 1613).

[91] Ibid.

oversee the legality of ordinary criminal trials. Writing in the *Third Institute*, Coke said that "the Court ought to see, that the Indictment, Trial, and other Proceedings be good and sufficient in law . . . ."[92] Describing a manuscript account of an Old Bailey sessions held in the summer of 1616, John Baker remarks that "although there are no arguments by counsel . . . the judges nevertheless concerned themselves all the time with legal and procedural refinements."[93] Chief Justice Hyde explained to John Twyn, a defendant being tried in 1663 for publishing a treasonable book: "[T]he court . . . are to see that you suffer nothing for your want of knowledge in matter of law; I say, we are to be of counsel with you."[94]

This duty to be counsel for the accused was in tension with the trial judge's other roles, such as his responsibilities for ruling on matters of law, probing suspect defensive evidence, advising the jury about how to apply the law, and summing up the evidence to the jury. Thus, when an accused being tried for forgery in 1698 asserted an interpretation of the governing law that the judge regarded as wrong, the accused "was fully answered and confuted by the Bench as to that Point [of law]."[95] When a trial judge suspected that witnesses for the accused were lying, he commonly cross-examined them vigorously.[96] Furthermore, in the course of exercising his power to comment on the evidence, the judge showed no reluctance to tell a jury that he found prosecution evidence persuasive.[97]

---

[92] Coke, *Third Institute* 137.

[93] J. H. Baker, "Criminal Justice at Newgate 1616–1627: Some Manuscript Reports in the Harvard Law School," 1973 *Irish Jurist* 307, 311 [hereafter Baker, "MS"].

[94] *R. v. John Twyn*, 6 *St. Tr.* 513, 516–17 (O.B. 1663).

[95] *The Trial of Edmund Audley . . . Together with the Trial of Awbry Price, for Counterfeiting an Exchequer Note* 1ʳ (London 1698) (Folger Libr., Washington, DC, shelfmark T2184.5). The court was rejecting the defendant's argument that merely altering the sum in a note, as opposed to fabricating a false instrument, did not amount to forgery.

[96] William Burridge, tried in March 1722 for stealing a horse, produced two witnesses to support his claim to have bought it. The trial judge cross-examined them carefully, concluding from errors in dates that their testimony "manifestly appear[ed] to be wilful and corrupt Perjuries . . . ." 1 *Select Trials* 139, 142. Another example: In the trial of John Hawkins and George Simpson for mail robbery, held in May 1722, the court examined a defense witness about the number of inks used in creating a document. The witness testified one, the court pointed out to the jury that the document evidenced two. Ibid. at 162, 168–70.

[97] For example, in a murder case tried at Essex Assizes in 1752, "the Judge summed up the Substance of what had been said with great Conciseness and Perspicuity, and observed in the Conclusion, that though the Evidence in the present Case was only circumstantial, yet it appeared to him perfectly strong and convincing; and though [the chief prosecution witness had a history of lying, his testimony in this case] . . . had been corroborated by so many strong Circumstances, related by Persons whose veracity had never been called in Question, that the Truth of what he had now alleged could not be disputed." *The Only True and Authentic Trial of John Swan and Miss Elizabeth Jeffreys for the Murder of Her Uncle . . . at the Lent Assizes Held at Chelmsford* 17 (London 1752); cf. *R. v. John Swann and Elizabeth Jefferys*, 18 *St. Tr.* 1194 (1752) (same case). For a further example of a judge exercising the power of comment adversely to the accused, see *infra*, Ch. 5, text at n. 337.

The law-fact distinction thus shaped both the rule against defense counsel and the scope of the court's responsibility to be counsel for the accused. Since "counsel learned in the law"[98] had no role in fact-finding, neither did court as counsel. As late as 1769, Blackstone emphasized that the accused's entitlement to court as counsel was limited to matters of law: "[T]he judge shall be counsel for the prisoner; that is, shall see that the proceedings against him are legal and strictly regular."[99]

Here, as elsewhere, the law-fact line was easy to state but hard to apply. Judges did feel a duty to probe prosecution evidence, hence to do a little of what counsel would later do in the name of cross-examination.[100] Discussing practice in the Old Bailey in the eighteenth century, John Beattie observes that the judges' responsibility to "protect defendants against illegal procedure, faulty indictments, and the like" did not import any obligation to help defendants "to formulate a defense or act as their advocates."[101] This refusal of the court to give tactical advice is illustrated in a larceny case tried at the Old Bailey in 1788. When the defendant was called upon to answer the prosecution case, he offered up a written statement for the jury. The trial judge asked him whether he wanted it read. The defendant said that he left that to the court's discretion. The judge at once replied: "No, it is not my duty to advise you as to what you offer in your defense."[102] Beattie remarks that the court-as-counsel rubric "perfectly expresses the view that the defendant should not have counsel in the sense that we would mean."[103] Even with the court serving as counsel, "accused felons had to speak in their own defense and to respond to prosecution evidence as it was given, and as they heard it for the first time. If they did not or could not defend themselves, no one would do it for them."[104]

The judges did intervene episodically to help the defendant in the realm of fact, for example, by cross-examining suspicious accusers when the defendant appeared ineffectual,[105] or by emphasizing shortcomings of

---

[98] A common phrase used to describe counsel, discussed *infra*, text at n. 120.

[99] 4 Blackstone, *Commentaries* 349.

[100] E.g., Denzell Holles, *A True Relation of the Unjust Accusation of Certain French Gentlemen, (Charged with a Robbery, of Which They Were Most Innocent)* 21, 22, 24 (London 1671) (Folger Libr., Washington, DC, shelfmark 140371q) (trial at bar in King's Bench; judge actively cross-examines).

[101] John M. Beattie, "Scales of Justice: Defense Counsel and the English Criminal Trial in the Eighteenth and Nineteenth Centuries," 9 *Law and History Rev.* 221, 223 (1991) [hereafter Beattie, "Scales"].

[102] John Duffey, *OBSP* (Sept. 1788, # 542), at 696.

[103] Beattie, "Scales" 223.

[104] Ibid. Cockburn writes in a similar vein of the period 1558–1625 that "judges did not assist defendants by pointing out inconsistencies in the evidence against them." Cockburn, "Introduction" 108.

[105] For example, in the case of Robert Dewar, prosecuted for the capital felony of forging a will, the trial judge mentioned that the accused had no counsel (the prosecution did have

the prosecution case when instructing the jury.[106] Indeed, the judges sometimes appear to have felt a deepened responsibility to assist defendants in this way in cases in which the prosecution was represented by counsel but the accused was not.[107] No accused could ever rely on the trial judge taking such initiatives, however. "Judges were only occasionally moved to engage in vigorous cross-examinations . . . . For the most part they took the evidence as they found it . . . . They certainly did not prepare in detail for examination and cross-examination; they were not briefed,"[108] in contrast to counsel, whom a solicitor would instruct by means of a brief reviewing aspects of the projected evidence favoring the client. Nor did anything prevent the judge from helping the prosecution. Sometimes we find trial judges disparaging defendants or defense witnesses whose statements the judge disbelieved. For example, at Surrey Assizes in 1738, in the case of John Heaford, who was tried for theft from a dwelling house, a character witness told the court that "I have known him three Months, and I know no Ill of him." The trial judge, Baron Carter, replied derisively: "That's a great Proof of his Righteousness. I have known him half a day, that's almost as long as you."[109]

In reported treason trials of the sixteenth and seventeenth centuries the bench was sometimes caustic in its treatment of defendants. The crown

counsel), and the judge vigorously cross-examined the prosecution witnesses. Robert Dewar, *OBSP* (Dec. 1783, #56), at 97, 98. (The jury convicted, and Dewar was sentenced to death.)

[106] For example, in the case of Margaret Lovelock, *OBSP* (Feb. 1762, #105), at 73, charged with theft from a dwelling house, "[t]he court were of the opinion that the taking [from] the lodgings was the act of the husband, and mentioned to the jury some circumstances in favor of the prisoner," who was acquitted. Ibid. at 74.

[107] For example, in the case of William Bird, *OBSP* (Sept. 1742, #102), at 42 (the jail keeper of the Roundhouse, prosecuted for the death of a prisoner who suffocated in cramped confinement), the defendant complained that half a dozen counsel whom he attempted to engage declined to represent him. Ibid. at 42. In summation, the trial judge appears to have argued the case for the defendant: "The Evidence being gone through, it was observed by the Court, on behalf of the Prisoner . . . ." Ibid. at 57. (The court directed a special verdict.) The following year, in a perjury prosecution, it was reported: "There were several Counsel for the Prosecution, but none for the Prisoner. It was therefore incumbent on the Court (who are of counsel for the Prisoner) to examine the Record, and there was a material variance found between that and the Indictment," which resulted in a directed verdict of acquittal. Joseph Ellis, *OBSP* (June–July 1743, #365), at 219. Regarding the problems of unrepresented persons in the dawning adversary system of the later eighteenth century, see *infra* Ch. 5, text at nn. 301–22.

[108] Beattie, "Scales" 233. As late as 1827 Baron William Garrow, a judge who had come to renown as an Old Bailey defense counsel in the 1780s and 1790s, explained to a grand jury that, although the judges were counsel for the defendants, "they could not suggest the course of defense [that] prisoners ought to pursue . . . ." Ibid. at 254 (quoting Garrow); regarding Garrow, see ibid. at 236–47; see also *infra* Chs. 4 and 5, *passim*.

[109] John Heaford, *Surrey Assize Papers* [hereafter *SAP*], (Mar. 1738), at 18, cited in Beattie, *Crime* 347, with other examples.

was deeply partisan in these prosecutions, and the judges held office at the pleasure of the crown.[110] "[T]he judiciary was still looked upon as a branch of the royal administration," and the judges "regarded themselves as advancing the royal policy . . . ."[111] In the trial of John Udall (1590), when the defendant asked for guidance about his right to challenge jurors, the judge is said to have replied: "Nay, I am not to tell you that. I sit to judge, and not to give you counsel."[112] In the case of John Twyn in 1663, Chief Justice Hyde told the jury at the end of the trial that they should believe the accusing witnesses: "I presume no man among you can doubt but the witnesses have spoken true; and for [Twyn's] answer you have nothing but his bare denial."[113] At Throckmorton's trial in 1554 the presiding judge, Bromley, urged the accused to confess, on the unlikely ground that "it will be best for you."[114] In John Lilburn's 1649 trial the presiding judge, Keble, having heard the prosecution case mounted by the Attorney General but not yet having heard Lilburn's defense, announced to the jury: "I hope the Jury hath seen the Evidence so plain and so fully, that it doth confirm them to do their duty, and to find the Prisoner guilty of what is charged upon him."[115] Most of us would hope that our defense counsel could do somewhat better by us.

At the end of the seventeenth century, the bias displayed against defendants by a subservient bench in the treason trials of the 1670s and 1680s provoked visible discomfort in the political classes (a main theme of Chapter 2 of this book). As one contemporary remarked, the judges who were meant to serve as counsel for the accused had "betrayed their poor Client, to please, as they apprehended, their better Client, the King . . . ."[116] The sense that the bench could not be trusted to be impartial in treason cases, hence that the courts had failed to be counsel for the defendants, was a precipitating factor in the movement to enact the Treason Trials Act of 1696, which allowed treason defendants to have the assistance of trial

[110] The Act of Settlement, 12 & 13 Wil. 3, c. 2, § 3 (1701), discussed *infra* Ch. 2, text at nn. 78–80, secured the judges against dismissal without cause.

[111] Keeton, *Jeffreys, supra* n. 50, at 21 (discussing Havighurst articles cited *infra* Ch. 2, nn. 40, 58).

[112] *R. v. John Udall*, 1 *St. Tr.* 1271, 1278 (Croydon Assizes 1590). The report is suspect, being a verbatim narrative of the trial supposedly written by the accused.

[113] *R. v. John Twyn et al.*, 6 *St. Tr.* 513, 534 (O.B. 1663).

[114] *R. v. Nicholas Throckmorton*, 1 *St. Tr.* 869, 877 (1554). The same report describes a one-sided summation. "Then the Chief Justice Bromley remembered particularly all the Depositions and Evidences given against the prisoner, and either for want of good memory, or good will, the prisoner's Answers were in part not recited: whereupon the prisoner craved indifferency, and did help the Judge's old memory with his own recital." Ibid. at 897.

[115] *R. v. John Lilburn*, 4 *St. Tr.* 1269, 1382 (1649). Lilburn's defense did not change Keble's mind. After hearing Lilburn, Keble told the jury that "you will clearly find that never was the like treason hatched in England." Ibid. at 1402. The jury acquitted.

[116] John Hawles, *Remarks upon the Tryals of Edward Fitzharris [et al.]* 22 (London 1689) [hereafter Hawles, *Remarks*].

counsel. The 1696 Act would be the first breach in the rule against defense counsel.

2. The Standard of Proof

Another justification for the rule denying trial counsel to persons accused of felony or treason was the contention that the standard of proof would suffice to protect the accused. We will see in Chapter 5 that the beyond-reasonable-doubt standard of proof for conviction in criminal cases developed at the end of the eighteenth century, in association with the ripening adversary system. But long before the courts articulated the beyond-reasonable-doubt standard, they were sensitive to the notion that in criminal adjudication, doubts should be resolved *in favorem vitae* (in favor of life). Coke evoked this tradition in his *Third Institute*, giving as a "reason" for the rule denying defense counsel that "in case of life, the evidence to convic[t] [the accused] should be so manifest, as it could not be contradicted."[117] Chief Justice Scroggs spoke in that vein in 1678 at the trial of the first of the Popish Plot defendants: "[T]he proof belongs to [the crown] to make out these intrigues of yours; therefore you need not have counsel, because the proof must be plain upon you, and then it will be in vain to deny the conclusion."[118] By this reasoning, the ostensibly high standard of proof, intended as a safeguard for the accused, was effectively turned against him, and used as a justification for denying him counsel.

3. The Accused's Advantage

An insistent strand of the justification for the rule denying defense counsel was the claim that the accused was better suited than counsel to respond to questions of fact. The juristic writers Staunford, Pulton, and Hawkins all argued that the accused should defend without the assistance of lawyers because the accused would know more about the facts alleged against him than any lawyer.[119]

In discussing the rule against defense counsel, these writers, as well as Coke in his *Third Institute*,[120] refer to counsel as "counsel learned in the law" or merely "counsel learned," a recurrent affectation, which underscores the contemporary fixation on the law-fact distinction. Counsel's

---

[117] Coke, *Third Institute* 137. Blackstone carried forward this argument from Coke, but he distanced himself from it, and from the rule against defense counsel, which he thought "to be not at all of a piece with the rest of the humane treatment of prisoners by the English law." 4 Blackstone, *Commentaries* 349.

[118] *R. v. Edward Coleman*, 7 St. Tr. 1, 14 (K. B. 1678), cited in 1 Stephen, *History* 382.

[119] Staunford, *PC, supra* n. 3, at 151ᵛ; Pulton, *De Pace, supra* n. 4, at 193; 2 Hawkins, *PC* 400.

[120] Coke, *Third Institute* 137.

learning ran to the law, not to what happened at the scene of the crime. Thus, says Pulton, "when the offender is put to answer to an indictment of treason or felony, he must answer it in proper person, and not by attorney, or counsel learned. For this plea of Not guilty doth tend to the fact, the which the party himself doth best know, and therefore he can best make answer unto it."[121] The argument was that counsel was on the wrong side of the law-fact line to be of any help to the accused.

A stronger form of this notion that counsel had nothing to contribute to the criminal trial was the argument that the accused's proximity to the events gave him a special advantage in defending himself at trial. Coke wrote that a defendant's plea of not guilty "goeth to the fact best known to the party . . . ."[122] Roger North, defending the denial of counsel to Stephen College in 1678, observed that criminal defendants "should not have any Assistance in Matters of Fact, but defend upon plain Truth, which they know best, without any Dilatories, Arts or Evasions."[123]

The definitive statement of this line of reasoning appears in 1721 in Hawkins' *Pleas of the Crown*. "[E]very one of Common Understanding may as properly speak to a Matter of Fact, as if he were the best Lawyer," wrote Hawkins. "[I]t requires no manner of Skill to make a plain and honest Defense," because "the Simplicity and Innocence, artless and ingenuous Behavior of one whose conscience acquits him, ha[s] something in it more moving and convincing than the highest Eloquence of Persons speaking in a Cause not their own."[124]

The fallacy in this reasoning[125] was the assumption that because the accused may have been close to the events, he is therefore adept at explaining the circumstances of his own conduct, or at cross-examining the testimony of mistaken or malevolent accusers. Beattie has described the pathetic ineptitude of criminal defendants attempting to conduct a criminal defense in an eighteenth-century trial: "[M]en not used to speaking in public who suddenly found themselves thrust into the limelight

---

[121] Pulton, *De Pace*, *supra* n. 4, at 193. Pulton's account closely follows Staunford's but without attribution. See Staunford, *PC*, *supra* n. 3, at 151ᵛ.

[122] Coke, *Third Institute* 137.

[123] Roger North, *The Life of the Right Honourable Francis North* 66–7 (London 1742), cited by James B. Thayer, *A Preliminary Treatise on Evidence at the Common Law* 168 n. 1 (Boston 1898) [hereafter Thayer, *Evidence*].

[124] 2 Hawkins, *PC* 400.

[125] Precociously identified by Robert Parsons, a Jesuit, who wrote in late Elizabethan times about the predicament of "a Man standing at the Bar for his Trial upon Life and Death," terrified about "what may happen unto him, . . . [and] astonished with the sight of such a Court and Company set against him . . . ." Parsons asked whether such a defendant, "especially if he be bashful and unlearned, in so short a time as there is allotted to him for answering of his Life, without help of a Lawyer . . . [to] direct, counsel or assist him," can conduct an effective defense, even though he be quite innocent. Parsons, *Memorial*, *supra* n. 7, at 250 (cited by Cockburn, "Introduction" 108).

before an audience in an unfamiliar setting—and who were for the most part dirty, underfed, and surely often ill—did not usually cross-examine vigorously or challenge the evidence presented against them."[126]

4. The Accused as an Informational Resource

The dubious claim that the rule against defense counsel worked to the advantage of the accused was in tension with a rather opposite concern—not the pretense that denying counsel helped the accused, but the frank recognition that allowing him counsel would work to his advantage by hampering the trial court's ability to convict him if he were guilty. Judges and juristic writers feared that counsel would tend to speak in place of the accused, and thereby diminish the accused as an informational resource for the court. There was also concern that counsel's defensive tactics would impair the court's ability to adjudicate accurately. We shall see in Chapter 5 that both concerns would turn out to be well-founded, when the barriers against defense counsel were relaxed and the implications of adversary criminal procedure began to emerge.

Writing in 1609, Pulton brooded that defense counsel might lead the jury astray. "[I]f counsel learned should plead [the defendant's] plea for him, and defend him, it may be that they would be so covert in their speeches, and so shadow the matter with words, and so attenuate the proofs and evidence, that it would be hard, or long to have the truth appear."[127] Pulton foresaw that defense counsel would not want "to have the truth appear." Presiding at a murder trial in 1651, Keble explained why he rejected the defendant's request for trial counsel: "[W]hen should we have any man answer? [W]hen would men be executed for robbing, and stealing, and killing?"[128]

These concerns found their classic expression in Hawkins' treatise in 1721. Only a decade before the judges began to lift the barriers to defense counsel in the 1730s, Hawkins was still contending that "the very Speech, Gesture and Countenance, and Manner of Defense of those who are Guilty, when they speak for themselves, may often help to disclose the Truth, which probably would not so well be discovered from the artificial

---

[126] Beattie, *Crime* 350–1. In 1824 during a debate in Parliament about allowing full defense of counsel there was reference to a petition from "certain Jurymen" at the Old Bailey, advising that "the prisoner's faculties, perhaps surprised by ... intimidation, are too much absorbed in the difficulties of his unhappy circumstances to admit of an effort towards his own justification against the statements of the prosecutor's counsel . . . ." David J. A. Cairns, *Advocacy and the Making of the Adversarial Criminal Trial 1800–1865*, at 89 (1998) [hereafter Cairns, *Advocacy*], citing 11 *Parliamentary Debates* 180–1 (1824).

[127] Pulton, *De Pace, supra* n. 4, at 193.

[128] *R. v. Christopher Love*, 5 *St. Tr.* 43, 61 (High Court 1651).

Defense of others speaking for them."[129] Thus, to his claim that "the Simplicity and Innocence" of the artless defendant helped the jury acquit the innocent, Hawkins added the argument that denying counsel helped the jury convict the guilty. The logic of the early modern criminal trial was to pressure the accused to speak, either to clear himself or to hang himself. Having to conduct his own defense obliged the accused to become an informational resource for the court. Allowing counsel to meddle with the fact-adducing process would interfere with the central dynamic of the trial. In the sentence just quoted, Hawkins uses the words "speak," "speech," and "speaking," epitomizing in contemporary discourse the image of what I have called the "accused speaks" trial. Later in this chapter I point to other aspects of the procedure that reinforced the pressure on the accused to respond in person to the substance of the charges and the evidence adduced against him.

5. The Contrast with Misdemeanor

The rule against defense counsel pertained "[w]here any person is indicted of Treason or Felony,"[130] but not in cases of misdemeanor, which were lesser offenses not punishable by death. At least as far back as the early decades of the seventeenth century, "it was apparently quite common for attorneys to act for individuals accused at quarter sessions of minor criminal offenses."[131] We have no particularly satisfying account of why contemporaries thought it appropriate to deny defense counsel in cases of serious crime while allowing counsel to represent persons accused of lesser offenses.

The category of misdemeanor included a variety of matters of a largely civil or regulatory character—for example, the liability of property owners and parishioners for the upkeep of the roads.[132] Questions touching property rights constituted the field in which lawyers were most prominent in civil practice; it would have been awkward to forbid counsel when an

---

[129] 2 Hawkins, *PC* 400.

[130] Coke, *Third Institute* 137.

[131] C. W. Brooks, *Pettyfoggers and Vipers of the Commonwealth: The 'Lower Branch' of the Legal Profession in Early Modern England* 190 (1986). Brooks also reports "demarcation disputes between barristers and attorneys over" the right of audience in such matters at provincial quarter sessions, a struggle that the barristers ultimately won. Ibid. at 190–1.

[132] E.g., *R. v. Corrock*, 1 *Strange* 187, 93 *Eng. Rep.* 463 (K.B. 1719) (indictment for not repairing a highway in alleged violation of an obligation attaching to tenure of a certain house); *R. v. Gamlingay*, 1 *Leach* 528, 168 *Eng. Rep.* 366 (K.B. 1789) (inhabitants of the parish of Gamlingay convicted on indictment for not repairing a highway). See generally Michael Dalton, *The Countrey Justice* 51–5 (London 1618) [hereafter Dalton, *Justice*]; 1 Sidney and Beatrice Webb, *English Local Government from the Revolution to the Municipal Corporations Act: The Parish and the County* 307–8 (1906) [hereafter Webbs, *Parish*].

archaic procedural form chanced to cast an issue that turned on property rights as misdemeanor rather than, say, civil trespass or nuisance.[133] Recent scholarship has shown that even misdemeanor actions for ostensible crimes of violence (assault and riot) were sometimes directed toward "obtaining compensation. These indictments were, in essence, civil suits."[134]

Some of the conventions of adversary criminal practice may have developed in misdemeanor trials during the centuries that defense counsel was forbidden in cases of serious crime.[135] In the nineteenth century it was observed that the misdemeanor courts, particularly quarter sessions, served as training grounds for young barristers who later went on to handle cases of serious crime.[136] That pattern was probably much older, and it helps explain why a criminal bar was at the ready when the judges lowered the barriers against defense counsel in cases of felony in the eighteenth century.[137]

Despite the overlap of misdemeanor and civil jurisdiction, these two forms of proceeding exhibited a radically different attitude toward the evidence of parties. The parties to civil litigation were disqualified from

---

[133] For example, John Baker has drawn attention to a manuscript report of misdemeanor proceedings held at the Old Bailey in 1625 on an indictment for nuisance. Baker "MS," *supra* n. 93, at 321–2. The indictment charged one Reuben Hunt with having newly erected a slaughterhouse in the Middlesex parish of St. Clement Danes, causing remnants and excrement from the slaughtered beasts to flow into the high street. Counsel appeared on both sides, and defense counsel's objections to the indictment resemble common law pleading on the civil side. Ibid. at 321.

[134] Landau, "Indictment," *supra* n. 50, at 508. Foremost among the obstacles to recovery in tort that would have made it attractive for an injured person to manipulate a misdemeanor charge as an alternative to a tort action was the testimonial disqualification of the tort plaintiff, discussed in Langbein, "Evidence" 1178–9. "However, as compensation was, in legal theory, not the goal of an indictment, a prosecutor could give evidence on an indictment." Landau, "Indictment", *supra* n. 50, at 534. The victim's ability to testify at trial must have enhanced the settlement value of his power to withdraw his misdemeanor action for compensation.

[135] For example, misdemeanor cases supply early evidence of the practice of solicitors instructing counsel by means of the so-called solicitor's brief. See, e.g., *The Tryal of John Giles . . . in the Old Bayly . . . July, 1680 . . . for . . . Attempt, to Assassinate and Murther John Arnold* 30 (London 1681) (Free Libr., Philadelphia, PA, Hampton Carson Collection, shelfmark LC9.85) (defense counsel opens, saying "if my Brief be true"). For discussion of the solicitor's brief in eighteenth-century felony practice, see Ch. 3 *infra*.

[136] "[C]ounsel usually begin to practice at sessions at the very commencement of their professional career . . . ." William Dickenson and T. N. Talfourd, *A Practical Guide to the Quarter Sessions and Other Sessions of the Peace* viii (3rd edn. London 1829).

[137] Allyson May has shown that Old Bailey counsel in the early nineteenth century led a second life, practicing in the civil courts, not in the superior courts (King's Bench and Common Pleas), where they appear to have been professional failures, but in the mayor's court and other small claims courts found in metropolitan London. Allyson N. May, "The Old Bailey Bar, 1783–1834, at 174 ff (unpub. Ph.D. thesis, University of Toronto, 1997) [hereafter May, "Thesis"].

testifying on account of their interest in the outcome.[138] In a criminal proceeding, by contrast, the parties were conceived to be the crown and the accused. The victim, although he served as the prosecutor, was merely a witness, and witnesses were ordinarily regarded as disinterested.[139] Accordingly, since the defendant was a party, he was only permitted to speak unsworn,[140] while his accusers, who were not parties, testified on oath. Disqualification for interest did not disturb the central dynamic of the criminal trial, the altercation between accuser and accused. In civil procedure, by contrast, disqualification wholly silenced the parties to litigation, limiting their participation at trial to the averments of counsel. Although the misdemeanor defendant was allowed to speak unsworn in his own defense as in a felony trial, the civil procedural tradition that parties were expected to be heard by counsel rather than in person may have helped shape the rule that full defense of counsel was allowed in the trial of misdemeanors.

Another factor that may have had an odd influence in limiting the rule against defense counsel to cases of felony and treason was the disparity in threatened sanctions. Whereas treason and felony were punishable with death, misdemeanors that touched property and regulatory affairs were punished mostly by fine. We might expect that this difference in sanctions

[138] See [Geoffrey Gilbert], *The Law of Evidence* 86 ff (Dublin 1754) (posthumous publication, written before 1726) [hereafter Gilbert, *Evidence*]; 2 Wigmore, Evidence §§ 575–6; Langbein, "Evidence" 1184–6; James Oldham, "Truth-Telling in the Eighteenth-Century English Courtroom, 12 *Law and History Rev.* 95, 107–17 (1994).

[139] There were some exceptions, noticed by Hawkins, in which the witness "is either to be a Gainer or Loser by the Event of the Cause," for example, the debtor in a case of usury, who "would in Effect swear for himself, by proving a Matter which may avoid his own Contract." 2 Hawkins, *PC* 433–4. We sometimes see exclusion enforced on this ground in forgery cases at the Old Bailey, e.g., Francis Cuff, *OBSP* (July 1770, #494), at 314, accused of forging a bill of exchange on John Weaver. The court ruled that "Weaver cannot be examined," ibid. at 315, even though excluding him resulted in acquittal. Similar cases: Edmond Bourk, *OBSP* (Oct. 1733, #23), at 213, 215 (forgery; defense counsel argues the law point that the prosecution witness should be disqualified for interest); William Russell, *OBSP* (Feb. 1738), at 53 (prosecution and defense counsel argue about whether to disqualify the prosecutor for his interest in the forged acquittance); Richard Jacobs, *OBSP* (Sept. 1773, #534), at 367 (forgery) ("as the holder of the note had not given [the proffered witness] a discharge for the note, her competency as a witness was objected to by the counsel for prisoner"); James Parry, *OBSP* (Apr. 1774, #357), at 193 (forgery of a promissory note in the name of Robert Gardner; "[t]here being no evidence other than [Gardner] and his wife, the Court were of opinion that they were both inadmissible").

Another circumstance that could result in disqualification was serving as a surety for the accused. For example, in a misdemeanor prosecution for riot, it is reported that "John Grice and another Witness appeared to this Prisoner's character, but as they had both been Bail for his Appearance at this Sessions, their Evidence was not taken." Robert Page *et al.*, *OBSP* (Oct. 1736, ##5–7), at 199, 202.

[140] According to the report of a mid-seventeenth-century trial, the court admonished a defense witness that "though you be not upon oath, you must speak the truth in the fear of God." "The Arraignment and Acquittal of Sir Edward Mosely," in 6 *Harleian Miscellany* 46, 49 (London 1810 edn).

would have had an opposite bearing on whether to allow defense counsel, since the defendant on trial for his life would seem to have had the greater need. But the thinking of the time was that in capital cases it was particularly important to restrain counsel from interfering with the court's access to the accused as an informational resource (recall Hawkins' concern that "the Truth ... probably would not so well be discovered from the artificial Defense of others speaking for them"[141]). That concern would have been less acute in the realm of misdemeanor, where lesser sanctions were at stake. In cases of capital crime, English criminal courts wanted to hear from the accused.

Whatever the reasons for allowing defense counsel in cases of lesser crime while forbidding such assistance to persons accused of serious crime, that contrast provoked considerable uneasiness. John March, an Interregnum tract writer, complained that "in the most petty, ordinary, and inconsiderable action that is, the Law allows a man counsel; why then should it be denied him in a case of the highest concernment to him that can be, his life? If he shall have Counsel in lesser things, why not in greater, where there is most need of it?"[142] A prominent tract published after the Glorious Revolution asked, "what Rule of Justice is there to warrant [the] Denial [of counsel in capital cases, when counsel is allowed] ... in a Civil Case of a Halfpenny Value ..."?[143] Similar sentiments were voiced even by Chief Justice Jeffreys, the notorious crown sycophant, whose mistreatment of treason defendants in the Bloody Assizes of 1685 (discussed below in Chapter 2) would figure importantly in the developments that led to the introduction of defense counsel in the Treason Trials Act of 1696. Presiding at a treason trial in 1684, Jeffreys observed that "it is a hard case, that a man should have Counsel to defend himself for a two-penny-trespass, and his witnesses examined upon oath; but if he steal, commit murder or felony, nay, high-treason, where life, estate, honor and all are concerned, he shall neither have Counsel, nor his witnesses examined upon oath."[144]

The Treason Trials Act of 1696 responded to these grievances, but only for treason defendants, not for persons accused of ordinary felony. As explained below in Chapter 2, the reformers of 1696 concluded that treason prosecutions entailed such special dangers to the accused that defense counsel should be allowed in trials for treason but not for ordinary felony. After 1696 the rule forbidding defense counsel in cases of felony, although insistently retained, became more anomalous, being

---

[141] 2 Hawkins, PC 400.

[142] John March, *Amicus Reipublicae: The Commonwealth's Friend. Or an Exact and Speedie Course to Justice and Right* 128 (London 1651) (Harvard Law Libr., shelfmark E M315a3 651).

[143] [Bartholomew Shower], *Reasons for a New Bill of Rights* 6 (London 1692).

[144] R. v. Thomas Rosewell, 10 St. Tr. 147, 267 (K.B. 1684).

sandwiched in the hierarchy of offenses between the extremes of treason and misdemeanor, for which the defendant had the right to defend by counsel. Another anomaly, not much understood,[145] is that in parts of British North America the rule against defense counsel was not followed.[146] (This departure from English practice was constitutionalized in the American Bill of Rights in 1789.[147])

D. The Marian Pretrial

Supporting the altercation of citizen accuser and citizen accused at the felony trial was a system of pretrial procedure that helped the victim (or other prosecutor) to prepare the prosecution. The pretrial investigation had been organized in the Marian Committal Statute of 1555[148] (named after Queen Mary, in whose reign it was enacted).

The Marian statute employed local magistrates, the justices of the peace (JPs), to conduct this work of reinforcing citizen prosecution. The JPs had the power to issue search and arrest warrants[149] for execution by local constables. (The constable was an ordinary citizen serving an unpaid term as a law enforcement officer in his locality.[150]) The JPs also had pretrial committal powers, that is, they could order accused persons to be

---

[145] For a starting point, see Felix Rackow, "The Right to Counsel: English and American Precedents," 11 *William and Mary Quarterly* 3 (3rd ser., 1954).

[146] Swift bristled with post-colonial rectitude when he explained: "We have never admitted that cruel and illiberal principle of the common law of England that when a man is on trial for his life, he shall be refused counsel, and denied those means of defense, which are allowed, when the most trifling pittance of property is in question." 2 Zephaniah Swift, *A System of the Laws of the State of Connecticut* 398 (Windham, 1795–6).

[147] "In all criminal prosecutions, the accused shall . . . have the Assistance of Counsel for his defense." U.S. Constitution, Amendment 6.

[148] 2 & 3 Phil. & Mar., c. 10 (1555). I have discussed the origins and operation of the Marian system at some length in John H. Langbein, *Prosecuting Crime in the Renaissance: England, Germany, France* 5–125 (1974) [hereafter, Langbein, *PCR*]; John H. Langbein, "The Origins of Public Prosecution at Common Law," 17 *American J. Legal History* 313 (1973) [hereafter Langbein, "Prosecution"].

[149] Warrant forms appear in Dalton, *Justice, supra* n. 132, at 313–15. Sir Thomas Smith describes the practice. Smith, *De Republica* 109.

[150] See generally Webbs, *Parish, supra* n. 132, at 26–9, 489–502. Although a constable had some power to act on his own motion or on citizen complaint, including the power to arrest at the scene of a felony or in hot pursuit, on most matters he was subordinated to the direction of the JPs. One of the many handbooks for constables counsels, "[y]our duty is to apprehend offenders, and not to determine offenses." *A Guide for Constables and All Peace Officers* iv (Birmingham 1779) (BL, shelfmark 518.c.23.5). For an account, based on quarter sessions depositions, of how these "legal officers and private citizens shared the responsibility for detection and arrest," see Cynthia Herrup, "New Shoes and Mutton Pies: Investigative Responses to Theft in Seventeenth-Century East Sussex," 27 *Historical J.* 811, 817 (1984) [hereafter Herrup, "Responses"]. For the special arrangements employed in early eighteenth-century London, see Beattie, *Policing* 114–207.

jailed until trial. The Marian statute required that when a suspect was apprehended and brought to the JP, the JP should, before committing him to pretrial detention, examine him and his accusers about the charges.

The Marian statute did not require the JP to investigate cases more widely, for example to seek out witnesses who were not among the "bringers" who showed up in his parlor at the time of the apprehension and commitment of the accused, but some JPs went beyond the letter of the statute and attempted to investigate more thoroughly.[151] The Marian statute required the JP to bind over (that is, to issue an order compelling) the victim and those accusing witnesses whose testimony would be "material to prove the . . . Felony" to attend the trial and to testify against the accused.[152] The JP would sometimes testify at trial about aspects of the pretrial investigation,[153] much as his successor in this role, the police detective, does in modern trials. (The coroners exercised a comparable role in homicide investigations.[154])

The Marian statute required the JP to "take the examination of such Prisoner, and information of those that bring him, of the fact and circumstance [of the crime, and shall summarize in writing] . . . as much thereof as shall be material to prove the felony . . ."[155] These documents, called pretrial depositions,[156] by recording the statements of accusers and accused when recollections were fresh, restricted the scope for subsequent

---

[151] Langbein, *PCR* 38–54, 77–97.

[152] 2 & 3 Phil. & Mar., c. 10 (1555).

[153] Langbein, *PCR* 38–54; Langbein, "Prosecution," *supra* n. 148, at 326–34; Cockburn, "Introduction" 110; 1 Stephen, *History* 376.

[154] See *supra* at note 8; cf. Pulton, *De Pace*, *supra* n. 4, at 252, discussing 1 & 2 Phil. & Mar., c. 13 (1554).

[155] 2 & 3 Phil. & Mar., c. 10 (1555).

[156] The JP handed in his pretrial examinations (of the accused and of the accuser and accusing witnesses) to the trial court. Sir Thomas Smith indicates that the accused's examination was routinely read in evidence at his trial. Smith, *De Republica* 113. A generally reliable manual about assize procedure dating from the early Restoration period says that the JPs routinely surrendered the pretrial examinations to the clerk of assizes, who studied each, "and if it be Evidence for the King, [the clerk] readeth it to the Jury." *The Clerk of Assize* 14 (London 1660) [hereafter *Clerk of Assize*] (This work is the predecessor of the manual cited as *Office of Clerk of Assize*, *supra* n. 54, published in 1682; the 1682 print was the second edition under that title; the first appeared in 1676.)

By the mid-eighteenth century the pretrial examinations were not being read at trial routinely, see Langbein, "Ryder" 82–3, partly as a consequence of the "best evidence" notion that preferred the oral evidence of the victim and the other accusing witnesses, whom the Marian statute required the JP to bind over to testify at trial. The pretrial examinations continued to be available at trial for impeachment and for exceptional circumstances, for example, to be read in the event that the victim or witness died before the trial. In the early nineteenth century MacNally was still emphasizing that "[t]he confession of the defendant himself, taken upon an examination, in writing, before justices of the peace, in pursuance of the statutes of Philip and Mary . . . is legal evidence against the party confessing." 1 Leonard MacNally, *The Rules of Evidence on Pleas of the Crown* 37 (Philadelphia 1811) (1st edn. Dublin 1802).

vacillation.[157] (In the argot of modern criminal justice, contemporaneous recording has been described as "freezing" the evidence, in the sense of keeping it fresh for trial.[158]) When our sources begin to supply fairly regular accounts of what happened at felony trials in London (from the end of the seventeenth century onward), we find incessant reports of cases in which the Marian pretrial examination, by eliciting a confession, proved to be decisive. For example, in the trial of Mary Everton, prosecuted at the Old Bailey in 1715 for the theft of clothing, "[t]he Prosecutor swore, That having lost his Goods, he suspected the Prisoner, and took her before Justice Ward, before whom she confessed it, and [she] did not deny it at her Trial, whereupon she was found Guilty . . . ."[159] William Wingfield, charged with theft from a dwelling house in 1721, "denied the Fact at the Bar, but his Confession before the Justice being read in Court, the Jury found him guilty . . . ."[160]

The Marian pretrial procedure also had the effect of circumscribing the autonomy of the private prosecutor in cases of felony.[161] The Marian JP who bound over the private prosecutor to testify at trial effectively stripped the victim of his discretion not to prosecute.[162] By injecting an element of official support and supervision into a system of prevailingly private prosecution, the Marian system organized a species of public prosecution for cases of serious crime.[163] But the Marian system mainly

---

[157] For example, Rowley Hanson, convicted at the Old Bailey in October 1755 for stealing a watch in a highway robbery, contended that the prosecutor gave him the watch as a bribe in exchange for Hanson's promise not to prosecute him for supposedly making homosexual advances to Hanson. It was proved that when examined by the JP, Hanson said he had never before seen the prosecutor. Hanson was convicted, sentenced to death, and executed. OBSP (Oct. 1755, #370), at 329, 330. Other instances in which the trial court explored discrepancies between the pretrial deposition and the trial testimony include Edward Flanagan et al., OBSP (July 1771, ##432–4), at 303, 305 (burglary); Joseph Bowman, OBSP (Feb. 1772, #299), at 136 (burglary); Richard Coleman, OBSP (Feb. 1788, #172), at 257 (burglary).

[158] Mirjan Damaska, "Evidentiary Barriers to Conviction and Two Models of Criminal Procedure: A Comparative Study," 121 Univ. Pennsylvania L. Rev. 506, 520 (1973).

[159] Mary Everton, OBSP (Feb. 1715), at 5 (theft of clothing valued above 20s.). The jury downvalued, finding her "Guilty to the value of 10d." Ibid. As a result, she was convicted of misdemeanor rather than felony, and she was sentenced to be whipped. Ibid. at 6. On the significance and prevalence of downvaluing, see infra, text at nn. 234–44.

[160] William Wingfield and Mary Harman, OBSP (Dec. 1721), at 1. The jury downvalued the goods, to 4s., 10d., which brought the offense beneath the 5s. ceiling on the clergyable amount, thus rescuing Wingfield from capital punishment. "The Evidence not reaching Harman, she was acquitted." Ibid.

[161] Discussed in Langbein, PCR 35; John H. Langbein, "Albion's Fatal Flaws," Past and Present (no. 98) 96, at 103–4 (Feb. 1983) (discussing the example of a prosecutor who defaulted, then petitioned to be excused from the £40 fine, on grounds of hardship).

[162] In Essex in the later eighteenth and early nineteenth centuries King found that about 10% of the persons bound over to prosecute at assizes and quarter sessions defaulted, on account of illness, death, or otherwise. Only about 10% of these, hence 1% of the total cohort, were fined. King, Crime 43–4.

[163] The theme of Langbein, "Prosecution," supra n. 148. For the court of quarter sessions in

helped perpetuate private prosecution. By limiting the role of the public officer to that of assisting the private prosecutor to build his case, the Marian statute channelled the English pretrial procedure away from Continental-style public prosecution. Centuries later the French observer Cottu still marvelled that the English authorities "make no efforts to obtain proofs of the crime, confiding its punishment entirely to the hatred or resentment of the injured party . . . ."[164]

The Marian system made the JP a partisan rather than a truth-seeker. The Marian statute directs the JP to assemble not the whole case, but only the prosecution case. The JP should bind over "all such . . . as do declare anything material to prove the . . . Felony . . . *against* such Prisoner . . . to appear at the next [sitting of the assize court] . . . to give evidence *against* [him]."[165] The one-sidedness of the Marian pretrial system endured through the eighteenth century. Barlow's JP manual, published in 1745, explains that although the JP ought not to suppress evidence favorable to the accused when such evidence is part of the statement of a prosecution witness, the JP ought not to "examine Witnesses that expressly come to prove the Offender's Innocence."[166] At an Old Bailey trial in 1787, when the judge asked a defense witness if she had given the same evidence at the pretrial examination, defense counsel (by then allowed) interjected: "The Magistrates at Bow Street never receive evidence for prisoners, only for prosecutors."[167]

The Marian system imparted a strong prosecutorial bias to English pretrial procedure. The JP's job was to help the accuser build the prosecution case, rather than to serve as a neutral investigator seeking all the evidence, inculpating and exculpating. This one-sidedness of the Marian system powerfully shaped the Anglo-American conception of the state's role in criminal investigation. "Magisterial questioning functioned as police interrogation does today; it offered the government an opportunity to get whatever information it could from an uncounseled, and frequently frightened and confused, defendant."[168] (Later in this chapter I discuss

the early seventeenth century, where lesser offenses were prosecuted, Cynthia Herrup depicts a similar overlay of private initiative reinforced by the local JPs and constables. Herrup, "Responses," *supra* n. 150.

[164] Cottu, *Administration* 37. He added (with evident disapproval): "Thus the business of prosecution, instead of being performed on the behalf of the public by an officer appointed expressly for the purpose, is committed entirely to the hands of the injured party, who, by this means, becomes the arbiter of the culprit's fate . . . ." Ibid. at 38.

[165] 2 & 3 Phil. & Mar., c. 10, § 2 (1555) (emphasis supplied).

[166] Theodore Barlow, *The Justice of Peace: A Treatise Containing the Power and Duty of that Magistrate* 190 (London 1745).

[167] Darcy [sic; sometimes D'Arcy] Wentworth, *OBSP* (Dec. 1787, #8), at 15, 19. For discussion of changes in pretrial investigation in eighteenth-century London, see *infra*, text at nn. 181–5; and Ch. 5, text at nn. 100–19.

[168] William J. Stuntz, "The Substantive Origins of Criminal Procedure" 105 *Yale L.J.* 393, 417 (1995) (characterizing English practice in the eighteenth century).

the question of why contemporaries were so insensitive to the seeming one-sidedness both of the Marian pretrial and of the altercation trial.)

The Marian pretrial procedure fed into the clerical establishment at the trial court. The victim, now bound over to prosecute, would consult with the JP's clerk (if he had one) or with the clerk of the trial court (assizes, Old Bailey, quarter sessions for lesser offenses) to have the charges framed as a bill of indictment.[169] The clerks charged fees for drafting indictments and for other paperwork. The system of private prosecution assimilated these costs to the model of civil procedure and charged them to the prosecutor, as though he were a civil plaintiff. The resulting disincentive to prosecute was a constant irritant to the authorities and commentators who wanted to make the criminal justice system more effective.[170] Only in the second half of the eighteenth century did the

[169] After the grand jury was seated, the clerk of assize was expected to call "the Parties, that are bound to prosecute by their Recognizances put in by the Justices [of the Peace], that they may get their bills made against the Prisoners, and be sworn unto them . . . and sent to the grand Jury with a Bailiff to give their evidence." *Clerk of Assize, supra* n. 156, at 6–7. Cockburn reports that "a majority of the indictments tried at assizes during [the period 1558–1625] were drafted in court by the Crown-side associate [i.e., one of the clerks of assize] or his clerk, on the instructions of individual prosecutors." Cockburn, "Introduction" 75. Working from quarter sessions sources for the next reign, Barnes found that indictments processed at that court, mostly misdemeanor, were usually drafted by an assistant to the clerk of the peace, sometimes working from Marian pretrial examinations when the offense in question had been serious enough to provoke a JP's investigation. Thomas G. Barnes, *The Clerk of the Peace in Caroline Somerset* 20 (1961). The clerks worked from collections of indictment forms that circulated in manuscript and from published form books, e.g., W. Stubbs and G. Talmash, *The Crown Circuit Companion: Containing . . . Useful Modern Precedents of Indictments* (London 1738).

[170] Sheppard wanted "a more easy way [to] be devised for Conviction, and Trial of offenders; and that it be without charge to the Prosecutors." Sheppard, *Balme, supra* n. 7, at 23. The Hale Commission recommended in 1653 an "allowance from the court" for the expenses of both prosecutor and witnesses, provided that their personal worth was less than £100. Hale Commission § 18, at 237, in 6 *A Collection of Scarce and Valuable Tracts* (Walter Scott ed.) (2nd edn. London 1809–15) (13 vols.) [hereafter *Somers Tracts*]. Regarding the Hale Commission and its proposals, see Donald Veall, *The Popular Movement for Law Reform: 1640–1660* (1970); M. Cotterell, "Interregnum Law Reform: The Hale Commission of 1652," 83 *English Historical Rev.* 689 (1968); G. B. Nourse, "Law Reform under the Commonwealth and Protectorate," 75 *Law Quarterly Rev.* 512 (1959).

Hale wrote in his treatise that it was "a great defect in this part of judicial administration, . . . that there is no power to allow witnesses their charges, whereby many times poor persons grow weary of attendance, or bear their own charges therein to their great hindrance and loss." 2 Hale, *HPC* 282. Henry Fielding, citing this passage from Hale, lamented that "the extreme poverty of the prosecutor" which "obstructs the prosecution of offenders." Henry Fielding, *An Enquiry into the Causes of the Late Increase of Robbers* (London 1751), in *An Enquiry into the Causes of the Late Increase of Robbers and Related Writings* 61, 157 (Malvin R. Zirker, ed) (1988) [hereafter Fielding, *Enquiry*]. Fielding regarded both the 2s. needed for the indictment and the expense of several days attendance at court, sometimes distant from home, to be hardships, and he favored public support. Ibid.

For discussion of costs in the seventeenth century, see J. A. Sharpe, "Enforcing the Law in the Seventeenth-Century English Village," in *Crime and the Law: The Social History of Crime in Western Europe since 1500*, at 97, 110–11 (1980). Regarding costs in misdemeanor prosecutions, see Robert B. Shoemaker, *Prosecution and Punishment: Petty Crime and the Law in London and Rural Middlesex, c.1660–1725*, at 140–2 (1991).

legislature begin to tinker with cost subsidies to lighten the burden on the prosecutor and supporting witnesses.[171]

A day or so before trial the grand jury would deliberate on whether to approve the prosecutor's bill. If the grand jury found it a "true bill", the accused was sent for trial by the petty jury. The prosecuting victim and other accusing witnesses would testify before the grand jury in support of the bill. The grand jury heard only accusing evidence.[172] Most bills of indictment were generated in the Marian pretrial procedure, but any citizen could appear and prefer a bill of indictment to the grand jury. The citizen prosecutor was not obliged to seek the pretrial assistance of the JP. Because the power to instigate charges belonged wholly to the private prosecutor, the system found it useful to maintain the grand jury as a filtering mechanism to dispose of groundless or insubstantial[173] prosecutions, sparing the defendant the peril and indignity of public trial in a transparently weak case.[174] For the years 1660–1800 Beattie found that the Surrey grand juries dismissed 11.5 percent of the bills of indictments for property offenses punishable by death and 17.3 percent of those brought for noncapital property offenses, 14.9 percent for murder, 27.4 percent for infanticide, 25.8 percent for wounding, 44.4 percent for rape.[175] Peter King reports that "between 1740 and 1805 at least one-seventh of the indictments brought before the grand jurors of Essex were dismissed . . ."[176] By serving this screening function, the grand jury survived the changes in demographics and governance in the later Middle Ages that had caused it to lose its original function as a jury of accusation, that is, as a panel that instituted criminal charges based on its own knowledge and investigation.[177]

---

[171] See supra n. 11.

[172] Discussed in Zachary Babington, Advice to Grand Jurors in Cases of Blood B2 (London 1677). The potential for abuse is emphasized in Hay, "Malicious Prosecution," supra n. 88, at 380–1.

[173] The question of the standard of proof appropriate for the grand jury to indict came into discussion in the later seventeenth century and remained contentious into the nineteenth century. See the valuable account in Barbara Shapiro, "Beyond Reasonable Doubt" and "Probable Cause": Historical Perspectives on the Anglo-American Law of Evidence 56 ff (1991) [hereafter Shapiro, BRD].

[174] The other safeguard against abusive private prosecutions was the tort of malicious prosecution, which was designed to deter the bringing of trumped-up prosecutions. See generally Hay, "Malicious Prosecution," supra n. 88.

[175] Beattie, Crime 402 and table 8.1 (assize and quarter sessions indictment files).

[176] King, Crime 231.

[177] It will be seen, infra nn. 181–5 and Ch. 5, text at nn. 101–19, that in the eighteenth century certain of the urban magistrates active in the London area began to exercise what amounted to pretrial dismissal powers over weak cases. This process of relocating the pretrial committal and dismissal power to the magistrates would intensify in the nineteenth century, rendering the grand jury obsolete and leading to its abolition in the twentieth century. "[T]he work of the grand jury became superfluous, for it merely duplicated the formal inquiry that was being conducted by the justices." Patrick Devlin, The Criminal Prosecution in England 8 (1958).

The JPs were mostly local gentlemen active in civic affairs.[178] They were commonly drawn from the higher social orders, typically gentry but not aristocracy. The JPs were, therefore, officers but not officials. They held crown appointments (in the commission of the peace for their county[179]), but they were not placemen or hirelings. JPs were substantial citizens who rendered unpaid parttime service in law enforcement and in other spheres of local government.[180] They were seldom lawyers, seldom legally trained. The office of magistrate was unpaid. The incentive to serve came from the JPs' interest in keeping local order and in reinforcing their stature in the community through the exercise of magistral authority.

It was a remarkable feature of the administration of justice in England that the responsibility for criminal investigation in cases of serious crime was lodged with these local amateurs. They brought local knowledge and local influence to their work, and they spared the crown the expense and administrative challenge of operating a professional magisterial or prosecutorial corps. But, as will be seen in Chapter 3, leaving the work of criminal investigation to the hit-or-miss efforts of amateur gentry entailed grievous shortcomings that, in the eighteenth century, would cause Anglo-American criminal procedure to turn down the path toward the lawyer-dominated trial.

The one-sidedness and amateurism of the Marian pretrial both presupposed and reinforced the centrality of oral public trial in English criminal procedure. The Marian JP was a local gentleman who helped a private accuser organize a private prosecution. By remitting the pretrial investigation to such persons rather than, as on the Continent, developing a reliable corps of professional magistrates capable of conducting a thorough investigation into the events, the Marian system was unable to resolve important matters in the pretrial. Into the eighteenth century the JPs had

---

[178] On the composition of the magistracy, see J. H. Gleason, *The Justices of the Peace in England: 1558 to 1640* (1969) [hereafter Gleason, *Justices*]; Norma Landau, *The Justices of the Peace: 1679–1760* (1984).

[179] Holdsworth reprints the full text of the commission of the peace as of the mid-eighteenth century. 1 William Holdsworth, *A History of English Law* 670–1 (1922–66) (16 vols.) [hereafter Holdsworth, *HEL*].

[180] In addition to the prosecutorial role in cases of felony, the JP's office had a further dimension, which was "adjudicative and legislative. He was empowered, usually on condition that he be joined by a minimum number of his fellow JPs for the county (a number that varied with the function), to adjudicate in a variety of matters that we would today regard as misdemeanor, local administration, and economic regulation. The main adjudicative forum was the court of quarter sessions, generally composed of all the JPs of the county. The JPs also sat in smaller panels that met more frequently for the minutiae of licensing orders and petty offenses." Langbein, "Ryder" 56. See generally John P. Dawson, *A History of Lay Judges* 136–45 (1960); Gleason, *Justices, supra* n. 178, at 96–122; Webbs, Parish, *supra* n. 132, at 294–305, 319–446.

no power to dismiss felony charges for insufficiency of the evidence.[181] It followed that virtually all decision-making had to be left for the convening of the two juries at or just before the sitting of the trial court. In the English system of criminal procedure, no systematic duty to search out the truth was assigned in the pretrial. One result was that an unjust accusation could occasion severe hardship in the form of harsh and lengthy pretrial detention. What passed for truth in English criminal procedure would have to emerge at trial, from the altercation of citizen accusers and citizen accused. The JP's job was to identify these persons and to compel their appearance at the trial court.

In London in the 1730s and in Middlesex by the 1750s and probably before, certain particularly authoritative JPs[182] began exercising some dismissal powers, especially for petty theft,[183] and then for more serious crime[184] in circumstances discussed below in Chapter 5.[185]

---

[181] Burn's JP manual, which became the dominant work of its sort in the second half of the eighteenth century, says: "If a felony is committed, and one is brought before a justice upon suspicion thereof, and the justice finds upon examination that the prisoner is not guilty, yet the justice shall not discharge him, but he must either be bailed or committed; for it is not fit that a man once arrested and charged with felony, or suspicion thereof, should be delivered upon any man's discretion, without further trial." Richard Burn, *The Justice of the Peace and Parish Officer* 207 (3rd edn. London 1756) (1st edn. 1755) [hereafter Burn, *JP*]. Burn cites Dalton's JP manual, at ch. 164, probably intending to refer to the passage in which Dalton, discussing homicide, advises that even in a case in which the examining JP thinks that the death was accidental or a suicide, it is "safest" for the JP "to commit the offender to Prison, or at least to join with some other [JP] in the Bailment of [the accused], (if the cause will suffer it) to the end the party may be discharged by a lawful Trial." Michael Dalton, *The Countrey Justice* 409 (London 1682 edn.). From its first edition, Dalton's manual emphasized the JP's lack of power to discharge. "[W]here any Felony be committed, and one is brought before the Justice of Peace upon suspicion thereof," the JP should commit the accused to stand trial, "though it shall appear to the Justice that the Prisoner is not guilty thereof. For it is not fit that a man once arrested and charged with Felony (or suspicion thereof) should be delivered by any man's Discretion, without further trial." Dalton, *Justice, supra* n. 132, at 260; see also ibid. at 40. Hale accords: JPs "cannot deliver a person by proclamation, as justices of gaol delivery may," but only on verdict. 2 Hale, *HPC* 46. The point is discussed in Langbein, *PCR* 7–8. Barbara Shapiro contends that the JPs must have exercised pretrial dismissal powers even in the sixteenth and seventeenth centuries; Shapiro, *BRD, supra* n. 173, at 151 ff., esp. 160, 162–3, but she does not offer evidence.

[182] The so-called "court JP" for Middlesex and his City equivalent, the "sitting alderman," whose work is discussed *infra* in Ch. 3, text at nn. 248, 281, and Ch. 5, text at nn. 100–7.

[183] See Beattie, *Crime* 268–81; Beattie, *Policing* 106–7; King, *Crime* 88.

[184] An instance evidenced in the *Sessions Papers*: In a case of alleged highway robbery tried at the Old Bailey in 1740, the JP testified that when the victim "came to him . . . he thought her a Person not fit to be believed, and would not take her Information." Patrick King and Patrick Branegan, *OBSP* (Sept. 1740, 372–3), at 213.

I have elsewhere reported that in the 1750s Henry Fielding, in his role as "Court JP" for Middlesex (discussed in Ch. 3 *infra*) appears to have been "discharging cases that would not stand up if sent on for trial, and in this respect he was the forerunner of the judicialized pretrial committal officer of the nineteenth century. Some of Fielding's discharges took the form of having the prosecutor withdraw the charge, which happily avoided the delicate question of whether JPs had the legal authority to dismiss felony charges, however ill founded." Langbein, "Ryder" 63 (footnotes omitted). In other cases, he seems to have

E. The "Accused Speaks" Trial

The one-sided Marian pretrial procedure delivered the accused to the courtroom. There he would confront the victim and other accusing witnesses, whom the JP had bound over to appear and testify against him at the oral public trial. The purpose of the altercation trial was to give the accused the opportunity to respond to this accusing evidence, hence our image of the "accused speaks" trial. I have emphasized that the rationale for the rule against defense counsel was to pressure the accused to serve as an informational resource at trial. So long as the accused lacked trial counsel, there was scarcely any possibility of distinguishing his roles as defender and as (unsworn) witness. Requiring him to conduct his own defense meant that he would need to respond in person to the charges and the evidence against him.

The denial of defense counsel was, however, only one of a number of attributes of early modern criminal procedure that put pressure on the accused to speak in his own defense. Various rules and practices reviewed below restricted the defendant's ability to construct an effective defense based on supporting witnesses. By impeding the accused's ability to locate and to summon defense witnesses, and by weakening the credibility of defense witnesses, the procedure kept the trial focused on what the accused could say. And by collapsing the sentencing decision into the proceeding for determining guilt, the trial procedure placed the accused under further pressure to speak in his own defense.

1. Pretrial Detention

The Marian procedure presupposed the routine use of pretrial detention[185]

dismissed without that stratagem. Thus, in January 1752 an issue of his paper, the *Covent Garden Journal*, reported that "on Friday and Saturday last [Fielding was] engaged above Twenty Hours in taking Depositions concerning [a murder in Essex], when a Person who had been suspected of being privy, at least, to the Murder, made his Innocence appear so evident, that he was very honorably discharged." *Covent Garden Journal* (28 Jan. 1752), in *The Covent Garden Journal and a Plan of the Universal Register Office* 402 (Bertrand A. Goldgar ed.) (1988). But Fielding was uneasy about his authority. The next month he expressed his irritation that "[b]y the Law of England, as it now stands, if a Larceny be absolutely committed, however slight the Suspicion be against the accused, the Justice of Peace is obliged in strictness to commit the Party; especially if he have not Sureties for his Appearance to answer the Charge. Nor will the trifling Value of the Thing stolen, nor any Circumstance of Mitigation justify his discharging the Prisoner. Nay Mr. Dalton says, that where the Felony is proved to have been done, should the Party accused appear to a Demonstration innocent, the Justice cannot discharge him, but must commit or bail. And however absurd this Opinion may appear, my Lord Hale hath thought fit to embrace and transcribe it in his History of the Pleas of the Crown." *Covent Garden Journal* (1752), ibid. at 409–10, discussed in Langbein, "Ryder" 63 n. 240. (The references to Dalton and Hale that Fielding would have had in mind are those cited *supra* n. 181.)   [185] *Infra* Ch. 5, text at nn. 100–19.

for persons accused of felony. The statute of 1555 that organized the procedure became known as the Marian committal statute, because it directed the JP to conduct his examination "before he . . . shall commit or send such Prisoner to Ward . . . ."[186] The JPs had some authority to authorize pretrial release under bail,[187] but not when a person accused of felony was seriously suspect.[188] The incessant use of the term "prisoner," even in official sources,[189] to describe any felony defendant underscores the expectation that the accused would be jailed until trial.

Because the provincial trial courts (assizes) sat only twice a year, in the spring and late summer, it was possible for an accused who was committed to pretrial detention just after the summer assizes to spend eight and a half months in jail awaiting the next sitting of the court.[190] The conditions of pretrial confinement were appalling; severe overcrowding and malnutrition were commonplace. Cockburn has compiled astonishing data showing that during the period from 1558 to 1625 at least 1,291 prisoners died in the jails of the Home Circuit (the five counties surrounding London).[191] Some died of starvation, most died from "what was known as 'gaol fever,' which was a particularly virulent form of typhus carried by lice and spread by contact and thus at its worst in crowded conditions."[192] An outbreak in the London jail of Newgate, adjacent to the Old Bailey, in April 1750 spread to the court and (according to a contemporary report) killed two judges, various court staff, the Lord Mayor of London, and "[o]f less note, a Gentleman of the Bar, two or three Students . . . and about Forty other Persons, whom business or curiosity had brought thither."[193] Another outbreak in Newgate reported in March 1755 killed a fifth of the persons awaiting trial.[194] These episodes occurred despite the peculiar architecture[195] of the eighteenth-century Old Bailey, which was designed as a partially open-air amphitheatre (see Fig. 1.1), probably in order to reduce the risk of contagion as well as to spare the court from the odor of the prisoners.

---

[186] 2 & 3 Phil. & Mar, c. 10 (1555).

[187] Discussed in Langbein, *PCR* 6–15; Langbein, "Prosecution," *supra* n. 148, at 320–1; Beattie, *Crime* 281–3.

[188] Beattie, *Crime* 282.

[189] E.g., Prisoner's Counsel Act, 6 & 7 Wil. 4, c. 114 (1836), extending the right to full defense of counsel to persons accused of felony.

[190] Beattie, *Crime* 309, refers to "examples every year of men and women committed within a few days or weeks of the conclusion of the Summer assizes who had to wait in jail through the winter before their trials came on."

[191] Cockburn, "Introduction" 36, 38–9.

[192] Beattie, *Crime* 301; regarding jail conditions, see ibid. at 298–309.

[193] Foster, *Crown Law* 75.

[194] 25 *Gentleman's Magazine* 135 (Mar. 1755) (eleven of fifty reported killed).

[195] The architectural history of this structure is discussed in Gerald Howson, *Thief-Taker General: The Rise and Fall of Jonathan Wild* 315–16 (1970).

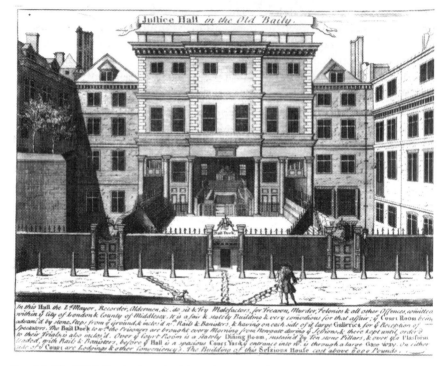

FIG. 1.1. *The Old Bailey in the early eighteenth century.* This partially open-air structure was meant to protect the court from the foul odor and risk of disease emanating from the prisoners. The building was closed up with sashes in 1736 and replaced in 1774.

Pretrial detention affected defensive opportunity in two ways. Jail conditions were physically disabling. Beattie's account, already noticed, of the ineptness that many felony defendants displayed when attempting to defend themselves at trial, links their predicament in part to the horrific jail conditions. "[M]en not used to speaking in public who suddenly found themselves thrust into the limelight before an audience in an unfamiliar setting—and who were for the most part dirty, underfed, and surely often ill—did not usually cross-examine vigorously or challenge the evidence presented against them."[196] The degradation and distraction of confinement continued into the courtroom; defendants were kept in leg irons until called for trial.[197]

The isolation of pretrial detention also interfered with the accused's ability to prepare a defense. Locked away without disclosure of the

---

[196] Beattie, *Crime* 350–1.

[197] E.g., John Waite, *OBSP* (Feb. 1743, #162), at 102 (theft) (court refused his request to have leg irons removed while awaiting his turn for trial).

precise charges against him,[198] or of the nature of the prosecution evidence, the accused had considerable difficulty locating defense witnesses or otherwise preparing to defend himself. Even in State Trials, in which defendants of the gentle classes usually received rather better treatment in pretrial detention (in part because they could afford to pay the jailer for it), we find constant lament about how confinement hindered preparation for trial.[199] The harder it was for the criminal accused to obtain defense witnesses, the more he was constrained to speak from his own knowledge about the charges and the evidence against him.

2. Restrictions on Defense Witnesses

In the age of the altercation trial, prosecution witnesses were privileged over defense witnesses in two ways. First, whereas the prosecution had compulsory process to require the appearance of its witnesses, the accused did not. That is, the Marian JP issued orders binding over the victim and the material accusing witnesses to appear at trial and testify, but there was no comparable means of compelling the participation of defense witnesses. Second, because prosecution witnesses testified on oath,[200] their testimony benefited from the enhanced credibility of

[198] As indicated above, *supra*, text at n. 88, the defendant was forbidden to have a copy of the indictment that specified the charges against him, not only in advance of trial, but even at trial. A clerk translated the indictment (from the Latin) to the defendant at the arraignment. The Treason Trials Act of 1696 abrogated the rule denying the accused the text of the indictment, but only for cases of treason. 7 & 8 Wil. 3, c. 3, §§ 1, 9, discussed *infra*, Ch. 2, text at nn. 125–34. For ordinary felony cases, the rule withholding the indictment endured, see, e.g., 2 Hawkins, *PC* 402, although it interfered with the defendant's ability to prepare his defense with precision. For discussion of the practice into the early nineteenth century, see Hay, "Malicious Prosecution," *supra* n. 88, at 343, 352.
    Another nondisclosure practice that the Treason Trials Act of 1696 eliminated, but only for cases of treason, was nondisclosure of the venire, that is, of the list of prospective jurors. 7 & 8 Wil. 3, c. 3, § 7. The reform was meant to facilitate the exercise of the defendant's challenge rights. In cases of ordinary felony challenge rights were virtually never exercised. Langbein, "CTBL" 275–6; Beattie, *Crime* 340. Without counsel and with such restricted opportunity for defensive preparation, such as investigating potential jurors, it is not surprising that challenge rights were of little use. I suspect that the exercise of challenge rights by the ordinary felony defendant was regarded as an affront to the challenged jurors, who were commonly the social superiors of the accused, and that the defendant understood that he ought not to risk offending the remaining jurors by striking some of their peers.
[199] E.g., *R. v. Nicholas Throckmorton*, 1 *St. Tr.* 869, 872 ("my grievous imprisonment"); ibid. at 886 ("I have been in close prison these 58 days"); *R. v. Edward Fitzharris*, 8 *St. Tr.* 243, 328 (K.B. 1681); *R. v. Stephen College*, 8 *St. Tr.* 549, 569 (1681) ("I have been kept a close prisoner in the Tower ever since I was taken: I was all along unacquainted with what was charged upon me. I knew not what was sworn against me, not the persons that did swear it against me, and therefore I am wholly ignorant of the matter").
[200] In some cases the requirement that prosecution witnesses be sworn worked to the advantage of the accused, particularly in cases of rape in which the victim was disqualified from testifying on account of infancy. For instances of acquittals in which the child victim was unable to testify, see, e.g., William Kick, *OBSP* (May–Jun. 1754, #341), at 215; Thomas

having been sworn. Defense witnesses, by contrast, were forbidden to be sworn.

The rule forbidding defense witnesses to testify on oath was criticized at least from the time of Coke, who contended in the *Third Institute* that the prohibition lacked authority.[201] During the Interregnum, the Hale Commission proposed legislation to overcome it[202] but without effect. Among the reforms of the Treason Trials Act of 1696 was the defendant's right to have witnesses testify on oath.[203] An Act of 1702 extended that reform to cases of felony, probably not for the purpose of enhancing the defensive posture of defendants, but in order to expose defense witnesses to prosecution for perjury.[204]

After 1702, although defense witnesses testified on oath, the defendant continued to be disqualified from testifying, ostensibly to spare him from being put to the choice of defending himself and damning his soul by committing the sin of perjury.[205] Thus, even though the central purpose of the criminal trial was to hear the accused speak, he spoke unsworn. In England this disqualification endured until 1898;[206] it was lifted a few

---

Crosby, *OBSP* (Dec. 1757, #17), at 8, 9 ("The Child being but nine years old, and not being examined upon oath, he was acquitted . . ."). Child rape cases are further discussed in Ch. 4 *infra*, text at n. 102. Cases involving Quaker accusers could have the same outcome, e.g., Francis Talbot, *OBSP* (Jan. 1772, #181), at 99 (burglary) ("The prisoner was taken in the fact, but the constable who apprehended him being a Quaker, and refusing to take an oath, he was acquitted"); Elizabeth Williams, *OBSP* (Sept. 1776, #713), at 421 (prosecutor, "one of the people called Quakers . . . would not take the oath, and his affirmation could not be admitted").

[201] "[W]e never read in any Act of Parliament, ancient Author, Book case, or Record, that in Criminal cases the party accused should not have witnesses sworn for him; and therefore there is not so much as *scintilla juris* against it . . . . And when the fault is denied, truth cannot appear without witnesses." Coke, *Third Institute* 79. Coke pointed with approval to an Act that provided for the trial in England of felonies committed across the Scottish border and allowed defense witnesses to be examined on oath "for the better information of the consciences of the Jury and Justice." Ibid., citing 4 Jas. 1, c. 1, § 6 (1606). The Act is discussed in Michael R. T. Macnair, *The Law of Proof in Early Modern Equity* 208–9 (1999), drawing on *The Parliamentary Diary of Robert Bowyer: 1606–7*, at 300–64 (David H. Willson ed.) (1931); and in George Fisher, "The Jury's Rise as Lie Detector," 107 *Yale L.J.* 575, 609–15 (1998) [hereafter Fisher, "Jury"].

[202] "[A]ny credible witnesses produced by the prisoner shall hereafter deliver their testimonies upon oath." *Several Draughts of Acts* (1653), 6 *Somers Tracts, supra* n. 170, at 177, 234 ("Touching Criminal Causes"), § 6 at 235.

[203] 1696 Act, § 1.

[204] 1 Anne, Stat. 2, c. 9, § 3 (1702), requiring defense witnesses to be sworn and declaring that such witnesses, "if convicted of any wilful Perjury in such Evidence, shall suffer all the Punishments" then in effect for perjury. Ibid. Beattie observes that this measure was part of an omnibus Act, doubtless government-inspired, whose title evidences its predominantly repressive purpose: "An Act for punishing of accessories to felonies, and receivers of stolen goods, and to prevent the wilful burning and destroying of ships." Beattie, *Policing* 319, quoting the title of the Act.

[205] See 2 Wigmore, *Evidence* § 576, at 686–93.

[206] Criminal Evidence Act, 61 & 62 Vict., c. 6 (1898).

decades earlier in most American states,[207] although it endured in the state of Georgia until 1961.[208]

The seventeenth century also saw a change in attitude toward the grant of compulsory process for defense witnesses. As late as 1649 John Lilburn was refused his request for "subpoenas" for defense witnesses, whom he complained "will not come in without compulsion."[209] At the arraignment of John Twyn, a printer charged in 1663 with publishing a treasonable book,[210] we find the bench accommodating such requests. Chief Justice Hyde told Twyn: "If you have any witnesses on your part, let's know their names, we will take care they shall come in."[211] At the arraignment of Fitzharris for treason in 1681, the defendant was denied his request to have access to a solicitor to help him send for witnesses, on the ground that he needed no solicitor to have his witnesses summoned. Fitzharris then requested "a rule of court to make my witnesses appear," which was granted.[212]

For treason cases, the 1696 Act removed the matter from judicial discretion by expressly granting compulsory process to defendants.[213] Felony defendants were placed on an equal footing in the eighteenth century, when the courts construed the Act of 1702, which authorized defense witnesses to testify on oath in felony cases, as impliedly authorizing compulsory process.[214]

Until these reforms at the end of the seventeenth and the beginning of the eighteenth centuries, however, the restrictions on oath and compulsory process diminished the availability and the effectiveness of defense witnesses. Impeding defense witnesses increased the burden on the defendant to defend on his own, hence to speak from his own knowledge about the charges and the evidence against him.

3. Excluding Defense Witnesses?

The restrictions on defense witnesses were real enough, but it is important

[207] See the intriguing suggestion in Fisher, "Jury," *supra* n. 201, at 662–97, that the American development was driven by sectional tensions about race relations.
[208] *Ferguson v. Georgia*, 365 U.S. 570 (1961).
[209] *R. v. John Lilburn*, 4 St. Tr. 1270, 1312 (1649) (treason).
[210] *R. v. John Twyn*, 6 St. Tr. 513 (O.B. 1663). Among its crimes, the book was alleged to have argued "that the supreme magistrate is accountable to the people," and still more seriously, that the people should revolt and kill the King. Ibid. at 513 n.
[211] Ibid. at 516.
[212] *R. v. Edward Fitzharris*, 8 St. Tr. 243, 330 (K.B. 1681). Other aspects of the court's conduct of the case, discussed *infra* in Ch. 2, figured among the grievances that led to the Treason Trials Act of 1696.
[213] 1696 Act, §§ 1, 7, discussed *infra* Ch. 2.
[214] 2 Hawkins, *PC* 434–5; for discussion, see Peter Westen, The Compulsory Process Clause, 73 *Michigan L. Rev.* 71, 90 n. 73 (1974).

not to exaggerate them. In some accounts of early modern criminal procedure, it is said that there was a rule forbidding defense witnesses.[215] There was not. The claim that there was such a rule rests upon the evidence of two incidents reported in sixteenth-century sources and reprinted in the *State Trials*. In the trials of Throckmorton in 1554[216] and Udall in 1590,[217] the reports (both suspect in their reliability[218]) depict the judges refusing each defendant's request to hear witnesses who were present and willing to testify. In the report of Throckmorton's trial the bench gives no reason for refusing his proffered witness, John Fitzwilliams. "Go you ways, Fitzwilliams," one of the trial judges tells him, "the court hath nothing to do with you; peradventure you would not be so ready in a good cause."[219] The judge who presided at Udall's trial is said to have invoked the dignity of the sovereign in refusing Udall's witnesses. "[T]he witnesses offering themselves to be heard, were answered, that because their Witness was against the queen's majesty, they could not be heard."[220]

---

[215] Blackstone thought there was, and he was so embarrassed about it that he blamed it on the Europeans. 4 Blackstone, *Commentaries* 352 (rule "derived from the civil law"). Stephen and Thayer also thought that there had been a rule against defense witnesses. 1 Stephen, *History* 350; Thayer, *Evidence* 157. Holdsworth followed them; see 5 Holdsworth, *HEL* 192. Recently, to the same effect, see Fisher, "Jury," *supra* n. 201, at 603 ("we may safely [conclude] . . . that the defendant could call no witnesses").

[216] *R. v. Nicholas Throckmorton*, 1 *St. Tr.* 869, 884–5. The *State Trials* report comes from the Elizabethan chronicle, Raphael Holinshed, *The Third Volume of Chronicles . . . to the Yeare 1586*, at 1104–17 (London 1587). Blackstone emphasized a passage in Holinshed in which Throckmorton supposedly argued that Queen Mary, "when she appointed Sir Richard Morgan chief justice of the common pleas [in 1553], . . . enjoined him, 'that notwithstanding the old error, which did not admit any witness to speak, or any other matter to be heard, in favor of the adversary, her majesty being party, her highness' pleasure was, that whatsoever could be brought in favor of the subject should be admitted to be heard . . . .' " 4 Blackstone, *Commentaries* 352–3, quoting Holinshed, *supra*, at 1112, reproduced as 1 *St. Tr.* at 887–8. I think this legend is apocryphal. Holinshed does not disclose where he obtained this information about supposed events that occurred decades before he wrote. It is unlikely that the monarch would have taken an interest in such a detail of courtroom practice, or that if she had, she would have dealt with it by issuing a ukase on a ceremonial occasion, as opposed to conveying her views to the judges circumspectly. Neither in subsequent practice nor in the legal authorities can we trace this supposed royal decree.

[217] *R. v. John Udall*, 1 *St. Tr.* 1271, 1281, 1304 (Croydon Assizes 1590) (charged with libelling the Queen).

[218] The report of Udall's trial, being attributed to the defendant ("Wrote by Himself"), 1 *St. Tr.* at 1271–2, is particularly problematic. On the defects of the early *State Trial* reports, see G. Kitson Clark, *The Critical Historian* 92–114 (1967). Of the report of Throckmorton's trial, Clark observes that it "seems to slanted in favor of Sir Nicholas who is credited in it with many telling legal points and much piety of expression . . . ." Ibid. at 94. Furthermore, because "[t]he trial took place sixty or seventy years before any practicable system of shorthand was available," the verbatim narrative must have entailed "a good deal of reconstruction . . . ." Ibid. at 94–5. Annabel Patterson presents reasons for thinking that the report may have been the product of notes made by one or more observers, which were thereafter enriched from the notes that Throckmorton had taken to prepare for his own defense. Annabel Patterson, *Reading Holinshed's Chronicles* 164 (1994).

[219] 1 *St. Tr.* at 885.   [220] 1 *St. Tr.* at 1281.

These two episodes, even if accurately reported, do not in my view justify inferring that a rule against defense witnesses had formed in early modern criminal procedure. Had so important a point of practice as this supposed prohibition been in effect, it would have been evidenced in the legal literature. The same practice manuals (Staunford, Pulton, Coke) that expound the rule against defense counsel would also have told us about any rule against defense witnesses. Yet Coke, it will be recalled, gives us a critique of the rule forbidding defense witnesses to testify upon oath,[221] an argument that would have been pointless if those witnesses could not be heard in any event.

I am aware of no evidence that a rule against defense witnesses was ever applied in a trial for ordinary felony. The trials of Throckmorton and Udall were State Trials, the former for treason, the latter for libelling the queen. Supposing the exclusions reported in those trials actually to have occurred, the question would remain whether they evidence a rule of excluding defense witnesses. Recall that in the major State Trials there had been an extensive pretrial investigation conducted by the Privy Council and the law officers of the crown. The judges' hostility to defense witnesses popping up for the first time at the trial stage may reflect the view that the accused ought to have produced defense witnesses at the Concilliar pretrial, where their evidence could have been investigated. By contrast, in cases of ordinary felony, because the amateur Marian pretrial investigation was not designed to ventilate defensive evidence, trial was where the accused was expected to initiate the consideration of such evidence.

The exclusion of defense witnesses in the trials of Throckmorton and Udall also reminds us that the discretion of the trial bench over the conduct of criminal trials was quite unfettered in Elizabethan times. If a bullying trial judge, cowering under the glare of crown oversight, excluded a defense witness from a political trial, the defendant had no remedy. (Below in Chapter 2, discussing seventeenth-century treason trials, I shall have more to say about the pressures that the crown brought to bear on the bench in treason trials, until judicial independence was secured in the eighteenth century.)

We have no reported instance of defense witnesses being refused audience after the supposed events in Udall's trial in 1598. If the judges had been exercising a discretion to exclude defense witnesses, which I doubt, they would soon have learned that the practice was counterproductive, because it risked offending trial jurors. According to the report in the trial of Throckmorton, the defendant called the jury's attention to the unfairness of the court's excluding his witness: "Since this gentleman's

---

[221] Coke, *Third Institute* 79, discussed *supra* n. 201.

Declaration may not be admitted, I trust you of the Jury can perceive, it was not for any thing he had to say against me; but contrariwise . . . it was feared he would speak for me."[222] Throckmorton was acquitted.

By the seventeenth century[223] the sources evidence the opposite practice. Defense witnesses were routinely heard. Dalton's influential JP manual, first published in 1618, says that assize judges "will often hear Witnesses and Evidence which goeth to the clearing and acquittal of the Prisoner, yet [the judges] will not take [it] upon oath, but do leave such Testimony and Evidence to the Jury to give credit to or think thereof, as they shall see and find cause."[224] At a felony prosecution tried in 1632, "divers witnesses were produced by the defendant which were heard, without oath."[225] The diary of Henry Townsend, a Worcestershire JP active in the 1660s, mentions instances in which assize judges heard defense witnesses.[226] Indeed, recent scholarship has turned up some indications that defense character witnesses were being heard at a much earlier time, in trials of the early fourteenth century.[227]

Accordingly, in assessing the burdens under which the accused labored at trial, we should not exaggerate a situation whose reality was bleak enough. Until the later seventeenth century the defendant could not compel the testimony of unwilling witnesses, and until the Treason Trials Act of 1696 and the legislation of 1702, he could not have his witnesses sworn, but there was never a rule forbidding the court to hear defense witnesses.

4. The Burden of Proof Inchoate

The beyond-reasonable-doubt standard of proof for criminal adjudication was not precisely articulated in English law until the last quarter of the eighteenth century,[228] although there had long been intimations that

---

[222] 1 *St. Tr.* at 885.

[223] Thayer thought there had been a change in attitude towards defense witnesses, evidenced in an Act of 1589, which made it a felony to "embezzle" the Queen's armor and ordinance. The Act authorized the accused to defend such a charge by lawful proofs, including witnesses. Thayer, *Evidence* 159 n., citing 31 Eliz. 1, c. 4 (1589).

[224] Dalton, *Justice, supra* n. 132, at 412 (1619 edn.).

[225] *Tyndal's Case*, Cro. Car. 291, 292, 79 *Eng. Rep.* 855, 856 (K.B. 1633), cited by Thayer, *Evidence* 159 n.

[226] "The Judges usually hear evidence on the behalf of the prisoner, but not upon oath, yet with a charge to speak the truth before God as upon oath; so Sir Robert Hyde at Worcester Assizes, 22 August 1661 in Hurdman's case, and Sir Waddam Windham, 5 March 1662; and then leave the same to the Jury." "Henry Townshend's 'Notes of the Office of a Justice of Peace,' 1661–3" (R. D. Hunt ed.) in *Miscellany II*, at 68, 95 (1967) (Worcestershire Historical Society, NS, vol. 5.).

[227] Anthony Musson, *Public Order and Law Enforcement: The Local Administration of Criminal Justice, 1294–1350*, at 205 (1996).

[228] Discussed *infra* Ch. 5, text at nn. 35–63.

doubt should be resolved in favor of the criminal defendant. In Chapter 5 of this book I review evidence about the formulation of the beyond-reasonable-doubt standard in the last decades of the eighteenth century. The present point is that in earlier times the imprecision of the standard of proof was another of the many factors that put pressure on the accused to speak in his own defense about his knowledge of the charges and the events. Stephen remarked: "When the prisoner had to speak for himself, he . . . could not, without a tacit admission of guilt, insist on the inconclusiveness of the evidence against him, and on its consistency with his innocence. The jury expected from him a clear explanation of the case against him; and if he could not give it, they convicted him."[229] Thus, the defendant who was denied counsel to probe the prosecution case also lacked the protection of the modern judicial instruction on the standard of proof, which encourages jurors to probe the prosecution case. As Beattie observes of the eighteenth-century sources, "if any assumption was made in court about the prisoner himself, it was not that he was innocent until the case against him was proved beyond a reasonable doubt, but that if he *were* innocent he ought to be able to demonstrate it for the jury by the quality and character of his reply to the prosecutor's evidence."[230] For example, a group of accused horse thieves tried at the Old Bailey in 1684, "not being able to bring any proof, where they were at the time the Robbery was Committed . . . were found guilty . . . ."[231] Beattie points to the case of a defendant being tried for larceny in Surrey in 1739, who responded to the prosecution case by saying, "I am no thief." The trial judge replied: "You must prove that."[232] This was, Beattie remarks, "plainly the situation that every prisoner found himself in."[233]

5. Trial as a Sentencing Proceeding

The sentencing practices of the later seventeenth and eighteenth centuries were a powerful source of pressure on the defendant to speak at his trial. Our modern expectation is that sentencing will occur in a separate post-verdict phase, after the trial has determined guilt. Furthermore, in jury-tried cases, we expect the judge, not the jury, to exercise whatever sentencing discretion the law might bestow. In early modern times, however, these divisions of function in sentencing matters between trial and post-trial, and between jury and judge, were less distinct. The trial jury exercised an important role in what was functionally the choice of

---

[229] James F. Stephen, *A General View of the Criminal Law of England* 194–5 (London 1863) [hereafter Stephen, *General View*].
[230] Beattie, *Crime* 341 (emphasis original).
[231] James Watts *et al., OBSP* (Dec. 1684), at 5.
[232] Durham, *SAP* (Lent 1739), at 20, cited by Beattie, *Crime* 349.   [233] Ibid.

sanction, through its power to manipulate the verdict by convicting on a charge that carried a lesser penalty. (A vestige of this power to mitigate the sentence survives in modern practice, when the jury convicts of a lesser included offense, or when it convicts on fewer than all the counts that are charged and proved.)

The practice of juries convicting only of a lesser charge, or "downvaluing" stolen goods in order to make the offense less serious,[234] and especially in order to mitigate against the death penalty, was immortalized in Blackstone's phrase as "pious perjury."[235] The historical literature has settled on the term "partial verdict" to describe these verdicts that convicted the defendant but reduced the sanction.

In the Elizabethan-Jacobean period partial verdicts were relatively uncommon.[236] It was the development of alternatives to the death penalty in the eighteenth century, especially the system of transportation to the New World for a term of penal servitude,[237] that allowed partial verdicts to burgeon. Transportation became the sanction for offenses that fell within the rubric of benefit of clergy,[238] giving the jury an effective choice between convicting an offender in a manner that would lead to the imposition of capital punishment or in a way that would result in transportation.[239] For example, if the jury convicted a defendant of burglary, the punishment was death; but if, on the same facts, the jury convicted of the clergyable offense of mere theft, the convict would be transported. Not all partial verdicts involved transportation: When the jury valued stolen goods at less than a shilling (invariably at 10d.), the offence became petty rather than grand larceny, for which the common sanction was whipping.[240] In a sample of London cases from the Old Bailey in the 1750s I

---

[234] Discussed in Beattie, *Crime* 419–30; Beattie, *Policing* 303–12, 339–46, 435–48; Langbein, "Ryder" 47–55; King, *Crime* 231–7; see also 1 Radzinowicz, *History* 83–106, 138–64.

[235] 4 Blackstone, *Commentaries* 239.

[236] Cockburn, "Introduction" 114 (5% of verdicts were partial). Precursors of this jury-operated system of mitigation can be traced back into the medieval common law. Green, *Verdict* 97–102.

[237] The Transportation Act, 4 Geo., c. 11 (1718), was the decisive step. On the development of transportation and its ramifications upon the criminal justice system, see Beattie, *Crime* 500–19, 538–48, 592–601, 619–21; Beattie, *Policing* 427–48.

[238] For a capsule history of benefit of clergy, see Langbein, "Ryder" 37–41.

[239] Beattie writes: "The scope for discretion in the administration of the law had arisen because the law was dominated by capital punishment; yet it was widely accepted that not every prisoner charged with a capital offense or even convicted of a capital offense would in fact be hanged. A large part of the business of administering the so-called Bloody Code was the selection of those who were to be hanged as examples. And in that selection, key roles were played by the jury, through its power to reduce a capital to a noncapital charge, and by the judge, through his right to reprieve condemned offenders and recommend them for a royal pardon." Beattie, "Scales" 231. The clemency system and its bearing on the "accused speaks" trial is discussed *infra*, text at nn. 245–9; *infra* Ch. 5, text at nn. 348–52.

[240] For example, in the case of a woman charged with theft of clothing from her lodging house, which the indictment valued at several pounds, "[t]he Prisoner did as good as

found that the juries returned partial verdicts in nearly a quarter of the cases.[241] For a few offenses, like picking pockets, the juries all but invariably downvalued, expressing a social consensus that the capital sanction was virtually never appropriate.[242] At the opposite end of the spectrum were a few property crimes, especially highway robbery and gang-style burglary, that were regarded as so menacing that juries virtually never mitigated the capital sanction.[243] Across the broad range of property crimes, however, jury discretion held sway. In deciding whether to return verdicts of mitigation, juries distinguished, first, according to the seriousness of the offense, and second, according to the conduct and character of the accused.

The jury's power to mitigate sanctions profoundly affected the purpose of the criminal trial for those many offenses in which the jury might return a partial verdict. Only a small fraction of eighteenth-century criminal trials were genuinely contested inquiries into guilt or innocence. In many cases, perhaps most, the accused had been caught in the act or with the stolen goods or otherwise had no credible defense. To the extent that trial had a function in such cases beyond formalizing the inevitable conclusion of guilt, it was to decide the sanction. Because the main purpose of defending such a case was to present the jury with a sympathetic view of the offender and of the circumstances of the crime that would encourage a verdict of mitigation, the criminal defendant labored under an enormous practical compulsion to speak in his own defense. By structuring sentencing as an incident of the trial, the procedure foreclosed the defendant from participating in what was in function his sentencing hearing unless he spoke about the circumstances of the offense. To be sure, character witnesses could and did carry some of this burden for the defendant in some cases; it was not impossible to remain silent and still obtain jury leniency. But it was a grave risk that few defendants had the stomach to undertake. Thus, the same factors that caused the procedure to prefer trials over guilty pleas[244] also induced criminal defendants at trial to speak to their knowledge of the events.

The partial verdict system abated slowly, toward the end of the eighteenth century and during the early decades of the nineteenth century, as

---

Confess the Fact, and said it was Poverty that constrained her to Commit that wicked Act, etc. So that she was found Guilty to the value of 10*d*." Elizabeth Wooly, *OBSP* (Sept. 1686), at 2. She was ordered whipped.

[241] See Langbein, "Ryder" 52. From a much larger sample of Surrey cases, including lesser crime as well as felony, Beattie found comparable partial verdict rates (24.9%) in the period 1700–39, then a decline to 12.7% for the period 1740–79, and 7.5% for the years 1780–1802. Beattie, *Crime* 419 and n. 32.

[242] Further discussed *infra* Ch. 5, at n. 387.

[243] See Beattie, *Crime* 427–9; King, *Crime* 231–3; Langbein, "Ryder" 53.

[244] Discussed *supra*, text at nn. 45–53.

the sanction of imprisonment replaced transportation. The modern system of post-verdict judicial sentencing arose in response to many factors. The movement to revise the substantive criminal law by consolidating and rationalizing the categories of offenses invited the grading of sentences according to severity. This development was deeply connected to the appearance of imprisonment as the routine punishment for cases of serious crime. The older sanctions, death and transportation, had lent themselves to jury manipulation, because they came as "either-or" choices. Because the new sanction of imprisonment for a term of years was all but infinitely divisible, it invited the concept of the sentencing range, which transferred to the judge the power to tailor the sentence to the particular offender. Until imprisonment began to displace transportation, however, the jury-operated system of mitigation by partial verdict placed an enormous premium on the defendant's willingness to talk to the jurors at trial about the charges and the evidence against him.

6. The Clemency System

The trial judges at assizes and the Old Bailey exercised discretion to recommend clemency to the crown.[245] The exercise of the royal pardon power on recommendation of the trial judges was a regular feature[246] of the criminal procedure. Henry Fielding, writing in 1753, underscores the reliance upon these post-verdict proceedings:

And yet, if after all this Precaution [of the trial procedure] it should manifestly appear, that a Person hath been unjustly condemned, either by bringing to Light some latent Circumstance, or by discovering that the Witnesses against him are certainly perjured, or by any other Means of displaying the Party's Innocence, the Gates of Mercy are still left open, and upon a proper and decent Application,

---

[245] For discussion of the judicially dominated pardon process as a routine aspect of criminal procedure in the eighteenth century, see Beattie, *Crime* 430–49; Beattie, *Policing* 287–304, 346–69, 448–62; 1 Radzinowicz, *History* 107–37; King, *Crime* 297–333; Langbein, "Ryder" 19–21; Douglas Hay, "Property, Authority and the Criminal Law," in *Albion's Fatal Tree: Crime and Society in Eighteenth-Century England* 17, 40–9 (D. Hay *et al.*, eds.) (1975); John H. Langbein, Albion's Fatal Flaws," 98 *Past and Present* 96, 109–14 (1983); see also Simon Devereaux, "The City and the *Sessions Paper*: 'Public Justice' in London 1770–1800," 35 *J. British Studies* 466 (1996) (use of the *Sessions Papers* in reporting to the monarch for clemency review). Gatrell follows pardon practice into the nineteenth century. V. A. C. Gatrell, *The Hanging Tree: Execution and the English People: 1770–1868*, at 543–65 (1994).

[246] Jurors' awareness of the prevalence of post-verdict clemency proceedings may occasionally have affected trial outcomes. A tract-writer reported that in a case tried in 1715, a juror who was inclined to acquit the accused admitted that the likelihood of pardon influenced him to acquiesce in the majority's decision to convict. "He did not think it worthwhile to differ in Opinion with them, because he knew the Gentleman [defendant] had such Interest at [the royal] Court, that he would not die for it." Anon., *Capt. Leeson's Case: Being an Account of His Tryal for Committing a Rape* (London 1715) (Folger Libr., Washington, DC, shelfmark DA 501 L4 C2 Cage). Leeson was reprieved for pardon.

either to the Judge before whom the Trial was had, or to the privy Council, the condemned Person will be sure of obtaining a Pardon, or preserving his Life, and of regaining both his Liberty and Reputation.[247]

In administering the pardon process, the judge depended upon information gleaned at trial for his view of the offender. We have seen[248] that a main reason that judges discouraged guilty pleas in seventeenth- and eighteenth-century criminal trials was the wish to learn about the offender at trial, in the event that clemency were later sought. A Surrey assize judge sitting in a case in 1751 explained that he hanged a man who had pleaded guilty because the guilty plea had shut the judge "out from all evidence and circumstances favorable and disfavorable which might have appeared."[249] Thus, the hope of influencing the post-verdict clemency system contributed yet another incentive for the accused to speak to the charges and the evidence against him at trial.

7. No Privilege against Self-Incrimination

The system of procedure rooted in the "accused speaks" trial allowed no room for any privilege against self-incrimination. It will be seen in Chapter 5 that the development of the privilege against self-incrimination was intimately connected to the appearance of defense counsel in the eighteenth century. Without defense counsel, the right to be silent was simply the right to forfeit all defense.[250] In the age of the altercation trial an opposite dynamic was at work, not promoting the accused's silence but pressuring him to speak.

F. The Plight of the Accused

I have emphasized in this chapter that securing the accused as an informational resource was the central preoccupation of the early modern criminal trial. This policy motivated the rule against defense counsel and many other incidents of the trial procedure. English criminal courts were determined to hear the accused speak in person and unaided at oral

---

[247] Henry Fielding, *A Clear State of the Case of Elizabeth Canning* (London 1753), in Fielding, *Enquiry* 281, 285.

[248] Supra, text at nn. 52–3.

[249] Quoted in John M. Beattie, "Crime and the Courts in Surrey: 1736–1753, in *Crime in England: 1550–1800*, at 155, 173 (J. S. Cockburn ed.) (1977).

[250] The theme of John H. Langbein, "The Historical Origins of the Privilege against Self-Incrimination at Common Law," 92 *Michigan L. Rev.* 1047 (1994) [hereafter Langbein, "PASI"], substantially republished in R. H. Helmholz et al., *The Privilege against Self-Incrimination: Its Origins and Development* 82 (1997).

public trial about the charges and the evidence adduced against him. Structuring the trial with so many burdens on the accused entailed the serious risk of convicting an innocent person who had been mistakenly or wantonly accused of capital crime. Why was there not greater contemporary sensitivity to the dangers inherent in the altercation trial?

1. Unpreparedness as a Virtue

The first great historian of the early modern criminal trial, Sir James Fitzjames Stephen, although aware of the shortcomings of the procedure,[251] undertook to defend it anyhow. "The trials were short and sharp," Stephen wrote. "[T]hey were directed to the very point at issue, and, whatever disadvantages the prisoner lay under, he was allowed to say whatever he pleased; his attention was pointedly called to every part of the case against him, and if he had a real answer to make he had the opportunity of bringing it out effectively and in detail."[252]

The crux of Stephen's argument is that the altercation trial exhibited a crude fairness. That argument is undoubtedly true, in the sense that an even more unfair procedure could have been devised. But Stephen's argument proves too little. The question is why English criminal procedure tilted the balance of advantage as heavily against the accused as the altercation trial in fact did. Why did the legal system insist on practices that so hampered innocent persons from defending themselves? Recall Beattie's image of criminal defendants brought to trial in eighteenth-century Surrey: "[M]en not used to speaking in public who suddenly found themselves thrust into the limelight before an audience in an unfamiliar setting—and who were for the most part dirty, underfed, and surely often ill—did not usually cross-examine vigorously or challenge the evidence presented against them."[253] Granting that Stephen was correct to see a crude fairness in these proceedings, the question remains, why be crude? Why did the system not make the trial fairer by relieving against some of the practices that disadvantaged the accused?

Oddly, at least part of the answer is that contemporaries appear to have believed that subjecting the accused to the pressures and hardships that I have described was actually truth-promoting. Speaking of the rationale for the one-sidedness of the Marian pretrial investigation, Beattie captures what he calls the contemporary "conception of trial" when he says: "[I]t was believed that the truth would be most clearly revealed if the prisoner was confronted with the evidence only in the courtroom so that the jury could judge the quality of his immediate, *unprepared*

---

[251] 1 Stephen, *History* 350.   [252] Ibid. at 355.   [253] Beattie, *Crime* 350–1.

response."[254] Keeping the defendant ignorant of the accusing evidence and then requiring him to reply to it "unaided by a lawyer . . . was thus not mere indifference to his feelings . . . ."[255] Rather, it helped the accused to prove "his innocence to the jury by the force and sincerity of his denials."[256] The systemic unpreparedness of the accused, which the modern observer sees as a grievous and truth-impairing defensive disadvantage, was understood by contemporaries as a truth-serving effort to enhance the spontaneity of the accused's account—recall Hawkins' celebration of "the Simplicity and Innocence, artless and ingenuous Behavior of one whose conscience acquits him . . . ."[257] The insistent orality of the English criminal trial[258] extended this emphasis on spontaneity to witnesses as well as the accused.[259]

This effort to justify the apparent one-sidedness of the altercation trial on the ground that it protected the freshness of the defendant's statements underscores the complete dependence of sixteenth- and seventeenth-century trial courts on identification evidence and character evidence (varieties of evidence whose unreliability has since become a byword[260]). We shall see in Chapters 2 and 3 how this naive faith in the truth-serving virtues of defensive unpreparedness came to be undermined at the end of the seventeenth and across the eighteenth centuries.

2. The Historical Dimension

A certain historical perception about the balance of advantage in early

[254] Ibid. at 271 (emphasis supplied). [255] Ibid.
[256] Ibid. at 272. [257] 2 Hawkins, PC 400.
[258] Sir Thomas Smith contrasted the striking orality of English criminal jury trial with the written criminal procedure then common on the Continent. "[I]t will seem strange to all nations that do use the civil Law of the Roman Emperors, that for life and death there is nothing put in writing but the indictment only." Smith, De Republica 114–15. For a modern comparison of English and Continental traditions on this point, see Tony Honoré, "The Primacy of Oral Evidence?," in Crime, Proof and Punishment: Essays in Memory of Sir Rupert Cross 172 (C. F. H. Tapper ed.) (1981).
[259] In an Old Bailey trial in 1736, the judge interfered when the victim of a theft, prosecuting the accused thief and the receiver of the stolen goods, began to read his testimony. The victim explained that he had "committed the Thing to writing, that I might not forget any Thing material, nor trouble the Court with any Thing that was trifling. This I did when the Thing happened." The judge replied: " 'Tis not usual Sir to read a Testimony. You may use your Papers to refresh your memory, but it has always been the Custom for Witnesses to give their Evidence viva Voce." Elizabeth Borroughs and Bryan Carney, OBSP (July 1736, ##69–70), at 182, 183–4. For a similar case half a century later, see John Langford and William Annand, OBSP (Jan. 1788, #137), at 177, 178 (court stops prosecution witness from reading his memorandum of the events of the crime).
[260] Regarding identification evidence, see, e.g., Elizabeth F. Loftus and James M. Doyle, Eyewitness Testimony: Civil and Criminal (3rd edn. 1997); regarding character evidence, see Federal Rules of Evidence, Rule 404(a), Advisory Committee's Note, 56 Federal Rules Decisions 219, at 221, quoting the California Law Revision Commission, that "[c]haracter evidence is of slight probative value and may be very prejudicial."

modern criminal procedure may also have contributed to the seeming insensitivity to the plight of the accused.

The altercation trial emerged at the end of the Middle Ages from the wreckage of an earlier system of criminal procedure. The jury-based criminal procedure of the twelfth and thirteenth centuries operated on radically different premises from Sir Thomas Smith's altercation trial. In medieval times both the jury of accusation (the forerunner of the grand jury) and the trial jury were self-informing. Jurors "were men chosen as being likely to be already informed."[261] The vicinage requirement, that jurors must be drawn from the immediate neighborhood where the crime had occurred, was meant to produce jurors who already knew what had happened, or whose communal relations would enable them to find out on their own.[262] It was their duty, "so soon as they have been summoned, to make inquiries about the facts of which they will have to speak when they come before the court. They must collect testimony; they must weigh it and state the net result in a verdict."[263] Medieval jurors came to court more to speak than to listen.

Across the fourteenth and fifteenth centuries this reliance upon juries of close neighbors who could inform themselves about the circumstances of a crime broke down. The medieval jury system presupposed a static populace and forms of communal agricultural organization whose dissolution probably began in earnest with the vast social dislocations of the Black Death of 1348–9. By Sir Thomas Smith's day both the grand and petty juries meeting at a county assize court were drawn not from the neighborhood of the events, but from the entire county.[264]

As the juries lost their proximity to the persons and events of the cases brought before them, they lost their capacity to inform themselves. They became the passive triers to which we are now accustomed, ignorant of the events in issue. Jury trial changed character, becoming an instructional proceeding for the purpose of educating the jurors about the matters they were about to determine.

The altercation trial took shape in response to this passivization of the jury. The seeming one-sidedness both of the Marian pretrial investigation and of the altercation trial reflects the strains that the legal system had

---

[261] Thayer, *Evidence* 90.

[262] Ibid. at 91.

[263] 2 Frederick Pollock and Frederic W. Maitland, *The History of English Law* (2nd edn. 1898) (2 vols.) 624–5 [hereafter Maitland, *HEL*].

[264] On the county-wide grand jury, see 4 Blackstone, *Commentaries* 299 ("gentlemen of the best figure in the county"). I have discussed the rules for the selection of petty jurors in John H. Langbein, "The English Criminal Trial Jury on the Eve of the French Revolution," in *The Trial Jury in England, France, Germany: 1700–1900*, at 13, 24–9 (Antonio Padoa Schioppa ed.) (Comparative Studies in Continental and Anglo-American Legal History) (1987) [hereafter Padoa Schioppa, *Trial Jury*].

experienced in responding to the loss of the self-informing trial jury. As the jury became ignorant of the events in issue, contemporaries may have seen the advantage shifting to the accused. He likely knew some or all of what happened, having been close enough to the events to get himself prosecuted, whereas the jury was now ignorant. Both the Marian pretrial examination and the pressures associated with the "accused speaks" trial were directed to overcoming the accused's informational advantage by inducing him to disclose what he knew.

Seen, therefore, in the light of then recent historical experience, the unfairness of the altercation trial may not have been evident to those who constructed and operated it in the sixteenth and seventeenth centuries. The English would need to learn from experience just how dangerous this mode of criminal trial could be to persons wrongly accused. Those experiences are the subject of Chapters 2 and 3 of this book.

Another epochal change in the conduct of criminal justice that occurred in the transition from medieval to early modern times may also have affected contemporary perceptions about the appropriate balance of safeguard. Into the later Middle Ages trial of any sort was reserved largely for cases of clandestine crime. Someone caught in the act or in flight from a serious crime was put to death on the spot, without trial. "[W]ithout being allowed to say one word in self-defense, he will be promptly hanged, beheaded or precipitated from a cliff," Maitland wrote.[265] By the end of the Middle Ages this lynch justice had been brought under control, and all accused persons were being brought to trial. In the eyes of Sir Thomas Smith's contemporaries, the altercation trial must have represented a vast enhancement in defensive safeguard for persons who previously would have been executed without being allowed to mount any defense.

Moreover, by processing to full jury trial large numbers of hopeless cases of persons manifestly guilty, this change in the case cohort must have inured contemporaries to the expectation that not many defendants would have anything material to say in their defense, thus dulling sensitivity to the danger that the procedures of the altercation trial could in some circumstances hamper an innocent person from making a genuine defense.

Understanding the criminal trial as a dynamic form that had already undergone profound changes by the time we encounter it in Sir Thomas Smith's account helps us to see why in Smith's day and for so long thereafter the shortcomings of the altercation mode of trial were not apparent. Neither the operatives who processed the cases nor the

politically significant classes who had the power to change the procedures had any inkling of what was wrong with contemporary criminal procedure. Those lessons would first dawn upon them in the last quarter of the seventeenth century, with the treason trials of the later Stuarts.

2

The Treason Trials Act of 1696:
The Advent of Defense Counsel

The first great breach in the rule against defense counsel occurred with the enactment of the Treason Trials Act of 1696.[1] The Act authorized treason defendants to have the assistance of counsel both at trial and in the

---

[1] An Act for Regulating of Trials in Cases of Treason and Misprision of Treason, 7 Wil. 3., c. 3 (1696) [hereafter 1696 Act].

pretrial, and it made other reforms to improve the defensive opportunities of persons accused of treason. The Act was a charter of defensive safeguard in criminal procedure, and as such, a turning point in the history of
Anglo-American criminal procedure. Adversary criminal trial traces to
the 1696 Act.

A striking peculiarity of this landmark legislation is that it was limited
to cases of treason, which was a rare but momentous offense. Treason[2]
entailed taking or plotting against the life of the monarch, or raising
armed rebellion.[3] The drafters of the 1696 Act were reacting to devastat-
ing miscarriages of justice that had occurred in a series of treason trials
held across the decade from 1678 to the Glorious Revolution of 1688–9.
For reasons to be discussed, the drafters thought that the problems
revealed in those cases were particular to treason. The 1696 Act authorized what amounted to a special form of procedure, the lawyer-
conducted criminal trial, for the handful of trials that arose in this
troublesome and atypical enclave of the law. Indeed, part of what
emboldened the drafters to undertake their reforms was the understanding that the Act was limited to treason. They had no reason to know that
they were laying the groundwork for routine adversary trial in cases of
ordinary crime. Decades later, in circumstances described in Chapter 3,
this lawyerized criminal procedure would burst the bounds that had been
carefully designed to confine it to treason, enter the trial of ordinary
crime, and transform Anglo-American criminal justice.

In this chapter I review the main treason trials of the later Stuarts. I
relate the agenda for procedural reform that emerged in the contemporary critique of the trials to the provisions of the Act, and I devote particular attention to the drafters' rationale for restricting their reforms to
cases of treason. The chapter concludes by examining how the restriction
to treason deflected attention away from the two central shortcomings of
adversary procedure, the combat effect and the wealth effect.

A. The Treason Trials of the Later Stuarts

The 1670s and 1680s were a period of notable instability in English polit-

---

[2] The term used in the Act is "high treason," which excludes petty treason. Petty treason
was the murder of a master by a servant, or of a husband by his wife. See 4 Blackstone,
Commentaries 75, 203; 1 Radzinowicz, *History* 209–13. Cases instancing conviction of murdering wives are discussed *infra* n. 51, and *infra* Ch. 5, n. 336.

[3] See *supra* Ch. 1, n. 15, for citation to the juristic literature on the definition of treason.
The offense acquired a statutory basis, earlier than most other offenses, in 25 Edw. III, st. 5,
c. 2 (1352), and subsequent legislation. See generally John G. Bellamy, *The Law of Treason in
England in the Later Middle Ages* (1986).

ical life.[4] The monarchy had been only recently restored in 1660 after the Interregnum (1649–60), which followed the execution of Charles I. In the political community there was deep uneasiness about the prospect that Charles II, who had no lawful descendants, would be succeeded by his Roman Catholic brother James, the future James II. James, it was feared, would use the monarchy to subvert the Anglican Church[5] and align the country with the Catholic powers, France and Spain. Resentment at the religious persecutions under Mary (1553–8), the last Catholic monarch, and fear of renewed religious strife under James, were acute. Charles II dissolved Parliament in 1681, undertook to rule without it, and did not call another during his reign. This program had the effect of channeling some of the factional strife from Parliament to the law courts, in the form of prosecutions for political crime.

A series of major treason trials occurred across the decade from 1678 to the outbreak of the Revolution of 1688–9. These trials—arising from the Popish Plot (1678), the Rye House Plot (1683), and Monmouth's Rebellion (1685)—would prove to be landmark events in the subsequent movement for procedural reform. As the treason trials wore on, the perception became widespread that innocent persons of the politically significant classes had been convicted and suffered traitors' deaths for want of the ability to defend effectively against baseless prosecutions. These perceived miscarriages of justice provoked a movement for enhanced defensive safeguards that resulted in provisions of the Declaration of Rights and the ensuing Bill of Rights of 1689, then led to the Treason Trials Act of 1696, and culminated with the reform of judicial tenure in the Act of Settlement of 1701.

1. The Popish Plot

The Popish Plot was an alleged conspiracy on the part of Catholics, including prominent courtiers, "to murder Charles, set fire to London (again), raise a catholic army and incite a foreign invasion . . . ."[6] James' secretary, Edward Coleman, was alleged to be a ringleader. The plotters intended that Jesuits disguised as Presbyterians would be sent to Scotland

---

[4] On the background, see J. H. Plumb, *The Growth of Political Stability in England: 1675–1725* (1967).

[5] For the view that James had in mind nothing more than securing tolerance for English Catholics, but so misplayed his hand that he gave the appearance of seeking to upset the Anglican Church, see the incisive account in G. V. Bennett, "The Seven Bishops: A Reconsideration" [hereafter Bennett, "Reconsideration"], in *Religious Motivation: Biographical and Sociological Problems for the Church Historian* 267, 274–75 (Derek Baker ed.) (1978). (I owe this reference to Henry Horwitz.)

[6] J. R. Jones, *Country and Court: England, 1658–1714*, at 199 (1978 edn.) [hereafter Jones, *Country*].

FIG. 2.1. *The Popish Plot*. A credulous depiction (from a tract published in 1681, just after the main Popish Plot trials of 1678–80) shows the Jesuits supposedly organizing an assassination attempt on Charles II.

to stir a revolt, while French troops assisted a rebellion in Ireland. Twenty thousand Catholics were to slay 100,000 Protestants in London.[7]

[7] John Miller, *Popery and Politics in England, 1660–1668*, at 156 (1973).

The main accusations were made by Titus Oates, a failed Anglican clergyman who admitted to having sojourned on Jesuit charity in France,
where he claimed to have overheard details of the plot. These sensational
revelations induced another perjurer, William Bedloe, to come forward.
He confirmed and embellished Oates' charges. As the resulting treason
prosecutions wore on, a few other false accusers chimed in, either to share
the limelight or to settle scores.[8] Further waves of allegations implicated
the Catholic nobles Lords Castlemaine and Stafford. As usual in cases of
state crime, the charges were investigated by the Privy Council; the law
officers of the crown assisted in the investigations and prosecuted at trial.

Coleman, the first victim of Oates' false witnessing, was a well-chosen
target, because he was prominently known "as a catholic lobbyist at
Westminster."[9] His papers were seized and revealed "detailed schemes to
dissolve Parliament, establish toleration and advance catholic interests."[10]
These documents seemed to confirm Oates and Bedloe's trumped-up allegations of impending regicide, massacre, and invasion. Hysteria worsened when a London magistrate (JP), Sir Edmund Berry Godfrey, before
whom Oates had sworn his information, mysteriously disappeared and
was later found dead in circumstances indicating murder, which seemed
to confirm the plot.[11] Coleman, Castlemaine, Stafford, various Jesuit
priests, and a variety of other defendants accused of being intending
assassins or helpers were prosecuted in trials that lasted from 1678 into
1680. Stephen describes these trials as "six memorable failures of justice,
involving the sacrifice of no less than fourteen innocent lives . . . ."[12]

Suspicions about Oates' veracity surfaced as the trials wore on.[13] His
web of falsehoods became uncontrollable, and after he was detected, he
was prosecuted and convicted of perjury in 1685.[14] The trial judge and

[8] See John Kenyon, *The Popish Plot* (1972) [hereafter Kenyon, *Plot*], for a careful, chilling
account of how Oates and Bedloe ratified each other's accusations and inspired bit players
(Dugdale, Prance, and Dangerfield in London, and Bolron and Mowbray in the north) to
further perjury.

[9] Jones, *Country*, *supra* n. 6, at 201.

[10] Ibid.

[11] Discussed in Kenyon, *Plot*, *supra* n. 8, at 264–70.

[12] 1 Stephen, *History* 392; accord, Kenyon, *Plot*, *supra* n. 8, at 179–80.

[13] For example, Sir John Reresby, a royalist MP and Middlesex JP, recorded in his diary
having encountered Oates at a dinner at the table of the Bishop of Ely in December 1680.
Oates made remarks "running down the Duke [of York, the future James II] . . . which
showed himself both a fool and a knave," but "nobody dar[ed] to contradict him (for fear of
being made a party to the Plot) . . . ." *Memoirs of Sir John Reresby* 208–9 (Andrew Browning
ed.) (2nd edn. 1991) [hereafter Reresby, *Memoirs*]. In the Plot-linked treason trial of Miles
Stapleton, held at York Assizes, the counsel for the King challenged a prospective juror,
happily named Christopher Tankard, on the ground that Tankard "disparaged the evidence
of the Plot and called his dogs by the names of Oates and Bedlow [sic]." *R. v. Miles Stapleton*,
8 *St. Tr.* 501, 503 (1681). Stapleton was acquitted despite judicial pressure to convict. Ibid.
at 526.

[14] *R. v. Titus Oates*, 10 *St. Tr.* 1079 (K.B. 1685).

sentencing officer in the perjury proceedings was the soon-to-be-reviled George Jeffreys, then Lord Chief Justice, about whom more below. Perjury was a misdemeanor, hence not punishable by death, although Jeffreys called Oates' perjury a "crime infinitely more odious than common murder."[15] Bristling at "[t]he destruction of poor innocent persons, by false accusations, by the pernicious evidence of perjured witnesses in a court of justice,"[16] Jeffreys sentenced Oates to be heavily fined, repeatedly pilloried, whipped, imprisoned for life, and defrocked of his clerical office.[17] Oates was savagely whipped and pilloried before a crowd that was reckoned to number 10,000 people (Fig. 2.2).[18]

Some Whig believers never conceded the falsity of the Popish Plot. After the Revolution of 1688–9 complaints about the severity of Oates' punishment were among the grievances that led to Article 10 of the Declaration of Rights, proscribing excessive fines and cruel and unusual punishments.[19] Oates was released from prison and "petitioned for relief as a victim of the unpopular Jeffreys."[20] The Houses of Parliament disagreed about whether to reverse his conviction, the Lords refusing.[21] William III pardoned him and pensioned him off. Oates' conviction and punishment, as well as the subsequent controversy about him, kept the miscarriages of justice associated with the Popish Plot trials in public recollection for a decade after the events, fueling the movement for treason trial reform.

Shorthand reporters attended and transcribed the Popish Plot trials and published contemporaneous pamphlet reports, which were later republished in the *State Trials*. Reading these accounts two centuries later, Stephen observed about the fantastic allegations of Oates and the other accusers: "Their evidence has every mark of perjury about it. They never would tie themselves down to anything, if they could possibly avoid it. As soon as they were challenged with a lie by being told that witnesses were coming to contradict them, they always shuffled and drew back, and began to forget."[22]

---

[15] Ibid. at 1300.   [16] Ibid.
[17] Ibid. at 1316–17.   [18] Kenyon, *Plot, supra* n. 8, at 257.
[19] Lois G. Schwoerer, *The Declaration of Rights, 1689,* at 93 (1981) [hereafter Schwoerer, *Declaration*]. It was emphasized that a secular court lacked jurisdiction to meddle with clerical office, even as a criminal sanction. Ibid. at 93–4. See also Anthony F. Granucci, " 'Nor Cruel and Unusual Punishments Inflicted': The Original Meaning," 57 *California Law Rev.* 839, 858–60 (1969)
[20] Kenyon, *Plot, supra* n. 8, at 259–60. The House of Lords refused to reverse his conviction, see Schwoerer, *Declaration, supra* n. 19, at 272–4.
[21] Schwoerer, *Declaration, supra* n. 19, at 272–4.
[22] 1 Stephen, *History* 385.

Fig. 2.2. *Titus Oates in the pillory for perjury.* Oates, the main prosecution witness in the Popish Plot trials, was convicted of perjury and publicly pilloried in 1685, underscoring for contemporaries the likelihood that the Plot trials had condemned many innocent defendants.

2. Fitzharris and College

In 1681, with the Popish Plot trials barely concluded, two further treason trials occurred that would figure prominently in the post-Revolutionary discussions about reforming treason procedures: Edward Fitzharris,[23] an Irish adventurer caught in his own web of intrigue; and Stephen College,[24] a staunch Protestant critic of Charles II, who was convicted of conspiring to murder the King.[25]

Awaiting trial, College petitioned the Privy Council to be allowed to consult with his solicitor, Aaron Smith, and his counsel, Robert West. "[H]is majesty was pleased to order" that College be allowed "to converse with them as often as he shall desire in presence and hearing of the warder . . . ."[26] When College was brought to trial, however, his papers were taken from him by "Mr. Murrell, the jailer, and Sewell, the King's messenger."[27] According to the well-known tract by Sir John Hawles, published in the months immediately after the Glorious Revolution, Murrell and Sewell acted "as the King's Counsel directed them."[28] College asked the court to order his papers returned, as they "were papers that concerned my defense, [including] some directions and instructions how to manage myself in that defense."[29] North CJ responded, "How comes any body to give you papers? Nobody can solicit for one that is under an accusation of High-Treason, unless [the solicitor] be assigned so to do by the court."[30] The Attorney General, Sir Robert Sawyer, one of the prosecuting counsel, protested Smith's role in advising College and in providing him with written guides. Sawyer complained that College's solicitor was effectively evading the rule against defense counsel, because he was acting as an intermediary between accused and counsel. If a solicitor is "permitted to go up and down and ask counsel of persons, and bring it in papers to the prisoner, it is the same thing as if

---

[23] *R. v. Edward Fitzharris*, 8 *St. Tr.* 243 (K.B. 1681).

[24] *R. v. Stephen College*, 8 *St. Tr.* 549 (1681). Most contemporary sources, including the report published in the *State Trials*, spell the name "Colledge." Here and in other instances in which there are variant spellings of a name, I follow when possible the usage of the *Dictionary of National Biography.*

[25] The trial included some of the Popish Plot witnesses—Dugdale for the crown, but Oates, Bolron, and Mowbray for College.

[26] 8 *St. Tr.* at 552 (extracting the order).

[27] Ibid. at 576.

[28] Hawles, *Remarks* 22. A lawyer who was an MP from 1689 to 1710, Hawles served as solicitor general from 1695 to 1702. The *State Trials* publishes extracts from Hawles' tract following each of the trials that Hawles criticized, e.g., following the trial of Stephen College, 8 *St. Tr.* at 723. My citations are to the first edition of the pamphlet.

[29] 8 *St. Tr.* at 570.

[30] 8 *St. Tr.* at 571. The term "assign" in this usage meant simply to authorize or permit the representation, a point discussed *infra*, text at nn. 144–53.

counsel came to him. Here is a busy solicitor, and he gets advice from counsel, and then he delivers it to the prisoner . . . ."[31]

The judges ordered College's papers to be seized and shared with the prosecution counsel,[32] who then changed their evidence, withdrawing witnesses whom College had been prepared to cross-examine or to refute.[33] Stephen was still indignant about this maneuver two centuries later, calling it "one of the most wholly inexcusable transactions that ever occurred in an English court . . . ."[34] Writing in 1689, only a few years after the events, Hawles said: "If it was lawful for the Prisoner to have [pretrial] Counsel, and to have Advice in Writing, it was very unlawful . . . [for] the King's Counsel to order his Papers to be taken away . . . ."[35] College was convicted and executed.

3. The Rye House Plot

The treason trials arising from the Rye House Plot (1683) resulted in the conviction and execution, among others, of two leading Whig figures, Lord William Russell, their leader, and the political theorist Algernon Sidney. In the historical literature these prosecutions have been described as "Stuart revenge" on the Whigs, who had welcomed the Popish Plot as an opportunity to depict the supporters of Charles II and the future James II as Catholic saboteurs.[36] The destruction of Russell and Sidney was a precipitating event in attracting Whig support to the movement for defensive safeguard in treason trials.

The Rye House Plot was a supposed conspiracy among Whig extremists determined to prevent James from acceding to the throne. Unlike the Popish Plot, which was a total falsehood, the Rye House Plot was rooted in actual events. Discussions did take place among key Whigs, Russell included, about forcibly preventing a Catholic succession.[37] Still, there

---

[31] 8 *St. Tr.* at 583.

[32] 8 *St. Tr.* at 584. "If I am ignorant what questions to ask of the witnesses," College argued, why not let my friends help me formulate them? Ibid. at 585. Chief Justice North gave the stock reply, invoking the court-as-counsel rubric (discussed *supra* in Ch, 1, text at nn. 90–116). "We will sift out the truth as well as we can, you need not fear it." 8 *St. Tr.* at 585.

[33] Hawles, *Remarks* 22.   [34] 1 Stephen, *History* 406.

[35] Hawles, *Remarks* 25.

[36] James R. Phifer, "Law, Politics, and Violence: The Treason Trials Act of 1696," 12 *Albion* 235, 239 (1980) [hereafter Phifer, "Act"].

[37] Regarding the evidence that there was indeed a plot to assassinate the King and provoke an insurrection, see Richard Ashcraft, *Revolutionary Politics and Locke's Two Treatises of Government* 338–40 (1986); Melinda Zook, *Violence, Martyrdom, and Radical Politics: Rethinking the Glorious Revolution, in Politics and the Political Imagination in Later Stuart Britain* 75, 77–80 (Howard Nenner ed.) (1997). Russell may have been the victim of some trumped-up evidence, but his participation in the discussions was probably enough to make him guilty of treason under the law. Lois G. Schwoerer, "The Trial of Lord William Russell (1683): Judicial Murder?," 9 *J. Legal History* 142 (1988) [hereafter, Schwoerer, "Russell"].

were "close parallels between this Rye House Plot ... and the earlier Popish Plot. Much of the evidence by the informers was false and fabricated . . . . Hearsay and accomplices' evidence ... was admitted. Defendants were not given sufficient time to prepare their defence or to summon witnesses."[38] The Rye House Plot prosecutions had more governmental direction than the Popish Plot cases, which, although investigated and prosecuted by the crown, depended on the fortuitous accusations of Oates and the other perjurers.

4. The Bloody Assizes

On the death of Charles II in 1685, the Duke of Monmouth, Charles' illegitimate son, led a Protestant uprising in the west of England, attempting to prevent James' accession. Loyal forces put down Monmouth's Rebellion at the battle of Sedgemoor. Captured rebels, numbering nearly 1,400,[39] were charged with treason. They were tried under a special assize commission with Chief Justice Jeffreys presiding. The trials came to be known as the "Bloody Assizes,"[40] on account of the large number of persons executed.

The Stuart bench reached its nadir in the imperiousness and venality that Jeffreys displayed in the Bloody Assizes. He is alleged to have sold pardons,[41] including one to the wealthy family of Edmund Prideaux, for the then astounding sum of £14,500, which Jeffreys pocketed.[42] Jeffreys advised the King that reprieved rebels would fetch £10 to £15 a head if sold for transportation into indentured servitude in the New World, and "courtiers competed to be given consignment of them."[43] Writing a few years later, in 1689, Hawles alluded to Jeffreys' caprice in deciding whom to reprieve, referring to "the late Practice in the West, where many Men were hanged for having old Jewish [first] Names, as Obediah, or the like,

---

[38] Jones, *Country, supra* n. 6, at 223.

[39] G. W. Keeton, *Lord Chancellor Jeffreys and the Stuart Cause* 329 (1965) [hereafter Keeton, *Jeffreys*]. The precise number is uncertain. Lists of the persons tried appear in J. G. Muddiman, *The Bloody Assizes* 195–225 (1929).

[40] The name originated in Whig martyrologies published immediately after the Revolution, which contain embellished accounts of the trials. See Melinda Zook, " 'The Bloody Assizes:' Whig Martyrdom and Memory after the Glorious Revolution," 27 *Albion* 373, 375–7 (1995) [hereafter Zook, "Bloody Assizes"]. Havighurst observes that "only after the Revolution were these trials treated as outrages. In 1685 they attracted little attention and few, if any, expressions of horror or pity." Alfred F. Havighurst, "James II and the Twelve Men in Scarlet," 69 *Law Quarterly Rev.* 522, 527 (1953) [hereafter Havighurst, "James II"].

[41] Technically, the crown and not the bench had the power to pardon, but the convention was that the crown accepted the trial judge's recommendation to pardon. For discussion, see *supra* Ch. 1, text at nn. 245–9, and *infra* Ch. 5, text at nn. 348–52; Beattie, *Crime* 431–49.

[42] Keeton, *Jeffreys, supra* n. 39, at 326; see also Schwoerer, *Declaration, supra* n. 19, at 96.

[43] Schwoerer, *Declaration, supra* n. 19, at 97.

with a Jest that their Godfathers hanged them."[44] Over 200 rebels were executed in six towns.[45] "[T]he full punishment for high treason was carried out. Rebels were hanged until unconscious, disembowelled, beheaded, and quartered. Their remains were then boiled in brine, covered in black tar and set up on poles and trees and lampposts" for a year until James II ordered the display ceased.[46]

The most celebrated victim of the Bloody Assizes was Lady Alice Lisle, a deaf widow in her seventies, who appeared not to understand much of what went on at her trial. Her late husband had been among the regicides who sent Charles I to death back in 1649. Her alleged treason[47] consisted of harboring one of the vanquished rebels who fled in the aftermath of Monmouth's defeat. She had long known the man, one Hicks, as a dissenting minister. At her trial her defense was that she did not know that Hicks was among the rebels, nor had she observed anything in his dress or behavior to suggest that he had been on the battlefield. Jeffreys took it upon himself to rebut her defense, telling the jury (if the report is to be believed[48]) that all "those lying, snivelling, canting Presbyterian rascals . . . one way or other had a hand in the late horrid conspiracy and rebellion."[49] The jury initially resisted convicting,[50] but yielded to Jeffreys. He sentenced Alice Lisle to be burned at the stake (the punishment of the day for treason[51] when committed by a woman). James II commuted the sentence to beheading.[52]

---

[44] Hawles, *Remarks* 25.

[45] Keeton estimates 200 persons executed, most of the rest transported. Keeton, *Jeffreys*, supra n. 39, at 329.

[46] Zook, "Bloody Assizes," *supra* n. 40, at 382–3.

[47] *R. v. Lady Alice Lisle*, 11 *St. Tr.* 297 (Winchester Assizes 1685).

[48] Whereas the other important treason trials of the period that are compiled in the *State Trials* derive from contemporaneous pamphlet reports, "[n]o report of Mrs. Lisle's trial was ever printed before 1719, when the first edition of *State Trials* was published . . . ." J. G. Muddiman, *State Trials*, and Robert Blaney, 155 *Notes and Queries* 111, 149, at 149 (1928) (2 parts). Muddiman attributes the report of Alice Lisle's trial to the manuscript of a Whig barrister, Robert Blaney, who had earlier been arrested in connection with the Rye House Plot, ibid. at 111, and who "desired to discredit . . . Jeffreys, as well as to convey the impression that the trial was unfair . . . ." Ibid. at 150.

[49] 11 *St. Tr.* at 359.

[50] 11 *St. Tr.* at 371.

[51] Including petty treason, for the murder of one's husband, see n. 3, *supra*. The penalty was enforced. For example, "[a]t Lent Assizes, Worcester, 8 March 1661, one Ursula Corbett condemned to be burnt and execution done for poisoning her husband. So at Lent Assizes 1662 another woman burnt for stabbing her husband." "Henry Townshend's 'Notes of the Office of a Justice of Peace,' 1661–3" (R. D. Hunt ed.) in *Miscellany II*, at 68, 103 (1967) (Worcestershire Historical Society, NS, vol. 5). Townshend, the JP who made note of these cases, observed that Corbett had only been married for three weeks at the time of the murder, and he observed: "An ill fate certainly attends when parents enforce their children to marry against their liking." Ibid. at 103 n. 1. An eighteenth-century petty treason case involving a murdering wife is noticed *infra* Ch. 5, n. 336.

[52] 11 *St. Tr.* at 379.

5. Addendum: The Seven Bishops

Mention needs also to be made of the most celebrated of the political prosecutions of the later Stuarts, the *Seven Bishops Case* (1688),[53] although it
differed from the great treason trials of the period in three important and
interrelated ways: (1) the offense charged was not treason, but rather seditious libel; (2) because the offense was a mere misdemeanor, the defendants were allowed counsel, who functioned with great effectiveness; and
(3) all the defendants were acquitted. The defendants, the Archbishop of
Canterbury and six other Anglican prelates, refused to read from their
pulpits the declaration of indulgence by which James II attempted to
suspended enforcement of the laws against religious dissenters. They
were prosecuted for seditious libel for a petition[54] of protest to James,
which disputed his authority to dispense with legislation. Defense counsel, "move[d] the argument on to a general attack on James for acting ille-
gally to promote the Romish religion. Eventually the lord chief justice
broke with all established legal precedent by actually putting it to the jury
to decide whether in point of law the bishops' petition amounted to a
seditious libel. Their acquittal had thus much of the character of a capitu-
lation to organized public opinion . . . ."[55] The acquittal of the Seven
Bishops was the event that sealed James' fate and triggered the
Revolution of 1688–9.

One lesson that contemporaries took from the *Seven Bishops Case* as
they began the process of trying to repair treason trial procedures in the
1690s was the demonstration that defense counsel could be hugely effective in resisting an unjust political prosecution.

B. The Critique of the Treason Trials

The treason trials of the later Stuarts became the subject of intense discussion in the years after the Revolution of 1688–9. In pamphlet literature
and in parliamentary proceedings, attention was directed to understanding why the procedures followed in these trials had allowed the conviction of so many innocent defendants. This critique set the agenda to

[53] 12 *St. Tr.* 183 (K.B. 688). Literature on the case is conveniently collected in Thomas A.
Green, "The English Criminal Trial Jury and the Law-Finding Traditions on the Eve of the
French Revolution," in Padoa Schioppa, *Trial Jury* 41, 54 n. 44.

[54] On the framing of the petition, see Roger Thomas, "The Seven Bishops and their
Petition, 18 May 1688", 12 *J. Ecclesiastical History* 56 (1961).

[55] G. V. Bennett, *The Seven Bishops: A Reconsideration, in Religious Motivation and
Sociological Problems for the Church Historian* 267, 284 (1978) (Ecclesiastical History Soc.).
"Because the bench divided on the question of whether the petition constituted a libel, that
question was left, de facto, to the jury." Green, *Verdict* 320.

which the Treason Trials Act of 1696 and the Act of Settlement of 1701 would respond. Three main grievances emerged: the partiality of the bench, the hampering of defensive preparation in the pretrial, and the denial of defense counsel.

1. Partiality of the Bench

Jeffreys' treatment of the pathetic Alice Lisle came to symbolize the excesses of the Stuart bench, but he was not alone in his partisanship. Chief Justice Scroggs, presiding at the Popish Plot trials, displayed astonishing bias. "[H]e checked and sneered at the prisoners when on their trial."[56] At the trial of Jesuit priests in the Popish Plot cases, Scroggs hooted at the defendants: "They eat their God, they kill their King, and saint the murderer!"[57]

"[T]he parliamentary Opposition's distrust of the judiciary . . . began as early as 1667 and became for the Whigs in 1680 an issue second in importance only to Exclusion [of the future James II], and when Exclusion failed, of first importance."[58] Revulsion at the behavior of the Stuart judiciary was a high theme of the Revolution of 1688–9. The opening sentence of the Declaration of Rights of February 1689[59] blamed the Revolution on James II and his "Evil Counsellors, Judges, and Ministers . . . ."[60] (The Declaration was soon to be codified as the Bill of Rights of 1689.) With the change of monarchs following the Revolution, the entire Jacobean bench was replaced: "None of the judges in office at the end of the reign continued or were ever reappointed."[61]

The criticisms of the judiciary that came to expression after the Revolution extended well beyond the judges' behavior in treason trials. There was particular resentment at the bench for having upheld the monarch's claim to possess a dispensing power over the laws.[62] (James

---

[56] 1 Stephen, *History* 395.

[57] Kenyon, *Plot*, *supra* n. 8, at 128.

[58] Schwoerer, *Declaration*, *supra* n. 19, at 87. Havighurst links the growing distrust of the late Stuart bench to the parliamentary agitation against the judges for fining jurors, which led to the ruling in *Bushell's Case, Vaughan* 135, 124 *Eng. Rep.* 1006 (1670), ending the practice. Alfred F. Havighurst, "The Judiciary and Politics in the Reign of Charles II" (pts. I and II), 66 *Law Quarterly Rev.* 62, 229, at 75 (1950) [hereafter, Havighurst, "Charles II"]. Regarding *Bushell's Case*, see *infra* Ch. 5, text at nn. 346–7; regarding the parliamentary background, see Green, *Verdict* 212–21; Langbein, "CTBL" 298–300.

[59] The Declaration contains a preamble, a list of thirteen grievances, and a further list of thirteen resolutions. The full text, which is not widely available, is reproduced as app. 1 of Schwoerer, *Declaration*, *supra* n. 19, at 295–8. In this book I cite it by grievance number or resolution number to Schwoerer's version [hereafter, *Declaration*].

[60] *Declaration*, *supra* n. 59, preamble.

[61] Havighurst, "James II," *supra* n. 40, at 523.

[62] The Declaration's opening complaint, *Declaration*, *supra* n. 59, grievance 1.

had asserted the authority to excuse noncompliance with the laws enforcing adherence to the Anglican faith, the claim that triggered the *Seven Bishops Case*.) The Declaration of Rights also complained of the judges' imposition of excessive bail, excessive fines, and illegal and cruel punishments.[63] The Bill of Rights of 1689 then forbade these practices[64] (in language that would be replicated a century later in the American Bill of Rights[65]). Responding to Jeffreys' conduct of the Bloody Assizes, the Declaration of Rights resolved against "[g]rants and promises of fines and forfeitures of particular persons before conviction."[66] The Bill of Rights tracked this measure as well.[67]

Jeffreys died in prison in 1689. Later that year Parliament attainted him, stripping him of "estate and honor."[68] Speaking in the House of Commons, Colonel Thomas Tipping, the nephew of Lady Alice Lisle, said of Jeffreys: "He has his Hand in Lord Russell's and Col. Sidney's Blood . . . . Innocent Blood he sought for, and condemned; as Mrs. Lisle, for harboring a Traitor knowing him to be such, and he knew he was not. He has raised his Estate on the ruin of the Laws." Obsequious[69] figures such as Scroggs and Jeffreys did not by accident become chief justices under the later Stuarts. The crown not only had the power to appoint judges, it also had the power to dismiss them without cause. The power to dismiss had become controversial under Charles I, who promised the Long Parliament in 1641 not to exercise it.[70] In the 1670s Charles II resumed the practice of sacking judges whose rulings displeased him.[71] In the 1670s and 1680s judges were dismissed for political reasons, and others were appointed though "wholly unfit for the post."[72] Hence, "by the end of

---

[63] Ibid. at 10–12, resolutions 1–2, 10–11.

[64] "That excessive Bail ought not to be required, nor excessive Fines imposed, nor cruel and unusual Punishments inflicted." 1 Wil. &. Mar., 2d Sess., c. 2 (1689). On the English Bill of Rights and its sources, see generally Richard L. Perry and John C. Cooper, *Sources of Our Liberties: Documentary Origins of Individual Liberties in the United States Constitution and Bill of Rights* 222–50 (1959).

[65] "Excessive Bail shall not be required, nor excessive fines imposed, nor cruel and unusual punishments inflicted." U.S. Constitution, Amendment 8.

[66] *Declaration, supra* n. 59, resolution 12. On the background, see Schwoerer, *Declaration, supra* n. 19, at 96–7. "[I]t was during the trials following Monmouth's Rebellion in 1685, Whig propaganda stressed, that the most blatant examples of granting or promising fines and forfeitures before conviction occurred." Ibid. at 97.

[67] "[A]ll Grants and Promises of Fines and Forfeitures of particular persons before Conviction are illegal and void." 1 Wil. & Mar., 2d Sess., c. 2 (1689).

[68] 9 Anchitell Grey, *Debates of the House of Commons from the Year 1667 to the Year 1694*, at 399 (1769) (10 vols.) (6 Nov. 1689) [hereafter Grey, *Debates*].

[69] When elevated to the office of serjeant in 1680, Jeffreys had his ring inscribed with the motto, "A deo rex, a rege lex" (from God the King, from the King the law). H. Montgomery Hyde, *Judge Jeffreys* 98 (1948 edn.)

[70] C. H. McIlwain, "The Tenure of English Judges," 7 *American Political Science Rev.* 217, 222 (1913) [hereafter McIlwain, "Tenure"].

[71] Ibid. at 223.   [72] 6 Holdsworth, *HEL* 507–8.

1683, after no less than eleven judges had been arbitrarily removed in the course of eight years, the king had a judiciary just about to his liking."[73] "In the four years of James' reign alone some thirteen were removed .... Four were removed in one day in 1686 for refusing to decide for the dispensing power .... "[74]

After the Revolution William III, the new monarch, marked out the path of the future by making his judicial appointments conditioned only on good behavior.[75] Because the structure of the judiciary was not a treason-specific issue, it fell outside the Treason Trials Act of 1696 and had to be dealt with on its own terms. Indeed, one strand of opposition to treason trial reform was the view that reforming the bench alone would suffice. In a debate in the House of Commons in November 1691 on a forerunner of the 1696 Act, George Treby, the Attorney General for the new regime of William and Mary, reflecting on the causes of "the hardship in the late times, in Trials for Treason," claimed that "[t]he fault was not in the Law, but in the Men." Since "their present Majesties ... will never permit such Men to come into Places of Judicature," Treby questioned the need for reforming the procedures for treason trials.[76]

Parliament was not content to follow either branch of this advice. "Good Kings, good Lawyers, and good Judges, are perishable commodities," another speaker warned the Commons.[77] Parliament reformed the procedures for treason trials in the 1696 Act, and a few years later the Act of Settlement of 1701 recast the terms of judicial office. Under the Act of 1701 judicial service ceased to be at the pleasure of the crown, and was

---

[73] Havighurst, "Charles II," *supra* n. 58, at 247.

[74] McIlwain, "Tenure," *supra* n. 70, at 223–4. The diarist Sir John Reresby, although quite active in the crown's service, recorded the event with evident disapproval. "[S]everal of those turned out were knowing and loyal gentlemen, and their crime was only this, that they would not give their opinions (as most of the rest had done) that the King by his prerogative might dispense with the taking of the test to Roman Catholics." Reresby, *Memoirs, supra* n. 13, at 421.

[75] Jane Garrett, *The Triumphs of Providence: The Assassination Plot, 1696*, at 182 (1980). Although William made his judicial appointments run for life (during good behavior), his court party forced deletion from the Bill of Rights of a measure mandating such appointments. D. A. Rubini, "The Precarious Independence of the Judiciary, 1688–1701," 83 *Law Quarterly Rev.* 343, 344 (1967). Lemmings notices that William's advisers resisted regularization of judicial salaries, in order that the judges not become "'too stiff; viz Honest and Independent.'" David Lemmings, "The Independence of the Judiciary in Eighteenth-Century England," in *The Life of the Law: Proceedings of the Tenth British Legal History Conference* 125, 130–1 (Peter Birks ed) (1994) [hereafter Lemmings, "Independence"]. The Act of Settlement of 1701 did not address judicial compensation. "An Act of 1760 first established judicial salaries, and provided that they should be made a permanent charge upon the Civil List. In 1799 legislation established judicial pensions." Shimon Shetreet, *Judges on Trial* 11 (1976), citing 1 Geo. 3, c. 23 (1761), 39 Geo. 3, c. 110, § 7 (1799).

[76] 10 Grey, *Debates, supra* n. 68, at 173–4 (18 Nov. 1691).

[77] 9 ibid. at 171 (Sir Charles Sedley, 18 Nov. 1691).

instead conditioned upon good behavior.[78] However, even after that Act, judicial appointments continued to expire with the monarch. Incoming regimes exercised the power to refuse to reappoint judges at the accession of new monarchs in 1702, 1714, and 1727.[79] Legislation in 1761 ended this practice,[80] finally establishing the principle of life tenure for judicial office.

This movement to insulate the judges from high politics[81] entailed a change not only in the conditions of judicial tenure, but in the conception of judicial office. G. W. Keeton observes of the late Stuart period that "the judiciary was still looked upon as a branch of the royal administration," and the judges "regarded themselves as advancing the royal policy . . . ."[82] Jeffreys said from the bench in a sedition trial in 1684 that "I hope I shall never lose my heart nor spirit to serve the government . . . ."[83] Across the eighteenth and nineteenth centuries, following the Revolution of 1688–9 and the Act of Settlement, the judiciary gradually "retired from the political arena, although the Lord Chief Justice of the King's Bench remained a member of the ministry until the end of the eighteenth century."[84] The judges grew in public esteem, but the debacle of the late Stuart bench remained firmly in the recollection of the political classes, cautioning the judges to distance themselves from partisanship—including the partisanship of the ever more lawyer-dominated criminal trial of the later eighteenth and early nineteenth century.

---

[78] 12 & 13 Wil. 3, c. 2, § 3 (1701). See Barbara A. Black, "Massachusetts and the Judges: Judicial Independence in Perspective," 3 *Law and History Rev.* 101, 103–12 (1985). The Act was made effective with the next reign, which turned out to be the Hanoverian succession of 1714. Actual practice predated the Act: "all the patents [for judicial appointment] under William and Mary and William III ran during good behavior and there were no removals." McIlwain, "Tenure," *supra* n. 70, at 224.

[79] Lemmings, "Independence," *supra* n. 75, at 126, 136–7.

[80] 1 Geo. 3, c. 23 (1761).

[81] Governments continued to exercise influence through control of judicial selection, seeking to appoint persons disposed to the crown's interests. Lemmings argues that government influence on the judicial career line followed a different pattern after the Revolution. Crown patronage was used "to develop a class of court lawyers who were trained in crown service from an early age in their careers, who became eligible to serve as judges because they were politically 'safe.' " Lemmings, Independence, *supra* n. 75, at 128. This career increasingly entailed a period of parliamentary service in support of the crown before advancement to the bench. Ibid. at 129–44.

[82] Keeton, *Jeffreys, supra* n. 39, at 21. As evidence for the view that "the judiciary was considered an integral part of Charles II's administration," Havighurst points to the "numerous duties of the judges outside the court room . . . [including their service in matters of] "[s]ewer administration, problems arising from former crown and church lands . . . [and especially] the service of the judges on the commission established to settle differences between landlords and tenants in London after the Great Fire of 1666." Havighurst, "Charles II," *supra* n. 58, at 66.

[83] *R. v. Samuel Barnardiston*, 9 St. Tr. 1333, 1355 (1684).

[84] Keeton, *Jeffreys, supra* n. 39, at 95.

Although the reform of the bench followed a separate track from the reform of treason trial procedure, the misbehavior of the judiciary in the late Stuart treason trials had a pervasive influence on the contents of the Treason Trials Act of 1696. The familiar justification for denying defense counsel—that the court would be counsel for the accused—had been tested and found wanting in these trials. Hawles expressed this sentiment in his tract of 1689: The judges who presided at the trials of Stephen College and others "did not make the best of their Client's Case; nay, generally [they] have betrayed their poor Client, to please, as they apprehended, their better Client, the King."[85] Lady Alice Lisle, convicted and executed at the Bloody Assizes, was said to have complained, "I have been told, the court ought to be counsel for the prisoner, instead of which, there was evidence given from thence"[86] against her. Court-as-counsel having proved to be an unworkable aspiration in treason prosecutions, the Treason Trials Act of 1696 resolved to permit counsel-as-counsel in these cases.

2. Restrictions on Pretrial Preparation

William Ireland, one of the Popish Plot defendants charged with plotting the assassination of Charles II, spoke at trial about his inability to prepare a defense when imprisoned and unaided. He named alibi witnesses who could prove that he was in Staffordshire, far from the scene of Oates' and Bedloe's allegations. "[O]n calling his first witness he observed, 'It is a hundred to one if he be here, for I have not been permitted so much as to send a scrap of paper.' "[87] His witnesses did not appear, and Ireland and his codefendants were convicted and executed.

Stephen College also complained at trial about the effect of pretrial confinement: "I have been kept a close prisoner in the Tower ever since I was taken. I was all along unacquainted with what was charged upon me. I knew not what was sworn against me, nor the persons that did swear it against me, and therefore I am wholly ignorant of the matter."[88] Reflecting on these trials, Stephen regarded it as a "real grievance"[89] that the precise charges were not disclosed to the defendant until he was arraigned on the indictment. (Arraignment took place close to or at the time of the trial.) The accused was invariably locked away in pretrial detention. When, as was common, the accused was also denied the

---

[85] Hawles, *Remarks* 22.
[86] 11 *St. Tr.* at 380 (but see *supra* n. 48, regarding doubts about the credibility of the report).
[87] 1 Stephen, *History* 388, citing *R. v. William Ireland*, 7 *St. Tr.* 79, 121 (O.B. 1678).
[88] 8 *St. Tr.* at 569.
[89] 1 Stephen, *History* 399.

assistance of solicitors or counsel while detained,[90] he could neither orga-nize his own defense nor have it done by lawyers.

The 1696 Act would provide for the right to consult lawyers in the pretrial for the purpose of developing defensive proofs, and for advance disclosure of the indictment and the names of prospective jurors.[91] The Act did not, however, call for the disclosure of information about prose-cution witnesses or their projected testimony, the step now known as pretrial discovery of the prosecution case. (Discovery of this sort would long be resisted, ostensibly for fear that persons allied with the defendant might intimidate or otherwise interfere with the accusing witnesses.)

3. Denial of Counsel

The most insistent theme in the post-Revolutionary critique of the late Stuart treason trials was the need for defense counsel. The arguments for counsel emphasized three unique aspects of treason prosecutions. One was the concern, already discussed, that the bench was unreliable in cases of such direct importance to the crown.

The second line of argument was the unfairness of denying counsel when the crown invariably employed lawyer prosecutors. Hawles wrote: "[A]s many Counsel as can be hired are allowed to be against him, none for him . . . . [I]t is a wonder how any person escapes; it is downright tying a man's hands behind him, and baiting him to death . . . ."[92] Speaking of the trial of Stephen College, he added: "The truth is, upon the whole, what College said was true; they took away all helps from him for defend-ing himself, and therefore they had as good have condemned him without a Trial."[93] Hawles linked this imbalance to intimations of prose-cutorial misconduct. He concluded that various of the accusing witnesses against College had been paid off,[94] hence that crown counsel promoted or acquiesced in suborning perjury. As Alexander Shapiro has observed, Whig "critics were disturbed that in a trial system already heavily weighted in favor of the prosecution, the government was abusing its advantage."[95]

The implicit remedy for this one-sidedness, and the route that would be mapped out in the Treason Trials Act of 1696, was two-sidedness. The preamble to the Act would trumpet the principle of equalizing the

---

[90] "If any Person advise or solicit for [the accused], unless assigned by the Court, by which he is Tried, they are punishable." Hawles, *Remarks* 32.

[91] Discussed *infra*, text at nn. 136–40, 156–8.   [92] Hawles, *Remarks* 32.

[93] Ibid. at 43.   [94] Ibid. at 37.

[95] Alexander H. Shapiro, "Political Theory and the Growth of Defensive Safeguards in Criminal Procedure: The Origins of the Treason Trials Act of 1696," 11 *Law and History Rev.* 215, 222 (1993) [hereafter Shapiro, "Treason Act"].

defense, a principle that the Act would implement most fundamentally by allowing the defendant to have access to counsel both in the pretrial and at trial. Persons accused of treason would be allowed to defend themselves in the way the state prosecuted them, with lawyers. The accused would be allowed the help of lawyers to prepare defensive evidence in the pretrial, to examine defense witnesses and cross-examine prosecution witnesses, and to serve as advocates at trial.

The third strand to the claim that treason defendants had a special need for defense counsel was the concern, prominently voiced in the post-Revolutionary critique of the trials of Russell and Sidney, that the legal complexity of the offence of treason merited the assistance of counsel. The prosecution of Sidney rested heavily upon the contents of his notes for a book. Russell contended that the conversations for which he was prosecuted amounted at most to misprision (concealment), not treason. Russell claimed that the prosecution was applying an overbroad concept of what conduct constituted the offense of treason, and he accused the prosecution of relying upon notions of "constructive treason" to overcome the requirement of the substantive law that there be two eyewitnesses to an overt act of treason.[96] Russell also contended that the two-witness requirement in treason cases was not satisfied unless the two testified about the same act, whereas the court construed it to mean the same course of treason.[97] Disputes about the law of treason were discussed in the post-Revolutionary debates,[98] and the 1696 Act made some adjustments in the substantive law.[99] These disputes about the correct application of the substantive law also influenced the movement to allow defense

[96] Regarding which, see L. M. Hill, "The Two-Witness Rule in English Treason Trials: Some Comments on the Emergence of Procedural Law," 12 *American J. Legal History* 95 (1968); 7 Wigmore, *Evidence* §§ 2036–9, at 263–72.

[97] Schwoerer, *Russell, supra* n. 37, at 160.

[98] In the House of Commons deliberations of 9 Apr. 1689, on a forerunner of what became the 1696 Act, Richard Hampden said, referring to the convictions of Russell and Sidney: "This thing of constructive Treason was set on foot in King Charles II's time. If there were not overt Acts, yet it was construed to be Treason." 9 Grey, *Debates, supra* n. 68, at 207. Colonel Thomas Tipping told the same session, "I have been always against making words Treason; for passion, or a man in drink, or a mistake of a word, may put our lives into our servants' hands, who may swear Treason against us." Ibid. at 206. Discussing a later draft of the Act, on 28 Nov. 1692, Sir Thomas Clarges said: "The hardships the Nation endured in constructive Treason was one of the greatest motives and inducements to the late change [of monarchs]." 10 ibid. at 285.

[99] The Act sustained the interpretation of the judges in *Russell's Case* that the two witnesses might testify either "to the same Overt Act, or one of them to one, and the other of them to another Overt Act of the same Treason," 1696 Act, § 2, but the Act also attempted to tighten this standard by requiring, ibid., § 4, "that if two or more distinct Treasons of divers Heads or Kinds shall be alleged in one Bill of Indictment, one Witness produced to prove one of the said Treasons, and another Witness produced to prove another of the said Treasons, shall not be deemed or taken to be two Witnesses to the same Treason, within the Meaning of this Act."

counsel in treason cases. The "increased reliance on constructive treason began to center some treason cases on legal interpretation."[100] By comparison with cases of ordinary crime, treason raised issues of considerable legal difficulty, and thus, treason defendants had a particular need for the guidance of counsel learned in the law. This sense that the substantive law of treason posed special hazards allowed the drafters of the 1696 Act to think that the line between treason and other offenses was one of intrinsic principle,[101] which justified limiting the grant of defense counsel to treason alone.

C. The Provisions of the Act

Although proposals to reform treason trial procedure surfaced immediately in the aftermath of the Revolution of 1688–9,[102] the legislation took the better part of a decade to negotiate the two Houses of Parliament. In the House of Lords the reform of treason trial procedure became entangled with the effort to change the rules governing the composition of the Court of the Lord Steward for the trial of peers.[103] The ostensible purpose of this measure was to make it harder for the crown to stack that court.[104] The House of Commons resisted the Lords[105] in several votes on this matter across the years but finally yielded in order to get the Treason Trials Act of 1696 enacted.[106]

---

[100] Shapiro, "Treason Act," *supra* n. 95, at 224.

[101] This argument was still being made a century and a half after the Treason Trials Act of 1696. In evidence submitted to the Criminal Law Commissioners in 1836 Serjeant Spankie contrasted the intricacies of treason with ordinary felony, in which the issues were, in his view, *ius gentium* and commonsensical. "The cases of difficulty are comparatively rare, and these turn upon questions of evidence," he told the Commissioners. *Second Report from Her Majesty's Commissioners on Criminal Law* (Parliamentary Papers vol. 36) (London 1836) 103 [hereafter *1836 Report*].

[102] Article 17 of the 2 Feb. 1689 draft of the "Heads of Grievances," a predecessor draft of the Declaration of Rights of 12 Feb. 1689, lists as a topic for relief: "Constructions upon the statutes of treason, and trials and proceedings and writs of error, in cases of treason, to be regulated." Schwoerer, *Declaration, supra* n. 19, at 300.

[103] "Trial of Peers Bill" (26 Feb. 1689), in Historical Manuscripts Commission, *The Manuscripts of the House of Lords: 1689–1690*, at 31 (1889) (12th Report, app., pt. 6) [hereafter HMC, *Lords MSS*] *The Portledge Papers* 59 (R. . Kerr and I. C. Duncan eds.) (1928) (entry for 9 Feb. 1689); Phifer, "Act", *supra* n. 36, at 244; Henry Horwitz, *Parliament, Policy and Politics in the Reign of William III*, 74 (1977).

[104] A. S. Turberville, *The House of Lords in the Reign of William III* 106–12 (1913) [hereafter Turberville, *Lords*].

[105] When the "Bill from the Lords, for the regulation of Trials was read first time" in the House of Commons in March 1689, Sir Thomas Lee sounded the theme of the opposition, that "this Bill [would] . . . let the Peers do all they please with impunity." 9 Grey, *Debates, supra* n. 68, at 172, 173.

[106] Turberville, *Lords, supra* n. 104, at 111–12.

The parliamentary activity has been carefully studied[107] and can be summarized for present purposes in a few particulars. The main features of what would become the 1696 Act were settled by 1691,[108] although the final language was polished across the years as the proponents groped for their political moment. That moment came in January 1696, with support from both Whig and Tory MPs, particularly from the country factions of each party, whose numbers increased in the parliamentary election of 1695.[109] Reaction to the crown's overzealous prosecution of yet another dubious treason plot, the Lancashire Plot of 1694, helped crystallize support. In that case, the Solicitor of the Treasury, Aaron Smith (Stephen College's onetime solicitor), was discovered to have fabricated evidence. "[O]bservers began to grasp that the alleged plot was entirely contrived, and that the government had political reasons for prosecuting those supposedly involved."[110] Moreover, "the behavior of the prosecution counsel . . . [frightened] contemporaries [who] were convinced that the government had once again overstepped its bounds by encouraging and elaborating upon questionable testimony."[111] "[T]he prosecution's apparently unscrupulous attempt to gain an advantage [by using] corrupt witnesses"[112] raised the chilling specter of a renewal of Stuart-style political prosecutions, precipitating the enactment.[113]

The right to defense counsel was the centerpiece of the Act, but the Act made several related reforms. The discussion in this chapter largely follows the sequence within the Act, but disregards some provisions not directed to the trial procedure.[114]

---

[107] On the dispute between the Houses, see Turberville, *Lords, supra* n. 104, at 106–12 (1913). Regarding the political dynamics of enactment, see Phifer, "Act," *supra* n. 36, which supersedes the earlier study, Samuel Rezneck, "The Statute of 1696: A Pioneer Measure in the Reform of Judicial Procedure in England," 2 *J. Modern History* 5 (1930). An important account of changes in the underlying political theory is Shapiro, "Treason Act," *supra* n. 95, discussed *infra*, text at nn. 121–4.

[108] Phifer, "Act," *supra* n. 36, at 245.   [109] Ibid. at 251.

[110] Ibid. at 253.

[111] Shapiro, "Treason Act," *supra* n. 95, at 247. A manuscript account of the proceedings has been published in a local record society volume: "An Account of the Tryalls at Manchester, October 1694," in *Remains Historical and Literary Connected with the Palatine Counties of Lancaster and Chester* (1864) (Chetham Society, vol. 61). The trial jury acquitted all the defendants, ibid. at 41.

[112] Shapiro, "Treason Act," *supra* n. 95, at 248.

[113] Shapiro also points to disquiet about the crown's having "commenced a policy of prosecuting libels" as treason in 1693. Ibid. at 249. He points to Hamburger's work "demonstrat[ing] that the Crown's libel policy was cut short by the unexpected passage of the Trials Act in 1696, which made the constructive treason of words more difficult to prove." Ibid. at 250, citing Philip Hamburger, "The Development of the Law of Seditious Libel and the Control of the Press," 37 *Stanford L. Rev.* 661, 722–3 (1985).

[114] Provisions not discussed in text: refinements made to the "overt act" requirement of substantive treason law, 1696 Act, §§ 2, 4; the summoning of peers for treason trials in the House of Lords, ibid. § 11; periods of repose (limitations), ibid. §§ 5, 6; a provision about

1. The Preamble: Innocence and Equality

The Act opens with a preamble, remarkable for the change in attitude displayed toward treason defendants. Recall Stephen's account of the treatment of the defendants in the Popish Plot trials: "[T]he sentiment continually displays itself, that the prisoner is half, or more than half, proved to be an enemy to the King, and that, in the struggle between the King and the suspected man, all advantages are to be secured to the King . . . ."[115] The preamble to the 1696 Act bespeaks quite a different view. It envisions that the defendant may be innocent, and thus the importance of his need for procedural equality with the prosecution. "[N]othing is more just and reasonable," the preamble announces, "than that Persons prosecuted for High Treason . . . should not be debarred of all just and equal means for the defence of their Innocencies in such Cases . . . ."[116] The series of procedural reforms propounded in the Act were meant to vindicate this changed conception of the accused as a potential victim rather than as the foregone villain. Having discovered how little safeguard the inherited procedure had afforded to an innocent accused, the reformers set about fashioning safeguards responsive to what they thought had miscarried.

Although the provisions of the 1696 Act and its preoccupation with vindicating innocence can be traced to grievances arising from the treason trials of the later Stuarts, the change in attitude toward treason defendants also reflects a change in the underlying political theory. Older notions of the citizen's duty of deference to the crown were losing their force. In the sixteenth century, as Lacey Baldwin Smith observed in a celebrated essay, "ideas concerning a subject's duty towards his sovereign and his society"[117] encouraged an eerie resignation on the part of treason defendants, even the innocent persons who had been framed to facilitate the marital adventures of Henry VIII. "Even those who were the victims of the most completely fabricated evidence admitted their guilt . . . ."[118] Anne Boleyn's

---

outlawing fugitives, ibid. § 3; the exclusion of impeachment and other parliamentary proceedings from the reach of the Act, ibid. §§ 9–10; and a clarification regarding the property requirement for jury service, ibid. § 10. This last measure redressed a grievance voiced at the trial of Lord Russell. He had complained that some of the men seated on the jury were not freeholders. The trial court held that the freehold requirement did not apply to an urban venue in which leasehold conveyancing was the norm. Schwoerer, "Russell," *supra* n. 37, at 160. The Declaration of Rights insisted on freeholders, see *Declaration, supra* n. 59, grievance 9, resolution 10; so did the Bill of Rights, 1 Wil. & Mar., 2d Sess., c. 2 ("jurors which pass upon men in trials for high treason ought to be freeholders"). Section 10 of the Treason Trials Act of 1696 redeemed this pledge.

[115] 1 Stephen, *History* 397.   [116] 1696 Act, preamble.
[117] Lacey Baldwin Smith, "English Treason Trials and Confessions in the Sixteenth Century," 15 *J. History Ideas* 471, 483 (1954).   [118] Ibid. at 476.

brother, prosecuted on a trumped-up allegation that he had been conducting an incestuous affair with her, declared: "I was born under the law, and I die under the law . . . . [F]orasmuch as it is the law which hath condemned me . . . I deserve death . . . ." [119] Reflecting on these sources, Smith wrote: "The victims of Tudor tyranny may have felt themselves innocent of the crimes immediately ascribed to them, but if the law, administered as the will of the King, deemed them worthy to die, then the prisoners considered themselves guilty, deserving death as men no longer useful to society."[120]

This subordination of the subject to the crown abated across the seventeenth century. The pattern of deference was thoroughly shaken in the Interregnum. Thereafter, the exclusion crisis of the 1670s and 1680s frightened many of the political elite, who feared that a Catholic monarch might attempt to undo the Reformation settlement, realign the country's foreign alliances, and provoke menacing instability. The distrust of Charles II and especially James II undermined older notions of political obligation that presumed the correctness of crown governance. In the tract literature of the 1670s and 1680s Alexander Shapiro has traced contrary ideas—hostility to the crown, suspicion of the crown's handling of judicial proceedings, and a new "theme of equality between Crown and subject . . . throughout many of the contemporary appraisals of trial procedure . . . ."[121] For example, Andrew Marvell wrote in 1677 that "we have the same right . . . in our propriety that the Prince hath in his regality; and in all cases where the king is concerned, we have our just remedy as against any person of the neighborhood, in the courts of Westminster Hall."[122] The King, reasoned Marvell, is no different from other litigants in the neighborhood. Shapiro also points to the spread among radical Whigs of the claim to "a fundamental principle of natural law . . . that man had a right to self-preservation or self-defense."[123] Shapiro quotes Sir Richard Grahme, defending himself in a treason trial in 1691: "I am bound in duty to myself . . . to insist upon all advantages I can have by law."[124] Grahme was rejecting the notion of subordination to the monarch's will that had been so salient in the Tudor trials.

With the monarchy having been brought into disgrace under James II,

---

[119] Quoted ibid. at 477.

[121] Shapiro, "Treason Act," *supra* n. 95, at 232.

[123] Ibid. at 233.

[120] Ibid. at 488.

[122] Quoted ibid. at 232.

[124] Ibid. at 240, citing Richard Grahme *et al.*, 12 *St. Tr.* 645, 661–2 (O.B. 1691). Shapiro notices, "Treason Act," *supra* n. 95, at 241, that in the first important treatise on the common law of evidence, Baron Gilbert links this idea to the notion that would become the privilege against self-incrimination: "Our law . . . will not force any Man to accuse himself; and in this we do certainly follow the law of Nature, which commands every Man to endeavor his own Preservation." Gilbert, *Evidence* 99. Regarding the history of the privilege, see *supra* Ch. 5, text at nn. 120–50.

the 1696 Act was drafted at an opportune moment for substituting notions of equality of procedural opportunity in place of subordination to the monarch. The preamble to the 1696 Act calls for treason defendants to be "justly and equally tried" and "not . . . debarred of all just and equal means for the defence of their Innocencies . . . ." The Act's chosen instrument to achieve this equality was defense counsel, fortified by other changes in trial procedure.

2. Disclosure of the Indictment

The first of the Act's reforms was a provision granting the treason defendant the right to obtain "a true Copy of the whole Indictment, but not the names of the Witnesses . . . five Days at the least before" the trial.[125] Disclosing the indictment to the accused responded to the complaint of treason defendants such as Stephen College about the defensive disadvantage of being put on trial without adequate notice. College, it will be recalled, told the court that because he had been locked up in the Tower until the moment of trial, he was "unacquainted with what was charged upon me."[126] He sought what the Treason Trials Act would later grant: "I do humbly desire that I may have a copy of the indictment, and a copy of [the names of the members of] the jury that is to pass upon me, and that I may have counsel assigned me . . . ."[127]

Letting the accused have an advance copy of the indictment was not as simple a step as might be imagined. In the parliamentary deliberations the concern was voiced that the timetable of the provincial assize system did not allow for much notice, because trial followed so rapidly upon indictment. In routine assize practice the grand jury deliberated and returned indictments on the first day or days of the assize, and the indictments went immediately to trial on those or the next days.[128] An assize session lasted only a few days, after which the judges rode off to preside at the long-scheduled assizes in the next county. Hence, said Heneage Finch in the House of Commons in a debate in 1691 concerning a forerunner of the Act, the proposed ten-day interval between delivering the indictment and trying the accused would effectively restrict the trial of treason to London: "[I]t is good in Middlesex . . . but not in Country Assizes, which cannot stay so long."[129] The point surfaced again a year

---

[125] 1696 Act, § 1.   [126] 8 *St. Tr.* at 569.

[127] Ibid. Regarding the meaning of "assigning" counsel, see *infra*, text at nn. 144–53.

[128] For example, at the summer 1754 assizes in Chelmsford (Essex), trials began at 4 p.m. on 7 August upon indictments that the grand jury returned earlier that afternoon. Langbein, "Ryder" 117.

[129] 10 Grey, *Debates*, *supra* n. 68, at 173 (18 Nov. 1691). This was Heneage Finch the younger, the son of Lord Nottingham (1621–82).

later, when Sir John Lowther, opposing the bill in Commons, protested the ten-day interval: " '[T]is impossible in our County [Westmorland] where the Assizes are but once a year, and [if another year had to elapse until trial] witnesses may be dead, or tampered with, or the Criminal may escape, and so not be punished."[130] In the final Act, the interval was reduced to five days, a period roughly as long as some provincial assize sessions.

The measure allowing the treason defendant to have a copy of the indictment was subject to a qualification, that the names of prosecution witnesses be withheld. What is odd about this provision is not the continuing refusal to allow discovery of the prosecution case, but the framing of that point as a restriction on the defendant's newly granted right to a copy of the indictment. These seemingly unrelated topics were linked in the drafters' thinking, I suspect, because in routine court practice the clerk recorded on the back of the parchment the names of the witnesses who testified in support of the indictment before the grand jury.[131] The Act was clarifying, therefore, that the new entitlement to disclosure of the terms of the indictment did not extend to disclosure of the names of prosecution witnesses whom the clerk had scheduled on the dorse.

Another limitation occasioned by the decision to allow the treason accused the right to a copy of the indictment was a provision of the Act that prevented him from raising any errors of spelling or "false or improper Latin" contained in the indictment as the basis for a motion to quash a conviction.[132] In a criminal trial the indictment was a matter "of record," for which the writ of error would lie in the event of a defect. The danger was that disclosure of the indictment would allow a conviction to be subsequently voided because of a technicality in the paperwork.[133] The rule of judicial practice denying the accused a copy of the indictment had

---

[130] 10 ibid. at 249 (18 Nov. 1692) In truth, prosecutions for high treason were seldom tried at county assizes. They were usually tried in London, on a special commission of oyer and terminer. But not always: as in the example of the Bloody Assizes, rebels would be tried and executed locally, where the rebellion was put down.

[131] See Cockburn, "Introduction" 86. At trial, "the Clerk of Assize direct[ed] the Cryer to call the Witnesses as they be subscribed to the Indictment," that is, in that order. *The Office of the Clerk of Assize* 49 (London 1682). The grand jury may not have heard all the scheduled witnesses. Counsel in a prominent forgery case told the court: "Although twenty witnesses appear upon the back of an indictment, if one witness satisfies the Grand Jury that the man ought to be tried, they often proceed no further in examining witnesses . . . ." *R. v. William Dodd, OBSP* (Feb. 1777), at 94, 103 (forgery).

[132] 1696 Act, § 9.

[133] The danger was well understood. In one of the Popish Plot trials, the accused was allowed counsel on a law point, and counsel argued that he was entitled to a copy of the indictment. "I do not say, that every one may demand a copy of his indictment *to find faults*; but upon a special plea, and particularly upon this, I humbly conceive he ought to have a sight and a copy of his indictment." *R. v. Edward Fitzharris*, 8 *St. Tr.* 243, 263 (K.B. 1681) (emphasis supplied).

effectively prevented such outcomes.[134] Thus, when the Treason Trials Act of 1696 granted the treason defendant a copy of the indictment for the purpose of disclosing the charges against him, it made a compensating adjustment to prevent him from taking advantage of clerical errors to defeat the verdict.

The close tailoring of the language of the Treason Trials Act to these small details of trial practice reflects, in my view, the influence of the judiciary, whose hand in the drafting can be reliably inferred from the House of Lords records.[135]

3. Assistance of Counsel in the Pretrial

The 1696 Act linked the grant of a copy of the indictment to a further safeguard, the pretrial assistance of counsel. The reason for disclosing the indictment to treason defendants was "to enable them . . . to advise with Counsel thereupon, to plead and make their Defense . . ."[136] The reference to pleading indicates that the drafters had in mind the arraignment phase of the procedure, which occurred in advance of trial (sometimes on an earlier day, sometimes as a preliminary to the trial but in a continuous proceeding). The arraignment was the phase at which the defendant was asked whether he contested the charges in the indictment, which he commonly did by pleading not guilty. Arraignment was the occasion for the defendant to raise an objection to the legal sufficiency of the indictment—an objection that would, if accepted by the court, preclude the trial.

The rule against defense counsel in cases of felony and treason was a rule of trial procedure. In the arraignment (pleading) phase, the defendant was in theory allowed to be represented by counsel, at least when

---

[134] The indictment exemplars that survive from early modern times often contain factual and spelling errors. Cockburn, "Introduction" 76–84. Without the right to a copy of the indictment, the accused had no practical way to raise objections, nor were the judges ordinarily willing to raise them. Cockburn points to a few cases in which judicial sympathy for the accused may explain why the judge took account of an indictment drafting defect and quashed the indictment. Ibid. at 85.

[135] The Lords summoned the entire bench to its deliberations on the Act in 1692 and 1694. "Ordered, That all the Judges do attend this House on Tuesday next, at Twelve of the Clock; at which Time the House will proceed upon the Bill, entitled, 'An Act for Regulating of Trials in Cases of Treason.' " 14 *Journals of the House of Lords* 664 (28 Nov. 1691); again, 15 ibid. 376 (22 Feb. 1694). The drafting process began in 1689; the surviving rough draft from that year is in the hand of Sir Creswell Levinz. See HMC, *Lords MSS, supra* n. 103, at 31. Levinz, author of the King's Bench reports reprinted in 63 *Eng. Rep.*, had been crown counsel and then attorney general in the Popish Plot cases and justice of common pleas from 1681. Dismissed under James II in 1686, he was one of the counsel for the Seven Bishops in 1688. Edward Foss, *Biographia Juridica: A Biographical Dictionary of the Judges of England* 406 (1870).

[136] 1696 Act, § 1.

raising a point of legal difficulty.[137] Thus, Stephen College was not being particularly aggressive when he asked the court in 1681 to "have counsel assigned me, to advise me, whether I have not something in law pleadable in bar of this Indictment."[138] However, in the period before the 1696 Act, practical difficulties hampered the accused in employing counsel to raise legal objections at arraignment. It was hard to engage counsel from conditions approaching solitary confinement. Recall College's complaint that "I have been kept a close prisoner in the Tower ever since I was taken: I was all along unacquainted with what was charged upon me."[139] The 1696 Act responded by mandating that "Counsel shall have free Access [to the defendant] at all seasonable Hours, any Law or Usage to the contrary notwithstanding."[140] Furthermore, even when counsel was waiting in the wings at arraignment, it was difficult for him to prepare legal objections when he had to respond on the spot to an indictment that was written in Latin and summarized by the clerk in English with whatever accuracy. Thus, the 1696 Act intended the right to an advance copy of the indictment as a measure that would enhance the effectiveness of defense counsel in probing the legal sufficiency of the prosecution case.

4. Trial Counsel

The landmark reform of the Treason Trials Act of 1696, already extensively discussed in this chapter, was the grant of defense counsel at trial. The Act allowed the accused "to make his . . . full Defense,[141] by Counsel learned in the law . . . ."[142] The seemingly innocuous term "full defense" would become a point of contrast with the more limited right to defense counsel in cases of ordinary felony that the judges began to allow in the 1730s. Parliament would have to intervene again, in the Prisoner's Counsel Act of 1836,[143] to extend full defense of counsel to felony trials.

The 1696 Act requires the trial court "or some Judge of that Court" upon the defendant's "Request, to assign to" him "such and so many Counsel, not exceeding Two, as the [defendant] shall desire . . . ."[144] This

---

[137] Discussed *supra*, Ch. 1, text at nn. 80–7.   [138] 8 *St. Tr.* at 569.
[139] Ibid.   [140] 1696 Act, § 1.
[141] In the eighteenth and nineteenth centuries the term "full defense of counsel" came to be contrasted with the more limited role of examining and cross-examining witnesses that was allowed to defense counsel from the 1730s onward. Until the Prisoner's Counsel Act of 1836, defense counsel was not allowed to make an opening statement to the jury nor to sum up nor to comment on the evidence at the end of the trial. These steps were known as "addressing the court." The campaign to extend defensive representation to include addressing the court (discussed in Ch. 5 of this book) came to be cast as the movement for full defense of counsel, echoing the language that appeared in the Treason Trials Act of 1696.
[142] 1696 Act, § 1.   [143] 6 & 7 Wil. 4, c. 114 (1836).
[144] 1696 Act, § 1.

provision can mislead the reader,[145] because the term "assign" counsel has changed meaning. In later usage,[146] "assigned counsel" has come to refer to a lawyer who is designated to represent an indigent defendant. Assigned counsel serves without compensation or for nominal compensation from public funds. The 1696 Act had quite a different purpose—not to supply defense lawyers for indigents, but to legitimate the service of defense lawyers as a professional activity that might otherwise be treated as conspiracy in the alleged treason.[147] In the late Stuart treason trials there had been occasional intimations that such "assignment" was needed to protect defense lawyers. At the arraignment of Edward Fitzharris, his wife told the court that she had been unable to engage a solicitor. "I hope your lordship will give leave for a solicitor; without your lordship's leave none will dare to venture."[148] At the trial of Stephen College, North CJ said to the accused, in the course of the celebrated transaction in which papers prepared by his solicitor were taken from him: "How comes any body to give you papers? Nobody can solicit for one that is under an accusation of High-Treason, unless [that solicitor] be assigned so to do by the court."[149] Fitzharris asked the court to assign a number of prominent counsel, whom he had not yet retained, to help him raise a plea to the jurisdiction. The presiding judge, Pemberton CJ, replied: "[W]e will not enjoin any counsel to serve you farther than they are willing themselves."[150] He nevertheless ordered: "Let them be assigned of counsel for him."[151] The effect of assigning counsel to an accused[152] was, therefore,

---

[145] E.g., William M. Beaney, *The Right to Counsel in American Courts* 12 (1955); Note, "An Historical Argument for the Right to Counsel during Police Interrogation," 73 *Yale L.J.* 1000, 1028–9 (1964).

[146] See, e.g., the subchapter "Assigning Counsel" in David Bentley, *English Criminal Justice in the Nineteenth Century* 110–15 (1998), discussing arrangements for providing counsel to indigent defendants in the nineteenth century.

[147] Seipp reports two examples of defense counsel being assigned in yearbook cases from 1340 and 1486, both cases involving political crime. For evidence of this practice from fourteenth- and fifteenth-century yearbook sources, see David J. Seipp, "Crime in the Year Books," in *Law Reporting in England* 15, 28 (Chantal Stebbings ed.) (1995).

[148] *R. v. Edward Fitzharris*, 8 *St. Tr.* 243, 256 (K.B. 1681).

[149] *R. v. Stephen College*, 8 *St. Tr.* at 571. Hawles confirms the report, saying that College was told that neither counsel nor solicitor "is allowed in Treason, unless assigned by the Court." Hawles, *Remarks* 22.

[150] 8 *St. Tr.* at 252.   [151] Ibid.

[152] This usage also appears in connection with engaging prosection counsel. In 1642, at the outbreak of the Civil War, Charles I instructed the assize judges to keep order in various ways while on circuit. As part of that responsibility, he commanded them to "assign . . . some of the ablest lawyers who ride that circuit to be of counsel for us, to assist in such pleas of the crown that may be most necessary for our service, in the execution and punishment of notorious delinquents." *The Kings Majesties Charge, Sent to all the Judges of England* (London, 26 July 1642), reprinted in 4 *A Collection of Scarce and Valuable Tracts* 464, 465 (2nd edn. 1810) (Walter Scott ed.) (2nd edn. London 1809–15) [hereafter *Somers Tracts*]. (The published version of the letter was addressed to the Home Circuit judges, but the title indicates that comparable instructions were to be sent to the judges on the other circuits.)

not to subsidize but merely to authorize the engagement. A quarter century after the Treason Trials Act, Hawkins was still cautioning that for ordinary felony "it is not safe for any one to be either Counsel or Solicitor to one in Prison for a capital Crime, in order to prepare him for his Trial, without an Assignment from the Court."[153]

5. Solicitors

We have seen that defense solicitors were engaged in some of the late Stuart treason trials, although crown counsel sometimes sought to hamper their work. In authorizing defense counsel, the 1696 Act also legitimated defense solicitors—mostly by implication, although the Act expressly mentions attorneys and other agents in its provision granting the accused the right to a copy of the indictment. The Act envisioned that the copy would be prepared at the request of the accused's "Attorney or Attorneys, Agent or Agents," upon their "paying the Officer [that is, the clerk] his reasonable fees for writing thereof, not exceeding Five Shillings for the Copy of every such Indictment . . . ."[154] (This passage also under-scores that subsidizing indigent defendants was not among the objectives of the Act.)

At the time of the 1696 Act the division of function in the English legal profession between solicitors and attorneys, on the one hand, and counsel (that is, barristers), on the other, was already evident.[155] In civil practice the solicitor dealt with the client, prepared pleadings and paperwork, investigated facts, located and prepared witnesses, and transmitted the fruits of his fact-gathering efforts to counsel. I shall have more to say in Chapter 3 about the growing role of solicitors in eighteenth-century criminal procedure for felony. In both civil and criminal procedure, counsel alone had the right of audience before the court. The solicitor's investigative work, summarized for counsel in a "brief" or set of "instructions," would enable counsel to strategize, to make effective use of defense witnesses, and (depending on what the solicitor was able to learn about the likely prosecution evidence) to cross-examine prosecution witnesses more effectively.

Beyond the mention of the attorney arranging for the copy of the indictment, the 1696 Act may also have contemplated solicitors for the defense in another provision, which grants the treason defendant the right to a copy "of the Panel of the [trial] Jurors . . . two Days at the

---

[153] 2 Hawkins, PC 401.   [154] 1696 Act, § 1.
[155] See generally 6 Holdsworth, HEL 432–57. On the attorneys, see C. W. Brooks, *Pettyfoggers and Vipers of the Commonwealth: The 'Lower Branch' of the Legal Profession in Early Modern England* (1986).

least before" trial.[156] The purpose of this measure was to allow some investigation of prospective jurors' backgrounds, in order to allow the accused to exercise his challenge rights in an informed way.[157] This sort of investigative work would routinely have fallen to solicitors.[158]

6. Defense Witnesses

We saw in Chapter 1 that until practice began to change in the second half of the seventeenth century, a criminal defendant was not entitled to compulsory process, meaning that he had no means to compel the attendance of witnesses who were unwilling to testify voluntarily (an understandable reluctance in treason cases, since volunteering to testify for an accused traitor would antagonize the crown). Prosecution witnesses were routinely bound over to testify either by the Privy Council or under the Marian committal procedure. The 1696 Act, striving to put the accused on an equal footing with the prosecution, granted the accused compulsory process. The language of the Act on this point echoes the concern sounded in the preamble about equalizing defensive opportunity. Persons accused of treason "shall have the like process of the Court where they shall be tried, to compel their Witnesses to appear for them at any such Trial or Trials, as is usually granted to compel Witnesses to appear against them."[159]

Until the 1696 Act defense witnesses were not allowed to testify on oath, hence they were less credible than prosecution witnesses, who were sworn. Experience in the late Stuart treason trials caused the testimonial disqualification of defense witnesses to be challenged. In his 1689 tract Hawles reviewed the testimony of the witnesses for and against Stephen College and concluded that the merits were a draw. "Now if College's Witnesses were credited, it was impossible [that] the King's Witnesses could be credited; that was agreed by the court to be true upon the Trial. The answer on the Trial was, that the King's Witnesses were on their Oaths, the Prisoner's were not; which was a Reason but in words and not in sense."[160] Consistent with the Act's central theme of equalizing the accused and the crown, defense witnesses were made as credible as prosecution witnesses by placing both on oath. The Act authorizes the treason

---

[156] 1696 Act, § 7.

[157] The point was made in Hawles' tract, written in 1689, that challenge rights are of little value unless the accused is given the opportunity to have the prospective jurors investigated in advance. Hawles, *Remarks* 31–2.

[158] Regarding the contemporary expectation that an imprisoned accused would engage a solicitor to investigate and gather defensive evidence, see ibid. at 24.

[159] 1696 Act, § 7.

[160] Hawles, *Remarks* 39.

defendant "to make any Proof that he . . . can produce by lawful Witness or Witnesses, who shall then be upon oath . . . ."[161]

The 1696 Act left untouched the rule that disqualified the accused from testifying on oath. Although the central purpose of the "accused speaks" trial was to have the accused serve as an informational resource, he was not considered a witness, and hence he spoke unsworn. This prohibition endured until lifted by statute for all criminal defendants—in England not until 1898,[162] a few decades earlier in most American jurisdictions.[163]

D. The Restriction to Treason

The conception that animates the 1696 Act is captured in its title and in its contents. This charter of defensive liberties was not a criminal procedure code, but a treason act. The reforms were carefully restricted to cases of treason. The enacting clause applied the Act to "every Person . . . accused and indicted of High Treason . . . ."[164] Why were the drafters of the 1696 Act so insistent upon limiting these extensive safeguards to political crime? Because the legislative materials do not discuss the point, we are left to try to understand it from context.

The restriction to treason would be easy enough to understand as a manifestation of the self-interest of the political classes. Since treason was the branch of the criminal law that might predictably touch the members of the political community, perhaps they legislated procedural safeguards only for themselves, callously leaving the lower orders to suffer the injustice of the unreformed procedure. Stephen actually voiced this view, derisively explaining the drafters' thinking that the safeguards of the 1696 Act were

so great a favor that [they] ought to be reserved for people accused of crime for which legislators themselves or their friends and connections were likely to be prosecuted. It was a matter of direct personal interest to many members of Parliament that trials for political offense should not be grossly unfair, but they were comparatively indifferent as to the fate of people accused of sheep-stealing, or burglary, or murder.[165]

Elsewhere in his *History* Stephen returned to this theme, remarking that "[t]here must have been plenty of Oateses and Bedloes [the perjured witnesses in the Popish Plot trials] at the assizes and quarter sessions who

---

[161] 1696 Act, § 1.
[162] Criminal Evidence Act, 61 & 62 Vict., c. 6 (1898).
[163] Regarding the American development, see *supra*, Ch. 1, text at nn. 207–8.
[164] 1696 Act, § 1.
[165] 1 Stephen, *History* 226.

have never been heard of, and no doubt scores or hundreds of obscure people suffered for common burglaries and robberies of which they were quite as innocent as [the Popish Plot defendants]."[166] Under this view, the Treason Trials Act of 1696 was an unprincipled piece of class legislation.

There is, however, considerable evidence that the drafters of the 1696 Act understood the restriction to treason to be principled, whether or not they were mistaken. In responding to the treason trials of the late Stuarts, the drafters thought the lesson was that treason cases presented distinctive problems that required special procedures. Four aspects of treason prosecutions appeared to contemporaries to demarcate treason trials as a procedural world of their own, remote from ordinary crime: (1) the prosecutorial imbalance; (2) the subservience of the bench; (3) the complexity of the offense of treason; and (4) the rarity of treason cases. Collectively, these attributes seemed to justify particular procedures, in order to even up for the advantages of the prosecution.

1. Prosecutorial Imbalance

Writing in 1721, a quarter century after the 1696 Act allowed counsel to treason defendants, Hawkins undertook to justify the rule against defense counsel in felony trials. Treason was different. "Experience" had shown the framers of the 1696 Act that there were "great Disadvantages from the want of [defense] Counsel, in Prosecutions of High Treason against the King's Person, which are generally managed for the Crown with greater Skill and Zeal than ordinary Prosecutions . . . ."[167] "Skill and Zeal" was code language. By "Skill," Hawkins was referring to the crown's use of lawyer prosecutors in treason cases. "Zeal" signalled the prosecutorial abuses that had occurred in the Stuart trials.

A central theme that emerged in the critique of the late Stuart treason trials was the sense of imbalance between the lawyer-prosecutor and the unaided accused. The uneasiness stemmed partly from alleged prosecutorial misconduct, such as suborning perjured witnesses, but, more fundamentally, the Stuart trials made observers aware of the structural inequality of the procedure. Recall Hawles' emphasis in his critique of College's trial, that "as many Counsel as can be hired is allowed to be against [the accused], none for him ."[168] Looking back from the middle of the eighteenth century, Michael Foster wrote in his *Crown Law* that the 1696 Act wisely allowed defense counsel in treason cases, because such trials "are carried on by the Weight of the Crown and too often in the Spirit of Party, and are generally conducted by Gentlemen of High

---

[166] Ibid. at 415.   [167] 2 Hawkins, *PC* 402.   [168] Hawles, *Remarks* 32.

Rank at the Bar" (a reference to the Attorney General and Solicitor General).[169]

In the ordinary criminal trial, prosecution was the work of the victim or other citizen accuser. The resources of the crown were not routinely poured into finding and preparing prosecution witnesses; at best, the lay JP and the lay constable aided the victim to build his case in the Marian pretrial procedure. The victim was allowed to engage prosecuting counsel, but virtually never did. Thus, in the 1690s the prosecution of felony was still thought to be the province of the rustic, lawyer-free, altercation-type trial that Sir Thomas Smith depicted in the 1560s. Only treason proceedings needed equalizing, because only in treason prosecutions was prosecution counsel characteristic.

2. Judicial Bias

The subservience of the bench in the late Stuart treason trials was also perceived as a problem special to treason, even though the main cure, judicial independence, could not be treason-specific and had to be addressed outside the 1696 Act, in the Act of Settlement of 1701.[170]

The judges who presided over the great treason cases were usually handpicked for the particular trial. Most of the trials took place in London, under the eye of the crown. The crown had an acute interest in the outcome of treason trials, whereas it had no direct interest in whether some accused was found guilty of stealing sheep or picking pockets. The drafters of the 1696 Act saw no particular reason to question the court-as-counsel rubric or to doubt the fairness of the judges in the routine administration of criminal justice. It was the special dynamic of the treason trial that led Hawles to contend that the judges "betrayed their poor Client, to please, as they apprehended, their better client, the King."[171]

3. Complexity of Treason

The sense that the bench was untrustworthy in treason cases interacted with another concern that was thought to be unique to treason, the legal complexity of the offense. The 1696 Act undertook to clarify a few of the substantive law issues that had arisen in the trials of the 1680s by tightening the overt Act requirements,[172] but ascertaining the line between loyal opposition and treason would continue to present difficult issues about the legal characterization of a defendant's knowledge, conduct, and intent. Accordingly, there was a particular hazard about having a hostile bench interpret so malleable a legal standard.

---

[169] Foster, *Crown Law* 231.   [170] *Supra*, text at n. 78.
[171] Hawles, *Remarks* 22.   [172] 1696 Act, §§ 2, 4, discussed *supra*, n. 114.

Even in the realm of fact, there was a sense that treason raised issues of special complexity. In cases such as the Popish Plot trials, or the prosecution of Russell's alleged intrigues, the sole crime was talk. The Popish Plot trials underscored the danger of false witnessing, and hence, the need for careful probing of accusing testimony. By contrast, the citizen accusers who prosecuted ordinary crime were untainted by the intense political factionalism that surrounded treason cases. Moreover, ordinary crime was assumed to involve more reliable proofs. Stealing sheep or shop goods, committing burglary or murder or highway robbery, involved conduct that might be witnessed or leave physical evidence. It will be seen in Chapter 3 that these assumptions about the greater reliability of the evidence in cases of ordinary crime would be called into question in the 1730s, when new prosecutorial initiatives raised new doubts about the reliability of prosecution evidence.

4. No Systemic Consequences

The drafters of the 1696 Act must have found reassurance in the knowledge that treason cases occurred so infrequently. Contemporaries sensed the danger that defense counsel might interfere with the traditional "accused speaks" trial. Commenting in the House of Commons in 1691 upon an early draft of what became the 1696 Act, Heneage Finch warned: "As for being allowed Counsel, in every Treason, it would make Trials long; and all Men's Cases are alike, when dressed up by Art of Counsel."[173] The danger was evident that the intermediation of defense counsel might cause the defendant to lose his distinctive voice, and by diminishing him as an informational resource, undercut the "accused speaks" trial.

Restricting the reforms of the 1696 Act to cases of treason removed any danger of impairing the routine administration of criminal justice. No matter how severe the dislocations wrought by defense counsel might prove to be in treason trials, such cases would remain predictably scarce. Moreover, most treason prosecutions followed an extensive pretrial examination of the accused and of the events, typically conducted by the law officers of the crown and members of the Privy Council. The fruits of that investigation would shape the evidence at trial even if the reforms introduced in the 1696 Act resulted in defense counsel silencing the accused at trial.

Venue also walled off most treason trials from ordinary criminal justice. Important treason trials were usually tried to a court specially

---

[173] 10 Grey, *Debates, supra* n. 68, at 174 (18 Nov. 1691).

convened for the particular case,[174] usually in London, rather than being sent to trial at routine Old Bailey or assize sittings.

5. Evening Up

Among those responsible for the administration of criminal justice, there was as yet no sense of dissatisfaction with the balance of safeguard in ordinary criminal procedure. Indeed, the decade of the 1690s was a period in which the main tendency of governmental policy in the criminal law was not safeguard but repression.[175] A new Dutch monarch sat precariously on the English throne. Various initiatives designed to reinforce and toughen the administration of the criminal law stem from this period. "[T]he reigns of William and Anne saw the introduction of about a hundred bills and the passage of a dozen statutes dealing in broad terms with the criminal law. The most important of these statutes aimed to strengthen the courts in their dealing with felonies, particularly with crime against property."[176] The series of reward statutes (whose untoward consequences would figure centrally in the extension of adversary trial procedure to ordinary crime) commence in 1692.[177] Also in these years the government finally succeeded in developing transportation as an alternative to capital punishment, an initiative whose purpose and effect was to increase the conviction rate for major property crimes by providing a milder sanction more in accord with public (and juror) sentiment.[178] Thus, the restriction to treason in the 1696 Act helped reconcile this measure of defensive safeguard with the dominant trend of the times toward greater repression in the administration of criminal justice.[179]

---

[174] Under a commission of oyer and terminer. For the Tudor-period practice, see John Bellamy, *The Tudor Law of Treason: An Introduction* 132–3 (1979).

[175] The theme of Beattie, *Policing passim*.

[176] J. M. Beattie, "The Cabinet and the Management of Death at Tyburn after the Revolution of 1688–1689," in *The Revolution of 1688–89: Changing Perspectives* 218 (Lois G. Schwoerer ed.) (1992).

[177] 4 & 5 Wil. & Mar, c. 8, § 2 (1692). The reward system is discussed *infra* Ch. 3, text at nn. 206–47.

[178] On the origins of transportation, see Beattie, *Crime* 470–83, 500–11; Beattie, *Policing* 424–62.

[179] Commenting on a prepublication draft of this chapter, Alexander Shapiro observes: "In ways that the ordinary criminal trial did not and could not, the treason trial represented in microcosm the struggle of crown and subject that was being addressed on a broader level in political theory and in the other reforms of the Williamite era. The treason trial was thus *sui generis*, not simply because of its unique procedural elements, but also because of its political significance . . . . It was only natural . . . [that the reformers would concentrate on] the politically charged institution of the treason trial itself, rather than on the general institution of the criminal trial, and that they would fail to, or refuse to, draw the connection between their reforms and the daily practice of the criminal courts." Letter from Alexander H. Shaprio, 7 May 2002.

The sense that the Act was evening up for the special advantages of the treason prosecution shows up in the language of equalization: in the preamble, with its manifesto that treason defendants "should not be debarred of all just and equal means for Defense of their Innocencies in such Cases;"[180] and in the compulsory process clause, empowering the accused to have "the like Process of the Court [for compelling their witnesses] . . . as is usually granted to compel Witnesses to appear against them."[181] All the principal reforms of the 1696 Act—the right to defense counsel, the enhanced pretrial disclosure, the swearing of defense witnesses, and compulsory process for defense witnesses—imitated prosecutorial practice for the purpose of rectifying imbalance.

The suggestion that the use of prosecution counsel should give rise to a right to defense counsel was not a wholly novel idea in the 1690s. During the Interregnum a committee chaired by Matthew Hale recommended abridging the rule against defense counsel in any criminal case in which counsel appeared for the prosecution.[182]

The mission of evening up, that is, of correcting for the special hazards of the treason prosecution, is what unites both the safeguards granted in the 1696 Act and the restriction to treason. The logic of evening up for prosecution advantages, especially the advantages of prosecution lawyers, would resurface: in the 1730s, in the developments that led the courts to extend the assistance of defense counsel to persons accused of ordinary felony; and again in nineteenth century, in the campaign that eliminated the last restrictions on the role of defense counsel in 1836.

E. Of Aristocrats and Paupers: Treason's Legacy for Adversary Criminal Justice

The oddity that adversary criminal procedure was originally devised for the exceptional circumstances of treason cases helps illumine the two characteristic shortcomings of adversary procedure, the wealth effect and the combat effect.

1. The Wealth Effect

Adversary criminal procedure privatizes the investigation and presenta-

---

[180] 1696 Act, preamble.   [181] Ibid., § 7.

[182] "[A]s well in matters of fact as law, where . . . any person plead as of counsel against the prisoner, in such case the prisoner may have counsel; and any credible witnesses produced by the prisoner shall hereafter deliver their testimonies upon oath." *Several Draughts of Acts* (1653), reprinted in 6 *Somers Tracts, supra* n. 152, at 177, 234 ("Touching Criminal Causes"), § 3, at 235.

tion of evidence. Such a procedure is intrinsically skewed to the advantage of wealthy defendants, who can afford to hire the most skilled counsel and to pay for the gathering and production of defensive evidence.

Treason in an aristocratic age was overwhelmingly the turf of the affluent. Treason defendants in seventeenth-century England were persons active in high politics. They were likely to be persons who possessed substantial wealth, or who were connected to the wealthy by ties of family or patronage.[183] If placed on trial for their lives, such persons could afford to hire counsel and to pay for investigative work. The drafters of the Treason Trials Act of 1696 presupposed that paying for adversary justice was not going to be an obstacle for the clientele that the Act meant to benefit. It is no mystery, therefore, why the drafters could disregard the wealth effect that is such a striking feature of the procedural regime they were devising.

In the next century, when the judges extended adversary procedure to cases of felony, a procedural regime meant to serve the needs of aristocrats would become generalized to a class of legal business (serious crime) that has always been uniquely the province of the poor. Maitland's remark, made with reference to quite a different chapter of English legal history (he was speaking about the spread of seal in contracting) resonates: "[I]n England . . . the law for the great became the law for all . . . ."[184] In 1696 no one had any reason for concern that a criminal procedure for the great might not be well suited to the circumstances of paupers.

2. The Combat Effect

The other defining shortcoming of adversary criminal procedure is its subordination of truth-seeking. Because adversary procedure remits to partisans the work of gathering and presenting the evidence, each side operates under an incentive to suppress and distort unfavorable evidence, however truthful it may be.

Why were the drafters of the Treason Trials Act of 1696 not more alert to the dangers inherent in combat justice? Part of the answer, I would suggest, is that the late Stuart treason trials left the drafters numb to

---

[183] There were, of course, exceptions. One of the codefendants in the trial of John Twyn, a printer in 1663 tried for publishing a treasonable book, was Nathan Brooks, a bookbinder. He was charged only with misdemeanor and was told that he had the right to counsel. He replied: "I am a poor man, I have not money to get counsel; I hope I shall not want that that belongs to me by law, for want of money." *R. v. John Twyn*, 6 *St. Tr.* 513, 519 (O.B. 1663). Another codefendant in the case, Dover, was allowed to inspect the indictment. He told the court that he was unable to read Latin. Chief Justice Hyde told him to hire his own clerk. 6 *St. Tr.* at 518.

[184] 2 Maitland, *HEL* 224.

partisanship. They had just experienced in the Stuart law courts an epoch of venomous political combat, in which the contending factions had employed trumped-up treason prosecutions to send each other to death. In attempting for the future to restrain and moderate these political and dynastic struggles, the drafters of the Act took for granted that treason trials would be highly partisan. What the drafters could not have foreseen is that this procedural form, which they so insistently confined to treason, would escape the bounds of the Act and inject into the administration of ordinary criminal justice the combat ethos of the newly lawyerized treason trial.

In the light of hindsight, the design of the 1696 Act can be seen as having come at the price of alternatives that might have proven wiser. Instead of employing partisans for the defense to even up for the partisanship of the prosecution, one could wish that the drafters of the fateful 1696 Act had explored institutional reforms to encourage greater neutrality in the work of investigating, charging, prosecuting, and trying criminal cases. But the drafters worked within the institutional and procedural tradition that they inherited. In crimes of state the law officers of the crown and their hirelings had been little better than henchmen;[185] in cases of ordinary crime the investigating and charging functions remained largely privatized, in the hands of the victim. Thus, the English had scant experience upon which to draw for constructing a system of impartial public prosecution. Their experience with prosecution was too primitive to inspire confidence that prosecution could be made principled.

Likewise, the drafters of the 1696 Act inherited a stunted conception of the judicial role. Judges had neither the responsibility nor the resources for investigating the merits of the cases coming before them. With the bench in disgrace for its misbehavior in the late Stuart treason trials, there could not have been a worse moment to confront the central shortcoming of the English conception of judicial office, the failure to make judges responsible for truth-seeking. The year 1696 provided no opening for rethinking the English tradition of judicial administration, no occasion to

---

[185] Macaulay's portrait of prosecution counsel in the late Stuart treason trials captures (from the Victorian armchair) the image that was left in historical recollection, of "a band of able, experienced, and unprincipled lawyers, who could, by merely glancing over a brief, distinguish every weak and every strong point of a case, whose presence of mind never failed them, whose flow of speech was inexhaustible, and who had passed their lives in dressing up the worse reason so as to make it appear the better. Was it not horrible to see three or four of these shrewd, learned, and callous orators arrayed against one poor wretch who had never in his life uttered a word in public, who was ignorant of the legal definition of treason and of the first principles of the law of evidence, and whose intellect, unequal at best to a fencing match with professional gladiators, was confused by the near prospect of a cruel and ignominious death?" 6 T. B. Macaulay, *The History of England from the Accession of James II*, at 2111 (C. H. Firth ed.) (1914) (1st edn. 1849–61).

contemplate expanding the responsibilities of the bench to include thorough and impartial investigation into the merits of criminal cases. English judges would continue to process cases whose truth, if any, lay elsewhere—with the accuser and accused, the witnesses, and the jury. For the drafters of 1696, convinced that the problem of safeguard was special to treason, it was easier to summon a new participant, defense counsel, as protagonist for the treason accused, than to undertake fundamental reform of the institutions whose weaknesses had permitted the late Stuart treason trials to become a slaughter of innocents.

Consistent with their goal to remedy the miscarriages in treason trials, the drafters of the 1696 Act carefully confined defense counsel to treason. They had no way of knowing that a generation later defense counsel would free himself from that tether, enter the ordinary trial, and work a revolution in common law criminal procedure.

3

The Prosecutorial Origins of Defense Counsel

In the 1730s the judges began to depart from the rule forbidding defense counsel in cases of ordinary felony. We find the judges allowing the defendant to have the assistance of counsel at trial for the limited purpose of examining and especially cross-examining witnesses. This fateful step sent our procedure down the path toward what would become the adversary criminal trial.

Stephen described this development as "[t]he most remarkable change" that took place in English criminal procedure from the time of its happening down to his own day.[1] Working from the handful of felony

---

[1] 1 Stephen, *History* 424.

cases reported in the *State Trials*, Stephen thought that the appearance of defense counsel to examine and cross-examine witnesses began in the second half of the eighteenth century.[2] Some years ago I was able to place the historical development a generation earlier, in the mid-1730s.[3] I worked from a set of pamphlet sources not known to Stephen, the *Old Bailey Sessions Papers*,[4] which are described in some detail in Chapter 4 of this book.[5] The *Sessions Papers* supply synoptic accounts of the London felony trials held at the Old Bailey, the main felony trial court for London. Using similar pamphlet sources for Surrey Assizes, John Beattie has documented the appearance of defense counsel in that court in the same period, including a case that occurred in 1732.[6]

Why did the judges of the 1730s depart from the rule against defense counsel, a rule they had enforced so determinedly and for so long? Unlike the Treason Trials Act of 1696, which allowed treason defendants to be represented by counsel, the change in practice in the 1730s was not embodied in legislation. Accordingly, we are missing the characteristic traces that help us to understand the origins of an enactment. We have no statutory text, no preamble, no journals of the two Houses, no papers of the parliamentarians. Although the change occurred in judicial practice, it did not arise from adjudication, and thus the judges did not leave decisional law to explain their thinking. The change in judicial practice is so poorly evidenced for its early decades that legal historians have been able to document it only through the study of obscure pamphlet trial reports that were all but unknown until the present generation. Lacking,

---

[2] Ibid. Accord, Glanville Williams, *The Proof of Guilt: A Study of the English Criminal Trial* 8 (1955).

[3] Langbein, "CTBL" 311–12.

[4] In the early years the title wanders before settling on a variant of *The Proceedings on the King's Commissions of the Peace, Oyer and Terminer, and Gaol Delivery . . . in the OldBailey, on [certain dates]* (trial reports for the City of London and the county of Middlesex, from c.1674 to 1913).

[5] *Infra* Ch. 4, text at nn. 7–52.

[6] Beattie, *Crime* 356–7, drawing upon the *Surrey Assize Papers* (*The Proceedings at the Assizes . . . for the County of Surrey . . . on [certain dates]*) [hereafter *SAP*]. The *SAP* survive irregularly from 1688 into the 1770s. See Beattie, *Crime* 23–5 and n. 31. The county of Surrey, extending south from the Thames, included part of metropolitan London. A small run of comparable pamphlets for Essex (1680 to 1774) and one for Kent (1766) are identified in King, *Crime* 222 n. 2.

The publishers seemed to have tested the market for comparable series in the mid- to late 1770s. In the endpapers to the April 1774 *Sessions Papers*, the shorthand reporter Joseph Gurney advertises separate sessions pamphlets for the "last Assize[s]" at Hertford, Essex, Kent, and Surrey. There was a series for York in the 1770s, of which six exemplars from 1775 to 1778 survive in the York Minster Library. (I owe this reference to John Styles.)

Provincial assize courts sat only twice a year, whereas the Old Bailey sat eight times a year, usually with a heavier caseload per sitting. Accordingly, the provincial pamphlet reports were never as extensive as the *Old Bailey Sessions Papers*, and far fewer have survived.

therefore, any authoritative account of the rationale for the judges' action, we are left to try to infer the purposes from the circumstances.

The theme of this chapter is that in admitting defense counsel the judges were responding to a complex set of developments in the patterns of prosecution. These developments were centered in London and its environs, where urbanization was particularly intense. The urban population of England, estimated to have been 5.25 percent in 1520, rose to 17 percent by 1700 and reached 21 percent in 1750. At the end of the eighteenth century it stood at 27.5 percent.[7] In 1520 London was a cluster of wards and villages with a population of 55,000 (2.25 percent of the English population). London's population increased to 200,000 in 1600 and to 575,000 in 1700. At the end of the eighteenth century it stood just short of a million (960,000 people, or 11 percent of the country's population).[8] This burgeoning urban population was notably transient; in the eighteenth century perhaps two thirds of the people living in London had not been born there.[9] Most of the growth, both in population and in crime, occurred not in the ancient City of London, but in the surrounding environs of Middlesex.[10]

The problems of crime and criminality associated with the social relations of the metropolis strained the inherited institutions of communal law enforcement, provoking considerable experiment with ways of organizing and paying for police.[11] Communal law enforcement yielded across the nineteenth century to the paid, uniformed police and the system of police-conducted prosecution.[12] The prosecutorial initiatives of the early eighteenth century that are emphasized in this chapter were, in the light of hindsight, way stations on that path. There were two main lines of development, whose ramifications would prove deeply unsettling to the eighteenth-century criminal trial: the use of lawyers to prepare and conduct criminal prosecutions, and the development of new incentives for prosecution that greatly increased the danger of perjured testimony.

---

[7] E. A. Wrigley, "Urban Growth and Agricultural Change: England and the Continent in the Early Modern Period," in *The Eighteenth-Century Town: A Reader in English Urban History 1688–1820*, at 45 (table 2) (1990).

[8] Ibid.

[9] W. A. Speck, *Stability and Strife: England, 1714–1760*, at 66 (1979 edn.)

[10] Paley reports "that by 1748 only 4% of metropolitan cases on the Crown Side of the [King's Bench] originated from the City; the rest were from Middlesex." Ruth Paley, " 'An Imperfect, Inadequate and Wretched System'? Policing London before Peel," 10 *Criminal Justice History* 95, 127 n. 18. (1989) [hereafter Paley, "Policing"].

[11] See Beattie, *Policing* 114–207.

[12] See generally Philips, "Engine"; Elaine A. Reynolds, *Before the Bobbies: The Night Watch and Police Reform in Metropolitan London, 1720–1830* (1998); Clive Emsley, *The English Police: A Political and Social History* (2nd edn. 1996); Stanley H. Palmer, *Police and Protest in England and Ireland: 1780–1850* (1988); T. A. Critchley, *A History of Police in England and Wales* (1967); 3 Radzinowicz, *History, passim*.

Both trends entailed drastic departures from the altercation trial, that is, from the sixteenth- and seventeenth-century model of the trial as a contest of citizen equals.

Prosecution Lawyers

Across the eighteenth century, solicitors came to play an ever increasing role in the work of investigating criminal cases, shaping criminal charges, and preparing evidence for trial, a role whose essentials survive in modern English practice. I emphasize in this chapter the work of solicitors for what I call institutional prosecutors (the Mint, the Bank of England, the Treasury, and the Post Office), as well as the growing use of solicitors by private prosecutors. Further, I point to the reinforcement for private prosecution that resulted from the development of associations for the prosecution of felons, voluntary societies that were intimately aligned with the solicitor's profession. The use of prosecution solicitors was associated with a perceptible increase in the use of counsel to prosecute felony cases at trial, further exaggerating the imbalance between the unaided accused and a lawyer-conducted prosecution.

This chapter also takes note of the growing use of solicitors for the defense. The rule against felony defense counsel was a rule of trial practice that did not impede solicitors from pretrial work. There were shady figures who practiced in London, mostly but not entirely for the defense, who were known disparagingly as "Newgate solicitors." (Newgate was the prison that held persons awaiting trial at the Old Bailey.[13]) By the 1730s there was considerable alarm about the ability of Newgate solicitors to falsify or to tamper with evidence in ways that judge and jury might be unable to detect at trial.

Prosecution Perjury

In the same period that solicitors and barristers were bringing legal-professional reinforcement to a range of criminal prosecutions, the government launched a sustained effort to increase the levels of criminal prosecution by offering monetary rewards for the successful prosecution of offenders who committed certain of the more serious property crimes. The reward statutes called forth a mercenary proto-police, the thieftakers, who lived close to the London underworld on which they preyed. The reward system turned out to be fraught with incentives for false witnessing.

---

[13] According to Foster, the commission of gaol delivery for the county of Middlesex ran "singly for the prison of Newgate. And therefore if a prisoner be in the Tower or in any other gaol in the county and is to be tried at Old Bailey, he must be removed by habeas corpus to Newgate." Foster, Hale MS 160, citing a decision of Holt CJ in *R. v. Beshall* (K.B. 1695).

Reward-seekers who received £40 (in some circumstances £140) per conviction had no intrinsic interest in distinguishing the guilty from the innocent. This deep flaw of the reward system came sharply to public attention in the Waller scandal of 1732, discussed below, just when the bench was making its epochal decision to allow defense counsel. Further scandals involving false prosecution for bounty plagued the reward system across the eighteenth century and beyond.

The judges who decided to admit defense counsel in the 1730s were also aware from the trials transpiring before them that a another great prosecutorial initiative was under way in London, a practice that, like the reward system, created ineradicable incentives for perjured testimony. Key magistrates in London had aggressively developed the technique now known as the crown witness prosecution (in American parlance, allowing the accused to turn state's evidence). The magistrate offered immunity to a suspect in return for his cooperation in testifying against his accomplices. It came to be understood that the crown witness system harbored incentives to false witness perhaps as dangerous as those of the reward system. Just as a reward-seeking prosecutor had no intrinsic interest in whether his £40 or £140 bounty came from convicting the guilty or the innocent, neither did a crown witness who testified to save himself from the noose.

Defense Counsel: Evening Up

This chapter advances the view that these innovations in prosecutorial practice precipitated the judges' decision in the 1730s to allow the criminal defendant to have the assistance of counsel for the purpose of probing the prosecution evidence presented at trial. The judges' move resembled that taken by Parliament in the Treason Trials Act of 1696, when treason defendants were permitted counsel to even up for the imbalance that had opened up between the crown and the accused. By the 1730s a similar dynamic was playing out in cases of felony. The judges responded as Parliament had a generation before, attempting to rebalance the trial by allowing the defendant to have counsel to assist him in probing the increasingly suspect prosecution evidence.

Even as the judges abridged the prohibition on felony defense counsel, they undertook to restrict counsel's role in felony trials in a way that would preserve the "accused speaks" trial, by confining counsel to the work of examining and especially cross-examining witnesses. Counsel was not allowed to "address the jury," that is, to present the defendant's version of the events. This compromise was meant to maintain the pressure on the accused to speak in his own defense, and thus to preserve the accused as an informational resource for the court. We shall see in Chapter 5 of this book how felony defense counsel undermined the

restrictions on his role. This experiment with restricted defensive representation lasted a century, until legislation in 1836 implemented another
round of evening up, extending to felony defendants the right to "full
defense of counsel."[14]

A. Prosecution Lawyers

By the early decades of the eighteenth century the historical sources allow
us to glean some evidence that solicitors were undertaking the role to
which they later became accustomed in English criminal procedure, as
pretrial investigators and managers. We see solicitors seeping into the
criminal prosecution, successfully offering their services to the nascent
government departments and other institutional prosecutors, to citizen
prosecutors, and to and through the justices of the peace and their clerks.

1. The Profession of Solicitor

Little has been written about the role of the solicitor in the history of criminal procedure.[15] The profession of solicitor was still taking shape in the
early eighteenth century.[16] Solicitors were only then securing their ascen-
dancy over the older profession of attorney, which they came to
subsume.[17] (The attorney had been associated with the work of a single
court, in connection with his role in entering pleadings.[18] Attorneys also

---

[14] Prisoner's Counsel Act, 6 & 7 Wil. 4, c. 114, preamble, § 1 (1836).

[15] Both the standard works of reference (Stephen, *History*; Holdsworth, *HEL*) and the
monographs on the history of the solicitor's or attorney's profession omit the topic. See, e.g.,
Michael Birks, *Gentlemen of the Law* (1960) [hereafter Birks, *Gentlemen*]; Harry Kirk, *A History
of the Solicitor's Profession, 1100 to the Present Day* (1976); Robert Robson, *The Attorney in
Eighteenth-Century England* (1959). C. W. Brooks, *Pettyfoggers and Vipers of the Commonwealth:
The 'Lower Branch' of the Legal Profession in Early Modern England* (1986). Geoffrey Holmes'
history of the professions includes a chapter treating lawyers that contains one passing
mention of solicitors in criminal practice. Speaking of the period about 1730 Holmes identifies four men as "attorneys specializing in criminal cases, [who] were among eighteen leading London practicers who had chambers, and in some cases lodgings, in the Inner Temple."
Geoffrey Holmes, *Augustan England: Professions, State and Society, 1680–1730*, at 150 (1982).
No source is cited, and I have not been able to trace the claim.

[16] Parliament supplied the regulatory base for the profession in the Act of 2 Geo. 2, c. 23
(1729) ("for the better regulation of attorneys and solicitors"). The Act allowed only persons
enrolled with one of the courts to sue out any writ or process, or to carry on any proceeding. See 12 Holdsworth, *HEL* 52–7. This registration requirement produced records that
make it possible to estimate the extent of the profession. It has been reckoned that London
in 1730 had over 1,500 attorneys, or one to every 383 inhabitants. Philip Aylett, "A
Profession in the Marketplace: The Distribution of Attorneys in England and Wales
1730–1800," 5 *Law and History Rev.* 1, 3 (1987).

[17] 6 Holdsworth, *HEL* 456–7.   [18] Ibid. at 453.

gathered evidence for use at trial.[19]) The solicitor first appeared in the fifteenth and sixteenth centuries, both to manage multi-jurisdictional litigation,[20] and in connection with the fact-finding needs of the "new courts and councils," especially Chancery, Star Chamber, and Requests.[21]

Indeed, into the nineteenth century "the solicitor was associated principally with the court of Chancery."[22] Chancery (like the defunct Tudor courts of Star Chamber and Requests) adjudicated without jury trial, basing judgment on the evidence that the parties gathered by means of interrogatories and the discovery of documents. Accordingly, these courts had a vastly larger appetite for investigation into matters of fact than did the common law courts, which exhibited an opposite tendency. From the later Middle Ages into early modern times the common law courts attempted to correct for the dangers of civil jury practice by narrowing their range of factual inquiry, employing such clumsy devices as single-issue pleading and the insistent preference for seal and record evidence.[23] The testimonial disqualification of the parties at common law[24] also greatly diminished the ability of the common law courts to find facts.

The initial development of the profession of solicitor, and the solicitor's subsequent displacement of the attorney, occurred as part of the larger saga of Chancery's "conquest"[25] of common law. The movement of solicitors into the work of investigating and managing criminal prosecutions was another manifestation of the expansion of the solicitor's profession from its base in Chancery. Having first appeared as evidence gatherers and litigation managers in Chancery and the prerogative courts, the solicitors gradually extended that model of legal representation into other jurisdictions, reaching the criminal courts in the decades under study in

[19] A practice manual admonished the attorney preparing a civil case for trial to "be sure that you instruct your Counsel sufficiently ... [a]nd have your Witness or other proofs in readiness." Thomas Powell, *The Attourneys Academy: Or, The Manner and Forme of Proceeding Practically* 135 (1623).

[20] Birks, *Gentlemen, supra* n. 15, at 88.

[21] 6 Holdsworth, *HEL* 453–4.

[22] Ibid. at 453.

[23] I have discussed these matters in Langbein, "Evidence" 1181–6, 1194–5 (1996).

[24] Chancery purported to follow the common law rule of testimonial disqualification of the parties, see 9 Holdsworth, *HEL* 194–5, but Chancery largely overcame the effects of the rule by facilitating party interrogatories and other discovery against parties.

[25] The expression is from Stephen N. Subrin, "How Equity Conquered Common Law: The Federal Rules of Civil Procedure in Historical Perspective," 135 *Univ. Pennsylvania L. Rev.* 909 (1987). The title of solicitor is said to have had a superior cachet to that of attorney, as a result of the solicitor's association with Chancery practice, where the clientele was wealthier. Birks, *Gentlemen, supra* n. 15, at 144. For evidence from the period 1789–91 that Chancery litigation involved far larger amounts than suits at common law, see Douglas King, "Complex Civil Litigation and the Seventh Amendment Right to a Jury Trial," 51 *Univ. Chicago L. Rev.* 581, 606 (1984).

this article. Because these trends in the history of the solicitor's profession have not been much studied, we lack a background historical literature to help us relate the developments in criminal procedure to the larger pattern.

The sources evidencing the investigative and preparatory work of the solicitor in eighteenth-century criminal cases are now quite meager. In general, contemporaries saw little reason to retain solicitors' investigative files or briefs to counsel. The useful life of such documents was short, especially on account of the dramatic finality of the criminal trial. If the felony defendant was acquitted, he could never be retried;[26] if he was convicted capitally and the trial judge did not reprieve him, he was executed with dispatch.[27] In either event, investigative documents generated by solicitors in the pretrial process had no further value and could be discarded.[28] Enough scattered evidence survives, however, to permit us to sketch the solicitor's growing presence. The present account draws upon archive sources from a variety of governmental prosecutors, references culled from the *State Trials* and the *Old Bailey Sessions Papers*, and contemporary tract literature.

2. Prosecuting Solicitors

The prosecuting solicitor emerges most visibly in the service of a new breed of prosecuting authority. A number of government departments or entities fielded an officer, actually labelled the solicitor, whose responsibilities included investigating and prosecuting criminal cases on behalf of the department. The Solicitor to the Mint, the Treasury Solicitor, the Solicitor to the Bank of England, and the Solicitor to the City of London left scraps of evidence about their prosecutorial activity. The Solicitor to the Post Office, whose office dates from 1683,[29] was also engaged, but his

---

[26] See 2 Hawkins, PC 368, § 1 (discussing *autrefois acquit*).

[27] Giving evidence to the Criminal Law Commissioners in 1835, the prominent defense solicitor James Harmer recalled "a case where, in a little more than 48 hours, enough could have been shown to justify a suspension of the judgment, but the men were executed before I had time to investigate." *Second Report from Her Majesty's Commissioners on Criminal Law* 88 (London 1836) (Parliamentary Papers vol. 36) [hereafter *1836 Report*]. A reprint edition of this work was published in the Irish University Press Series of British Parliamentary Papers: "Reports from the Royal Commission on the Criminal Law with Appendices and Index 1834–41," 3 *Legal Administration Criminal Law* 71–202 (1971).

[28] Many local record offices have holdings of solicitors' papers, usually deposited after a firm wound up its business. I have examined several such sets of papers. They contain abundant evidence of transactional and conveyancing work, but I have not found solicitors' briefs or other documents bearing on the criminal work in the first half of the eighteenth century. Michael Miles has found some traces of criminal practice in solicitors' records from later in the century, discussed *infra*, text at nn. 72–3.

[29] Roger Williams, "The Post Office: 300 Years of Prosecuting," 13 *The Retainer: The Journal of the Prosecuting Solicitors Society of England and Wales* 13 (Apr. 1984).

records do not survive until later.[30] I have not been able to locate evidence of the prosecutorial work of the East India Company and the South Sea Company until the 1740s.[31]

The appearance of these institutional prosecutors reflects important developments well beyond the law, including the changes in technology and in economic organization that produced the Post Office and the Bank of England, as well as the greater elaboration of governmental departments from the Restoration onward. These institutions found themselves with an agenda to enforce parts of the criminal law. The Post Office needed to protect the mails both from robbers and from pilfering employees. The Bank of England prosecuted the forgery of its banknotes. The Royal Mint defended the currency against clipping and counterfeiting. The Treasury Solicitor exercised a general superintendence over royal interests in criminal prosecutions, especially in cases of sedition.[32]

Several circumstances distinguished the task of the institutional prosecutor from Sir Thomas Smith's prototypical citizen prosecutor, who was the victim of a robbery. Since counterfeiting and offenses against the coin did not victimize particular persons, the authorities could not expect ordinary citizens to shoulder the work of law enforcement. Furthermore, crimes such as embezzlement from the mails or forgery and alteration of banknotes entailed legal complexity, because the culprit often came into

---

[30] The earliest solicitor's brief that I have been able to locate is for *R. v. Squat*, P74/253 (1774), Post Office Archives, Mount Pleasant Street Sorting Office, London. Squat, a postal employee, was subsequently tried at the Old Bailey in July 1774 for having stolen money from the mails. At the trial, "Mr. Parkin, Solicitor to the Post-office" testified about his pretrial investigation in the case. *OBSP* (Jul. 1774, #548), at 401. (Squat was acquitted on one indictment but convicted and transported on another.) Post Office prosecutions appear decades earlier in the *Sessions Papers*, but the accounts are not detailed enough to show us the hand of the solicitor. E.g., Samuel Snow, *OBSP* (Mar. 1720) 6 (mail robbery; "Counsel for the King, in opening the Indictment, set forth" a narrative of the events); John Hawkins and George Simpson, *OBSP* (May 1722) (correct date; pamphlet is misprinted April 1722), at 2–3 (highway robbery of the mails; crown witness case in which the accomplice's confession was made to Mr Carteret, Post Master General, by whose "directions the Prisoners were taken," ibid. at 3; neither solicitor nor counsel disclosed).

[31] William Oliver, *OBSP* (Dec. 1740, #35), at 9–10 (theft of more than 400 pounds of pepper from the East India Co.; prosecution counsel evident); John Waite, *OBSP* (Feb. 1743, #162), at 102 (theft of bonds from the East India Co.; three prosecution counsel and four defense counsel noticed); Winifred Jackson and Judith Mayers, *OBSP* (Feb. 1744, ##167–8), at 80 (defrauding the East India Co. in the surrender of a bond; prosecution and defense counsel); Hugh Pelling, *OBSP* (Jan. 1747, #103), at 58 (forgery in fraud of the South Sea Co.; prosecution and defense counsel); William Martin, *OBSP* (Oct. 1747, #383), at 277 (theft from East India Co.). (The *Sessions Papers* also show a burst of prosecutions, mostly conducted by the attorney general and/or the solicitor general, in excise (smuggling) cases in the years 1747–8; defense counsel is disclosed to have been present in virtually all of them.)

[32] Beattie has found that a second Treasury solicitor's post had been created in 1696 to prosecute treason and coining. Beattie, *Policing* 232. From October 1714 two undersecretaries of state were named in the Middlesex Commission of the Peace, doubtless in order to give them the examining powers of magistrates. Ibid. at 384–91.

initial possession lawfully.[33] Legal skill was needed to arrange for proper drafting of the indictment, and to identify and prepare witnesses to prove the elements of these offenses.

Institutional prosecutors dealt with crimes that often required determined investigation to identify and apprehend the culprits, and to gather, preserve, and present the evidence of their deeds. Prosecuting in these circumstances required skill, effort, and resources, which is just what the institutions supplied. They arranged for a legally knowledgeable solicitor to administer what amounted to an enforcement budget.

(a) What Solicitors Did: The Mint

The most useful archival record of early eighteenth-century prosecutorial activity that has come to my attention[34] is that of the Royal Mint. A class of document called Mint Office Record Books preserves periodic financial accounts from the Mint Solicitor from 1713. Because these accounts itemize steps taken in criminal cases that caused the Solicitor to incur charges for which he claimed reimbursement,[35] they supply a window on his prosecutorial work.

---

[33] On the development of the substantive law on these matters, see Jerome Hall, *Theft, Law and Society* 3–36 (1935). For example, in a prosecution in 1745 for embezzling from the Bank of England, "the Counsel for the Prisoner insisted on a point of law, relating to the meaning and construction of the word 'embezzle,' and that the Prisoner did not come within the intent and meaning of the act of parliament; which being fully argued [by counsel] on each side, it was the opinion of the Court that the Prisoner was within the intent and meaning of the said act." Robert Scruton, *OBSP* (Sept. 1745), at 231, 235.

[34] I acknowledge the kindness of John Beattie in suggesting these sources to me. John Styles also pointed to them in his essay " 'Our Traitorous Money Makers': The Yorkshire Coiners and the Law," 1760–83, in *An Ungovernable People: The English and Their Law in the Seventeenth and Eighteenth Centuries* 172, 183–6 (John Brewer and John Styles eds.) (1980) [hereafter Styles, "Coiners"], a work that I overlooked when I first wrote about these sources in John H. Langbein, "The Prosecutorial Origins of Defence Counsel in the Eighteenth Century: The Appearance of Solicitors," 58 *Cambridge L. J.* 314 (1999) [hereafter Langbein, "Prosecutorial Origins"]. Douglas Hay has also pointed to early Mint prosecutions in Staffordshire. Douglas Hay, "Crime, Authority and the Criminal Law: Staffordshire 1750–1800," at 342–4 (unpub. Ph.D. thesis, University of Warwick, 1975) [hereafter Hay, Thesis]. See also Beattie, *Policing* 236–7, 239–40, 243–5 (coining prosecutions of the 1690s).

[35] *Mint Office Record Book*, vol. 8 (1699–1713), Public Record Office [hereafter PRO], Mint 1/8, at 115–20 ("An Account of Expenses and Disbursements in the Prosecution and Conviction of Counterfeiters and Debasers of the Current Coin of this Kingdom and some others for uttering false Money knowing the same to be Such and other Law Charges attending the same in and about London, Westminster, Southwark, Essex and Kingston Assizes for two years, from Michaelmas 1713 to Michaelmas 1715") [series hereafter *Mint Books*].

The Mint records also evidence criminal investigations conducted on behalf of the Mint but not expressly attributed to the Mint Solicitor. "The Memorial of Henry Smithson," dated 25 Mar. 1714, recites "[t]hat the said Henry Smithson hath been for near 14 years employed by the late and present Warden of the Mint in the apprehending and prosecuting" of counterfeiters. *Mint Book*, vol. 7 (1699–1728), at 64. Smithson was asking to have his bill paid. His "Account of [his] charges and Expenses" contains entries such as "Charges and expenses for

The Mint Solicitor had an illustrious predecessor in his prosecutorial work, Isaac Newton. Serving as Warden of the Mint in the years 1696–9,[36] Newton found himself taking a leading hand in criminal investigations.[37] He chafed under this work and urged that it be assigned to lawyers. " 'Tis the business of an Attorney and belongs properly to the King's Attorney and Solicitor General, and they are best able to go through it especially with such assistance as they can procure."[38] Later, as Master of the Mint, Newton acted on his inclination to lodge the work of criminal investigation and prosecution with lawyers. "In 1706 he secured a standing and larger allocation of public funds for the Mint's police work, and in 1715 he made its conduct less amateur by appointing a legally qualified man as extra clerk . . . . This Deputy Warden became Solicitor to the Mint . . . ."[39]

The Mint Solicitor's main work was to investigate crime and gather evidence for trial. Sometimes the Solicitor investigated on his own, sometimes he worked with or through helpers. In developing the case against John and Elizabeth Barker, tried at the Old Bailey in 1714 for coining, the Solicitor, Richard Barrow, spent money "attending the justices [that is, the magistrates, the justices of the peace who conducted the pretrial committal proceedings] and the witnesses who lived at Wapping and other far places."[40] He spent more "in inquiring after the [suspects] and giving money to persons for Information." Barrow then "[p]aid the constable for looking after the [seized counterfeiting] tools and letting them lie in his house," and "for a Box and a Basket Lock and Key" to secure them. He incurred additional "Expenses in going several times to Newgate to Speak to the persons to see if they would make discovery." In another case in 1715 Barrow's successor, Calverly Pinckney, claimed expenses "[f]or going into Surrey, finding out and taking Proofs from several Witnesses against" certain suspects, and for having "[p]aid one Woodward . . . towards enabling him to make out his pretended Discoveries."[41]

---

my self, assistants and Horses in the pursuing and taking of Elizabeth Metcalfe, Francis Buckle . . . with others on Suspicion, of whom Elizabeth Metcalfe was convicted and executed and others fined and imprisoned . . . ." Ibid. at 65.

[36] See John Craig, "Isaac Newton and the Counterfeiters," 18 *Notes and Records of the Royal Society of London* 136 (1963) [hereafter Craig, "Newton"].

[37] Newton's investigations are extensively evidenced in PRO, Mint 15/17, a collection of more than 500 "Depositions against or by counterfeiters sworn before Wardens, Mayors or Justices of the Peace, May 1698–May 1706, with a few letters and appeals to mercy to Wardens."

[38] Letter to the Commissioners of the Treasury, (No. 553), Jul.–Aug. 1696, in 4 *The Correspondence of Isaac Newton: 1694–1709*, at 209, 210 (J. F. Scott ed.) (1967).

[39] Craig, "Newton," *supra* n. 36, at 143.

[40] *Mint Books*, *supra* n. 35, vol. 8, at 118.

[41] Ibid. at 122, 123.

The Mint Solicitor's efforts at detection and evidence-gathering led seamlessly into the work of preparing witnesses, framing and procuring indictments, and arranging for prosecution at trial. Barrow recorded that he prosecuted William Strange and James Robinson at Essex Assizes in March 1713 "for putting off counterfeit money." He paid the justices' clerk "for drawing the information and binding the Evidence over" and for drafting the two indictments. Barrow paid for the "expenses of Witnesses during the time of Trial at the Assize," and he "[g]ave the witnesses" a further £1 10s. In this case Barrow engaged counsel, whom he paid both to advise on the indictments ("to peruse them"[42]) and to prosecute the defendants at the trial.

These four categories of expenditure—for investigation, for fees to clerks and other functionaries, for witnesses, and for counsel—recur in the Mint records across the eighteenth century. We also find the Solicitor's work evidenced in the *Sessions Paper* reports,[43] when he testified at Old Bailey trials about how he investigated or apprehended accused coiners.[44]

Locating and preparing witnesses

By mid-century the Mint accounts sometimes supply more detail about the Mint Solicitor's involvement with prosecution witnesses. In a counterfeiting case pending in Stafford in 1756, the Solicitor charged for "[a]ttending [five named persons] and other Witnesses to take the Substance of their Evidences," and then "[a]ttending [another named] witness to take the heads of His Evidence and service of a Subpoena on him."[45] These contacts with witnesses were directed beyond detection,

---

[42] Ibid. This expression appears often in the Mint accounts and elsewhere. In the Corporation of London Record Office (hereafter CLRO) there survives a draft indictment in the case of Elizabeth Nichols, which was sent for review to counsel, John Tracey. Nichols was charged with malicious prosecution. Tracey suggested some changes, then wrote at the end of the draft, "I have perused and do approve of the draft of this indictment." His signature is dated 30 Nov. 1743. CLRO, *London Sessions Papers 1744*, at 9. Tracey suggested a few drafting changes. At one point he inserted the words "with force and arms." In the margin he explained, presumably to the instructing City Solicitor: "I know there are precedents without those Words as well as others with them but as the Inserting cannot possibly do any Hurt and the leaving them out may furnish some little objection I thought it safer to Insert them." Ibid. at 6. (I owe the reference to this file to John Beattie.)

[43] For discussion of these sources, see *infra* Ch. 4, text at nn. 7–52.

[44] E.g., Mary Haycock and Ann Haycock, *OBSP* (Jul. 1734, ##19–20), at 147–9 (Solicitor North testifying); Catherine Bougle (Jul. 1734, #27), at 152, 155 (North testifies about his tactics in "keep[ing] the Information secret as long as I could" while searching for others); John Irons, *OBSP* (Apr. 1737, #555), at 110, 112 (North testifies about the counterfeiting technology at issue in the case); Judith Murray *et al.*, *OBSP* (Apr. 1738, ##14–16), at 63, 65–6 (North testifies to his follow-up at the scene); Jonathan Thomas, *OBSP* (Sept. 1738, #22), at 130, 134 (North testifies about apprehending him and searching his premises); Patrick Kelly *et al.*, *OBSP* (Jan. 1743, ##116–19), at 70, 73 (North testifying again).

[45] *Mint Books, supra* n. 35, vol. 11 (1752–64), at 84 (account for 1755–6).

toward what we now recognize as the characteristic lawyer's role of selecting and preparing witnesses for trial.

Cooperation with the magistrates

In some cases the Mint Solicitor worked through the London magistracy, rather than conduct an investigation independently. In the case against John and Elizabeth Barker for coining in 1714, previously discussed, the Solicitor recorded having attended the London magistrates. In later decades, when the so-called court JP system was in operation in Middlesex, the Solicitor made use of it. At least by the third decade of the century, and perhaps earlier,[46] the central government took to designating one of the Middlesex JPs to render special service in criminal investigation and prosecution. This agent became known as the "court JP," "court" in this usage referring to the central government. He received financial support, both in the way of compensation and in order to defray expenses.[47] Sir Thomas DeVeil, an ex-soldier who entered the Middlesex commission of the peace in 1729, served as the court JP until his death in 1746. Whether DeVeil had predecessors in the office has not been established. DeVeil was succeeded by Henry Fielding, the novelist, who died in 1754, and then by Henry Fielding's half-brother, the renowned blind magistrate, Sir John Fielding. All three kept their office at Bow Street—the origins of the Bow Street magistrate's court, which endures to the present.[48] The Mint Solicitor made ready use of the Bow Street magistrate. For example, in the investigation of Henry Lightouler and others in 1756, we find the Solicitor turning to John Fielding, the court JP, for the arrest warrant. The Solicitor "examin[ed] him and [wrote up] his Information whereby he charged" various others. The Solicitor then "[a]ttend[ed] Justice Fielding when [Lightouler] was further examined . . . and committed."[49] On occasion the initiative flowed the other way. In the case of John Domine, for passing off counterfeit guineas, the Solicitor recorded: "On motion from Mr. Fielding, attend him when Defendant was examined and Committed."[50]

---

[46] An anonymous author claimed to trace the court JP system through various supposed seventeenth-century incumbents back into Elizabethan times, but on insubstantial evidence. Anon., *Memoirs of the Life and Times of Sir Thomas DeVeil, Knight* 22–34 (London 1748) [hereafter *DeVeil Memoirs*]. The Webbs repeat this tale. 1 Sidney and Beatrice Webb, *English Local Government from the Revolution to the Municipal Corporations Act: The Parish and the County* 337–8 (1906).

[47] Regarding the court JP system, see Langbein, "Ryder" 60–1.

[48] 3 Radzinowicz, *History* 29 n. 2; see generally Anthony Babington, *A House in Bow Street: Crime and the Magistracy in London 1740–1881* (1969).

[49] *Mint Books*, *supra* n. 35, vol. 11 (1752–64), PRO, Mint 1/11, at 90 (account for 1755–6). Further dimensions of this case are discussed in Styles, "Coiners," *supra* n. 34, at nn. 178–81, 184, 190–1, 230–3.

[50] *Mint Books*, *supra* n. 35, vol. 11, at 97.

Financing criminal investigation

Part of what the Mint Solicitor contributed to investigation and prosecution was money. In Domine's case, the Solicitor paid for having the suspect's lodgings searched, where coining tools were found.[51] Thus, Mint funds flowed through to support the Bow Street magistrate's band of thieftakers and constables, who amounted to a quasi-police force in the decades before London policing received a recognized basis.[52] In later periods as the Mint caseload grew, the Solicitor increasingly delegated the work of investigation and trial management to outside solicitors hired for each case.[53]

Instructing counsel

During the early years of the eighteenth century the Mint Solicitor did not invariably employ counsel in the cases that he brought to trial.[54] He was sometimes content to rely upon the witnesses to tell their own tales in the familiar fashion of the altercation trial. But by the 1730s employing trial counsel in solicitor-directed cases became routine.[55] Lawyerization of the pretrial promoted lawyerization of the trial. The solicitor who built a criminal prosecution by locating, selecting, and preparing witnesses

[51] Ibid.

[52] The Mint was not alone in subsidizing the Bow Street force on a case-by-case basis. In the slender Bank of England archive there survives for the year 1779 a bill from the Bow Street officers for their services in arresting the culprit and going to retrieve silver stashed at his mother's dwelling in Oxford. *R. v. J. Matthison*, Bank of England, F2/190 (1778–9). This case is the subject of a contemporary pamphlet account. Anon., *Memoirs of the Life of John Matthieson [sic], Executed for a Forgery on the Bank of England* 17 (London 1779) (Yale Law Libr. shelfmark RB SSP M512 c.1), discussed in another connection *infra* Ch. 5, n. 306.

[53] By the 1840s the Mint Solicitor had become a prosecutorial administrator, who placed most of the forensic work with outsiders. See *Report of the Commissioners Appointed to Inquire into the Constitution, Management, and Expense of the Royal Mint* (London 1849) (copy preserved as PRO, Mint 2/17). Joseph Blunt, Solicitor of the Mint, testified to a Parliamentary committee about the work of his office. Ibid. at 183. He reported steadily increasing prosecutions and prosecution costs from the 1780s to the 1840s. In 1786 the Mint brought twenty-two prosecutions at a cost of £1,325. In 1842 the Mint prosecuted 457 cases at a cost of £10,744. Ibid. at 184. Blunt testified that he did not attend pretrial examinations or trials. He worked from the pretrial examinations taken by magistrates' clerks in order to "prepare briefs for the counsel. I draw a short analysis of the case, as a kind of brief, to attract the attention of counsel to the evidence, because without that they would have to hunt out what the different points were." Ibid. at 189. The Mint hired local solicitors to manage the prosecutions. "[W]e usually prefer employing the gentleman who sends up the information; he is commonly the magistrate's clerk, and then if he is [an experienced] person . . . I correspond with him about any deficiency in the evidence." Ibid. at 192. For more on the overlap between magistrate's clerk and practicing solicitor, see *infra*, text at nn. 100–13; see also *infra* n. 176.

[54] For example, none is recorded in the case against John and Elizabeth Barker, *supra*, text at nn. 40–1.

[55] E.g., Mary Haycock and Ann Haycock, *OBSP* (July 1734, ##19–20), at 147–9; Elizabeth Tracey and Ann Knight, *OBSP* (July 1734, 21–2), at 149–52; Catherine Bougle (July 1734, #27), at 152–5.

wanted a legal professional to lead those witnesses at trial. (I recur to this subject below, when discussing the growing use of prosecution counsel.)

(b) Prosecution by the Executive

The monarch and the government also provided episodic reinforcement for criminal prosecution in the early eighteenth century.

In 1722 John Woodburne and Arundel Coke were convicted at Bury St. Edmunds of slitting the nose of Edward Crispe, a contemporary cause célèbre reported in the *State Trials*.[56] The *State Papers* reveal that the King was offended at this "barbarous" offense (which had dignitary overtones). Concerned that the culprits might otherwise "escape unpunished," he directed the Attorney General to see to it "that able Counsel and a proper Solicitor be employed to attend that prosecution" at the King's expense.[57] The Attorney General commissioned Nicholas Paxton[58] to be the prosecuting solicitor. The two defendants were convicted. Paxton ran up a bill for £85, which doubtless included counsel fees. The Secretary of State directed the Treasury Solicitor to pay it.[59]

A year later the King intervened to arrange for lawyers to prosecute the suspected killers of a woman named Anne Bristol, whose violent death became a notorious case in the metropolis. Four men were charged with murdering her, allegedly in a gang rape. They denied the charges and contended that she had probably been killed when run over accidentally by a wagon.[60] The King, "having much at heart that the four Watermen who murdered Anne Bristow [*sic*] on Smalbury Green in so barbarous a manner Should not escape unpunished," directed the Attorney General to "take this Prosecution under your Care, and appear at their Trials at the Old Bailey."[61] The Secretary of State told the Treasury Solicitor of the

---

[56] *R. v. John Woodburne & Arundel Coke*, 16 St. Tr. 53 (Suffolk Assizes 1722). The offense had been made felony without benefit of clergy under 22 & 23 Car. 2, c. 1, § 7 (1670).

[57] *State Papers Domestic Entry Book*, PRO, SP 44/81 at 24 (entry for 5 Feb. 1722).

[58] Paxton acted on behalf of the crown in another matter in 1722, advancing money to bring a prisoner down to London from the North. Ibid. at 139. A prosecution brief from Paxton dated June 1729 in an unrelated seditious libel case survives in the Treasury Solicitor's archive, PRO, TS 11/424/1290. In the 1730s Paxton appears to have been active on behalf of the crown in King's Bench prosecutions, e.g., PRO, SP 44/82, at 68, 69, 71, 72, 74, 76. Beattie mentions Paxton's work in this case and identifies him as the assistant treasury solicitor. Beattie, *Crime* 354; Beattie, *Policing* 389 n. 62. For Paxton's role in prosecuting under the Black Act, see E. P. Thompson, *Whigs and Hunters: The Origin of the Black Act* 212–13 (1975), noted in Beattie, *Crime* 354 n. 92; Beattie, *Policing* 386–7. Beattie has also found evidence that Paxton managed the trial of Jonathan Wild, ibid. at 382 n. 39; on Wild, see *infra*, text at nn. 222–3, 260–2.

[59] *State Papers Domestic Entry Book*, PRO, SP 44/81 at 69, 119, 171.

[60] George Smith *et al.*, *OBSP* (Apr. 1723), at 1. Two medical experts testified in rebuttal to the defensive theory.

[61] *State Papers Domestic Entry Book*, PRO, SP 44/81 at 189, Townshend to Attorney General, ibid. at 189 (entry for 11 Mar. 1723).

King's pleasure "that you take care to procure the necessary Proofs, and to lay the same before Mr. Attorney General, who is directed to take this Prosecution under his Management, and to appear at their trials at the Old Bailey."[62] Despite the lawyers' efforts in the case, the jury was uncertain about what had happened and acquitted the defendants.[63]

Government intervention of this sort in noteworthy criminal cases unrelated to affairs of state is well evidenced for the 1750s. In the case of John Swan and Elizabeth Jefferys, tried in 1752 at Chelmsford Assizes for the murder of Jefferys' uncle, "the Attorney General . . . received Orders to prosecute at the Expense of the Crown . . . ."[64] The government also took charge of prosecuting the celebrated murder case of Mary Blandy,[65] who was convicted at Oxford in 1752 of having poisoned her father in order to overcome his opposition to her romance. The prosecution brief survives among the Treasury Solicitor's papers,[66] showing that Bathurst, the prosecuting counsel, spoke literally when he told the jury in his opening statement that "I am counsel in this case for the King, in whose name, and at whose expense, this prosecution is carried on . . . ."[67] Comparison of the published trial report with the solicitor's brief shows that counsel's opening statement closely tracked the solicitor's summary of the case in the brief, sometimes verbatim.[68] Douglas Hay has pointed to further cases in the 1750s (one involving a poisoner, another a gang of robbers) in which the government took over the prosecution of heinous crimes.[69]

We see in these cases the theme that Beattie has emphasized,[70] the growing interest taken by the central authorities in the enforcement of the criminal law in the decades after the Revolution of 1688–9. For present purposes the instructive point is that when the central authorities wanted to strengthen a criminal prosecution, they did it by sending in the lawyers. They employed solicitors to investigate and to plan the prosecution, and barristers to take the case to trial. As in the practice of the

---

[62] Ibid. at 189, Townshend to Cracherode.

[63] *OBSP* (Apr. 1723), at 3. The *Sessions Paper* account, which extends across portions of three folio pages, its an exceptionally detailed report for the condensed format of these years. The report summarizes the testimony of prosecution and defense witnesses but does not disclose the participation of the prosecution counsel.

[64] Foster, *Crown Law* 104. Foster presided at the trial, see 18 *St. Tr.* 1193, 1197 (Chelmsford Assizes 1752).

[65] *R. v. Mary Blandy*, 18 *St. Tr.* 1118, 1120 (Oxford Assizes 1752).

[66] PRO, TS 11/854/2948 (the prosecution brief and copies of the depositions from the pretrial committal proceeding).

[67] 18 *St. Tr.* at 1120.

[68] For example, counsel's statement at 18 *St. Tr.* at 1126–7 contains verbatim paragraphs from the brief, PRO, TS/11/864/2948, at 1–14.

[69] Hay, Thesis, *supra* n. 34, at 346.

[70] Beattie, *Policing, passim*; J. M. Beattie, "The Cabinet and the Management of Death at Tyburn after the Revolution of 1688–1689," in *The Revolution of 1688–89: Changing Perspectives* 218 (Lois G. Schwoerer ed.) (1992).

from an Original Painting

Mifs MARY BLANDY

Aged 33 and Executed at OXFORD - April 6, 1752, for poisoning her Father.

Fɪɢ. 3.1. *The execution of Mary Blandy.* The trial of Mary Blandy and her lover in 1752 for the murder of her father (who had opposed her marriage) was among several celebrated cases in which the government engaged solicitors and counsel to prepare and conduct the trials.

specialized institutions such as the Mint and the Bank, so in the episodic interventions of the central authorities, criminal prosecution was increasingly understood to be lawyers' work. In the light of this growing lawyerization of prosecution, Hawkins' claim that criminal defense "requires no manner of Skill"[71] must have looked ever more hollow.

(c) Solicitors Conducting Private Prosecutions

The lawyers' role in criminal prosecution in the early decades of the eighteenth century is harder to trace in cases brought on behalf of ordinary citizens. Citizen prosecutors lacked the resources and incentives to employ lawyers as routinely as the institutional prosecutors, nor did citizens share the interest or the capacity that the nascent bureaucracies were developing for preserving their papers.

By mid-century there is evidence of seemingly routine prosecutorial work in the financial ledgers of a prominent Bradford solicitor, John Eagle, who was active in the decades after 1759. We learn that he brought six substantial criminal cases during his career.[72] "In April 1765 he handled a prosecution case against three defendants for stealing shalloons [wool lining material], malt, and silver spoons. He examined witnesses and drew the brief. The defendants were convicted at Pontefract Sessions and sentenced to be transported."[73] Public officers such as constables cooperated with privately engaged prosecution solicitors. For example, the pamphlet report of a murder trial held at the Old Bailey in 1769 chances to preserve the testimony of the constable that he "endeavored to collect all the evidence together . . . and gave it [to] the prosecutor's solicitor to make what use of it he pleased."[74] There is every reason to suspect that solicitors were investigating and managing criminal prosecutions earlier in the century, but the historical sources have not yet surfaced.[75]

---

[71] 2 Hawkins, *PC* 400.

[72] Michael Miles, " 'Eminent Attorneys': Some Aspects of West Riding Attorneyship *c*.1750–1800" (unpublished Ph.D. thesis, University of Birmingham, 1982) [hereafter Miles, Thesis], at 257. The account in text follows Miles; I have not examined his sources.

[73] Ibid. at 257 n. 2. The extract quoted in text is the only one of the six cases Miles identified that he describes.

[74] John Barrett, *OBSP* (Oct. 1769, #560), at 423, 427.

[75] The understanding that solicitors were by this time characteristically used to gather prosecution evidence is voiced in a pamphlet published in 1768 by an acquitted criminal defendant, James Oliphant. Oliphant was a surgeon who had been prosecuted for the murder of a servant girl whom he contended drowned accidentally. Oliphant alleges in the pamphlet that a vindictive coroner insisted on charging him and his wife with murdering the girl. Describing the coroner's exceptional industry in preparing the case against the Oliphants, the pamphlet complains "that he had become as a *solicitor* in this *prosecution*; that he had gone a hunting into the country after other witnesses than those who were examined on the inquest, to give

The most valuable window that I have found on the activity of solicitors working for private prosecutors in the early decades of the eighteenth century is an anonymous tract published in London in 1728, titled *Directions for Prosecuting Thieves without the Help of Those False Guides, the Newgate Sollicitors* [sic] (hereafter *Directions*).[76] Although the author tells his readers that his "profession is not directly the Law,"[77] he was close enough to the London legal scene to dedicate the pamphlet to the influential recorder of London, Sir William Thompson;[78] and he was knowledgeable enough about criminal practice to devote the back half of the pamphlet to an exposition of the rudiments of criminal practice derived from Hawkins' *Pleas of the Crown*.[79] A main theme of *Directions* is the superiority of counsel as an advisor in a criminal matter by comparison with a solicitor. Even though the tract is hostile to solicitors, it underscores the contemporary perception that solicitors were becoming increasingly important in organizing and preparing prosecution cases at the Old Bailey and in the lesser London criminal courts.

The author's announced "Design" is "to detect and put a Stop to the oppressive and dishonest Practices of the Tribe of Solicitors, in Prosecutions for Felony about this City . . . ."[80] He laments the expense of engaging solicitors to prosecute at the Old Bailey. By driving up the cost, these "Newgate solicitors" worsen the victim's disincentive to prosecute.[81] Because the victim is ignorant of the system, "the Matter is undertaken on the Solicitor's Terms," even though the solicitor's eventual "Bill is more unreasonable than a Tailor's . . . ."[82] (The undertone that pervades

---

evidence against the prisoners on their trial . . . ." Anon., *The Case of Mr. James Oliphant, Surgeon, Respecting a Prosecution which he . . . Underwent in the Year 1764*, at 49 (Newcastle 1768) (emphasis supplied) (Yale Univ., Beinecke Libr., shelfmark British Tracts 1768 Ol 4).

Another pamphlet, from the previous decade, describes the investigative work of a provincial attorney, Edward Wise, and his London agent, in detecting a false civil action under the statutes of hue and cry, and successfully prosecuting the culprit criminally. Edward Wise, *The Remarkable Tryal of Thomas Chandler, Late of Clifford's Inn, London, Gent., Who Was Tried and Convicted at the Lent Assizes at Reading, 1750, before Mr. Baron Clive, for Wilful and Corrupt Perjury, in Swearing That He Was Robbed of Fifteen Bank Notes of the Value of £960, 5 Guineas in Gold, 20s. and Upwards in Silver, and a Silver Watch . . . in Berkshire, in the Road to Reading, by Three Men on Foot* (Reading 1751).

[76] Anon., *Directions for Prosecuting Thieves without the Help of Those False Guides, the Newgate Sollicitors* [sic] (London 1728) (Oxford Univ., Bodleian Law Libr. shelfmark L.Eng.B.62.e.93) [hereafter *Directions*], discussed in Langbein, "Ryder" 109 n. 441, 127–9 n. 511; Langbein, "Prosecutorial Origins," *supra* n. 34, at 335–8, 348 (from which the discussion above in text derives); Beattie, *Policing* 395–8.

[77] *Directions, supra* n. 76, at ii.   [78] On whom, see Beattie, *Policing* 424–48.
[79] *Directions, supra* n. 76, at 14–27.   [80] Ibid. at ii.   [81] Ibid. at 2.
[82] Ibid. at 4. The tract sets forth a sample bill from a solicitor for managing the case, mostly for pretrial work, which amounts to £3 8s. 9d. Ibid. at 10. If "you do your Business without a Solicitor, the whole Prosecution of a Thief will cost you no more than two Shillings and four Pence." Ibid. at 11. This sum, which is not explained, probably represents the clerk's fee for drafting the indictment.

this tract, that solicitors are duplicitous and disreputable, reflects an important strand of contemporary concern, discussed below in connection with the phenomenon of so-called "Newgate solicitors.")

Directions depicts London solicitors as eager to sell their services. "[A] Solicitor makes Application to the Party robbed"[83] to represent him. "When it gets into the public Papers that such a Person was robbed . . . he is not many Hours without some of these officious Persons to advise him . . . ."[84] The solicitor's early steps prepare for framing of the indictment. "[T]he Solicitor pulls out a Pocket-Book, takes the Name of the Prosecutor, the Parish of which he is an Inhabitant, and the Value of the Goods stolen . . . ." and he takes special care to get the goods and the accused accurately described.[85] Once again, the pamphlet deprecates the solicitor's contribution, asserting that anybody can do this work: "this, and much more, may be done without the Help of one of these Harpies . . . ."[86]

The tract indicates something of the solicitor's role in preparing witnesses for trial. The "next Step is to make a great Stir in summoning all those together, who are to be Witnesses at the Trial of the Prisoner, and to direct who shall speak first, and how they shall deliver themselves to the Judge and Jury . . . ."[87] We find in this account a confirmation of the inference drawn above on the basis of prosecution briefs and other archive sources, that solicitors were already in this period taking an active hand in selecting, preparing, summoning, and sequencing the witnesses for trial.

Although *Directions* disparages the solicitor's pretrial activity as make-work, that view seems nostalgic and unpersuasive. The author contends that the solicitor's preparation of witnesses is counterproductive: "[N]othing pleases the Judges more, than to hear Truth told with the utmost Simplicity and Plainness," rather than to have to preside over "the Proceedings and Villainy of sharping Solicitors . . . ."[88] Only "silly People are so ignorant as to believe they cannot be brought into Court, without being introduced by a Solicitor, nor be heard if they do not speak his Language more strictly than their own Sentiments . . . ."[89] Indeed, "what is easier than to speak Truth, and what you know and saw, but not what

---

[83] Ibid. at 2.   [84] Ibid. at 2–3.   [85] Ibid. at 3.
[86] Ibid. In a similar vein, the author advises the victim "to give Instructions to the Person who draws up the Indictment," ibid. at 7, who is said to be a clerk at the Guildhall or at Hick's Hall or in Westminster Hall. Ibid. at 9, 27. The clerk "will readily assist you" if you give him the right information. Ibid. at 9. The prosecutor is better off without using a solicitor to inform the clerk, because (1) the clerks are more deferential to solicitors, who tend to get the facts wrong; (2) solicitors are "perpetually tippling at the Expense of silly People" who hire them; and (3) "the Solicitor may be in Fee with your Prisoner to entangle you at the same time that he takes your Money, promising to exert the utmost of his Talents to [convict] the Prisoner . . . ." Ibid. at 9–10.
[87] Ibid. at 3.   [88] Ibid. at 5.   [89] Ibid.

others said, for that is no Evidence . . . ."[90] These passages seem to echo
for the prosecution Hawkins' argument about why the accused needs no
counsel—that any defendant "of Common Understanding . . . may as
properly [defend himself] as if he were the best Lawyer," hence that "it
requires no manner of Skill to make a plain and honest Defense . . . ."[91]

Directions does not describe solicitors instructing counsel, nor does it
mention counsel acting at trial. The pamphlet implies that the role of prosecuting counsel at trial was still slight in 1728. The trial judge is depicted
as the examiner at trial,[92] an expectation that would endure for decades.[93]
The pamphlet contains a sample bill[94] from the solicitor to the prosecuting client that itemizes the solicitor's services. The bill shows no entry for
engaging counsel, although it records the solicitor charging for initial
advice, for "examining and cautioning the Witnesses," for obtaining
subpoenas (presumably to compel the attendance of prosecution
witnesses), for "attending on the Prisoner to bring him to Confession," for
"waiting at Hicks Hall" (a reference to the process of drafting the bill of
indictment and securing its approval from the grand jury), and for
"attending at the Old Bailey."[95] According to this source, therefore, the
prosecuting solicitor in a victim-prosecuted case at the Old Bailey in 1728
was not yet routinely briefing counsel. It will be seen that the evidence of
the *Old Bailey Session Papers* accords with this account.[96]

We see in this unique tract further support for the view that the main
engine of lawyerization of prosecution in the early decades of the eighteenth century was the solicitor, not the barrister, and that the main
sphere of influence for lawyers was in the pretrial rather than at trial.
Directions contends that the trend that it deplores to have solicitors
manage criminal prosecution has become prevalent enough to sustain a
full-time corps of London-area professionals.[97]

Although the tract's model bill of charges for services presupposes that
the solicitor would not ordinarily employ trial counsel, the author does
recommend consulting counsel "when a Matter of great Consequence is

---

[90] Ibid. at 6.   [91] 2 Hawkins, *PC* 400.

[92] Because prosecutors come to court nervous and long-winded, the judges must "draw
the Circumstances of the Fact from them by a mild and gentle Method . . . ." *Directions, supra*
n. 76, at 13.

[93] Dudley Ryder, newly minted as the Chief Justice of King's Bench and unfamiliar with
Old Bailey practice, confided to his diary in 1754 that he planned "to come late some days
at Old Bailey on purpose to be present when a trial being on, I may hear how the judge sums
up and examines witnesses." Ryder, "Assize Diary" 18.

[94] *Directions, supra* n. 76, at 10, discussed *supra* n. 82.   [95] Ibid.

[96] *Infra*, text at nn. 195–6.

[97] "I have known some Fellows," the author writes, "who have had nothing else to
support them for some Years, but what they perfectly extorted from People [i.e. prosecutors]
for Advice (and what may properly be called *Mismanagement*) at Guildhall, Hicks Hall, and
the Old Bailey, in the time of the Sessions." *Directions, supra* n. 76, at 12 (emphasis original).

to be tried [and] Advice is necessary."[98] The author asserts that "Counsel learned in the Law" will do the client "all the Justice the Merits of the Cause will admit of, yet the Charge will in the end be found less than employing a Newgate Solicitor, who in effect does nothing at all, but what might have been as well done, and very often much better, without him."[99] The implication in this passage that solicitor and counsel were competitors in rendering "Advice" about how to try the case sheds valuable light on the role of lawyers in criminal procedure in this period. Although the author is partial to counsel and hostile to solicitors, he makes no mention of counsel's having any right of audience at trial, an advantage over the solicitor that we would expect this author to have trumpeted had it mattered. I take the author's silence on this point as evidence that he still understood the lawyer's role in the prosecution of ordinary felony to be the job of pretrial management. The prosecution witnesses were still expected to speak at trial under the guidance of the judge and without the intermediation of counsel.

(d) Magistrates' Clerks as Prosecuting Solicitors

The suggestion in *Directions*[100] that solicitors came into initial contact with potential clients on the prosecution side by following up newspaper reports, whether or not accurate in some events for London, is not likely to have typified the patterns of engagement. A more regular channel for connecting the prosecutor with the solicitor was the magistrate, that is, the justice of the peace (JP), discussed in Chapter 1, to whom a victim would first come to report the crime and instigate proceedings. The magistrate often put the clerk in charge of the paperwork arising from the initial steps in bringing a criminal prosecution, which included transcribing the pretrial examinations of the prosecutor and his witnesses, issuing warrants, and taking recognizances.[101] It was common for the magistrate to employ as his clerk a person who practiced privately as a solicitor or attorney.[102] This early and official contact with inexperienced victims positioned the clerk on the inside track to be employed as the prosecutor's solicitor.

---

[98] Ibid.   [99] Ibid.

[100] Ibid. at 2–3, discussed *supra*, text at n. 84.

[101] Burn's JP manual supplies model forms for (*a*) the pretrial examination of an accused felon, (*b*) the pretrial examination of an accusing witness, (*c*) binding over a witness to give evidence at trial, (*d*) binding over a complainant to prosecute, and (*e*) summoning a potential witness for pretrial examination by the JP. Burn, *JP* 208–9.

[102] "All but one of the justices' clerks active [in Kent] in the last quarter of the [eighteenth] century are included in lists of attorneys resident in the counties—lists published for the first time in 1775." Norma Landau, *The Justices of the Peace: 1679–1760*, at 229 n. 50 (1984).

Michael Miles observed a little of this practice of the solicitor appropriating business from the JP's parlor in sources for the later decades of the eighteenth century. Miles examined the records of the Yorkshire solicitor John Howarth, who was appointed clerk to the magistrate Joshua Horton in December 1769 and served him for a quarter century until Horton died in 1793.[103] Howarth "was often the first person to be consulted on a whole host of complaints and problems,"[104] including potential prosecutions. Howarth's cash books from his solicitor's practice show that he assisted one prosecutor in developing a case for violation of the game laws, taking the pretrial examinations of prosecution witnesses.[105] In another case Howarth charged for preparing advertisements growing out of a robbery investigation (probably a case of highway robbery, hence advertising the reward).[106] Miles reports that "Howarth's annual number of Quarter Sessions cases rose from nine in 1769 to 23 in 1770 on being appointed a Justice's clerk,"[107] and that "Howarth's yearly profits from conducting these prosecutions rose from an average of £6 in 1768 [before he was named magistrate's clerk] . . . to as much as £34 between 1770 and 1780."[108]

When serving as the prosecuting solicitor, Howarth was exploiting an overlap that the system tolerated[109] between the responsibility of the magistrate's clerk to develop the case ex officio and the solicitor's role as a service provider for hire. Howarth seems sometimes to have obtained the prosecutor as a client when the prosecutor approached him in his capacity as the magistrate's clerk. "[I]n these prosecutions, the person who made the accusation often approached Howarth first with details and witnesses, and [Howarth] then drew up the information or issued search warrants before going to the Justice . . . ."[110] Curiously, Howarth

---

[103] "Howarth's yearly emoluments from this source ranged from £68 in 1770 to as much as £151 in 1778." Miles, Thesis, *supra* n. 72, at 267 (drawing upon Howarth's ledgers, called cash books).

[104] Ibid. at 267. Howarth also advised potential civil and criminal defendants who had been summoned before other magistrates. Ibid. at 268.

[105] Ibid. at 268.   [106] Ibid.

[107] Ibid. at 270. "His Assizes business, however, increased only slightly." Ibid.

[108] Ibid.

[109] Barnes noticed the private practice of the magistrates' clerks in the first half of the seventeenth century. Thomas G. Barnes, *The Clerk of the Peace in Caroline Somerset* 37 (1961). But see *infra*, text and notes at nn. 167–8, 174, regarding the London Grand Jury Presentment of 1733, which denounced as an abuse the practice of the magistrate's clerk charging a fee to a citizen prosecutor for steps taken as part of the magistrate's duties under the Marian pretrial procedure.

[110] Miles, Thesis, *supra* n. 72, at 270. Thus, "[i]n August 1771 John Ferguson, an Halifax linen draper, came to Howarth with witnesses when Mary Firth had been detected in his shop stealing silk handkerchiefs. Howarth drew the informations [that is, the Marian pretrial examinations] of Ferguson and the two women witnesses and then went to Horton [the JP] at Howroyd." Ibid. at 270 n. 3 (citing Howarth's MS day books). George Fisher

did not regard himself as precluded from doing defense work. Miles reports that "Howarth's Day Books reveal him advising both plaintiffs and the relatives of defendants in prosecutions for theft, coining, poaching and malicious damage, as well as conducting proceedings on their behalf."[111]

The pattern of having the magistrate's clerk serve as the prosecuting solicitor also occurred in institutional practice, where it lasted deep into the nineteenth century. The Mint Solicitor told a Parliamentary committee in the 1840s that "we usually prefer employing [as the solicitor to prosecute a case] the gentleman who sends up the information; he is commonly the magistrate's clerk . . ."[112] Stephen wrote in 1863 that "the attorney for the prosecution . . . is most frequently the clerk to the magistrates . . . ."[113]

John Howarth was not alone in serving sometimes as a solicitor for the defense. During the decades that solicitors were assuming an increasingly important role in the prosecution of crime, the profession also developed a role in defending criminal cases. Once again, the sources are too thin to permit us to learn about the frequencies, but we can see the phenomenon in outline. The rule forbidding counsel to the criminal defendant was a rule of audience in the trial court. For the out-of-court pretrial work of the solicitor no such prohibition took hold, although in the treason trials of the later Stuarts (where the law reports first notice[114] the defense solicitor), we

reports that in the year 1786 about a dozen attorneys, mostly JPs' clerks, got most of the reimbursement money paid for prosecutors' expenses at Salford Quarter Sessions (Manchester) in theft cases (131 reimbursements in that year). By 1796 one of these attorneys was receiving over 80% of the reimbursements (over 200 in that year, averaging more than £5 each). George Fisher, "The Birth of the Prison Retold," 104 *Yale L.J.* 1235, 1250–1 (1995). Regarding the series of statutes from 1752 onward that reimbursed some prosecution costs under various conditions, see 2 Radzinowicz, *History* 76–7. King reports that more than half of prosecutors for property crime received subsidies in Essex in the late 1780s. King, *Crime* 49–52 and fig. 3.1.

[111] Miles, Thesis, *supra* n. 72, at 270. "For instance, he advised John Holroyd of Marsden about the mode of prosecuting a person on suspicion of maiming three of his tups [male sheep]. In January 1770 Luke Dewhurst of Turvin was arrested for diminishing the coin, whereupon his wife consulted Howarth for advice. Similarly, he advised Mr. Taylor of Golcar Hill on his son being accused of killing fish. He also advised his tenant whose brother had been accused of coining and he appeared as his defence attorney at York Assizes in March 1770." Ibid. at 270 n. 2.

[112] Report of the Commissioners Appointed to Inquire into the Constitution, Management, and Expense of the Royal Mint (London 1849), discussed *supra* n. 53, at 192.

[113] Stephen, *General View* 155. "The *Law Times* frequently and violently condemned the practice 'of magistrates' clerks acting as attorneys against such persons as are committed by the magistrates for whom they act.'" Philip B. Kurland and D. W. M. Waters, "Public Prosecutions in England, 1854–79: An Essay in English Legislative History," 1959 *Duke L.J.* 493, 495 n. 10, quoting the 2 *Law Times* 259 (1843), with further citations.

[114] In addition to the *State Trials* reports discussed next in text, there is a pamphlet report of a trial held at the Old Bailey in 1680, in which counsel in his opening remarks refers to his brief, that is, to the solicitor's brief instructing him in the case. "[I]f my brief be true, I make

see considerable mistrust of solicitors who aided accused traitors.[115] The eighteenth-century *State Trials* show the courts voicing no objection to the defendant's use of a solicitor. Among the cases in which the report mentions the defendant having a solicitor are Richard Noble in 1713 for murder;[116] John Matthews in 1719 for treason in printing a libel;[117] and Christopher Layer in 1722 for treason.[118] From the 1730s onward, when the pamphlet reports of Old Bailey trials become more detailed, they occasionally show defense solicitors taking some action, such as explaining to the court the absence of witnesses or counsel.[119]

The institutional prosecutors could also find themselves fielding a solicitor for the defense when an agent or an officeholder found himself prosecuted for conduct in the line of duty.[120] Indeed, as an inducement to

no question but to satisfy your Lordship and the jury . . . that [the defendant] had no hand in this Bloody Action." (The defendant had counsel because the offense was charged as misdemeanor.) Anon., *The Tryal of John Giles at the Sessions House in the Old Bayly* 30 (London 1681) (for attempted murder on John Arnold, a JP for Monmouth and MP) (Lincoln's Inn Libr., shelfmark Trials 216, no. 3).

[115] Discussed *supra* Ch. 2, text at nn. 26–35, 147–53.

[116] *R. v. Richard Noble et al.*, 15 *St. Tr.* 731 (Surrey Assizes 1713). "Mr. Lindsey, one of the attorneys concerned for the prisoners (for they had many) deposed that he" had drafted a subpoena for a witness, and sent a messenger to serve it in London, who had not yet returned. Ibid. at 732.

[117] *R. v. John Matthews*, 15 *St. Tr.* 1323 (O.B. 1719). Defense counsel Ketelbey, who was allowed to conduct a full defense under the Treason Trials Act of 1696, made an opening statement in which he referred to the solicitor's brief. "[W]e shall, according to our instructions, be able to produce a great number of witnesses to contradict what these witnesses have sworn . . . ." Ibid. at 1368–9.

[118] *R. v. Christopher Layer*, 16 *St. Tr.* 93 (K.B. 1722). Hungerford, defending, objected to the threatened reading of some papers by the prosecution, "though for my part I know not what they are, for there is no hint of them in my brief . . . ." Ibid. at 199. Regarding the extensive latitude given to the defense solicitor in the notable trial of Edward Arnold in 1724 for malicious wounding, see *infra*, text at nn. 317-19. *R. v. Edward Arnold*, 16 *St. Tr.* 695 (Surrey Assizes 1724).

[119] For example, in the case of William Kitchinman, *OBSP* (Sept. 1737, #8), at 165, accused of stealing calico cloth, his solicitor, Mr. Lutwych, tried unsuccessfully to have the trial postponed, telling the court, "The Prisoner's Sister gave me Money for Counsel and Subpoenas against tomorrow," and that "I gave Subpoenas to Mr. Dottery and his Wife, but I did not imagine his Trial would have been till tomorrow." Ibid. at 166. In the case of John Latour, *OBSP* (Sept. 1736, #75), at 186, the defendant told the court that "his Attorney had engaged Counsel in his Cause; but the Prosecutor sent notice to him last Night, that the Matter was compromised, and that this was the Reason he had no body to appear for him." Ibid. at 188. Mr. Compton, identified as Latour's attorney, confirmed this account and "was much surprised when I found Mr. Latour was called to his Trial; if I had known it, I should have feed [that is, paid a fee to, meaning hired] Serjeant Haywood. I had Instructions to call [a witness to speak to a key issue of fact] if I had been prepared." Ibid.

[120] An 1803 committee of inquiry into the work of the City of London Solicitor traced the office back to 1545 and reported that "he has been employed to defend the magistrates and officers of this city in proceedings instituted against them for acts done in the execution of their respective offices and the discharge of their several duties . . . ." *Report in Relation to the Nature, Duties, and Emoluments of the Office of City Solicitor*, CLRO, Papers, Acts and Reports (PAR), book 13 (Common Council, 27 July, 1803), at 3.

zeal on the part of officers, the authorities occasionally trumpeted their willingness to defend citizen officeholders against civil and criminal suit, for example, when the monarch ordered a crackdown on street crime in Covent Garden in 1742.[121]

The *Sessions Papers* also supply an occasional window on the defensive work of solicitors, discussed below in connection with the so-called "Newgate Solicitors."[122]

3. Associations for the Prosecution of Felons

Another channel of engagement that placed criminal prosecutions under the management of solicitors was the association for the prosecution of felons. These remarkable organizations were formed in uncounted profusion through most of England. The earliest known examples date from the 1690s.[123] The organizations were especially characteristic of the decades

---

The Post Office archive, discussed *supra* n. 30, contains a brief titled "The King against Read: For Felony. Brief for the Prisoner," P74/271, prepared in 1793 by Parkin & Lambert, the solicitors' firm of Anthony Parkin, who was then the Post Office Solicitor. The Post Office was defending an employee, a guard on the Exeter mail coach, who had fired a weapon in purported defense of the coach. The *Sessions Paper* reports the trial and the acquittal of the defendant but does not disclose the appearance of the defense counsel whom the Post Office Solicitor briefed. Patrick Read, *OBSP* (Jan. 1793, #128), at 199.

[121] In December 1742 the King had Newcastle write to the chairman of Westminster Sessions, to convey royal interest in cleaning up the Covent Garden area. He wrote that "Covent Garden is infested with great Numbers of reputed Thieves, Pick-Pockets and other desperate Persons, who have formed themselves into Bodies, so that it is hazardous and dangerous for Persons of Quality to pass and repass to the Playhouses and other Parts thereabouts, without being assaulted and robbed. His Majesty, who is desirous to encourage the Suppressing of such wicked Disorders, has commanded me to acquaint you, that Orders shall be given to the Solicitor of the Treasury to defend, at his Majesty's Expense, all Constables, and other Peace Officers of the said City and Liberty in any vexatious actions, or Suits at Law, that may be brought against them, for what they shall do in the faithful Discharge of the Duty of their Offices, in putting in Execution the Warrants issued to them by the Justices of the Peace, for the purposes aforementioned." PRO, SP 44/82, *Criminal Book,* 17 Dec. 1742, at 188. Newcastle hoped "that the apprehension of Trouble and Expense on this Account may not discourage them from carrying on a Service so important to the Peace and Security of his Majesty's Subjects." Ibid. at 189.

[122] *Infra,* text at nn. 179–94.

[123] See the chronological table of associations in David Philips, " 'Good Men to Associate and Bad Men to Conspire:' Associations for the Prosecution of Felons in England 1760–1860" [hereafter Philips, "Associations"], in Hay and Snyder 113, 161–6. Regarding the Maghull, Lancashire, association, formed in 1699, see *infra,* text at n. 130. Douglas Hay has found evidence of an association against horse thieves that was formed in Stoke on Trent in 1693. Hay, Thesis, *supra* n. 34, at 355. He suggests the possibility "that such associations were not uncommon among wealthier farmers and tradesmen in the first half of the [eighteenth] century," but "because the provincial press developed largely after the 1730s," they cannot be traced through the advertising of rewards and stolen property, which is the way that many later associations have been documented. Ibid. "No evidence has been found for other associations in Staffordshire earlier than 1763." Ibid. at 356.

after 1770.[124] They declined in the middle of the nineteenth century, when official policing and police prosecution effectively displaced them. Estimates of the total number of prosecuting associations range from 1,000[125] to as many as 4,000.[126] Many associations were short-lived,[127] others functioned for decades; indeed, a handful still survive as provincial dining societies.

Among the reasons for taking an interest in the associations is that they help correct for the London bias of much of the rest of the sources for the history of criminal prosecution in the eighteenth century. Although some prosecuting associations formed in cities,[128] most operated in provincial areas and had a special emphasis on crimes such as the theft of horses and other livestock—for example, the 1770 "Articles of Association and agreement . . . by several Gentlemen, Tradesmen, Farmers and others of the County of Nottingham, To prosecute Horse Stealers for offenses committed in the said county."[129]

The associations aspired to promote the enforcement of the criminal law by spreading the costs of investigation and prosecution among the membership. One of the earliest surviving association agreements, from Maghull, Lancashire, recited in 1699 that the association was being formed in response to the danger that persons who committed serious crimes might "escape prosecution and punishment by reason of the charge and expense that would be occasioned in case the owner of the goods stolen should prosecute such felons by due and legal courts of law."[130]

---

[124] Philips, "Associations," *supra* n. 123, at 161–6. For Staffordshire, Hay reports a handful of formations in the 1760s, thirty-eight in the 1770s, and thirty-three more in the 1780s. Hay, Thesis, *supra* n. 34, at 356–7.

[125] Philips, "Associations," *supra* n. 123, at 120.

[126] P. J. R. King, "Prosecution Associations and their Impact in Eighteenth-Century Essex" [hereafter King, "Essex"], in Hay and Snyder 171, 173 n. 8.

[127] Ibid. at 180 (in the studied Essex sample "half of those formed before 1785 do not seem to have survived the century").

[128] Instances of the work of the London Society for Prosecuting Felons from the year 1795 are discussed in Ch. 5, *infra*, text at nn. 283–4.

[129] Nottingham County Record Office, DD.T. 25/1 (24 Oct. 1770).

[130] Maghull Agreement for the Prosecution of Felons, dated 21 July 1699, extracted in Adrian Shubert, "Private Initiative in Law Enforcement: Associations for the Prosecution of Felons, 1744–1856," in *Policing and Punishment in Nineteenth Century Britain*, at 25, 26 (Victor Bailey ed.) (1981) (attributed to Lancashire Record Office, PR 2814/1) [hereafter Shubert, "Initiative"].

Shubert describes a similar statement of purposes from the Bretherton Association in 1744. Its articles recite that "diverse burglaries and felonies have of late years been committed," yet "prosecutions are not carried on against the offenders with so much vigor as ought to be on account of the great expense attending such prosecutions . . . ." Ibid. at 26, citing Lancashire Record Office 2851/12/1. The result is that "persons from whom goods are stolen often acquiesce and do not endeavor to find out or prosecute offenders by reason of the great expense attending such prosecutions, by which means they go unpunished." Ibid.

The associations have begun to attract the attention of legal histori-ans.[131] Although the link between the associations and the solicitor's profession has not been a central concern of this literature, enough has been learned to permit us to see that the associations were a main conduit for the lawyerization of criminal prosecution in the eighteenth century. Unfortunately, little is known about the work of the associations in the early decades of the century, the period of particular interest in the present chapter. The archival record is extremely thin until the second half of the century, and thus, our picture is mostly drawn from sources that are later than we would wish.

As the name implies, the prosecuting associations were voluntary organizations of a sort now sometimes characterized as mutual benefit insurance societies. Members who pay a subscription fee become entitled to scheduled benefits. My automobile club, for example, will tow my car or charge the battery if the breakdown occurs within the period of my subscription. The association not only provides these specialist auto repair services, it also serves an insurance function. Because not all members will actually require the covered services, the association oper-ates as a risk pool, spreading the cost of the services it performs across the larger number of persons covered. This cost-spreading feature allows the association to deliver the services well below unit cost to the members who receive them.

The association for the prosecution of felons was a benefit society for the purpose of bearing some of the costs associated with the risk of being victimized by a serious crime. Members adopted articles of asso-ciation and paid a subscription. When a member suffered a crime of a type covered in the articles, the association would pay the expenses of criminal investigation and prosecution. It would advertise stolen goods and offer rewards for the return of goods and the apprehension of culprits. Sometimes the articles of the association contained a schedule of rewards payable to persons "giving such information against such offenders as shall lead to his or their conviction . . . ."[132] (These private rewards must be distinguished from the rewards paid by the crown for certain offenses pursuant to legislation, discussed later in this chapter.) Some of the associations also functioned as indemnity funds, insuring members against part of the loss that resulted when the stolen goods

---

[131] Philips, "Associations," *supra* n. 123, centered on the period 1760–1860, is particularly illuminating. See also King, "Essex," *supra* n. 126; and Shubert, "Initiative," *supra* n. 130. Douglas Hay's unpublished doctoral dissertation of 1975 supplies data on the Staffordshire associations. Hay, *Thesis, supra* n. 34, at 355–94.

[132] *Rules and Orders of the Binbrook Association for the Prosecution of All Persons Who Shall be Guilty of Felonies, Thefts, Crimes, or Misdemeanors* (Louth 1820) (printed handbill) (exemplar in Lincolnshire County Record Office, classmark 4 BM 5/5/2/2).

were not recovered.[133] Finally, when the culprits were identified, the association absorbed part or all of the costs[134] of gathering evidence and bringing prosecutions. Comparable associations developed in the eighteenth century to deal with another endemic concern—the challenge of preventing, fighting, and recompensing losses from fires.[135]

The feature of particular interest for present purposes is that by the second half of the eighteenth century (when the sources become ample) the associations were routinely managed by solicitors. The association's secretary or treasurer was usually a solicitor, often named in the articles of association.[136] Although some associations left it to the member to institute prosecution and seek reimbursement for expenses incurred,[137]

---

[133] E.g., *Rules and Orders of the Fakenham Association against Horse-Stealers*, at 8–9 (Norwich 1782) (Yale Univ., Lewis Walpole Libr., shelfmark 767So5) (providing that three months after the loss occurred the association would pay the value of the horse, to a ceiling of £20). The Nottingham association, discussed *supra* n. 129, paid the owner half the value of the horse to a ceiling of £13, one year after the loss. Nottingham County Record Office, DD.T. 25/1, art. 5 (24 Oct. 1770).

[134] Sometimes the association's articles provided general authority for reimbursement, for example, in *Rules of the Linton, Hildersham, Bartlow and Hadstock Association for the Detection and Prosecution of Felonies and Misdemeanors* (20 Nov. 1818), art. 2: "All reasonable Expenses which may be incurred in apprehending and prosecuting Offenders against Subscribers to this Association, shall be paid out of the Common Stock . . . ." Cambridgeshire Record Office, L95/18/1. Other associations devised preset reimbursement schedules. The Binbrook Association, *supra* n. 132, art. IV, at 4 (1820), promised to reimburse members 4*d*. per mile "[f]or every prosecutor's and witness's horse-hire in going to any magistrate or court," 5*s*. per day "[f]or every male witness's time, trouble, and expenses," and 4*s*. per day "[f]or every female witness's time, trouble, and expenses . . . ."

[135] Experience with the Great Fire of 1666 spurred the development. The fire caused losses "which exceeded £10 million, a sum equivalent perhaps to a full quarter of the national income at that date." Because there was no insurance industry, it was a case of "100% underinsurance . . . ." 1 Clive Trebilcock, *Phoenix Assurance and the Development of British Insurance: 1782–1870*, at 4 (1985). By the late eighteenth century the surviving evidence shows that the Phoenix was taking a hand in the prosecution of arson. The company "would distribute handbills in the vicinity of fires, advertise in newspapers and offer rewards; they also frequently assisted with prosecution expenses." Ibid. at 141. "Between 1782 and 1800 Phoenix filed suit against no less than seventeen individual arsonists." Ibid. at 142 (some appear to have been civil cases). Bow Street runners (thieftakers employed by the court JP) tracked one culprit to Frankfurt and were paid 25 guineas in 1787. Ibid. at 143. For the extensive trial report of an arson prosecution conducted by another London insurer, the Sun Fire Office, see David Clary and Elizabeth Combert, *OBSP* (Apr. 1788, #270), at 367.

[136] For example, the articles of the Nottingham association, *supra* n. 129, designated the solicitor Job Brough as the person to whom members should report a covered loss, ibid., art. 3, and directed him to invest any surplus funds "on Government Security." Ibid., art. 6. When Brough died in 1795, the association's journal recorded that "Messrs Pocklington and Company, Bankers in Newark" would replace him as treasurer; and that Edward Smith Godfrey and Benjamin Joseph Smith were "appointed Agents and Solicitors to the Association." Ibid., entry for 1795.

[137] Shubert reports that the articles of the Turton Association in Lancashire were careful to spell out that the prosecutor was left "to take upon himself all the trouble of prosecuting and providing all the proper evidence . . . as if prosecuting at his own charge." Shubert, *Initiative*, *supra* n. 130, at 32 (citing Lancashire Record Office, UDTu19). Philips dates the

the model that prevailed recast the association as the service provider, by providing that the association's managing solicitor would conduct the investigation and prosecution. For example, the Binbrook (Lincolnshire) Association's articles designated Thomas Rhodes of Market Rasen as treasurer "and also secretary and solicitor for conducting prosecutions," and allowed him to pay himself "out of the funds of this Association his fees of office, and all other reasonable charges for extraordinary trouble relating to the affairs of this Association."[138] David Philips, summarizing a study of more than 200 sets of association records dating mostly from 1760 or later, observes: "The solicitors invariably benefited most financially from the associations: they received a regular retainer from the society, and they handled all its business, taking members' reports of offenses committed and handling the subsequent prosecutions, advertising the society and its members, and collecting subscriptions."[139] Entries like the following, from the annual bills filed by the solicitor to a Bedfordshire association active from 1799, abound: "Paid printer and distributing bills [regarding] . . . Mr. Burton's Mare." "Clerk's Journey to Newport to learn the names and residences of two Men who were suspected to have stolen the mare." "Journey to Turvey to examine Evidence as to Bacon stolen from Mr. Brattams by Thomas Norman." "To Counsel and Clerk with Brief in the Prosecution of Thomas Hawkins for Stealing Wheat Stacks from Mr. B. Brooks of Emberton." "Attending Mr. Griggs and others and taking instructions to prosecute Marshall for stealing Meal." "Paid Expenses of the several Witnesses to and from and at Aylesbury on the prosecution of Marshall."[140] Philips remarks: "Reading through [such] itemized accounts (each interview at 3s. 4d. or 6s. 8d. a time, which quickly mounted up) one sees how good associations were for [the solicitor's] business."[141]

In these association records we see the lawyers taking over an important segment of the work of criminal investigation and prosecution in the provinces. From the standpoint of the solicitor, a prosecuting association was a dream client. The solicitor fed off the retainer for the society's routine administration, and he then charged piece rates for performing its investigating and prosecutorial work. The association also brought the solicitor into steady contact with the substantial citizens who constituted the association's membership, among whom he could prospect for other

---

founding of the Turton Association to the year 1789. Philips, "Associations," *supra* n. 123, at 163.

[138] Binbrook Association, *supra* n. 132, art. 11, at 7–8 (1820).

[139] Philips, "Associations," *supra* n. 123, at 136–7.

[140] Olney, Turvey and Harrold Association, Bedfordshire Record Office, GA 1108 (solicitor's bills, loose pages, filed by date from 1799), entries for 1799, 1800, 1808.

[141] Philips, "Associations," *supra* n. 123, at 137.

business. Indeed, there is every reason to believe that much of the initiative in creating these associations passed from the citizenry to the solicitors' profession. John Styles has reported in this connection that "a Yorkshire attorney's precedent book from the 1750s includes . . . an agreement [establishing an association to prosecute felons], suggesting that they were already part of an attorney's work at that date."[142] Philips noticed indications that solicitors "were the most active promoters of associations, urging local property-owners to set them up; and many [solicitors] acted as solicitor to more than one association."[143]

To conclude: The associations for the prosecution of felons are traceable from the 1690s. By the second half of the eighteenth century they were serving as important conduits for the lawyerization of criminal investigation and prosecution in provincial centers and in the countryside. The archival record for the early decades of the eighteenth century is too thin for us to know when this phenomenon became significant. If by the 1730s the associations were already beginning to influence the criminal prosecutions coming before the courts, their contribution to the legal-professional transformation of criminal prosecution would have been among the factors that the judges were weighing as they rethought the rule against defense counsel.

4. "Newgate Solicitors"

Already in the 1730s, when the English bench made its epochal decision to allow defense counsel to probe prosecution evidence at trial, there was a growing uneasiness about the reliability of the evidence that the lawyers were generating, both for the prosecution and for the defense.

Disquiet about the potential for solicitors to defeat the truth can be found in the English tract literature as early as 1681, when an anonymous broadside published in London complains that "[t]here is much cunning in procuring and tampering with witnesses, and much art in packing of Jurors . . . ."[144] The writer poses the question "May not a man meddle with or question a Witness?" The answer given is, "Yes, But with certain limitations. Otherwise a Witness may be made or corrupted, Judges and Jurors abused, and the Innocent utterly destroyed."[145] The writer wrestles with the boundaries of correct professional practice, approving of pretrial

---

[142] John Styles, "Print and Policing: Crime Advertising in Eighteenth-Century Provincial England" [hereafter Styles, "Advertising"], in Hay and Snyder 55, 64.
[143] Philips, "Associations," *supra* n. 123, at 137. King reports that the Essex "attorney, William Mason . . . acted as clerk to at least five prosecution associations in the north-east of Essex." King, "Essex," *supra* n. 126, at 192.
[144] *Seasonable Cautions for Juries, Solicitors and Witnesses; To Deterre from Man-Catching*, 1ʳ (London 1681) (Huntington Libr., San Marino, CA, shelfmark 133509).
[145] Ibid.

investigation but voicing concern lest the solicitor suborn the witnesses. "A Solicitor ... may not instruct, threaten or bribe [witnesses] to swear this or that."[146]

Directions, the 1728 pamphlet critical of London prosecuting solicitors, warns of the danger that in cases in which there is a statutory reward for conviction, solicitors would strain to exaggerate the evidence in order to bring the offense within the rewardable category. Thus, "by the Insinuations of the Solicitor, and the Covetousness of the Prosecutor, Truth would be perverted . . . ."[147] Isaac Newton, writing to the Treasury in 1696, complained that his prosecutorial work as Warden of the Mint exposed him to the "calumnies of ... Coiners and Newgate Solicitors," who made "false reports and oaths and combinations against me."[148]

(a) Misbehaving Solicitors

In September 1732, in the prosecution of Peter Buck for highway robbery,[149] we find the script that the author of *Directions* warned about, namely, a solicitor orchestrating a false prosecution for gain. Joseph Fisher, the ostensible victim, testified that Buck forcibly stopped him in Chancery Lane and robbed him of his snuff box. The defendant's sister testified that the prosecution resulted from a failed shakedown organized by one "Lawyer Grimes," who "solicits in this court." In advance of the trial Grimes had met with her and introduced her to Fisher as "a Man that will swear a Robbery against [her brother]." (Highway robbery was an offense for which a £40 reward was payable to the persons who convicted the offender,[150] as well as a further £100 by royal proclamation.[151]) Grimes told the sister that, if she "would save [her] Brother's Life," she needed to pay off both Grimes and Fisher. Grimes wanted £3 in payment of a supposed debt that the brother owed Grimes, and a further 2 guineas for Fisher. Fisher told her that "if you'll satisfy Lawyer Grimes, and give me 2 Guineas, I'll make it up," that is, drop the prosecution.[152] Another witness testified that Fisher admitted ruefully to her a few days before

---

[146] Ibid. The passage in text continues: "He may discourse with them, and enquire whether they have any thing to say to this or that point, in order to save the Court a trouble; but he ought not to work them by hope of reward, or fear of harm to say more, or less than they are inclined to . . . ." After framing the issue in this way, the writer devotes the remainder to sermonizing about the evils of false witness.

[147] *Directions*, *supra* n. 76, at 4. The author gives the example of overcharging as highway robbery what "was only a Quarrel between the Prosecutor and the Prisoner." Ibid.

[148] Letter to the Commissioners of the Treasury, *supra* n. 38, at 210.

[149] *OBSP* (Sept. 1732, #53), at 210.

[150] 4 & 5 Wil. & Mar., c. 8, § 2 (1692), discussed *infra*, text at n. 206.

[151] For the proclamation practice in the 1730s, see Beattie, *Policing* 401–2 and table 8.1.

[152] *OBSP* (Sept. 1732, #53), at 210.

that he had sworn falsely against Buck, and that "Lawyer Grimes put me upon it."[153]

The trial judge ordered Grimes brought into court, "reprimanded him, and forbade him ever to Practice in that Court for the future."[154] The jury acquitted Buck on the spot, but discussion of Grimes continued. One of the jurors told the court: "My Lord, we have taken Notice of his being very busy with the Witnesses all this Sessions." Someone named Robert Nash told the court that Grimes "makes it his Business to set People together by the Ears and foment Law-Suits," and that Nash had paid off Grimes to spare a lawsuit. Someone identified as "A Juryman's Wife" volunteered that "Lawyer Grimes keeps a public Bawdy-House in Church Yard Alley . . . ."[155] The trial judge replied to these allegations that "Those who know these Things should indict him as a common Barretor, and for keeping a common Bawdy-House."[156]

Grimes was a hard man to put out of business, however. A few days later, the reporter tells us, "Mary Tompson, a Juryman's Wife, informed the Court upon Oath" that Grimes approached her outside the court-house door, took her aside, and talked to her about the case of Henry Davis, who was to be tried for burglary (another of the offenses for which legislation promised a £40 reward for conviction[157]). Grimes told her: "[W]hisper your Husband to tell the rest of the Jury, that if they will find [Davis] guilty of the Indictment, they shall have two Guineas a piece."[158] The report continues: "Upon this the Court immediately granted a Warrant for apprehending the Lawyer."[159]

The same September 1732 sessions of the Old Bailey that heard these reports of Grimes' efforts to bring a false prosecution and to bribe a jury also dealt with a case involving the abuse of coaching witnesses. In the case of James Lewis,[160] for forging a will, prosecution counsel appeared and stated the case against him. It was alleged that Lewis was a money-lender to sailors, and that such moneylenders commonly required the sailor to make a will in favor of the moneylender before making the loan. In this case, prosecution counsel claimed, the accused forged a sailor's

---

[153] *OBSP* (Sept. 1732, #53), at 211.

[154] Ibid. The report identifies Grimes as having the alias John Graham, regarding which, see *infra* n. 159.

[155] Ibid.   [156] Ibid.

[157] 10 & 11 Wil. 3, c. 23, § 2 (1699).   [158] *OBSP* (Sept. 1732, #53), at 211.

[159] Ibid. The events were also reported in 2 *Gentleman's Magazine* 975 (Sept. 1732) (entry for 11 Sept). Grimes was involved in yet another questionable prosecution in the September 1732 sessions, under his alias as John Graham. In the case of Ann Foster, *OBSP* (Sept. 1732, #20), at 180, who was accused of stealing a pocketbook containing promissory notes, the prosecuting victim had advertised the lost items. He told the court that he had Foster arrested and prosecuted after John Graham came to him and told him that Foster had his pocketbook. Foster was acquitted after presenting evidence that she found the items.

[160] *OBSP* (Sept. 1732, #17), at 178.

will after the death of the sailor. Witnesses were brought to testify about when the will was signed. One Joseph Wass, apparently serving as the prosecution solicitor, was overheard telling one of the witnesses to say that the decedent signed the will on 30 November. An unidentified "Officer" interrupted the trial and advised the court, "My Lord, here's this Man, Joseph Wass, [who] prompts the Witnesses."[161] An unidentified "Gentleman," apparently a bystander who overheard Wass, volunteered the same information. The judge ordered them sworn and asked them what they heard Wass say. Each testified that Wass told them what date to testify to. Wass defended himself: "Suppose I did, I hope there was no Harm in that." The judge exploded: "No harm, Sir? When a Man's Life is at Stake, are you to put Words in the Witnesses' Mouths, and direct them what to swear? Officer, take him into Custody."[162] Here, on the eve of the judges' decision to admit defense counsel to cross-examine witnesses, is an Old Bailey judge recognizing the danger that solicitors may "put words in the Witnesses' Mouths, and direct them what to swear . . . ."

We have seen that *Directions*, the 1728 pamphlet critical of solicitors, complained of the duplicity of solicitors at the Old Bailey. The author contended that the prosecuting solicitor "will often, for a Fee from the Prisoner, advise the Prosecutor to compound the Felony before Sessions, or not to appear at the [trial], for which [the prosecutor is himself theoretically] liable to a Prosecution . . . ."[163] Some years later, in 1741, the *Sessions Papers* disclose such a case, a prosecution for highway robbery in which the victim, Parish, testified that after the robbery, "I not knowing how to proceed, a Fellow, one Baker, offered me his Assistance as an Attorney, and got a Bill of Indictment drawn according to his own Way of Thinking; I paid him 2 shillings for it, and he has dropped me, and keeps the Indictment."[164] Later in the trial Baker appeared as a defense witness, claiming that Parish had been unable to identify the culprits at the time of the crime. "The Court severely reprimanded Baker for his Conduct in this Affair."[165]

---

[161] Ibid. at 179.

[162] Ibid. The judge ordered Wass sent to Newgate, where we lose trace of him.

[163] *Directions, supra* n. 76, at 14.

[164] George Stacey and Matthias Dennison, *OBSP* (Jan. 1741, ##24–5), at 11, 12 (highway robbery).

[165] Ibid. at 13. The two defendants were convicted and sentenced to death. This case also evidences, ibid. at 12–13, the earliest appearance in the *Sessions Papers* of Stephen Macdaniel (here, Macdonnel, sometimes McDonald or McDaniel), who would figure in as the chief villain in 1754 in the great reward scandal noticed *infra*, text at nn. 236–7, discussed in detail in Langbein, "Ryder" 110–14. Macdaniel appeared as a crown witness, testifying against his former accomplices. As in his later exploits, this was a case of highway robbery, for which legislation offered a reward of £40 per head to the persons who prosecuted and convicted offenders. The reward system is discussed *infra*, text at nn. 206–47. Paley reports that in this case Parish, Macdaniel, and six others split £80 in statutory reward money for convicting the

The Old Bailey trial sources also contain allegations about solicitors absconding, for example, the pitiful James English, accused in 1736 of stealing clothes, who was apparently believed and acquitted when he told the court: "I have not any Witnesses, for I gave all my Money to one Mac ____ something, a Newgate solicitor, to manage my Cause, and he is run away with the Money and has done nothing."[166]

(b) The 1733 London Grand Jury Presentment

In September 1733 the London grand jury returned an extraordinary presentment, complaining that "many Vexatious and litigious Prosecutions have appeared before us . . . ."[167] The document points to two abuses. First, magistrates' clerks (who often practiced as solicitors in their own right) were charging fees for the performance of the magistrates' public duties, hence confusing private employment and public office.[168] Second, "Clerks and Solicitors in Confederacy with a set of People calling themselves informing Constables, Newgate Solicitors and others . . . [were acting] as Solicitors and Agents . . . [in] encouraging and Abetting ignorant and weak People to" bring insubstantial prosecutions, and consequently, "getting that Money from them which they stand in Need of for the Support of themselves and [their] poor families."[169]

The London grand jury's concern with vexatious prosecution needs to be understood in the light of a striking shortcoming of the early modern

two offenders. Ruth Paley, "Thieftakers in London in the Age of the McDaniel Gang, c.1745–1754" [hereafter Paley, "Thieftakers"], in Hay and Snyder, at 319.

[166] James English, *OBSP* (Jul. 1736, #13), at 154.

[167] CLRO, London Sessions Papers, September 1733, doc. unnumbered [hereafter 1733 Grand Jury Presentment]. The presentment was contemporaneously printed as a two-sided bill; a copy is found bound with the September 1733 trial pamphlet in the collection of *Old Bailey Sessions Papers* belonging to the University of Chicago Law Library, and is cited in Langbein, "Ryder" 109 n. 441.

[168] The Presentment says that "Divers Persons, Clerks or Servants to many of his Majesty's Justices of the Peace within this City, do under Color and in the Execution of their Office Exact and Take from all Persons accused and others bound to Prosecute Several Sums of Money under Pretence for Warrants, Commitments, Recognizances, Discharges and other Matters Incident to the Duty and Office of a Justice of Peace, contrary to the known Laws of this Realm, In Violation of public Justice and to the great oppression of his Majesty's Subjects." 1733 Grand Jury Presentment, *supra* n. 167, at 1ʳ.

An Old Bailey case from 1738 illustrates the kind of thing the grand jury was complaining about five years earlier. In the prosecution of Joseph Golding, *OBSP* (Apr. 1738, # 22), at 66, for highway robbery, a witness told of having gone to Justice Farmer's to give an information. Farmer's clerk, Warrener, refused to take it without being paid a Guinea. "The Court expressed their Resentment of Mr. Warrener's behavior; and declared it to be the duty of all who serve as Clerks under Gentlemen in the Commission of the Peace, to be always ready to execute their Office without Exaction." Ibid. at 67.

On the tension between the clerk's magisterial and private practice, see *supra*, text at nn. 101–13.

[169] 1733 Grand Jury Presentment, *supra* n. 167, at 1ʳ.

criminal justice system. Into the eighteenth century the procedure lacked an effective pretrial screening mechanism to weed out insubstantial cases until the eve of trial, when the grand jury reviewed evidence in support of proffered bills of indictment and dismissed insubstantial cases.[170] This "dependence on prosecutions initiated by private individuals," Ruth Paley has remarked, invited "vexatious actions."[171] Indeed, the bare threat to institute a groundless prosecution was terrifying enough that it could be used to extort money. Thomas Neaves, a "Noted Street-Robber" active in the 1720s, boasted of his success at this technique.[172] False charges of sodomy (sodomy was then a felony) were particularly feared for their reputational injury.[173] Behind the London grand jury's presentment is the

---

[170] Discussed *supra* Ch. 1, text at nn. 172–7.

[171] Paley, "Thieftakers," *supra* n. 165, at 312. Paley has traced the activities of several gangs of London thieftakers active in the 1740s and 1750s, showing that they took advantage of the ease of charging to institute malicious prosecutions. Ibid. at 312–13 and n. 39.

[172] He would "step to a Justice of the Peace, and having given some formal Account of a Robbery, sometime or other committed, he generally procured a Warrant, which he carried along with him, till he had an Opportunity of securing . . . [his victims, unless they paid him off. Otherwise,] they were certainly charged in Custody, and sent to Prison on suspicion till he could (as he often pretended) find an Adversary to prosecute them." Anon., The Life of Tho[mas] Neaves, the Noted Street-Robber 26 (London [c.1729]), discussed in Langbein, "Ryder" 109–10.

In at least one case, Neaves apparently did more than threaten false prosecution, he successfully conducted one. We learn of it from the report of Neaves' execution at Tyburn in February 1729, following his conviction for theft of shop goods. In December 1727 Neaves had testified against Richard Nichols, who was convicted for stealing ten watches from a shop. Nichols was executed on 20 May 1728. When it came Neaves' turn to be executed, "the Father and Wife of Richard Nichols, who was hanged on Neaves's Evidence, came into the Cart, and asked Neaves, if the evidence he had given against Nichols was true. Neaves declared, that it was not, that Nichols was innocent, and that he had never seen him till the Day he was taken up." 3 Select Trials at the Sessions-House in the Old Bailey 175 (London 1742 edn.) (4 vols.) [hereafter Select Trials].

[173] E.g., the case of Thomas Elmes, tried in 1720 for highway robbery, whose defense was that the prosecutor falsely charged him with the robbery after Elmes observed the prosecutor committing sodomy. Elmes was not believed and was convicted of the robbery. 1 Select Trials 10, 11.

At Bristol Assizes in 1734 two men were prosecuted for sodomy on the evidence of one Burgess. They were acquitted after introducing evidence that Burgess had been a crown witness in another sodomy case a few months earlier at the Old Bailey, and that Burgess had "offered to decline giving his Evidence for [a payment of] 2 Guineas . . . ." 4 Gentleman's Magazine 509 (Sept. 1734).

The details of another such case, in 1751, are captured in the title of the pamphlet that reports it: A Full and Genuine Narrative of the Conspiracy Carried on by Cather, Cane, Alexander, Nixon, Paterson, Falconer, Smith, Which Last Was Executed at Tybourn with McLeane, against the Hon. Edward Walpole, Esq., Charging Him with the Detestable Crime of Sodomy, in Order to Extort a Large Sum of Money from Him, together with an Account of Their Remarkable Trial and Conviction before the Rt. Hon. the Lord Chief Justice Lee, in the Court of King's Bench, Westminster, July 5th, 1751 (2nd edn. London [1751]) (Yale Univ., Beinecke Libr., shelfmark British Tracts 1751 F 95).

Two such cases that came before Lord Mansfield in the 1770s are discussed in James Oldham, "Truth-Telling in the Eighteenth-Century English Courtroom," 12 Law and History Rev. 95, 107–8 (1994) (R. v. Foote (1776) (unreported), and R. v. Donnally, Leach 199, 188 Eng.

discomfort that contemporaries felt that solicitors specializing in criminal prosecutions had at their fingertips the ability to subject citizens to the danger, expense, and humiliation of defending against criminal charges.[174]

The image of the prosecuting solicitor as a figure of menace endured across the decades. It surfaced again, for example, in 1773 in Robert Holloway's vituperative tract, *The Rat-Trap*,[175] which caricatures the London magistrate's clerk as a "petty-fogging attorney: a rascal so branded with infamous practices, that he is rendered too despicable for any employment but solicitor to a rotation office. This miscreant [has the power to] convict, or acquit, just as the prosecutor will pay, or the thief bribe . . . ."[176] Holloway purports to describe "a certain Old Bailey solicitor, who . . . [after being dismissed] from the Bow Street Office [where Henry and then John Fielding served as the court JP], has met with such singular success in Litchfield Street [another magistrate's office], that he shares five hundred pounds per annum from indictments; and that from hanging and transporting innocent men at the price of five guineas each."[177] Holloway concludes with a flourish that "an Italian assassin would demand double the wages for stabbing single-handed, that our bravo [solicitor] requires for a volume of sheer perjury."[178]

Rep. 199 (1779)). Mansfield brooded that such cases were "a specious mode of robbery of late grown very common . . . ." Quoted in Oldham, *supra*, at 108.

Evidence of a solicitor's involvement in a trumped-up sodomy case appears in the Old Bailey prosecution of George Sealey and Thomas Freeman, *OBSP* (Sept. 1736, ##78–9), at 188. Freeman testified that the prosecutor "got acquainted with one Cuttings, a Solicitor in the Old Bailey, and [Freeman and Cuttings] gave . . . Directions to draw the Bill for Sodomy against me." Ibid. at 190. In *R. v. Thomas Jones*, 1 Leach 139, 168 *Eng. Rep.* 171 (O.B. 1776), the Twelve Judges sustained a conviction and death sentence for highway robbery, deemed to have been committed by extorting money from the victim on the threat of falsely charging him with sodomy. Regarding the Twelve Judges procedure, see *infra* Ch. 4, text at n. 153.

[174] The *Gentleman's Magazine* reported that, in addition to the presentment discussed in text, "the Grand Jury presented 4 noted Solicitors for infamous Practices, in fomenting and carrying on Prosecutions against innocent Persons for the sake of Rewards, &c, whereupon the Court returned Thanks to the Grand Jury and assured them that the Offenders should be rigorously prosecuted." 3 *Gentleman's Magazine* 493 (Sept. 1733). Beattie has traced this report in the London records and identified the four solicitors. Beattie, *Policing* 398–400. The Old Bailey made an ineffectual regulatory response to the presentment, decreeing that the ranks of solicitors practicing at the court would be restricted to persons "that have been admitted Sworn Attorneys in some of the Courts at Westminster and are amenable to Justice for Such their Practice." 1733 Grand Jury Presentment, *supra* n. 167, at 1ᵛ. This response echoes the 1729 legislation for requiring the enrollment of solicitors, *supra*, n. 16.

[175] Robert Holloway, *The Rat-Trap, Dedicated to the Right Hon. Lord Mansfield, Chief Justice of England; Addressed to Sir John Fielding, Knight* (London 1773) (Lincoln's Inn Libr., shelfmark Law Pamphlets 29, no. 5).

[176] Ibid. at 15–16 n. He continues: because "there is a good understanding kept up between the amiable trio, justice, solicitor, and thief-catcher, it is almost impossible to determine in many cases which ought to receive the reputation of hanging the innocent or screening the guilty." Ibid. at 16 n.

[177] Ibid.   [178] Ibid.

(c) Newgate Defenders

Contemporary concern about the ability of solicitors to impair the reliability of the evidence that would be presented at trial was not confined to the prosecution. There was considerable fear of the Newgate solicitor's ability to concoct false alibis for defendants. Writing in 1751, Henry Fielding warned that hardened criminals "have for their last Resource some rotten Members of the Law to forge a defense for them, and a great number of false Witnesses to support it."[179] An alarming example occurred in the prosecution of Thomas Gray, alias MacCray,[180] for highway robbery in 1735.[181] MacCray had been arrested near the scene of the robbery. The prosecuting victim, a clergyman, testified that he was quite certain of the identification. The moonlight at the scene of the holdup had been good, and the clergyman had seen the culprit full face. When arrested, MacCray had in his possession a lock and key that the prosecutor identified as part of the stolen loot.

Against this powerful case, the accused mounted a defense of alibi. Prosecuting counsel, mistrustful of the defense witnesses, asked to have them excluded from the courtroom during each other's testimony, explaining that "We fear some bad Practices . . . ."[182] MacCray contended that the prosecution was a frame-up growing out of election hostilities, and that he had alibi witnesses placing him at a pub in Holborn on election business at the time of the robbery. His first witness, Gilbert Campbell, identified himself as an attorney, and testified that he took MacCray with him to the pub on a client's business. Two further witnesses corroborated Campbell's story, one Ruffhead, a butcher, and Julian Brown. Brown's appearance stirred Sir Thomas DeVeil, the court JP,[183] who was sitting with the trial bench, to recollect that Brown had been prosecuted for a robbery four years earlier, and had been lucky to be acquitted because the evidence against him was very full. Nevertheless, confronted with three unrebutted alibi witnesses, the jury acquitted MacCray.

The contemporaneous report of MacCray's case in the *Old Bailey Sessions Papers* underscores the reporter's distrust of the alibi witnesses. A footnote identifies Campbell as having been a defense witness in another felony case a few months before.[184] Another footnote cites readers to the

---

[179] Fielding, *Enquiry* 75, 77.
[180] MacCray was the leader of a gang of London criminals who figured in a number of Old Bailey cases in the period around 1735, and who are being studied in current research by Heather Shore.
[181] *OBSP* (Jul. 1735, #22), at 89.   [182] Ibid. at 90.
[183] Discussed, *supra*, text at n. 48.   [184] Ibid. at 90.

1731 report of the prosecution of Brown.[185] A posthumous biography of DeVeil, published in 1748, claims that a notorious solicitor, William Wreathock, masterminded the false alibis that saved MacCray.[186] Wreathock was renowned as the attorney with the effrontery to bring the so-called *Highwayman's Case* in the Exchequer in 1725. That suit asserted a dispute about the profits of a joint venture. When the court discovered that both parties were highway robbers contesting their shares in stolen loot, the case was dismissed and Wreathock fined £50 for contempt of court.[187] In 1735 Wreathock was convicted at the Old Bailey of highway robbery[188] and sentenced to death but reprieved for transportation and ultimately pardoned. He returned to London, and resumed practicing as a solicitor; he was finally struck off the solicitors' rolls in 1758.[189]

The biography of DeVeil also contends that the MacCray gang, alarmed at DeVeil's investigations of their "remarkable villainies," had planned in October of 1735 to have Julian Brown assassinate DeVeil, but that Brown became frightened and warned DeVeil. Among the MacCray gang, the pamphlet says, "were retainers to the law, who understood all the dark arts that qualified Newgate solicitors, and these fellows provided and managed every thing, and that too with such dexterity, that there was nothing they could not prove, or disprove upon very short notice."[190] (This concern that London criminal gangs could call upon the skills of solicitors also troubled the reward system, discussed below.) MacCray himself appears to have been a sometime solicitor. He appeared as the prosecuting victim in one of the earliest known cases in which defense counsel appeared at the Old Bailey, in December 1734. Cross-examined about his business, MacCray replied, "I practice the Law—'tis what I was bred to."[191]

[185] Ibid. at 91, citing Julian Brown, *OBSP* (Sept. 1731, #7), at 11. Brown was prosecuted the following October and acquitted of the rape of an 11-year-old girl. Julian Brown, *OBSP* (Oct. 1735, #35), at 161.

[186] Wreathock "had managed the whole scene of perjury, by which Maccray came off in Middlesex, and a very bold attempt of the same nature, by which it was endeavored to get him acquitted likewise in Surrey, though that miscarried." *DeVeil Memoirs, supra* n. 46, at 38. (I owe the reference to this passage to Heather Shore.) Regarding DeVeil and this pamphlet biography, see Langbein, "Ryder" 59–60.

[187] The case, which arose on a bill in the equity side of the court of Exchequer, is unreported. The archive sources are discussed and extracted in "Note, The Highwayman's Case (*Everet v. Williams*)," 9 *Law Quarterly Rev.* 197–9 (1893).

[188] William Wreathock *et al.*, *OBSP* (Dec. 1735, ##67–71), at 18. He boasted to the court in his defense that "I have been an Attorney these 18 Years, and have acquired in this Capacity a small Fortune." 4 *Select Trials* 139, 145.

[189] Birks, *Gentlemen, supra* n.15, at 135, 149; 12 Holdsworth, *HEL* 59.

[190] *DeVeil Memoirs, supra* n. 46, at 34–5.

[191] Margaret and Hester Hobbs, *OBSP* (Dec. 1734, #29), at 16 (privately stealing from the person). The prosecution was brought by Thomas Gray, identified by the alias MacCreagh, that is, MacCray. He claimed the two women stole some money from him. Their defense

So ill was the repute of solicitors at the Old Bailey in these years that the anonymous author of a measured tract[192] about the case of Thomas Carr, a solicitor who was convicted and executed in 1737, argued that prejudice against solicitors had influenced the jury to return a mistaken verdict. Carr was convicted of committing a robbery at knife point. The author, after discussing the evidence that pointed to Carr's innocence, speculated that the jury's error resulted in part from hostility to solicitors.[193]

As of the mid-1730s, therefore, events had made the public and the bench increasingly aware of the danger that some solicitors in criminal practice would employ unscrupulous means to "prove . . . or disprove"[194] whatever the case needed for victory. The judges' decision, taken in these years, to allow defense counsel to cross-examine witnesses at trial was, in my view, motivated in considerable part by their growing realization of the potential for distortion and fabrication that inhered in the increasingly lawyer-dominated pretrial that lay behind the trials over which they presided.

(5) Prosecution Counsel

In the same years that the prosecution solicitor was entrenching himself in the pretrial process in cases of serious crime, lawyerization was spreading

---

was that the case was a grudge prosecution, deliberately orchestrated by the gang. The jury acquitted.

[192] Anon., *Some Observations on the Trial of Mr. Thomas Carr, who was Executed at Tyburn, January 18, 1737* (London 1737) (Lincoln's Inn, shelfmark Trials 101, no. 1).

[193] "A common Prejudice against Mr. Carr's profession, especially in the Way he was sometimes unhappily engaged in [it, together with] A particular personal Prejudice against him, on his general Character of leading an irregular Life, and upon the Report of his having been concerned in the defense of certain Persons and Causes not altogether to his Credit, added to the seeming Consistence [sic] of the Prosecutor's well seamed Story, might sway, and prepossess their minds against him." Ibid. at 6. The case is reported as Thomas Car [sic] and Elizabeth Adams, *OBSP* (Oct. 1737, ##4–5), at 204. The jurors seem also to have been irritated at defense counsel's aggressive questioning of a prosecution witness. They are said to have requested that the trial judge "would please to ask the Questions that are proper, and that the [witness] may not be interrupted." Ibid. at 206. According to another account, Carr was involved "with a certain knot of People who were concerned in procuring Evidence on particular Causes, when, and whenever such Assistance was necessary; to which detestable Practice, if Mr. Baron Thompson, and other worthy Magistrates had not opposed themselves, it must by this Time have swelled to an enormous Height. As it was, Mr Carr had a great share in the Success which for some time that Practice met with . . . ." 4 *Select Trials* 254, 272 (extract from the Ordinary of Newgate's account, appended to the trial of Thomas Carr and Elizabeth Adams, Sept. 1737). Regarding the Ordinary's accounts, narratives of the lives of condemned criminals prepared and published by the Anglican priest who ministered to them while they awaited execution, see generally Peter Linebaugh, "The Ordinary of Newgate and his Account," in *Crime in England: 1550–1800*, at 249 (J. S. Cockburn ed.) (1977) [hereafter Linebaugh, "Ordinary"].

[194] *DeVeil Memoirs, supra* n. 46, at 35.

from pretrial to trial. The sources evidence a growing use of prosecution counsel to conduct felony cases at trial, further distancing the eighteenth-century criminal trial from Sir Thomas Smith's lawyer-free altercation of citizen accuser and citizen accused. From the later 1710s and into the 1720s the *Sessions Papers* contain a trickle of cases, about one a year, in which the appearance of prosecution counsel is disclosed.[195] Such cases are reported with increasing frequency in the early 1730s. For the year 1734, in which the *Sessions Papers* disclose the first appearance of defense counsel, there were eight cases in which prosecution counsel is identi-fied.[196]

The use of prosecution counsel in prosecutions by the Mint Solicitor has already been mentioned.[197] In the early years of the eighteenth century the Solicitor sometimes did not employ counsel, relying instead upon the witnesses to tell their tales unaided in the fashion of the altera-tion-style trial. Across the century, however, the employment of trial counsel became routine. Having built a criminal prosecution by locating, selecting, and preparing witnesses, the Solicitor wanted counsel to lead the witnesses at trial. In this way, lawyerization of the pretrial facilitated lawyerization of the trial.

The division between the two branches of the English legal profession prevented the solicitor who had built the case from presenting it at trial. Only counsel (the barrister) had the right of audience at trial.[198] Accordingly, the solicitor who managed the pretrial proceedings needed to transmit his work product to the counsel who would present the case. This process of informing the barrister about the case came to be known as instructing or briefing counsel. The convention developed, which endures to the present, that the solicitor would prepare a document called a brief that summarized the case for counsel.

Prosecution briefs from the early decades of the eighteenth century are quite rare in the surviving archives. As with other evidence of the solici-tor's pretrial work, the function of the brief was fulfilled at the trial, and thereafter no one had much incentive to preserve it. The Mint accounts sometimes show payments for preparing prosecution briefs.[199] Among

---

[195] Discussed in Langbein, "CTBL" 311.   [196] Ibid. at 312 and n. 160.

[197] *Supra*, text at n. 55.

[198] Investigating solicitors did on occasion testify about their pretrial work. In the cele-brated case against Samuel Goodere for murdering his brother, the prosecution solicitor, Jarrit Smith, was the first witness to be examined. Samuel Goodere *et al.*, 17 *St. Tr.* 1003, 1017–26 (Bristol Assizes 1741). For cases evidencing the testimony of the Solicitor of the Mint in counterfeiting cases, see *supra* n. 44.

[199] For example, in the case of Sarah Harris, the Mint Solicitor "paid for briefs and copies on trial." *Mint Books*, *supra* n. 35, vol. 8, at 116 (Kingston Assizes, 1713). In the prosecution of Amy Healy at York, Lent 1756 Assizes, for uttering counterfeits, the Mint Solicitor entered a payment for "Drawing brief." Ibid., vol. 11, at 82–3.

the records of other institutional solicitors, a few briefs exist. The Bank of England archives preserve some documents, including the brief, from the case of Robert Minor, accused in 1719 of presenting a forged bill of exchange. The Bank's directors ordered Minor prosecuted "if Mr. Woodford [the Bank's solicitor] shall think proper" (an indication of the internal delegation of authority to the solicitor characteristic of the increasingly complex organizations that appear as institutional prosecutors).[200] Woodford's two-page brief[201] to counsel summarizes the indictment, then provides a short statement of the charges, styled "The Case." The main section, headed "To prove which Case," sets forth a series of factual propositions, for example, "To prove the handwriting of [the payee]," "To prove the forged bill is like the handwriting of Minors," and "To prove the tender of the bill." Alongside these propositions the solicitor entered the names of the witnesses who would testify in support of each point.[202] A still earlier brief, from 1702, in the records of the City of London Solicitor, instances a more primitive version of this format.[203]

Prosecution briefs became more elaborate across the century. On occasion the solicitor used the brief to advise the barrister on trial tactics. In a case for criminal malicious prosecution brought in 1741, the City of London Solicitor, Peterson, warned counsel about the danger that the defense "will produce the Record of [the prosecution witness' prior] Conviction for Conspiracy for which he was sentenced to stand in the Pillory. Please therefore against this to guard as much as possible. If in General they should attempt to impeach his character, we say that in such dirty work as a Conspiracy 'tis supposed None but persons of indifferent Characters are Consulted, and therefore such only can be produced as witnesses."[204] Peering through this rare window into early lawyer-driven criminal trial tactics, we see that lawyers inclined even then to the partisanship in gathering and presenting facts that is such a troublesome feature of the modern adversary system. The City Solicitor hoped to suppress the truth about his witness, but if that failed, he suggested a line of argument for downplaying the defect.

---

[200] *Bank of England v. Robert Minors*, Bank of England F4/38/1 (1719). The file also contains a copy of the indictment, F4/38/2, and a copy of Minors' pretrial examination, taken before William Thomson, the recorder of London. F4/38/3.

[201] F4/38/5 (1719).

[202] Ibid. at 2.

[203] *R. v. Savage*, CLRO, *London Sessions Papers 1702*, Miscellaneous Documents file (a case of criminal libel). (I owe this reference to John Beattie.)

[204] CLRO, *London Sessions Papers, September 1744* (the quoted brief dates from 1741 but is filed with documents from 1744 involving the same matter).

B. Prosecution Perjury

In the same years that uneasiness was growing about the ability of solicitors to compromise the integrity of the evidence in criminal trials, the judges were becoming increasingly aware that two other pillars of early eighteenth-century prosecutorial practice—the reward system and the crown witness system—were rife with incentives for false witness. By admitting defense counsel in the 1730s for the primary purpose of probing prosecution testimony on cross-examination, the judges were responding to the increasingly manifest danger of perjury[205] in prosecution evidence.

1. The Reward System

Beginning in 1692,[206] Parliament enacted a series of statutes that offered rewards up to £40[207] to persons who would apprehend and convict offenders who committed serious property crimes: highway robbery, burglary and housebreaking, coining, theft of livestock, and certain other offenses.[208] The first reward statutes were part of a broader program designed to stiffen law enforcement under William III, reflecting the concern of the government in the aftermath of the Revolution of 1688–9 that urban disorder could imperil the new monarch's grip.[209] The weak point in the received policing and prosecutorial practice was the neglect of the investigatorial function,[210] that is, seeking information when the facts of a crime were not fairly obvious. The Marian system left that work to the victim or to the amateur JP, but if they were not able or disposed to do it, it did not get done. The reward statutes created incentives for others to take up the job.

---

[205] Disquiet about perjury in civil and criminal cases was pervasive in the eighteenth century. In 1786 the judges "met at Lord Mansfield's chambers and proposed a bill that would make the crime punishable by death." 2 Oldham, *Mansfield* 1066; see generally ibid. at 1066–1106.

[206] 4 & 5 Wil. & Mar., c. 8, § 2 (1692).

[207] £40 was the reward for both highway robbery and burglary. 2 Radzinowicz, *History* 57–9. For coining and theft of livestock, the offer was £10. Some of the statutes offered, in addition to or in place of cash rewards, so-called "Tyburn tickets," negotiable certificates of immunity from parish and ward offices that traded freely in the aftermarket. Ibid. at 155–61.

[208] See the list compiled in Patrick Colquhoun, *A Treatise on the Police of the Metropolis* 390–2 (7th edn. London 1806) (1st edn. London 1795) [hereafter Colquhoun, *Police*]. Modern accounts appear in Beattie, *Policing* 376–417; Beattie, *Crime* 50–9; 2 Radzinowicz, *History* 57–60; Langbein, "Ryder" 106–14.

[209] Beattie, *Policing* 376–417; see also Robert B. Shoemaker, "Reforming the City: The Reformation of Manners Campaign in London, 1690–1738," in *Stilling the Grumbling Hive: The Response to Social and Economic Problems in England: 1689–1750*, at 101 (Lee Davison *et al.* eds.) (1992) [hereafter Davison, *Hive*] (efforts against petty crime, including the King's proclamation of 21 Jan. 1692, against blasphemy, profanity, drunkenness, etc.).

[210] Beattie, *Policing* 226.

Offering a financial inducement to encourage volunteers to engage in law enforcement was a device that already had a long history in England when the legislation of the 1690s extended it to felony. In a variety of regulatory matters Parliament authorized *qui tam* actions, under which informers shared in the penalty imposed upon the violator.[211] (In the 1730s there would be an extensive and controversial effort to enforce the Gin Acts by such means.[212]) The primitiveness of the public institutions of law enforcement in England left the authorities little alternative but to privatize enforcement. When the authorities thought that revenge or other motives would not achieve sufficient levels of enforcement, they sometimes used enforcement bounties to encourage greater prosecution.

In addition to the statutory rewards, the government episodically offered rewards by proclamation, mostly directed against highway robbery or murder in the metropolis, sometimes worth as much as £100.[213] When a statutory reward overlapped a proclamation, prosecuting highway robbers could be worth £140 a head,[214] or indeed, £280 when the

---

[211] See, e.g., Langbein, *PCR* 44; Margaret Gay Davies, *The Enforcement of English Apprenticeship: 1563–1642* (1956) (apprenticeship regulation under the Statute of Artificers, 5 Eliz. 1, c. 4 (1563)); Mark Goldie, *The Hilton Gang and the Purge of London in the 1680s*, in *Politics and the Political Imagination in Later Stuart Britain* 43 (Howard Nenner ed.) (1997) (enforcing the Conventicles Acts against Quakers). See generally "Note, The History and Development of *Qui Tam*," 1972 *Washington Univ. L.Q.* 81, 83–91.

[212] Lee Davison, "Experiments in the Social Regulation of Industry: Gin Legislation, 1729–1751," in Davison, *Hive*, *supra* n. 209, at 25, 36 ("4,000 claims by informers for rewards"); see also Jessica Warner and Frank Ivis, "Vox Populi and the Unmaking of the Gin Act of 1726," 33 *J. Social History* 299 (1999).

[213] Beattie, *Crime* 52–3. Radzinowicz traced these proclamations well back into the seventeenth century and concluded that they inspired the later statutory system. 2 Radzinowicz, *History* 84–8.

[214] Paley, "Thieftakers," *supra* n. 165, at 324. The sense that £140 was the going rate in London rather than the base statutory reward of £40 appears in the statement at trial of one of the defendants, William Booth, in a highway robbery case prosecuted in 1733. Denouncing the accomplice witness appearing against him, Booth says, "I set down a Candle by him at the King's Arms, and it happened to burn his Wig, upon which he swore that Job should fetch him £140." John Ackers *et al.*, *OBSP* (Jan. 1733, ##34–6) at 44, 45. James Shaw, also prosecuted with accomplice testimony from a crown witness in 1722, complained to the court that the crown witness "had been proved perjured in Court before, and that now he swore his Life away, for the sake of £140 Reward." James Shaw and Richard Norton, *OBSP* (Jan. 1722), at 3, 4. (The crown witness system is discussed below in this chapter.) Beattie thinks that royal proclamations offering the supplementary £100 for offenses committed within five miles of London were continuously in force for highway robbery and burglary in London from the 1720s until 1745, see Beattie, *Policing* 379–80; and again in the years 1749–50, see ibid. at 414 n. 142. Dudley Ryder, who was appointed Chief Justice of King's Bench in 1754, and had to learn about the reward system in preparation for his first assizes that summer, recorded in his diary: "There was not long ago a further reward of £100 given per proclamation to the takers of highwaymen within five miles of London payable per Treasury, but this is expired." Ryder, "Assize Diary" 1.

The Surrey Assize Paper for 1738 shows a successful prosecutor, Tobias Wall, the victim of a highway robbery, calculating the £140 gross for convicting the robber. The trial judge

prosecutor could convict a pair, or £420 for a three-person gang. The *Gentleman's Magazine* reported in May 1732 that "[f]our hundred Pounds were paid at the Treasury to the persons that apprehended [four named men who were] executed at Guildford."[215] These were stupendous sums at a time when a craftsman earned about £20 per year and a laborer less than £15.[216] Local authorities sometimes offered further rewards, as did private persons and the associations for the prosecution of felons.[217] The trial judges became intimately familiar with the administration of the reward system, because the statutes put them in charge of apportioning the reward among the persons who claimed to have participated in procuring the conviction.[218] Peter King has computed that at Essex Assizes in the second half of the eighteenth century, "16 percent of Essex prosecutors obtained rewards . . . ."[219]

(a) Inviting Perjury

The reward system was meant to combat what was perceived to be endemic underprosecution of serious property crimes. Henry Fielding attributed "the Remissness of Prosecutors" to a variety of causes, including laziness, modesty about appearing in a public court, aversion to the

---

told Wall that he "would give him a Certificate for [Wall's share of half the £40 reward]. Mr. Wall said he believed there were other Advantages besides the £40, the Robbery being done within 5 Miles of London, and there was a Proclamation offering £100 for convicting any one." Samuel Caton, *SAP* (Mar. 1738) at 4, 5.

[215] 2 *Gentleman's Magazine* 772 (May 1732).

[216] E. H. Phelps Brown and Sheila V. Hopkins, "Seven Centuries of Building Wages," in 2 *Essays in Economic History* 168, 177 (table 1) (E. M. Carus-Wilson ed.) (1962).

[217] See 2 Radzinowicz, *History* 98–137. On the activity of the associations in advertising rewards, see Styles, *Advertising, supra* n. 142, at 60–2. Owners of stolen goods also advertised rewards for the return of the goods and the apprehension and conviction of the culprits. Examples from the *London Gazette* are discussed in Malcolm Gaskill, "The Displacement of Providence: Policing and Prosecution in Seventeenth- and Eighteenth-Century England," 11 *Continuity & Change* 341, 348–9 (1996). The so-called Jonathan Wild Act, 3 Geo. 1, c. 11 (1717), threatened heavy fines for offering no-questions-asked payments for the return of stolen goods.

[218] Apportionment is discussed in Beattie, *Policing* 401–5; Langbein, "Ryder" 107–8; Paley, "Thieftakers," at 317–18. The 1692 Act directed the trial judge to issue a certificate authorizing the sheriff to pay the reward, "and in case any Dispute shall happen to arise" in cases involving more than one claimant, the judge was empowered to allocate the money "in such share and proportions as to the said Judge . . . shall seem just and reasonable." 4 Wil. & M., c. 8, § 1 (1692). These documents came to be known as "blood money certificates," and some have survived in various archives. CLRO, Misc. MS 152.5 ("Sessions: Certificates for Reward for Apprehending Highwaymen and Housebreakers, 1732," 8 items); PRO, E 407/27–30 (blood money certificates, 1649–1800, several hundred loose documents). For the text of a model certificate, see W. Stubbs and G. Talmash, *The Crown Circuit Companion* 30–1 (London 1738). The Treasury records of sheriffs' accounts in the PRO evidence the payment process; examples are cited in Langbein, "Ryder" 107 n. 431 (Old Bailey cases 1754–6).

[219] King, *Crime* 48. "[A] further 4 percent were eligible for a Tyburn ticket." Ibid.

death penalty, unwillingness to bear expenses of prosecution, compounding the felony (that is, accepting payment for nonprosecution), and intimidation by gang threats.[220] But in creating incentives to overcome these hazards, the reward system risked, as the economists would say, overincentivizing. The system called forth a mercenary proto-police, the thieftakers, who lived close to the London underworld on which they preyed. The thieftakers who responded to the reward offers had no particular interest in distinguishing between the innocent and the guilty. The danger, as described in a tract published in 1737, was that reward-driven prosecutors might "perjure themselves to accuse innocent Persons, when they are sure to get forty or fifty Pounds for each Convict."[221] A defendant who was tried at the Old Bailey in 1723 on the testimony of the notorious "thieftaker general" Jonathan Wild[222] complained: "There is not a greater villain upon God's Earth than Jonathan Wild. He makes it his business to swear away honest Men's lives for the sake of the Reward, and that is what he gets his Livelihood by."[223]

There was persistent concern that juries, sensing this danger, would discredit reward-based prosecutions. As early as 1696, only months after the enactment of a statute offering rewards for convicting counterfeiters and coiners, Isaac Newton, serving as the Warden of the Mint, wrote to the Treasury that "the new reward of forty pounds per head has now made Courts of Justice and Juries so averse from believing witnesses and Sheriffs so inclinable to empanel bad Juries that my Agents and Witnesses are discouraged and tired out by the want of success and by the reproach of prosecuting and swearing for money."[224]

---

[220] Fielding, *Enquiry* 154. In addition to defending the reward system and its attendant thieftakers, ibid. at 151–4, Fielding urged the provision of public subsidy when needed to offset "the extreme Poverty of the Prosecutor." Ibid. at 157.

[221] Anon., *An Enquiry into the Causes of the Encrease and Miseries of the Poor of England* (London 1738) (Yale Univ., Beinecke Libr., shelfmark CP 1020).

[222] On whom, see Gerald Howson, *Thief-Taker General: The Rise and Fall of Jonathan Wild* (1970) [hereafter Howson, *Wild*]; Andrea McKenzie, entry for Wild, in *New Dictionary of National Biography* (forthcoming 2004).

[223] William Duce, who was prosecuted to his death for highway robbery. 1 *Select Trials* 357, 360–1 (Jul. 1723). (I owe this reference to Andrea McKenzie.) The *Sessions Paper* reports of Duce's two trials (for separate offenses) do not contain the quoted language. William Duce and James Butler, *OBSP* (Jul. 1723), at 6.

Howson reports that in 1720 the Privy Council consulted Wild about how to reduce highway robberies, and that Wild recommended that the crown offer a further £100 by proclamation, in addition to the statutory £40. Howson, *Wild, supra* n. 222, at 125. Wild migrated into prosecuting for reward from his earlier business of mediating between thieves and victims for the return of stolen property. Some of his seventeenth-century forerunners in this line of work are traced in Tim Wales, "Thief-takers and Their Clients in Later Stuart London," in *Londinopolis: Essays in the Cultural and Social History of Early Modern London* 67 (Paul Griffiths and Mark S. R. Jenner eds.) (2000); and Beattie, *Policing* 226 ff.

[224] Letter to the Commissioners of the Treasury (no. 553), July–Aug. 1696, in 4 *The Correspondence of Isaac Newton: 1694–1709*, at 209 (J. F. Scott ed.) (1967). The concern voiced

Prosecuting for bounty, even prosecuting real offenders, was not a very attractive line of work, and it did not call forth genteel types. Henry Fielding, who collected a small force of thieftakers around his Bow Street office, lamented that they were "in Danger of worse Treatment from the Populace than the Thief."[225] In her study of the thieftakers active in London in the decade from the mid-1740s, Ruth Paley found that "all had strong ties to the capital's criminal communities. Almost all had some kind of criminal record."[226] Many were linked to criminal gangs, which engaged in extortion and blackmail as well as prosecutions for reward. Paley exaggerates, but not by much, when she contends that "the major effect of the provision of £40 rewards was to provide an incentive not to the detection of crime but to the organization of thief-making conspiracies . . . . [T]hief-takers were in business not to detect crime but to commit it."[227]

(b) The Reward Scandals

The long-festering suspicion that the reward system might provoke false prosecutions was confirmed in 1732, when the first of the great reward scandals broke. One John Waller was convicted at the Old Bailey of a misdemeanor in attempting to prosecute a person falsely for a highway robbery in order to collect the reward. Evidence was adduced that Waller had succeeded in bringing such prosecutions in other counties. He was convicted and sentenced to be pilloried.[228] When he was exposed in the pillory at the Seven Dials (today's Cambridge Circus), Edward Dalton, the brother of one of his victims[229] set upon him and beat him to death.

by Newton was still troubling the authorities a half century later. A memorandum in the State Papers written in 1750 reports that "[t]he Encouragement of the lower Class of People with large rewards has proved strong temptations to Perjury insomuch that the Juries have been rather inclined to acquit than condemn, when the chief motive for Apprehending [defendants] has appeared to be for the sake of the Reward." 2 Radzinowicz, *History* 97 n. 65, quoting Memorandum, "Precedents, etc.," S.P. 37/15 (1750).

[225] Fielding, *Enquiry* 151.
[226] Paley, "Thieftakers," *supra* n. 165, at 304.
[227] Ibid. at 323.
[228] John Waller, *OBSP* (May 1732, #89), at 146–8.
[229] The victim, James Dalton, was convicted in April 1730 of having robbed Waller the previous November. James Dalton, *OBSP* (Apr. 1730), at 13; 3 *Select Trials* 167 (same case). Waller claimed to have left a pub in Dalton's company, after which Dalton supposedly pistol whipped him and took money, clothing, and a quantity of tea. Waller identified Dalton, who was detained in Newgate for another matter. Dalton was well selected as a plausible culprit, having recently admitted to a long criminal career. These disclosures of former crimes were probably made as part of a crown witness bargain, and were published in confessional pamphlets. *A Genuine Narrative of All the Street Robberies Committed Since October Last, by James Dalton, and His Accomplices, Who Are Now in Newgate, to Be Try'd Next Sessions, and against Whom, Dalton (Called Their Captain) is Admitted Evidence . . . Taken from the Mouth of James Dalton* (London 1728) (BL shelfmark 1080.m.32.2); *The Life and Actions of James Dalton,*

DICK SWIFT,

Thieftaker, Teaching his Son the Commandments.

FIG. 3.2. *The ill repute of thieftakers.* This cartoon, from about 1765, reflects the uneasiness contemporaries felt about the growing role of the unsavory thieftakers in the prosecution of serious crime in the metropolis. The thieftaker Swift is shown instructing his disreputable-looking son in the text, "Thou shalt steal."

Thereafter, Edward Dalton was tried at the Old Bailey, convicted of Waller's murder, and sentenced to death.[230] This veritable Greek tragedy caused a sensation. The title of a contemporary pamphlet account suggests the horror that it evoked: *The Life and Infamous Actions of that Perjur[e]d Villain John Waller, who Made his Exit in the Pillory, at the Seven-Dials, on Tuesday, the 13th Day of This Instant June. Containing All the Villainies . . . Which He Practised . . . in Swearing Robberies against Innocent Persons to Take Away Their Lives, for the Sake of the Rewards Granted by Act of Parliament.*[231]

A few months after the Waller affair, another false prosecution for reward came to light at the Old Bailey. At the September sessions, Bartholomew Harnet prosecuted William Holms for highway robbery. Harnet claimed that Holms had stopped Harnet for directions, decoyed him to a secluded spot, and then robbed him (in cahoots with an armed accomplice who escaped). In selecting Holms as his victim, Harnet made a serious mistake. Holms was not a friendless youth, the sort of person

---

(The Noted Street-Robber.) Containing All the Robberies and Other Villanies Committed by Him (London 1730) (BL shelfmark 615.b.29.3). At his trial for robbing Waller, Dalton denounced Waller as "a Fellow of a vile Character, a common affidavit Man, who has found out a new Method of Living, by Swearing away the Lives of others . . . ." 3 *Select Trials* 167, 168; accord, *OBSP* (Apr. 1730), at 13. Although insisting that he was falsely prosecuted by Waller on this occasion, Dalton admitted that he was guilty of another robbery for which he had been tried and acquitted in January 1730. Howson traces James Dalton's criminal career, Howson, *Wild, supra* n. 222, at 125, 139–40, 167, 211, 221, 243, 247, 310. We learn from another source that Waller's successful prosecution of Dalton was his second try. Waller is said to have initially sworn the robbery against Dalton at a time when Dalton was in jail. When he discovered his miscalculation, he "dropped that prosecution," waited "about a month after . . . Dalton had obtained his Liberty, [and then] again swore the aforementioned robbery against him." *The Life and Infamous Actions of That Perjur[e]d Villain, John Waller, Who Made His Exit in the Pillory, at the Seven-Dials, on Tuesday, the 13th Day of This Instant June. Containing All the Villa[i]nies . . . Which He Practised . . . in Swearing Robberies against Innocent Persons, to Take Away Their Lives, for the Sake of the Rewards Granted by Act of Parliament* 15 (London 1732) (BL shelfmark 518.e.20.10) [hereafter *Waller Pamphlet*]. Had Dalton been allowed counsel to cross-examine Waller about Waller's earlier activities prosecuting for reward, of which Dalton accused him at the trial, Dalton would probably have been acquitted, especially if Waller's earlier false allegation against Dalton had been brought out. Accordingly, this was a case in which lawyering of the sort that the judges were about to allow might well have detected and defeated the perjured prosecution. At his execution, Dalton admitted his life of crime but again insisted that "he was entirely innocent" of the crime of which he had been convicted, and that "John Waller had sworn his Life away merely for the sake of the Reward given by Act of Parliament." Ibid.

[230] Edward Dalton *et al.*, *OBSP* (Sept. 1732, ##86–8), at 219, 221.

[231] *Waller Pamphlet, supra* n. 229, at 29 (mob pulled down the pillory, broke Waller's skull, and trampled his body). The pamphlet recounts other false prosecutions that Waller brought for reward, ibid. at 15–20. The events were followed in the *Gentleman's Magazine*: see 2 ibid. (May 1732) 774 (entry for 29 May), reporting Waller's conviction and trial, and remarking "that he had made it his common Practice to go [around] the [assize] Circuits, and swear against innocent Persons for the sake of the Reward"); 2 ibid. 823 (entry for 13 June) (reporting Waller's death in the pillory at the hands of the mob).

typically targeted for these false prosecutions. Rather, he was a married man, employed by a concerned master, and he had a locktight alibi, having been a dinner guest in the company of several respectable people at the time Harnet swore that he was committing the robbery in a distant spot. Holms was acquitted,[232] and the court ordered Harnet held for prosecution for perjury. Harnet was subsequently tried, convicted, and sentenced to be pilloried; he was then transported.[233]

Word of the Waller and Harnet scandals must have reached the King. The *Gentleman's Magazine* reported in October 1732 that "His Majesty having been informed, that Perjuries and other ill Consequences are the Effects of granting the large Reward for apprehending Highwaymen and Street Robbers, has ordered that for the future the said Bounty be subject to the Discretion of the Rt. Hon. Lord Mayor, and of the Judge who tries the Convict."[234]

Waller was an individual entrepreneur at the business of false prosecution, not connected to a gang. His tactics were primitive compared to the frame-ups staged by gangs in later decades. He would pretend to have been robbed outside a pub, where he identified some hapless person as the supposed attacker.[235] At the trial it was Waller's word against the innocent accused. Groups[236] such as the Macdaniel gang (active from the 1740s,[237]

---

[232] William Holms, *OBSP* (Sept. 1732, #37), at 189, 191.

[233] Bartholomew Harnet, *OBSP* (Dec. 1732, #84), at 24; the affair was noticed in 2 *Gentleman's Magazine* 1123 (Dec. 1732) (entry for 11 Dec.), remarking the "[p]arallel to . . . Waller's Case . . . ."

[234] 2 *Gentleman's Magazine* 1029 (Oct. 1732) (entry for 9 Oct.). The "the large Reward for apprehending Highwaymen and Street Robbers" refers to the supplementary £100 reward offered by royal proclamation for convicting robbers of offenses committed within five miles of London. See *supra*, text and nn. 213–19. The Lord Mayor of London (a nonlawyer who served in the office for a year) presided together with the trial judges at Old Bailey trials.

[235] John Waller, *OBSP* (May 1732, #89), at 146, 148.

[236] E.g., John Warwick *et al.*, *OBSP* (Jan. 1737, ##33–5), at 52, who were convicted of perjury in conspiring falsely to charge John Drinkwater with a highway robbery. Drinkwater testified at the perjury trial that a lawyer managed the spurious prosecution for highway robbery: "I was moved from Chelmsford to Hartford jail, by one Campbell, who calls himself an Attorney." Ibid. at 53.

[237] Some of Macdaniel's activities at the Old Bailey can be traced in the *Sessions Papers* from 1741 onward:

(1) George Stacey *et al.*, *OBSP* (Jan. 1741, ##24–6), at 11–14 (highway robbery). Macdaniel testified as an accomplice. Regarding the crown witness system, see *infra*, text at nn. 249–82.

(2) Samuel Ellard, *OBSP* (Oct. 1744, #468), at 261 (returning from transportation, a capital and rewardable offense under 16 Geo. 2, c. 16, § 3 (1743)). Macdaniel, acting as the thieftaker, also produced a certificate evidencing the former conviction.

(3) William Taylor, *OBSP* (Jan. 1745, #145), at 77 (privately stealing, i.e., picking pockets). Taylor contended that Macdaniel (spelled "Mcdonald"), operating with another thieftaker, Charles Remington, "is the person who took the handkerchief out of the gentleman's pocket, and now he wants to push it upon me. They are the greatest rogues and thief-takers in the world; they do it for the sake of the reward." Ibid. Taylor said that Macdaniel "has been an evidence [that is, a crown witness, testifying against former confederates in crime], and hanged two or three people." Macdaniel at once replied, altercation style: "I was an evidence here, and

detected and prosecuted in 1754[238]) perfected better techniques for false witnessing in reward prosecutions. They employed several persons to give seemingly corroborative evidence—apprehenders of the accused robber, sometimes a feigned victim for the staged crime, and sometimes other supposed witnesses.[239] The gangs were also cunning in their selection of victims. "Those entrapped were invariably young and inexperienced and were often newcomers to the capital . . . [d]enied counsel and faced with what was in effect a professional prosecution conducted without regard to truth . . . ."[240] As one such victim, John Busk, told the Old Bailey at his trial for burglary in February 1736: " 'Tis the Practice of these Thieftakers to take up young Fellows, make them drunk, and get them to say what they would have them, that they may take their Lives away for the sake of the Reward."[241] In Busk's case, the jury, perhaps uneasy about the reward motive, returned a partial verdict.[242] The jury acquitted him of the

have made myself an honest man. I have been indicted indeed. I have left it off these five years [i.e., I have not been committing crimes for the past five years]." Ibid. The jury convicted Taylor but downvalued the goods, not only sparing him from capital punishment but also denying Macdaniel and Remington the reward. This practice is discussed *infra*, text at nn. 243–4.

(4) Priscilla and Ann Saunders, *OBSP* (Oct. 1745, ##389–90), at 250–1 (highway robbery). Macdaniel ("McDonald") and an associate, Stephen Berry, testified against them. The jury acquitted. (Berry was active in the gang's false prosecutions of Kidden and others, which were detected in the 1754 scandal. He was pilloried with Macdaniel in 1756, discussed in Langbein, "Ryder" 112.)

(5) Felix and Anthony Matthews, *OBSP* (Sept. 1746, ##314–15), at 248–50 (highway robbery). They were convicted and sentenced to death. Macdaniel ("McDonald") was the thief-taker. Felix Matthews claimed that Macdaniel planted ammunition on him.

(6) Elizabeth May, *OBSP* (Sept. 1747, #338), at 234 (highway robbery). She was acquitted. Macdaniel ("McDonald") was present when she was apprehended, ibid. at 235.

(7) Thomas Dunkin and Edward Brusby (July 1749, ##486–7), at 106–7 (highway robbery). Macdaniel ("McDonald") was the purported victim. The jury acquitted.

(8) Randolph Branch and William Descent, *OBSP* (Sept. 1752, ##487–8), at 268–72 (highway robbery and murder). The offense was genuine. Macdaniel ("Macdonald") as thieftaker testified to arresting both men. Both Macdaniel and the examining JP testified about the attempt of each accused to be designated as a crown witness against the other. Ibid. at 270. (The significance of such crown witness competitions for the development of the law of evidence is discussed in Ch. 4, *infra*.) Both the accused were convicted and sentenced to death.

Cox, the high constable who unmasked the Macdaniel gang in 1754, published an account of the gang's activities in 1756. He claimed to have traced their hand back to a false prosecution that miscarried some eighteen years before his publication date, which would have been 1738. Joseph Cox, *A Faithful Narrative of the Most Wicked and Inhuman Transactions of That Bloody-Minded Gang of Thief-Takers, Alias Thief-Makers, Macdaniel . . .* 57 ff (London 1756).

[238] Extensively discussed in 2 Radzinowicz, *History* 326–32; Langbein, "Ryder" 110–14; Paley, "Thieftakers," *supra* n. 165, at 331–7. The unmasking of the gang in 1754 caused a sensation, discussed in Langbein, "Ryder" 112–14.

[239] E.g., the McDaniel gang's prosecution of Joshua Kidden, *OBSP* (Jan. 1754, #129), at 71, discussed in Langbein, "Ryder" 110.

[240] Paley, "Thieftakers," *supra* n. 165, at 328.   [241] *OBSP* (Feb. 1736, #50), at 78.

[242] The phenomenon of partial verdicts is discussed *supra* Ch. 1, text at nn. 234–44. See Beattie, *Crime* 419–30; Langbein, "Ryder" 41–3, 47–55; King, *Crime* 231–7; see also 1 Radzinowicz, *History* 83–106, 138–64 (1948).

burglary, but convicted him of the noncapital felony of theft above a shilling's value, for which he was sentenced to transportation. Because he had not been convicted of the rewardable offence of burglary, the prosecutors could collect nothing. Henry Fielding, who as court JP for Middlesex was trying to build a proto-police force funded in part from reward money,[243] chafed at such "foolish Lenity of Juries . . . . [B]y acquitting the Prisoner of the Burglary, and finding him guilty of the simple Felony only, or by finding the Goods to be less than the Value of 5s.[,] both often directly contrary to Evidence, [the verdict] take[s] the case entirely out of [the reward provisions] of the Act of Parliament . . . ."[244]

The Waller and Harnet scandals would have been much on the minds of the judges in the early 1730s, when they began to admit defense counsel to assist criminal defendants in probing prosecution evidence. The judges had learned how profoundly the reward system could compromise the integrity of the prosecution evidence in the trials coming before them. This hazard loomed large, in my view, among the concerns that contributed to the judges' decision to allow defendants to have the assistance of counsel in probing prosecution evidence. The reward system may also have contributed indirectly to the increased use of prosecution solicitors and counsel in the eighteenth century. A prosecutor looking to pocket a reward of £40, £140, or multiples more, had a financial inducement to invest in legal services to enhance the prospects of conviction.[245]

The potential unreliability of reward-based prosecutions remained a nightmare for the courts until the reward system was abolished in 1818.[246] It will be seen in Chapter 5 that questioning the reliability of prosecution evidence in reward-driven prosecutions became a staple of the work of defense counsel. Allowing defense counsel was not, of course, a sufficient corrective for the dangers of reward-induced perjury. Counsel could not unmask every reward abuse, and in any event many of the victims of these false prosecutions were commonly too poor to afford counsel (the "wealth effect" of adversary criminal procedure). Moreover, counsel's skills were not limited to the service of the innocent. "[M]any notorious

---

[243] Discussed in Langbein, "Ryder" 60–7.

[244] Fielding, *Enquiry* 152.

[245] E.g., Daniel Tipping, *OBSP* (July 1732, #23), at 160 (highway robbery), a crown witness prosecution for a rewardable offence, in which prosecution counsel managed the case. Ibid. at 163.

[246] The scandal that finally precipitated abolition of the reward system is recounted in *The Whole Four Trials of the Thief Takers and Their Confederates . . . Convicted at Hicks Hall and the Old Bailey, Sept. 1816, of a Horrible Conspiracy to Obtain Blood Money* (London 1816) (BL shelfmark 6497.b.17). The repealing legislation, Bennet's Act, 58 Geo. 3, c. 70 (1818), is discussed in 2 Radzinowicz, *History* 74–82. The repeal of the statutory system did not, of course, prevent the later episodic offer of government and private rewards, e.g., in 1840, for the murder of Lord William Russell, discussed in David Mellinkoff, *The Conscience of a Lawyer* 27–8, 82–6, 92–3 (1973).

offenders often escape justice" in cases where there are rewards, Colquhoun wrote at the end of the century, because counsel had become so effective at impairing the credit of prosecution evidence in reward-based prosecutions.[247]

The judges of the 1730s began to allow the accused to have the assistance of counsel at trial, not because they thought that counsel would be a cure for the hazards of the reward system, but because this adjustment in trial procedure was the one response that lay within easy reach. The judges had no means of addressing the systemic shortcomings of the pretrial, which resulted from the persistent failure of English governments to confront the need for policing and prosecutorial institutions appropriate to a commercial metropolis.

2. Crown Witness Prosecutions

Another great prosecutorial initiative that came into full vigor in the early eighteenth century was the crown witness system for securing accomplice testimony. A magistrate (often the court JP[248] in Middlesex or the "sitting alderman"[249] in the inner City of London) would grant immunity from prosecution[250] for a culprit who agreed to testify against his former confederates in crime.

[247] Colquhoun, *Police, supra* n. 208, at 393.

[248] Discussed *supra*, text at nn. 46–8. In the *Sessions Paper* accounts, the court JP is sometimes shown testifying about his activities in administering the crown witness system. For example, in the case of William Brown and Moses Davis, *OBSP* (Jan. 1742, ##1–2), at 22–3, accused of stealing pheasants from John Crew, the court JP, Sir Thomas DeVeil, described his interview with Davis. "I told him, if he would be an Evidence concerning my Lord Essex's Pheasants [another theft], I would on Account of his Family admit him to be [the crown witness], but he absolutely denied that he knew any Thing of that Robbery, upon which I committed him . . . ." Ibid. at 23. Other instances of testimony by or about the investigative work of DeVeil and the Fieldings are discussed in Ch. 4, *infra*, text at nn. 105–14.

[249] Aldermen serving as JPs sat in a rotation system operated from a central location, where they conducted pretrial examinations, dismissed weak cases, and issued committal orders. Regarding the system in the 1750s, see Langbein, "Ryder" 76–81. Beattie has traced the origins of the sitting alderman procedure to the mid-1730s. See Beattie, *Policing* 91–113, 417–20. Beattie emphasizes that, unlike the Fieldings sitting at Bow Street as Middlesex court JPs, "[t]he City aldermen did not make detection part of the public work of magistrates," Beattie, *Policing* 420, nor did they "develop as 'police courts,'in which fully professional magistrates, leading a group of professional constables, took up the investigation and prosecution of serious crime." Ibid. at 419. The daily turnover of magistrates in the City rotation would have made it difficult to lead such a force. The City had less crime, less territory, less population, and better crime prevention through the system of paid watchmen organized at the ward level. Regarding the paid watch and paid constables in the City, see ibid. at 155–7, 172–207. Because the Fieldings lived from a central government subsidy and were effectively in the service of the government, theirs was a role that was hard to adapt to the jealous independence of the City authorities. Ibid. at 419–21.

[250] I have elsewhere explained how language in Lord Mansfield's opinion in *R. v. Rudd*, 1 *Leach* 115, 168 *Eng. Rep.* 160 (K.B. 1775) has misled historians into describing the crown witness system as one that promised pardon for the crown witness. Pardon was the back-up

At provincial assizes the bench exercised some supervisory review over grants of crown witness immunity by the provincial magistrates. In the course of the arraignment proceedings in the celebrated forgery case of Dr. William Dodd, Willes J had occasion to describe his role in crown witness cases on assize:

The clerk of assize has come to me on the circuit, and said such a justice of peace has committed this matter, and wishes, if you have no objection to it, that one prisoner may be admitted an evidence against the other. Then I always pay that deference to the discretion of the justice, unless the circumstances make it improper to do as he has desired. Sometimes the clerk of assize has brought me the informations taken by the justice of peace. I look them over carefully and exercise my discretion, whether such a person ought or not to be admitted an evidence against a co-defendant, and if I see there is no probability of convicting him by the assistance of that evidence, then I never admit him.[251]

In the same proceeding, Gould J discussed another pattern, in which the initiative for designating a crown witness came from the provincial grand jury rather than from a JP. "They came to me, I remember, at Lancaster particularly three or four instances. They said, here are such persons committed, and without the evidence of one or the other it will be impossible to find the bill. Then upon reading the depositions and informations, I have ordered that man to be admitted an evidence."[252]

Matthew Hale, writing some time before his death in 1676, expressed unease about crown witness testimony. "I have always thought, that if a person have a promise of a pardon, if he gives evidence against one of his own confederates, this disables his testimony"[253] on the ground of disqualification for interest. However, that question had been decided oppositely, over Hale's dissent, even before he wrote.[254] Another indication that the

---

remedy, as Mansfield explained in *Rudd*, but it was virtually never needed, because in routine circumstances the crown witness was not prosecuted and thus suffered no conviction needing pardon. See Langbein, "Ryder" 91–5. The forgery prosecutions that gave rise to *Rudd* are cited *infra*, n. 290; see also *infra* Chapter 4, text at n. 172 and fig. 4.1.

[251] William Dodd, *OBSP* (Feb. 1777, #161), at 94, 103–4 (forgery). Dodd was raising, through defense counsel, a challenge to the indictment based upon the claim that the grand jury had heard from a witness who was improperly before it. The trial judges referred the point to the Twelve Judges, who decided it unanimously against Dodd. Their opinion on the point is reported in *OBSP* (May 1777), at 244. For the saga of *Dr. Dodd's Case*, see Gerald Howson, *The Macaroni Parson: A Life of the Unfortunate Dr. Dodd* (1973) [hereafter Howson, *Dodd*].

[252] *OBSP* (Feb. 1777, #161), at 104.   [253] 2 Hale, *HPC* 280.

[254] 1 ibid. at 304. Hale mentions that he and another judge were in the minority, but he does not identify the case or date. The question of whether the crown witness should be disqualified for interest was argued as late as 1708. Defending against a prosecution for matricide, counsel for the defendant (who was allowed to appear to raise the law question) "argued, That a Man that is persuaded to become an Evidence by the Promise of a Pardon, cannot be a good Evidence . . . ." Anon., *The Truth of the Case: Or, a Full and True Account of the Horrid Murders, Robberies, and Burnings, Committed at Bradforton and Upton-Snadsbury, in*

refusal to disqualify the crown witness in felony cases was a close call as a matter of doctrinal principle is that virtually the identical question arose with regard to *qui tam* actions (in which the crown split the fine with the informer who brought the charges), where it was resolved oppositely, the informer being disqualified for interest from testifying.[255]

The crown witness system operated in close association with the reward system, in cases in which accomplice testimony was used to convict persons accused of rewardable offenses. Indeed, several of the main reward statutes contained provisions promising pardons to accomplices who convicted former confederates,[256] but these measures appear not to have been much employed, doubtless because the device of simple nonprosecution was easier for the prosecuting authorities to administer and more credible to the accomplice.

Crown witness "evidence was very common in trials at Surrey assizes from the late seventeenth century."[257] At the Old Bailey we can identify fourteen crown witness prosecutions in the year 1721 alone.[258] There were five such cases in a single sessions in September 1722.[259] Most crown

the County of Worcester 21 (London 1708) (Lambeth Palace Libr., shelfmark OB.55.8.27). The assize judge, Sir John Powell, rejected the argument, saying that "such Witnesses were frequently admitted at the Old Bailey. That the Practice was countenanced by the late Act, for the better Discovery of Burglaries, &c., and that unless Accomplices were admitted for Evidence, and promised Pardon, none of these secret Murders and Villainies could be found out . . . ." Ibid. Powell was referring to 10 Wil. 3, c. 5 (1698), which made the culprit who convicted two or more accomplices "entitled to His Majesty's most Gracious Pardon." Writing in 1721, Hawkins treated the point as "long settled" in favor of accomplice testimony. 2 Hawkins, *PC* 432; cf. ibid. at 434, § 25.

[255] *R. v. Shipley*, temp. 4 Anne (Q.B. 1705), reported in Anon., *A Collection of Select Cases Relating to Evidence: By a Late Barrister at Law* 11 (London 1753) (attributed to Sir John Strange). The same source also cites *R. v. Cobbold*, 12 Anne (Q.B. 1713).
[256] Discussed in John Fielding, *Extracts from the Penal Laws* 316–20 (London 1768 ed.).
[257] Beattie, *Crime* 366.
[258] The cases: (1) William Spigget and Thomas Phillips, *OBSP* (Jan. 1721), at 6–7 (highway robbery); (2) William Barton, 1 *Select Trials* 33 (Apr. 1721) (highway robbery); (3) Barbara Spencer, 1 *Select Trials* 40 (May 1721) (coining); (4) William Wade, 1 *Select Trials* 44 (May 1721) (highway robbery of the mails), (5) Mary Roberts *et al.*, 1 *Select Trials* 54 (Jul. 1721) (privately stealing, i.e., picking pockets); (6) James Reading, *OBSP* (Sept. 1721), at 6 (highway robbery); same, 1 *Select Trials* 66 (misdated Aug. 1721); (7) John Wigley, *OBSP* (Sept. 1721), at 7 (highway robbery); same, 1 *Select Trials* 67 (misdated Aug. 1721); (8) John James, *OBSP* (Oct. 1721), at 2 (highway robbery); same, 1 *Select Trials* 88; (9) William Courtney, *OBSP* (Oct. 1721), at 3 (burglary); (10) John Dikes, *OBSP* (Oct. 1721), at 4 (highway robbery) ("Jonathan Wild deposed, that he being informed [about] Dikes and [the crown witness] . . . took them together; that Dikes told him that he could make a Discovery against [the crown witness] of some Triffles, but no great sums"); same case, 1 *Select Trials* 91; (11) William Field, *OBSP* (Oct 1721), at 6–7 (theft of goods from a dwelling house) (acquitted on evidence including the testimony of Jonathan Wild that Wild heard the crown witness say "that she would stick the Prisoner if she could get into his Company," ibid. at 7); (12) John Beton and Richard Farthing, *OBSP* (Dec. 1721), at 5; (13) Butler Fox, *OBSP* (Dec. 1721), at 6 (highway robbery); same, 1 *Select Trials* 111; (14) James Wright, *OBSP* (Dec. 1721), at 8 (highway robbery).
[259] Arthur [Hughs] and John Casy, *OBSP* (Sept. 1722), at 2 (highway robbery); Robert

witness cases entailed charges of highway robbery, burglary, coining, horse theft, or theft from a shop, for which rewards were payable upon conviction, underscoring that both inducements to perjury could affect the same case. Of the fourteen Old Bailey cases in 1721, the underworld thieftaker Jonathan Wild was active in six.[260] A pamphlet published at the time of Wild's downfall in 1725 contended that he extracted protection money from London robbers, and that he would arrange for false crown witness testimony to exterminate any who would not pay, collecting a reward for the conviction while he was at it.[261] We recall the lament of one of Wild's victims that Wild made it "his business to swear away honest Men's lives for the sake of the Reward . . . ."[262]

The crown witness testified under a material incentive to commit perjury, because, in the words of an accused who was defending himself against such a prosecution, the accomplice "will say anything to save his own life."[263] "The danger," as a Victorian judge would express it, "is that when a man is fixed, and knows that his own guilt is detected, he purchases impunity by falsely accusing others."[264] Instances of perjury were occasionally revealed in crown witness trials. For example, John Tent was prosecuted at the Old Bailey in 1715 for burglary on the evidence of "one Moses Whittle, an Accomplice, [who] swore, That he and the Prisoner [and others] . . . broke the House, and stole the

---

Wilkinson and James Lincoln, *OBSP* (Sept. 1722), at 4 (same; in addition to the testimony of the crown witness, others testified to having identified the culprits in a lineup procedure at Newgate prison involving "14 or 15 prisoners"); John Dyer, *OBSP* (Sept. 1722), at 5 (privately stealing); Joseph Bury and Thomas Williams, *OBSP* (Sept. 1722), at 6 (charged with shop theft above the clergyable amount; the jury convicted but valued the goods at 10*d.*, which rescued them from death for transportation); William Peters, *OBSP* (Sept. 1722), at 6–7 (theft of slate, jury convicted but valued the goods at 10*d.*).

[260] Cases 6–8, 11, 13–14 in n. 258, *supra*.

[261] If robbers who refused to pay Wild were arrested, but the "Evidence was wanting to convict them, it was customary for him to take up [i.e., arrest] one of his Fellows, whose Life was always in his Power, and make him swear himself into some of the Robberies of which the others were suspected, whereby their Evidence might obtain some credit with the Jury, and [Wild] was entitled to the Reward if he was the person who took them." Anon., *The History of the Lives and Actions of Jonathan Wild, Thief-Taker* 15 (3rd edn. London [1725?]) (BL shelfmark 10825.aa.16); see also H.D. ["late Clerk to Justice R____"] *The Life of Jonathan Wild From His Birth to His Death* 18 (London 1725) (BL Shelfmark 1419.i.26) (another version). For Wild's trial and conviction for receiving stolen goods, see Jonathan Wild, *OBSP* (May 1725), at 5–7.

[262] The complaint of William Duce in the trial of William Duce and James Butler, 1 *Select Trials* 357, 360–1 (July 1723), discussed *supra*, text at nn. 222–3. Beattie has suggested that it was the crown's policy, instituted in 1720, of increasing rewards for burglary and highway robbery to £140 per conviction, which induced Wild to move from his original enterprise of locating stolen property for victims willing to pay him a fee, into his new line of work fingering criminals for reward. Beattie, *Policing* 379–82.

[263] Richard Munday, *OBSP* (Apr.–May 1756, #203), at 169, 170.

[264] Lord Abinger, speaking in *Regina v. Farler*, 8 C. & P. 106, 108, 173 Eng. Rep. 418, 419 (Worcester Assizes 1837), cited in 4 Wigmore, *Evidence* § 2057, at 358; § 2059, at 362.

Goods."[265] Tent, however, had learned (perhaps as the result of his solicitor's inquiries) that Whittle, when examined by the magistrate, Justice Fuller, at the Marian pretrial hearing, had denied that he knew Tent. At the trial, Tent "called Justice Fuller's Clerk to justify [that is, to confirm Whittle's pretrial statement]; whereupon [Tent] was acquitted."[266] John Davis, apprehended for highway robbery and murder in 1731, attempted to have himself designated as the crown witness by "pretending that one Nathaniel Gravett was concerned with him in [the crime] . . . ." In this case, evidence from the prosecutor defeated the maneuver. He testified that "I have seen Gravett, and am sure that he was not the Man who was with the Prisoner when I was robbed."[267]

A spectacular demonstration of the potential for perjured testimony in crown witness cases occurred in a prosecution for burglary tried at Surrey Assizes in Croydon in 1745. The accomplice, Henry Simms, admitted on the stand that he had falsely accused the defendants. "I know nothing of the Robbery," he now said. "The Prisoners are all innocent, and the Information I made [in the pretrial examination] is wrong. I was persuaded to do it by Will H____, a Thief-Catcher." Simms said that the thieftaker had initially threatened to prosecute him unless he agreed to testify as the crown witness in some street crimes that Simms admitted having committed. "But these were not sufficient, for [the thieftaker] came to me a second Time, and told me that I . . . must . . . [testify against the defendants in the present case] or I should not be saved. I then went a second Time before Sir Thomas [DeVeil, the court JP for Middlesex], and made an Information of that Robbery, but it is not true."[268] The astonished trial judge asked, "Is nothing in this Information true, Simms?" "Not a word of it," he replied. "I have perjured myself. I did it to save my own Life."[269]

The inducement to perjury was intensified when the authorities pitted two or more captured criminals against each other in a competition to be

[265] John Tent, *OBSP* (Feb. 1715), at 2 (burglary).   [266] Ibid.

[267] 3 *Select Trials* 269, 270.

[268] William Cavenagh *et al.*, *SAP* (Mar. 1745), at 3, 7 (burglary). The reporter suppressed the name of the alleged instigator, rendered as "Will H____." I suspect this was done to prevent any civil libel risk. The *Old Bailey Sessions Papers* exhibited a similar caution for decades, e.g., H.____ J.____, *OBSP* (May–June 1723), at 6 (declining to publish the name of an acquitted rape defendant).

[269] *SAP* (Mar. 1745), at 8. The court directed an acquittal of the defendants and ordered Simms prosecuted for perjury. Ibid. at 9, 10. Whether Simms committed perjury in charging the defendants in the pretrial, or at the trial in retracting the charges, cannot be known. Simms was subsequently convicted at the Old Bailey for theft from a dwelling house. Henry Simms, *OBSP* (May 1745, #241), at 172–4. He insisted at that trial, apparently successfully, that his earlier confession to DeVeil could not be used against him, because it had been taken under oath (to be used against others). See ibid. at 173, where Simms is quoted as saying, "A man can't swear against himself."

named the crown witness. Occasionally the trial judge expressed displea-
sure at the outcome of the competition, when the authorities allowed the
greater villain to testify against the lesser. In one such case, a prosecution
for coining in 1746, the trial judge told the jury that "I could have wished
that the [crown witness] might have been prosecuted, and this poor
[defendant] made an Evidence . . . ."[270] The jury took the hint and acquitted the defendant.   The competition to be made the crown witness
sometimes erupted into a sort of bidding war, in which the prize of
nonprosecution would be awarded to the candidate who offered to testify
against the largest number of alleged culprits. We see this competition in
the trial of John Hill for highway robbery in 1744. When arrested he implicated his confederates Waters and Gascoign. Hill "desired the constable
to intercede with the Justice [of the Peace], that he might be admitted the
Evidence, and he promised that he would make an ample discovery."[271]
When Waters was taken, "he begged that he might be admitted the
Evidence," and being told that Hill had already accused him and
Gascoign, "when he was before the Justice he said he could impeach nine
people . . . ."[272] William Udal, captured for highway robbery in 1739 on
the evidence of his accomplice Thomas Mann, "wanted to have been
made an Evidence against Mann, and said he could put three or four more
into his Information."[273] Humphrey Anger, a highway robber tried at the
Old Bailey in 1723, disclosed that he kept a journal "of all the Robberies
he had committed," preparing for the day when he might need to outbid
his fellow culprits.[274] The inflationary impulse in these situations, that is,
the competitive advantage of being able to accuse more persons than
one's competitor(s), was a further inducement to false witness.

---

[270] Anne Wilson, *OBSP* (Apr. 1746, #191), at 137, 140.

[271] John Hill, *OBSP* (Dec. 1744), at 7 (highway robbery).

[272] Ibid. (testimony of Miles Carrol, a thieftaker). The magistrate was not bound to choose
the winner of this auction. Other factors, such as the ages and degrees of culpability of the
offenders, were also taken into account in relevant cases. For example, at a burglary trial in
1753, the crown witness was Joseph Stevens, a 15-year-old, who told why the magistrate
preferred him over one of the two defendants, Hamilton. "Mr. Withers said I was the
youngest, he'd make me evidence." Paul Wood & Samuel Hamilton, *OBSP* (July 1754), at
232, 233. Withers' clerk testified that Withers had another reason: knowing that Hamilton
"had been an evidence here in the January sessions, and cast five persons for transportation
[that is, gave testimony that caused the five to be convicted and sentenced to transportation],
he would not admit him, but admitted the other." Ibid. at 233.

[273] William Udal, *OBSP* (Feb. 1739, #143), at 46 (the passage quoted in text is the trial testimony of the constable, who also explained that "as [Udal] had been admitted an Evidence
several Times before, his Request was denied").

[274] "Being asked by the Court what was his Design for keeping a Journal, whether it was
[that] upon the Perusal of his Robberies he might the more particularly repent of them, he
replied, 'No, but it was for his own Safety, that he might be the more exact when he should
have the Opportunity to save himself by becoming an Evidence.' " Humphrey Anger, *OBSP*
(Aug. 1723), at 7; same case, 2 *Select Trials* (Aug. 1723), at 1–14. This incident is noticed in
Linebaugh, "Ordinary," *supra* n. 193, at 265 (spelling Anger as Angier).

The magistrate running the competition[275] not only selected the winner who would testify as the crown witness against the loser, he also arranged for the loser's admissions, made in his unsuccessful effort to be chosen as the crown witness, to be used against the loser at trial.[276] We shall see in Chapter 4 that these competitions were common, and that they would ultimately bring the crown witness system into collision with the confession rule, one of the earliest branches of the dawning law of criminal evidence.[277]

For much of the eighteenth century the crown witness system was practically the only resort of the London-area authorities in dealing with gang crimes.[278] Writing in 1721, Serjeant Hawkins observed that "[i]f no accomplices were to be admitted as witnesses, it would be generally impossible to find evidence to convict the greatest offenders."[279] Henry Fielding observed in 1751 that "[t]he Method of discovering [persons who have committed street robberies] is generally by means of one of the Gang, who being taken up, perhaps for some other Offense, and, thinking himself in Danger of Punishment, chooses to make his Peace at the Expense of his Companions."[280] The cycle of crime and betrayal that played out in crown witness prosecutions became so familiar to contemporaries that Hogarth used it as a motif in his "Industry and Idleness" series.[281]

---

[275] The magistrate was not obliged to defer to the wishes of the prosecutor. In the case of William Kelley *et al.*, *OBSP* (July 1745, #327–9), at 193, 194 (highway robbery), the prosecutor testified that "I did design to admit . . . [one of the three defendants] an evidence, but I was told my recognizance would be estreated, and I must prosecute." He was referring to the recognizance called for under in the Marian pretrial procedure, by which the examining magistrate would bind over the victim to prosecute at trial. For discussion, see *supra* Ch. 1, text at n. 152.

[276] For example, in a case of highway robbery in 1751, the two robbers, Brown and Vincent, competed to be named the crown witness. Henry Fielding chose Brown, then arranged for another witness to testify at the trial that Vincent tendered his "confession of this fact, in Bow Street, Covent Garden. He wanted to have been made an evidence, and mentioned several robberies, especially this." William Vincent, *OBSP* (Jan. 1751, #136), at 55.

[277] See *infra* Ch. 4, text at nn. 197–217.

[278] Both Fieldings say as much in their tracts, as does their fellow Middlesex magistrate Saunders Welch. Henry Fielding described using government funds to pay an informant "to betray [certain gang members] into the hands of a set of thieftakers, whom I had enlisted," and he reported "examining . . . and taking the depositions against them . . . [for] whole days, nay, sometimes whole nights, especially when there was any difficulty procuring sufficient evidence to convict them." Henry Fielding, "Introduction," in *The Journal of a Voyage to Lisbon* 17, 20 (2nd edn. London 1755). See also John Fielding, *A Plan for Preventing Robberies within Twenty Miles of London* (London 1755), at 10–11; Saunders Welch, "A Letter upon the Subject of Robberies, Wrote in the Year 1753," in *A Proposal to Render Effectual a Plan to Remove the Nuisance of Common Prostitutes from the Streets of This Metropolis* 61 (London 1758).

[279] 2 Hawkins, *PC* 432. "In a sample of twenty Essex Assizes 1772–1800, 3.4% of offenders held awaiting trial were crown witnesses." King, *Crime* 49 n. 3.

[280] Fielding, *Enquiry* 158.

[281] Plate 10 of the series sets the scene for the downfall of the criminous "idle apprentice" in a pretrial examination before the sitting alderman (the London equivalent of the

We shall see in Chapter 4 that the unreliability of crown witness prosecutions became so worrisome that, at least by the 1740s and probably
earlier, it caused the judges to fashion one of the earliest rules of the law
of criminal evidence, the corroboration rule excluding accomplice testimony not confirmed by other evidence. When, therefore, the judges
began to allow felony defendants to have the assistance of counsel to
probe prosecution evidence at trial in the 1730s, the judges were acting
with an acute awareness that both the reward system and the crown
witness system harbored potent incentives for false witnessing. Yet, "in
the absence of regular police and detective forces, immunity from prosecution (along with the offer of rewards) gave the authorities their only
means of securing evidence, especially against members of gangs."[282] The
courts had neither the means nor the mission to remedy the inadequacies
of the pretrial. The responsibility for designing police and prosecutorial
institutions appropriate to the needs of an urban society lay elsewhere.
The law courts were left to grope for ways to adjust at the trial for the
dangers inherent in crown witness prosecutions.

The judges' response was to allow the defendant to have some help in
probing the prosecution evidence, the help of defense counsel. Allowing
defense counsel to examine and cross-examine witnesses was hardly a
cure-all. The defendant might not be able to afford counsel, and cross-
examination might not always unmask perjured prosecutions. But allowing defense counsel to assist the defendant was the response that lay close
to hand. The judges had only to adapt for felony trials the existing practice in cases of misdemeanor[283] and (since 1696) treason.

Middlesex court JP). As Hogarth's caption tells it, the idle apprentice is "Impeached by his
Accomplice." An accomplice—a confederate in crime who has been shown in the previous
plate being captured along with the idle apprentice—is depicted being admitted as the
crown witness. He is shown swearing to a confession in which he implicates the idle apprentice. Hogarth's audience would have known that the crown witness would repeat the
confession at the trial of the idle apprentice at the next sessions of the Old Bailey, sealing his
doom (which is depicted in Plate 11, showing the convicted idle apprentice being carted to
the gallows at Tyburn). See 2 Ronald Paulson, *Hogarth's Graphic Works*, pl. 180–91 (1965) for
the series; see 1 ibid. at 200 for detail regarding pl. 10. Preliminary drawings for pl. 10 are
reproduced in 2 Ronald Paulson, *Hogarth: His Life, Art, and Times* 69 (1971). Paulson dates the
series to c.1747. Ibid. at 75. (I wish to acknowledge the kindness of Peter Linebaugh, who
first drew to my attention Hogarth's use of the crown witness.)

By the 1740s the sitting alderman operated from dedicated premises, the so-called Justice
Room in the Matted Gallery of the Guildhall. Hogarth's depiction of the chamber is ideal-
ized, departing from what is known about the actual premises. For discussion, see Langbein,
"Ryder" 78, 84; Beattie *Policing* 108–9.

[282] Beattie, *Crime* 369.

[283] For example, in forgery cases, which had been mostly misdemeanor until 1729, the
judges had seen defense counsel in action in cases of evidentiary complexity; e.g., Elizabeth
Wartly, *OBSP* (Oct. 1715), at 2 (perjury) (defense counsel presents defense witnesses to
contradict prosecution witnesses' testimony about what the defendant testified in a civil
proceeding, resulting in an acquittal in the criminal case).

C. Making Forgery Felony

Another development that may have influenced the bench in its decision to allow felony defendants to have the assistance of counsel in matters of fact was the abrupt change in the substantive law of forgery that has been brought to light in the historical scholarship of Randall McGowen.[284]

In 1729 Parliament made the crime of forging private financial instruments, previously a misdemeanor,[285] into a felony,[286] in order to make it punishable by death.[287] In consequence, the misdemeanor defendant's traditional right to counsel was suddenly removed[288] from an offense in which the complexity of the proofs[289] made it especially difficult for the defendant to serve as his own cross-examiner or to lead his own rebuttal witnesses. Moreover, solicitors and counsel were routinely employed to

---

[284] Randall McGowen, "From Pillory to Gallows: The Punishment of Forgery on the Age of the Financial Revolution," *Past and Present* 107 (no. 165) (Nov. 1999) [hereafter McGowen, "Gallows"]; Randall McGowen, "Knowing the Hand: Forgery and the Proof of Writing in Eighteenth-Century England," 24 *Historical Reflections* 385 (1998) [hereafter McGowen, "Proof"]; Randall McGowen, "Forgery Discovered: Or the Perils of Circulation in Eighteenth-Century England," 1 *Angelaki* 113 (Apr. 1994) [hereafter McGowen, "Perils"].

[285] A few particular forms of forgery, such as forging Bank of England paper, had been made felony in the later 1690s. See McGowen, "Gallows," *supra* n. 284, at 111. For an instance, see the trial of Frederick Schmidt, *OBSP* (Feb., Mar.–Apr. 1724), at 7 (capitally convicted of forging a Bank of England banknote; prosecution counsel appeared).

[286] 2 Geo. 2, c. 25 (1729).

[287] The background: "[T]he growing use of notes by consumers was a comparatively recent phenomenon. It was brought about in large part by the rapid increase in banks, not only in London, but more especially throughout the country." McGowen, "Perils," *supra* n. 284, at 117. By the 1780s it was not uncommon for such provincial notes to be offered by strangers to shopkeepers. "Society was becoming more dependent upon paper instruments. Yet the traditional safeguard of only accepting notes from a person one knew well was rendered obsolete by the anonymity of consumer-oriented exchange." Ibid. at 121.

[288] "Down to 1729 most forgeries were tried as misdemeanors, and defendants in such cases had a right to counsel." McGowen, "Proof," *supra* n. 284, at 390.

[289] Forgery commonly entailed exceptionally difficult proofs, about the identity of the note, its signatures, and its possession in circulation and acceptance by the victim. See McGowen, "Perils," *supra* n. 284, at 122–6 (discussing a dozen Old Bailey cases for the years 1777–85). "A successful prosecution demanded the full and accurate description of the note and a full history of its location from the time of offer to the day of the trial. Such details were difficult to provide; a successful tradesman might slip a bill into a drawer full of other notes, with which it might be confused," or to which other persons might have access. Ibid. at 125. "A vigorous defense, such as was becoming the rule in forgery trials by the 1780s, played upon these difficulties with skill and enthusiasm." Ibid. Another indication of the difficulty of forgery cases is that they sometimes led to the use of special verdicts, a device employed in a case of legal difficulty to transfer responsibility for applying the law from the jury to the judge (who often sought the views of other judges before deciding). For example, John Seal, *OBSP* (Oct. 1715), at 2 (forgery) ("a Point of Law arising, the Court directed the Jury to bring it in Special"); Richard Warner, *OBSP* (Jan. 1746, #85), at 57–8 (forgery) (special verdict); James Gibson, *OBSP* (Jan. 1766, #109), at 81, 89 (forgery) (special verdict on whether the conduct was within the act).

prosecute forgery cases, both because of the complexity of the proofs, and because the victim was commonly a bank or a merchant. Thus, forgery cases were far removed from the old altercation trial that pitted citizen accuser against citizen accused. After 1729 the typical forgery trial featured solicitors and counsel prosecuting an accused whose former right to full defense of counsel had recently been stripped away as an incidental consequence of Parliament's determination to escalate the threatened sanction.

Forgery defendants were usually higher up the social ladder than accused footpads or burglars, because forgery was an offense of the literate. Accordingly, defendants were more likely to be able to afford counsel, either from their own means, or by virtue of connections to persons of means.[290] McGowen comments: "It may well have seemed unfair, especially given the usual class of the accused, to deprive defendants of this privilege after the crime became capital."[291]

Thus, the typical forgery case involved a relatively sympathetic criminal defendant, prosecuted by lawyers, in a case that entailed difficult mixed questions of fact and law, in which the defendant had been entitled to full defense of counsel in misdemeanor procedure until 1729. The changed position of the forgery defendant put further pressure on the old justifications for denying defense counsel, at just that moment when the lawyerization of the prosecution and the dangers associated with reward and crown witness prosecutions were weighing ever more heavily on the bench.

D. Defense Counsel Enters the Felony Trial

The rule forbidding counsel to assist a felony defendant on a matter of fact had been premised, it will be recalled, on the view that the accused

---

[290] Some defendants were con artists, but most were clerks, merchants, tradesmen, or persons of gentle class who had yielded to financial pressure or temptation. The most celebrated was the society priest, Dr. Dodd, whose trial and execution in 1777 for forging a note in a moment of panic became a turning point in the decline of public support for capital punishment for property crimes. William Dodd, *OBSP* (Feb. 1777, #161), at 94, discussed in 1 Radzinowicz, *History* 450–72; Howson, *Dodd, supra* n. 251. Another forgery case of comparable notoriety involving gentle culprits who were well represented was the Perreau–Rudd affair, discussed in Donna T. Andrew and Randall McGowen, *The Perreaus and Mrs. Rudd: Forgery and Betrayal in Eighteenth-Century London* (2001). The proceedings gave rise to Lord Mansfield's well-known dicta on the nature of the crown witness system, *R. v. Rudd*, 1 Leach 115, 168 *Eng. Rep.* 160 (K.B. 1775), discussed in Langbein, "Ryder" 91–6.
[291] McGowen, "Proof," *supra* n. 284, at 390.

did not need counsel. Serjeant Hawkins wrote in his treatise that the accused "may as properly speak to a Matter of Fact, as if he were the best Lawyer . . . it requires no manner of Skill to make a plain and honest Defense . . . ."[292] By the 1730s experience with the new prosecutorial techniques canvassed in this chapter caused the judges to conclude that too many of the criminal trials over which they presided were ceasing to resemble Sir Thomas Smith's altercation of unaided victim and accused. Especially in London, prosecution for major property crimes was becoming ever more the province of (1) lawyers, (2) an unsavory corps of reward-seeking thieftakers, and (3) confessed culprits testifying as crown witnesses to save their necks. These determined operators increased the danger that the prosecution evidence coming before the courts could be unreliable.

By allowing defense counsel to cross-examine prosecution witnesses, the judges of the 1730s undertook to correct for the imbalance that had opened between the unaided accused and a criminal prosecution that increasingly reflected the hand of lawyers and quasi-professional thieftakers. The bench was tacitly acknowledging that prosecution evidence needed probing of a sort that itinerant trial judges processing huge caseloads were not able to do. The judges relaxed the rubric of court as counsel in favor of counsel as counsel.

Defense counsel entered the felony trial without fanfare. Because the *Old Bailey Sessions Papers* and other pamphlet trial reports upon which we mostly depend omit mention of some appearances of counsel,[293] we cannot quantify the presence of counsel. Nevertheless, the sources permit us to see that "the rule prohibiting the defendant to have counsel gave way suddenly."[294] There is reason to think that the change may have been occurring as early as 1730.[295] The earliest unambiguous sighting occurred

---

[292] 2 Hawkins, *PC* 400, discussed *supra* Ch. 1, text at n. 124.

[293] Langbein, "Ryder" 23–4 and n. 80 (identifying four cases from the years 1754 and 1756 in which the trial judge's notes evidence defense counsel not disclosed in the published pamphlet reports); see also *supra* n. 63, observing that the extensive *Sessions Paper* report of the evidence in a celebrated murder case tried in 1723 omits mention of the prosecution counsel whom we know from other sources to have been active in the case.

[294] Beattie, *Crime* 357.

[295] I suspect that defense counsel was at work in the February 1730 trial of Sir Francis Charteris, a celebrated rake (on whom, see sources cited in Langbein, *CTBL* 296 n. 96). He was convicted at the Old Bailey of raping a servant girl, Anne Bond, and sentenced to death. The King later pardoned him. The *Sessions Paper* reports only the outcome of the trial, explaining: "So great a Variety of uncommon Circumstances occurring in the Course of this Trial, the Publisher is obliged to suspend Publishing them till the [spring] Assizes in the several Counties are ended, and the Judges returned to Town, that it may be printed in a true and impartial Manner." *OBSP* (Feb. 1730), at 17. The publisher made good on this undertaking, publishing an account of the trial (and the Pardon) as a separate pamphlet. *The Proceedings at the Sessions of the Peace and Oyer and Terminer for the City of London . . . in the Old Bailey . . . upon a Bill of Indictment Found against Francis Charteris, Esq.; for Committing a Rape*

in Surrey in 1732.[296] At the Old Bailey "[i]n 1734–1735 there occur unmistakable instances of lawyers examining and cross-examining for the defense; and already in the year 1736 nine cases are reported."[297] Beattie reports nine cases from Surrey Assizes in the years 1738–42, mostly in cases of robbery and burglary.[298]

Despite the imperfections in the sources, it seems clear that defense counsel was employed only in a relative trickle of cases until the last decades of the eighteenth century. This pattern of seeming insignificance may have lulled the judges into thinking that the introduction of defense counsel would leave the old order disturbed.[299] Beattie has done a careful count from the *Old Bailey Sessions Papers*, which are the only usable sources, but which are intrinsically unreliable for quantitative study, because the compilers had so little interest in reporting the participation of lawyers. Beattie concluded "that not more than ten percent of defendants are likely to have had counsel through the middle decades of the eighteenth century."[300] For some years as late as the 1770s he found

on the Body of Anne Bond, of Which He Was Found Guilty (London 1730) (BL shelfmark 1379.g.25). Bond, a maid in Charteris's house, testified that he summoned her to his room, bolted the door, and whipped and raped her. The reason I suspect that Charteris was allowed defense counsel at the trial is that the cross-examination of Bond was quite hostile and was conducted on the basis of information about prior relations between victim and accused that the court would not have known. The cross-examination is reported in the passive voice, concealing who was doing it. Had the accused himself been cross-examining, the report would have said so, as in contemporary *Sessions Papers* trials.

> She being cross-examined, was asked, If she was not acquainted with the Prisoner at Cockeram in Lancashire? She denied it.
> She was asked, If when she came to live with the Prisoner, she did not bring him a Letter? She denied it.
> She was asked, If she had not lain in the same Bed with the Prisoner? She said, No.
> She was asked, If she did not lie in the Truckle-Bed in the same Bed-Chamber, and just by the Bed of the Prisoner? She owned she lay there four Nights, that the fifth Night he had another Maid Servant in Bed with him, and he called to her to come to him, that he might lie in State (as he expressed it) but she said she refused it, and never lay in the Truckle-Bed after that . . . .
> She was asked, If she did not accept of a Mother of Pearl Snuff-Box from him after his tempting her to lie with him? She said, he forced her to accept it.

Ibid. at 6–7. The pamphlet does not disclose counsel on either side. It does disclose that the victim, Bond, had the help of one Mr. Biss, perhaps a solicitor, in helping her get the bill of indictment drawn. He testified at the trial about her being brought to him by a co-worker shortly after the attack. He said the bill of indictment "was at first drawn for an Assault, with an Intent to Ravish her, but that the grand Jury on examining her, thought it a Rape, and [had] the Indictment altered accordingly." Ibid. at 8. (See *infra* Ch. 5, n. 214, for discussion of why rape cases were commonly charged merely as attempted rape.)

[296] Beattie, *Crime* 356–7, discussed *supra*, text at n. 6.
[297] Langbein, "CTBL" 312–13 and n. 161.
[298] Beattie, *Crime* 356–7.
[299] This point is further discussed *infra* in Ch. 5, text at nn. 11–19.
[300] Beattie, "Scales" 227 (table 1).

defense counsel reported in only 1 or 2 percent of cases.[301] Not until the 1780s, when there was a spurt in the reported use of defense counsel, did adversary combat come to typify the seriously contested criminal trial.[302] "By the end of the century, between a quarter and a third of defendants at the Old Bailey had the benefit of counsel, and a substantial proportion of prosecutors."[303]

1. Preserving the "Accused Speaks" Trial

We have seen in Chapter 1 that the logic of the altercation trial was to provide an opportunity for the accused to respond in person to the charges and the evidence produced against him, hence that he would serve as an informational resource for the court. The rule against defense counsel had been driven by the fear that counsel would interfere with this "accused speaks" trial. We recall the response of Keble J, presiding at a murder trial in 1651, explaining why he rejected the defendant's request for trial counsel: "[W]hen should we have any man answer? [W]hen would men be executed for robbing, and stealing, and killing?"[304] In a like

---

[301] He reports 1.1% in 1750, 2.1% in 1770 and 1775. Ibid. (table 1).

[302] Beattie reports defense counsel in 12.8% of trials in the year 1782, 17.6% in 1784, 20.2% in 1786, and a high of 36.6% in 1795. Ibid. Feeley and Lester also counted the appearance of lawyers in the *Old Bailey Sessions Papers*, the source for Beattie's data, but at twenty-year intervals, leaping over the period 1775–95 when the spurt in defense counsel seems to have occurred. For the year 1795, they show a graphed figure for what they call "defense attorney" that is just under 40%, hence in accord with Beattie's 36.9%. Malcolm Feeley and Charles Lester, "Legal Complexity and the Transformation of the Criminal Process," in *Subjektivierung des justiziellen Beweisverfahrens: Beiträge zum Zeugenbeweis in Europa und den USA* (18.–20. Jahrhundert) 337, 341 (fig. 5) (André Gouron *et al.* eds.) (1994). Landsman, also working from the *OBSP* pamphlet reports, tabulates materially higher figures for cases containing appearances by defense counsel in the one year, 1782, for which both he and Beattie provide a count. He identifies defense counsel in 21.37% of that year's cases, nearly twice Beattie's figure of 12.8% for the same year. Stephen Landsman, "The Rise of the Contentious Spirit," 75 *Cornell L. Rev.* 497, 607 (table II) (1990) [hereafter Landsman, "Spirit"]. The discrepancy probably arises because Landsman counts cases in which he thinks "the nature of the proceedings (i.e., highly developed line of cross-examination or extensive legal argument) strongly suggested [to Landsman] that a lawyer participated." Ibid. at 519 n. 100.

[303] Beattie, "Scales" 228. Allyson May reports comparable figures for the first three decades of the nineteenth century, also based upon the risky but unavoidable technique of counting appearances recorded in the *Old Bailey Sessions Papers*. She finds that defense counsel appeared somewhat more often than prosecution counsel: in 25.7% of cases in 1805, declining to 12.9% in 1810 and 14.8% in 1820 before returning in 1825 to 25.2% and in 1830 to 27.7%. She counts prosecution counsel in 22% of cases in 1805, declining to 6% in 1810, increasing back to 10.7% in 1820, then hovering at about 8% in the 1820s. May, Thesis 91–2 and table 3.1. Charles Phillips, the leading criminal defense lawyer of the 1820s and 1830s, claimed to a committee of the House of Lords in 1836 that he was singlehandedly doing better than that. "In the year 1828 it fell my lot to defend no less than 800 prisoners at the Old Bailey and on the Oxford Circuit . . . . In the September Sessions [at the Old Bailey] of that year I had 110 separate briefs . . . ." Quoted in Cairns, *Advocacy* 102.

[304] *R. v. Christopher Love*, 5 St. Tr. 43, 61 (High Court 1651), cited *supra* Ch. 1, text at n. 128.

voice, Hawkins' treatise of 1721 exulted that the "Guilty, when they speak for themselves, may often help to disclose the Truth, which probably would not so well be discovered from the artificial Defense of others speaking for them."[305]

When the judges admitted counsel to the ordinary criminal trial in the 1730s, they attempted to do it in a way that would preserve the "accused speaks" trial. The judges permitted counsel to assist the defendant in examining and cross-examining witnesses, but they forbade him to "address the court," that is, to comment on the evidence or to narrate the accused's version of the events. "I am very well apprised that I have no right to argue upon matters of fact,"[306] defense counsel told the Old Bailey in 1750, by which time the contours of the practice were well settled. In an Old Bailey trial in 1766, when the judge called upon the accused at the end of the prosecution evidence, the accused said, "I leave it to my counsel."[307] The judge told him at once: "Your counsel cannot speak for you. You must do that yourself, if you have anything to say."[308] In the words of another Old Bailey judge to a felony defendant in 1777, "if your defense arises out of a matter of fact, you must yourself state it to me and the jury."[309] In a case tried at the Old Bailey in 1783, counsel explained to his client, one Macnamara, that "I cannot say anything for you though I have your story here in my brief" (a reference to the solicitor's brief instructing counsel).[310] The trial judge then drew the implication for the accused: "Mr. Macnamara, it is now your time to make your defense . . . . [Y]our counsel . . . cannot make a defense, he can only examine witnesses and observe on points of law."[311]

2. Evening Up

In deciding to allow defense counsel in the 1730s, the judges surely took comfort from the precedent established by the Treason Trials Act of 1696. Hawkins, it will be recalled, intimated in 1721 that a main reason that the Act's grant of defense counsel was limited to treason defendants was because in those cases lawyers appeared for the crown. Treason

---

[305] 2 Hawkins, *PC* 400, cited *supra* Ch. 1, text at n. 129.

[306] The Trial of William Baker for Forging an East-India Warrant . . . at the Old-Bailey 13 [on 9 Dec. 1750] (2nd edn. London 1751).

[307] Joseph Trout, *OBSP* (Dec. 1766, #23), at 11, 12 (theft from a dwelling house). Regarding the later history and significance of this increasingly formulaic utterance, see *infra* Ch. 5, text at nn. 64–85.

[308] *OBSP* (Dec. 1766, #23), at 12.

[309] Russen, *OBSP* (Oct. 1777), at 374 (rape), cited in Landsman, "Spirit," *supra* n. 302, at 534 n. 183.

[310] William Macnamara, *OBSP* (Sept 1783, #641), at 857, 858 (theft of shop goods).

[311] Ibid. at 858.

prosecutions, he wrote, "are generally managed for the Crown with greater Skill and Zeal than ordinary Prosecutions . . . ."[312]

By the 1730s the lawyer's hand had become increasingly apparent in these "ordinary Prosecutions." Much as Parliament in the 1696 Act had undertaken to even up for the advantages of the insistently lawyerized treason prosecution by allowing full defense of counsel, the judges of the 1730s began allowing defendants to have the help of counsel to probe the sometimes menacing evidentiary product of prosecutions that were increasingly lawyer-driven and perjury-prone.

Although both treason trial reform in the 1690s and felony trial reform in the 1730s were episodes of procedural evening up, the role of the bench in the two cycles was strikingly different. We have seen in Chapter 2 that the judges of the Stuart bench were among the main villains against whom the 1696 Act had been directed. The judges of the 1730s were the reformers who abridged the rule against counsel in felony trials for the purpose of enhancing defensive safeguard. How could judicial attitudes have changed so profoundly in a generation? The starting point in answering that question, in my view, is to avoid overdrawing the contrast between the villainous Stuart judges and their virtuous successors. The subservience of the bench in the Popish Plot or the Bloody Assizes was not typical of the routine administration of criminal justice, in which the judges were not under career pressure to side with the prosecution. Furthermore, judicial independence, which was largely secured in the Act of Settlement of 1701,[313] distanced the judges from responsibility for the government's agenda and supplied the framework for a changed attitude of greater tolerance for the accused. The most important connection between the reforms of the 1690s and the 1730s is that the judges of the 1730s understood the enduring lesson of the Stuart treason trials—that there might lurk within common law criminal procedure the potential for convicting the innocent.

3. The Juridical Basis

The role of the judges as instigators of the change in felony trial practice in the 1730s raises another puzzle, about the source of the judges' authority. In 1696 Chief Justice Holt had taken the position that allowing defense counsel in the fashion authorized under the Treason Trials Act of 1696 was so completely beyond the judicial power that the courts could not extend the grant to a treason defendant whose trial occurred one day before the effective date of the Act. Holt told the defendant, Sir William

---

[312] 2 Hawkins, *PC* 402, discussed *supra*, Ch. 2, text at n. 167.
[313] Discussed *supra*, Ch. 2, text at nn. 78–80, where important qualifications are noticed.

Parkyns: "We must conform to the Law as it is at Present, not to what it will be Tomorrow. We are upon our Oaths to do so."[314] If the judges of 1696 felt themselves powerless to allow counsel in a transitional case so completely within the statutory purpose, on what authority did the judges of the 1730s ameliorate the rule against defense counsel in cases so far removed from treason?

We do not know how the judges came to work the change in felony procedure. If the judges or some of them deliberated about the change and came to a collective decision to alter the practice, they left no record of it. Had their decision arisen in the course of adjudication, the legal sources of the time are likely to have evidenced it. Indeed, to speak of the judges making "a decision" to admit defense counsel in the 1730s may be misleading. The change seems to have been implemented in the practice of individual judges, exercising the trial judge's traditional discretion in the conduct of trial business. "The decision" may have been to experiment with such exercises of discretion. Another line of experiment, reported by Hawkins in 1721, was that "by Leave of the Court Prisoners have sometimes been indulged the Assistance of Counsel, not only to advise them in Prison, but also to stand by them at the Bar.[315] A knowledgeable observer wrote in 1733 that "of late the counsel for prisoners are allowed to sit by them and instruct them how to make their defense."[316]

The earliest departures from the rule against defense counsel may have occurred as special-purpose exceptions, without intent to alter the rule. We have record of an example from 1724, in the case of Edward Arnold,[317] a deranged defendant tried for malicious wounding. The trial judge effectively allowed the defendant's solicitor to conduct his defense at trial.[318] The solicitor cross-examined a prosecution witness (the magistrate who conducted the pretrial committal hearing) and presented the

---

[314] Foster, *Crown Law* 232. Another version: *R. v. William Parkyns*, 13 *St. Tr.* 63, 72–3 (1696).

[315] 2 Hawkins, *PC* 401.

[316] *Reports on the Laws of Connecticut by Francis Fane, K.C., Standing Counsel to the Board of Trade and Plantations* 73 (Charles M. Andrews ed.) (1915). The quoted language is from Fane's report regarding a Connecticut Act that would have denied defense counsel in criminal cases. Fane advised the Board that he "doubt[ed] whether it be a laudable or even a justifiable practice" to deny defense counsel, especially in view of the new English practice described in the passage quoted in text. Ibid. (I owe this reference to Robert Stevens.)

[317] *R. v. Edward Arnold*, 16 *St. Tr.* 695 (Surrey Assizes 1724). The judge's instruction to the jury in this case became an early milestone in the development of the insanity defense. See 1 Nigel Walker, *Crime and Insanity in England: The Historical Perspective* 53–7 (1968).

[318] At the arraignment, Arnold's counsel referred to the client's impaired circumstances and asked that Arnold "may have a solicitor by him to call his witnesses only." 16 *St. Tr.* at 697. Serjeant Cheshire, for the crown, opposed the request, invoking the familiar rubric of court as counsel. "Your lordship is of counsel for all the prisoners, who by law can have none, as this man can't have any." 16 *St. Tr.* at 697. Three other crown counsel endorsed Cheshire's view, 16 *St. Tr.* at 697–8.

defense case.[319] (Arnold was convicted and sentenced to death, but his sentence was commuted to life imprisonment.)

The sense that defense counsel's right of audience lay within the discretion of the trial judge is an idea that persisted long after the change in practice in the early to mid-1730s. In December 1738 one Old Bailey judge was still resisting counsel. When a felony defendant told the court that "I have feed counsel" (that is, engaged counsel by paying his fee), the trial judge, echoing Hawkins' rationale for excluding defense counsel, responded: "But here is no Point of Law; and you know Matters of Fact as well as your Counsel."[320]

Doubt about the force of the new rule allowing defense counsel to examine and cross-examine witnesses was voiced by prosecution counsel in 1741 in the trial of Samuel Goodere for murder at Bristol.[321] When the trial judge[322] asked the defendant whether he wished to cross-examine a main witness, his counsel intervened to ask the court to "indulge counsel to put his questions for him . . . ."[323] Prosecution counsel still thought it worth his while to object, emphasizing in this striking passage his understanding of the extent of judicial discretion about whether and how to allow defense counsel to cross-examine:

This, I apprehend, is a matter purely in the discretion of the Court, and what can neither in this or any other court of criminal justice be demanded as a right. The judges, I apprehend, act as they see fit on these occasions, and few of them (as far as I have observed) walk by one and the same rule in this particular: some have gone so far, as to give leave for counsel to examine and cross-examine witnesses; others have bid the counsel propose their questions to the Court; and others again

---

[319] E.g., ibid. at 714–15, 717. The "Solicitor for the Prisoner" called the accused's brother to testify about his mental state. The trial judge examined the witness, and prosecution counsel cross-examined. Ibid. at 717–18. Most of the questioning seems to have been done by the judge on the solicitor's motion, e.g., "My lord, I desire this witness may be asked" this or that, ibid. at 737 (two instances), but on occasion the solicitor took over and conducted the examination himself, e.g., ibid. at 740–2.

Notice that although Arnold had counsel, it was the solicitor whom the court allowed to assist Arnold in presenting his case. This episode is interesting as an illustration that as late as 1724 the exclusion of solicitors from audience at trial was not as firm in English criminal practice as it subsequently became.

[320] Robert Andrews, *OBSP* (Dec. 1738, #16), at 9, 11.

[321] *R. v. Samuel Goodere*, 17 St. Tr. 1003 (1741).

[322] Michael Foster was presiding, as recorder of Bristol, soon to become a King's Bench judge (1746–63). In his *Crown Law*, published in 1762, Foster was still hostile to counsel's new role in criminal defense. "I am far from disputing the Propriety of [the] Rule" that "[a]t Common-Law no Counsel was allowed upon the issue of Guilty or Not guilty in any Capital Case whatsoever, except upon questions of Law. And then only in Doubtful, not in Plain Cases." Foster, *Crown Law* 231. Foster's views were not likely to have been softer back in 1741, when the departure was more recent, hence prosecution counsel's effort to get him to refuse audience to Goodere's counsel. (Foster conceded the wisdom of allowing defense counsel in treason cases under the 1696 Act. Ibid, discussed *supra*, Ch. 2, text at n. 169.)

[323] 17 St. Tr. at 1022.

have directed that the prisoner should put his own questions: the method of practice in this point, is very variable and uncertain; but this we certainly know, that
by the settled rule of law the prisoner is allowed no other counsel but the Court
in matters of fact, and ought either to ask his own questions of the witnesses, or
else propose them himself to the Court.[324]

This contention that the assistance of defense counsel lay "purely in the
discretion of the Court," and that "few of [the judges] . . . walk by one and
the same rule," supports the view that the change in practice did not take
the form of an authoritative decision or directive, but rather emerged
from the judges' exercise of their residual discretion over trial management.

A similar recollection was preserved in remarks uttered a decade later
in the course of a trial held pursuant to English procedure in the colony
of Antigua. Tried for murder in 1753, the defendant asked to be "allowed
counsel on my defense, not only to matters of law, but also to matters of
fact, and to make my defense in the fullest manner." He represented that
this request was "no new thing, it being, as I am informed, usual in
England . . . ."[325] Prosecution counsel, recently arrived from England and
serving as Solicitor General, advised the court that the defendant had
mischaracterized the English practice. "[I]t has gone no farther than to
permit counsel to examine and cross-examine witnesses," which "though
at first a pure indulgence, yet now seems to be so far grown into a right, that
I . . . readily consent to the granting of it on behalf of the crown."[326] He
emphasized that defense counsel had "never" been allowed "to make
observations on the evidence; or to draw arguments or inferences from it
to the point in issue; or to do any thing else in the way of a formal or full
defense."[327]

As late as 1769 Blackstone was uneasy that in theory the right to have
the assistance of defense counsel in felony rested on the discretion of the
individual trial judge. After criticizing the rule against defense counsel as
being "not at all of a piece with the rest of the humane treatment of prisoners by English law,"[328] Blackstone happily observed that "the judges
themselves are so sensible of this defect in our modern practice, that they
seldom scruple to allow a prisoner counsel to stand by him at the bar, and
instruct him what questions to ask, or even to ask questions for him, with
respect to matters of fact . . . ."[329] "But still," continued Blackstone, "this
is a matter of too much importance to be left to the good pleasure of any
judge, and it is worthy [of] the interposition of the legislature . . . ."[330]

---

[324] Ibid.   [325] *R. v. John Barbot*, 18 *St. Tr.* 1229, 1231 (1753).
[326] Ibid. (emphasis supplied).   [327] Ibid.
[328] 4 Blackstone, *Commentaries* 349.   [329] Ibid. at 349–50.
[330] Ibid.

The discretionary character of the change in practice that allowed trial counsel to assist the criminal defendant in matters of fact was still remembered in the 1780s, the period in which the use of defense counsel appears to have increased materially. In an Old Bailey case heard in 1786 the defense counsel, William Garrow, objected when the trial judge, Heath J, allowed a prosecution witness who was mute to be examined through an interpreter. According to a manuscript report of the exchange, Garrow persisted after the court overruled his objection. Heath then upbraided him, reminding him: "What you do here is by *permission of the Court in a Criminal* Case."[331]

We also find instances in the Old Bailey pamphlet reports in which a trial judge exercised discretion to relieve against the remaining restrictions against defense counsel, permitting broader representation. In a prosecution for mail robbery in 1771, the accused was unwell when tried. "The judge said, that as the prisoner was ill he would permit his counsel to state his defense to the jury."[332] In 1783, presiding over the trial of a German defendant accused of the theft of some jewelry, the judge permitted defense counsel to state the accused's defense, on the ground that the accused was a foreigner, even though a German-speaking interpreter was being employed.[333]

As the submission from Goodere's counsel in 1741 hints, there is some indication that the patterns of retreat from the rule against defense counsel may have been shaped on a court-by-court basis, rather than entirely in the discretion of the particular judge. In an exceptionally well-reported Old Bailey case from July 1742, defense counsel referred to his understanding that there was a "Course of the Court at the Old Bailey" regarding the scope of defense permitted to counsel.[334] Such court-specific

---

[331] Manuscript bound with the Harvard Law Library's exemplar of the *Old Bailey Sessions Papers* for January 1786, following the case of William Bartlett, *OBSP* (Jan. 1786, #151) at 247. The quoted language appears at 1ᵛ, (emphasis original).

[332] William Davis, *OBSP* (Dec. 1771, #40), at 16, 25.

[333] Charles Bairnes, *OBSP* (Feb. 1783, #197), at 292 (judge to defense counsel: "As the prisoner is a foreigner, though I cannot consistent with the practice of the court allow you to make a speech for him, yet you may state your facts to me").

[334] Counsel said that "he knew by the Course of the Court at the Old Bailey, he was not at Liberty to observe upon the Prosecutor's Evidence," but he was allowed to open (that is, introduce) the defense case "without making any Observations upon it." James Annesly and Joseph Redding, *OBSP* (July 1742) (supplementary pamphlet), at 19 (murder). The case also appears at 17 *St. Tr.* 1093, 1113 (O.B. 1742).

A sense of hesitancy about the Old Bailey rule shows up in another case in the same year, in which the accused is recorded asking permission for counsel to serve. "I have Counsel, and beg that Gentleman may ask the Questions for me." William Remue, *OBSP* (Dec. 1742, #44), at 32 (rape).

variations[335] further underscore that the rule against defense counsel was probably not altered in one authoritative pronouncement, but rather in piecemeal departures.

There is a special irony about this course of development. The trial judge was so dominant that he could admit defense counsel as an act of grace—an "indulgence" in the term of the Antiguan Solicitor General. But the power to admit defense counsel could not remain perpetually in judicial discretion as the precedents accreted. As the Antiguan Solicitor General explained, over time it grew into a right. The judges of the 1730s who turned common law criminal procedure down this path had no way of knowing that defense counsel would overcome the limitations that the judges placed upon him, indeed, that defense counsel would recast the dynamic of the criminal trial so fundamentally that the judges would ultimately cede mastery of the criminal trial to counsel. On the contrary, the judges who engineered the change in practice in the 1730s must have prided themselves on the deftness of the compromise they had devised. They had responded to the increased dangers associated with prosecutorial power by allowing the accused to have the assistance of counsel, yet they had preserved the "accused speaks" trial by limiting counsel to the role of examining and cross-examining witnesses. The accused would still need to speak in his own defense if his version of the events were to be presented, or if weaknesses of the prosecution case were to be confronted, or if the accused hoped to present the court with a view of his character and circumstances that could motivate the jury to return a partial verdict or allow the judge to recommend executive clemency.

It will be seen in Chapter 5 how defense counsel overcame these bounds and commandeered the trial. Defense counsel would ultimately end the altercation trial, silence the accused, marginalize the judge, and break up the working relationship of judge and jury. Before taking up that story, however, I turn in Chapter 4 to examine the other great effort at enhancing defensive safeguard initiated by the eighteenth-century bench, the law of criminal evidence. The judges developed rules to exclude particularly problematic classes of evidence. At the core of this new body of law were the corroboration and confession rules, which the judges devised for the same reason that they decided to allow defense counsel into the felony trial: out of concern that the prosecutorial initiatives traced in this chapter raised ever greater dangers of mistaken conviction of innocent defendants.

---

[335] Small differences in the role allowed to prosecution counsel also persisted among the assize circuits into the nineteenth century. See *1836 Report* 10 n. (discussing circuit differences on whether prosecution counsel could preview the expected prosecution evidence for the judge and jury in an opening statement).

4

The Law of Criminal Evidence

Allowing defense counsel to cross-examine the testimony of prosecution witnesses was one of two great initiatives taken by the bench to enhance the reliability of the evidence in eighteenth-century criminal trials. The other response to the dangers that emerged from prosecutorial practice in this period was to devise rules of evidence that excluded certain problematic types of proof. These rules ultimately coalesced into a body of law that for a time was thought of as a distinct field, the law of criminal evidence,[1] but which has since been largely subsumed in the general law

---

[1] E.g., Leonard MacNally, *The Rules of Evidence on Pleas of the Crown* (1st edn. Dublin 1802); I cite the American edition (Philadelphia 1811) [hereafter, MacNally, *Evidence*]; Henry Roscoe, *Digest of the Law of Evidence and Practice in Criminal Cases* (1st edn. London 1835); I cite the Sharswood edition (George Sharswood ed.) (3rd Am. edn. from 3rd London edn.

of evidence. Although the creation of the law of criminal evidence was the work of the bench, it played into the hands of the lawyers, who would find in the exclusionary principle one of the levers that would help them wrest control of the criminal trial.

Four main rules of evidence were articulated in the criminal trials of the eighteenth century. Three were distinctive to the criminal trial: the character rule, the corroboration rule, and the confession rule. The fourth, the hearsay rule, was shared with civil practice, but when applied in criminal cases, was viewed in the treatises as part of the law of criminal evidence.[2]

The *character rule* prevented the prosecution from introducing evidence of the defendant's bad character, especially evidence of former crimes, except by way of rebuttal. The mature rule of the eighteenth century provided that "the prosecutor cannot enter into the defendant's character, unless the defendant enable him to do so, by his calling witnesses to support it, and even then the prosecutor cannot examine to particular facts."[3]

The *corroboration rule* was directed at crown witness testimony, that troubling prosecutorial innovation discussed in Chapter 3. Responding to the danger of perjury that inhered in the testimony of an accomplice, the corroboration rule required evidence in addition to that of the accomplice in order for the jury to convict. In the 1780s the rule was softened to a mere rule of caution or recommendation to the jury, in developments that are discussed in this chapter.[4]

The *confession rule* excluded evidence that the accused had made an out-of-court confession of the crime, unless the confession was voluntary. The mature rule excluded evidence of a confession "forced from the mind by the flattery of hope, or by the torture of fear . . . ."[5]

The *hearsay rule* rejected testimony by one person about what another person said when that testimony was offered to prove the truth of the out-of-court statement. Three main reasons were given for disapproving hearsay: (1) that accepting someone else's report of a statement was inconsistent with the best evidence rule, which preferred the best obtainable evidence of the fact being proved; (2) that because the out-of-court declarant had not testified on oath, that testimony lacked the enhancement to

---

Philadelphia 1846) [hereafter Roscoe, *Criminal Evidence*]. This tradition continues in Adrian Zuckerman, *The Principles of Criminal Evidence* (1989).

[2] E.g., Roscoe, *Criminal Evidence*, supra n. 1, at 22.
[3] Leach's formulation in 4 Hawkins, *PC* § 206, at 457 (Thomas Leach ed.) (7th edn. 1795) (citing Buller's *Nisi Prius* for authority, on which, see *infra* n. 150).
[4] In *R. v. James Atwood and Thomas Robbins*, 1 Leach 464, 168 *Eng. Rep.* 334 (1788) [sic; 1787], discussed *infra* text at nn. 148–69.
[5] *R. v. Jane Warickshall*, 1 Leach 263, 263–4, 168 *Eng. Rep.* 235 (1783).

veracity that resulted from swearing a witness in court; and (3) that the out-of-court declarant had not been subjected to cross-examination. Only in the middle of the nineteenth century did the consensus form that the doctrinal basis of the hearsay rule was to promote cross-examination. The three rationales for the hearsay rule pertained equally in civil cases, and to the interests of plaintiffs and prosecutors as well as defendants. Accordingly, the hearsay rule was not particularly oriented to safeguarding criminal defendants against prosecutorial abuse, which was the concern that motivated the core rules of the eighteenth-century law of criminal evidence, the corroboration and confession rules.

Wigmore, the pioneering scholar whose work still shapes our understanding of the history of the law of evidence, misunderstood both the timing and the causes of the appearance of these rules. Working from the *State Trials* and other published law reports, he placed the character rule and the hearsay rule too early (in the seventeenth century) and the corroboration and confession rules too late (in the last decades of the eighteenth century).[6] The present account is drawn prevailingly from the *Old Bailey Sessions Papers*, the series of pamphlet reports of London trials already used in earlier chapters of this book. These sources, which were unknown to Wigmore (or to his predecessors Stephen and Thayer) allow us to be more precise about when and how the rules of criminal evidence formed, and to gain a better understanding of the forces that caused the judges to embark on this remarkable program of excluding relevant evidence from the trial juries.

A. The View from the *Sessions Papers*

Because the findings in this chapter derive so heavily from the *Old Bailey Sessions Papers*,[7] it is important to bear in mind some of the attributes and the weaknesses of these sources.

---

[6] *Infra*, text at nn. 54–6, 116–17, 133, 171–5, 219, 225–8, 242.

[7] The title of the series wanders but is, after the early years, a variant of *The Proceedings on the King's Commissions of the Peace, Oyer and Terminer, and Gaol Delivery . . . in the OldBailey, on [certain dates]*. Regarding comparable pamphlet reports for a few other counties, see Ch. 3, *supra*, at n. 6. I have described the *Sessions Papers* of the early decades in Langbein, "CTBL" 267–72, and those of the mid-eighteenth century in Langbein, "Ryder" 3–5, 10–18, 21–6. Regarding the series in the later eighteenth century, see Simon Devereaux, "The City and the *Sessions Paper*: 'Public Justice' in London, 1770–1800," 35 J. British Studies 466 (1996) [hereafter Devereaux, City]; id, "The Fall of the *Sessions Paper*: Criminal Trial and the Popular Press in Late Eighteenth-Century London" (1999 draft) (*Criminal Justice History*, forthcoming) [hereafter Devereaux, "Fall"].

1. The Skew to London

The *Sessions Papers* necessarily impart an urban slant to the historical inquiry that is based upon them. More theft of shop goods and less theft of livestock was prosecuted at the Old Bailey than at provincial assizes. Because the London-area caseload was so much larger, the Old Bailey sat more frequently, eight sessions per year; assizes met twice a year. The Old Bailey had a permanent judge, the recorder of London, who supplied some continuity and direction to its work,[8] in addition to the royal judges who rotated in and out.

I have emphasized in Chapter 3 how the distinctive problems of detecting and prosecuting criminals in a metropolis as yet lacking a police force gave rise to two seriously flawed prosecutorial initiatives, the reward system and the crown witness system. The judges' decision to allow defendants to have the help of counsel in presenting and cross-examining witnesses was in part a response to the dangers of perjury inherent in these new prosecutorial techniques. A main theme of the present chapter is that the same concern shaped the development of the two most distinctive rules of criminal evidence, corroboration and confession. These new principles of proof were the work of a tiny national bench, composed of about a dozen judges at any one time. The judges alternated their service at the Old Bailey with tours on the assize circuits.[9] Hence, while the special problems of the metropolis shaped the trial procedure that we see in the Old Bailey, there was no means of confining the developments to London.[10] What was created was not London law but English law.[11]

---

[8] Discussed in Beattie, *Policing* 424–62, with particular reference to the efforts and influence of Sir William Thomson, who served from 1715 to 1739; compare the hostile biography in 8 Edward Foss, *The Judges of England* 173–6 (London 1864).

[9] See Langbein, "Ryder" 115–23; for the calendar of Old Bailey and assize sessions for a typical year, 1755, see ibid at 12 n. 29. Eighteenth-century assize practice for the county of Surrey is described in Beattie, *Crime* 267 ff.

[10] A similar point can be made about the pressures that led to the reworking of the sanction of transportation into an effective alternative to capital punishment in the early decades of the eighteenth century. Beattie has shown how heavily City of London interests influenced this development, see Beattie, *Policing* 427–62, but the Transportation Acts applied nationwide.

[11] For example, in a series of pamphlet trial reports for York assizes, published in the 1770s, discussed in Ch. 3, *supra*, at n. 6, there is extensive evidence of the application of the confession rule, whose development is traced in this chapter from the Old Bailey sources. The confession rule cases from York are cited in Langbein, "Evidence" 1198 n. 147. Likewise, the *Surrey Assize Papers* (*SAP*), which run from the 1680s to the 1770s, routinely confirm that the developments discussed in this chapter were simultaneously occurring at provincial assizes. The *SAP* are discussed in Ch. 3, n. 6; and especially in Beattie, *Crime* 364–73.

2. Evolution of the Series

The *Sessions Papers* originated close to an earlier genre of popular literature, the sensation-mongering chapbooks, which were pamphlet crime
reports that date back to Elizabethan times.[12] The chapbooks were
produced for sale to the general public. Each pamphlet recounted the
detail of a recent crime, together with (typically) the ensuing investigation, trial, conviction, and execution. The earliest exemplars of the *Old
Bailey Sessions Papers* survive from the 1670s.[13] They have as their subject
the trials occurring at a single sessions of the Old Bailey; such sessions
were held on average about every six weeks. The pamphlets were quite
selective, recounting only a few cases likely to have the most popular
interest. The early *Sessions Papers* also exhibit the moralizing tone that was
characteristic of the chapbooks ("And because from the Female Sex
sprung all our Woes and bad Inclinations at first, we may begin with The
Trial of three very young Women . . . ."[14]).

From these beginnings the *Sessions Papers* were published in a substantially continuous series for nearly two and a half centuries.[15] The series

---

[12] Discussed in Langbein, *PCR* 45–54.

[13] The earliest exemplar that has come to my attention is Anon., *The Truest News from
Tyburn, or, An Exact Account of the Tryal, Condencation* [sic; Condemnation] *and Execution, of the
Syrurgion* [sic; Surgeon], *and Butcher, and the Rest . . . Sentenced to be Hang[e]d for Their Several
and Respective Offences Herein Particularly Specified. At Justice-Hall in the Old Bailey, the 12th of
Decemb[er] 1674* (London 1674). This and more than a dozen other rare pamphlets from the
1670s are bound together with contemporary chapbooks in the Guildhall Library, London,
under shelfmark A.5.4, no. 34. The producers' sense of the novelty of their enterprise is
reflected in the preface to the April 1676 pamphlet (also in the Guildhall volume), at page 3,
which observes that former pamphlets "having proved very acceptable, we have thought
good to continue their publications; this Sessions being as remarkable as others . . . ."
A similar impulse was being felt in this period on the Home Circuit, but it did not find a
sustaining market. A pamphlet account of a few trials conducted at the July 1676 Hertford
Assizes was published contemporaneously in London, with a hopeful preface that refers to
other such ventures. "Whereas Narratives of the chief Proceedings at several Assizes, have
of late been published, and well received by divers ingenious inquisitive men, as tending not
only to divertize Readers with the Novelty of the Relations, but likewise to forewarn innocent people of the subtle practices of Villains . . . [the anonymous author has decided] to
present the world with the following Account or Abstract of the several notorious
Malefactors' Trials, at the Assizes holden for the County of Hertford, July the 15th and 16th,
1676." Anon., *A True Narrative of the Proceedings at the Hertford Assizes, This Instant July 1676*,
at 2–3 (London 1676) (Huntington Libr., San Marino, CA, shelfmark 54791 (no. 13)).
Because these early pamphlets are so unrevealing about the issues of criminal procedure
that I have been researching, I have not devoted much effort to finding more of them, or to
learning whether earlier examples exist.

[14] Anon., *A True Narrative of the Proceedings at the Sessions-House in the Old Bayly* (Aug.
1676), at 3 (Guildhall Libr. shelfmark A.5.4, no. 34).

[15] The series terminates in April 1913, with a curt two-page account of the notable trial of
the woman's suffrage leader, Emmeline Pankhurst, for conspiracy in the bombing of Lloyd
George's house. For context, see Martin Pugh, *The Pankhursts* 258–61 (2001). Across the
years I have worked with substantial collections of the *Sessions Papers* at five libraries: the

underwent incessant change in size, format, content, and function. From their origins as episodic chapbooks they became a periodical, published immediately after each of the eight annual sessions of the court, and sold separately for a few pence. In the 1680s the pamphlets became semi-official, under license from the City of London;[16] by the later eighteenth century the City was subsidizing the publication.[17] Instead of limiting themselves to a selection of higher-profile cases, the *Sessions Papers* began to report increasing numbers of the mundane property crimes that comprised the bulk of the court's caseload. Crude sensation-mongering died out from the title pages,[18] and moral instruction disappeared from the accounts. The series came to operate under an obligation of completeness; at least the outcome of every trial held at the particular sessions was noted.[19] As the eighteenth century wore on, the *Sessions Papers* lost interest in street-corner sales and became a stodgy, quasi-official crime calendar, published under license of, and ultimately with financial support from, the City of London.

3. Scope and Reliability

Into the 1710s most accounts of individual trials in the *Sessions Papers* were quite compressed and thus not very revealing about the procedural detail of what had transpired. From the middle of that decade some cases are reported in greater detail,[20] summarizing the individual testimony of the prosecutor and of witnesses, as well as the accused's responses. The eighteenth-century *Sessions Papers* were the product of shorthand

Bodleian Law Library, Oxford; the British Library; the Guildhall Library (London); the Harvard Law School Library; and the University of Chicago Law School Library. The *Sessions Papers* for the years 1714–1834 were commercially microfilmed by the Harvester Press, Sussex, using Harvard and Guildhall originals, under the title *Old Bailey Proceedings, 1714–1834* (38 reels, 1984). A project to digitize the *Sessions Papers* from the 1670s to 1834 in a word-searchable on-line database is being conducted by Robert Shoemaker and Tim Hitchcock at the University of Sheffield. A portion of the database, to 1788, is projected to be available by December 2002. For description, see <www.shef.ac.uk/uni/academic/D-H/hri/bailey.htm>.

[16] Beattie, *Policing* 3 n. 6.

[17] Devereaux, 'City', *supra* n. 7, at 468.

[18] The April 1682 issue is among the last with a sensation-seeking title page. It trumpets in large and partially bold-face type that one of the trials was "In Relation to the Person Accused for Getting his Daughter With-Child."

[19] When the January 1742 issue neglected some cases, the February issue reported them with the following preface: "The Trials of the five following Persons having been omitted in the last Sessions-Book for want of Room, they are here inserted to obviate any Surmise that they were left out with any Design or sinister View whatsoever." *OBSP* (Feb. 174[3]), at 42.

[20] Beattie would link the greater detail of the *Sessions Papers* after 1714 to heightened concern about the threat of violent crime in the early years of the Hanoverian succession. Beattie, *Policing* 370–6.

reporters who attended the trials[21] and then edited their notes for immediate publication. In the 1730s we find the pamphlets occasionally narrating question-and-answer sequences, in the manner of a stenographic
transcript. (It is from these passages that it has been possible to detect the
entry of defense counsel in the 1730s, the development discussed in
Chapter 3.) As the reports grew in detail, they also grew in heft. The
customary four-page folio editions of the early years gave way to eight-
page folios in the later 1710s and the 1720s, then in the 1730s to twenty-
page quarto-sized pamphlets.[22] In the 1730s a single sessions commonly
required two (occasionally three) pamphlets of twenty pages. By the
1780s ten such pamphlets were sometimes needed to chronicle a single
sessions.[23] This massive enlargement, from four pages of synopsis to as
much as 200 pages of sometimes verbatim proceedings per sessions,
reflected (in addition to larger caseloads) the change in character of the
Sessions Papers away from lay literature toward officially sponsored quasi
law reports.

[21] As a result, it became common practice to use the reporter as a prosecution witnesses
in a perjury trial to prove the testimony that the defendant had given at the prior trial; e.g.,
James Payce, OBSP (Oct. 1751, #609), at 311; Thomas Ashley, OBSP (Apr. 1752, #268), at 148;
Moses Henericus, OBSP (Jan. 1758, #95) at 83; Henry Myers, OBSP (June 1758, #255), at 256;
John Luthwart and John Simpson, OBSP (Apr. 1763, ##193–4), at 136, 137 (alleged perjury
committed at Admiralty sessions, which were held as an adjunct to Old Bailey sessions);
Mary Heather, OBSP (Jan. 1764, #124), at 88; Edward Smith, OBSP (Feb. 1771, #230), at 152;
Elizabeth Young, OBSP (Dec. 1773, #98), at 43; Thomas Chalkley, OBSP (Apr.–May 1775,
#389), at 207 (Gurney's clerk testified that Gurney was then occupied "taking down the
arguments on an appeal in the House of Lords; but I remember perfectly, without referring
to Mr. Gurney's notes [what] the prisoner swore . . ."); Henry Harvey, OBSP (Sept. 1785,
#909), at 1152, 1154.
[22] The change in format took effect in the 1730 mayoral year. A preface to the pamphlet
for December 1729 (the first sessions of that mayoral year) announced the change in format
and explained that it was meant to make it easier to collect and bind the reports into annual
sets. OBSP (Dec. 1729) at 2. Henceforth, the publisher would publish "a Complete Annual
Register of these Proceedings," that is, an index for each year's reports; readers were recommended to bind the year's pamphlets with the index in "a Handsome Volume." Ibid. The
publisher expressed the further hope that encouraging readers to collect the Sessions Paper
pamphlets into annual sets in this way would kill the market for volumes of selected trials,
since it would no longer be "worth any one's while to reprint [the trial reports] in Volumes,
which has been done at extraordinary Rates [i.e. prices], and which could only be necessary
by the Destruction of those [former issues of the Sessions Papers that were] Printed on bad
Paper, and in the Sheet Size . . . ." Ibid. The format change was undertaken with the further
purpose of increasing the amount of detail that would be reported regarding "the Crime, the
Evidence, and the Prisoner's Defense." Ibid. The first index is bound with some surviving
sets of the Sessions Papers, e.g., that in the Guildhall Library, headed "An Alphabetical List
of All the Persons tried . . . in the Year 1730." The following year the series began to be
continuously paginated for the year, rather than by the sessions as before, doubtless to facilitate the annual indexing. A further reference tool, assigning a number to each defendant,
began with the 1733 mayoral year, starting in December 1732. (In citing Sessions Paper cases,
I preserve these numbers in parentheses with the date of the report.)
[23] From 1783 to 1790 the Sessions Papers ran to a minimum of eight and sometimes ten
issues per session. Devereaux, "Fall," supra n. 7, text at n. 57.

The greatest shortcoming of the *Session Papers* as historical sources is their tendency to compress the trials they report, and to do it in ways that do not allow us to be confident that we know what was being deleted or why. In the 1730s, for example, a single sessions lasted two to five days and processed fifty to 100 felony cases, yet all the trials were reported in two or sometimes three twenty-page pamphlets. By the 1780s, when the *Sessions Papers* achieved their greatest detail, they were still omitting most of what was said at most of the trials they reported. Much of what the *Sessions Papers* omitted occurred in the many squib reports, which summarized entire cases in a few lines. For example, the proceedings in a forgery prosecution conducted in 1763 are reported in their entirety in one sentence. "Upon the counsel's opening the indictment, there appeared no foundation to convict them, and without going into the evidence they were Acquitted."[24] Events of considerable juridical interest produced this result, but the report bleaches them out. Omission in *Sessions Paper* accounts also took the form of compression within the more fully reported cases. Hence, even extensively reported cases were not necessarily fully reported. It follows that quantitative analysis from such incomplete data is exceptionally problematic,[25] and that negative inferences are hazardous. We cannot safely infer that something was not happening at these trials solely because the pamphlets do not report the happening. On the other hand, we need not worry about fabrication or invention of content. The regularity and the increasingly official character of the reports means that they were unlikely to have tolerated fiction. Some years ago I reported on having cross-checked *Sessions Paper* trials from the mid-1750s against an exceptionally detailed set of judge's notes taken by Sir Dudley Ryder, who, as Chief Justice of King's Bench, was one of the judges who presided at the trials.[26] The comparison showed that much had been omitted from the published reports, but that nothing contained in the reports had been fabricated. I concluded that if the *Sessions Paper* "report says something happened, it did; if the ... report does not say it happened, it still may have."[27]

---

[24] John Deschamps and Sarah Tompson, *OBSP* (Jan. 1763, ##91–3), at 58.

[25] See *supra*, Ch. 3, text and notes at nn. 300–3.

[26] "Law Notes of Sir Dudley Ryder" (1754–56), doc. nos. 12–17, Harrowby Manuscripts, Sandon Hall (judge's notes) (typescript transcript, copies on deposit at Lincoln's Inn Libr; Univ. Chicago Law Libr., shelfmark KA 29.R96A4.1973) [hereafter Ryder, "Judge's Notes"; all citations are to doc. no. 14, the notes for Ryder's four Old Bailey sessions, unless another volume is indicated]. For more on Ryder's notes, see Langbein, "Ryder" 8–10; Langbein, "Evidence" 1176–78. Regarding the genre, see James Oldham, "Eighteenth-Century Judges' Notes: How They Explain, Correct and Enhance the Reports," 31 *American J. Legal History* (1987).

[27] Langbein, "Ryder" 25. Another technique for validating the *Sessions Papers* in some respects is to compare the trials they report with the surviving public records in the local archives, which sometimes contain indictments, recognizances of persons bound over to

From the standpoint of the legal historian trying to understand the development of criminal procedure and the law of evidence, the *Sessions Papers* are particularly frustrating on account of the reporters' prevailing lack of interest in our subject. The *Sessions Papers* were primarily crime reports, resolutely focused on the circumstances of crime, detection, and punishment. The publishers had relatively little interest in the institutions, procedures, and personnel of the criminal justice system. For example, the *Sessions Papers* took no notice of the judges' decision to allow counsel to assist defendants in the 1730s.[28] It has been possible to detect the appearance of defense counsel in the *Sessions Papers* of those years only because the reports attribute a few scattered lines of questioning to persons identified as counsel.[29]

The publishers of the *Sessions Papers* came under recurrent financial pressure to reduce the size of the publication, pressure to which they responded by stripping out legal procedural detail of the sort we would most have wanted to see preserved. Thus, in September 1742 the reports began a period of printing only the answers "to Questions put to the Witnesses; which Questions are omitted for Brevity sake, the Answers denoting what they were."[30] Later in the 1740s the *Sessions Papers* returned to showing some questions, but often unattributed (identified only as "Q."), which can prevent us from knowing who (judge, prosecution or defense counsel, perhaps others) were posing them. During the 1749 and 1750 mayoral years a notice ran in each issue assuring "The Public" that throughout that mayor's term of office "the *Sessions Book* will be constantly sold for four-pence, and no more, and that the whole Account of every Sessions shall be carefully comprised in One such Four-penny Book, without any farther Burden on the Purchasers."[31] In the 1772 mayoral year the Lord Mayor of London ordered a ceiling of two pamphlets per session.[32] In the years 1774–7 a large fraction of the cases, particularly acquittals, were reported in cursory "squib" accounts, apparently in order to hold down the size and hence the cost of publishing the series.

---

prosecute, jail calendars of persons to be tried, jury lists, and pretrial examinations (depositions) for the reported trials. See ibid. at 50–1 n. 193. These records are now kept in the Corporation of London Record Office (Guildhall) and in the Greater London Record Office. Furthermore, as has been seen in Ch. 3, various classes of central archives, especially the State Papers and Treasury records, supply information on some of the prosecutorial initiatives and on the post-verdict clemency process in some of the cases reported in the *Sessions Papers*.

[28] Even though contemporaries sensed the potential for a market among legal professionals: An advertisement for the first (1735) edition of the *Select Trials* compilation, which was based on *Sessions Paper* accounts asserts that "[these] trials are . . . very necessary for all Lawyers, Justices of the Peace, Clerks of the Indictments, and other Persons concerned in Prosecutions . . . ." *OBSP* (Apr. 1735), at 81, 82.

[29] Discussed *supra* Ch. 3, text at nn. 293–8.   [30] *OBSP* (Sept. 1742), at 26 n.

[31] *OBSP* (Dec. 1749), at 1.   [32] *OBSP* (Dec. 1771), at 32.

For long stretches of the eighteenth century the *Sessions Papers* were particularly unrevealing about the views of the judges. During these periods of repression, the pamphlets reported rulings without rationales, even in circumstances in which it seems highly likely that the judges would have been explaining why they were ruling as they did.[33] It turns out that for some years the editors of the *Sessions Papers* pursued a deliberate policy of suppressing what the judges were saying. We learn about this practice from a chance disclosure in the issue for January 1769, whose docket included a cause célèbre—the *Brentwood Elections Case*, a murder trial of two defendants charged with having clubbed to death a rival political supporter at the polls.[34] The report of the case was exceptionally detailed, and it was published in two parts. The second pamphlet contains an endnote explaining that, on account of the great public interest in the case, the publisher had hastened to publish the first pamphlet, which included some remarks attributed to the judges.[35] The reporter, Thomas Gurney,[36] "confesses [that it] has not been usual to [publish the judges' remarks] without their permission or supervision," and he apologized for having done it in this case.[37]

This reluctance to publish the judges' views probably arose from the conventions of contemporary law reporting in the superior courts, where the practice was for the reporter to submit to the judge an advance text of the reporter's rendering of the judge's oral opinion, which the judge could revise and polish before the publication of that volume of reports.[38] This leisurely pace would have interfered with the rapid publication schedule of the *Sessions Papers*, which were printed and circulated immediately after the sessions. It appears that Thomas Gurney had been resolving this tension for the *Sessions Papers* by expunging the judges' remarks—the worst possible solution from the standpoint of the historical record. That practice appears to have ceased shortly after we learn of it, when there was a change of proprietorship in the *Sessions Papers*. Under the new

---

[33] For example, in *R. v. Timothy Murphy*, 19 *St. Tr.* 693 (O.B. 1753), a forgery prosecution published as a separate pamphlet by Thomas Gurney, the *Sessions Paper* reporter, and subsequently incorporated in the *State Trials*, the pamphlet preserves the arguments of four prominent counsel, two on each side, addressing the question of whether a crown witness should be disqualified for interest, ibid. at 702–9. The judge's ruling, refusing to disqualify, is summarized in a single sentence, bracketed to show that the judge's remarks were not being quoted. Ibid. at 709. The case is discussed in another connection, *infra*, text at n. 161.

[34] Laurence Balfe and Edward McQuirk, *OBSP* (Jan. 1769, ##108–9), at 66–100.

[35] Ibid. at 74–6.

[36] Regarding whom, see Langbein, "Ryder" 12.

[37] *OBSP* (Jan. 1769), at 100.

[38] W. T. S. Daniel, *The History and Origin of the Law Reports* 66, 102 (1884). Holdsworth attributes to Sir James Burrow's King's Bench Reports (5 vols., 1756–71) the first major break with the convention that a reporter needed to have the license of the judges in order to publish reports of their judgments. 12 Holdsworth, *HEL* 112–13.

reporter, Joseph Gurney, who took over from his father in 1770, the sensi-tivity about not disclosing the judges' remarks was overcome. Already in Joseph Gurney's first issue there were several cases in which the judges' views were attributed.[39]

In December 1778 Gurney reversed the trend to compression, increas-ing the size of the session's issue to four twenty-page pamphlets. He attributed the decision to the City's governing bodies, the "Court of Aldermen and Common Council, [which have] recently resolved that the Trials at the Old Bailey shall, in future, be printed at large, as well in cases where the prisoners are acquitted, as when they are convicted . . . ."[40] (The City was by then supporting the *Sessions Papers* financially; in the year 1795 the subsidy reached £105 per year.[41])

In the 1780s the *Sessions Papers* entered their short golden age. During the reportership of Edmund Hodgson, which commenced in September 1782 and ceased in December 1790, the pamphlets reported many cases in exceptional detail. Hodgson sometimes printed lengthy question-and-answer transcripts of cross-examinations, and he sometimes reported motions and arguments of counsel together with the judges' rulings. Simon Devereaux has suggested that the *Sessions Papers* of this period were compiled with particular concern to facilitate the administration of the pardon process, providing detail about the circumstances of capital crimes in order to aid the recorder, the Privy Council, and the monarch in their deliberations about whom to execute and whom to spare.[42]

Hodgson routinely identified counsel by name; indeed, the suggestion has been made that he was attempting to develop a market for the *Sessions Papers* as a species of law report.[43] The leading Old Bailey barrister of the 1780s, William Garrow, appears to have owned a set of *Sessions Papers*. A copy of the volume for the 1784 mayoral year, now in the collection of the University of Chicago Law Library,[44] contains corrections and annota-tions in Garrow's hand, indicating that Garrow was using it as a reference

---

[39] E.g., John Higgs, *OBSP* (July 1770, #467), at 309, 310; Higham Solomon, *OBSP* (July 1770, #491), at 313; Frances Cuff, OBSP (July 1770, #494), at 314, 315.

[40] *OBSP* (Dec. 1778), at 40; ibid. at 60. See also Devereaux, "City," *supra* n. 7, at 468, report-ing that a City committee insisted in 1778 "that the *Sessions Paper* should provide a 'true, fair and perfect narrative' of all the trials at the Old Bailey. It was after this year that the length of most trial accounts began to increase substantially."

[41] Devereaux, "Fall," *supra* n. 7, text at n. 28.

[42] Devereaux, "City," *supra* n. 7, at 471–81.

[43] "Hodgson's pursuit of the legal market may also account for the fact that it is his editions of the *Sessions Paper* which first mention *all* of the names of the counsel who appeared at the Old Bailey." Devereaux, "Fall," *supra* n. 7, text at n. 73. Devereaux reports that "lawyers were so important a factor in Hodgson's sales that they constituted a distinct category of purchasers in two of the accounts which he submitted to the City. An account of 1786 notes sales to 'counsel,' while one of 1790" names several of the counsel, including William Garrow, as purchasers. Ibid., text at n. 81.

[44] Shelfmark K2025.C9L85/1783–84) [hereafter 1784 Chicago Volume].

work.[45] The next year a trial report depicted Garrow using his copy of the 1784 volume in court. Defending a smuggler, Garrow raised a law point about the construction of a term in the statute. He "hand[ed] up to the Court the opinion delivered by themselves in [a] preceding case," which the reporter identified in a footnote as "the Volume of *Sessions Papers* in Alderman Peckham's Mayoralty."[46] (Robert Peckham was Lord Mayor of London in 1784.)

Across the last decades of the eighteenth century the *Sessions Papers* lost their popular market to competition from the London daily press, and to the City's inability or unwillingness to enforce its purported claim to a licensing monopoly over the reporting of Old Bailey trials.[47] "The *Sessions Paper* ceased to be a publication aimed at a popular audience. By the end of the [eighteenth] century, it was being produced almost entirely with administrative purposes in mind."[48] (The series limped on throughout the nineteenth century, ceasing publication on the eve of the First World War.)

---

[45] He annotated many rulings on points of law, inserting a topic heading above or alongside the printed report, suggesting that he wanted to be able to find his way back to the report in future cases dealing with that topic; e.g., "Interested Witness," ibid. at 344; "Burglary," ibid. at 744; "Application to Put off Trial:" at 747; "Excise—19.G.2" (a statutory citation) at 991; "Murder—Duel," at 1033. Garrow sometimes underlined language from a ruling, e.g., at 1047, or inserted statutory citations, ibid. at 1059, 1070; or added a note about a subsequent case on point, ibid. at 1071.

Several of Garrow's notes improved upon the reporter's accounts of the trials. In the case of Kyrin Ryen, *OBSP* (Sept. 1784, #827), at 1146 (forging a will), Garrow expanded on the argument attributed to him in the report. "This objection [that is, the report of its objection that Garrow had taken at the trial] is miserably stated." He then gave his version, adding that in the subsequent "case of John Murray, December Sess[ions] 1784, I made a like objection. Lord Loughborough and the Recorder were of opinion that this offense might be committed in taking a false oath [remainder illegible from trimming of the page in binding]." Ibid. at 1146. The reference would have been to John Murray, OBSP (Dec. 1784, #198), at 222. (The published report in that case records neither Garrow's objection nor the ruling of the judges.) Alongside the report in Elizabeth Shaw, *OBSP* (Sept. 1784, #924), at 1219 (coining), Garrow explained the court's rationale, which the *Sessions Paper* omitted: "Mr. Recorder held this to be a fatal variance between the Record and Evidence, but the Witness [a thieftaker] as appeared by what followed mended his Testimony to ma[tch?] the fact charged." 1784 Chicago Volume, *supra* n. 44, at 1219.

Some of Garrow's entries have a purely diaristic tone. Having served as defense counsel for John Lucas, *OBSP* (May 1784, #540), at 736, who was acquitted in a burglary prosecution on a law ground, Garrow recorded in the margin the further adventures of his client: "Lucas was tried Feb[ruary] Sess[ions] 1785 for a Burglary in the House of Thomas Knott and convicted." 1784 Chicago Volume, *supra* n. 44, at 736. To the report of the trial of Lorentz Greenhome, *OBSP* (Sept. 1784, #818), at 1133 (highway robbery), in which Garrow served as defense counsel, he made a note about hot air of a different sort than normal at the Old Bailey. "During this Trial Mr. Lunardi passed over London in view of the Sessions house in a Gallery attached to a Balloon filled with inflammable Air—the first which ascended in England." 1784 Chicago Volume, *supra* n. 44, at 1135.

[46] George Cossans (alias George Teapot), *OBSP* (May 1785, #600), at 772, 780.

[47] Devereaux, "Fall," *supra* n. 7, text at nn. 39–43.

[48] Ibid., text between nn. 31–32.

The exceptional detail of the *Sessions Papers* of the 1780s presents interpretive problems of its own. When, for example, we find a burst of reported activity by counsel for prosecution and defense in those years,[49] are we seeing an increase in the level of lawyerization, or an illusion brought about by the improvement in the sources, or both? The quality of reporting in the *Sessions Papers* declined sharply after Hodgson. The accounts of individual trials became more compressed, and legal detail was again bleached out. For the two years beginning in December 1790 the *Sessions Papers* under Hodgson's immediate successor, Manoah Sibley, ceased reporting acquittals.[50] This experiment, reviving and intensifying the trend to minimize reports of acquittals that we noticed in the mid-1770s under Joseph Gurney, may have been a response to the concern expressed by some City officials that publishing details of successful defenses encouraged imitation and inspired strategies for defense perjury.[51] Of course, diminishing or eliminating coverage of acquittals, that is, of cases in which the activities of defense counsel were likely to have been most influential, severely impairs the value of the reports as historical sources for procedural and evidentiary developments in those years.

When I first began using the *Sessions Papers* in work published a quarter century ago, I cautioned that relying upon these problematic sources for the history of criminal procedure was "a perilous undertaking, which we would gladly avoid if superior sources availed us," but I concluded that "on the present state of our knowledge about the surviving sources, it has to be said that the [*Sessions Papers*] are probably the best accounts we shall ever have of what transpired in ordinary English criminal courts before the later eighteenth century."[52] Nothing has come to light in the interval to cause me to modify that assessment. The view from the *Sessions Papers*, however obstructed, is irresistible.

B. The Character Rule

Speaking about the proceedings in a criminal trial held in 1653 and reported in the *State Trials*, Stephen observed that "at this time it was not considered irregular to call witnesses to prove a prisoner's bad character

---

[49] *Supra* Ch. 3, text at n. 302.
[50] Devereaux presents some evidence that city officials, who by then were subsidizing the publication, had become concerned that the *Sessions Papers* were schooling potential criminal defendants in how to secure acquittals. Devereaux, "Fall," *supra* n. 7, text at n. 57.
[51] Ibid., text at n. 31.
[52] Langbein, "CTBL" 271.

in order to raise a presumption of his guilt."[53] Wigmore noticed a similar case from 1669,[54] but thought that the trials of John Hampden in 1684[55] and Henry Harrison in 1692[56] established the rule that has endured, disapproving the use of character evidence.

Hampden was prosecuted in King's Bench for the misdemeanor of seditious assembly. Defense counsel (allowed in misdemeanor) offered a witness to impeach the credibility of a prosecution witness, Lord Howard, on the asserted ground that Lord Howard was an atheist. The court refused to hear the witness, with one judge remarking that in a recent forgery prosecution the King's Bench had refused to allow the prosecution to "give evidence of any other forgeries . . . because we would not suffer any raking into men's course of life, to pick up evidence they cannot be prepared to answer to."[57] In the trial of Harrison, for murder, Chief Justice Holt refused to allow a prosecution witness to testify about other allegedly felonious conduct of the accused some three years before the homicide. Holt asked rhetorically, "Are you going to arraign his whole life? Away, away, that ought not to be; that is nothing to the matter."[58] In these seventeenth-century cases, therefore, the judges voiced concerns about whether evidence of character was material, and about whether such evidence unfairly surprised the witness. They did not raise the policy that is considered central to the rule of exclusion of character evidence in modern times, which is the concern that such evidence is unduly prejudicial to the accused,[59] because it distracts the jury from attention to the facts in the present case.

---

[53] 1 Stephen, *History* 368, discussing *R. v. Benjamin Faulconer*, 5 *St. Tr.* 323, 354–6 (Upper Bench 1653) (perjury).

[54] *R. v. Robert Hawkins*, 6 *St. Tr.* 921, 935, 949 (Buckingham Assizes 1669) (theft), discussed in 1 Wigmore, *Evidence* § 194, at 646 n. 1. As indicated in the table of abbreviations to this book, I cite Wigmore's treatise to the third edition, which was published in 1940, the last that he wrote. Later editors have updated the book for reference purposes; it is now undergoing an extensive revision under the general editorship of Professor Richard D. Friedman of the University of Michigan Law School.

[55] *R. v. John Hampden*, 9 *St. Tr.* 1053, 1103 (K.B. 1684) (sedition).

[56] *R. v. Henry Harrison*, 12 *St. Tr.* 833, 864, 874 (O.B. 1692) (murder) (Holt CJ, excluding a witness who would testify to alleged felonious conduct three years before the offense in question, asks, "Are you going to arraign his whole life?").

[57] 9 *St. Tr.* 1053, at 1103.

[58] *R. v. Henry Harrison*, 12 *St. Tr.* 833, 864 (O.B. 1692). Wigmore attributes to his report of the language from Holt that I quote above in text a further sentence that I do not find in the report: "How can he defend himself from charges of which he has no notice?" 1 Wigmore, *Evidence* § 194, at 647.

[59] 1 *McCormick on Evidence* § 186, at 649 (John W. Strong ed.) (5th edn. 1999) (2 vols.) [hereafter McCormick, *Evidence*] (character evidence "almost always has some probative value, but in many situations, the probative value is slight and the potential for prejudice large").

1. Old Bailey Practice

The *Sessions Papers* show us that the state of the law on using character evidence was far from being as settled as Wigmore thought. In October 1683 Elizabeth Hare was tried for coining; it "appear[ed] that she had been an Old Offender, and [had been] pardoned about Three Years since, the Jury found her Guilty."[60] In 1684, the year of the decision in *Hampden's Case*, which Wigmore saw as the turning point in disapproving the use of character evidence, we find Old Bailey cases in which character evidence was not only admitted, but was said to have been central to the outcome. In July 1684 Thomas Brown, charged with the theft of a silver tankard from a pub, blamed somebody else, "but he having been burnt in the Hand before, and other bad Circumstances against him, he . . . was found Guilty."[61] In December of that year Anne Gardener, charged with obtaining silk by fraud, denied it, "but being known to be a notorious cheat and shoplift, she was found Guilty . . . ."[62] At the next sessions, in January 1685, Abraham Biggs was convicted of burglary; "having been a frequent inhabiter of Newgate [Prison], and [his explanation of how he obtained the goods being] looked upon as an artifice, he was found guilty . . . ."[63] Across the next thirty years the *Sessions Papers* report a steady stream of such cases.

Sometimes, as in the case of Thomas Brown just noticed, the report says that the accused had been previously burned in the hand or branded on the thumb. Branding was a step that occurred as part of the system of mitigated sanctioning called "benefit of clergy," by which a person convicted of a less serious crime was spared capital punishment.[64] In 1685 William Sims, charged with a theft, "appearing to be an old Offender, and Burnt in the Hand, having no Evidence in his Defense, was thereupon brought in Guilty by the Jury."[65] At the trial of Samuel Presby, tried in 1685 for stealing £36 worth of cloth, there was evidence that he had admitted the offense. "It farther appearing, he had formerly been Branded in his Hand, he was brought in Guilty."[66] John Thacker and two others, accused in 1687 of stealing pewter plates that were discovered in the their lodgings, gave "a slender account of themselves, and [two of them] having been formerly branded in the Hand, they were all found Guilty."[67]

---

[60] Elizabeth Hare, *OBSP* (Oct. 1683), at 4.
[61] Thomas Brown, *OBSP* (July 1684), at 4.
[62] Anne Gardener, *OBSP* (Dec. 1684), at 5.
[63] Abraham Biggs, *OBSP* (Jan. 1685), at 3.
[64] I have provided a summary account of the origins and eighteenth-century mechanics of benefit of clergy in Langbein, "Ryder" 37–43.
[65] William Sims, *OBSP* (July 1685), at 1.
[66] Samuel Presby, *OBSP* (Oct. 1685), at 2.
[67] John Thacker *et al.*, *OBSP* (Feb. 1687), at 3.

A defendant who was branded on the thumb had been tried and convicted of a felony, but excused from capital punishment as a first-time offender, under the rubric of benefit of clergy. Branding was an afflictive sanction, because it was applied to the offender's body, and also a dignitary sanction, because by stigmatizing the convict it exposed him to social ostracism. Branding also meant to prevent the convict from pleading benefit of clergy again should he be convicted of another felony. In an era before centralized criminal record-keeping, branding caused the convict to bear physical evidence upon himself that he had already taken advantage of his once-in-a-lifetime privilege to invoke the doctrine of benefit of clergy.[68] But benefit of clergy operated in arrest of sanction, not verdict. Technically, the question of whether the accused was disqualified to claim benefit of clergy because he had already claimed it for another offense should have been none of the trial jury's business. That question should have arisen after verdict, when the judge went to impose sentence for the new felony. Because the convict carried upon his body in an exposed place physical evidence of the former conviction,[69] it may have been hard to keep the jury from observing it or being told about it. Yet the judges could have devised, had they cared to, a routine for keeping defendants' hands out of jurors' sight. The recurrent *Sessions Paper* reports that juries regarded branding as salient when convicting a defendant of the new offense seem to show that no effort was being made to keep this information from them.

Old Bailey juries routinely received testimony about the accused's bad character in cases that did not involve branding. The *Sessions Paper* for May 1696 reports the trial of Hannah Westcot, who was charged with stealing pewter plates. "[T]he Constable of the Parish appear[ed] against her, and gave evidence that he took the Plates in her custody, and that she was a person of bad life and conversation; and having little to say in her

---

[68] Even then, "[t]he burned thumb was not . . . a legal record; it warned the court officers to counterplead the prayer of clergy by producing the record of the previous conviction." John Baker, "Criminal Courts and Procedure at Common Law 1550–1800, in *Crime in England: 1550–1800*, at 15, 41–2 (J. S. Cockburn ed.) (1977).

In an Old Bailey prosecution in 1717 for murder, testimony that the defendant had been previously branded was received. Since the offense was not clergyable, the testimony must have been admitted as evidence of the accused's character. "[A] record was produced in Court of his having been Convicted at Hertford Assizes, and burnt in the Hand, for robbing the Lady Butterfield; and several persons came many miles to do him and themselves justice, in ridding themselves of so troublesome and dangerous a Neighbor." Joseph Sill, *OBSP* (Feb.–Mar. 1717), at 2–3 (murder). Sill was convicted.

[69] For a few years, from 1699 to 1706, branding was applied to the cheek rather than the thumb, as an afflictive sanction designed both to maim and to shame the offender. See Beattie, *Policing* 330–4. For this cohort of old offenders, concealing the brand would have been impractical.

own defense, she was found Guilty."[70] At the next sessions John Cope was prosecuted for stealing a coat from a parked coach. The *Sessions Paper* explains that, in addition to the testimony of an eyewitness, the defendant "having been in Bridewell [Prison] for a former offense, he was found Guilty of the Felony."[71] Cases of this sort continue into the early eighteenth century. Thomas Dickson, charged with burglary in 1707, "could say little in his Defense, and being an old Offender, the Jury found him guilty of the Indictment."[72] Against another group of burglary defendants in that year, "the evidence being very clear, and the Prisoners Old Offenders, the Jury found them all Guilty . . . ."[73] John Read, charged at the same sessions with stealing a horse, "could say little in his defense, and being an old Horse Stealer, the Jury found him Guilty."[74] (Since horse-stealing was a capital offense not subject to benefit of clergy, it was unlikely that Read had actually been convicted of it in the past. The evidence being summarized in the *Sessions Paper* is likely, therefore, to have been a witness's allegation that Read had stolen other horses.) Three men accused of stealing shop goods were convicted in December 1708; "being old Offenders, and saying little for themselves, the Jury found them all guilty of the Indictment."[75]

The *Sessions Papers* continued to report cases of this sort into the 1710s;[76] six are reported in the 1714 year.[77] Thereafter they became quite rare. Because the *Sessions Papers* were becoming more detailed in these years, I think it is reasonable to infer from the decline that the rule against

---

[70] Hannah Westcot, *OBSP* (May 1686), at 4.

[71] John Cope, *OBSP* (July 1686), at 4.

[72] Thomas Dickson, *OBSP* (Apr. 1707), at 1 (burglary).

[73] John Hall *et al.*, (Dec. 1707), at 2, 3 (burglary).

[74] John Read, *OBSP* (Dec. 1707), at 3.

[75] Joseph Hatfied *et al.*, *OBSP* (Dec. 1708), at 3.

[76] E.g., Peter Cartwright, *OBSP* (May 1711), at 2 (highway robbery) ("being an old Offender"); Josiah Wilson, *OBSP* (May 1711), at 2 (breaking and entering) ("being an old Offender"); Alice Mills, *OBSP* (Jan. 1712), at 1 (theft of shop goods) ("she being an old Offender"); John Appleton, *OBSP* (Feb. 1712, at 2 (theft) ("being an old Offender (though but a lad)").

[77] Anthony Grey, *OBSP* (Apr. 1714), at 1, 2 (robbery) ("he was known to be an old Offender, having received Her Majesty's most Gracious Pardon but last summer[,] whereupon he was found guilty of the indictment"); Elizabeth Boyle, *OBSP* (Apr. 1714), at 5 (theft from dwelling house, her second trial of the sessions) ("She had nothing material to offer in her Defense, and is known to be a very notorious Offender; so she was found Guilty of this Indictment also"); Katherine Kirk, *OBSP* (May 1714), at 2 (theft) ("She denied herself to be the Person, and said she was taken by mistake, another being accused before; but there was nothing of Truth in that, and she was known to be an old Offender, whereupon she was found guilty of the Indictment"); Mary Skinner, *OBSP* (May 1714), at 3 (theft) ("She pretended the Prosecutor lent them to her; but she appeared to be an old Offender, and was found guilty of Felony"); James Powell, *OBSP* (July 1714), at 2 (burglary) ("known to be an old Offender"); William Dyer, *OBSP* (July 1714), at 4 (two indictments for burglary, theft) ("He was known to be an old Offender, and found Guilty of both Indictments").

character evidence was finally taking hold at the Old Bailey about 1715. Thus, even though the rule and something of its rationale were stated clearly enough in the cases of 1684 and 1692 on which Wigmore relied for the claim that the character rule was established by that time, the Old Bailey sources show persistent inattention to the supposed rule in the most important criminal trial court in England for decades thereafter. Indeed, even after the rule against character evidence seems to have taken hold, the *Sessions Papers* show lapses. I have noticed instances of seeming departure from the rule in trials held in 1717,[78] 1721,[79] and 1726.[80] In 1732 at the trial of John Waller for perjury (the prosecution arising from the first of the great reward scandals, discussed above in Chapter 3), the underclerk of the Norfolk assize circuit was allowed to testify about inquiries he made after Waller's activities fell under suspicion following a prosecution that Waller brought at Cambridge. The assize judge "ordered me to inquire into his Character. I inquired of a Gentleman at Thetford. 'Waller,' says he, 'why he's the wiliest Fellow living. He makes a Trade of swearing away Men's Lives for the Sake of the Reward granted for convicting Robbers.' "[81] The next year, in a crown witness prosecution at the Old Bailey, someone identified as "A Turnkey" was allowed to testify that the defendant had been a crown witness (hence a confessed but unprosecuted felon): "[H]e was an Evidence last Summer against 5 young fellows, who were all capitally convicted, but were afterwards transported."[82] As late as February 1743, in the trial of John Wyth for stealing iron goods, the prosecutor was apparently allowed to testify without disapproval that "I understand the Prisoner has been five Times in New Prison for these Practices."[83] (Such testimony also alerts us to the failure to enforce any rule against hearsay, a subject discussed later in this chapter.) As late as December 1747 we find a report that an accused pickpocket "was known to be an old offender."[84]

Generalizing from these cases, we may say that it appears that enforcement of the character rule at the Old Bailey was indifferent for the thirty

---

[78] Jacob Shoemaker, *OBSP* (Jan. 1717), at 2 (fraud, pawning a brass cup washed with silver, vouching it to be Sterling) ("there were other Testimonials of the like Practices committed by him; so the Jury found him Guilty").

[79] Richard Browne, *OBSP* (July 1721), at 2 (theft) ("The evidence being very positive, and he being an old Offender, the Jury found him Guilty").

[80] William Marjoram, *OBSP* (Oct. 1726), at 2 (privately stealing from the person) ("The Prisoner was an old Offender, he had been an Evidence against Blewit and his Gang, and had not been a Week out of Gaol when he was taken for this Fact. The jury found him Guilty . . .").

[81] John Waller, *OBSP* (May 1732, #89), at 146, 148.

[82] William Norman, *OBSP* (Feb. 1733, #58) at 71 (breaking and entering, theft from a dwelling house).

[83] John Wyth, *OBSP* (Feb. 1743, #151), at 91.

[84] William Clark, *OBSP* (Dec. 1747, #37), at 13.

years from 1684 to 1714, and not fail-safe for another thirty-odd years. Thus, it seems that in this formative era of the law of evidence, even after a consensus had formed that a practice such as admitting character evidence was unwise, individual judges retained for a time some discretion to depart from such a "rule"; or else departures occurred without a theory of justification, simply because there was as yet no effective means of remedy against a trial judge's "error." Unless defense counsel had been engaged (and we recall that defense counsel appears to have been relatively uncommon until the 1780s[85]) there was nobody to detect, deter, or protest error. In this sense, although the early rules of criminal evidence developed without counsel, the presence of counsel may have been needed to complete the work of transforming rules of practice into rules of law.

2. The Rebuttal Exception

The rule against character evidence was subject to an important limitation, which survives to the present,[86] and which was already well developed in the Old Bailey sources of the mid-eighteenth century. The defendant was permitted, indeed encouraged, to offer witnesses to support his good character, but if he did, he opened himself to rebuttal witnesses testifying about his bad character. Thus, the rule against character evidence as finally shaped became and has remained a defensive option, not a prohibition. "[T]he prosecutor cannot enter into the defendant's character, unless the defendant enable him to do so, by his calling witnesses to support it . . . ."[87] The rebuttal exception shifted from the prosecution to the defendant the power to decide whether or not the court would consider prosecution evidence of the defendant's character.[88] Because there was such pressure on defendants to adduce evidence of good character,[89] the rebuttal exception materially diminished the reach of the character rule.

---

[85] *Supra* Ch. 3, text at n. 302.

[86] See 1 McCormick, *Evidence, supra* n. 59, § 191, at 673.

[87] Leach's formulation in 4 Hawkins, *PC* § 206, at 457 (Thomas Leach ed.) (7th edn. 1795).

[88] In Continental criminal procedure, by contrast, the court inquires about the background and circumstances of the accused at the outset of the criminal trial, without regard to the preferences of prosecution or defense. I have discussed the German practice in John H. Langbein, *Comparative Criminal Procedure: Germany* 71–2, 76–7 (1977).

[89] For example, in a case in 1784 the trial judge told Mary Higgins, accused of the theft of shop goods, what the expectations were: "Have you anybody to speak for you, to give you the character of an honest woman?" "I have not a friend in the world," she answered, "my husband is a tailor, he was gone into the country to look for work." Replied the judge: "If you were an honest woman, there are people that know you, you might have a character[.]" Mary Higgins, OBSP (Mar. 1784, #454), at 623, 627.

We find prosecution counsel insisting on the rebuttal exception in several mid-century Old Bailey cases. In a smuggling case tried in 1748 crown counsel is reported moving the court: "As the Prisoner has entered into his character, I beg leave to call one witness,"[90] who then testified that "the character he bore was as a smuggler."[91] In a forgery case in 1761 prosecution counsel said: "As the prisoner has made his character part of his defense, we have a right to call witnesses to his character likewise,"[92] which was done. In 1767, in a trial for theft, prosecution counsel invoked the rebuttal exception, saying: "As the prisoner has called to his character, I have a witness here that can give an account of the prisoner."[93] We find other instances in which character evidence was used in rebuttal settings, although the sources do not spell out that the evidence was heard on the basis of the rebuttal rule.[94] After Jervis Rhodes, who was tried for highway robbery in 1729, adduced character witnesses in his behalf, the *Sessions Paper* tells us: "An Officer in Court [perhaps a constable] being called by the Prosecutor, deposed, That he knew nothing of the Prisoner himself, but when he has been towards Covent Garden, where the Prisoner was known, he had heard People say, as the Prisoner passed along, 'There goes Jervis Rhodes, the greatest Rogue in England.' The Jury found him guilty of the Indictment. Death."[95] (We see again the astonishing insensitivity to hearsay evidence, which will be discussed below.)

When character evidence was allowed under this exception, it was limited to general expressions of opinion, as opposed to evidence of particular past acts.[96] This subrule against particulars responded to the concerns about materiality and lack of notice that we saw in Chief Justice Holt's early formulation of the rationale for the rule against character evidence. We see that rationale expressed from the bench in the trial of John Tomkins in 1734, accused of breaking and entering and of stealing a large sum of money. A witness, apparently testifying for the prosecution in rebuttal, is recorded saying, "I convicted the prisoner 12 or 14 years ago for stealing a Pair of Silk Stockings." The judge stopped him, saying, "You must not speak to Particulars, for it is not to be supposed that the Prisoner is prepared to answer them."[97] We see the rule against particulars some

---

[90] Samuel Childers and Robert Scott, *OBSP* (Jan. 1748, #103–4), at 70, 73.

[91] Ibid. at 74.

[92] Nicholas Campbell, *OBSP* (Jan. 1761, #66), at 72, 85.

[93] William T. Gilliard, *OBSP* (Feb. 1767, # 187), at 133, 135.

[94] E.g., John Smith, *OBSP* (Jan. 1735, #53), at 34, 40 (theft) ("some Soldiers came after him one Day, and said he belonged to Col. Churchill's Regiment, and was a Deserter"); John Busk and Eleanor Wingfield, *OBSP* (Feb. 1736, ##50–51), at 78 ("I know Willford has a very ill Character, and has been tried before this, at Kingston Assizes"); Robert Rhodes, *OBSP* (Apr.–May 1742, #38), at 80 (forging a sailor's will).

[95] *OBSP* (Dec. 1729), at 24.   [96] 3 Wigmore, *Evidence* § 979, at 532–8.

[97] John Tomkins, *OBSP* (Dec. 1734, #23), at 13.

years later in the case of an accused smuggler, James Watling, tried in 1748. Defense counsel called one Samuel Barber to impeach the character of a prosecution witness, John Leader. "Pray what character does [Leader] bear?" defense counsel asked Barber. "He bears a very bad character, with respect to stealing poultry and other things," Barber replied. Prosecution counsel at once objected, effectively rephrasing defense counsel's question: "You must not go into that. What is his general character?" Barber replied, "It is very bad."[98] In 1783 in the trial of a defendant charged with stealing fifty pounds of wood, prosecution counsel undertook to cross-examine the defendant's character witness. "Did you ever hear of the prisoner stealing wood?," he asked. Defense counsel interrupted, saying, "That ought not to be asked." The trial judge agreed: "That is an improper question."[99]

Because the rule against character evidence did not restrain the defendant's option to raise doubts about the character of the prosecutor and other prosecution witnesses, it offered no obstacle[100] to the practice of putting the victim's character in issue in prosecutions for rape. Rape cases were sometimes reported in exceptional detail in the *Sessions Papers*, especially in the early decades of the series when the publishers were still cultivating a popular market, doubtless on account of the appeal to the salacious. In a case prosecuted in 1735 the victim, a young girl,[101] claimed to have been a virgin, and to have contracted venereal disease from the attack.[102] The defendant's half-brother was allowed to testify regarding

---

[98] James Watling, *OBSP* (May 1748, #291), at 186, 189 (smuggling). Defense counsel continued to press, eliciting from Barber that Leader had been committed to prison.

[99] Francis Hall, *OBSP* (Sept. 1783, #667), at 893, 896.

[100] Rebuttal character witnesses were allowed on her behalf, of course, and awareness of that played a role in defense counsel's tactical decision about whether to malign her. In the rape prosecution of Daniel Lackey, *OBSP* (Apr. 1757, #187), at 156, prosecution counsel served notice that "[w]e have several witnesses to [the victim's] character; if they attack that, we shall call them." Defense counsel replied: "We don't intend to attack it." Ibid. at 166.

[101] Edward Jones, *OBSP* (Dec. 1735, #84), at 36. Sexual intercourse with a girl under the age of 10 was made a nonclergyable felony in the sixteenth century, clarifying earlier legislation. 18 Eliz. 1, c. 7 (1576).

[102] The significance of this fact pattern is developed in a paper by Antony E. Simpson, "Vulnerability and the Age of Female Consent: Legal Innovation and Its Effect on Prosecutions for Rape in Eighteenth-Century London," in *Sexual Underworlds of the Enlightenment* 181 (G. S. Rousseau and Roy Porter eds.) (1987). Simpson identifies fifty-seven rape cases that were prosecuted at the Old Bailey in the years 1730–1830 that involved victims under 10. Ibid. at 188 and table 1. The dark figure of unreported or otherwise unprosecuted cases must have been materially larger. I summarize a few of these child rape cases from *Sessions Paper* accounts, *infra* nn. 276–7; another, in which the defense adduced evidence that the child had not contracted venereal disease, was Thomas Slade, *OBSP* (Sept. 1734, #6), at 174. For another, from 1758, in Mansfield's assize notebooks, see 2 Oldham, *Mansfield* 1397–9. Simpson compares the quantity of these cases arising at the Old Bailey with the materially lower figures that he finds on the assize circuits, concluding that child rape cases "seem[] to have been primarily a Metropolitan phenomenon." Simpson, *supra*, at 192. Further, Simpson points to evidence that the levels of venereal disease were much

the victim that, "I have heard she is a loose Girl, and kept company with a Barber that was Poxed [that is, who suffered from venereal disease]." Mary Proctor, another defense witness, testified that "I have heard that she is a wicked vile base lying Girl, that she used to lie out till twelve or one in the Morning, and that a Barber gave her the Pox."[103] The jury acquitted the defendant; what role this (hearsay) character evidence played in the outcome we cannot say. (I shall have more to say about rape cases, in connection with the steady use of hearsay evidence about the victim.)

3. Delayed Application to Magistrates

The *Session Paper* cases disclose a notable and unexpected departure from the rule against character evidence. Until about 1770 the Old Bailey exhibited a seemingly unrestrained tolerance for character evidence against the accused emanating from the magistrate who had conducted the pretrial examination (that is, the Marian JP, especially in his Middlesex iteration as the court JP). The Old Bailey received such character evidence both in cases in which the magistrate narrated it, and in cases in which third persons testified about the magistrate's pretrial investigation. At the trial of Mary Eagan in 1734, who was charged with murder for a homicide that occurred during some horseplay in a pub, the JP testified: "She has a most infamous Character . . . . I have had several Informations against [her and certain companions]; they make it their common practice to lie in Highgate Lane, and expose their Bodies to all comers for a Penny or Two pence a time."[104]

Sir Thomas DeVeil, who served as court JP from 1729 until his death in 1746,[105] routinely sat with the bench[106] at Old Bailey trials. The reports of

higher in London than in the provinces, and he directs attention to the folk notion, said by a contemporary to be widespread "'among the lower people, both male and female, that if they have [sexual] commerce with a sound person, they will get rid of the disease.'" Ibid. at 193.

Simpson's suggestion is that the high level of child rapes in London and its environs is to be explained, at least in part, as the result of infected culprits seeking cure. Simpson's essay derives from his Ph.D. thesis, Antony E. Simpson, "Masculinity and Control: The Prosecution of Sex Offenses in Eighteenth-Century London" (unpub. Ph.D. thesis, New York University 1984).

[103] *OBSP* (Dec. 1735, #84), at 37–8.
[104] Mary Eager, *OBSP* (Sept. 1734, #4), at 170, 171.
[105] DeVeil is discussed *supra*, Ch. 3, text at nn. 48, 183, 190.
[106] DeVeil held office in the Middlesex commission of the peace. Beattie reports that as late as 1717 the Middlesex JPs were not named in the Old Bailey jail delivery commission, and thus were not seated on the bench, which they resented. Beattie, *Policing* 13–14, 16. I do not know when the convention against Middlesex justices eased; John Beattie has suggested to me that the circumlocution about the "Gentleman upon the Bench" indicates that DeVeil was not still not formally seated ex officio in his capacity as a Middlesex justice.

cases sometimes identify him speaking about his role in the pretrial, and in other cases he is identified simply as "a Gentleman upon the Bench." DeVeil appears to have had complete license to disparage the character of an accused (or anyone else) without regard to the rule against character evidence. At the trial of Marmaduke Bignell and Richard Ford for stealing money from a customer in Bignell's pub, the victim–prosecutor (doubtless with advance connivance) was reported "desiring a Gentleman upon the Bench might be asked if he knew the Prisoners." The "Gentleman," probably DeVeil, launched into the following screed (riddled with hearsay and irrelevancy):

[H]e deposed, That he knew them both, and that their characters were the very worst, in all the City and Liberty of Westminster. That the House Bignell kept (the Rose) was a notorious, infamous, thieving House; that he had known both the Prisoners many Years; that they had been brought before him several Times, upon Charges for Felony; that the Woman he called his Wife, one Rose Malone, was an infamous Person, both he and she having been several Times charged with Felonies, which they afterwards compounded; that Rose Malone had been tried for Felony, and that the House they kept was the worst House in Westminster, except that which was kept by Eastmead, Bignell's Master.[107]

In this case the court allowed the "Gentleman" to ignore the rule against character evidence and its subrule against particulars. Two sessions later, in a pickpocketing case, the "Gentleman upon the Bench deposed . . . that he knew [the defendant] to be a most notorious Pickpocket, and that both she and her Husband had been several Times committed for Felony, which they afterwards had compounded."[108] In the case of James Hanns, tried for highway robbery in 1743, "[o]ne of the prosecutors desired Col. DeVeil," who had testified earlier in the trial about the recovery of the stolen goods, "to give an account of" a defense witness named Newberry whose testimony gave Hanns an alibi. DeVeil replied that "[h]e was sorry he was asked that Question, but he was obliged to declare that Mr. Newberry is a Person of a most infamous Character, and not to be believed in any Court in the World."[109]

In other cases the tolerance for character evidence from or associated with the magistrates took the form of trial testimony (often hearsay) about what had been said at the pretrial hearing. Ann Serjeant was charged in 1743 with picking the pockets of Robert Morgan in a pub. At trial Morgan testified how he had a constable arrest her and take her "before Col.

[107] Marmaduke Bignell and Richard Ford, *OBSP* (Feb.–Mar. 1740, ##159–60), at 89, 91. The same "Gentleman . . . declared farther, that the Characters of several of the Prisoners' Witnesses were no better than their's . . . [and] that Mills, in particular, had been several Times brought before him for Felony." Ibid. at 91.

[108] Margaret Newel, *OBSP* (Apr. 1740, #197), at 105, 107.

[109] James Hanns, *OBSP* (Sept. 1743, #379), at 221, 228.

DeVeil [where] . . . there was a Woman, who said the Prisoner was a very honest Woman; but the Colonel said, he had seen [Serjeant] at least eight or nine Times,"[110] meaning that she had been brought before him recurrently on other charges. The next year, in the trial of Samuel Goodman for highway robbery, the husband of the prosecuting victim testified that at the pretrial hearing the JP recognized Goodman, saying, "Oh, my old Friend, where have you been all this while; what, ain't you hanged yet?"[111] Goodman was represented by defense counsel, who cross-examined the victim and her husband about their reward motive in bringing the charges, but who is not reported to have voiced any objection to the prejudicial character hearsay related by the husband.

In the 1760s and into the year 1770 we find more of these cases, with the evidence of bad character emanating from pretrial proceedings before Sir John Fielding, the court JP of the day. Edward Hull was tried in 1767 for stealing shop goods. Joseph Levi, who had seized him at the scene, told the trial court of having taken Hull "before Sir John Fielding. He was well known there. Sir John's clerk said, 'you had the luck to escape last sessions, but you will not the next.' "[112] Roger Prat, tried for commercial fraud in 1770, had been the subject of a pretrial hearing before Fielding. At the Old Bailey trial the prosecutor testified about the proceedings before Fielding. "There were about thirty-six of us with these complaints against him . . . . [T]here were for what I know a hundred people in court that he had got goods of in that manner."[113] At the trial of John Martin for burglary in 1768 the victim testified that at the pretrial hearing before Fielding, Martin "wanted to be admitted an evidence; and said he would make very great discoveries. Sir John said [that Martin] was an old offender and would not admit him."[114] (We see in this case not only the character hearsay from the pretrial hearing being reported to the trial court, but evidence of what the accused confessed in a failed attempt to escape being prosecuted by being made a crown witness. Cases involving admissions made in such circumstances form an important part of the history of the confession rule, discussed below in this chapter.)

Cases that allowed JPs or persons who had dealt with JPs to testify about the accused's character in disregard of the rule against such evidence appear to die out after 1770. I am unable to say with confidence on what doctrinal basis the cases tolerating such evidence until 1770

---

[110] Ann Serjeant, *OBSP* (June–July 1743, #344), at 207. She was acquitted.
[111] Samuel Goodman, *OBSP* (Dec. 1744, #69), at 34, 36.
[112] Edward Hull, *OBSP* (June 1767, #282), at 181.
[113] Roger Prat, *OBSP* (Jan. 1770, #127), at 100, 101.
[114] John Martin, *OBSP* (Dec. 1768, #13), at 7, 8. For another such case, in which it was reported to the trial court that Fielding would not make the accused a crown witness because the accused "was an old offender," see Moses Lyons, *OBSP* (June 1770, #385), at 231, 232 (burglary).

rested. It is possible but unlikely that these cases instance some then declared but now lost exception to the character rule, excusing testimony about proceedings before the JPs from the reach of the rule. Mention of such a formal exception would have found its way into the juristic literature, but we do not in fact find such a doctrine in the law reports or the treatises.[115] It will be seen in connection with the hearsay rule that for long years after the rule was formulated, the courts exhibited a broad tolerance for hearsay evidence arising from testimony about how an accused was detected or detained, evidence of a sort that I call "pursuit hearsay." I have wondered whether there was a similar notion of pursuit character evidence.

In cases in which the testifying JP was the repeat player DeVeil, who routinely attended Old Bailey sessions, and who probably reviewed the trial calendar with the judges in advance of trial, it would have been awkward for the judges to exclude his testimony. Indeed, in some of these cases in which DeVeil spoke to the bad character of the accused, he may not in the technical sense have been testifying—that is, he may not have spoken in the capacity of a witness sworn for the trial; rather, he may simply have volunteered from the sidelines or from the bench. But no such explanation is available for the cases in which third parties testified at the trial about what the JP had said in the pretrial. I am inclined to think, therefore, that until 1770 or so the trial judges exercised a residual discretion not to enforce the character rule in circumstances in which the court thought the character evidence to be particularly authoritative.

To summarize: The rule against character evidence, although formulated in the 1680s, needed three decades or so to take hold in the most important English criminal court, where notable indications of nonenforcement persist into the mid-1710s. An enduring exception for rebuttal character evidence was recognized, and a puzzling exception for character evidence arising from pretrial proceedings lingered until about 1770. But these lapses aside, from early in the eighteenth century testimony about the accused having been an old offender and the like receded from Old Bailey trials, sparing the accused from the risk of prejudice inherent in such evidence.

The rule against character evidence was a safeguard for criminal defendants that predated the lawyerization of the felony trial. It follows that the initiative must have come from the judges, rather than in response to demands from defense counsel. In the years following, when the judges created the other two distinctively criminal rules of evidence, the corroboration rule for accomplice testimony and the confession rule, they would

---

[115] Even though other aspects of the use of pretrial statements at trial are discussed in the treatises, e.g., 2 Hawkins, PC 429–30.

be following a path that they had already developed with the rule against character evidence—excluding probative information from the jury for the ostensible purpose of enhancing the reliability of the verdict.

C. The Corroboration Rule

The corroboration rule (also called the accomplice rule) was a judicially developed safeguard for cases involving the testimony of crown witnesses. The workings of the crown witness system have been described in Chapter 3. An apprehended criminal was excused from prosecution in exchange for testifying against former confederates. Because the crown witness saved his neck by agreeing to convict others, he testified under a potent incentive to commit perjury. I have explained in Chapter 3 why I think that the judges' alarm about that danger was one of the driving forces that motivated their decision in the 1730s to allow felony defendants to have the assistance of counsel in probing prosecution evidence at trial.

The corroboration rule was another response to the danger of perjured crown witness testimony. The judges understood that allowing defense counsel to cross-examine the crown witness was hardly a foolproof remedy against a careful and determined perjurer; and in any event, many defendants would have been too poor to have been able to afford counsel. Defense counsel was meant to bring the skills of professional cross-examination to bear on the crown witness, and thus to probe his testimony for falsehood. The corroboration rule, by contrast, undertook to identify a particular subset of crown witness cases—those with no other evidence of the defendant's culpability—as too problematic for the jury to be allowed to convict.

1. Exclusion or Mere Caution?

Wigmore thought that the corroboration rule dated from 1780s, the period when it appeared in the published law reports.[116] Moreover, he insisted that it "amount[ed] to no rule of evidence, but merely to a *counsel of caution* given by the judge to the jury," which the jury "might or might not regard . . . ."[117] Wigmore was wrong on both points. The corroboration rule came into force in the 1740s, not the 1780s, and as a rule of exclusion, not a mere caution. The rule of caution that Wigmore encountered in the law reports

---

[116] 7 Wigmore, *Evidence* § 2056, at 313 and n. 3 (corroboration rule implemented at "the end of" the eighteenth century).
[117] Ibid. at 315 (emphasis original).

of the 1780s embodied what amounted to an overruling of the earlier rule of exclusion.

Although judicial disquiet about the dangers of crown witness testimony goes back at least to Hale (d. 1676),[118] and there are occasional cases in which doubt about the credibility of a particular uncorroborated crown witness prosecution figured in a jury's decision to acquit,[119] it seems clear from the *Sessions Papers* that into the year 1744 no corroboration rule was being applied in the Old Bailey.[120] In that year we find four reasonably well-reported cases, two each from January[121] and

---

[118] Hale voiced the concern that would lead the courts to develop the corroboration rule, saying that "it would be hard to take away the life of any person upon such a witness, that swears to save his own, and yet confesseth himself guilty of so great a crime, unless there be also very considerable circumstances, which may give the greater credit to what he swears." 1 Hale, *HPC* 305.

[119] E.g., Simon Jacobs, *OBSP* (Oct. 1722), at 3, 4 (breaking and entering with intent to commit burglary) ("There being no Evidence against the prisoner but Lock [the crown witness], who was one of a Scandalous Character, the Jury acquitted the prisoner"); Susan Bean and Christian Smith, *OBSP* (Dec. 1731), at 3, 4 ("There being no Evidence to affect the Prisoners but that of Bess Willoughby, the jury acquitted them").

[120] Crown witness prosecutions before 1744 resulting in conviction, in which no evident corroboration appears from the *Sessions Paper* accounts, include:

(1) Peter Cartwright, OBSP (May 1711), at 2 (highway robbery). "Jewell, a Person concerned in the Fact ... plainly proving both [robberies] upon the Prisoner, and he being an old Offender, the Jury found him guilty ...."

(2) Stephen Nott, *OBSP* (Sept. 1714) at 1 (theft of four geese). "The Witness was one concerned in the Robbery, who swore, That the Prisoner and he and another, lifted up a Board of the Prosecutor's Stall, and took the Geese ...."

(3) Mary D'Arbieau, *OBSP* (Apr. 1722), at 5 (burglary). The accomplice "deposed that himself, the prisoner, and" another committed the burglary, but "the Truth of the Fact entirely depending on [the crown witness'] Evidence, the Jury found her guilty of Felony only." Ibid. Thus, in this instance, the jury appeared to have doubts about convicting on uncorroborated accomplice evidence, which were resolved by returning a partial verdict. She was convicted of mere theft rather than burglary, with the result, ibid. at 6, that she was transported rather than hanged.

(4) Thomas Smith, *OBSP* (May 1722), at 5 (misprinted as 6) (burglary). "William Falkner deposed, that the prisoner and himself did the Fact." "The prisoner said in his Defense, that he never was concerned in any Robbery, and that [Jonathan] Wild and Falkner spited him, and swore they'd hang him. Guilty." Regarding Jonathan Wild, see *supra* Ch. 3, text at nn. 222-3, 258-62.

(5) William Cady, *OBSP* (May 1738, #34), at 95–6 (highway robbery). The accomplice, one Stephen Horsenail, offered the only testimony of Cady's guilt. The case was a reward-driven prosecution organized by the thieftaker Joseph Barnes, who testified about going to Bristol to arrest Cady.

[121] Thomas Talbot and Patrick Gaffney, *OBSP* (Jan. 1744, ##104–5), at 43–4 (theft of a wig from a shop); Joseph Isaacs, *OBSP* (Jan. 1744, #116), at 50–2 (burglary). In the former case, the *Sessions Paper* report takes the trouble to record that there was suspicion about the testimony of the crown witness. An asterisked footnote to the account of the testimony by the crown witness John Hawkins draws attention to an inconsistency between what Hawkins said about having participated with the two defendants in the theft on the evening of 29 Nov. 1743, and Hawkins' testimony as crown witness in an earlier prosecution at the same sessions, at which Hawkins had said that "he did not know he committed any other robbery that night." Ibid. at 43.

May,[122] in which uncorroborated accomplice testimony seems to have been sufficient to convict.

An exchange between crown witness and accused at one of the January 1744 trials highlights the brutal dynamic of betrayal that drove crown witness prosecutions. Joseph Isaacs, tried for burglary, complained about the crown witness. "You do this to save your own life and take away mine. Pray, my Lord, enquire into his character." The crown witness replied, without reported objection or comment from the court: "Your character is like mine, I have proved myself a rogue and so have you, for you were an evidence [in two other cases], so you cannot brag of your honesty any more than I can of mine."[123]

Suddenly, in December 1744, the *Sessions Paper* reports three acquittals in which the only disclosed ground was want of corroboration. At the trial of James Leekey and William Robinson for the theft of silver and clothing from a dwelling house, their alleged accomplice, Joseph Uptebake, testified about how the three of them stole and fenced the loot. No other evidence bearing on the culpability of the defendants is disclosed. The report concludes: "There being no other evidence upon this indictment but the accomplice, the prisoners were acquitted."[124] Next, Edward and John Hill were tried for highway robbery on the accomplice testimony of Joseph Waters. "The Prosecutor not being posi- tive to either of the Prisoners, and there being no other proof against them, but the evidence of the accomplice, they were acquitted."[125] In the third case it is reported: "There being no other evidence but the accom- plices, the prisoners were Acquitted."[126]

In each of the three cases the report indicates that the want of corrobo- ration caused the acquittal, but because these are summary rather than verbatim reports, they do not disclose precisely how the corroboration rule was formulated or applied. The verdicts in these cases could have

---

[122] Robert Hodges *et al.*, OBSP (May 1744, ##244–5), at 107 (theft of goods from anchored vessels; receiving); Robert Rockett, OBSP (May 1744, #273), at 126–9 (highway robbery). Against the accused receiver in the former case, two witnesses were allowed to offer hearsay character evidence, one that "People used to talk, that he got coals and corn in a clandestine manner," the other that he "has been suspected of these practices [i.e., receiving stolen goods]; I have heard several times that people found their things there." OBSP (May 1744), at 109.

[123] Joseph Isaacs, OBSP (Jan. 1744) at 50, 51.

[124] James Leekey and William Robinson, OBSP (Dec. 1744, ##10–11), at 5.

[125] Edward Hill and John Hill, OBSP (Dec. 1744, ##26–7), at 9, 10. Both men, father and son, were tried on another indictment, where they were reported represented by counsel. Edward Hill and John Hill, OBSP (Dec. 1744, ##24–5), at 8–9. Counsel is reported cross- examining the prosecutor about her reward motive ("Was you not directed to go into the King's Road in order to be robbed?" "Did you not receive a shilling for that purpose?"), but the report does not attribute the invocation of the corroboration rule to counsel.

[126] James Ruggles *et al.*, OBSP (Dec. 1744, ##93–5), at 48, 49.

been reached under a rule of caution or under a mandatory corroboration rule enforced by directed verdict. Across the next few years the *Sessions Papers* report many examples of acquittal for want of corroboration in crown witness cases,[127] without disclosing whether the rule was mandatory or advisory. (The *Sessions Papers* of these years also report cases of conviction on accomplice testimony in which corroboration is not disclosed.[128] The sources do not permit us to say whether in some of these cases the trial judge rejected or neglected to apply the corroboration rule, or whether in all of them the *Sessions Papers* simply neglected to preserve mention of the corroborating evidence.)

We find decisive clarification on the nature of the corroboration rule of the time in Henry Fielding's tract *An Enquiry into the Causes of the Late Increase of Robbers*, published in 1751. Serving as the court JP for Middlesex, Fielding chafed under the corroboration rule and wanted it altered. Indeed, the corroboration rule is virtually the only subject Fielding treats in a chapter ostensibly devoted to the whole of trial procedure. Fielding complains that even "though the Evidence of the Accomplice be ever so positive and explicit, nay ever so connected and

[127] E.g., Sarah Lambert, *OBSP* (July 1745, #300), at 179 (burglary) ("There being no other positive evidence, but that of the accomplice, to affect the Prisoner, she was acquitted"); John Stephens and John Jennings, *OBSP* (July 1746, #242–3), at 185 (highway robbery); John Lawrence and William Prossey, *OBSP* (Jan. 1747, ##94–5), at 54 (theft of coals) ("As there was no other Evidence but the Accomplice, Miller, they were acquitted . . ."); Thomas Lane and William Clark, *OBSP* (Apr.–May 1747, #214–15) (theft of hats from a shop), at 150, 151 ("as there was no other Evidence but Brown the Accomplice, nor none of the Goods found, the Prisoners were acquitted . . ."); William Grace, *OBSP* (June 1747, #137), at 171, 172 ("As there was no other Evidence but the Accomplice Butler, the Prisoner was acquitted . . ."); John and Miles Nutbrown, *OBSP* (Jan. 1751, ##116–17), at 52, 53.

[128] The most troublesome is the conviction of Robert Grane, *OBSP* (Apr. 1745, #197), at 105, 106 (theft of jewelry, household silver, and clothing from a dwelling house), on the testimony of Joseph Uptebake, the same crown witness whose testimony against Leekey and Robinson in December 1744 was rejected for want of corroboration. In this case, he accused Grane of participating with those two in another theft. Not only is there no reported corroboration, but Uptebake effectively admitted that this was a spite prosecution. Grane asked Uptebake, "Had you any design to put me into your information, till you was desired to do it by the high constable?" Uptebake replied that he "put [Grane] into my information" only after learning that Grane was "the principal instrument of my being taken up . . . ." Ibid. at 106. The *Sessions Paper* reporter in an asterisked footnote points to discrepancies between Uptebake's trial testimony and his pretrial statement before the examining JP. Ibid.

Other instances of successful crown witness prosecutions in these years in which corroboration is not evident include John Short and George Thomas, *OBSP* (July 1746, ##266–7, 268–9 [two cases]), at 202–10 (highway robbery); John Pagon, *OBSP* (Sept. 1746, #305 [two cases]), at 242 (theft) (defense counsel was present); Richard Clay and John Mathews, *OBSP* (Dec. 1746, ##1–3 [two cases]), at 2–5 (burglary); Thomas McLane, *OBSP* (Feb. 1747, #139), at 92–3 (theft of silver buckles) (11-year-old recidivist sent to service upon a naval vessel in lieu of transportation); John Hudson and William Blankflower, *OBSP* (Apr.–May 1747, ##210–11), at 146 (burglary) (one convicted, one acquitted). The case reported immediately following *Hudson and Blankflower* was *Lane and Clark*, cited *supra* n. 127, in which the corroboration rule was applied to acquit both defendants.

probable, still, unless it be corroborated by some other Evidence, it is not sufficient."[129] Speaking of the difficulty of prosecuting highway robbers under the rule, he continues:

Unless therefore the Robbers should be so unfortunate as to be apprehended in the Fact, (a Circumstance which their Numbers, Arms, &c. renders ordinarily impossible) no such Corroboration can possibly be had; but the Evidence of the Accomplice standing alone and unsupported, the Villain, contrary to the Opinion, and almost direct Knowledge of all present, is triumphantly acquitted, laughs at the Court, scorns the Law, vows Revenge against his Prosecutors, and returns to his Trade with a great Increase of Confidence, and commonly of Cruelty.[130]

This passage leaves little doubt that the corroboration rule that Fielding confronted in his prosecutorial work was a requirement enforceable by directed verdict.[131] When "the Evidence of an Accomplice [is] not suffi-cient to put the Prisoner on his Defense . . . the Jury are directed to acquit him . . . ."[132] Fielding wanted the evidence in crown witness cases to reach the jury, which is where a mere-caution rule would have been sending them.[133]

Conceivably, Fielding misunderstood the corroboration rule in force in his day and misdescribed it in his tract, but that possibility must appear

---

[129] Fielding, *Enquiry* 158.

[130] Ibid. at 159.

[131] There is no doubt that the technique of directed verdict was in use at this time. In the case of Mary Sawhagen, *OBSP* (Oct. 1754, #469), at 306 (theft of household goods), we learn from the notes of the trial judge, Dudley Ryder, otherwise Chief Justice of King's Bench, that he "told the jury this [prosecution] could not be felony because the goods came to posses-sion of the prisoner by consent. I directed the jury to find her Not Guilty . . . ." Ryder, "Judge's Notes" 15. In a tort action for assault that same year, Ryder recorded that "I directed the jury that they must find for the plaintiff, but could not find too small damages as the defendant was the cause of the whole." *Fish v. Chappel* (1754), in Ryder, "Judge's Notes" 1, 3. In an action for money had and received arising from the sale of a leasehold, Ryder records: "I summed up for plaintiff and directed the jury to find for plaintiff. Verdict for [plaintiff] £30." *Fisher v. Perrif* (1754), Ryder, "Judge's Notes" 19, 21.

Oldham directs attention to the point that the "directed verdict" of these decades "differ[ed] from the modern concept of a directed verdict as a final determination. The eigh-teenth century jury was considered to have a moral obligation to follow the direction of the judge and his construction of applicable laws, but there was no legal obligation to do so. Nevertheless, trial judges did frequently direct juries to find for one party or the other, and juries ordinarily complied." 1 Oldham, *Mansfield* 150. The modern American directed verdict, in which the court effectively enters the verdict, emerged only in the second half of the nineteenth century. William W. Blume, Origin and Development of the Directed Verdict, 48 *Mich. L. Rev.* 555 (1950); Frank W. Hackett, "Has a Trial Judge of a United States Court the Right to Direct a Verdict," 24 *Yale L.J.* 127, 137–41 (1914).

[132] Fielding, *Enquiry* 160.

[133] Fielding also wanted to treat the accomplice's testimony as shifting the burden of production and perhaps of persuasion to the accused. "I intend no more than that such Evidence shall put the Prisoner on his Defense, and oblige him either to controvert the Fact by proving an Alibi, or by some other Circumstance; or to produce some reputable Person [to] his Character." Ibid. at 162.

highly unlikely. As the court JP for Middlesex, Fielding had more reason than anyone else in England to know the law governing crown witness testimony. Wigmore wrote his history of the corroboration rule in ignorance of Fielding's tract. Understandably, Wigmore had no particular reason to think of extending his research on the corroboration rule to the nonfiction writings of Henry Fielding. If he had, and if he had understood why Fielding spoke with such authority on crown witness matters, he would have formed a materially different view of the history of the corroboration rule. Wigmore would have concluded that a mandatory corroboration rule was already in force in 1751 when Fielding published the *Enquiry*, rather than the counsel-of-caution rule that Wigmore found in the 1780s.

The *Sessions Papers* supply us with some milestones on the path from the binding corroboration rule of the 1740s to the advisory rule of the 1780s. For a dozen years or so after Fielding's tract the practice at the Old Bailey appears to have been congruent with Fielding's description. Cases continued to be reported in which acquittals were explained on the ground that the testimony of the accomplice was "not . . . supported by any person of credit."[134] Indeed, because these results occurred with such monotonous regularity, it seems slightly puzzling that prosecutors continued to bring these doomed cases to trial. The most likely explanation is that they hoped that further evidence would emerge, or perhaps that an unrepresented accused would make an admission in the course of conducting his defense that would supply corroboration. The magistrates who bound over some of these cases for trial may also have wished to subject the accused to the unpleasantness of pretrial detention and the fright of trial, even though acquittal was predictable.[135]

We cannot exclude the possibility that the corroboration rule was less

---

[134] Andrew Gray and William Corning, *OBSP* (Jan. 1753, ##65–6), at 47; accord, Paul Kenady et al., *OBSP* (Apr.–May 1754, ##267–9), at 137 (accomplice's "evidence standing unsupported by any evidence of credit, they were all three acquitted"); Thomas Tailor and John Russel, *OBSP* (Jan. 1761, #47), at 59 ("There being no other evidence of credit to confirm [the accomplice], who owned himself to be a guilty person, they were Acquitted"); Thomas Davis, *OBSP* (Dec. 1761, #10), at 7, 18 ("The accomplice being unsupported by any witness of credit . . . the prisoner was acquitted"); Humphrey Millar and William Gabriel, *OBSP* (Jan. 1763, ##75–6), at 43 (accomplice's "evidence not supported by any witness of credit"); John Oberend et al., *OBSP* (Jan. 1763, ##90–3), at 58 (accomplice's "account being unsupported by any other witness of credit"); Joseph Davis and Robert Addison, *OBSP* (Apr. 1763, ##141–2), at 112 ("there being no other witness to support [the accomplice's] evidence"); John Swift and Dennis McCarty, *OBSP* (May 1763, ##251–2), at 163 (accomplice testimony "not supported by any witness of credit"); Samuel Beeton, *OBSP* (July 1763, #299), at 182 (accomplice "unsupported by any evidence of credit"); John Robinson and Rowland Jones, *OBSP* (Sept. 1763, ##423–4), at 229 ("[t]here being no evidence to the fact . . . except" the accomplice").

[135] For a modern analogue, see Malcolm M. Feeley, *The Process Is the Punishment: Handling Cases in a Lower Criminal Court* (1979).

consistently applied than our sources suggest. The *Sessions Papers* of these years report some convictions in crown witness trials in which we cannot detect corroborating evidence from the information reported.[136] These are commonly squib accounts, cases reported in only a few lines, but even in cases that are more fully reported, the reports are so compressed (that is, they omit so much) that we cannot draw any inference that corroboration was actually lacking. The more likely explanation is simply that corroborating evidence was presented but that the reporter had no particular interest in preserving mention of it.

2. Accomplice Exclusion

Beginning in 1764, the *Sessions Papers* show the corroboration rule being enforced in the Old Bailey with even greater intensity than the practice that irked Henry Fielding in 1751. Fielding described a corroboration rule enforced by a directed verdict of acquittal in the event that the accomplice's testimony went uncorroborated. In the practice traceable from 1764, some judges refused to hear the crown witness at all unless the prosecution established at the outset that evidence of corroboration would be offered. The earliest of these cases that I have noticed is the trial of Richard Hitchins for theft in February 1764. The victim–prosecutor, Wright, testified about his loss and about his contact with the crown witness, Parsons. Wright tendered Parsons to testify that Parsons and Hitchins had committed the theft. The trial judge, Baron Perrot, asked Wright: "Have you any witness of credit that can confirm the account [that Parsons] can give?" Wright replied that he had "no other witness." Perrot then asked Wright if he had personal knowledge of Hitchins' involvement, to which Wright again said that he did not. The report concludes: "The court did not think it proper to examine Parsons. Acquitted."[137] For the next several years, into 1770, the *Sessions Papers* disclose a number of cases of this sort, which I shall call accomplice exclusion cases. At the trial of two men in January 1766 for stealing cheeses, "[t]he only evidence to the fact was ... [the] accomplice, and without going into the evidence, they were Acquitted."[138] In April of that year James Muffin was tried before James Eyre, the Recorder of London, for

[136] Examples from 1751 (the date of Fielding's *Enquiry*) to 1764, when, as explained below, the corroboration rule took its next turn: William Hatton, *OBSP* (May 1751, #374), at 173; John Briant *et al.*, *OBSP* (Dec. 1753, ##20–2), at 6; John Mason and John Welch, *OBSP* (Dec. 1753, ##46–7), at 12–14; Michael Kelley *et al.*, *OBSP* (Apr.–May 1754, ##275–8), at 139–42; Michael Taraham, *OBSP* (May 1755, #248), at 220; William Gold and Thomas Shervil, *OBSP* (Jan. 1756, ##68–9), at 66; William Page, *OBSP* (Feb. 1758, #135), at 133–5; George Warren, *OBSP* (Sept. 1762, #266), at 190–2.
[137] Richard Hitchins, *OBSP* (Feb. 1764, #182), at 133, 134.
[138] John Currant and James Cunningham, *OBSP* (Feb. 1766, ##192–3), at 131, 133.

the theft of silver and jewelry from a dwelling house. "There was no evidence to the fact but Jones the accomplice; he was not examined. Acquitted."[139]

Two more accomplice exclusion cases were reported in 1767,[140] and five in 1770.[141] Years later, in May 1784, we find a discussion of the rationale for accomplice exclusion in one of the detailed *Sessions Paper* reports of the Hodgson years, the trial of William Dunbar in May 1784. Dunbar was accused of forging a Bank of England banknote. Prosecution counsel, William Fielding (Henry's son), told the court that he planned to call a certain accomplice. "I am aware," Fielding said, "that there is a common objection to calling an evidence [that is, an accomplice] first . . . ."[142] The judge responded: "I do not conceive there is any rule to put it out of the power of the Court in any case . . . it has always been considered as discretionary. Different Judges hold different practices, but I am clearly convinced that the better way is not to examine the accomplice first, for this reason: The Jury ought not to receive impressions from evidence, of which ultimately they may not be at liberty in point of law to believe."[143] Dunbar's counsel, William Garrow, immediately endorsed this rationale. "My Lord, I am not fond of the jury hearing what they are afterwards told to forget."[144] Judging from the cases reported in the *Sessions Papers* across the 1770s and 1780s, however, I have the impression that the practice of excluding the accomplice as endorsed in *Dunbar's Case* in 1784 was not widely followed, and that most judges enforced the corroboration rule only after the accomplice had been heard, by directing a verdict or directing the jury to disregard the uncorroborated testimony.[145]

---

[139] James Muffin, *OBSP* (Apr. 1766, #274), at 170.

[140] Joseph Fletcher, *OBSP* (July 1767, #368), at 242, 243 ("the court did not think proper to examine [the accomplice] as there was no evidence of credit to support his testimony"); Samuel Randall, *OBSP* (Jan. 1768, #149), at 75, 76 (the accomplice "was not examined, as there was no evidence of credit to support or corroborate his account. Acquitted.").

[141] William Moody, *OBSP* (Jan. 1770, ##107–9), at 84, 88 (burglary); John Lister and Isaac Pemberton, *OBSP* (Jan. 1770, #117–18), at 95, 96 (convicted on first indictment for an unrelated offense; on second indictment; "[t]here being no evidence of credit to confirm or corroborate the account [that the accomplice] could give, he was not examined. Both acquitted"); James Smith and Thomas Abet, *OBSP* (Feb. 1770, ##157–8), at 114 (burglary); two indictments for unrelated offenses, same accomplice witness, George Memory; Memory was heard on the first case "but his account not being supported by any evidence of credit, the prisoners were both acquitted"; on second indictment, there being "no evidence of character to corroborate the evidence of Memory, Memory was not examined"); Shepherd Strutton and William Ogilvie, *OBSP* (Apr.–May, 1770, ##230–1), at 159 (burglary); James McDonald and James Smith, *OBSP* (June 1770, ##338–9), at 210, 211 (burglary).

[142] Joseph Dunbar, *OBSP* (May 1784, #656), at 836.

[143] Ibid. at 836–7.   [144] Ibid. at 837.

[145] By way of example, consider a year's worth of cases, from September 1770 through September 1771: William Moreton and Catherine Graham, *OBSP* (Sept. 1770, ##502–4 [two cases]), at 320 (theft, receiving) ("There being no evidence to bring the charges home to the prisoners, but that of Tailor the accomplice, they were all three [*sic*] acquitted"); John

The rationale for the accomplice exclusion cases that emerges from *Dunbar's Case* underscores that the corroboration rule as it stood in 1784 was still a mandatory rule—the rule described and criticized in 1751 by Henry Fielding, not the mere counsel-of-caution rule that Wigmore knew. The judge's explanation in *Dunbar* that he favored excluding the accomplice in order to prevent the jury from "receiv[ing] impressions from evidence, of which ultimately they may not be at liberty in point of law to believe," was a reference to the judge's power to direct the jury to disregard the testimony for want of corroboration. The judge viewed excluding the witness as a superior way to administer the mandatory corroboration rule. Neither mode of enforcement—the direction to the jury to disregard or the refusal to hear the witness—was consistent with Wigmore's claim that the corroboration rule "amount[ed] to no rule of evidence, but merely to a *counsel of caution* given by the judge to the jury," which the jury "might or might not regard . . . ."[146] If the jury had been free to disregard the caution, the judge would have had no basis either for removing the jury's "liberty in point of law to believe" the accomplice or for preventing the jury from hearing the testimony

Later in this chapter I shall return to Garrow's approving remark in *Dunbar's Case* that he was "not fond of the jury hearing what they are afterwards told to forget."[147] It reflects the concern that dawned in the 1770s and 1780s that a law of evidence premised upon excluding relevant information from the jury needed to confront the problems of making exclusion workable.

Simpson, *OBSP* (Sept. 1770, #550), at 333 (burglary) (same phrase); Benjamin Murphy *et al.*, *OBSP* (Sept. 1770, ##583–6), at 341 (burglary) (same phrase); William Cox and Richard Prarie, *OBSP* (Sept. 1770, ##599–600), at 344, 345 (theft, receiving) (same phrase); George Humphreys, *OBSP* (Oct. 1770, #680), at 376, 377 (receiving) (same phrase); Solomon Wood, *OBSP* (Dec. 1770, #28), at 17 (burglary) ("There was no evidence to prove the charge upon the prisoner, excepting that of James Hebert the accomplice. Acquitted"); Samuel Davis, *OBSP* (Jan. 1771, #88), at 77 (burglary) (same phrase); Nicholas Murphey, *OBSP* (Apr. 1771, #235), at 162 (burglary); John Moody *et al.*, *OBSP* (Apr. 1771, ##257–9), at 168 (burglary) (the trial judge is reported saying, "Here is not a circumstance against either of these prisoners but the evidence of the accomplice"); William and Jane M'Cloud, *OBSP* (July 1771, ##447, 449), at 314 (theft from dwelling house) ("There was no evidence . . . to bring the charge home to the prisoners, but that of Thomas Younger, the accomplice"); Matthew Holland and Joseph Lyon, *OBSP* (July 1771, ##483–4), at 334 (burglary) ("There was no evidence to affect the prisoners, but that of Patrick Finley, the accomplice"); William Thwaits, *OBSP* (July 1771, #509), at 392, 393 (highway robbery) (similar phrase); William Chesterman *et al.*, *OBSP* (Sept. 1771, ##535–7), at 403 (highway robbery) ("There was no evidence to bring the charge home to the prisoners but the accomplice's"); John Richardson, *OBSP* (Sept. 1771, ##633–6), at 486 (burglary) (similar phrase).

[146] 7 Wigmore, *Evidence* § 2056, at 315 (emphasis original), quoted *supra*, text at n. 116.

[147] *OBSP* (May 1784), at 837, *infra*, text at n. 311.

3. Retrenching in *Atwood and Robbins*

The corroboration rule underwent a drastic revision, in what became the leading case, styled *R. v. Atwood and Robbins*,[148] decided in 1787.[149] *Atwood and Robbins* reduced the corroboration rule to a rule of caution. This revision of the rule was precipitated by Francis Buller, a common pleas judge and author of the notable civil practice manual Buller's *Nisi Prius* (1772),[150] who tried *Atwood and Robbins* at first instance on the Western Assizes. The case grew out of a highway robbery. Three men waylaid the prosecutor at night and took his money by force. He could not identify them because of the dark, but at the trial he produced a man purporting to be one of the three to testify as an accomplice against the other two. The accomplice was not corroborated. Buller, however, neither excluded the witness nor instructed the jury to disregard his testimony when corroboration did not materialize. Rather, Buller admitted the accomplice "to give his testimony; and [the accomplice] deposed, That he and the two prisoners at the bar had, in the company of each other, committed this robbery."[151] The jury convicted. Rather than sentence the two convicts, Buller respited judgment (that is, he ordered them back to jail pending sentence) while he "submitted [the case] to the consideration of the Twelve Judges."[152]

Submitting a case to the Twelve Judges was a practice that functioned as a species of appellate review. When a point of difficulty arose that a trial judge was reluctant to decide on his own, especially when capital sanctions were involved and the convict would otherwise be promptly executed, the judge could defer sentencing and refer the question to a

---

[148] James Atwood and Thomas Robbins, 1 *Leach* 464, 168 *Eng. Rep.* 334 (1788) [*sic*; 1787].

[149] The case is known in the legal literature from Leach's report, see *supra* n. 148, which dates it to 1788. However, the December 1787 *Sessions Paper* establishes that the case was decided in 1787. See John Durham and Edward Crowther, *OBSP* (Dec. 1787, #38), at 52 (burglary), discussing and applying *Atwood and Robbins*. The trial judge in *Durham and Crowther*, Baron Perryn, referred to the holding in *Atwood and Robbins* as the ground for refusing a motion made by Garrow as defense counsel to exclude the testimony of an accomplice. Perryn told Garrow that "on the very first day of this term, Mr. Justice Buller tried a person for a felony, and he was convicted on the evidence of the accomplice only; he [Buller] referred the case to the twelve judges, and the ten judges that were there present were unanimously of opinion, that it only went to his credit, and not his competency, and that he might be received." Ibid. at 53.

[150] Francis Buller, *An Introduction to the Law Relative to Trials at Nisi Prius* (London 1772) [hereafter Buller, *Nisi Prius*]. There were later editions in 1773, 1775, 1781, 1785, 1790, 1793, and 1817. 1 *Sweet & Maxwell's Legal Bibliography* 335 (2nd edn. 1955). Buller's *Nisi Prius* was actually a revision of [Henry Bathurst], *The Theory of Evidence* (London 1761) [hereafter Bathurst, *Evidence*]. Bathurst was Buller's uncle; serving as Lord Chancellor (1771–8), he appointed Buller a judge of King's Bench at the age of 32. *Biographical Dictionary of the Common Law* 36–7, 87–9 (A. W. B. Simpson ed.) (1984). Bathurst expanded and republished his work in [Henry Bathurst], *Introduction to the Law Relative to Trials at Nisi Prius* (London 1767) (2nd edn. Dublin 1768). Buller took over that title.

[151] 1 *Leach* at 464, 168 *Eng. Rep.* at 334.   [152] Ibid.

meeting held back in London of all the judges, commonly twelve, of the three common law courts.[153] Their decision would resolve the case, and the precedent would clarify future practice. In *Atwood and Robbins* the report gives no indication that the defendants had trial counsel, hence it appears that Buller referred the case to the Twelve Judges on his own motion. He explained that "a doubt arising in my mind respecting the propriety of this conviction, I thought it proper to refer [the] case to the consideration of the Twelve Judges."

Behind this genteel expression of uncertainty was the reality that Buller had deliberately provoked a conflict with existing practice under the corroboration rule, obtained a verdict inconsistent with the rule, forced it on the agenda of the English bench, and was about to succeed in getting the judges to overrule the established rule, materially weakening the protection for accused persons in future crown witness cases. We do not know what inclined Buller in this direction, nor who else may have shared the dissatisfaction with the corroboration rule that led Buller to instigate the reconsideration that occurred in *Atwood and Robbins*. We do know that at least since Henry Fielding's *Enquiry* in 1751, there was a strand of thought that the corroboration rule was overly solicitous of criminal defendants in crown witness cases.[154] That theme had been echoed only a couple of years before *Atwood and Robbins* in Martin Madan's bloodthirsty tract, *Thoughts on Executive Justice* (1785), which expressed misgivings about the accomplice rule as part of its general critique of excessive leniency in the administration of the criminal law.[155]

The Twelve Judges rested their decision in *Atwood and Robbins* on a false syllogism between competency and credit, which careened away from the real policies that were at stake in balancing the needs for repression and for safeguard in crown witness prosecutions. In reporting the results of the Twelve Judges' deliberation, Buller seems to say that it was his doing to frame the question in that way. "My doubt was, Whether the evidence of an accomplice, unconfirmed by any other evidence . . . was sufficient to warrant a conviction? And the Judges are unanimously of opinion, that an accomplice alone is a competent witness; and, that if the Jury, weighing the probability of his testimony, think him worthy of belief, a conviction supported by such testimony alone is perfectly legal."[156] This emphasis on competency resonated in contemporary civil

---

[153] "Whether a point was reserved was entirely in the discretion of the trial judge," and the judges varied in their propensity to refer. D. R. Bentley, *Select Cases from the Twelve Judges' Notebooks* 13, 14 (1997).

[154] *Supra*, text at n. 130.

[155] [Martin Madan], *Thoughts on Executive Justice, with Respect to our Criminal Laws, Particularly on the Circuits* 151–67 (1st edn. London 1785) [hereafter Madan, *Thoughts*].

[156] 1 *Leach* at 465, 168 *Eng. Rep.* at 334.

practice, in which disqualification for interest loomed large; indeed, Buller's treatise on civil trial practice discussed the subject at length.[157] But Buller misstated the question that arose under the corroboration rule when he characterized it as one of competency. The competency of the accomplice in crown witness prosecutions had been long settled, and *Atwood and Robbins* did not in fact disturb the law on that point. We saw in Chapter 3 that the testimonial competency of the accomplice, although doubted by Matthew Hale in the seventeenth century, had been decisively resolved against Hale's position in Hale's lifetime.[158] Under the corroboration rule as it had been practiced across the eighteenth century until *Atwood and Robbins*, the accomplice's unconfirmed testimony had been rejected not for want of competency but for want of reliability. The fear was that, even though competent, his testimony might still be perjured.

The topic of the accomplice's competency resurfaced in the Twelve Judges' rationale in *Atwood and Robbins*, not because it was in doubt, but as a foil to be contrasted with the concept of credit in the false syllogism that the corroboration rule had to embody one of those two concepts. According to Buller's report of the Twelve Judges' decision, they were "unanimously of opinion, that an accomplice alone is a competent witness; and that, if the Jury, weighing the probability of his testimony, think him worthy of belief, a conviction supported by such testimony alone is perfectly legal." Buller's account then continues:

The distinction between the competency and the credit of a witness has long been settled. If a question be made respecting his competency, the decision on that question is the exclusive province of the Judge; but if the ground of the objection go to his credit only, his testimony must be received and left with the Jury, under such directions and observations from the Court as the circumstances of the case may require, to say whether they think it sufficiently credible to guide their decision on the case. An accomplice, therefore, being a competent witness, and the Jury in the present case having thought him worthy of credit, the verdict of Guilty, which has been found, is strictly legal, though found on the testimony of the accomplice only.[159]

In short: since the accomplice is competent, (1) the only potential objection to his testimony would be an objection to his credit, and (2) since matters of credit are the sole province of the jury, albeit subject to judicial comment, it follows that (3) anything not excluded for competency must

---

[157] Buller, *Nisi Prius, supra* n. 150, at 279–87. The subject of disqualification for interest dominated the treatment of oral evidence in the leading eighteenth-century treatise, Gilbert, *Evidence* 86–94. On the prominence of disqualification questions in the civil trials conducted by Dudley Ryder, see Langbein, Evidence 1184–6.

[158] *Supra* Ch. 3, text at nn. 253–4.

[159] 1 Leach at 465–6, 168 *Eng. Rep.* at 334–5.

be admissible. This formulation overlooked the middle ground, long since developed in the contemporary character and confession rules as well as in the received corroboration rule, that the trial judge could exercise a power to exclude particular evidence of a concededly competent witness. The rationale in *Atwood and Robbins* has as its premise the wholly undefended assumption that competency is the only ground for excluding evidence, hence that all competent evidence is admissible.

Atwood and Robbins was not the first case to make this blunder. We find the same idea a century earlier, in 1670, in a case in which the King's Bench refused to exclude hearsay from a civil trial, saying that a witness may testify to an out-of-court declarant's statement, even though that declarant "might not be admitted as a Witness at the Trial," because the statement "is but matter of Evidence, and [it] is left to the Jury how far they will give credit to [the statement], and it is lawful for one that is admitted as a Witness to give any thing in Evidence which may concern the Matter in Question."[160] Anything that a competent witness says is admissible. We find the same claim invoked by prosecution counsel in 1753 in a well-reported forgery case, the trial of Timothy Murphy:[161] "There are always two ways in which objections to evidence are made; one is to the competency of a witness, which is a total rejection of his testimony; and the other is to his credit, which is proper only for the consideration of the jury."[162] A passage in Hale's seventeenth-century treatise, contrasting competency with credit, may have contributed to this confusion;[163] it attracted the attention of later writers.[164] Another source of the confusion between competency and credit in *Atwood and Robbins* may have been the practice that we have observed in some crown witness cases (from *Hitchins* in 1764 to *Dunbar* in 1784), in which the judge administered the corroboration rule by excluding the accomplice from testifying unless corroboration was initially assured. Excluding a witness was how

---

[160] 1 John Lilly, *The Practical Register; or, A General Abridgment of the Law* 549 (1719), citing an unidentified case temp. "22 Car. B.R.").

[161] Timothy Murphy, 19 *St. Tr.* 693 (O.B. 1753) (forgery).

[162] 19 *St. Tr.* at 707.

[163] 1 Hale, *HPC* 305 (although an accomplice "be admissible, as a witness in law, yet the credibility of his testimony is to be left to the jury").

[164] Henry Fielding invoked the passage from Hale in his critique of the corroboration rule in 1751; see Fielding, *Enquiry* 160. Although critical of Hale's disdain for accomplice testimony, Fielding seized upon Hale's seeming admission "that the credibility of [the accomplice's] Testimony is to be left to the Jury, and so is the Credibility of all other Testimonies." Ibid. Fielding makes the obvious reply: "[S]urely, if the Evidence of an Accomplice be not sufficient to put the Prisoner on his Defense, but the Jury are directed to acquit him, . . . the Credibility of such Testimony cannot well be said to be left to a Jury." Ibid. Madan, writing in 1785, also cited and refuted Hale on this point; his argument tracks Fielding and was probably lifted from the *Enquiry*. Madan, *Thoughts, supra* n. 155, at 158–9. Both defense counsel (Nares, Davy) in *Murphy's Case* invoke the passage from Hale, see 19 *St. Tr.* at 703–4, 706. Burns JP manual also cites Hale for the distinction between competency and credit. Burn, *JP* 203.

disqualification worked. However, accomplice exclusion was intended not as a rule of competency, but simply as a more effective technique for implementing the exclusion of uncorroborated testimony.

It is astonishing that in *Atwood and Robbins* a panel composed of all the common law judges of England could have made such an elementary error, contradicting their current practice under the character rule, the confession rule, and the hearsay rule, as well as the established understanding of the corroboration rule. The Twelve Judges announced themselves unable to distinguish between a rule of evidentiary exclusion and the exercise of a judicial power to comment on the credibility of evidence. That confusion may give us something of a clue about the origins of the rules of evidence. Exclusionary rules such as the character rule and the corroboration rule had their beginnings in the exercise of the judicial power of comment. Such guidance was discretionary, both in the sense that not all judges may have held or expressed the same views, and in the sense that the judge's advice did not bind the jury to which it was given. But as the consensus on a particular point grew stronger among the judges, the principle tended to find expression as a norm from which neither judge nor jury ought to depart—a rule of law, hence a rule of exclusion removed from the discretion of either.

This process of turning fact into law has been remarked for other fields of law in the eighteenth and nineteenth centuries, and it is not surprising that we should see it at work in the norms of proof for cases of serious crime—that is, in the law of criminal evidence. Brian Simpson has spoken of "the progressive dethronement of the jury" in the course of the nineteenth century as the courts produced legal rules in spheres of substantive law such as contract "where before there was little or none."[165] John Baker has written in a similar vein that "in truth there was very little law of contract at all before the [nineteenth] century, because there was no machinery for producing it and most of the questions were left to juries as questions of fact."[166] Formal jury instruction was the main mechanism that recast matters of fact into questions of law;[167] and directions to exclude evidence were part of this broader pattern.

[165] A. W. B. Simpson, "The Horwitz Thesis and the History of Contracts," 46 U. Chicago L. Rev. 533, 600 (1979); 1 Oldham, *Mansfield* 223.

[166] John Baker, Book Review of Patrick Atiyah, 'The Rise and Fall of Freedom of Contract (1979),' 43 *Mod. L. Rev.* 467, 469 (1980), remarked in 1 Oldham, *Mansfield* 222–3. Baker has made a similar point about criminal jury practice: "[T]he law of evidence and the substantive criminal law . . . were aspects of decision-making which the judges managed to keep from the laymen. . . . [B]y enlarging the scope of the substantive law the judges were able to tell the jurors what conclusion followed if they found certain facts to be true." John Baker, "The Refinement of English Criminal Jurisprudence, 1500–1848," in *Crime and Criminal Justice in Europe and Canada*, 17, 19 (Louis A. Knafla ed.) (1981).

[167] This theme is discussed in Florian Faust, "*Hadley v. Baxendale*—an Understandable Miscarriage of Justice," 15 *J. Legal History* 40, 54–65 (1994).

Our sources indicate that the practice of requiring corroboration for accomplice testimony had crossed the line from a mere usage to a rule of law by the 1740s, yet in 1787 the Twelve Judges were able to squirm out of the corroboration rule by treating it as a mere precept of caution.[168] The judges must have had policy grounds,[169] sound or not, for wanting to cut back on the scope of the corroboration rule, but instead of bringing those reasons into discussion, the opinion in *Atwood and Robbins* fell back on an archaic and inaccurate account of how evidence law worked. The opinion denies the possibility of rules requiring the exclusion of testimony from a competent witness. We see in the Twelve Judges' opinion an indication of how primitive the theoretical basis of the law of evidence remained as late as 1787. The centrality of competency to the thinking in *Atwood and Robbins* also reflected the world of contemporary civil practice that the judges mostly inhabited, where the testimonial disqualification of parties and other witnesses for interest (competency) played such a prominent role in restricting the receipt of oral evidence at trial.

The judges who developed the law of criminal evidence in the eighteenth century had little appreciation of what they were creating. As late as *Atwood and Robbins* in 1787 they appear not to have recognized the commonality of the rules, that is, they seem not to have understood that the corroboration rule was part of a larger doctrinal enterprise, including the character, confession, and hearsay rules. Only in the nineteenth century did it come to be understood that these rules shared a common purpose, a theory, which is that accuracy in adjudication can be promoted by excluding from the trier certain types of testimony, even though competent and material, in the service of various competing policies.

---

[168] With the result that for another century the corroboration rule generated a mass of conflicting precedents, conveniently reviewed in Christopher J. W. Allen, *The Law of Evidence in Victorian England* 43–7 (1997) [hereafter Allen, *Evidence*]. Allen concludes: "The state of the law [as of the middle of the nineteenth century] was that in a case where the sole evidence against a prisoner was that of an uncorroborated accomplice, a judge *did* have an unreviewable discretion to withdraw the case from the jury, leave it to them with a warning, or leave it to them with no warning at all." Ibid. at 47.

[169] For example, I suggest below, text at nn. 211–17, that the extension of the confession rule in the 1770s to eliminate an important class of what had previously been regarded as corroborating evidence in accomplice cases increased the reach of the corroboration rule, and hence its interference with law enforcement. Contemporaries sensed an exceptionally high level of gang crime in the London area in the mid-1780s, in the period of demobilization following the American war. Beattie, *Crime* 224–5; cf. ibid. at 584–5. Furthermore, the Gordon riots highlighted the shortcomings of policing in London, yet Parliament remained stalemated over proposals to enhance policing. "The numerous public disturbances which eighteenth-century London experienced, culminated in the Gordon riots of June 1780, when much of the center of London was in the hands of rioting crowds for a number of days, prisons were burned down, attacks were mounted on institutions like the bank of England, and the houses of magistrates, judges and other prominent people were attacked and demolished." Philips, "Engine" 164. Regarding the political stalemate that prevented enactment in 1785 of government-supported legislation to create a police force, see ibid. at 165–8.

D. The Confession Rule

Whereas the rebuttal exception narrowed the character rule, and *Atwood and Robbins* gutted the corroboration rule, the confession rule that took hold in the eighteenth century steadily expanded its reach across the nineteenth century. In the twentieth century the Americans would adapt and partially constitutionalize the confession rule for the work of controlling police interrogation practices.[170]

The confession rule disapproved evidence that the defendant had confessed the crime, unless that confession had been voluntary, a concept whose meaning became expansive and artful. Working from Leach's *Crown Cases*, published in 1789, Wigmore attributed to Lord Mansfield in *Rudd's Case* in 1775 "the first judicial utterance limiting the admissibility"[171] of confessions, even though the passage from Mansfield on which Wigmore relied indicated that the confession rule was already in force.[172] Wigmore concluded that it was not until *Warickshall's Case*[173] in 1783 that "the modern rule received a full and clear expression, and confessions not entitled to credit because of the promises or the threats by which they had been obtained were declared inadmissible in evidence."[174] From *Warickshall* came the pithy formulation that excluded a confession "forced from the mind by the flattery of hope, or by the torture of fear."[175]

The *Sessions Papers* make it clear that the confession rule long predated *Warickshall*. Indeed, the rule was formulated in the early 1740s and settled by the 1760s.

In the early decades of the eighteenth century the sources indicate no sensitivity to the dangers of confession evidence. Thus, at the trial of Margaret Wilson in 1722 for theft from a dwelling house, her pretrial confession was proved and she was convicted although she claimed that the prosecutor "told her if she'd confess they'd forgive her."[176] In later practice the judges would ventilate such a claim and exclude the confession on the ground that it had been induced by "hope of favor," but in 1722 the Old Bailey is reported as having paid no attention to her allegation. We

---

[170] Regarding the modern American confession rule, see 2 Wayne R. LaFave *et al.*, Criminal Procedure §§ 6.1–6.10, at 435–629 (1999 & Supp.) (6 vols.).

[171] 3 Wigmore, *Evidence* § 819, at 237.

[172] "The instance has frequently happened," said Mansfield in *Rudd*, "of persons having made confessions under threats or promises; the consequence as frequently has been that such examinations and confessions have not been made use of against them on their trial. *R. v. Margaret Caroline Rudd*, 1 *Leach* 115, 118, 168 *Eng. Rep.* 160, 161 (K.B. 1775), quoted in 3 Wigmore, Evidence § 819, at 237.

[173] *R. v. Jane Warickshall*, 1 *Leach* 263, 168 *Eng. Rep.* 234 (O.B. 1783).

[174] 3 Wigmore, Evidence § 819, at 238.

[175] 1 *Leach* at 263–4, 168 *Eng. Rep.* at 235.

[176] Margaret Wilson, *OBSP* (Jan. 1722), at 5.

Engraved for The Malefactor's Register.

Codd delin   *Judd sculp.*

Mrs MARGARET CAROLINE RUDD *on her* TRIAL
at the New Sessions House, in the Old Bailey.

FIG. 4.1. *The trial of Mrs. Rudd. Rudd's Case* in 1775 produced important precedents on both the confession rule and the corroboration rule. The trial took place in the courtroom in the new Sessions House, which was built in 1774.

also find cases in which the court disregarded the other branch of what would become the confession rule—the defendant's claim that he confessed in fear.[177]

Beginning in the later 1730s we detect signs of change. Prosecution witnesses are quoted as reciting that pretrial confessions were voluntary, an indication that the issue was in play.[178] Beattie has drawn attention to a case reported in 1738 in Surrey, in which an employer induced his female servant to confess a felony upon the promise of impunity; he then used the confession to prosecute her. Willes CJ, presiding at the trial, denounced the employer's behavior and said that the confession should "have no Weight with the Jury . . . ."[179] Thus, in 1738 the defect still affected credit, or "Weight with the Jury," as Willes put it. The jury in that case acquitted. By contrast, no such instruction was given in a comparable case two years later at the Old Bailey. In the April 1740 trial of Rachel Poole for theft of silver from the dwelling house where she lodged, the prosecutor admitted that "I made her promise, in Order to get my Goods again." He said he did not promise her a pardon, whatever that meant; "I only promised to be favorable, so as the Law would run."[180] No instruction to exclude is reported to have been given, and she was convicted.

Suddenly, in July 1740, the confession rule pops out, in another case of theft from a dwelling house. At the trial of Tobias and Rachel Isaacs, the prosecutor testified that Rachel "denied it with Earnestness for 2 Hours; but upon my promising to be a Friend to her, and that I would not hurt [her], she confessed."[181] The report continues: "The Prosecutor was not allowed to proceed; and another Witness afterwards offering to give an Account of what she had confessed to him, was likewise stopped; because a Confession obtained on a Promise of Friendship, or by false Insinuations (which was the latter Case) ought not to be given in Evidence against a Prisoner."[182] Thus, a concern that had led to a recommendation about weight in Surrey[183] in 1738 was expressed as an exclusionary rule at the

---

[177] E.g., John Kelly, *OBSP* (July 1736, #27), at 157, 159, who was convicted without judicial inquiry into his allegation that "I was not in my right Senses when I made that Confession, and was frighted into it."

[178] E.g., John Maxworth, *OBSP* (July 1736, #15), at 155 (burglary); George White, *OBSP* (Sept. 1740, #380), at 218, 219 (highway robbery) (confession recites that "he voluntarily" signed it); Richard Welch, *OBSP* (Sept. 1740, #391), at 226 (theft) (confession recites that it was made "voluntarily and without any menaces").

[179] Ann Wilcox, *SAP* (Aug. 1738), at 6, extracted in Beattie, *Crime* 346–7.

[180] Rachel Poole, *OBSP* (Apr. 1740, #200), at 107, 108.

[181] Tobias and Rachel Isaacs, *OBSP* (July 1740, ##324–5), at 193–4.   [182] Ibid.

[183] Beattie sees the period around 1740 as the turning point in the Surrey sources. "I have not found (in the admittedly skimpy Surrey assize reports) much concern being expressed in court before the 1730s about the way confessions had been obtained . . . . But by 1740 confessions were often scrutinized by the bench and were from time to time disallowed as evidence because they had not been made voluntarily. Inducements (in the form of promises of favor or forgiveness) or threats were frequently held to be fatal." Beattie, *Crime* 365.

Old Bailey in 1740. Two years later, however, in July 1742, we find the trial judge in a skimpily reported Old Bailey case formulating the confession rule once again as a mere rule of caution: if the defendant had "any promises of Indulgence before he confessed . . . the Jury will consider that."[184] A year and a half later, at the December 1743 sessions, in the burglary prosecution of Samuel Moses and two others, we find an egregious instance of improper inducement, with no judicial response. There was uncontested evidence that at the pretrial examination the JP told Moses that "if he would make an ingenuous Confession of all the Robberies they had committed, he should have Favor . . . ."[185] Moses' incriminating disclosures in response to this invitation were proved at trial, apparently without caution or direction to exclude, and the three defendants were convicted.

We see, therefore, that various judges were following three irreconcilable approaches to the problem of potentially unreliable confession evidence in the early 1740s: exclude, caution, or admit without caution. The rule of exclusion (the later confession rule) was not as yet a rule of evidence; it did not bind the judges. Across the later 1740s and the 1750s we have examples of both attention[186] and inattention[187] to the dangers of coerced or improperly induced confessions. By the 1760s, however, the rule of exclusion appears to have prevailed. Departures cease to be reported, practice had become law. James M'Locklin, tried in 1761 for stealing a huge quantity of sugar, was acquitted because "[t]here was no evidence that could convict the prisoner, exclusive of that of his own

---

[184] Richard Fill, *OBSP* (July 1742, #10), at 3 (theft).

[185] Samuel Moses *et al.*, *OBSP* (Dec. 1743, ##74–6), at 30, 31 (burglary). What the JP had in mind by the promise of "favor" is not disclosed; if the favor were to be chosen the crown witness, the case would fall into the crown witness competition group discussed below.

[186] For example, Elizabeth Goodsense and Mary Delforce, *OBSP* (Feb. 1746, ##117–18), at 82, 83 (theft), in which it was testified that a 15-year-old girl confessed to the JP after her mother "beat her till she was in a Gore of Blood." The report explains that "the Girl being so young, and the Confession seeming to be extorted from her, they were both acquitted." We also find evidence of the bench probing for infirmities in confessions, e.g., John Wickham, *OBSP* (Sept. 1746, #283), at 224, 225 (breaking and entering) ("Was there any Promise of Pardon before the Justice?"); John Preston and John Dison (Dec. 1754, ##16–17), at 10, 11 ("Were there any threats or menaces, or the like, made use of in order to bring him to a confession?").

[187] Ann Humphrys, a publican, lost a silver tankard. She knew and suspected the accused, Ann Perry, and sent for her. Perry confessed the theft and told where she pawned it. Perry was tried for theft from a dwelling house. At the trial, the pawnbroker and the broker's servant identified the accused. At the close of the trial, Humphrys revealed that "I did promise the Prisoner before she confessed the thing, that if she would acknowledge it, I would not hurt her, and that I would not send her to Newgate." There is no indication of judicial response to this disclosure, and the jury convicted, although the jury downvalued the tankard from the £7 charged in the indictment, to 39s., which spared her from the capital sanction that applied for theft from a dwelling house above the value of 40s. Ann Perry, *OBSP* (May, 1748, #281), at 172, 173.

confession, which was made in expectation of favor promised him."[188] Benjamin March, a journeyman peruke (wig) maker, tried in 1764 for stealing 4 guineas from his employer, had confessed the deed and returned the money after the employer confronted him with the words, "You know very well you have robbed me this morning of four guineas. Deliver it up and no creature shall know of it." The report concludes: "As his confession was drawn out of him with a promise of forgiveness, he was acquitted."[189] Since there was no doubt that March had committed the offense, the acquittal could not have resulted from a rule of weight or credit; March's confession was disregarded despite compelling evidence of its reliability. The next year John Flint was tried for theft. The report: "There being no evidence against the prisoner, besides his confession, which was drawn out of him by a promise that he should not be hurt, he was Acquitted."[190]

Another acquittal under the rule in circumstances in which reliability was not in question occurred in the trial of Samuel Knock in 1767, a journeyman carpenter, for stealing tools. Several pawnbrokers with whom he pawned various of the tools identified Knock. His entire defense as reported in the Sessions Paper was: "They told me if I would tell where the tools were they would let me go." The prosecutor then "acknowledged they did make him the promise he mentioned. Acquitted." The report supplies an observation that (in view of the Sessions Papers' reluctance in these years to attribute language directly to the judges) must have been the rationale of the judge: "Note, It is hoped this will warn prosecutors not to draw out confessions with promises of favor."[191] The following year the Sessions Paper explained another acquittal on the ground that the case rested on "his own confession, which was obtained from him by a promise, which in law could not be received . . . ."[192] In the Brentwood Election Case of 1769, previously discussed in connection with the reporter's apology for violating his normal circumspection about publishing "what he understood to fall from the Judges,"[193] we find unmistakable confirmation that exclusion had become a rule of law, no longer subject to judicial discretion. Gould J said that "where a man is intimi-

[188] James M'Locklin, OBSP (Sept. 1761, #258), at 331.

[189] Benjamin March, OBSP (Feb. 1764, #155), at 110. The prosecutor did not want the case to go forward, but he had called in a constable to help him search for the money, who insisted on taking the case before the JP for a pretrial examination. The JP in turn insisted on binding the defendant to trial.

[190] John Flint, OBSP (Feb.–Mar. 1765, #186), at 107.

[191] Samuel Knock, OBSP (Jan. 1767, #86), at 63.

[192] Plymouth Jumboe and Henry Pullen, OBSP (Oct. 1768, ##609–10), at 366 (emphasis supplied).

[193] Laurence Balfe and Edward McQuirk, OBSP (Jan. 1769, ##108–9), at 66, 100, discussed supra, text at n. 34.

dated with menaces, or drawn in by promises of favor, in that case no court of justice will ever permit such a confession; it is against the very genius of the law of England to be given in evidence."[194] Indeed, in the 1780s we find judges saying that they were bound by the confession rule ("it would be too much now to vary it"[195]) even though they thought it overbroad.[196]

1. Crown Witness Confessions

As the judges developed the confession rule across the 1750s and 1760s, they displayed one remarkable blind spot in its application. They did not apply the rule to the confession uttered by a person who made the confession for the purpose of persuading the authorities to designate him as the crown witness, with the result that he would escape prosecution. In such cases, evidence was presented at trial that the defendant had confessed to a constable or to a JP while negotiating to be designated the crown witness. I have noticed cases of this sort as early as the 1710s and 1720s;[197] thereafter they appear for almost half a century. Here are some examples:

(1) In the prosecution of a group of women for shoplifting in 1726, the JP, Vaughan, testified about examining them at the pretrial hearing. Jane Holms "would fain have been an Evidence, and named I believe near 40 Robberies, that she had been concerned in, but she having been transported, I could not admit her. Then [Sarah] Turner offered to become an Evidence, and confessed that she had committed several Felonies in Company with [Katherine] Fitzpatrick," another of the defendants.[198] All three women were convicted on the testimony of a fourth, Mary Burton, also an accomplice.

---

[194] Ibid. at 69.

[195] Samuel Chesham and James Sherrard, *OBSP* (Jan 1788, #135), at 170, 172 (per Wilson J) (theft).

[196] In the same case Baron Eyre said: "I rather think that for the sake of public justice, it were to be wished, that the principle should not be extended quite so large as it has been." Ibid. at 172.

[197] E.g., John Savil and William Tibbs, *OBSP* (Dec. 1714), at 3 (convicted of breaking and entering, theft of housewares) ("[t]he Evidence against Savil was his own Confession in Newgate when taken up for a Robbery on the Highway, by which he thought to make himself an Evidence"); Thomas Butler, *OBSP* (Jan. 1721), at 4 (highway robbery) (he had confessed everything when detected, "saying it signified nothing to conceal any thing, for he was to be an Evidence. The Jury found him Guilty. Death"); John Dikes, *OBSP* (Oct. 1721), at 4 (highway robbery) ("Jonathan Wild deposed, that he being informed [about] Dikes and [the crown witness] . . . took them together; that Dikes told him that he could make a Discovery against [the crown witness] of some Triffles, but no great sums").

[198] Jane Holms *et al.*, *OBSP* (Aug.–Sept. 1726), at 2–4 (multiple entries for Holms and related defendants); the quoted language is from Katherine Fitzpatrick and Sarah Turner, *OBSP* (Aug.–Sept. 1726), at 4.

(2) William Newell, tried in 1731 for the theft of silk, complained that
     "I made an Information [that is, a confession] in Expectation of
     being an Evidence." The report then quotes the court JP, DeVeil,
     that he "endeavored to make the Prisoner confess his Accomplices,
     he was obstinate at first, but next Day he sent to me and discovered
     three Persons, who have since been tried and found Guilty. I would
     have had him to have been an Evidence then, but was informed
     [that] a Bill [of indictment had already been] found against him, so
     that it proved too late."[199] Even assuming it were true that DeVeil
     lost his ability to arrange for nonprosecution once Newell was
     indicted, it hardly followed that DeVeil should have testified about
     a confession elicited under representation of immunity. In truth an
     indicted person could testify. Hawkins wrote in 1721: "it hath been
     often ruled, That Accomplices who are indicted, are good
     Witnesses for the King until they be convicted."[200]

(3) Thomas Faxton and Thomas Smith were tried for highway robbery
     in 1732. Both the JP, Norris, and another witness, Dennis (perhaps
     Norris' clerk), testified about the pretrial examination of Faxton.
     Dennis said: "When Faxton was before the Justice he was advised
     to confess in order to be made an Evidence. Upon which he fell on
     his knees, and confessed the Fact . . . ." Norris testified that Faxton
     "confessed the Fact before me, and as far as I know, it was volun-
     tary."[201]

(4) Charles Orchard was prosecuted in 1737 for a highway robbery on
     the evidence of his accomplice. The thieftaker testified that at the
     pretrial examination, Orchard "begged I would desire Justice
     Farmer to permit him to be an Evidence, for says he, 'I can hang
     five men, and can knock down the other Evidence, because he has
     not put all the Robberies in his information, that I was concerned
     in. I committed a Robbery,' says he 'between Rag Fair and the
     Triple-house, and he has mentioned nothing of that.' "[202] Orchard
     was convicted and sentenced to death.

(5) John Hill, tried for highway robbery in 1744, implicated his confed-
     erates Waters and Gascoign when he was arrested. "Hill desired
     the constable to intercede with the Justice [of the Peace], that he
     might be admitted the Evidence, and he promised that he would
     make an ample discovery." Subsequently, Waters was examined
     and "begged that he might be admitted the Evidence." Told that

---

[199] William Newell, *OBSP* (Dec. 1731), at 15.
[200] 2 Hawkins, *PC* 432 (citing cases from the *State Trials* and the nominate reports).
[201] Thomas Faxton and Thomas Smith, *OBSP* (Feb. 1732, ##36–7), at 87–9.
[202] Charles Orchard, *OBSP* (Feb. 1737, #24), at 69.

Hill had already accused him and Gascoign, "when [Waters] was before the Justice he said he could impeach nine people . . . ."[203]

What strikes us as problematic about the crown witness confession cases is not simply that the courts were rewarding deception by admitting evidence obtained under false pretenses, but also that the courts did not recognize that confessions elicited in this way exemplified the "hope of favor" branch of the confession rule that was then developing. In crown witness cases, there was a powerful incentive (remarked above in Chapter 3,[204] and exemplified in the last two cases) for a suspect to outbid competitors by confessing to ever more crimes, and to implicate as confederates ever more persons, whether or not truthfully. Precisely this dynamic is what motivated the courts to develop the corroboration requirement for accomplice testimony, but in cases in which the confession was used against the person confessing rather than against his accomplices, the courts seem for a time not to have made the connection. That is, they seem not to have understood that the danger of perjury was quite comparable.

Henry Fielding, whose enthusiasm for crown witness evidence and whose hostility to the corroboration rule we have already noticed, figured in several of these crown witness confession cases in the early 1750s,[205] as did his successor, John Fielding, in the 1760s and as late as 1770.[206] Indeed, in some cases, evidence of the defendant's confession made in the hope of being made the crown witness seems to have supplied the confirmation needed under the corroboration rule to support the testimony of the accomplice who won the competition.[207]

Finally, in the 1770s the tension between the confession rule and the crown witness competition was squarely acknowledged and resolved in

---

[203] John Hill, *OBSP* (Dec. 1744, #23), at 7, 8 (highway robbery). I have previously referred to this case in Ch. 3, *supra*, text at n. 271, in connection with the perverse incentives of the crown witness system.

[204] *Supra* Ch. 3, text at nn. 270–4.

[205] Thomas Lewis and Thomas May, *OBSP* (Apr. 1750, ##307–8), at 68 (highway robbery); William Vincent, *OBSP* (Jan. 1751, #136), at 55 (highway robbery); Thomas Quinn *et al.*, *OBSP* (May 1751, ##369–71), at 171 (highway robbery).

[206] Thomas Jacob, *OBSP* (Sept. 1766, #400), at 260 (burglary); John Martin, *OBSP* (Dec. 1768, #13), at 7, 8 (burglary) (prosecutor testifies that Martin "wanted to be admitted an evidence; and said he would make very great discoveries. Sir John said, he was an old offender, and would not admit him"); Moses Lyon, *OBSP* (June 1770, #385), at 231, 232 (burglary).

[207] For example, in the case of Humphry Millar, *OBSP* (Jan. 1763, #75), at 43, convicted of stealing hay, the only evidence to corroborate the accomplice was the prosecutor's testimony that the defendant confessed to the JP, hoping to made the crown witness. The JP chose the accomplice rather than Millar to be the crown witness, despite the prosecutor's request that Millar be chosen. Millar was then tried and acquitted on two other indictments involving the accusing testimony of the same accomplice; in these cases Millar had not tendered a confession.

favor of exclusion under the confession rule. There had been signs of disquiet well before. As early as 1743, in the trial of Mary Williams for a highway robbery that she allegedly committed on a drunken prosecutor, she was acquitted despite her confession; "considering [that] there was no other Evidence against her but her own voluntary Confession (and that amounting only to the receiving Goods knowing them to be stolen), on the Hopes she had of being made an Evidence, the Jury Acquitted her."[208] (This precise statement of the jury's rationale for acquittal probably reflects the *Sessions Paper* reporter's understanding of the trial judge's recommendation or instruction to the jury.) At the trial of Edward Ward for burglary in 1751, a witness testified about the pretrial examination before Henry Fielding, where the accused and a co-defendant both confessed in an effort to be designated the crown witness. "[T]he prisoner ... told the whole case, what method they used to get in, and how they robbed the house." The trial judge was initially inclined to disapprove the testimony: "As [the pretrial confession] was done under an expectation of being admitted an evidence, that cannot be taken as evidence here."[209] But, perhaps because it was testified that Ward had made the confession "before he came to the justices,"[210] the judge backed off and the jury convicted him. In October 1770 William Brent was tried for the theft of jewelry and banknotes from a dwelling house. He attempted to avoid his confession by saying that he had been promised "that if I would confess I broke open the house, they would admit me an evidence." The trial judge immediately probed the point with the JP, Clay, who had examined him: "Was any thing said to him about being admitted an evidence?" Clay responded: "It is not true, my Lord."[211] The implication from the judge's interest in the defendant's claim is that he may have been prepared to disapprove the use of a crown-witness-type confession. The following year, at the trial of a gang of accused burglars and receivers, a witness testified that one of them had asked when apprehended to be made the crown witness, and said "he could impeach sixteen or more that were in the gang, and tell where every thing was." The court was suspicious, asking if anyone had "persuade[d]" the accused "to tell this[.]" The witness replied that the accused had been urged to "tell the truth, and if you can be admitted an evidence, you shall." The court replied, "Then you should not have made use of it, it is not right."[212] Yet revealingly, the judge did not follow through on this view and exclude the evidence. All the defendants were convicted.

[208] Mary Williams, *OBSP* (Jan. 1743, #113), at 69, 70.
[209] Edward Ward, *OBSP* (Apr. 1751, #311), at 140.
[210] Ibid.
[211] William Brent, *OBSP* (Oct. 1770, #684), at 377, 383.
[212] Luke Cannon *et al.*, *OBSP* (Feb. 1771, #136–40), at 104, 111.

The turnaround to a rule of exclusion of crown witness confessions uttered under the "hope of favor" branch of the confession rule is clearly evidenced in the September 1773 sessions. At the trial of Thomas Ashby and two others for a burglary, the victim, Bailey, began to testify that "Ashby wanted to turn evidence and he said—." The court interrupted: "Had you before that recommended it to him to turn evidence?" Bailey replied, "Yes." The court ruled: "Then you must not mention any thing that he said in consequence of that."[213] Another witness, a neighbor named Lucas, who had observed Ashby at the scene and was active in his arrest the next day, also testified that "Ashby confessed that what I swore was nothing but truth." Lucas was then asked whether "you had before advised him to turn evidence?" He answered, "Yes." The court replied: "Then we cannot hear that evidence against the prisoner."[214] In December 1773 the principle of exclusion was again announced, in a case in which a man taken with others for highway robbery had confessed in response to an invitation from Sir John Fielding to be the crown witness. When Fielding found that the man had lied, he had him prosecuted. When this came out at the trial, the judge said: "What he said at the time he was admitted as an evidence for the crown is not to be made use of against him afterwards,"[215] and he was acquitted. By contrast, in the similar case of Joseph Everett a few months later the trial judge did not disapprove the use of such evidence. At the trial the arresting constable testified: "When I took [Everett] he said if Sir John [Fielding] would admit him an evidence he would discover some persons that had committed several robberies . . . Sir John said he would not admit him an evidence till the other people were apprehended . . ."[216] When Everett's leads proved fruitless, he was prosecuted, found guilty, and sentenced to death. After this case, however, I have noticed no departures from the new understanding that the confession rule applied to confessions tendered in the hope of being made a crown witness. In a case in October 1775 the court reiterated the principle ("Don't mention any thing he said when under the expectation of being admitted an evidence"[217]), and thereafter the phenomenon of crown witness confession prosecutions simply disappeared from the reports—evidence, I take it, that the London magistrates and constables quickly learned not to employ such evidence.

[213] Thomas Ashby et al., OBSP (Sept. 1773, ##512–14), at 353, 354.
[214] Ibid. at 354.
[215] John Rann et al., OBSP (Dec. 1773, ##1–4), at 3 (highway robbery). Accord: Joshua Coster and Peeling Herne, OBSP (Jan. 1774, ##157–8), at 85, 86 (highway robbery, confession tendered in response to a magistrate's undertaking to "do all that lay in his power for them," judge rules it "ought not to be given in evidence against them").
[216] Joseph Everett, OBSP (May 1774, #421), at 229, 231–2 (burglary).
[217] William Archer and Charles Reading, OBSP (Oct. 1775, ##775–6), at 574, 576 (burglary).

I have wondered whether the extension of the confession rule to crown witness cases in the 1770s may have been a factor contributing to the judges' decision in *Atwood and Robbins* in 1783, the case that suddenly reduced the corroboration rule from a rule of exclusion to a mere caution. Since Henry Fielding's day there had been persistent disquiet about the corroboration rule in prosecutorial circles, and we could well imagine that the further impairment of the crown witness system as a result of the extension of the confession rule may have contributed to the pressure to redraw the corroboration rule. I have not, however, found sources bearing on the question.

2. *Warickshall* and the Poison Tree

Wigmore, it will be recalled, understood *Warickshall's Case* (1783), which he knew from the report in Leach's *Crown Cases*,[218] to be the defining precedent for the confession rule. Wigmore took *Warickshall* to be the foundational statement of the extent and rationale of the rule. (*Warickshall* was an Old Bailey case, hence also reported in the *Sessions Papers*,[219] but those sources were not known to Wigmore and the other writers on the history of the law of evidence.) In truth, the account of the confession rule in *Warickshall* was a mere restatement of the rule that we have seen firmly in force since the 1760s. The precise holding of the case was directed to a subsidiary question—whether the confession rule operated to exclude evidence other than the confession, when that evidence had been discovered as a result of the confession. Nares J held that evidence "obtained in consequence of an extorted confession" should be welcomed if "fully and satisfactorily proved, without calling in the aid of any *part of the confession* . . . ."[220] The position in *Warickshall* became broadly accepted.[221] (In late twentieth-century American practice, as the confession rule became oriented to deterring misconduct by police and professional prosecutors, some courts preferred the opposite rule, excluding such "fruits of the poisonous tree."[222])

Nares dismissed as "a mistaken notion" the idea that the confession rule rested upon a "public faith," by which I think he was rejecting the view (which remains contentious to this day[223]) that the integrity of the

---

[218] *R. v. Jane Warickshall*, 1 *Leach* 263, 168 *Eng. Rep.* 234 (O.B. 1783).
[219] *Sub nom.* Thomas Littlepage *et al.*, *OBSP* (Apr. 1783, #254), at 370.
[220] 1 *Leach* at 264, 168 *Eng. Rep.* at 235 (emphasis supplied).
[221] The case law of the next two decades is discussed in 2 Edward Hyde East, *A Treatise of the Pleas of the Crown* 657–8 (London 1803) [hereafter East, *PC*].
[222] E.g., *Commonwealth v. Prater*, 651 N.E.2d 833 (Mass. 1995); *People v. Bethea*, 493 N.E.2d 937 (N.Y. 1986). The United States Supreme Court has waffled. *Oregon v. Elstad*, 470 U.S. 298 (1985).
[223] See 1 McCormick, *Evidence*, *supra* n. 59, § 156, at 552–4.

criminal justice system should require the courts to abstain from processing deceptively obtained prosecution evidence. Reliability was the only policy to which Nares would admit in his discussion of the confession rule. Grounding the rule on the objective criterion of reliability was easier than trying to articulate the dimensions of a notion of "public faith."

In describing the reliability policy, Nares framed it in an odd way: the issue, he said, was whether particular confessions "are or are not entitled to credit." This use of the concept of "credit" to describe the basis for an exclusionary rule of evidence illustrates once more (in the same year as *Atwood and Robbins*) the tendency to characterize the rules restricting the receipt of oral evidence under the rubric of credit, simply because they fell outside the then most characteristic category of excluded oral evidence, which was competency.

3. Questioning the Policy

Confession evidence has long been welcomed at common law, for manifest reasons. Innocent persons do not voluntarily bring serious criminal sanctions upon themselves by confessing to crimes that they have not committed. When genuinely voluntary, a defendant's confession virtually eliminates the risk of error that always abides when a court must decide that a defendant who protests innocence is guilty. Moreover, because a confession effectively resolves the case, it spares the time and effort required to adjudicate a contested case.

Writing in 1721, Serjeant Hawkins expressed unrestrained enthusiasm for confession evidence. "[T]he Confession of the Defendant himself, whether taken upon an Examination before Justices of Peace, in pursuance of [the Marian procedure, or in concilliar procedure for crimes of state] . . . or in Discourse with private Persons, hath always been allowed to be given in Evidence against the Party confessing . . . ."[224]

Wigmore, who understood the value of confession evidence, was savagely critical of some of the strained applications of the confession rule that he found in the early nineteenth-century law reports, especially cases arising under the "hope of favor" branch of the rule. He thought the English bench had developed "a general suspicion of all confessions, a prejudice against them as such, and an inclination to repudiate them upon the slightest pretext."[225] Trying to fathom this seeming "sentimental irrationality,"[226] Wigmore speculated that patterns of English social deference underlay the confession rule. The judges may have been concerned that "half-respectful and half-stupid" persons of the "lower

[224] 2 Hawkins, *PC* 429.   [225] 3 Wigmore, *Evidence* § 820, at 238.
[226] Ibid. § 865, at 351.

classes" allowed themselves to be intimidated by "social superiors"; these ancient patterns of deference were "especially marked, though not solely found, among the peasantry and towards the squires and other landed superiors on whose will hangs the tenant's fortune."[227] Wigmore continued: "We may believe that rationally a false confession is not to be apprehended from the normal person under certain paltry inducements or meaningless threats; but we have here perhaps a person not to be tested by a normal or rational standard."[228]

Thin as Wigmore's conjecture otherwise was, it seems especially unhelpful on the matter of timing. Social stratification was centuries old, and the further back the more striking. Why then did the judges first appear to become alarmed about it in the reign of George III? Wigmore's instincts, as so often, were sound, but he was off target in the application. What he missed was that the confession rule was not generated in rural venues populated by "half-stupid" peasants fawning before squires, but in metropolitan London, then the largest urban center in the world. The typical confessant was a young and vulnerable domestic servant (often female),[229] or an apprentice, hireling, or lodger, often far from the support of home and family, charged with taking food, clothes, housewares, tools, or stock of the trade. Cases in which a suspect was overawed into confessing a crime of which he or she was completely ignorant were no doubt rare, but it was plausible for contemporaries to have been concerned that a frightened and bewildered servant, mistakenly accused of a crime by the master upon whom the servant depended for daily bread, might confess to something the servant had not done, if that is what the master insisted, especially when the master promised impunity or forgiveness (the "hope of favor" branch of the rule). Moreover, there were a few occasions in which alleged crimes arising out of domestic or workplace settings were ambiguous, in the sense that the servant had a tenable claim of entitlement to the allegedly stolen goods as part of an understanding about the terms of service.[230] Such cases were not smash-and-grab

---

[227] 3 Wigmore, *Evidence* § 820, at 353.   [228] Ibid.

[229] Beattie presents evidence that almost 40% of persons accused of property offenses in City of London cases tried at the Old Bailey across the years 1670–1750 were women, and that in the years 1690–1713 more men than women were accused. Beattie, *Policing* 63–71 and table 1.4. Regarding contemporary concern about theft by domestic servants, see id. at 37–8.

[230] Linebaugh treats such cases as a mainspring of criminal justice. Peter Linebaugh, *The London Hanged: Crime and Civil Society in the Eighteenth Century* (1991). In truth, such cases occurred quite rarely, see John H. Langbein, "Culprits and Victims," *Times Literary Supp.*, 11 Oct. 1991 (reviewing Linebaugh). Though rare, such cases did occur. Beattie has pointed to the trial of William Hayward, a coachman prosecuted by his vengeful former employer for the theft of an old harness that the employer had replaced with a new one. Under cross-examination by Garrow, the prosecutor admitted that Hayward had reason to believe the harness was his as a perquisite of the job. William Hayward, *OBSP* (Jan. 1790, #228), at 230, cited in John M. Beattie, Garrow for the Defense, *History Today* (Feb. 1991), at 49. Another

break-ins, but workplace disputes. The danger was that the master might determine to win the dispute with a three-step minuet: first instigating or threatening criminal prosecution, then promising impunity if the servant confessed stealing what the servant had taken without criminal intent, and then reneging on the promise not to prosecute the servant on the confession.

Another factor that motivated the expansive application of the "hope of favor" branch of the confession rule was the ever growing aversion to capital punishment for relatively minor crimes of theft.[231] Several of the statutes that had removed benefit of clergy from particular offenses were targeted at domestic and workplace offenders, including theft from a dwelling house of goods valued above 40s. and from a shop above 5s.[232] Although the increasing use of the sanction of transportation to the New World as an alternative to the death penalty for many offenses steadily reduced the penal death rate across the eighteenth century,[233] English criminal law still threatened vastly more executions than the authorities were prepared to inflict. A central objective of the eighteenth-century criminal justice system was to winnow down the number of applications of the capital sanction. I have discussed this phenomenon in Chapter 1, in connection with the encouragement given to juries to manipulate the values of stolen goods in order to rescue offenders for transportation (the partial verdict system), and I return to the topic in Chapter 5, when discussing why contemporaries showed such tolerance for the truth-defeating tendencies of adversary criminal trial. The present point is simply that in a system of criminal law that felt pressure to reduce the number of capital verdicts, there was less concern that the confession rule was somewhat error-prone. The rule was mostly applied to less serious felonies committed by less serious criminals, commonly young servants who had yielded to temptation or need. The judges who shaped the confession rule knew that the hardened gang criminals whom contemporaries most feared were not in general the people who were tendering confessions on a "hope of favor." Gang criminals were the main target of the crown witness system; and we have seen that the same judges who were extending the confession rule were simultaneously cutting back (in

instance: the East India Company prosecuted an employee, Hugh Doyle, for theft of pepper from its warehouse. Doyle was acquitted after Garrow, cross-examining, got the key prosecution witness to agree that it was "common [for such a worker] to have some of the pepper corns about your person when you go home at night[.]" Hugh Doyle, *OBSP* (Sept. 1784, #805), at 1119, 1120.

[231] Discussed in Ch. 5, *infra*, text at nn. 386–400; see generally 1 Radzinowicz, *History* 301–96, 450–607.

[232] Beattie, *Policing* 329, 335–7.

[233] A central theme of Beattie, *Crime* 471 ff; see esp. 620 and fig. 11.1; see also ibid. at 506–19, 530–48, 560–9, 582–601, 619–21; Beattie, *Policing* 427–62.

Atwood and Robbins) on the scope of protection against potentially perjured crown witness testimony.

The confession rule can also be linked to the two great prosecutorial initiatives of the age, the crown witness system and the reward system. We have already seen that, after some reluctance, the judges recognized that confessions uttered in the expectation of being made a crown witness fell squarely within the prohibitions of the "hope of favor" branch of the confession rule. For rewardable offenses such as burglary and highway robbery, the dangers of the reward system were also in the background. The entrepreneurial thieftakers, operating under the temptation of rewards as high as £140 per conviction, were capable both of rough stuff and of deception. Foster was hinting at this concern when he recorded his distrust of "hasty Confessions made to Persons having no Authority to examine," confessions that he called "the Weakest and most Suspicious of All Evidence. Proof may be too easily procured, Words are often Misreported . . . ."[234] Moreover, Foster continued, "this Evidence is not in the Ordinary Course of Things to be Disproved by that Sort of Negative Evidence by which the Proof of plain Facts May be and often is Confronted."[235] Moreover, even magistrates who did have authority to examine may not have been wholly beyond suspicion of rough stuff. No less a figure than Henry Fielding, in his work as court JP for Middlesex, boasted of the oppressive conditions in his effort to procure confessions. He told of "examining . . . and taking the depositions" of suspected gang members in sessions lasting "whole days, nay, sometimes whole nights, especially when there was any difficulty procuring sufficient evidence to convict them."[236]

We find a splendid illustration of the sort of thing that Foster was worried about in an Old Bailey case that arose in 1747, more than a decade before Foster's book, hence early enough in the development of the confession rule that the thieftaker was not yet aware that admitting to deception in procuring a confession could defeat the case. In the trial of George Welden for highway robbery in 1749, the thieftaker, Smith, boasted of his cleverness in deceiving the suspect during their pretrial encounter. "I said to him if you will confess, I'll discharge you from your confinement." Welden hesitated, asking Smith, "[W]ill you be trust to me?" Smith again assured him. Welden again probed, "[G]ive me your Hand and swear to be true to me." Smith persevered: "I gave him my Hand and Oath. I said, by God, if you will confess the Robbery, I'll discharge you from your Confinement."[237] Welden confessed, upon which Smith promptly had him

---

[234] Foster, *Crown Law* 243.   [235] Ibid.
[236] Henry Fielding, "Introduction," in *The Journal of a Voyage to Lisbon* 17, 20 (2d. ed. London 1755).
[237] George Welden, OBSP (Apr./May 1747, #179), at 124, 125.

locked up for trial. At the Old Bailey the trial judge before whom Smith testified about his duplicity sputtered in amazement: "What, to swear by your Maker, that if a Man will discover, you will discharge him . . . then . . . to bring him here for the Reward . . . ." The case arose before the confession rule had been settled, and the judge contented himself with pointing out that the jurors had no reason to credit Smith's testimony at trial. "You are telling them that you have no regard to an Oath."[238] The judge appears to have followed through on his inclination to treat the matter as one of weight or credit rather than excluding the evidence. The *Sessions Paper* tells us, probably ascribing the judge's instruction as the jury's rationale, that "[t]he jury acquitted the Prisoner, paying no regard to [Smith's] Evidence, who in so wicked and notorious a Manner, had forsworn himself, in order to extort a confession from [Welden], with an Intent, as it appeared to the Jury, to entitle himself to the Reward."[239]

I conclude, therefore, that the "hope of favor" branch of the confession rule was not an expression of the judges' "sentimental irrationality."[240] In forty years time, from the 1720s to the 1760s, English law had moved from Hawkins' ringing endorsement of confession evidence to Foster's view that confession was "the Weakest and most Suspicious of All Evidence." The new hostility to confession evidence was grounded in precisely those concerns about the potential unreliability of prosecution evidence that had motivated the corroboration rule, and that had led to the decision in the 1730s to allow defense counsel. These measures of safeguard developed in judicial practice to even up for the dangers and defensive disadvantage that had developed as a result of the prosecutorial initiatives discussed in Chapter 3.

E. Unfinished Business: The Hearsay Rule

The eighteenth-century *Sessions Papers* also give us an early window on what would become the central enterprise of the mature Anglo-American law of evidence, the hearsay rule. Unlike the three rules distinctive to the criminal trial (character, corroboration, and confession), the hearsay rule was shared with civil practice. And unlike the corroboration and confession rules, the hearsay rule did not have any particular connection to the shortcomings of pretrial criminal procedure. The ultimate rationale for the hearsay rule (serving the process value of promoting cross-examination) was not settled[241] until well into the early nineteenth century.

---

[238] Ibid. at 125.   [239] Ibid. at 126.

[240] 2 Wigmore, Evidence, § 865, at 353, cited *supra*, text at n. 226.

[241] The suggestion has been made that the difficulty in establishing the policy bases of the

Wigmore, who based his historical account on the *State Trials* and on civil cases reported in the nominate law reports, thought that the hearsay rule was forming through the later seventeenth century. He thought he found "by the beginning of the 1700s, a general and settled acceptance of [the hearsay] rule as a fundamental part of the law."[242] There were indeed cases in which hearsay was disapproved in the seventeenth and early eighteenth century, but Wigmore was mistaken in reading these cases as having settled the rule. I have already directed attention in this chapter to notable examples of hearsay evidence being received without objection in eighteenth-century Old Bailey trials.[243] Reported instances of hearsay evidence abound in the *Sessions Papers*[244] and other pamphlet sources. I have elsewhere discussed the picture that emerges from Dudley Ryder's extensive judge's notes for the civil trials over which he presided in 1754–6.[245] Counsel seldom objected to hearsay, and Ryder received it

hearsay rule as well as the continuing dissatisfaction about the proper scope of the rule trace to the confusion of hearsay with what is known in American constitutional parlance as the confrontation policy, that is, the right of the criminal accused "to be confronted with the witnesses against him . . . ." U.S. Constitution, Amendment 6 (1789). On the overlap between the two concepts, and on the English historical background to the confrontation policy, see Richard Friedman, "Confrontation: The Search for Basic Principles," 86 *Georgetown L. Rev.* 1011, 1022–5 (1998); id., "Anchors and Flotsam: Is Evidence Law 'Adrift'?," 107 *Yale L.J.* 1921, 1938–9 (1998) (review of Mirjan Damaska, *Evidence Law Adrift* (1997)).

I have been puzzled at the failure of the English common law to identify and develop the confrontation policy as a matter of doctrine. Even though the confrontation policy had not been adhered to in some notable Tudor State Trials, especially *R. v. Nicholas Throckmorton*, 1 *St. Tr.* 869 (1554), and *R. v. Walter Raleigh*, 2 *St. Tr.* 1, 14–15, 18 (1603), the policy was well understood by the later seventeenth century. See especially Hale's account of the rationale for "[t]he Excellency of this open Course of [hearing] Evidence to the Jury in Presence of the Judge, Jury, Parties and Counsel, and even of the adverse Witnesses . . . . [Where] there is Opportunity of confronting the adverse Witnesses . . . great Opportunities are gained for the true and clear Discovery of the Truth." Matthew Hale, *The History of the Common Law of England* 163–4 (Charles M. Gray ed.) (1971) (1st edn. 1713) [hereafter cited as Hale, *Common Law*] [posthumous publication, Hale died in 1676]. Interestingly, Hale emphasizes the importance of cross-examination in implementing the confrontation policy, but does not yet treat cross-examination as distinctively associated with counsel. "[T]here is Opportunity for all Persons concerned, *viz.* The Judge, or any of the Jury, or Parties, or their Counsel or Attorneys, to propound occasional Questions, which beats and bolts out the Truth much better than when the Witness only delivers a formal [statement] without being interrogated . . . ." Ibid. at 164. Hale was contrasting common law trial procedure in civil matters with the practice of the English civilian (i.e., ecclesiastical and university) courts, and perhaps the equity courts as well.

242 5 Wigmore, *Evidence* § 1364, at 26.

243 *Supra*, text at nn. 83, 95, 103, 106, 111, 114; *infra* n. 277.

244 I have discussed examples appearing in the *Sessions Papers* from the 1670s into the 1730s in Langbein, "CTBL" 301–2. Further examples from those sources in 1710s and 1720s are remarked in Stephan Landsman, "The Rise of the Contentious Spirit: Adversary Procedure in Eighteenth Century England," 75 *Cornell L. Rev.* 565–7 (1990) [hereafter Landsman, "Spirit"]. Examples from the 1750s are noticed in Thomas P. Gallanis, "The Rise of Modern Evidence Law," 84 *Iowa L. Rev.* 499, 514–15 (1999) [hereafter Gallanis, "Iowa"].

245 Langbein, "Evidence".

aplenty.[246] Lord Mansfield's notebooks in the 1780s[247] provide further instances of hearsay in civil trials. Goebel and Naughton reported similar findings from manuscript and pamphlet sources in criminal cases in colonial New York: "[A] good deal of testimony which would today be excluded as hearsay was regarded as admissible in the eighteenth century."[248]

We find greater sensitivity to what a modern Anglo-American lawyer would identify as hearsay on the criminal side. Beginning in the 1730s, the *Sessions Papers* began to report cases in which the court resisted such evidence.[249] In these cases of the 1730s and 1740s the judges did not speak of hearsay; rather they disapproved on the ground that the testimony was "no evidence." "What another told you is not evidence."[250] "What his Father told you is no Evidence."[251] "What one or the other told you is no Evidence. Is either of them here?"[252] "That's no Evidence. You must not swear what you heard, but only what you know."[253] "You must not swear what the Mother-in-Law told you—'Tis no Evidence."[254] "What her Fellow Servant told you is nothing; did you see her?"[255] Because the *Sessions Papers* underwent a change of format and enhancement of detail in the 1730 mayoral year,[256] it is certainly possible that the development being disclosed in the reports in the years just thereafter was occurring somewhat earlier but went unrecorded in the sources.

1. "No Evidence"

A helpful example of these early cases is the trial in 1732 of George Mason for taking a hat and 2s. from a woman in circumstances alleged to have

---

[246] Ibid. at 1186–90.

[247] James Oldham, "Truth-Telling in the Eighteenth-Century English Courtroom," 12 *Law and History Rev.* 95, at 104–5 and nn. 46–7 (1994) [hereafter cited as Oldham, "Truth-Telling"].

[248] Julius Goebel Jr. and T. Raymond Naughton, *Law Enforcement in Colonial New York: A Study in Criminal Procedure (1664–1776)*, at 642 (1944); see ibid. at 643–4 for discussion of instances of hearsay in prominent eighteenth-century trials.

[249] Beattie also cites a pair of such cases from the Surrey assize papers in 1739. Beattie, *Crime* 364 n. 123, citing Cobbing, *SAP* (Summer 1739), at 19; Edmundson, *SAP* (Lent 1759), at 7.

[250] Joseph Pearson, *OBSP* (Dec. 1732, #80), at 23 (rape).

[251] John Bennett, *OBSP* (Jan. 1733, #3), at 31 (murder).

[252] George Sutton and William Simonds, *OBSP* (June 1733, ##46–7), at 191, 193 (highway robbery).

[253] Mercy Hornby, *OBSP* (Apr. 1734, #22), at 108, 109 (infanticide).

[254] Christian Brown and Sarah Thursby, *OBSP* (Dec. 1734, #69), at 17–18 (theft of clothing).

[255] Mary Pope, *OBSP* (Oct. 1746, #357), at 293 (infanticide).

[256] Mayoral years began in December of the preceding year, hence in this instance the change in format effective with the 1730 year commenced in December 1729. The change in format in 1729–30 is discussed in Beattie, *Policing* 373–4; Langbein, "CTBL" 270.

constituted highway robbery. The case grew out of events in a pub, the Cow's Face. At his trial Mason defended by attacking the prosecutor's motives and perception, asserting that the prosecutor was so drunk that neither the female publican nor "her Man" (an employee) would let the prosecuting victim have any more. Three witnesses then testified on the defendant's behalf "that [t]he Man at the Cow's Face told me the same thing," whereupon a constable testified, apparently in reply, that "the same Man told me . . . that the Prisoner and his two Companions were three notorious rogues, and that he would draw them no more drink, but turned them out of Doors, for he would not have a Disturbance in his House." At this point the court appears to have had enough hearsay and is quoted as saying: "What was said by the Man or Woman at the Cow's Face is no Evidence on either side, except they were here to swear it themselves."[257]

We see in the court's intervention in *Mason's Case* traits that would characterize the judicial treatment of hearsay in criminal cases for decades. The court did not speak of hearsay, but rather disapproved of the testimony on the opaque ground that it was "no Evidence." As late as 1753 the *Sessions Paper* reporter was so unfamiliar with the term "hearsay" that he misspelled it. "This here-say is not evidence, and should not have been printed," he said in an apologetic footnote to certain testimony, explaining that it was needed to give coherence to the rest of the report.[258] (The implication that the reporter may have had a systematic bias for underreporting hearsay is another warning about the unpredictable selectivity of *Sessions Paper* reports.) Because the court in *Mason's Case* is not reported to have excluded the testimony, in the sense of directing the jury to disregard it, the judge's intervention is more likely to have been meant as an exercise of the judicial power to comment on the evidence than as an instruction to exclude.

The idea that something is "no Evidence" suggests that the court knows what evidence is. This formulation resonates with an older meaning of the concept of evidence, growing out of the pleading of civil cases, in which the question was constantly raised of whether particular facts were sufficient to sustain the plaintiff's writ. That question was a matter of substantive law, hence remote from the central task of the modern law of evidence, which is to control the fact-adducing process at trial. (In criminal practice the parallel question, as framed in Hawkins' treatise, was "What Evidence maintains an Indictment."[259]) This earlier conception of the law of evidence endured throughout the eighteenth century—in the

---

[257] George Mason, *OBSP* (Dec. 1731), at 13, 14. The defendant was convicted. Landsman extracts the key language of the case, see Landsman, "Spirit," *supra* n. 244, at 567–8.

[258] James Bignall, *OBSP* (Sept. 1753, #414), at 253 (theft of money).

[259] 2 Hawkins, *PC* 428, further expounded ibid. at 435–8.

abridgements, such as Viner[260] and Strange;[261] in Gilbert's *Evidence*, the dominant eighteenth-century treatise;[262] and in Buller's *Nisi Prius* (1772),[263] which was the standard guide to civil-side assize practice.

This older conception of what was meant by the term "evidence" would die out in the nineteenth century, as the modern convention of organizing substantive law by doctrinal categories such as tort and property replaced the old writ-based scheme that attempted to arrange substantive law along lines suggested by procedure and pleading. What linked the two concepts of evidence law and permitted the same word to be used to describe such disparate phenomena as rules of substantive law and rules of proof is the notion of materiality, that is, the court's power to refuse to waste time hearing pointless evidence.[264] Evidence that is "no Evidence" on the matter in question is immaterial. The later law of evidence, understood as the rules governing the proofs at trial, extended the technique of refusing evidence from the ground of materiality to other policies that were thought to promote the accuracy of verdicts.

Beyond the label "no Evidence," the ruling in *Mason's Case* in 1732 supplied a further ground of decision. The judge explained that what was wrong with the testimony was that the out-of-court declarants were not present at trial "to swear it themselves," that is, they were not on oath. The hearsay evidence lacked that enhancement to veracity thought to arise from placing the declarant on oath. The judge did not refer to the other policy ground for excluding hearsay, the concern that hearsay permitted the out-of-court declarant whose statement was being reported to the court to escape cross-examination. There is case law on the civil side

---

[260] Viner's volume 12 was devoted all but entirely to collecting such cases. 12 Charles Viner, *General Abridgement of Law and Equity* (London 1741–175[7]) (23 vols.). Viner collected a few entries labelled "hearsay," most of which bear on sufficiency and are remote from modern hearsay conceptions. 12 ibid. at 118–119. (Viner's volume 12 was the last of the twenty-three volumes to be published; Holdsworth reckons that it actually appeared in 1757, the year after Viner died. 12 Holdsworth, *HEL* 165 n. 3.)

[261] Anon., *A Collection of Select Cases Relating to Evidence: By a Late Barrister at Law* (London 1754) (attributed to Sir John Strange).

[262] Gilbert, *Evidence* 113–99, discussing "the several Issues in each Particular Action . . . ," ibid. at 113. Gilbert died in 1726; the treatise was first published in 1754. Macnair believes that the book was written early in the 1700s, because "[a]ll citations after 1710 in the printed book are absent from the [surviving manuscript sources for the book]." Michael Macnair, "Sir Jeffrey Gilbert and His Treatises," 15 *J. Leg. Hist.* 252, 266–7 n. 107 (1994).

[263] Buller, *Nisi Prius*, *supra* n. 150, at 217–79.

[264] Modern accounts of the law of evidence continue to recognize the linkage between the requirement of materiality and the substantive law of the case. McCormick says: "If the evidence is offered to prove a proposition that is not a matter in issue, the evidence is immaterial. What is 'in issue,' that is, within the range of the litigated controversy, is determined mainly by the pleadings, read in the light of the rules of pleading and controlled by the substantive law." 1 McCormick, *Evidence*, *supra* n. 59, § 185, at 637.

invoking that concern as early as 1668.[265] Hawkins raised the point in his treatise in 1721, explaining that hearsay "is in Strictness no Manner of Evidence either for or against a Prisoner, not only because it is not upon Oath, but also because the other Side hath no Opportunity of a cross Examination . . . ."[266] But concern about the want of cross-examination remained a muted theme in criminal practice throughout the eighteenth century. The first judicial mention of that rationale for excluding what we would call hearsay that has come to my attention in the *Sessions Papers* turns up in 1789,[267] in the decade when the use of defense counsel was becoming more frequent.[268]

Despite the trend to disapprove of what we would recognize as hearsay, which appears to set in from the 1730s onward in cases at the Old Bailey, contrary cases occurred for decades. Chief Justice Lee remarked in 1744 that, despite the rule "that hearsay cannot be admitted, . . . it is notorious that from necessity [it has] been allowed."[269] As examples of such cases, Oldham has pointed to instances in which hearsay appears to have been allowed because the parties who could have given nonhearsay testimony were disqualified for interest.[270] Moreover, there was an expansive and longstanding notion that hearsay testimony was unobjectionable when it supplemented sworn testimony. Speaking of the two witnesses

---

[265] 2 *Rolle's Abridgment* 679, pl. 9 (London 1668), cited by Edmund M. Morgan, "Hearsay Dangers and the Application of the Hearsay Concept," 62 *Harvard L. Rev.* 177, 182 and n. 7 (1948).

[266] 2 Hawkins, *PC* 431.

[267] William Woodcock, *OBSP* (Jan. 1789, #98), at 95 (murder); *R. v. Woodcock*, 1 *Leach* 500, 168 *Eng. Rep.* 352 (1789) (same case). Baron Eyre, presiding, applied what is in modern parlance the dying declaration exception to the hearsay rule (on which, see 2 McCormick, *Evidence, supra* n. 59, §§ 309–12, at 305–11), and allowed testimony that the dying victim said that her husband, the defendant, beat her to death. Eyre contrasted this special case with the norm: "ordinarily legal evidence consists in the deposition [i.e., testimony] of witnesses, taken on oath, before the jury, administered in the face of the court where the prisoner is tried; and that evidence comes down to the jury, under all the advantages which examination and cross-examination give." *OBSP* (Jan. 1789), at 111.

In a similar case a few years earlier, the statement of an allegedly murdered boy was excluded. Baron Eyre and Nares J justified the exclusion entirely on the want of oath, not the want of cross-examination. William Higson, *OBSP* (Apr. 1785, #415), at 536. Narres told a witness who was about to quote the child: "I think you are not to tell us what the boy said . . . [Y]ou see, gentlemen of the Jury, that declaration was not upon oath . . . nor was [the boy] in that sort of state, to enforce what he said to be true; as for instance, the declarations of dying people not expecting to recover, have that influence on their minds and consciences at that time which makes them equal to an oath . . . ." Ibid. at 539. Eyre agreed: "All evidence against prisoners is to be on oath, with one exception, which is a declaration without oath by a person who conceives himself to be in a dying condition, as to the author of the injury he has received. And that is upon this ground, that the situation of such a party creates an obligation upon his mind to speak the truth, equal to the sanction of an oath." Ibid.

[268] *Supra* Ch. 3, text at n. 302.

[269] *Omychund v. Barker*, 1 *Atk.* 21, 46, 26 *Eng. Rep.* 15, 31 (Ch. 1744).

[270] Oldham, "Truth-Telling," *supra* n. 247, at 103–5, 113–17.

required in treason cases, Matthew Hale thought that "[t]hese witnesses must not be only by hearsay."[271] Hawkins explained that hearsay may be used "only by way of inducement or illustration of what is properly Evidence."[272] Gilbert wrote that although "Hearsay be not allowed as direct Evidence, yet it may be in Corroboration of a Witness' Testimony . . . ."[273] Christopher Allen observes about this steady use of hearsay that although contemporaries "had been aware of the weakness of hearsay evidence," they "had not thought themselves bound to reject it absolutely, and quite often had used it to introduce, explain, or corroborate more regular proof."[274] I suspect that this tolerance for supplementary hearsay was the justification for those recurrent cases that I have earlier referred to as "pursuit hearsay," in which hearsay was adduced about how an accused attracted suspicion upon himself or how a particular investigation had been conducted.[275]

The Old Bailey also tolerated flagrant hearsay in rape prosecutions involving a child victim who was not competent to testify because she was too young to appreciate the significance of her oath.[276] The judges

[271] Matthew Hale, *Pleas of the Crown: Or, a Methodical Summary of the Principal Matters Relating to that Subject* 262 (London 1694) (posthumous publication, written before 1676) (this work is different from Hale's treatise, the two-volume *History of the Pleas of the Crown*, which is cited as Hale, *HPC* in this book).

[272] 2 Hawkins, *PC* 431. This passage was cited to the court in *R. v. Mary Heath*, 18 St. Tr. 1 (K.B. Ireland 1744) (perjury). When the court interrupted a witness who was about to offer hearsay, counsel offering the witness referred the court to Hawkins' statement of the "rule, that hearsay evidence, that serves to illustrate what is the proper evidence to be given before the Court, shall be admitted." The court replied: "Hearsay-evidence may be made use of to introduce material evidence, but when a witness has said all that is material, we shall not admit that." Ibid. at 67.

[273] The passage in full: "Hearsay be not allowed as direct Evidence, yet it may be in Corroboration of a Witness' Testimony to show that he affirmed the same thing before on other Occasions, and that the Witness is still consistent with himself; for such Evidence is only in Support of the Witness that gives in his Testimony upon Oath." Gilbert, *Evidence* 108.

[274] Allen, *Evidence, supra* n. 168, at 24.

[275] *Supra*, text at n. 115. A notable example appears in the case of Thomas Edwards and others who were prosecuted for a highway robbery committed upon a clergyman in 1732. The victim gave in evidence a lengthy account, all of it hearsay, of how the robbers came under suspicion and were captured:

> On the Sunday following [the robbery], some Persons came from Rag-Fair to visit a Man in Swan-Alley, near my Brother's . . . Brewhouse, and they sent for a Pot of Beer, and so they fell into Discourse. "And how goes Trade your Way?," says one. "Why, truly, but so-so," says another, "but Robbing goes forward however." "Robbing?," says a third. "Ay," says the second, see what a pass the World is come to! We had a Clergyman robbed here last Wednesday Night between 12 and 1." "A Clergyman?," says the fourth to the first. "Why, did not we see some Fellows in Rag-Fair with a Parson's Hat?" "And so we did, now I think of it," says his Neighbor. The Alehouse-Man who was one of the Company alerted my Brother with what had passed, and the Prisoners were afterwards taken in Rag-Fair.

Thomas Edwards *et al., OBSP* (Feb. 1732, ##41–3), at 89, 90.

[276] Hale recommended hearing the child's testimony unsworn but requiring sworn corroboration evidence for the jury to convict, 1 Hale, *HPC* 634 (an application of the notion

were disposed to compensate by allowing the mother, a surgeon, or others to whom the child had spoken contemporaneously upon the happening of the events to give an account of what the child had then said.[277] Such cases appear in the *Sessions Papers* for almost a century, from

that hearsay was unobjectionable when merely illustrative of or corroborated by sworn testimony). Some judges adhered to this practice as late as 1775, when the Twelve Judges by split decision resolved against it, saying "that in criminal cases no testimony can be received except upon oath." *R. v. Powell*, 1 Leach 109, 168 *Eng. Rep.* 157 (1775); accord *R. v. Brasier*, 1 *Leach* 199, 168 *Eng. Rep.* 202 (1779), discussed *infra*, n. 278. The Twelve Judges' rationale was in tension with the rule allowing the criminal accused to speak unsworn (he was forbidden to testify on oath in England until 1898), but the problem was wished away by labelling— the accused was treated as defending rather than testifying.

As a matter of substantive criminal law, statute treated carnal knowledge of a child under 10 as rape without regard to whether she consented. 18 Eliz. 1, c. 7 (1576). In a case involving a child a few months older, an Old Bailey judge directed an acquittal on the ground of ambiguity about whether the child consented, "the prosecution not being able to prove a direct Force upon the Child." John Hunter, *OBSP* (Apr. 1747, #208), at 142, 145.

Acquittals such as this in what seem to be well-proven rape cases were astonishingly common in the eighteenth-century *Sessions Papers*, in part because, for reasons discussed, *supra* n. 102, victims too young to testify were a favorite target of offenders. Another factor is the sense that juries may have thought the capital sanction too hard, at least in some cases. This concern was voiced in a rape prosecution at Sussex assizes in 1786. After deliberating for half an hour, the jurors returned to ask the judge "whether there could be any medium" between acquittal and death. Told not, they acquitted. *The Trial of John Motherhill for Committing a Rape on the Body of Miss Catharine Wade* 35 (London 1786). For discussion of defense counsel's tactics in rape cases, see *infra*, Ch. 5, text and note at n. 214.

[277] In Langbein, "CTBL" 291–3, I have reproduced in full an early example, the trial of Stephen Arrowsmith, which is reported in exceptional detail in the pamphlet account of Old Bailey trials for December 1678. *Exact Account* 14–16. In that case the child victim and a playmate, aged 8 and 9 respectively, were heard unsworn, but later sworn and reexamined when the jury expressed uneasiness about their not being sworn. Hearsay was received from four witnesses (a midwife and a doctor who examined the victim, and two women who apparently had her in their care) about what she told them when the event was detected. The trial judge defended the use of hearsay on the ground that "such Offenders never call others to be by while they commit such actions," and that the victim was too young to be sworn. Ibid. at 16. When the jury resisted convicting, the judge changed his mind and had the victim and another child repeat their testimony under oath. (This case is discussed in another connection, *infra* Ch. 5, text at nn. 361–4.)

Further instances of such cases from the *Sessions Paper*:

(1) Adam White, *OBSP* (July 1726), at 7, was charged with ravishing his 11 year old daughter. The child testified (whether or not on oath is not disclosed) that the incident occurred in the house of her aunt where she lodged, and that she told no one for several weeks until the mistress to whom she was apprenticed became suspicious. The mistress then testified that "I found a disorder in her linen, she said she was gauld [sic; infected with venereal disease; from 'Gaul', the French disease]. I sent for Nurse Stevens, who said she believed that it was the foul Disease, and that her Father had given it her. For my part I did not Examine the matter myself, but I sent for a Surgeon, and he said she was not torn, he could not perceive there had been any Penetration, but only a running, though he could not say it was the foul Disease." Ibid. The report then concludes: "Neither the Aunt, the Nurse, or the Surgeon appearing to give a farther light into the Affair, the Jury Acquitted the Prisoner."

(2) Thomas Norris, *OBSP* (Dec. 1741, #54) at 17. The landlady of the house, the child's aunt, and a surgeon testified to what child said at the time; the child was also examined, although whether or not on oath is not disclosed. On cross-examination the surgeon admitted that he

the 1670s into the 1760s, but no formal exception to the hearsay rule developed for them, doubtless because they were too hard to reconcile with the core policy motivating the hearsay rule (be it oath or cross-examination). In 1779 the Twelve Judges pronounced against receiving the testimony unless the child were sworn.[278]

had doubts whether the offense could have been committed in the fashion the third claimed. Another surgeon, who had not examined the child but doubted her story, testified for the defendant. Two character witnesses testified for the accused. He was acquitted.

(3) John Birmingham, *OBSP* (May 1753, #217), at 147, a case in which the trial judge excluded the hearsay, telling the mother who was testifying, "You must not say any thing the girl told you." Ibid. at 148. The judge gave no reason (or if he did, the reporter did not preserve it).

(4) William Kick, *OBSP* (May–June 1754, #341), at 215. "There being no other evidence against the prisoner than the hearsay from the child's mother, it was not judged sufficient [directed verdict of acquittal?]; he was therefore acquitted, but detained to be tried on another indictment at Hicks Hall [Middlesex Quarter Sessions] for an assault with an intent to commit a rape ..." Ibid. at 216. Quaere here (and in the next case) whether the implication is that hearsay deemed insufficient to convict for felony rape might be sufficient upon a trial for misdemeanor.

(5) Thomas Crosby, *OBSP* (Dec. 1757, #17), at 8, 9. The child's mother testified about what the child told her. The report concludes: "The child being but nine years old, and not being examined upon oath, [the defendant] was acquitted; but detained to be tried next sessions for an assault upon the child, with an intent to commit a rape ..." Ibid.

(6) Isaac Spicer, *OBSP* (Dec. 1768, #78), at 33. The mother of the 6-year-old child testified about what the child told her. "The child being too young to be examined, he was acquitted."

(7) William Allam [sic], *OBSP* (Sept. 1768, #538), at 319. The mother of the 8-year-old child testified about what the child told her. He was acquitted.

Beattie discusses another such case that arose at Surrey assizes in 1739. Beattie, *Crime* 364 n. 122, citing Bromley, *SAP* (Lent 1739), at 22.

A pamphlet report of a trial conducted at Hertford assizes in 1753 supplies a further instance. Joseph Law, a surgeon, testified to having examined the 16-year-old victim and finding "that there had been a penetration; I examined the Girl concerning it, and she said, her Father had lain with her by Force, and she farther owned to me, that she felt something come from her father warm into her." Anon., *The Trial of Job Wells of Redburn in the County of Hertford* 6 (London 1753).

[278] *R. v. Brazier*, 1 *Leach* 199, 168 *Eng. Rep.* 262 (1779). The case arose at Reading Assizes and was referred to the Twelve Judges. The victim was under the age of 7. Her mother and a woman lodger testified about what the child said at the time of the event. The Twelve Judges said that even a 7-year-old might be sworn and admitted as a witness, if she could adequately appreciate "the nature and consequences of an oath," but that "no testimony whatever can be legally received except upon oath ...." Accordingly, "the evidence of the information which the infant had given to her mother and the other witness, ought not to have been received." Ibid. at 200, 168 *Eng. Rep.* at 202–3.

Michael Foster, who died in 1763, seems to have been inclining to this result. On blank pages interleaved in his copy of Hale's *Pleas of the Crown*, he wrote about the agonizing conflict of policies that arose "[i]n cases of foul facts done in secret and where the child is the party injured[.] I think the repelling of the evidence of children totally is in some measure denying them the protection of the law, which is every subject's birthright .... But that the levity and inexperience of children are undoubtedly circumstances that go greatly to their credit." Foster, Hale MS following 263. The same source shows that Foster compiled a list of eighteenth-century precedents respecting the admissibility of child witnesses, several from a source he describes as "Manuscript Denton." Oldham thinks the source was a manuscript

The Old Bailey sources show us that by the end of the eighteenth century the hearsay rule was firmly in place in criminal practice. Thomas Gallanis' extensive study confirms an equivalent development of the hearsay rule in the practice of the civil courts. Working from the published law reports and the treatise literature, Gallanis finds a significant increase in the frequency of hearsay objections in civil litigation of the 1780s and 1790s.[279]

2. Counsel's Influence

I said at the outset of this chapter that counsel does not appear to have played much of a role in the initial development of the law of criminal evidence. The character rule largely predates the change in practice that allowed defense counsel in felony trials. Counsel was still relatively uncommon in the 1740s and immediately thereafter when both the corroboration and confession rules took shape. In the early development of the hearsay rule, as we would now call it, we have one detailed instance of counsel protesting the hearsay and insisting on a curative instruction. In the trial of Samuel Goodere for murder at Bristol Assizes in 1741,[280] the prosecution solicitor was serving as a central fact witness. Under examination by prosecution counsel he related that the decedent told him that the accused, Samuel Goodere, the decedent's brother, had, at the time of their father's death, procured some people "to take away his life."[281] Defense counsel, Shephard, protested to the trial judge (Michael Foster, sitting as recorder of Bristol, who twenty years later would write Foster's *Crown Law*):

MR. SHEPHARD. I must submit it to the Court, that what [the decedent] said at that time is not matter of evidence.

MR. RECORDER. It is not evidence, but perhaps it is introductory to something Mr. Smith has further to say: if it be not, it should not have been mentioned. . . .

MR. SHEPHARD. Whether this be evidence, I insist upon it in point of law that it is not, and it may have an effect upon the jury.

MR. RECORDER. I will take notice to the jury what is not evidence. Go on, Mr. Smith.[282]

---

owned by Denton J (C.P. 1727–40), and he notes that Foster cited the manuscript in his published work, e.g., Foster, *Crown Law* 108, 185. Thus, Foster recorded a child "about nine admitted to prove a rape on herself by Holt" (O.B. 1705); "[o]ne under twelve admitted in [King's Bench in] 1709"; a child "of ten years and eleven months admitted at Old Bailey to prove a rape on herself" (O.B., Apr. 1704) (per Holt and Tracey JJ); "[c]hild of five or six refused [in] Stuart's case. One of seven refused by Raymond at Kingston [Assizes], April 1726." Ibid.

[279] Gallanis, "Iowa," *supra* n. 244, at 533.

[280] *R. v. Samuel Goodere*, 17 St. Tr. 1003 (Bristol Assizes 1741), discussed in another respect, *supra* Ch. 3, text at nn. 321–4.

[281] Ibid. at 1018.   [282] Ibid. at 1018.

We see in this passage that defense counsel raised the hearsay objection and successfully resisted the court's initial instinct to dismiss it under the exception for mere illustration or introduction.

The *Old Bailey Sessions Papers* do not let us detect the hand of counsel in pressing hearsay objections across the eighteenth century. We cannot say whether this is an illusion of the sources, reflecting the *Sessions Papers'* lack of interest in such housekeeping matters, or whether hearsay objections were rare. In the 1780s, however, we do catch one glimpse of pressure from defense counsel to apply and extend the rule, the force that would become ever more insistent in the nineteenth century. In the trial of William Jones for the theft of iron goods in 1783 we see William Garrow, who became the dominant Old Bailey barrister of the day, chipping away at the exception for pursuit hearsay. A constable narrating certain of the circumstances produced some of the stolen goods and said, "I asked Mrs. Dunn whose they were." Garrow, representing the defendant, interrupted the constable: "You must not tell us what she said." Opposing counsel protested: "He must tell his story." Garrow replied: "Then I will apply to the Court whether this man is to tell us what Mrs. Dunn and Mrs. Brett said." Said the judge: "No, certainly not."[283] In this revealing exchange we see the opposition between the older notion of the altercation trial ("He must tell his story") and the dawning system of filtering testimony through a counsel-administered web of evidence rules. The law of evidence may have been a judicial creation, but it had the effect of empowering counsel. Although the rules of evidence crystallized out of the judge's discretion over the conduct of trials in his courtroom, in the new setting of adversary combat the quest for advantage in the particular case would cause counsel to press to extend such potentially expansive principles as the hearsay rule.

Lawyerization had the long-term effect of putting pressure on the bench to turn discretionary practice into rule, not only because lawyers tended to push the logic of a rule to embrace new cases, but also because lawyers were a force for consistency in practice among the different judges before whom they appeared.[284] We see this process under way in

---

[283] William Jones, *OBSP* (Dec. 1783, #102), at 130, 131.

[284] There were, of course, other mechanisms of coordination, of which the Twelve Judges procedure was the most explicit. Moreover, all the common law judges were members of one of three collegial courts (King's Bench, Common Pleas, Exchequer), whose members sat together on civil matters (and in King's Bench, on the relatively few criminal cases that were tried at bar). The clerical establishment at the Old Bailey and on the assize circuits was also a source for guidance for the judges about prior practice. Leonard MacNally, an Irish barrister who became an Old Bailey practitioner in the 1780s, wrote a practice manual in which he depicted a clerk of the arraigns explaining to the Old Bailey in 1784 what the court's practice was in admitting pretrial confessions. MacNally, *Evidence, supra* n. 1, at 33. Because assize courts had no permanent seat, the clerk of assize for each circuit supplied the organizational continuity, which gave him a position of influence with the judges, whose service on the

FIG. 4.2. *Accommodating counsel in the Old Bailey.* This print, from the early years of the nineteenth century, shows how the Old Bailey, was reconfigured in the building erected in 1774 to accommodate the growing role of lawyers in the conduct of criminal trials. The interior shows, from left to right, below the elevated bench: the counsel's table, a witness (the woman standing) being examined, the jury box (three rows of four jurors), and the prisoner's dock. Public galleries are in the background above and are hinted in the center foreground.

another Old Bailey case in 1789. Garrow argued on behalf of an accused who had confessed to the arresting constable that the confession should be disallowed for violation of the "hope of favor" branch of the confession rule. The constable's words fell within "the language I remember of Mr. Justice Gross on our last circuit, [that the confessing suspect] 'must neither be influenced by hopes nor awed by fears.'"[285] Garrow was doubtless intrigued by the limitless potential of the term "influenced by hopes," which offered a means of extending the rule to his weak case. (The Old Bailey judge refused and allowed the confession.) Looking back from the mid-nineteenth century, the treatise writer William Best pointed to counsel's influence in the development of the law of evidence. "[T]he necessary consequence of [allowing defense counsel] was that objections to the admissibility of evidence were much more frequently taken, the attention of the judges was more directed to the subject of evidence, their judgments were better considered, and their decisions better remembered."[286]

circuit rotated. For example, in 1754 Dudley Ryder recorded a series of observations from the Home Circuit clerk of assize Jerome Knapp about how the recent statutes of 1752 and 1754 for subsidizing some costs of criminal prosecutions were being implemented. Ryder, "Assize Diary" 7, 13, 16, 25, which I have transcribed in part in Langbein, "Ryder" 122 n. 495.

[285] Michael Hay, *OBSP* (May 1789, #365), at 464, 469.

[286] William M. Best, *A Treatise on the Principles of Evidence and Practice as to Proofs in Courts of Common Law* 133 (London 1849), [hereafter Best, *Treatise*].

3. Cross-Examination as the Rationale

Concern to promote cross-examination became the central justification for the hearsay rule in later law. We can find that concern raised in an isolated civil case as early as 1668.[287] Hawkins made the point in his treatise in 1721, explaining that hearsay "is in Strictness no Manner of Evidence either for or against a Prisoner, not only because it is not upon Oath, but also because the other Side hath no Opportunity of a cross Examination . . . ."[288] Nevertheless, concern about the want of cross-examination remained a muted theme in criminal practice throughout the eighteenth century. The first judicial mention of that rationale for excluding what we would call hearsay that has come to my attention in the *Sessions Papers* turns up in 1789,[289] in the decade when the use of defense counsel was becoming frequent.[290]

Gallanis has examined the evidence treatises of the eighteenth and nineteenth centuries. He finds the turn of the century as the period in which the dominant rationale for the hearsay rule shifts from oath to cross-examination.[291] Concern about the absence of cross-examination "appeared first in Lofft's 1791 revision of Gilbert, although only in connection with criminal cases. By 1801, however, Peake's treatise

---

[287] See *supra* n. 265.

[288] 2 Hawkins, *PC* 431.

[289] William Woodcock, *OBSP* (Jan. 1789, #98), at 95 (murder); *R. v. Woodcock*, 1 *Leach* 500, 168 *Eng. Rep.* 352 (1789) (same case). Baron Eyre, presiding, applied what is in modern parlance the dying declaration exception to the hearsay rule (on which, see 2 McCormick, *Evidence*, *supra* n. 59, §§ 309–12, at 305–11), and allowed testimony that the dying victim said that her husband, the defendant, beat her to death. Eyre contrasted this special case with the norm: "ordinarily legal evidence consists in the deposition [i.e., testimony] of witnesses, taken on oath, before the jury, administered in the face of the court where the prisoner is tried; and that evidence comes down to the jury, under all the advantages which examination and cross-examination give." *OBSP* (Jan. 1789), at 111.

In a similar case a few years earlier, the statement of an allegedly murdered boy was excluded. Baron Eyre and Nares J justified the exclusion entirely on the want of oath, not the want of cross-examination. William Higson, *OBSP* (Apr. 1785, #415), at 536. Narres told a witness who was about to quote the child: "I think you are not to tell us what the boy said . . . . [Y]ou see, gentlemen of the Jury, that declaration was not upon oath . . . nor was [the boy] in that sort of state, to enforce what he said to be true; as for instance, the declarations of dying people not expecting to recover, have that influence on their minds and consciences at that time which makes them equal to an oath . . . ." Ibid. at 539. Eyre agreed: "All evidence against prisoners is to be on oath, with one exception, which is a declaration without oath by a person who conceives himself to be in a dying condition, as to the author of the injury he has received. And that is upon this ground, that the situation of such a party creates an obligation upon his mind to speak the truth, equal to the sanction of an oath." Ibid.

[290] *Supra* Ch. 3, text at n. 302.

[291] Gallanis, "Iowa," *supra* n. 244, at 533. Gallanis has pointed to the timing of this development as support for the suggestion that criminal trial practice was shaping the law of civil evidence. He is particularly persuasive in identifying data that barristers who had Old Bailey criminal practices were more aggressive in raising evidentiary objections. Ibid. at 543–50. On the same theme, see Langbein, "Evidence" 1201–2.

presented the two rationales on equal terms and for Evans in 1806 the lack of cross-examination was 'the stronger objection.' "[292] Early nineteenth-century practice books can be found that continue to treat oath as the basis for the hearsay rule, for example, Dickenson's quarter sessions manual in 1815,[293] but with the publication of Starkie's treatise on evidence in 1824,[294] a pivotal work, the primacy of the cross-examination-based theory was established.

Belief in cross-examination as "the most perfect and effectual system for the unraveling of falsehood ever devised by the ingenuity of mortals"[295] became a central argument for abolishing that pillar of the older law, the testimonial disqualification of parties for interest. Even Bentham, the most caustic contemporary critic of the early nineteenth-century English law of evidence, accepted cross-examination uncritically as the assumed pathway to truth in fact-finding. "Against erroneous or mendacious testimony, the grand security is cross-examination . . . ."[296] Underlying the movement from oath-based to cross-examination-based theories of safeguard in the law of evidence was a changed view of what promoted veracity. The oath-based system presupposed the witness's fear that God would damn a perjurer. In place of the former reliance upon the vengeance of God, the new order substituted its faith in the truth-detecting efficacy of cross-examining lawyers.

The puzzle about the ready acceptance of cross-examination as the guarantor of truth is that contemporaries were well aware how easily cross-examination could be abused for partisan and truth-defeating ends. In 1787 Sir John Hawkins, the prominent London magistrate, expressed the concern that fear of abusive cross-examination had become a deterrent to prosecution. Potential prosecutors worried, said Hawkins, that "[t]hey may be entangled or made to contradict themselves, or each other,

---

[292] Gallanis, "Iowa," supra n. 244, at 533, citing Thomas Peake, A Compendium of the Law of Evidence 7 (London 1801); William D. Evans, "On the Law of Evidence" 283, in 2 Robert J. Pothier, A Treatise on the Law of Obligations (W. D. Evans trans.) (London 1806) (2 vols.).

[293] Anon. [William Dickenson], A Practical Guide to the Quarter, and Other Sessions of the Peace. Adapted to the Use of Young Magistrates and Gentlemen of the Legal Profession, at the Commencement of Their Public Duties 221–2 (London 1815).

[294] Thomas Starkie, A Practical Treatise of the Law of Evidence, and Digest of Proofs in Civil and Criminal Proceedings 40 ff (London 1824), discussed in Gallanis, "Iowa," supra n. 244, at 516–23.

[295] The language of an anonymous American commentator writing in 1857: "Of the Disqualification of Parties as Witnesses," 5 American L. Register 257, 262 (1857), cited in Joel N. Bodansky, "The Abolition of the Party-Witness Disqualification: An Historical Survey," 70 Kentucky L. Rev. 91, 96 (1981–2).

[296] 5 Jeremy Bentham, Rationale of Judicial Evidence Specially Applied to English Practice 212 n. (London 1827) (5 vols.). Bentham is thought to have written the Rationale c.1802–12. A. D. E. Lewis, "The Background to Bentham on Evidence," 2 Utilitas 195, 203–10 (1990). Further instances of Bentham's reliance on counsel-conducted examination and cross-examination are noticed in Stephan Landsman, "From Gilbert to Bentham: The Reconceptualization of Evidence Theory," 36 Wayne L. Rev. 1149, 1181–2 (1990) [hereafter Landsman, "Wayne"].

in a cross examination, by prisoner's counsel . . . ."[297] In 1819 John Payne Collier spoke of the "abuses of the Bar" in cross-examining witnesses, which cause truthful testimony to "be defeated by those who have attained such skill in confusing what is clear, and involving [that is, making complex] what is simple."[298] Contemporaries knew that the purpose of cross-examination was to win, whether that entailed seeking or distorting the truth. I shall have more to say in Chapter 5 about the centrality of cross-examination in the dawning system of adversary criminal trial across the eighteenth century, and about some of the factors that caused the jurists of the nineteenth century to base the law of evidence upon so flawed a theory of truth-seeking.

F. Groping for the Lever: Excluding Evidence

Speaking in 1790 in a King's Bench case, Chief Justice Kenyon said: "All questions upon the rules of evidence are of vast importance to all orders and degrees of men . . . . [These rules] have been matured by the wisdom of ages and are now revered from their antiquity and the good sense in which they are founded . . . ."[299] Kenyon's opinion strikes us as questionable in several respects. We have seen that the law of evidence, at least in criminal cases, was in Kenyon's day still a fairly recent product, hardly a descendant from English "antiquity." Far from having "matured," the law of evidence was then still in its infancy. Furthermore, the importance that Kenyon attached to "the rules of evidence" seems quite out of proportion to the still frail body of law that has been described in this chapter, even if we also take into account the large and important set of rules about proving documents on the civil side.[300] Indeed, Kenyon's contemporary Edmund Burke seems to have been closer to the mark when he quipped a few years later in the House of Commons that the rules of "the law of evidence . . . [were] very general, very abstract, and comprised in so small a compass that a parrot he had known might get them by rote in one half hour, and repeat them in five minutes."[301]

---

[297] John Hawkins, *The Life of Samuel Johnson, LL.D.* 462 (Dublin 1787); see also *infra* Ch. 5, n. 216, regarding contemporary resentment of William Garrow's tactics of abusive cross-examination.

[298] John Payne Collier, *Criticisms on the Bar* 109–10 (London 1819), cited by Gallanis, "Iowa," *supra* n. 244, at 540 n. 298.

[299] *R. v. Inhabitants of Eriswell*, 3 Term Rep. 707, 721, 100 *Eng. Rep.* 815, 823 (K.B. 1790). The case concerned the question of whether it had been error for a panel of magistrates to have received hearsay testimony in a Quarter Sessions proceeding concerning the settlement of a pauper.

[300] Discussed in Langbein, "Evidence" 1173–4, 1181–4.

[301] Spoken in 1794, quoted in 12 Holdsworth, *HEL* 509 n. 7.

How could such knowledgeable figures hold such opposite views? The answer, it seems clear, is that each had in mind a different meaning of "evidence." Kenyon was speaking of the vast store of settled points of pleading law that had filled out the fine detail of the writ system—the old meaning of evidence as sufficiency of the evidence on particular points of substantive law.[302] Burke was thinking of the new law of evidence, the rules governing proof-taking at trial.

This continuing confusion about the very nature of the law of evidence at the end of the eighteenth century underscores how primitive and undertheorized the subject then was. Beyond the confusion arising from having two quite different bodies of law called "evidence," there was uncertainty about the rationale for what would become the most important of the new rules of evidence, hearsay. This uncertainty is reflected both in the transition from oath-based to cross-examination-based accounts, and in the longstanding confusion of the hearsay rule on the civil side with the best evidence rule.[303] Most importantly, the central concept that underlies the modern law as a system of rules restricting the admissibility of evidence had still not been worked out. Neither the doctrinal basis for exclusion nor the mechanisms to implement and enforce exclusion had been resolved at the end of the eighteenth century.

The want of a settled doctrinal basis for exclusion was exposed in *Atwood and Robbins* in 1787. The logical blunder in that case, it will be recalled, was that the court confused the function of excluding evidence with that of evaluating evidence. The court insisted that the only basis for excluding evidence was disqualifying a witness for competency, and that otherwise, any evidentiary objection to a witness affected "his credit only, [and hence] his testimony must be received and left with the Jury, under such directions and observations from the Court as the circumstances of the case may require, to say whether they think it sufficiently credible to guide their decision on the case."[304] This account misdescribed not only

---

[302] Thayer, who puzzled about Kenyon's remark, speculated that "Lord Kenyon doubtless included those numerous exclusions of evidence, running back into the Year Books, which go upon grounds of substantive law and pleading, and hold that what is offered does not maintain the issue." Thayer, *Evidence* 493 n. 1.

[303] "[I]f the Witness [that is, the out-of-court declarant whose remarks are reported as hearsay] is living, what he has been heard to say is not the best Evidence." Bathurst, *Evidence, supra* n. 150, at 111. Buller carries this line forward unchanged. Buller, *Nisi Prius, supra* n. 150, at 290. On the centrality of the best evidence rule in eighteenth- and early nineteenth-century thinking about the law of civil evidence, see Thayer, *Evidence supra* 489–97; William Twining, "The Rationalist Tradition of Evidence Scholarship," in *Rethinking Evidence: Exploratory Essays* 32, 56–7, 188 (1990); Langbein, "Evidence" 1173–4; Landsman, "Wayne," *supra* n. 296, at 1154. For the view that the best evidence rule still has much to recommend it as an organizing principle for the field, see Dale A. Nance, "The Best Evidence Principle," 73 *Iowa L. Rev.* 227 (1988).

[304] 1 *Leach* at 465–6, 168 *Eng. Rep.* at 335.

the earlier mandatory corroboration rule that *Atwood and Robbins* over-turned, but also the vibrant character and confession rules of the day, which plainly forbade (excluded) the affected evidence.

Another contemporary example of irresolution about the workings of exclusion occurred in 1789 in a dying declaration[305] case tried before Chief Baron Eyre, who left it to the jury to decide whether or not "the declarations were admissible."[306] Admitting or excluding evidence is a decision for the judge; jurors cannot exclude evidence from themselves.

In thinking about the puzzling opinion in *Atwood and Robbins*, it is help-ful to recall that the eighteenth-century *Sessions Papers* do not show us clear-cut directions to juries to disregard evidence that should have been excluded. Instead, the judge would rule that something was "not evidence," or he might use his power of comment to disapprove or coun-teract it. Not only was the concept of directing exclusion unfamiliar, so was another of the standard modern techniques for administering a system of rules that exclude evidence, which is to excuse the jury from the courtroom while the judge previews the evidence and rules upon its admissibility. According to Sylvester Douglas, later Lord Glenbervie, the compiler of two respected sets of late eighteenth-century law reports,[307] when judges determined questions of admissibility, they did so in the presence of the jury. "Perhaps it would be an improvement," Douglas mused in 1776, "when questions of admissibility are raised, that the jury, as well as the witnesses, should withdraw till the point was argued and determined."[308] We have already noticed the usually confident William

---

[305] The dying declarations doctrine, which modern evidence law classifies as one of the main hearsay exceptions, 2 McCormick, *Evidence*, supra n. 59, § 309, at 305, is older than the hearsay rule, see ibid., having originally taken shape as an exception to what in American parlance is now called the confrontation policy, requiring that witnesses testify in person. For the confrontation policy, see 2 Hawkins, *PC* at 428 ("no Evidence is to be given against a Prisoner but in his Presence"); cf. ibid. at 430; accord, Hale, *Common Law*, supra n. 241, at 164 (lauding "the Opportunity of confronting the adverse Witnesses" as a means "for the true and clear Discovery of the Truth"). On the link between the hearsay rule and the confrontation policy in modern law, see *supra* n. 241.

[306] *R. v. Woodcock*, 1 *Leach* 500, 504, 168 *Eng. Rep.* 352, 354 (O.B. 1789). The reporter, Leach, collects contrary authority from the years 1790–2, in a note. 1 *Leach* at 504, 168 *Eng. Rep.* at 354. (I owe this reference to Richard Friedman.)

[307] Wallace records Hargrave's praise for Douglas' "collection of excellent Reports on the law of parliamentary elections." John W. Wallace, *The Reporters* 453 (4th edn. 1882); see ibid. at 529 n. 1, regarding Douglas' King's Bench reports.

[308] "Notes on the Case of Cardigan," in 3 Sylvester Douglas [Lord Glenbervie], *Election Cases* 232 n. B. (2nd edn. London 1802) (1st edn. 1775–6). Remarkably, Wigmore knew this source and extracted it in part in a footnote in his treatise. 6 Wigmore, *Evidence* § 1808, at 275 n. Douglas was explaining why a parliamentary election committee should not address questions of the admissibility of evidence with "the same strictness" as the common law trial courts that sit with juries. In fuller text the passage reads: "It has often occurred to me, that, in trials at *nisi prius*, when evidence is objected to, there is an impropriety in allowing the counsel who offers it, to state what he means to prove in the hearing of the jury, and this for

Garrow groping to express the same thought in the Old Bailey in *Dunbar's Case* in 1784. He muttered to the court, "My Lord, I am not fond of the Jury hearing what they are afterwards told to forget."[309] Two months earlier Garrow faulted prosecuting counsel in another case for failing to have "contrived any way that the Jury should not have heard" a piece of evidence that the prosecuting counsel offered and that the court refused to "receive."[310] We see, therefore, that contemporaries were only just beginning to come to grips with the problems of implementing a system of excluding evidence—in these instances, the difficulty of attempting to get jurors to "unbit[e] the apple of knowledge."[311]

From the standpoint of modern comparative law, what is distinctive about the Anglo-American law of evidence is its exclusionary character, that is, its undertaking to deal with suspect classes of proof by excluding the evidence from the jury, rather than allowing such weaknesses to affect credit as in most modern Continental practice.[312] Mirjan Damaska reminds us of the insight from comparative law that the bifurcation of the Anglo-American trial court into separate spheres for judge and jury is the trait that enabled our law of evidence to develop its exclusionary mechanism. By contrast, he points out, in the "unitary" courts of the European continent, "a judge cannot keep inadmissible hearsay from the factfinder by a preliminary ruling [because] the same persons decide the admissibility of evidence and the weight it deserves."[313] As late as the end of the eighteenth century, however, our law of evidence had not yet articulated its distinctive exclusionary quality. Rather, the confusion about the premises of the field extended to the questions of whether and how to exclude. Because the jury was routinely present in court when the judge purported to rule on admissibility, and because the jury was not operating on clear directions to exclude what it should not have heard, there was as yet little practical difference between excluding hearsay (or other forbidden evidence) and admitting it with diminished credit.

The judges soon found their way out of the fallacy in *Atwood and Robbins*. Indeed, the way should have been clear from the canonical

---

the reason already mentioned; especially as jurymen are too apt to infer, that evidence so offered must be both true, and fatal to the party who objects to it, merely because it is objected to. Perhaps it would be an improvement, when questions of admissibility are raised, that the jury, as well as the witnesses, should withdraw, till the point was argued and decided." Douglas, *supra*, at 232–3.

[309] Joseph Dunbar, *OBSP* (May 1784, #656), at 836, 837.

[310] William Newland, *OBSP* (Feb. 1784, #276), at 333, 349.

[311] Mirjan Damaska, *Evidence Law Adrift* 50 (1997).

[312] See, e.g., Damaska's discussion of a 1987 decision of the German Supreme Court for nonconstitutional matters, the Bundesgerichtshof, in which the court held that the trial court had placed too much weight on hearsay witnesses. Mirjan Damaska, "Of Hearsay and its Analogues," 76 *Minn. L. Rev.* 425, 455–6 (1992).

[313] Ibid. at 427.

language of the eighteenth-century confession rule as formulated in *Warickshall* in 1783. The court there said: "[A] confession forced from the mind by the flattery of hope, or by the torture of fear, comes in so questionable a shape when it is to be considered as the evidence of guilt, that *no credit* ought to be given to it; and therefore it is *rejected*."[314] By treating the defect of evidentiary policy (confession, hearsay, whatever) as having the effect of denying all credit to the proffered testimony, the court was able to characterize the question as one of law rather than fact and hence to direct the jury to exclude the evidence from its deliberations and verdict ("no credit . . . rejected"). The path of the future lay here.

At several points in this chapter I have remarked on the process of turning fact into law that we see constantly at work in the emergence of evidence law. Precepts of judicial practice hardened into rules.[315] As late as Best's treatise in 1849 there was still a sense that the principles of hearsay and the other rules of evidence had only recently been "reduced . . . into a system [that] . . . vested them with the obligatory force essential to the steady and impartial administration of justice."[316] The hardening of the law of evidence not only stripped the judges of their former discretion to depart from what had been mere precepts of practice, it also came at the expense of jury discretion over fact, by recasting ever more issues and inferences arising from fact as questions of law on which the court would direct the jury.

I have emphasized in this chapter that the creation of the law of criminal evidence, like the decision to allow defense counsel to assist felony defendants in matters of fact, was the work of the judges. These pragmatic undertakings were meant to improve safeguard for criminal defendants, in response to the perception that the prosecutorial initiatives of the eighteenth century had unbalanced the trial and increased the risk of prosecution perjury. Although the law of criminal evidence was a judicial creation, it would turn out to be a bonanza for the lawyers. The law of evidence took matters of trial conduct that had previously been within the discretion of judge and jury and opened them to demand by counsel. In this way the law of criminal evidence became part of the process, discussed in Chapter 5, by which the lawyers, especially defense counsel, came to dominate the criminal trial.

---

[314] *R. v. Jane Warickshall*, 1 *Leach* 263, 263–4, 168 *Eng. Rep.* 234, 235 (O.B. 1783) (emphasis supplied), see *supra* text at n. 175.

[315] The sources reviewed in this chapter, which allow us to glimpse the unfolding of the law of criminal evidence in its earliest decades, supply no support for Macnair's suggestion that the English law of evidence instances doctrinal borrowing from the European *ius commune*. Michael R. T. Macnair, *The Law of Proof in Early Modern Equity* (1999).

[316] Best, *Treatise* 117–18, cited in Allen, *Evidence, supra* n. 168, at 24.

5

From Altercation to Adversary Trial

The felony criminal trial retained its lawyer-free character into the 1730s. Citizen accusers confronted the accused in altercation-style trial. Prosecution counsel was virtually never used; defense counsel was forbidden. The accused conducted his own defense, as a running bicker with the accusers. Replying in person to the charges and the evidence against him was the only practical means of defense that the procedure allowed. I have called this style of proceeding the "accused speaks" trial, to emphasize that its dominant purpose was to provide an opportunity for the jury to hear the accused in his own defense. The "accused speaks" trial took place under the general superintendence of the judge. The judge commonly questioned the participants to fill out the testimony they volunteered, and called upon the accused to respond. I have repeatedly evoked Serjeant Hawkins' account of the rationale for the "accused speaks" trial: The innocent accused will be as able to defend himself on "a Matter of Fact, as if he were the best Lawyer," whereas "the Guilty, when they speak for themselves, may often help to disclose the Truth, which probably would not so well be discovered from the artificial Defense of others speaking for them."[1] Hence, by speaking at trial, the accused would clear himself or hang himself.

Across the half century or so from the 1730s into the last quarter of the eighteenth century, the altercation trial gave way to a radically different style of proceeding, the adversary criminal trial. Lawyers for the prosecution and especially for the defense assumed commanding roles at trial. In the prototype of the fully lawyerized trial, solicitors gathered and prepared evidence in advance of trial; counsel then conducted the fact-adducing work at trial, examining and cross-examining witnesses and raising matters of law. As this style of proceeding took hold, counsel tended to supplant both the judge and the accused. By 1820 the French observer Cottu remarked that during the taking of proofs, the English judge "remains almost a stranger to what is going on," and that the accused did so little in his own defense that "his hat stuck on a pole might without inconvenience be his substitute at the trial."[2] In place of the "accused speaks" trial there had developed a new mode of trial, adversary trial, which largely silenced the accused. With it came a new theory of the purpose of trial, which endures into our day, that trial is primarily an opportunity for defense counsel to probe the prosecution case.

Although the importance of this transformation from lawyer-free to lawyer-dominated trial has been remarked in the historical literature,[3] not much has been known about how and why it occurred. Whereas Chapter 3, treating the factors that led to the admission of defense counsel, was

[1] 2 Hawkins, PC 400.   [2] Cottu, Administration 88, 105.
[3] 1 Stephen, History 424.

centered on the 1730s, this chapter focuses mainly on the last quarter of the eighteenth century, when the main features of the new style of trial emerge. Continuing to draw heavily on the *Old Bailey Sessions Papers*, those valuable but problematic sources that became particularly detailed in the later 1770s and 1780s,[4] I sketch the main themes of the transformation. After considering the pace of lawyerization, the chapter concentrates on the silencing of the accused, the ascendance of defense counsel, and the acquiescence of the bench. I point to the growing aversion to capital punishment as a factor that contributed to the willingness of contemporaries to tolerate the truth-impairing attributes of adversary procedure. I conclude with a glance at the path not taken, asking why the truth-seeking procedures of Continental criminal procedure held no interest for the English as an alternative to the dawning adversary system.

The judges of the 1730s who took the decisive steps to admit counsel to assist defendants in cases of felony had no inkling of the enormity of the changes in criminal procedure that were to ensue. The judges were attempting to make a modest adjustment in trial practice. As I have explained in Chapter 3, the judges relaxed the ban on felony defense counsel as a means of evening up for the growing use of prosecution lawyers, especially the use of solicitors to gather and prepare prosecution evidence; and as a corrective to the dangers of perjury in reward-driven and crown witness prosecutions.

When admitting defense counsel, the judges severely restricted the scope of counsel's activity, in order to keep pressure on the accused to continue to serve as an informational resource at trial. The judges declined to follow the broader path laid out by Parliament in the Treason Trials Act of 1696, which allowed the treason defendant "to make his . . . full Defense, by Counsel learned in the law . . . ."[5] Rather, the judges allowed defense counsel into the felony trial for the limited purpose of assisting the accused in examining and cross-examining witnesses. But felony defense counsel was not permitted to comment on the evidence or to narrate the accused's version of the events. At an Old Bailey trial in 1783 the judge reiterated to the defendant William Macnamara the limits on counsel that had been in effect since the 1730s: "[Y]our counsel . . . cannot make a defense, he can only examine witnesses and observe upon points of law."[6] Macnamara's counsel underscored the message: "I cannot say anything for you, though I have your story here in my brief."[7] A few years later William Garrow, the celebrated Old Bailey defender, stated the matter thus: "[A]ll that it is permitted to us who stand as counsel for

---

[4] Discussed *supra* Ch. 4, text at nn. 7–52.
[5] 1696 Act, § 1, discussed *supra* Ch. 2.
[6] William Macnamara, *OBSP* (Sept. 1783, #641), at 857, 858 (theft of shop goods).
[7] Ibid. at 858.

prisoners is to endeavor, by such questions as may occur to us, to impress on the minds of the Jury observations tending to excite distrust of the evidence . . . ."[8] Garrow was being less than candid, because, as we shall see, defense counsel had by Garrow's time developed techniques for evading to some extent the judges' efforts to confine him to the work of cross-examining, but Garrow's remark perfectly captures the judges' design. Counsel would be allowed to question, but the accused would still need to speak if the accused's version of the events were to be heard. Thus, at the close of the prosecution evidence in the notable forgery case of Dr. William Dodd in 1777, the court told the defendant (who was represented by counsel): "[T]his is the time for you to make your defense to what the witnesses have said . . . it is not the province of the counsel to open the case of a criminal in your situation [that is, defense counsel was not allowed to make an opening address to the jury], but you may contradict any thing that has been given in evidence against you . . . . I shall with great patience hear . . . any thing you have to urge in your defense."[9]

The judge-created restriction against defense counsel addressing the jury remained nominally in effect until Parliament intervened in 1836 to extend full defense of counsel to felony defendants,[10] but by then the unfolding dynamic of adversary criminal trial had largely undermined the "accused speaks" trial. In this chapter we shall see why the judges' design failed to contain defense counsel and to preserve the "accused speaks" trial.

A. Latency

A decisive factor in the advance of adversary procedure was the relatively slow pace of the development. This quality of latency lulled the bench into inaction until the lawyers had become entrenched. The consequences of admitting defense counsel took decades to become manifest. Had the full dimensions of adversary criminal procedure been apparent at the outset, the judges might have been able to react in time—to slam the door shut again on the opening that they had created for defense counsel.

---

[8] George Platt and Philip Roberts, *OBSP* (Dec. 1790, #35) at 60, 61 (highway robbery). Garrow was actually appearing for the prosecution when he made the remark quoted in text about the extent of defense counsel's role.

[9] William Dodd, *OBSP* (Feb. 1774, #161), at 106, 117 (perjury), discussed in Gerald Howson, *The Macaroni Parson: A Life of the Unfortunate Dr. Dodd* (1973) [hereafter Howson, *Dodd*]. Radzinowicz thought the conviction and execution of Dr. Dodd marked a turning point in the growth of sentiment against the death penalty. 1 Radzinowicz, *History* 450–72.

[10] 6 & 7 Wil. 4, c. 114 (1836). On the immediate background to the legislation, see Cairns, *Advocacy* 67–87.

Although defense counsel was allowed from the 1730s, most of the felony caseload remained lawyer-free throughout the eighteenth century[11] (and long beyond[12]). Then as now, most criminal defendants were paupers, unable to afford lawyers. The wealth effect of the adversary system was evident from the outset, and the judges made no serious effort to overcome it. They neither sought public subsidy for defense counsel nor encouraged Old Bailey counsel to serve without fee.[13] The *Sessions Papers* show us the occasional case in which defense counsel served *pro bono publico*[14] or was asked to volunteer,[15] but these were rare exceptions. (It may have been more common for young barristers to serve without compensation at provincial assizes, where criminal defense work was regarded as a training exercise.[16]) I shall have more to say about the

---

[11] Regarding the frequency of appearance of counsel, see *supra* Ch. 3, text at nn. 300–3.

[12] Regarding the unrepresented, see *infra*, text at nn. 300-22. Using the *Old Bailey Sessions Papers*, Allyson May has tabulated the frequency of appearance of prosecution and defense counsel at five-year intervals from 1805 to 1830 (omitting 1815 for which she found the sources too deficient). Prosecution counsel was reported in 22% of the cases in 1805, declining to 8.8% in 1830. Defense counsel appeared in 25.7% of cases in 1805 and in 27.7% in 1830. May, Thesis 91 and table 3.1. I have discussed the difficulties of relying upon the *Sessions Papers* to estimate the levels of representation, see *supra* Ch. 3, text and notes at nn. 300, 302. What can be measured in the *Sessions Papers* is not appearances of counsel as such, but the occasions on which the reporters cared to disclose such appearances. Figures for the nineteenth century also appear in Malcolm M. Feeley and Charles Lester, "Legal Complexity and the Transformation of the Criminal Process," in *Subjectivierung des justiciellen Beweisverfahrens: Beiträge zum Zeugenbeweir in Europa und den USA (18.–20. Jahrhundert)* 337, 341, and fig. 1 (A. Gouron *et al.* eds.) (1994). Other reservations about the handling of data in that paper have been discussed in Ch. 1, *supra*, at n. 40

[13] See *infra*, text at nn. 300–22.

[14] Garrow intervened seemingly quite spontaneously to serve *pro bono* in two reported cases. In 1783 in a case against two women charged with theft from a dwelling house above the clergyable amount, hence capital, "The Prisoners having no Counsel, Mr. Garrow undertook to cross-examine the Witness for them." Sarah Slade and Mary Wood, *OBSP* (Dec. 1783, #41), at 77, 78. His cross-examination of the thieftaker elicited that a piece of real evidence (a key) taken from the women had been out of the thieftaker's possession between the event and the trial. The jury acquitted. It is not apparent from the report what motivated Garrow to intervene in this case, as opposed to the thousands of others that were tried during his Old Bailey career in which defendants went unrepresented. Perhaps he spotted the evidentiary defect at once, or had a score to settle with the thieftaker.

In 1790, at the outset of the trial of a woman indicted for returning from transportation (a capital felony), Garrow is shown asking the court, "My Lord, as this poor woman has no Counsel, will you permit me, as Amicus Curiae, to ask [one of the prosecuting witnesses] a question or two?" The court agreed. Sarah Pearson, *OBSP* (Feb. 1790, #311), at 322. Garrow used his cross-examination to formulate the argument that the circumstances of her return were involuntary. He persuaded the jury, which acquitted her because "we think she was not at large without lawful cause." Ibid. at 323. On the phenomenon of defense counsel using cross-examination to evade the ban on addressing the jury, see *infra*, text at nn. 220–38, 274–5.

[15] Jacintho Phararo *et al.*, *OBSP* (Apr. [*sic*, Feb.] 1970, #329), at 367, 368 (murder), discussed *infra*, text at n. 290.

[16] Cottu reported in 1820 that it was "the general case" for the accused to have counsel "in the country, but very rare in London . . . ." Cottu, *Administration* 88. If his report was correct, it seems likely that some barristers were representing indigents without fee. A

phenomenon of unrepresented defendants (and prosecutors) later in this chapter. The present point is that the relatively low levels of lawyerization in the early decades of the experiment with allowing felony defense counsel was a factor that helped put the judges off guard, causing them to think that the option to engage defense counsel would not be much used. Only in the light of hindsight did it become clear that this was a miscalculation, both because the levels of representation later increased, and because principles that were developed in the lawyerized trial spread to trials in which counsel did not appear.

There was a long incubation period between the first appearances of felony defense counsel in the 1730s and the trend toward adversary domination of the trial,[17] which became visible in the last quarter of the eighteenth century. The perception that defense counsel was an important asset, hence that a criminal defendant who could not afford counsel was disadvantaged as a result, came to expression in *Sessions Paper* cases only in the 1770s.[18] Thus, by the last quarter of the eighteenth century, when the systemic consequences of lawyerization of the trial became pronounced, the defendant's right to engage trial counsel had become an entitlement of English criminal procedure.[19]

---

prominent criminal barrister active in the middle of the nineteenth century wrote: "The criminal courts of the assizes give the junior members of the bar an opportunity of ventilating their powers, and they almost invariably receive assistance and encouragement from the judges." 1 William Ballantine, *Some Experiences of a Barrister's Life* 63 (London 1882) (2 vols.) [hereafter Ballantine, *Experiences*]. The hint is that young barristers may have done ill-paid or unpaid work in order to obtain experience and develop a reputation. Allyson May directs attention to Twiss' account of Lord Eldon's early days in practice on the Northern Circuit. After Eldon's call to the bar in 1776, he had little business "except that which is usually entrusted to mere beginners—the defense of prisoners for petty felonies." 1 Horace Twiss, *The Public and Private Life of Lord Chancellor Eldon* 105 (London 1844) (3 vols.), cited in May, Thesis 229. May has other references to young barristers cutting their teeth on criminal work at assizes in the early nineteenth century, ibid. at 229–31. Serjeant Spankie, corresponding with the Criminal Law Commissioners in 1836, opposed the proposal to allow full defense of counsel. He cautioned that most felony defendants "would be in the hands of gentlemen, very young in the profession . . . ." *1836 Report* 104.

[17] In one Old Bailey case tried in 1737, not long after the change in practice, the jury complained to the court that counsel's cross-examination was a nuisance. "We desire his Lordship would please to ask the Questions that are proper, and that the [witness] may not be interrupted." Thomas Car [sic, Carr] and Elizabeth Adams, *OBSP* (Oct. 1737, ##4–5), at 204, 205–6 (highway robbery), discussed in another context, *supra* Ch. 3, text at nn. 192–3.

[18] Thomas Dempsey *et al.*, *OBSP* (Apr. 1776, ##367–72), at 231, 235 (murder) (Andrew Nihil, one of the accused, tells the court: "As I am not provided with counsel, I beg, my lord, you will take my case in hand"); Sarah Armstrong, *OBSP* (May 1777, #350), at 216, 217 (theft of shop goods) ("As I have no counsel, will your lordship please to hear what I have to say?"). These cases are further discussed, *infra*, text at nn. 306–16.

[19] See *supra* Ch. 3 n. 326, quoting the Antiguan Solicitor General regarding the English practice as of 1753: "[P]ermit[ing] counsel to examine and cross-examine witnesses . . . though at first a pure indulgence, yet now seems to be . . . grown into a right . . . ." *R. v. John Barbot*, 18 *St. Tr.* 1229, 1231 (1753).

B. Silencing the Accused

1. Production Burdens: The Prosecution Case

Anglo-American courts use the concept of the burden of production, also known as the burden of going forward with the evidence, to organize the parties' responsibilities to inform the court. In criminal procedure, setting aside some arcane matters involving affirmative defenses, the critical production burden is that of the prosecution. The court will dismiss a prosecution case without trial if the prosecution does not present sufficient evidence to allow the judge to conclude that a reasonable jury could decide the case in accordance with the charges in the indictment. (In European criminal procedural systems, since the court is responsible for gathering the evidence to inform its decision, there are no party production burdens.)

Writing in 1863 in a passage to which I have previously directed attention,[20] James Fitzjames Stephen pointed out why the burdens of production (and of proof) were so primitive in the days of the altercation trial. "When the prisoner had to speak for himself, he . . . could not, without a tacit admission of guilt, insist on the inconclusiveness of the evidence against him, and on its consistency with his innocence. The jury expected from him a clear explanation of the case against him; and if he could not give it they convicted him."[21] Allowing defense counsel had the effect of disentangling two strands of activity that had been merged in the hands of the unrepresented defendant: probing for whether the prosecution had presented a tenable case, and offering defensive evidence (including the statement of the accused) sufficient to rebut the prosecution's evidence. Defense counsel not only helped the defendant examine and cross-examine witnesses, he also insisted on asking the judge whether the prosecution had discharged its burden of adducing sufficient evidence (the prosecution case) to support a verdict in its favor, typically by making a motion for a directed verdict of acquittal at the conclusion of the prosecution evidence. Only if the judge overruled that motion would the defense have occasion to decide whether to present evidence of its own.

The concept of the prosecution's production burden was still inchoate in the days of the altercation trial. We recall that Sir Thomas Smith depicted trial in the sixteenth century as a relatively spontaneous bicker

---

[20] *Supra* Ch. 1, text at n. 229.

[21] Stephen, *General View* 194–5. For an exceptional instance of a defendant against whom there was very strong evidence attempting unsuccessfully to defend on the sole contention that the prosecution case was inadequate, see *The Trial of William Morgan, for the Murder of Miss Mary Jones* 13 (Gloucester 1772) ("All I can say, my Lord, is, they can't prove it against me").

between accusers and accused. We see that aspect of the procedure in a pamphlet account from 1647, which recounts the trial of Sir Edward Mosely for rape.[22] As the victim was narrating her account of the events, Mosely "interrupted her" with a long question that served to give his version of the events. The judge then began exploring the implications of what Mosely had said, asking the victim's husband about Mosely's allegations, to which question the victim rather than the husband replied. Later in the trial Mosely introduced a defense witness, Kilvert, who was about to testify that the victim had bragged to him of having previously threatened to bring a trumped-up rape case against an innocent clergyman in order to extort hush money. Before Kilvert could speak, the victim intervened to declare that "I hope no body will believe what this knave Kilvert will say, for he is a knave known to all the court, and all that hear him."[23] Speaking of cases published in the Surrey Assize pamphlets in the early decades of the eighteenth century, Beattie remarks that defendants' responses "very often took the form not of careful cross-examination but rather of denying the evidence as it was being presented."[24] Such trials had a formless or wandering quality that resembles ordinary discourse, a conversation of sorts, lacking the crisp division into prosecution and defense case that we now expect.

Failing to focus on whether the prosecution had met its production burden could disadvantage the accused. For example, in the trial of James Dixon for robbery at Chelmsford Assizes in 1680, a brief pamphlet report tells us that "[al]though the evidence was not so positive, yet by many credible circumstances he was thought Guilty, as not being able to give an account where he was during the time of the Robberies, so that he was upon [the jury's] weighing each particular brought in Guilty . . . ."[25] What appears to have happened is that the weak prosecution case ("evidence . . . not so positive") went untested, and Dixon's failure to offer alibi evidence (which would have belonged to the defense case) was treated as decisive. In later practice, had Dixon been represented by counsel, counsel would have moved for a directed verdict at the close of the weak prosecution case, preventing the jumbling of prosecution and defense cases.

The *Sessions Papers* indicate that the unstructured bicker passed out of practice in the second quarter of the eighteenth century, hence during the early decades of lawyerization. Although we still see some bicker-style

---

[22] *The Arraignment and Acquittal of Sir Edward Mosely* (London 1647), reprinted in 6 *Harleian Miscellany* 46 (London 1810 edn.) (1st edn. London 1744–6). Presumably, the original pamphlet report found its way to market on account of the salacious facts.

[23] Ibid. at 49.

[24] John M. Beattie, "Crime and the Courts in Surrey 1736–1753," at 155, 169, in *Crime in England 1550–1800* (J. S. Cockburn ed.) (1977).

[25] *The Full and True Relation of all the Proceedings at the Assizes Holden at Chelmsford, for the Countie of Essex* (1680). (Lincoln's Inn Libr., shelfmark Trials 215, no. 3).

trials in the 1730s,[26] by the 1750s the Old Bailey trials conducted by Sir Dudley Ryder show a consistently crisp division of testimony along partisan lines. In one case, Ryder recorded in his notebook an occasion when he policed the line. An accomplice testified against Abraham Davis in a crown witness prosecution for theft. "I called on Abraham Davis to ask any questions. He began by saying he would tell all and how he was drawn in, but I stopped him."[27]

Defense counsel often sought[28] and sometimes won[29] motions for directed verdict, but as Ryder's practice shows, the articulation of the criminal trial into prosecution and defense cases, once developed, did not require defense counsel to sustain it. The Old Bailey sources show us both cases in which counsel insisted on the production burdens,[30] and cases in which judges enforced them unprompted by counsel. In the 1746 trial of a case involving the theft of household linen, after hearing the prosecution evidence, the judge effectively told the accused, Mary Nutcher, that the prosecution had satisfied its production burden. "The Evidence seems presumptuous that you are the Person that stole the Goods, unless you can lay the Charge to somebody else; but you are to prove it, or bring

---

[26] E.g., in the trial of an accused highway robber in 1735, depicted replying seriatim to the testimony of accusing witnesses. Burton Brace, *OBSP* (Dec. 1735, #29), at 7, 8.

[27] Ryder, "Judge's Notes" 36, 37. The *Sessions Paper* report of the case discussed in text does not contain the quoted language. Abraham Davis *et al.*, *OBSP* (Oct. 1755, ##390–2), at 349.

[28] E.g., Elizabeth Parker, *OBSP* (May 1743, #253), at 163, 166 (theft of clothing from master's house) ("The Prisoner's Counsel pleaded that it could not amount to a Felony, because the Goods were put under the Prisoner's Care; but the Court were of a different Opinion"); William Price, *OBSP* (Feb. 1785, #393), at 492, 494 (theft of iron goods) (Garrow for the defense overruled on submission that "there is no ground to set the prisoner on his defense"); Mary Beck, *OBSP* (June 1785, #646), at 831, 833 (Garrow for the defense overruled on motion that "there is no evidence to put the prisoner on her defense"); Darcy [sic; sometimes D'Arcy] Wentworth and Mary Wilkinson, *OBSP* (Dec. 1787, #8), at 15, 19–20 (Wentworth for highway robbery, Wilkinson for receiving stolen goods) (Knowlys for the defense "submit[s] . . . that . . . there is nothing to call on Mary Wilkinson for a defense," because she was dominated by her companion, Wentworth; trial court overrules the motion, saying that "no person but a wife is entitled to that protection; as to a mistress she is not entitled to that protection. She cannot plead any coercion. She was at full liberty. She might have gone to a Justice of peace . . .").

[29] E.g., John Waite, *OBSP* (Feb. 1743, #162), at 102, 106–15 (taking of certain bonds from Bank of England by employee held not felony at the time of the offense); Moses Moravia, *OBSP* (Jan. 1744, #138), at 60, 64 (perjury) (only one prosecution witness, "which by opinion of the Court was not sufficient in law to convict [the defendant] of perjury, and he was thereupon acquitted"); Joseph West *et al.*, *OBSP* (Feb. 1771, ##152–4), at 120, 129 (murder) (directed verdict for one of three codefendants on counsel's motion "that as there is nothing proved against [him], he need not be put on his defense").

[30] For example, defense counsel in a murder case asked at the close of the prosecution case "[w]hether or no the prisoner need go into his defense?" The court refused, putting counsel to his case, which he began by saying, "I would not have it thought I decline going into his defense, which is a very full and a very clear one." Willy Sutton, *OBSP* (Feb. 1761, #97), at 107, 137.

Persons to your Character."[31] The situation more commonly discussed in the sources, however, was a determination that the prosecution had not met its burden. For example, in a coining case tried in 1771, we find the court holding: "Here is no evidence at all . . . that can render it necessary for the prisoner to go into any defense. The prosecutors have undertaken to prove that he coined a counterfeit quarter guinea. Neither of the witnesses are able to prove such a thing upon him."[32] In a prosecution of co-defendants in 1774, the court ruled that only one of them had to defend; "I shall not call upon [the other] for his defense, as there is no evidence to affect him."[33] In a well-reported case from 1783 the judge concluded that because the prosecution evidence did not adequately identify the accused: "there is nothing at all to affect the prisoner," hence "it is too slight evidence even to put the prisoner upon her defense . . . ."[34]

When a trial was resolved at the end of the prosecution case on the judge's determination that the prosecution had failed to satisfy its production burden, the accused was completely silenced. But even when the defense was put to its proofs, the recognition of the prosecution's burden, combined with the use of defense counsel to test whether that burden had been met, materially reduced the amount of speaking that the accused had to do in order to defend effectively. As counsel assumed the work of cross-examining prosecution witnesses and examining defense witnesses, the accused was remitted to making a statement after the close of the prosecution case, hence after the strengths and weaknesses of the accusing evidence had been fully disclosed.

2. Persuasion: Beyond Reasonable Doubt

The prosecution's production burden should be distinguished from the prosecution's burden of persuasion, that is, from the standard of proof. The beyond-reasonable-doubt standard of proof crystallized in the later eighteenth century,[35] but the underlying presumption of innocence (the idea that doubt should be resolved in favor of a criminal defendant) was

---

[31] Anne Gray and Mary Nutcher, *OBSP* (Jan. 1746, #59), at 37, 38. In response to Nutcher's claim the codefendant Gray was the culprit, the court told Nutcher that "you ought to have some Witnesses to prove that, or bring some Persons to your Character." Ibid. She did produce character witnesses and was acquitted.

[32] Samuel Byerman, *OBSP* (May 1771, #344), at 254, 256.

[33] John Ducret and James Musila, *OBSP* (Sept. 1774, ##617–18), at 432, 433 (theft from dwelling house). Leach reports a similar case, in which the court found that the prosecution had not carried its production burden with respect to one defendant, but had with respect to the other. *R. v. Thomas Tickner*, 1 *Leach* 107, 168, *Eng. Rep.* 196 (O.B. 1778) ("The evidence did not affect the prisoner Adams to put him upon his defense . . .").

[34] Mary Murrell (Dec. 1783, #33), at 59, 64 (shop theft).

[35] Discussed *infra*, text at nn. 51–7.

ancient. It was known from classical Roman law[36] and had been reinvigorated in the natural law literature of the seventeenth century.[37] English juristic writers subscribed to it, from Fortescue[38] to Coke[39] to Blackstone.[40] The beyond-reasonable-doubt standard emerged only in the second half of the eighteenth century. The historical literature long focused on a series of treason trials in Ireland in 1798 as the first appearance of the standard,[41] although more recent scholarship has found the beyond-reasonable-doubt standard in use in colonial Massachusetts (in the Boston Massacre trials) as early as 1770.[42]

In routine criminal adjudication at the Old Bailey we find scant indication of any standard of proof being the subject of jury instruction until the last quarter of the eighteenth century. Before then, many an Old Bailey case seems impossible to square with a high standard of proof. For example, Olander Boston was charged in 1686 with the theft of more than £38 worth of cloth goods from a warehouse. Although the prosecution was "not able to prove that he stole the Goods," which would have been grounds for dismissing the case under a properly articulated standard of proof, Boston was "found Guilty to the value of [10d.]."[43] Thus, doubts about his culpability were channelled into the sentence,[44] and Boston was

---

[36] Peter Holtappels, *Die Entwicklungsgeschichte des Grundsatzes "in dubio pro reo"* (1965).

[37] Joachim Hruschka, "Die Unschuldsvermutung in der Rechtsphilosophie der Aufklärung," 112 *Zeitschrift für die gesamte Strafrechtswissenschaft* 285 (2000).

[38] John Fortescue, *De Laudibus Legum Angliae* 65 (S.B. Chrimes ed. and trans.) (1942) [hereafter Fortescue, *De Laudibus*] (written *c*.1470) ("I should, indeed, prefer twenty guilty men to escape death through mercy, than one innocent be condemned unjustly").

[39] In cases of treason or felony, "the evidence to convic[t] [the accused] should be so manifest, as it could not be contradicted." Coke, *Third Institute* 137, see also id. at 29.

[40] 4 Blackstone, *Commentaries* 352 ("it is better that ten guilty persons escape, than that one innocent suffer"). By the end of the century, another commentator had raised the desired ratio to 100:1. Mr. Serjeant Kirby, *A Charge Delivered to the Grand Jury, at the Quarter Sessions of the Peace for the County of Southampton* at 6 (Winton 1793) ("innocence is always to be presumed, till guilt be made manifest—that it is better that a hundred guilty men should escape, than one innocent man should suffer unlawfully . . .").

[41] 2 *McCormick on Evidence* § 341, at 429 and n. 5 (John W. Strong ed.) (5th edn. 1999) (2 vols.), citing May, "Reasonable Doubt in Civil and Criminal Cases," 10 *American L. Rev.* 642, 656 (1876).

[42] Anthony A. Morano, "A Reexamination of the Development of the Reasonable Doubt Rule," 55 *Boston Univ. L. Rev.* 507, 516–19 (1975) [hereafter Morano, "Doubt"].

[43] Olander Boston, *OBSP* (Oct. 1686), at 1. The report also observes that Boston made "but a weak and frivolous defense . . . ." Ibid. Under the later developed production burdens, he would not have been called upon to make any defense to a prosecution case so flimsy.

[44] Such cases abound. In the same year a woman accused of stealing clothing valued at several pounds from her lodgings "denied the Fact, and produced several Witnesses on her Side, which availed but little, she being a person of very bad Character. Yet the matter being not positively proved against her, she was brought in Guilty only to the value of 10 pence" and whipped. Elizabeth Collins, *OBSP* (Sept. 1686), at 4. In a coining case tried in 1743, the jury convicted but recommended mercy because of misgivings about the bad character (and hence, presumably, the reliability) of the prosecution witnesses. Patrick Kelly *et al.*, *OBSP* (Jan. 1743, #116–19), at 70, 74. Later cases in which doubts about guilt affect sentence are noticed *infra*, text at nn. 60–1 and note 61.

convicted of mere petty larceny, for which the sanction was whipping. In 1714 Katherine Kirk was tried for stealing silver from the prosecutor's house. The silver was missed after Kirk left the house, but there was no direct evidence of her having committed the theft. "She denied herself to be the Person, and said she was taken by mistake, another having been accused before [that is, the prosecutor having previously accused someone else]; but there was nothing of Truth in that, and she was known to be an old Offender, whereupon she was found guilty of the Indictment."[45] Once again, a case that would in later times have been dismissed at the end of the prosecution evidence resulted in a conviction, apparently on account of character evidence that would later have been excluded under the rule against such evidence discussed in Chapter 4; and because the defendant mishandled her defense, asserting in error that the prosecutor previously charged the offense to someone else. Beattie has observed (in a telling passage to which I have already directed attention in Chapter 1) that the assumption "was not that [the accused] was innocent until the case against him was proved beyond a reasonable doubt, but that if he *were* innocent he ought to be able to demonstrate it for the jury by the quality and character of his reply to the prosecutor's evidence."[46]

The standard of proof remained crude into the later eighteenth century. "We must not presume guilt against a man trying for his life,"[47] explained one Old Bailey judge in 1770. In an extensively reported instruction in a murder case in 1776, Nares J used the still familiar formula that the jurors should convict if "fully satisfied in your conscience," but not "if a doubt remains in your mind about it . . . ."[48] In the treason trial of Lord George Gordon in 1781 Lord Mansfield still had no conception of the beyond-reasonable-doubt standard. He told the jury: "If the scale should hang doubtful, and you are not fully satisfied that he is guilty, you ought to lean on the favorable side and acquit him."[49] As late as 1783, in a meticulously reported murder case, Willes J told the jury that if, upon "considering the evidence that has been laid before you, and all the circumstances of the case, you should err on the innocent side of the question, I am sure your error will be pardonable."[50] Thereafter, however, we find a burst of instructions reported in the *Sessions Papers* of the next few years that home in on reasonable doubt: "If on viewing the evidence any

[45] Katherine Kirk, *OBSP* (May 1714), at 2.
[46] Beattie, *Crime* 341, (emphasis original), quoted *supra* Ch. 1, text at n. 230.
[47] Francis Cuff, *OBSP* (July 1770, #494), at 314, 315 (forging a bill of exchange).
[48] Joseph Bull, *OBSP* (Jan. 1776, #191), at 132, 140 (murder).
[49] Lord George Gordon, 21 *St. Tr.* 485, 647 (O.B. 1781) (Gordon riots).
[50] Daniel Macginniss, *OBSP* (Jan. 1783, #85), at 111, 127.

reasonable doubt remains . . . he will be entitled to your acquittal."[51] "[I]f you have any doubt,[52] you will acquit him."[53] "If you have doubts about [the case], of course you will acquit the prisoner."[54] "[I]f there is a reasonable doubt, in that case that doubt ought to decide in favor of the prisoner."[55] Acquit "if any doubt whatever remains in your minds . . . ."[56] "[I]f you see any reasonable doubt, you will acquit him."[57] Thus, the beyond-reasonable-doubt standard of proof was being applied in the Old Bailey more than a decade before the Irish treason cases.

The sources do not allow us to say whether the novelty in these cases of the mid-1780s is the articulation of the beyond-reasonable-doubt standard, or merely the disclosure of it (as a result of the greater detail of the *Sessions Papers* of the period). The beyond-reasonable-doubt standard had not yet become a rule of law, in the sense of being invariably applied, hence we still find different judges formulating the standard of proof differently. For example, Chief Baron Eyre, trying a highway robbery in the Old Bailey in 1789, told the jury to convict the two defendants "if you should be of opinion that the crime is sufficiently fixed upon them . . . ."[58] We also find cases in these years in which the instruction on the standard of proof went unreported, or in which none was given,[59] and there is sometimes indication in such cases that the jury convicted on evidence that would not have satisfied the beyond-reasonable-doubt standard. Thus, in 1790 an Old Bailey jury convicted William Ingham of burglary but asked the judge to "recommend him to mercy, not to suffer death . . .

---

[51] John Higginson, *OBSP* (Apr. 1783, #314), at 491, 499 (theft from the mails).

[52] Morano found four *State Trials* over the period 1744–95 in which the term "any doubt" was employed. Morano, "Doubt," *supra* n. 42, at 512 n. 43. He understands the term to invoke a standard of absolute certainty "that had been applied in English criminal trials for centuries." Ibid. at 513. Morano then concluded that the movement to "reasonable doubt" in the later eighteenth century entailed a "lowering of the burden of persuasion," ibid., which "had the effect of reducing the prosecutor's burden of proof in criminal trials." Ibid. at 514. I think this interpretation is mistaken. Morano presents no evidence for the claim that a standard of absolute certainty "had been applied in English criminal trials for centuries." The evidence of the State Trials, from *R. v. Nicholas Throckmorton*, 1 *St. Tr.* 869 (1554), into the Restoration, is contrary. From the Restoration into the mid-eighteenth century the reported jury instructions commonly spoke about the need for the jurors to achieve a "satisfied conscience" about the correctness of their verdict, hardly a synonym for absolute certainty. Barbara J. Shapiro, *"Beyond Reasonable Doubt" and "Probable Cause"* 19–21 (1991) [hereafter Shapiro, *BRD*]. Shapiro argues that "any doubt" implied "reasonable doubt." Ibid. at 21.

[53] Patrick Bowman, *OBSP* (Dec. 1783, #1), at 2, 5 (highway robbery).

[54] Samuel Newton, *OBSP* (Dec. 1783, #46), at 87, 89 (horse theft).

[55] Richard Corbett, *OBSP* (July 1784, #670), at 879, 895 (arson).

[56] William Higson, *OBSP* (Apr. 1785, #415), at 536, 547 (murder).

[57] Joseph Rickards, *OBSP* (Feb. 1786, #192), at 298, 309 (murder).

[58] Mary Wade and Jane Whiting, *OBSP* (Jan. 1789, #155), at 168, 172. The defendants, aged 10 and 14, were charged with stripping the clothes from an 8-year-old. The jury convicted.

[59] For an example of a detailed instruction, seemingly reported verbatim, with no mention of beyond-reasonable-doubt or any other standard of proof, see James Watts and Francis Hardy, *OBSP* (Dec. 1786, #3), at 22, 35–6 (highway robbery).

[b]ecause there was some doubts about the light [at the scene of the crime], and [about] the identity of the person of the man . . . ."[60] In this case doubts that would have been channelled towards acquittal under a beyond-reasonable-doubt standard of proof came to expression as grounds for mitigation. (Ingham did not have counsel.) Two years earlier another such case was reported, in which the jury returned a conviction but recommended mercy "as it is a very nice case."[61]

Our sources also leave us unable to say how the emergence of the beyond-reasonable-doubt standard was related to the growing lawyerization of Old Bailey trials in these years. The *Sessions Papers* depict the judges of the 1780s groping toward the beyond-reasonable-doubt standard without counsel playing much role in the process. We do not, for example, find defense counsel demanding greater precision in the standard of proof. It is surely possible that, as with the development of the rules of evidence discussed in Chapter 4, the initiative came from the bench rather than from counsel. At minimum, however, the presence of defense counsel was a force for consistency, as in the development of the law of evidence, helping transform judicial practice into an expectation of routine that would become a rule of law. Thus, by 1791 Garrow, the celebrated Old Bailey practitioner, can be found arguing on behalf of an accused murderer "that every man is presumed to be innocent till proved guilty."[62]

The rise of adversary criminal trial may have affected the development of the beyond-reasonable-doubt standard of proof in a different way, by disposing the judges to feel the need for further safeguard against the failings of adversary procedure. I have pointed to the fundamental structural flaws of adversary criminal procedure, the combat effect and the wealth effect, which were becoming apparent in the later eighteenth century. By the combat effect, I refer to the incentives to distort or suppress the truth, for example, by concealing relevant witnesses, withholding information that would help the other side, preparing witnesses to affect their testimony at trial (coaching), and engaging in abusive cross-examination. By the wealth effect I refer to the skewing of advantage away from the party

---

[60] William Ingham, *OBSP* (Feb. 1790, #334), at 384, 386.

[61] Joseph Taylor, *OBSP* (Sept. 1788, #521), at 670, 673 (burglary). As late as 1811 Sir Richard Phillips reported another such case: "I observe by the newspapers, that an Old Bailey Jury recommended a culprit to mercy; and on being asked the reason, they stated that they had doubts in regard to the evidence of one of the witnesses! This was a fair ground for acquitting the prisoner, but was not a ground for a Jury to take in a recommendation to mercy." Richard Phillips, *On the Power and Duties of Juries* 191 n. (London 1811) [hereafter Phillips, *Juries*].

[62] George Dingler, *OBSP* (Sept. 1791, #312), at 468, 482 cited in Beattie, "Scales" 249 and n. 77. Garrow was pressing as a purported objection of law the contention that the evidence did not sustain the indictment. This tactic is discussed, *infra*, text at nn. 262–9.

(usually but not always the defendant in criminal cases) who is less able to hire lawyers and to pay for pretrial investigation. The judges of the late eighteenth and early nineteenth centuries who found themselves articulating the beyond-reasonable-doubt standard of proof were former advocates, well acquainted with these weaknesses of the procedure. The question is whether, in developing the beyond-reasonable-doubt standard, the judges may have been motivated to some extent by their awareness of the truth-impairing tendencies that adversary trial procedure had revealed across the recent decades, especially in cases in which prosecution lawyers faced off against unrepresented defendants. By way of comparison, it is instructive to notice that in the still lawyer-free realm of summary jurisdiction for petty offenses, there was a substantially contemporaneous movement away from the beyond-reasonable-doubt standard of proof.[63] The key elements that distinguished summary jurisdiction from felony trial were lighter sanctions and the absence of adversary jury trial.

The emergence of the beyond-reasonable-doubt standard for felony criminal trials was a further factor that reinforced the accused in his growing disinclination to speak to the merits of the charges. Setting a high standard of proof and instructing the jury about it encouraged the jury to probe the prosecution case, rather than to focus on whether or how well the defendant answered.

3. "I leave it to my counsel"

It became possible in the second half of the eighteenth century for an accused to mount an effective defense without speaking to the merits of the charges and the evidence against him. Increasingly across the second half of the eighteenth century, when the judge asked the defendant to reply at the conclusion of the prosecution case, the defendant would utter a formulaic phrase: "I leave it to my counsel." Sometimes the defendant prefaced that line with an unsubstantiated denial. For example, William Horne, tried at Nottingham Assizes in 1760 for murder, said: "My Lord, I am accused of a crime I know nothing of. I am prosecuted maliciously by Persons who want my Life and Estate. The rest I leave to my Counsel and the Witnesses."[64] More commonly in these cases, the defendant said nothing at all to the merits. "My counsel are properly instructed in my case, and I leave myself to their judgment. I have a number of gentlemen to

---

[63] The theme of an important paper by Bruce P. Smith, "The Presumption of Guilt in Anglo-American Criminal Law" (Nov. 2001 draft) (forthcoming).

[64] A Genuine Account of the Life and Trial of William Andrew Horne 23 (3rd edn. London 1760). Horne was being belatedly prosecuted for the murder of an infant that he had fathered on his sister 35 years before. He was convicted and executed.

speak to my general character."[65] Sometimes the court cautioned the defendant about the hazard of this step: "Your counsel cannot speak for you; you must do that yourself, if you have anything to say."[66] Again: "Your counsel cannot speak for you. If you have any account to give of yourself to the jury, where you was; or if you have anything to observe on the evidence, you must do it yourself."[67] Sometimes in these cases the defendant appears to have had no practical avenue of defense; "leaving it to counsel" was little more than a display of hopelessness.[68] But in other cases in which the defendant left his defense to counsel, counsel mounted a vigorous affirmative defense, sometimes calling witnesses to contradict the prosecution case.[69] Acquittals in cases "left to counsel" were common.[70] By 1785 we find Baron Eyre addressing a defendant in terms that appear to express the expectation that the accused would defend in this way: "Now Sir, do you leave your defense to your counsel, or do you desire to speak yourself to the Jury?" The reply: "I leave my defense to my counsel, and your Lordship."[71]

In addition to these cases in which the defendant uttered the stock phrase "I leave it to my counsel," doubtless having been tutored by solicitor or counsel beforehand, we see the occasional case in which the reports depict counsel seeming to make an on-the-spot tactical adjustment to silence the defendant. In 1757 we find counsel for a pair of accused coiners telling them at the close of the prosecution case, "I, as your counsel, would advise you to rest the case on the evidence as it now stands."[72] (They did; the jury convicted one and acquitted the second.) In a case in 1784 Garrow is quoted telling his clients after the prosecution case, "Prisoners, if you take my advice, I advise you to leave the case where it is, it is in perfect good hands."[73] (They did and were acquitted.) A few years later we find Garrow responding to the court's question whether the defendant would speak. "No, my lord, I would not advise him to say any thing on this occasion."[74]

---

[65] James Gibson, *OBSP* (Jan. 1766, #109), at 81, 88 (forgery).

[66] Joseph Trout, *OBSP* (Dec. 1766, #23), at 11, 12 (theft from a dwelling house).

[67] Thomas Newton *et al.*, *OBSP* (Jan. 1790, #128), at 137, 139 (highway robbery).

[68] Charles Nangle and Mark Lowe, *OBSP* (Sept. 1774, ##635–6), at 440, 442 (forgery); William Lewis, *OBSP* (Oct. 1774, #709), at 467, 468 (forgery).

[69] E.g., George Whichcote, *OBSP* (Feb. 1773, #326), at 152, 158 (highway robbery).

[70] E.g., John White, *OBSP* (Jan. 1762, #73), at 47 (theft); Joseph Trout, *OBSP* (Dec. 1766, #23), at 11, 12 (theft from a dwelling house); Christopher Waring, *OBSP* (Jan. 1771, #59), 46, 55 (burglary); George Whichcote, *OBSP* (Feb. 1773, #326), at 152, 158 (highway robbery); Ralph Cutler (Sept. 1777, #522), at 321, 329 (rape).

[71] Samuel Holt, *OBSP* (Apr. 1785, #477), at 623, 625 (receiving).

[72] Joseph Wood and Jemima Wilcox, *OBSP* (Dec. 1757, ##47–8), at 24, 32.

[73] Thomas Isham *et al.*, *OBSP* (July 1784, #734), at 967, 968.

[74] D'Arcy [*sic*; sometimes Darcy] Wentworth, *OBSP* (Dec. 1789, #1), at 2, 4 (highway robbery) (acquitted).

In a handwritten note made in the margin of his copy of the 1784 *Sessions Papers* Garrow left revealing evidence of his thinking about the strategic advantage to the defendant of remaining silent. To the report of a forgery trial in which he had served as prosecution counsel and convicted the defendant, he added an observation (at the place where the report narrated the accused's statement): "This Prisoner was one of the innumerable Instances of Persons who by making a Speech occasion their own conviction."[75] Garrow knew (and was teaching his criminal defense clients) that adversary procedure had toppled the "accused speaks" trial. The criminal defendant was usually better served by keeping quiet and letting defense counsel refocus the trial on the asserted weaknesses of the prosecution case. By extinguishing the accused as an informational resource, lawyerization of the trial permitted combat to prevail over truth. This would prove to be an epochal step, or rather, misstep, for the Anglo-American procedural tradition. A truth-seeking trial procedure, such as in European and European-derived legal systems, does not create incentives systematically to deny itself access to the person who usually knows the most about what happened.

As adversary presentation became more regular across the eighteenth century, the judges are found encouraging represented[76] defendants to abstain from participating in any manner other than by making a statement at the end of the prosecution case. In the murder trial of Mary Blandy at Oxford Assizes in 1752, when she was tempted to ask "some questions" of a witness, the court told her: "You had better tell your questions to your counsel; for you may do yourself harm by asking questions."[77] In 1783 an Old Bailey judge told a murder defendant, Daniel Macginniss, that if there were "any questions omitted that you think proper to have your counsel ask, write them down and send them over . . . . [D]o not you put the question yourself, but hand it to your counsel."[78] Later that year another Old Bailey judge told a defendant, "God

---

[75] Garrow's note to the report of the trial of Thomas Freeman, *OBSP* (Oct. 1784, #1002), at 1336, 1345; Garrow's copy of the volume is discussed *supra* Ch. 4, text and nn. 44–5. In this case his note continued that the "strange prevarication" of a key prosecution witness "and the impossibility of relying on [that witness'] Account must have ensured an Acquittal," had not the accused thrown away this advantage by speaking at trial. Ibid. at 1345.

[76] Occasionally, remarks of a similar tenor were also made to an unrepresented defendant, although the meaning was not to encourage him to defer to counsel, but to beware making damaging admissions of a sort that defense counsel would have prevented. For example, in a case tried at the Old Bailey in 1770 the trial judge cautioned a defendant who was attempting to cross-examine a crown witness, "You will take care what you say, that you don't convict yourself." Peter Conoway and Michael Richardson, *OBSP* (July 1770, ##463–4), at 292, 294 (murder).

[77] *R. v. Mary Blandy*, 18 *St. Tr.* 1118, 1163 (Oxford Assizes 1752) (murder). The case is discussed *supra* Ch. 3, text at nn. 65–8.

[78] Daniel Macginniss, *OBSP* (Jan. 1783, #85), at 111, 118, 119.

forbid that you should be hindered from saying anything in your defense, but if you have only questions to ask, I would advise you to leave them to your Counsel."[79] In a case in 1788 the court twice stopped a defendant from speaking out of turn, explaining: "Though you are permitted to speak, it is greatly to your own disadvantage to begin your defense before they begin your charge."[80] Again: "[B]y entering into any part of your defense now, you give them an opportunity of applying their evidence to your answer."[81] Rather than promote truth-seeking in the style of the altercation trial, the judges of the 1780s were applying production burdens.

We also find the judges encouraging the defendant to consult with counsel about the substance of the defendant's statement. The court advised Macginniss: "Let your counsel see your defense before you read it, you do not know what is so proper to read as they do. Let them read it first."[82] Such advice bespeaks complete abandonment of Hawkins' view that the accused could defend himself on "a Matter of Fact, as if he were the best Lawyer."[83] Remarkably, it became common practice for defense counsel to ghostwrite the defendant's trial statement,[84] further removing the defendant as an informational resource. Sometimes the accused simply handed in the lawyer-prepared statement to be read to the jury by the clerk of the court. We see this drill in the case of Jane Butterfield, tried for murder at Surrey Assizes in 1775:

COURT. Prisoner, now is the time for you to make your defense. Do you choose to say anything, or leave your defense to counsel?
PRISONER. I have committed a few truths to paper, which I beg your lordship will order to be read.
COURT. Let it be read.
(The Prisoner's defense was read by the clerk of the arraigns . . . .)[85]

In such a trial, the participation of the accused had become nearly perfunctory.[86]

---

[79] Jacob Thompson, *OBSP* (Dec. 1783, #145), at 154, 159 (theft from a dwelling house).
[80] David Clary and Elizabeth Gombert, *OBSP* (Apr. 1788, #270), at 367, 368 (arson).
[81] Ibid. at 371.
[82] Daniel Macginniss, *OBSP* (Jan. 1783, #85), at 111, at 121.
[83] 2 Hawkins, *PC* 400.
[84] E.g., William Gansel, *OBSP* (Sept. 1773, #535), at 372, 384 (feloniously shooting).
[85] *The Trial of Jane Butterfield for the Wilful Murder of William Scawen* 36 (London 1775).
[86] James Harmer, a prominent criminal defense attorney of the early nineteenth century, told the Criminal Law Commissioners in 1836 that he sometimes ghosted defendants' statements. Harmer lamented that such a statement sometimes became unsuitable when the trial took an unforeseen turn after he prepared the statement. *1836 Report* 3. The Commissioners' report disparaged the prepared written defense, which "if prepared before the trial, will often be irrelevant and of little value to the Prisoner. If it be prepared while the trial is going on, it must obviously be very much hurried . . . . And in either case it is often read to the Jury very inefficiently by the officer of the court." Ibid. at 10–11.

Not only did defense lawyers diminish the role of the accused as an informational resource, but when the accused did speak, the lawyers were also affecting the content of what the accused said. Remarking on this phenomenon of represented defendants "having their statements prepared by, or in conjunction with, their legal advisers" in the early nineteenth century, Cairns observes:

The prisoner's lawyers reduced the "testimonial" content of the statement by carefully controlling factual disclosures . . . . [In a prominent murder case tried in 1828], for example, the prisoner's solicitor discussed prior to trial whether the jury would more favorably receive a story of suicide or provocation, and during the trial [the defendant] made changes to his statement on legal advice. Such a groomed presentation was a far cry from the unrehearsed explanation of events expected in the pre-counsel trial of the eighteenth century.[87]

By telling witnesses and accused what sort of statement might be helpful and what might be harmful, defense lawyers could effectively shape some of what the defendant and the defense witnesses said.[88] We see in this practice of coaching another manifestation of the combat effect, that is, of the tendency of the adversary system to interfere with truth-seeking. As the adversary dynamic took hold, the court's access to the accused and to the witnesses was filtered through partisan lawyers, whose interest was in winning, not in truth-seeking. The courts were encouraged to accept this new order in part on the ground that cross-examination of witnesses would detect and thus deter prevarication and hence promote truthful outcomes. But because the accused spoke unsworn and was not a witness, he was not subject to cross-examination. And in any event, reliance on cross-examination was at most an article of faith. Cross-examination was a blunt instrument, a hit-or-miss safeguard against the truth-bending and truth-concealing effects of placing partisans in charge of the production and presentation of the evidence.

Adversary criminal procedure undermined the "accused speaks" trial. By the 1780s, when the exceptional detail of the *Sessions Paper* sources give us an improved observation post, we see that defense counsel had largely

---

[87] Cairns, *Advocacy* 50, discussing the trial of William Corder (Bury St. Edmunds (Norfolk) Assizes 1828).

[88] An early instance of counsel allegedly coaching the accused arose in 1713, two decades before defense counsel had been granted audience on matters of fact. Richard Noble, tried for murder in 1713, was allowed counsel to raise a law point, which the court rejected. It seems that counsel also advised him on trial tactics. Noble was convicted. Asked whether he had anything to say in arrest of sentence, he blamed counsel for inducing him to lie at trial about a point of fact, on which he was subsequently refuted. "My counsel obliged me to say on my trial, that I heard Mr. Sayer's voice before he broke open the door," even though Nobel told counsel that the claim was false. "It was my misfortune, that what I said, as to hearing the decedent's voice, was turned to my disadvantage by the counsel against me . . . ." Richard Noble *et al.*, 15 *St. Tr.* 731, 747 (Surrey Assizes 1713).

achieved what the judges of the 1730s had feared and had tried to prevent with their restrictions on full defense: Counsel had largely silenced the accused. With counsel available to cross-examine prosecution witnesses, to examine defense witnesses, to raise evidentiary objections, and to insist on the prosecution burdens of production and proof, an effective defense no longer required the participation of the accused. Initially, the new procedure separated the two forensic roles that the defendant had performed when he had been denied counsel, that is, defending and informing, assigning only the work of defending to counsel. This change had the unforeseen effect of focusing the trial on the prosecution case and away from the objective that had preoccupied the old altercation trial, which was to see how the defendant responded to the prosecution case. In this way, the introduction of defense counsel transformed the very purpose of the criminal trial, recentering the trial on the prosecution rather than on the defendant. Trial became what it has remained, a proceeding whose primary purpose is to provide defense counsel with an opportunity to test the prosecution case.

To be sure, this new theory of the purpose of the trial had always been implicit in the old altercation trial,[89] in which the accused had been allowed not only to quarrel with his accusers, but also to question the sufficiency of their proofs. As a practical matter, however, few criminal defendants were sufficiently skilled and self-possessed to perform the latter feat effectively. As the Criminal Law Commissioners observed in 1836, the innocent accused "is surprised and confused by false evidence," especially in a case built upon circumstantial evidence, which "calls for the greatest exertion of the skill of the experienced advocate . . . ."[90] The imperilled and inexperienced defendant tended to offer abject denials rather than to question, analyze, and criticize the accusing evidence. By assuming the work of defending, defense counsel disentangled the criminal defendant from his former predicament of having to speak to the merits in order to make any defense.

---

[89] In discussing the antics of John Lilburn in his 1649 treason trial, I have elsewhere observed how the newer theory of the trial lay close to the surface in the old. Lilburn resolutely refused to answer a line of questioning about his asserted authorship of treasonous writings, demanding that the prosecution prove its case. *R. v. John Lilburn,* 4 St. Tr. 1269, 1340–1 (1649). If this had been a homicide or a theft, Lilburn would have hanged himself with such tactics. His ploy was designed to put the prosecution on trial. Without counsel, that risk could be taken only in a political case such as Lilburn's, in which the defendant had reason to suspect that he could evoke the sympathy of the jury. John H. Langbein, "The Historical Origins of the Privilege against Self-Incrimination at Common Law," 92 *Michigan L. Rev.* 1047, 1076 n. 131 (1994) [hereafter Langbein, "PASI"], substantially republished in R. H. Helmholz *et al., The Privilege against Self-Incrimination: Its Origins and Development* (1997) [hereafter Helmholz, *Privilege*], at 244–5 n. 123.

[90] *1836 Report* 3.

The change in the attitude of the bench regarding the silencing of the accused is particularly noteworthy. The concern to preserve the accused as an informational resource, which we have seen epitomized in Hawkins' treatise in 1721, and which had been an insistent theme in the juridical literature for two centuries before Hawkins,[91] appears to have been abandoned in the last quarter of the eighteenth century, when, as we have seen, the judges were facilitating adversary domination of the trial. I shall say more below about the change in the judges' attitude, about their acquiescence in adversary domination and its attendant silencing of the accused.

The legislation of 1836, which extended full defense of counsel to felony defendants, definitively abrogated the "accused speaks" trial, effectively abandoning the centuries-old emphasis on having the accused as an informational resource. The *Second Report from Her Majesty's Commissioners on Criminal Law*[92] of 1836, which underlies the reform legislation, devoted considerable energy to refuting one of the claims that we associate with Serjeant Hawkins' defense[93] of the rule against felony defense counsel—that an innocent accused could defend himself as well "as a skillful advocate."[94] The Commissioners said:

A party charged with a crime, though in full possession of all his faculties, must often, from a sense of the disgrace and danger to which he is exposed, and from ignorance of the forms of law, conduct his defense to great disadvantage. It . . . frequently happens, that an innocent person is surprised and confused by false evidence and rendered incapable of making an efficient defense by a forcible exposition of the improbabilities and discrepancies arising on a nice comparison of facts, which may be the only means of discovering the truth and rescuing an innocent man. To cope with a false charge so supported calls for the greatest exercise of the skill of the experienced advocate. It can seldom happen that an ordinary defendant can in such a situation possess the coolness and talent requisite for the task.[95]

---

[91] *Supra* Ch. 1, text at nn. 119-21, discussing Staunford and Pulton.

[92] Regarding the Commission, see Michael Lobban, *The Common Law and English Jurisprudence: 1760–1850*, at 202–6 (1991); Rupert Cross, "The Reports of the Criminal Law Commissioners (1833–49) and the Abortive Bills of 1853," in *Reshaping the Criminal Law* 5 (P. R. Glazebrook ed.) (1978).

[93] *Supra*, text at n. 1.

[94] *1836 Report* 2.

[95] Ibid. at 3. This passage tracks the argument of a noted defense solicitor, James Harmer, who wrote a tract in 1807 criticizing "[t]he hardship of depriving men charged with felony of the assistance of counsel to address the jury . . . ." James Harmer, *Murder of Mr. Steele: Document and Observations Tending to Show a Probability of the Innocence of John Holloway and Owen Haggerty, Who Were Executed on Monday the 23d of February, 1807, as the Murderers of the Above Gentleman* 63 (London 1807). Harmer wrote: "The most innocent of men could not avoid agitation, when put on his trial, in a crowded court, for an offence which not only impeaches his character, but affects his life. Nay, the more falsely he is sworn against, the greater his agitation, and the less is he master of his own powers." Ibid. Bearing in mind as well the defendant's ignorance of the law, Harmer asked, "Is a man, thus circumstanced, enabled to address the jury with effect?" Ibid.

This passage is ingenious in emphasizing circumstances (complex facts, false witness) in which counsel's skill might "rescu[e] an innocent man," but deficient for its failure even to acknowledge, much less respond to, the other branch of Hawkins' argument, his concern that lawyerization would silence the accused.[96] The only plausible explanation is that the Criminal Law Commissioners understood that Hawkins' concern was already archaic in 1836. Counsel had long since silenced the accused, except for the statement that the accused might make at the end of the prosecution case, and increasingly, as the Commissioners remarked, counsel had been molding that.[97] Indeed, the courts interpreted the 1836 legislation to work a needlessly drastic silencing of the accused. The rule became settled that the accused's decision to be heard by counsel precluded him from also making a statement in his own defense. "It was held, following the practice of misdemeanor cases,[98] that the defense was entitled to address the jury only once, and so had to choose between a prisoner's statement and a speech from counsel."[99]

4. Parallels in the Pretrial

The silencing of the accused at trial found an echo in developments in the pretrial process that occurred across the eighteenth and nineteenth centuries. The court JP for Middlesex and his City equivalent, the "sitting alderman,"[100] assumed powers to dismiss weak cases.[101] Beattie has found indications of pretrial dismissal in City practice as early as December 1729.[102] Indeed, he reckons that in the 1730s "almost half the felony cases [that one prominent alderman] heard concluded with the

---

[96] The report does have a response of sorts to Hawkins' claim that the guilty accused, if he has to speak unaided, will give himself away. 2 Hawkins, PC 400 ("the Guilty, when they speak for themselves, may often help to disclose the Truth, which probably would not so well be discovered from the artificial Defense of others speaking for them"). Said the Commissioners: "It frequently happens that hardened villains possess more coolness and composure than the innocent . . . [who] exhibit a degree of confusion which might seem to indicate a consciousness of guilt." 1836 Report 3.

[97] 1836 Report 10–11 (discussing counsel's ghostwriting of the accused's statement).

[98] E.g., The Trial of Henry Yorke for a Conspiracy 28 (York 1795) (York Assizes 1795) (Rooke J tells accused, "You may choose whether yourself or your counsel will address the Jury").

[99] Cairns, Advocacy 118, citing R. v. Boucher, 8 Car. & P. 141, 173 Eng. Rep. 433 (Gloucester Assizes 1837); R. v. Burrows, 2 M. & Rob. 124, 174 Eng. Rep. 236 (Exeter Assizes 1838). Other cases, including early cases resisting this result, are canvassed in Zelman Cowan and P. B. Carter, "Unsworn Statements by Accused Persons," in Essays on the Law of Evidence 205, 207 (1956).

[100] Discussed supra Ch. 3, text at n. 248; see also Ch. 3, n. 281.

[101] Regarding the lack of formal authority for the Marian JP to engage in pretrial dismissal, and the evident loosening of this restriction in the eighteenth century, see supra, Ch. 1, text at nn. 181–5.

[102] Beattie, Policing 107 and nn. 74–5.

FIG. 5.1. *The Bow Street office.* The magistrate's pretrial examination in cases of felony (a fixture of English criminal procedure from the 1550s) evolved in the middle of the eighteenth century toward the format of a public hearing, especially at the Bow Street office of Henry and John Fielding. Two or three JPs also sat as the court of petty sessions to adjudicate regulatory matters and minor offences.

accused being released without trial."[103] The pretrial examination "became something more than a procedure to gather the evidence that would prove the guilt of the accused at trial."[104] I have mentioned in Chapter 1 that Henry Fielding left unmistakable evidence of his exercise of pretrial dismissal powers in Middlesex. For example, he reported in the *Covent Garden Journal* in 1752 that he "very honorably discharged" a murder suspect after repeated examinations made the suspect's "Innocence appear so evident . . . ."[105]

At least in London, the magistrate's pretrial inquiry increasingly took on the trappings of a public hearing, which would ultimately come to be known as the preliminary hearing, in the sense of preliminary to trial.

---

[103] Beattie, *Policing* at 107.　　　　　　　　　　　　　　　　　[104] Ibid. at 106.
[105] *Covent Garden Journal* (28 Jan. 1752), in *The Covent-Garden Journal and A Plan of the Universal Register-Office* 402 (Bertrand A. Goldgar ed.) (1988), discussed *supra* Ch. 1, n. 184.

John Fielding at Bow Street[106] and the sitting alderman in the City[107] sat at regular times[108] in courtroom-style premises. As the format evolved, the hearing became an occasion at which a defense lawyer could challenge the prosecution case,[109] although he could not yet present defensive evidence. As late as 1787 an experienced Old Bailey barrister serving as defense counsel remarked in response to a question from the bench[110] that "[t]he Magistrates at Bow Street never receive evidence for prisoners, only for prosecutors."[111] The proactive solicitor can be glimpsed in the pretrial hearing before Sir John Fielding in the famous forgery case of the brothers Perreau and Mrs Rudd in 1775, in which Mrs Rudd's solicitor negotiated her designation as crown witness.[112] Cottu conveys the sense that by his day, in 1820, mastery of these proceedings had already passed to the lawyers. The prosecutor with his attorney "come[s] into court," as does the defendant, "accompanied by his solicitor, if he has the means of procuring one. The magistrate takes down in writing the prisoner's declaration, together with the depositions of the [prosecutor] and his witnesses, as they are respectively elicited by the prosecutor's or prisoner's solicitor."[113]

[106] Depicted in a contemporary engraving in the frontispiece to 3 *The Malefactor's Register; or, the Newgate and Tyburn Calendar* (London [1779]) (5 vols.), reproduced in Langbein, "Ryder" 74.

[107] Hogarth depicts an idealized version of the sitting alderman's hearing in plate 10 of the "Industry and Idleness" series, discussed *supra* Ch. 3, text and n. 281, reproduced in Langbein, "Ryder" 79;, and in Beattie, *Policing*, pl. 6, following 268. Regarding the actual chamber, see Langbein, "Ryder" 78, 84; Beattie *Policing* 108–9. Cottu says: "These examinations take place in London in a room open to the public, by the magistrates in Westminster, and by the aldermen in the City." Cottu, *Administration* 34.

[108] A hostile pamphleteer asked rhetorically of Fielding: "In what manner will you justify the practice [of holding public hearings] every Wednesday, at the expense of a set of miserable objects [that is, detained suspects], whose wretchedness becomes the sport of your unfeeling auditors and an abandoned rabble? After commitment, you [should] have no kind of business with them; they are not to suffer the torture of repeated examinations, but [should] stand over to the next sessions for acquittal or conviction. It is your endeavor always to prevent the former, and secure the latter; for this purpose a formal judicial enquiry is made every Wednesday." William A. Miles, *A Letter to Sir John Fielding, Kn[igh]t, Occasioned by His Extraordinary Request to Mr. Garrick, for the Suppression of the Beggar's Opera* 21–2 (London 1773). (I owe this reference to John Beattie.) A generation later, in 1820, Cottu described the practice of pretrial "examinations [that] take place in London in a room open to the public, by the Magistrates in Westminster, and by the aldermen in the City." Cottu, *Administration* 34.

[109] Beattie, *Policing* 106.

[110] The judge asked a witness who testified favorably for the accused whether she had given the same testimony at the Bow Street pretrial. Darcy Wentworth and Mary Wilkerson, *OBSP* (Dec. 1787, #8), at 15, 19 (highway robbery).

[111] Ibid. The counsel quoted in text was Newman Knowlys, a leader of the Old Bailey bar, on whom see May, Thesis 353.

[112] Discussed in Donna T. Andrew and Randall McGowen, *The Perreaus and Mrs. Rudd: Forgery and Betrayal in Eighteenth-Century London* 28 (2001). The case gave rise to Lord Mansfield's opinion in *R. v. Rudd*, 1 Leach 115, 168 Eng. Rep. 160 (K.B. 1775), discussed *supra* Ch. 3, nn. 250, 290; see also *supra* Chapter 4, text at n. 172 and fig. 4.1.

[113] Cottu, *Administration* 34.

We know as yet very little about the extent of the lawyers' activity in the eighteenth-century pretrial hearing, but it is likely that lawyerization of the pretrial had the same influence upon the accused as lawyerization of the trial, that is, encouraging the accused to silence. Cottu, contrasting the emphasis on interrogating the accused that characterized contemporary French practice, was struck by the orientation away from the accused in England. "Scarcely a single question is put to the defendant: if asked to give an account of himself, he answers, if he thinks proper . . . . Nor is he asked for any explanation of the charges resulting against him from the depositions."[114] As happened at the lawyerized trial, so in the lawyerized pretrial, the bench found itself facilitating the silencing of the accused.

Across the nineteenth century, as professional police increasingly assumed responsibility for gathering prosecution evidence, the urban magistrate's office would shed its prosecutorial cast. The magistrate's examination became the forerunner of the modern pretrial committal hearing.[115] As this development unfolded, there was "increasing official encouragement to persons accused of felony to remain silent during the pre-trial investigation,"[116] in stark contrast to the explicit pressure to speak in earlier practice.[117] The codifying legislation known as Sir John Jervis' Act of 1848[118] confirmed the magistrate's duty to warn the accused before taking a statement from him: "Having heard the Evidence, do you wish to say anything in answer to the Charge? You are not obliged to say anything unless you desire to do so, but whatever you say will be taken down in Writing, and may be given in Evidence against you upon your Trial."[119]

This saga of the lawyerization and judicialization of the pretrial is even less well documented than the parallel developments at trial, and it has yet to be the subject of sustained historical study. It bears mention here because it shows in a distinct phase of the procedure the same dynamic

---

[114] Ibid. at 37. Cottu marvelled that "[t]he English appear to attach no importance to a discovery of the causes which may have induced the prisoner to commit the crime," indeed, he remarked, they hardly seem to care whether they find him guilty. Ibid. Regarding this seeming disdain for truth, see *infra*, text at nn. 381–429.

[115] Remarked in Patrick Devlin, *The Criminal Prosecution in England* 7 (1958).

[116] Christopher J. W. Allen, *The Law of Evidence in Victorian England* 124 (1997) [hereafter Allen, *Victorian Evidence*].

[117] E.g., Thomas Parks *et al.*, *OBSP* (Jan. 1747, ## 84–6), at 50 (trial judge tells defendants at trial, "When you were examined before the Justice of the Peace [in the pretrial, you should have brought alibi witnesses] to prove that you were every Night at Home, or that you always kept good Hours"). The case is cited by Stephen Landsman, "The Rise of the Contentious Spirit: Adversary Procedure in Eighteenth-Century England," 75 *Cornell L. Rev.* 497, 521 (1990) [hereafter Landsman, "Spirit"].

[118] 11 & 12 Vict., c. 42 (1848); see also 11 & 12 Vict., c. 43. See generally David Freestone and J. C. Richardson, "The Making of English Criminal Law: Sir John Jervis and his Acts," 1980 *Criminal L. Rev.* 5.

[119] 11 & 12 Vict., c. 42, § 18 (1848), noted in Allen, *Victorian Evidence, supra* n. 116, at 124–5.

that our sources have shown us at trial, the tendency of adversary procedure to divide a criminal investigation into prosecution and defense
cases, with the concomitant silencing of the accused as an informational
resource.

5. The Privilege against Self-Incrimination

The reconstruction of trial procedure that resulted from the admission of
defense counsel was the precipitating event in developing what we now
recognize as the privilege against self-incrimination. The procedures of
the "accused speaks" trial stood in profound tension with the notion that
the accused had any entitlement to be silent at trial—that he not "be
compelled in any criminal case to be a witness against himself . . . ."[120] So
long as the rule against defense counsel required the accused to conduct
his own defense, there could be no effective privilege against self-incrimination. In common law criminal procedure, therefore, the privilege
against self-incrimination was the creature of defense counsel.

Historical understanding of the privilege against self-incrimination has
undergone considerable revision in recent years.[121] What became the
privilege had its origins as an effort by the common law courts, using the
writ of prohibition, to restrain practices of the ecclesiastical and prerogative courts, most prominently the Court of High Commission, in the
seventeenth century. High Commission dealt with affairs of the post-
Reformation Church and clergy and did not follow jury-based common
law criminal procedure. Rather, the judges of the court investigated and
adjudicated. Using so-called ex officio oath procedure, the court would
direct an accused to swear an oath to answer questions that the court
might subsequently put, on penalty of imprisonment or other sanctions
for contempt if he refused.[122] Puritans and other religious dissenters, who
were typically quite guilty of the nonconformist religious practices being
investigated, resisted submitting to ex officio oath procedure. They
dressed up their resistance with a Latin maxim, *nemo tenetur prodere seipsum*, liberally translated as "no one is obliged to accuse himself." We now
know that the maxim originated (for quite different purposes[123]) in the

---

[120] U.S. Constitution, Amendment 5 (1789).

[121] The principal work is Helmholz, *Privilege, supra* n. 89, publishing or republishing the
work of six authors, covering periods from the Middle Ages to the modern.

[122] See generally Mary H. Maguire, "Attack of the Common Lawyers on the Oath Ex
Officio as Administered in the Ecclesiastical Courts in England," in *Essays in History and
Political Theory in Honor of Charles Howard McIlwain* 199 (Carl Wittke ed.) (1936).

[123] It was meant to clarify the line between two spheres of Christian obligation, underscoring that the believer's duty of penitential confession did not require instituting criminal
proceedings against himself. The Christian could confess sin to a priest without being
obliged to confess punishable offenses to judge or prosecutor. See R. H. Helmholz, "Origins

law of the medieval Roman Church. In 1641, as part of the events that led to the civil war and the Interregnum, Parliament sided with the Puritans, abolished the courts of Star Chamber and High Commission, and forbade the ecclesiastical courts from using ex officio oath procedure.[124] These events, especially the fall of Star Chamber and High Commission, remain landmarks of English political and legal history.

The seventeenth-century struggles that made resistance to the ex officio oath part of the Anglo-American constitutional heritage had nothing to do with common law criminal procedure. At common law, the accused was not examined under oath, indeed, he was forbidden to testify on oath even if he wished. The issue on which the historical understanding has changed in recent times is the question of how the common law courts came to internalize a principle of hostility to self-incrimination, which they had originally developed to counteract the radically different, oath-based procedures of the ecclesiastical and prerogative courts. Wigmore, the most influential proponent of the older view, supposed that the common law courts lost sight of the distinction between their own procedures and those of the rival prerogative courts.[125] The newer scholarship focuses on the appearance of defense counsel. Without defense counsel, a criminal defendant's right to remain silent was the right to forfeit any defense; indeed, in a system that emphasized capital punishment, the right to remain silent was literally the right to commit suicide. Only when

of the Privilege against Self-Incrimination: The Role of the European Ius Commune," 65 *New York Uni. L. Rev.* 962, 982 (1990). substantially republished in Helmholz, *Privilege, supra* n. 89, at 26–7.

[124] 16 Car. 1, c. 11 (1640), revised at the Restoration as 13 Car. 2, c. 12 (1661).

[125] "It begins to be claimed, flatly, that *no man is bound to incriminate himself* on any charge (no matter how properly instituted) or *in any court* (not merely in the ecclesiastical or Star Chamber tribunals). Then this claim comes to be conceded by the judges . . . . By the end of Charles II's reign [that is, by 1685], there is no longer any doubt, in any court . . . ." 8 Wigmore, *Evidence* § 2250, at 289–90 (footnotes omitted) (emphasis original).

Wigmore based his case for a seventeenth-century privilege against self-incrimination at common law on some references to the maxim that one need not accuse oneself that appear in late seventeenth-century *State Trials* and other published law reports. I have elsewhere shown that the authorities on which Wigmore based this account do not support the claim that the common law courts recognized a general privilege against self-incrimination by the end of the seventeenth century. Langbein, "PASI," *supra* n. 89, at 1071–85, substantially republished in Helmholz, *Privilege, supra* n. 89, at 100–8. Five of the cases on which Wigmore relied were civil rather than criminal, mostly dealing with penalty issues in equity. In the eleven trials that were criminal, there was no sustained reliance on such a privilege; rather, in each, the defendant spoke persistently to the merits in his own defense. What Wigmore identified as evidence of the defendant invoking the privilege against selfincrimination was an isolated remark or exchange that occurred in a trial in which the defendant otherwise spoke constantly. In five of the eleven criminal trials, what Wigmore treated as evidence of the common law court's recognition of the privilege against selfincrimination was actually hostile behavior by the trial judge, refusing to allow the defendant to crossexamine an accusing witness. These were manifestations of what we now understand to have been the socalled witness privilege, discussed below.

defense counsel succeeded in restructuring the criminal trial to make it possible to defend a silent accused did a workable privilege against self-incrimination within common law trial procedure become possible.[126] The privilege that we know in modern Anglo-American law was fashioned across the nineteenth century, by extension of an earlier privilege that had protected third-party witnesses, but not the criminal accused.[127]

When we look for evidence of a privilege against self-incrimination in the practice of the Old Bailey and other common law criminal courts in the later seventeenth and eighteenth centuries, we find exactly what our understanding of the "accused speaks" trial would lead us to expect. I have examined most of the Sessions Paper reports from their beginnings in the 1670s through the 1780s. In these thousands of cases I have not noticed a single instance in which an accused refused to speak at trial on the asserted ground of a privilege to remain silent. There were instances in which the court refused to allow an accused's pretrial statement to be admitted when the JP had made the mistake of taking it on oath. In some such cases this step was justified on the ground that examination under oath entailed a species of unpermitted compulsion,[128] although the testimonial disqualification of the accused would have provided a sufficient independent ground. Thus, in the murder trial of Sarah Malcolm in 1733, the court excluded her sworn pretrial examination, saying that if it "is upon Oath it cannot be read [at trial], for Persons are not to swear against themselves; all Examinations ought to be taken freely and voluntarily, and not upon Oath, and then we can read them."[129] Beattie has pointed to a similar case a decade later at Surrey Assizes in 1743, in which the pamphlet report tells us that the defendant's pretrial "Confession was produced; but it being taken on Oath, it could not be read. If it had been

---

[126] The theme of Langbein, "PASI," *supra* n. 89, substantially republished in Helmholz, *Privilege, supra* n. 89, at 82 ff.

[127] The important finding of Henry E. Smith, "The Modern Privilege: Its Nineteenth-Century Origins," in Helmholz, *Privilege, supra* n. 89, at 145 ff [hereafter Smith, "Modern Privilege"]. Smith's work is confirmed and extended in John Witt, "Making the Fifth: The Constitutionalization of American Self-Incrimination Doctrine, 1791–1903," 77 *Texas L. Rev.* 825 (1999); Katherine B. Hazlett, "The Nineteenth-Century Origins of the Fifth Amendment Privilege against Self-Incrimination," 42 *American J. Legal History* 235 (1998).

[128] Nelson's JP manual spells out this linkage: "The Felon may be examined before he is committed, but not upon Oath, because *nemo debet seipsum accusare*." William Nelson, *The Office and Authority of a Justice of Peace* 253 (London 1718).

[129] Sarah Malcolm, *OBSP* (Feb. 1733), at 90–1, discussed in Langbein, "CTBL" 283 n. 58. In another Old Bailey case a generation earlier, the defendant may have been trying to raise this claim, but in a situation in which the examination had been properly taken, that is, unsworn. Seeking to avoid "his Confession, he said, That it was an old Maxim in the Law, that what a Person should confess before a Justice [of the Peace] should not be given in Evidence. But it was replied [that is, from the bench], That if there was such a Maxim, it was so old that it was forgotten; but was asked, If he could produce any such Record [that is, of the Maxim]?" He could not and was convicted. John Bellingham, *OBSP* (Oct. 1699), at 4 (forgery). Another example has been discussed *supra* Ch. 3, n. 269.

taken voluntarily it would have been admitted as good Evidence; but the law supposes that an Oath is a Compulsion; and consequently that no Man is obliged to swear against himself in Cases where it affects his Life."[130]

The preoccupation with oath in these cases was highly characteristic of early thinking about the privilege. "The history of the privilege, from the struggles over the authority of High Commission through at least the framing of the American Bill of Rights, is almost entirely a story of when and for what purposes people would be required to speak under oath."[131] The oath-centeredness of early thinking about self-incrimination is a main reason why the privilege had so little capacity to affect the treatment of the criminal defendant at trial, since he was not allowed to be sworn until 1898 in England (a few decades earlier in many American jurisdictions).[132]

Apart from these cases excluding sworn pretrial examinations, we do not see privilege-like concepts voiced to protect any supposed right of the accused to be silent in Old Bailey trials until the later 1780s, when the Sessions Papers report a couple of cases in which the court invoked the principle against self-accusation to explain to jurors why particular questions could not be put to the accused. At the trial of William Ludlum for a forgery in 1788 the judge explained to the jury that "[i]t would not be fair to press the prisoner with very sharp observations [about discrepancies] . . . in his defense; as to what he says now, if it does not make for him, it should make against him, because we do not ask him to accuse himself, but to defend himself."[133] The next year, in the trial of an accused highway robber, who was alleged to have had an accomplice, the jury is reported to have inquired "where the person is that was with him?" The trial judge replied: "We have no right to call on the prisoner to oblige him to say who the man was and where he is; to be sure, observations may arise in your minds and mine upon it."[134] These sources show slippage

---

[130] James Scate, SAP (Summer 1743), at 12, 13 (breaking and entering, theft from dwelling house), cited in Beattie, Crime 365. In an Old Bailey case in 1745 DeVeil, the court JP, took examination of Henry Simms on oath, preparing to use him as a crown witness; and an unsworn "confession, which was also signed freely and voluntarily." DeVeil subsequently prosecuted Simms after Simms recanted on a crown witness bargain in another case. The court ignored Simms' protest that "A man can't swear against himself," apparently treating the unsigned confession as the operative document, even though the Sessions Paper reprints the sworn confession. Henry Simms, OBSP (May 1745, #291), at 172, 173–74.

[131] Albert W. Alschuler, "A Peculiar Privilege in Historical Perspective: The Right to Remain Silent," 94 Michigan L. Rev. 2625, 2641–2 (1996), substantially republished in Helmholz, Privilege, supra n. 89, at 181, 187.

[132] Criminal Evidence Act, 61 & 62 Vict., c. 6 (1898); regarding the American developments, see George Fisher, "The Jury's Rise as Lie Detector," 107 Yale L.J. 575, 659–97 (1997).

[133] William Ludlum, OBSP (Jan. 1788, #116), at 134, 138.

[134] James Walton, OBSP (Jan. 1789, #137), 145, at 146. The court was inviting the jury to draw a negative inference from the defendant's failure to speak, the practice disapproved by the U.S. Supreme Court in the much criticized Warren Court precedent, Griffin v. California, 380 U.S. 609 (1965).

away from the oath-centeredness of the early privilege, since the defendant was not on oath. There was indeed a change in attitude toward questioning of the accused across the eighteenth century, a growing sense that it was inappropriate to question the accused's statement. As late as 1748 the *Sessions Papers* show us an Old Bailey judge engaged in fairly determined questioning of an accused's statement,[135] and I have noticed an isolated instance as late as 1772,[136] but Stephen was correct to say that "[i]n the eighteenth century," and particularly in the second half of the century, "the practice of questioning prisoners at their trial appears to have fallen into disuse . . . ."[137] We are unable to say whether this development was motivated by notions that later came to be associated with the privilege against self-incrimination.

The privilege against self-incrimination that we find in current law "developed through analogical extension of the witness privilege"[138] in the nineteenth century. In the eighteenth-century *Sessions Papers* we see this privilege for witnesses invoked to prevent defense counsel from

---

[135] In the case of John Morris, *OBSP* (Oct. 1748, #479), at 282, 283 (theft of a watch), the *Sessions Paper* reports detailed questioning of the accused about his claim to have purchased the watch from a sailor:

COURT [to accused following prosecution case]. Can you give an account how you came by this watch?
PRISONER. I bought it of a sailor, at the [T]hree [T]uns at Greenwich.
COURT. How long was it before you offered it [for sale] to this Gentleman [the last prosecution witness]?
PRISONER. About 12 o'clock in the day.
COURT. What was his [the sailor's] name?
PRISONER. I did not ask his name.
COURT. What ship did he say he belonged to?
PRISONER. [names one]
COURT. What day was it?
PRISONER. [Thursday a month ago.]
COURT. Are you sure it was upon a Thursday?
PRISONER. No, my Lord, it was upon a Tuesday.
COURT. What Tuesday?
PRISONER. It was a month yesterday.

The *Sessions Paper* drops a footnote at this point, saying: "The watch was not lost then, it was not lost till [a later date]." Ibid. at 283. Morris offered two witnesses to his version of buying it from a sailor. The court examined them closely, and after the jury convicted Morris (of theft, but not in the dwelling house, hence clergyable), the court ordered the two witnesses prosecuted for perjury.

Two years before in another Old Bailey trial, the court told the accused, charged with stealing a promissory note, "You must tell us how you came by the Note." John Smith, *OBSP* (July 1746, #270), at 210, 214. The accused was represented by counsel, who apparently made no objection. Questioning of the accused by court and prosecution counsel is reported in the trial of Dick Turpin at York Assizes in 1739. Derek Barlow, *Dick Turpin and the Gregory Gang* 406–7 (1973).

[136] Edward Barry, *OBSP* (June 1772, #435), at 214, 215 (highway robbery).

[137] Stephen, *General View* 194.

[138] Smith, "Modern Privilege," *supra* n. 89, at 146.

pursuing some line of questioning in the cross-examination of a prosecution witness.[139] For example, in the trial of Thomas Bambridge for theft in 1729, when one Wilkerson was offered to testify against him, Bambridge "desired [that Wilkerson] might be asked what Money he received and how long he had been maintained to be an Evidence against him, but was told by the Court that such a Question was not proper to be asked. If he could prove it he might."[140] In a case in 1744 one accused, Parker, called another, Randall, as a defense witness, saying, "I have no other witness but . . . Randall, he can clear me of this." The court "informed [Randall] that he might choose whether he would be sworn or not [meaning, in this setting, whether he would serve as a defense witness or not], because he was not obliged to answer any questions that might tend to accuse himself. He paused some time and then consented to be sworn."[141] Randall exonerated Parker, who was acquitted; Randall was then tried and convicted on a separate indictment.[142]

By the 1780s, when the *Sessions Papers* show us more of what the lawyers were doing at trial, we find counsel as well as court invoking the principle, and sometimes the explicit maxim, against forcing a witness to accuse himself. In the trial of Joseph Dunbar in 1784 for forging a bank note, Garrow for the defense began cross-examining a prosecution witness by asking him, "How long . . . have you been a smuggler?" Opposing counsel objected, "That is certainly an improper question." Garrow replied, "He has told us already that he is a smuggler." The court then intervened to clarify: "If he was asked as to any act of smuggling, the question would be contrary to law."[143] Answering questions about particular acts would require the witness to incriminate himself, as opposed to the question that Garrow was asking. Later in the same cross-examination, the judge again intervened to protect the witness, telling Garrow: "I must stop you in that question. A question that can be answered only one way without accusing himself, is not to be put."[144]

The *Sessions Papers* report several other cases in which the witness privilege was successfully invoked to shield a witness against aggressive cross-examination by Garrow. On behalf of a defendant tried in 1785 for

---

[139] Some other instances of this phenomenon were among the late seventeenth-century *State Trial* cases that Wigmore thought evidenced recognition of a general privilege against self-incrimination in that period, discussed *supra* n. 125.

[140] Thomas Bambridge, *OBSP* (Dec. 1729), at 17, 18.

[141] Thomas Parker, *OBSP* (Jan. 1744, #119), at 53, 54 (theft).

[142] William Randall, *OBSP* (Jan. 1754, #120), at 54, 56 (theft).

[143] Joseph Dunbar, *OBSP* (May 1784, #656), at 836, 839. (The case is discussed in another connection in Ch. 4, *supra*, text at nn. 142–7, 309.)

[144] Ibid. at 840. Notice that the point is expressed not as a privilege personal to the witness to decline to answer the question (the modern privilege), but as a prohibition of the question that would require the accused to invoke the privilege.

receiving stolen goods, Garrow tried to ask a prosecution witness whether in his testimony just concluded "he has confessed that he has perjured himself[.]" The court stopped Garrow and told him, "you may prove it but not ask it of himself."[145] Cross-examining a prosecution witness in a burglary case the next year, Garrow asked her whether what she had just said was true or false. The trial judge intervened, saying: "You have no right to make her accuse herself."[146] In three separate cases in the December 1787 sessions, the court spared a witness from answering questions from Garrow on cross-examination about whether the witness was a receiver of stolen goods.[147] The recorder of London summarized the witness privilege in the Old Bailey in 1784, saying that defense counsel "has a right to discredit the [prosecution] witness by any question the answer to which does not tend to criminate himself."[148]

To the extent that the witness privilege was the forerunner of the later and broader privilege against self-incrimination, we must notice the irony that in this early phase the privilege against self-incrimination was still not much associated with safeguarding the criminal accused. Rather, its main use was to limit the scope of cross-examination, which in the eighteenth century was nearly the only tool in defense counsel's kit.

The witness privilege had a dimension beyond protecting against self-incrimination. It was also understood to protect a dignitary or reputational interest against shameful disclosures. We see that concept discussed in a murder trial in 1784 that resulted from a brawl at a political rally. The celebrated advocate, Thomas Erskine, representing a criminal defendant, began to cross-examine a prosecution witness about having once been flogged. The trial judge halted him, telling Erskine that he had "no right to ask [the witness] for what he was flogged. I do not think a man is obliged to answer any question to his own turpitude." Erskine acknowledged that "no man is in a Court of Justice to be asked as to anything that may bring a prosecution upon him," but Erskine insisted that "in order to get at the veracity of a witness, and to see whether this man is really speaking truth or not, I have a right to ask him [about] an offense which is past and gone, and for which he cannot receive punishment again." The judge refused the distinction and

---

[145] Uziel Barrah, *OBSP* (Apr. 1785, #500), at 660, 663.

[146] Henry Thompson and Thomas Harris, *OBSP* (Feb. 1786, #211), at 346, 352.

[147] John Durham and Edward Crowther, *OBSP* (Dec. 1787, #38), at 52, 54–5 (burglary); Thomas Duxton, *OBSP* (Dec. 1787, #83), at 93, 94–5 (burglary); Joseph Percival, *OBSP* (Dec. 1787, #84), at 95, 96 (burglary) ("You cannot ask this woman whether she received stolen goods").

[148] Stephen Tissington, *OBSP* (May 1784, #655), at 843, 845 (forgery); accord, Mary Heath, 18 *St. Tr.* 1, 14 (K.B. Ireland 1744) (perjury) (court, admonishing prosecution witness in habeas corpus proceeding to declare the truth, advises: "You are not obliged to say anything to criminate yourself").

stopped the questioning, saying: "I have always understood that no man or woman is to be asked a question that tends to disgrace themselves. I have known a woman asked whether she ever had a bastard child, and it has always been stopped."[149] This strand of the witness privilege, protecting reputational interests, fell away in the mid-nineteenth century.[150]

To conclude: The slogan that a criminal defendant need not accuse himself (*nemo tenetur prodere seipsum*) emerged as a revered principle from the constitutional struggles of the mid-seventeenth century. It had been formulated to strike at the oath-based investigative procedures of the non-common law courts but had no determinate meaning when applied to the common law criminal trial, at which the accused was forbidden to speak on oath. The principle seeped into the common law trial primarily as a protection for witnesses rather than for the accused, especially to shield prosecution witnesses against the growing aggressiveness of cross-examination by defense counsel in the second half of the eighteenth century. The older "accused speaks" trial had no room for the counter-principle of silence, no means of vindicating an accused's right to silence. So long as the accused had to conduct his own defense, there could be no effective privilege against self-incrimination. Only after the rule against defense counsel was overcome was the privilege extended to protect the accused, a development overwhelmingly of the nineteenth and twentieth centuries. In this chapter I have emphasized the revolutionary importance of lawyerization of the trial in silencing the accused at trial. The privilege against self-incrimination embedded this silencing of the accused into the doctrinal structure of later criminal procedure.

C. Prosection Counsel

The main theme of this chapter is the influence of defense counsel in transforming the conduct of the criminal trial across the second half of the eighteenth century. Before turning directly to the work of defense counsel, it will be useful to cast a glance at his courtroom protagonist, prosecution counsel. Above in Chapter 3, treating the prosecutorial origins of felony defense counsel, I emphasized three major changes in prosecutorial practice in the early decades of the eighteenth century: the reward system, the crown witness system, and the use of prosecution lawyers, especially the use of solicitors to investigate and gather evidence in the pretrial. I pointed out that lawyerization of the pretrial tended to lead to the use of prosecution counsel at trial, particularly in cases brought by

---

[149] Patrick Nicholson *et al.*, *OBSP* (May 1784), at 649, 666.
[150] Smith, "Modern Privilege," *supra* n. 89, at 157–9.

institutional prosecutors such as the Mint and the Post Office. The combined effect of these prosecutorial innovations was to unbalance the old altercation trial, so disadvantaging the accused that the judges began to relent on the rule against defense counsel in the hope of better safeguarding the innocent accused.

These large shifts in prosecutorial practice did not, however, cause material change in the courtroom role of prosecution counsel. Prosecution counsel was still not much used. As late as 1834 a leading Old Bailey counsel estimated that prosecution counsel appeared in only one case in twenty.[151] Because prosecution counsel had long been allowed, his appearance in the felony trial was not a radical break with the past. Compared to the fundamental changes in the role and influence of defense counsel in the eighteenth century, the position of prosecution counsel changed less and mattered less.

1. The Solicitor's Influence

In most cases in which a solicitor investigated the case and selected and prepared the witnesses, the solicitor played a more important part in the prosecution than the counsel who presented the case at trial.[152] We occasionally see prosecution counsel refer to the solicitor's instructions at trial— sometimes incidentally,[153] sometimes more pointedly, in order to distance himself from a case that might,[154] or that already had[155] miscarried. (At

---

[151] May, Thesis 92 n. 6, citing MS letters from Charles Phillips to Lord Brougham, *Brougham Papers* nos. 28,437, 28,465.

[152] Regarding the relations of solicitor and prosecutor, see *supra* Ch. 3, text at nn. 55, 92–7, 195–204.

[153] E.g., William Bird, *OBSP* (Sept. 1742, #102), at 42 (murder) (prosecution counsel, opening, refers to how "the Case now to be laid before you is stated to me in my Instructions"); John Aikles, *OBSP* (Jan. 1784, #226), at 285,286 (theft of bill of exchange) (Garrow, prosecuting, refers to his instructions); Richard Wooldridge, *OBSP* (Feb. 1784, #357), at 480, 482 (clipping coin) (Garrow again refers to his instructions).

[154] For a case in which prosecution counsel, appearing to be uneasy about the strength of his case, emphasized that he was merely following instructions, see Henry Harvey, *OBSP* (Sept. 1785, #909), at 1152 (perjury). Harvey was being tried in September 1785 for having prosecuted a false highway robbery the previous February. The recorder of London, who had played a decisive role in obtaining royal reprieves and pardons for the two men convicted in February, presided at the September trial. He instructed the jury that the suspicious behavior that led him to instigate the pardons was that of the prosecutor in the former case, and not Harvey, a headborough (constable) who had assisted the man. Ibid. at 1176. In opening the case, prosecuting counsel, Morgan, repeatedly prefaced his summary of what the witnesses would say with the phrase, "I am instructed . . . ." Ibid. at 1153. For good measure he added that the jurors should acquit if they "have any doubt . . . ." Ibid. They did. Ibid. at 1179. For the antecedent prosecution, see Peter Newbery and William Iverson, *OBSP* (Feb. 1785, #292), at 340 (highway robbery).

[155] For example, in a prosecution for murder resulting from an election-related riot in 1784, after defense counsel's cross-examination discredited the main witness, a flustered prosecution counsel apologized to the court. "[Y]ou know I know nothing of this witness, therefore it is impossible [that] I can anticipate what they say. I can only go through the witnesses

least in cases touching the monarch, it appears that the employment of prosecution counsel could commence before trial, when counsel was used to lay the bill of indictment before the grand jury.[156])

The sources also show defense counsel sometimes referring to solicitors' instructions,[157] but because defense counsel was restricted in the realm of fact mainly to cross-examining witnesses, his role was more reactive than prosecution counsel and thus less amenable to advance direction by the solicitor. Moreover, in some circumstances the accused could engage defense counsel directly, without employing a solicitor.[158]

By comparison with the solicitor who prepared the case, the counsel on either side who presented it at trial often had only cursory familiarity with it. A barrister who had a significant Old Bailey and assize practice in the middle third of the nineteenth century recalled in his memoirs that

[scheduled in the solicitor's brief] and see what they will prove." William Wilkins, *OBSP* (Sept. 1788, #523), at 674, 684. Two decades before, in a prosecution arising from the Wilkes riots in 1768, Serjeant Glyn abandoned the case after the prosecution's witnesses failed to make out the case. "I am not now pressing this gentleman's conviction," he said, and the jury acquitted without hearing the defense. Samuel Gillam, *OBSP* (July 1768, #488), at 274, 283 (aiding and abetting unknown persons to commit murder).

[156] We learn of this work from a passage in the report of the Regicide Trials held at the Restoration in 1660. The judges framed some directions, including one dealing with the grand jury proceedings, in which they remarked that it was "usual in all cases that the prosecutors upon indictments are admitted to manage the evidence for finding the bill, and the king's counsel are the only prosecutors in the king's case [that is, in treason cases]; for he cannot prosecute in person." *Regicide Trials*, 5 *St. Tr.* 947, 972 (1660). In the *State Trials* report of that case, the editor notes (in connection with the point that evidence is presented to the grand jury in camera, that is, not in public) that in the prosecution of Thomas Hardy for treason in 1794, "the Solicitor for the Crown attended the Grand Jury for the purpose, at the desire of the Grand Jury and by leave of the Court." Ibid. at 972, citing information from a "Mr. Clarkson, the Attorney employed for Hardy." *R. v. Thomas Hardy*, 24 *St. Tr.* 199 (O.B. 1794).

An earlier example comes to us in a broadsheet about a pickpocket who was caught cutting a purse in the royal chapel at Whitehall on Christmas Day 1611. A week later Francis Bacon, the solicitor general, procured the indictment from a grand jury impanelled for the case. The accused pleaded guilty, begged mercy, was convicted and executed. *The Arraignment of John Selman* (London 1612) (Huntington Libr., San Marino, CA, shelfmark 30325).

[157] John Mattsham, *OBSP* (July 1774, #454), at 243 (highway robbery) (cross-examining defense counsel, probing prosecuting victim's identification of the defendant, cautions him, "I give you fair notice, I have instructions that you will be contradicted; was he one of the men or not?"). In treason cases, in which the 1696 Act permitted full defense of counsel, and in cases of misdemeanor, defense counsel was allowed an opening address. The reports of such addresses sometimes contain references to counsel's instructions, e.g., John Matthews, 15 *St. Tr.* 1323, 1368–9 (O.B. 1719) (treason) ("we shall according to our instructions, be able to produce a great number of witnesses to contradict what these witnesses have sworn"); Christopher Layer, 16 *St. Tr.* 93, 199 (K.B. 1722) (treason) (defense counsel objects to the threatened reading of some papers by the prosecution, "though for my part I know not what they are, for there is no hint of them in my brief"); William Hales, 17 *St. Tr.* 209, 219 (O.B. 1729) (forgery) (misdemeanor) ("I have nothing material in my instructions; therefore, I shall not trouble your lordships").

[158] Discussed in May, Thesis 103–6.

counsel was commonly instructed only on the eve of trial. On assize, it was the custom "for the judges to enter the town before the bar . . . ." Once the bar arrived, at most a day before the trials got under way, "[t]he attorneys were to be seen hurrying with the briefs destined for their fortunate recipients . . . ."[159] Such a system bespoke an expectation of scant pretrial preparation by counsel. Appearing without preparation was "daily experience" for barristers, since "well into the nineteenth century it was usual for a criminal brief not to be delivered to counsel until the day of the trial."[160] As between solicitor and counsel, therefore, if anybody did any investigating, or much thinking, it had to be the solicitor.

Lawyerization of the trial located responsibility for gathering the facts with the lawyers, but the division of function between solicitor and barrister largely exonerated the barrister from responsibility for what he urged on the court. In contrast to the *Aufklärungspflicht*, the duty to clarify, of the Continental judge, in England none of the trial participants was responsible for truth-seeking. The judge was growing ever more dependent on counsel, and counsel took his instructions from the solicitor, who had no audience before the court. In the trial of Lord George Gordon for treason arising from the Gordon riots of 1780, the Attorney General told the jury in his opening remarks that "I open to you from my instructions what is given me as facts, and where witnesses are put down to prove them, I am not answerable for the truth of them."[161]

2. The Duty of Restraint

In well-reported cases at the Old Bailey in the eighteenth century, prosecution counsel is commonly shown making an opening address, usually based on the information in the solicitor's brief. The opening summarized the charges against the accused, identified the witnesses to be called, and previewed their testimony. In the trial of Lord George Gordon the Attorney General continued with the opening remarks just quoted, saying: "God forbid that anything I mention unsupported by proof should turn to the prejudice of the prisoner at the bar."[162]

This studied tone of concern for the welfare of the accused in the opening address was in keeping with a peculiar notion, the so-called duty of

---

[159] 1 Ballantine, *Experiences, supra* n. 16, at 62. Cairns points to an instance in 1783 on the Midland Circuit in which three barristers were fined for being in an assize town before the Commission day. Cairns, *Advocacy* 37. "As late as 1863 Fitzjames Stephen said prosecution briefs were delivered 'to counsel generally speaking (at least in the country) in court on the day of trial.' " Ibid., citing Stephen, *General View* 156.

[160] Cairns, *Advocacy* 34, citing Henry Brougham, Lord Abinger, 1 *Law Review* 79 (1845).

[161] Lord George Gordon, 21 *St. Tr.* 485 (O.B. 1781).

[162] Ibid.

prosecutorial restraint, which developed to mitigate the unfairness of the continuing restrictions on the scope of defense counsel's activity in felony cases. Until the 1836 legislation prosecution counsel was allowed to make an opening statement to preview its case for the jury, but the defense was not. Likewise, prosecution counsel was permitted to address the jury at the close of the case, commenting on the evidence received and on the accused's defenses, but defense counsel was forbidden to make closing remarks (a restriction whose purpose was to pressure the accused to speak in his own defense). The duty of restraint expressed the idea that prosecution counsel "ought to confine himself to a simple detail[ing] of the facts which he expects to prove, because the prisoner has no opportunity of laying his case before the jury by his counsel . . . ."[163]

Cottu reported in 1820 that the prosecutor was expected to "guard[] himself . . . from every sort of invective against the prisoner . . . ."[164] Actually, seeming to be solicitous of the interest of the accused was probably quite an effective tactic of prosecutorial advocacy. Telling a jury that "you are not to be influenced by what I have stated, or what I have observed" (as was done in a murder prosecution in 1772[165]) hardly overcame the advantage inherent in being able to use the opening statement to impress upon the jury the structure of the prosecution case.

By the early nineteenth century, and probably earlier, there were discrepancies among the assize circuits about whether to allow the prosecution to make an opening address. "On the Northern Circuit the practice was for counsel 'always' to make an opening address to the jury . . . . On the Oxford Circuit counsel 'scarcely ever' began with a speech. On the Midland Circuit . . . counsel only opened in cases of intricate circumstantial evidence."[166] The Criminal Law Commissioners, reporting in 1836, spoke of the reluctance to allow an opening address on the Midland Circuit as an indication that the contrary practice elsewhere placed the accused "under great disadvantage, for want of the assistance of counsel . . . ."[167] The Commissioners also voiced concern that prosecutorial

[163] William Dickenson and T. N. Talfourd, *A Practical Guide to the Quarter Sessions and Other Sessions of the Peace* 350 (3rd. edn. London 1829) [hereafter Dickenson and Talfourd, *Guide*], cited by Cairns, *Advocacy* 39.

[164] Cottu, *Administration* 87. Perhaps contrasting French histrionics, Cottu observed that the prosecutor does not paint the accused "as a monster of whom the earth ought to be that instant rid . . . ." Ibid. at 89.

[165] *The Trial of William Morgan for the Murder of Miss Mary Jones . . . at the Assizes held at Glo[u]cester, on Wednesday the 11th of March 1772*, at 5 (Gloucester 1772) (B.L. shelfmark 115.h.32). For another well-reported example of a "restrained" opening address in a murder case, see Daniel Macginniss, *OBSP* (Jan. 1783, #85), at 111, 113–15 (William Fielding prosecuting) ("I shall not say a syllable to you to excite your indignation . . .").

[166] Cairns, *Advocacy* 8. May discusses Old Bailey practice and cites many examples. May, Thesis 133–4 and n. 125.

[167] *1836 Report* 10 n.

restraint was not always so restrained, because the supposed duty was hard to enforce. "Occasionally, even in trials for Murder, the whole skill of an expert advocate has been allowed to be exerted in his opening statement,"[168] they said, making a pointed reference to a "celebrated speech of Mr. Garrow, on opening the case against Patch on an indictment for Murder."[169] Cairns observes that "[t]here was never an authoritative expression of the duty of restraint, so it remained a matter of circuit etiquette, judicial discretion, and the 'good taste' and 'right feeling' of counsel in individual cases."[170]

The duty of prosecutorial restraint pertained only in felony cases. The logic was to offset the disadvantage under which defense counsel had been placed as a result of the prohibition upon his addressing the jury. An early nineteenth-century practice manual for the court of quarter sessions, where most serious misdemeanor cases were tried, observed: "In cases of misdemeanor, the prosecuting counsel is not thus restricted, because here the defendant is allowed to make a real defense by his counsel, and, therefore, here the counsel for the prosecutor may not only state his facts, but reason on them, and anticipate any line of defense which his opponent may probably adopt."[171] Allyson May has pointed to several misdemeanor trials at the Old Bailey in the period 1784–91 in which the behavior of prosecution counsel was "unrestrained. The case against the accused was argued much more forcibly, and references to 'my instructions' were no longer necessary. Instead, prosecuting counsel declared vehemently the certain guilt of the accused, and such addresses concluded with strong words to the effect that the miscreant must be punished."[172]

Only by hiring prosecution counsel could the victim or other prosecutor obtain the tactical advantage that inhered in being allowed to make an opening address. "Where no counsel is engaged for the prosecution there is, of course, no opening; for a prosecutor is never allowed personally to address the jury."[173] The early nineteenth-century manual that described the practice in that way undertook to justify it on the conceptualistic

[168] Ibid. at 10.

[169] Ibid. They were referring to Garrow's opening address in *The Trial of Richard Patch for the Wilful Murder of Isaac Blight* (London 1806). For discussion of Garrow's controversial imputation of motive to Patch in breach of the convention, see Cairns, *Advocacy* 41–4.

[170] Cairns, *Advocacy* 44.

[171] Dickenson and Talfourd, *Guide*, supra n. 163, at 350.

[172] May, Thesis 140, citing William Stevenson, *OBSP* (Sept. 1784, #843), at 1164, 1165; William Priddle et al., *OBSP* (Apr. 1787, #448), at 580, 581; Robert Jacques et al., *OBSP* (July 1790, #537), 614, 619 (Silvester prosecuting, says on opening, "I shall prove . . . that they are all guilty of this charge; and it is high time that justice should overtake these delinquents"); John Oliver, *OBSP* (Oct. 1791, #443), at 613, 614.

[173] Dickenson and Talfourd, *Guide*, supra n. 163, at 350.

ground that the prosecutor, who otherwise had complete control over the content of the prosecution case, was a mere witness like any other. "The case is not *his* cause, but that of the crown, though conducted at his instance, and therefore he can only be examined on his oath in the box like another witness."[174] A better explanation for restricting the privilege of making opening remarks to counsel was that the citizen prosecutor could not be trusted to observe the rule of advocacy that the opening address be limited to the projected scope of the proofs.[175]

The main responsibility of prosecution counsel was to adduce the evidence of the accusing witnesses, typically the victim and other witnesses to the events, but sometimes also experts (especially medical experts in cases turning on sanity,[176] or in cases involving murder[177] or rape[178]). In contrast to defense counsel, whose main function was to cross-examine prosecution witnesses, prosecution counsel concentrated on developing the prosecution case on examination-in-chief.[179] To be sure,

---

[174] Dickenson and Talfourd, *Guide, supra* n. 163, at 350 (emphasis original).

[175] On the rule against counsel claiming more in the opening than the evidence proves, see 6 Wigmore, *Evidence* § 1808, at 275 n.

[176] Nigel Walker's effort to quantify the frequency and success rate of insanity pleas in the eighteenth century was the first use of the *Old Bailey Sessions Papers* in legal historical work. 1 Nigel Walker, *Crime and Insanity in England: The Historical Perspective* 66–72, 284 (1968). Recent study suggests a growing subordination of medical experts to adversary control from the later eighteenth century onward, especially in cases turning on sanity, and that this pattern displaced a less partisan conception of the expert's role that had prevailed earlier in the eighteenth century. See Joel P. Eigen, *Witnessing Insanity: Madness and Mad-Doctors in the English Court* (1995); Stephan Landsman, 'One Hundred Years of Rectitude: Medical Witnesses at the Old Bailey,' 16 *Law and History Rev.* 445 (1998).

[177] E.g., George Smith *et al.*, *OBSP* (Apr. 1723), at 1, 3 (murder). Two prosecution medical experts testified in opposition to the defense claim that the victim had been accidentally run over by a wagon; the case, a cause célèbre, was prosecuted at crown expense at the direction of the King, see *supra*, Ch. 3, text at nn. 60–3.

Crawford reports from a sample of seventy-five homicide trials in eight years "surveyed systematically between 1729–30 and 1789–90 that "[medical evidence was heard at more than half the Old Bailey trials for homicide in each decade between 1730 and 1790, and dissections were performed for 26% of them. Practitioners who had treated a victim were usually asked for a description of the symptoms and an opinion about the cause of death." Catherine Crawford, "The Emergence of English Forensic Medicine: Medical Evidence in Common Law Courts 1730–1830," at 22, 43 (unpublished D.Phil. thesis, University of Oxford, 1987); see also Thomas Rogers Forbes, *Surgeons at the Old Bailey: English Forensic Medicine to 1878* (1985).

[178] E.g., Thomas Norris, *OBSP* (Dec. 1741, #54) at 17 (surgeons testify for prosecution and defense; defense surgeon had not examined the child victim but doubted her story).

[179] Cairns attributes to Lord Brougham an unsigned article published in 1845 reflecting in this regard upon Garrow's advocacy. Garrow's "real forte," Brougham thought, was "his examination in chief, which was unrivalled, and which is, indeed, a far more important and not less difficult attribute than the cross-examination which so captivates the ignorant." Cairns, *Advocacy* 8, quoting [Henry Brougham], "Mr. Baron Garrow," 1 *Law Review* 318, 320 (1845). On the attribution to Brougham, Cairns cites MS authority: Stewart to Brougham, Nov. 1844, Brougham Papers no. 23,878.

the conduct of cross-examination was sometimes critical to the prosecution case, especially when the defendant presented alibi witnesses. The
Sessions Papers show Garrow, serving as prosecution counsel, exposing
discrepancies in alibi defenses on cross-examination,[180] so effectively in
one case that the court immediately ordered the witness committed to
trial for perjury.[181] But the main advantage to having prosecution counsel
was the clarity and thoroughness that counsel brought to the work of
developing the prosecution case on examination-in-chief, by comparison
with the conventional practice in which the accuser and the witnesses told
their stories unaided. Furthermore, as defense counsel became increasingly influential, engaging prosecution counsel was a way to fight fire
with fire.[182]

D. Defense Counsel

1. Cross-Examination

The restrictions preventing defense counsel from addressing the jury
were meant to limit his new license in the realm of fact to the role of examining and cross-examining witnesses. Fact witnesses for the defense were
not very common or important in most eighteenth-century trials; medical
experts were sometimes called, for example, in rape cases.[183] Character
witnesses were often called, but adducing character evidence required
little from counsel. Thus, examination-in-chief was less significant in the
work of defense counsel than it was for prosecution counsel, who needed
to elicit from the mouths of event witnesses evidence sufficient to carry
the burdens of production and persuasion. Cross-examining prosecution
witnesses was the primary task for which the judges admitted defense
counsel to the felony trial.

　　At first the idea seems to have been that felony defense counsel would
supplement rather than supplant questioning by the court and the defendant. In the early years after the ban on defense counsel was relaxed, the
defendant continued to do some of his own cross-examining even when
he had defense counsel to assist him.[184] In the well-reported murder trial

---

[180] E.g., Edward Lowe and William Jobbins, *OBSP* (Oct. 1790, #705), at 904, 919–23 (arson,
theft) (Garrow cross-examining the alibi defense of John Jobbins, father of one the accused).
　　[181] George Platt and Philip Roberts, *OBSP* (Dec. 1790, #35), at 60, 73.
　　[182] See *infra*, text at nn. 283–4, noticing this dynamic in the decisions of the London Society
for Prosecuting Felons about whether to engage a prosecution solicitor.
　　[183] E.g., *R. v. Benjamin Russen*, 1 East, *PC* 438 (O.B. 1777) (rape; two surgeons testified for
the defense that penetration had not occurred; the jury disbelieved them and convicted).
　　[184] E.g., George Turner, *OBSP* (Sept. 1734, #5), at 171, 172 (murder) ("counsel" is not identified as prosecution or defense but attributed questioning appears to be defensive in

of John Swan and Elizabeth Jefferys in 1752, although counsel were present on both sides, the bench did most of the questioning of witnesses, much as in the days of the lawyer-free trial.[185] Across time, as the adversary dynamic unfolded and the altercation model of trial receded, it became ever more exceptional for the court or the defendant to play a direct role in cross-examining prosecution witnesses when the defendant was represented. In a rape case in 1775 the defendant is recorded asking the court's permission to pose "two or three questions" to the prosecutor, after the prosecutor testified to matter that "my counsel have no instructions about . . . ."[186] By the 1780s, we have seen, the court was telling the defendant that if there were "any questions omitted that you think proper to have your counsel ask, write them down and send them over . . . . [D]o not you put the question yourself, but hand it to your counsel."[187] Garrow did not need the judge to deliver that message. In a case in 1784 his client, the defendant, spoke up during Garrow's cross-examination of the accused, saying "I wish to put another question to [the prosecuting victim]." Garrow cut him off: "Send the question to me in writing," he said.[188]

I have explained in Chapter 3 why I think that disquiet about the danger of perjury in reward and crown witness prosecutions was a precipitating factor in the judges' decision in the 1730s to permit felony defendants to have the assistance of counsel in probing the testimony of prosecution witnesses. Our sources sometimes show defense counsel using cross-examination of an accomplice to remind the jury of the incentive for false witness. For example, in a case in 1760 counsel asked: "Then you made this discovery to save yourself?" (the accomplice's reply: "Yes").[189] In Garrow's hands the technique became more aggressive and derisive. Serving as defense counsel in a crown witness prosecution in 1788, Garrow heaped scorn on the accomplice. He interrupted prosecution counsel's examination-in-chief to caution him: "The gentleman [prosecution counsel] says you have been a bad boy, therefore, begin to amend."[190] Garrow began the cross-examination by addressing the

---

import); John Smith, *OBSP* (Jan. 1735, #53), at 34, 35 (theft); John Becket, *OBSP* (May 1735, #1), at 86 (theft); Robert Rhodes, *OBSP* (Apr.–May 1742, #38), at 80, 87 (forging a will); John Saunders, *OBSP* (May 1744, #248), at 110 (assault and robbery near the highway).

  [185] *R. v. John Swann and Elizabeth Jefferys*, 18 *St. Tr.* 1194 (Essex Assizes 1752).

  [186] William Priddle, *OBSP* (Feb. 1775, #175), at 99, 110.

  [187] Daniel Macginniss, *OBSP* (Jan. 1783, #85), at 111, 118–19 (murder), quoted in another context *supra* n. 78.

  [188] Humphry Moore, *OBSP* (Apr. 1784, #467), at 628, 633 (theft from dwelling house).

  [189] Thomas Shaw, *OBSP* (Sept. 1760, #269), at 276, 277 (breaking and entering dwelling house).

  [190] John Langford and William Annand, *OBSP* (Jan. 1788, #137), at 177, 182 (theft, receiving).

accomplice as his "honest friend." He remarked that it was "an unexpected pleasure to get you into this part of the Court"—meaning the witness stand rather than the prisoner's dock—and underscored that the accomplice was testifying "to get [him]self out of the scrape."[191]

In prosecutions for rewardable offenses, it was also common for cross-examination to be directed to showing the reward inducement. "Do you expect part of the Reward?"[192] " 'Tis for the sake of the great reward, I suppose, that you do this?"[193] "Was you not directed to go into the King's Road in order to be robbed?" "Did you not receive a shilling for that purpose?"[194] "Is not the reward an inducement to you to give testimony?"[195] "You have heard of the reward before now?"[196] In a well-reported coining case in 1788 defense counsel successfully insinuated through cross-examination that a thieftaker planted coins on the accused for the sake of the reward.[197] One thieftaker, Charles Jealous, who "belonged to Sir John Fielding's Office [for] many years,"[198] offered a feisty response when cross-examined about whether he expected to share in the reward for convicting an accused highway robber. "Yes," he told defense counsel, "you know that as well as you get your own fee."[199]

In the 1780s Garrow was particularly vigorous in cross-examining in reward cases. Representing an 11-year-old defendant accused of participation in a simple theft, which was not a rewardable offense, Garrow intimated by his questioning that reward-seeking drove the prosecution. He asked a prosecution witness: "Did you never hear there was a reward of forty pounds upon the conviction of that child?"[200] "[U]pon your oath did you never hear that you should be entitled to forty pounds as the price of that poor infant's blood?"[201] Defending in a case of alleged highway robbery that resulted from an incident of pickpocketing, Garrow used cross-examination to elicit that a thieftaker had counseled the prosecutor

[191] Ibid. at 183.
[192] Patrick Kelly et al., OBSP (Jan. 1743, ##116–19), at 70, 72 (coining).
[193] Samuel Goodman, OBSP (Dec. 1744, #69), at 34, 35 (highway robbery).
[194] Edward Hill and John Hill, OBSP (Dec. 1744, ##24–5) at 8–9.
[195] William Taylor, OBSP (Jan. 1745, #145), at 77.
[196] John Valentine and Broughton Birt, OBSP (Feb. 1783, #169), at 256, 257 (highway robbery).
[197] Samuel Dring, OBSP (Sept. 1788, #590), at 794, 795–6.
[198] James Roberts, OBSP (Dec. 1783, #2), at 5, 6 (highway robbery).
[199] Ibid. at 9. Another thieftaker, John Clark, had used much the same line in similar circumstances a few years earlier. Asked whether he expected some share of the reward, he replied, "As much as you do with your brief, sir . . . ." John Morgan et al., OBSP (Jan. 1782, ##100–3), at 146, 147 (coining). When the thieftaker took umbrage at being asked about the reward motive, the judge told him that cross-examination about "whether there is a reward, and do you expect a part of it . . . is no sort of imputation on your character. It is a proper question." Ibid. at 148.
[200] William Horton, OBSP (July 1784, #735), at 970 (theft).
[201] Ibid. at 971.

to testify that the accused had shoved the prosecutor, for the purpose of making the offense violent and hence rewardable as highway robbery.[202] Defending in another prosecution for highway robbery, he asked the thief-taker how many persons would divide the reward, and he asked another witness: "How much of the reward are you to have?"[203] On behalf of a defendant charged with a highway robbery, Garrow asked a prosecution witness whether "the thieftakers have thrown some gold dust in your eyes?"[204] Defending in a burglary case, Garrow used his cross-examination to raise the possibility that the witness had been seeking either a reward or a grant of nonprosecution under the crown witness system.[205] From the prosecutor in a highway robbery case, one Sheppard, Garrow elicited that Sheppard had twice before prosecuted for robberies to his person, convicting once. Sheppard denied having shared reward money in that case. Garrow then asked Sheppard: "Then you will not get above forty [pounds] if you convict now, my old friend, you will not get eighty this time?"[206]

The themes of cross-examination that we see in the reward cases—impugning the prosecutor's motives and probing for contradictions or other shortcomings in the prosecution evidence—were not, of course, confined to reward and crown witness cases.[207] We see defense counsel cross-examine to develop discrepancies between the pretrial statement and the trial testimony;[208] to shake the identification of persons[209] or property;[210] to question criminal intent;[211] and to explore base motiva-

---

[202] John M'Carty and Thomas Hartman, *OBSP* (Dec. 1787, #28), at 45, 45–7. The thieftaker "belonged to the public office [that is, the magistrate's office] in Bloomsbury"; the cross-examination established that he and another (a constable) prepared instructions for drawing the indictment, which the prosecutor gave to the clerk. The jury convicted the men of simple theft, rather than highway robbery, saving them from capital punishment and denying the prosecutors the reward. The case is discussed in John M. Beattie, "Garrow for the Defense," *History Today* (Feb. 1991) at 49, 51 [hereafter Beattie, "Garrow"].

[203] Thomas Gibbs, *OBSP* (Dec. 1788, #44), at 28, 29.

[204] William Eversall *et al.*, *OBSP* (May 1788, #333), at 436, 437 (highway robbery).

[205] Thomas Jones, *OBSP* (Dec. 1788, #76), at 48, 49 (burglary).

[206] Robert Mitchell, *OBSP* (Dec. 1784, #190), at 196, 198. Other cases in which Garrow emphasized the reward motive on cross-examination include Robert Horsely, *OBSP* (Dec. 1786, #83), at 100, 107 (burglary); Martha Cutler *et al.*, *OBSP* (Feb. 1788, #178), at 266, 268 (highway robbery).

[207] Beattie has drawn attention to the growing importance of cross-examination, particularly in the work of William Garrow, in the 1780s. Beattie, "Scales" 239–47; Beattie, Garrow, *supra* n. 202, at 49–53. Compare the adulatory account of cross-examination at the eighteenth-century Old Bailey in Stephan Landsman, "Spirit," *supra* n. 117, at 539–42, 548–57, with Cairns, *Advocacy* 34, arguing that cross-examination became counterproductive as it became more aggressive, especially in the nineteenth century.

[208] John Smallwood, *OBSP* (Jan. 1748, #86), at 55 (highway robbery).

[209] Elizabeth Robinson, *OBSP* (Oct. 1790, #764), at 980, 981–4 (theft from dwelling house).

[210] An early example: Peter Dayley, *OBSP* (Sept. 1748, #397), at 245, 246 (theft of money from dwelling house); James Scott (Jan. 1784, #216), at 262, 265 (Garrow attempting to establish "on behalf of the prisoner, that this is a property that cannot be identified").

[211] Elizabeth Wilson and Mary Williams, *OBSP* (Sept. 1784, #784), at 1079 (theft of shop

tions for bringing prosecutions[212]—for example, that the crown was paying the witness in a smuggling case ("How should I live else?," the witness said sheepishly).[213] Edelstein has pointed out how effectively counsel defended some rape cases by cross-examining to insinuate that the prosecution was the outgrowth of a failed effort to extort money from the defendant.[214] I have previously emphasized (in Chapter 4, discussing character evidence) cross-examination about the rape victim's prior sexual history. Both techniques were early manifestations of the defense strategy that has come to be known as "trying the victim."

The intensity and effectiveness of cross-examination grew at the Old Bailey across the eighteenth century as counsel became acclimated to criminal practice. The aggressiveness of William Garrow, who began appearing in the court in 1783,[215] seems to have been a turning point, on which contemporaries remarked.[216] Garrow's skill as a cross-examiner

goods) (Garrow and Silvester for the defense used cross-examination to challenge the prosecution contention that the women were caught in the act; the trial judge recommended acquittal, which followed, ibid. at 1084; neither defendant spoke in her own defense).

[212] William Bailey and Rebecca Brown, *OBSP* (Dec. 1744, ##40–1), at 17 (highway robbery) (grudge); Constantine Macguire, (Dec. 1744, #68), at 30, 31 (highway robbery) (grudge); William Clarenbolt, *OBSP* (July 1748, #338), at 215, 216 (attempted robbery); Anne Wallis (July 1766, #390), at 253 (servant's theft of a ring, cross-examination establishes an antecedent sexual relationship).

[213] Thomas Kemp, *OBSP* (Jan. 1748, #105), at 74.

[214] Laurie Edelstein, "An Accusation Easily to be Made? Rape and Malicious Prosecution in Eighteenth-Century England," 42 *American J. Legal History* 351 (1998). She points out that the victim's fear of abusive trial procedure may explain why so many rape cases were charged merely as attempted rape, a misdemeanor tried at quarter sessions. "Under a charge of attempted rape, it was not necessary to prove penetration, but only what the attacker had in mind. Cross-examination of the victim at trial, therefore, was not as extensive or as demanding as in a rape case." Ibid. at 378; accord Beattie, *Crime* 129–32.

The imputation that a prosecution was being brought because the accused had refused to pay the prosecutor not to do it (itself an offense, called compounding felony) was not limited to rape. See, e.g., William Askew, *OBSP* (Apr. 1746, #167), at 118, 120 (theft of silver from master's house), in which defense counsel cross-examined the prosecutor, "ask[ing] whether you have not offered any of the Prisoner's Friends, if they would give you any Thing, you would make it up?"

[215] Beattie, "Scales" 237.

[216] A pair of tracts reprove Garrow for his behavior in cross-examining. Matthew Concanen, *A Letter to William Garrow, Esq. on the Subject of his Illiberal Behaviour to the Author, on the Trial of a Cause . . . at the Lent Assizes, 1796, held at Kingston in the County of Surrey* (London n.d. [1796]) [hereafter Concanen, *Garrow*]; Thomas Hague, *A Letter to William Garrow, Esquire, in Which the Conduct of Counsel in the Cross-Examination of Witnesses and Commenting on Their Testimony is Fully Discussed and the Licentiousness of the Bar Disclosed* (London 1808) [hereafter Hague, *Garrow*]. Rowlandson caricatured Garrow's prowess in the print captioned "Being nervous and Cross-examined by Mr. Garrow," part of a series called "Miseries of Human Life" (London 1808), see fig. 5.2. It has previously been reproduced in Beattie, "Garrow," *supra* n. 202, at 49. From the sources it is hard to tell how much of a break with the past Garrow's tactics were. Highly effective cross-examination figured in the previous decade in the trial of Mrs Rudd. See Donna T. Andrew and Randall McGowen, *The Perreaus and Mrs. Rudd: Forgery and Betrayal in Eighteenth-Century London* 224–5 (2001), discussing *R. v. Margaret Caroline Rudd*, 1 Leach 115, 168 *Eng. Rep.* 160 (K.B. 1775).

was the basis of what a scornful contemporary acknowledged to be Garrow's "preeminence and celebrity."[217] There was a sense that Garrow's skill could affect the outcome of Old Bailey trials. In 1788 one John Davis, conducting his own defense in a highway robbery case, asked the prosecutor whether he had ever prosecuted anyone before. The prosecutor answered that on one prior occasion "I prosecuted two men, and they got off because a Mr. Garrow was their counsel."[218] I have mentioned in Chapter 4 that in 1787 Sir John Hawkins, the prominent London magistrate, expressed his concern that fear of abusive cross-examination deterred prosecution. He wrote that potential prosecutors worried that "[t]hey may be entangled or made to contradict themselves, or each other, in a cross examination, by prisoner's counsel . . . ."[219]

2. Evading the Restriction

We have seen that when the judges began allowing felony defendants to have the assistance of trial counsel in the 1730s, they forbade counsel to address the jury, which prevented counsel from stating the accused's defense or interpreting the evidence. These limitations upon defense counsel had been meant to oblige the accused to continue to speak in his own defense. A main reason for the primacy of cross-examination in the work of eighteenth-century defense counsel was that the prohibition on addressing the jury left counsel with so little practical alternative. "The denial of an address to the jury forced counsel to cross-examine for, put bluntly, he had 'either to cross-examine or do nothing.' "[220]

Throughout the century that the restriction was in force, defense counsel complained that it hampered them unfairly. Already in the 1740s we find counsel lamenting at an Old Bailey trial that "as to Matters of Fact, I am under very great Restrictions, and that is the Misfortune of the Prisoner."[221] Defending in a complex forgery case in 1786, Erskine remarked to the jury that he would have wished for them to understand "what I call my witnesses to [prove], but as I must not explain it, you Gentlemen of the Jury must pick out the defense as you can . . . ."[222] A

---

[217] Hague, *Garrow, supra* n. 216, at 6.

[218] William Chatwin and John Davis, *OBSP* (June 1788, #429), at 561, 562.

[219] John Hawkins, *The Life of Samuel Johnson, LL.D.* 462 (Dublin 1787), discussed *supra*, Ch. 4, text at n. 297.

[220] Cairns, *Advocacy* 47, quoting T. N. Talfourd, "On the Profession of the Bar," 1 *London Magazine* (NS) 323, 328 (1825).

[221] John Waite, *OBSP* (Feb. 1743, #162), at 102, 106 (forgery).

[222] Nathaniel Goodridge *et al., OBSP* (Jan. 1786, #123), at 156, 211 (forging a will).

FIG. 5.2. *"Being Nervous and Cross-examined by Mr. Garrow."* Rowlandson's cartoon, from a series titled "Miseries of Human Life" (1808), captures the dread that Garrow's courtroom behavior inspired in witnesses, whether perjured or truthful.

main theme in the movement to eliminate the restriction and permit full defense of counsel was the contention that forbidding counsel the opportunity to criticize the prosecution case could lead to the conviction of innocent persons.[223]

Not content to chafe under the restriction, defense counsel developed ways of evading its full force. "Contemporaries saw the felony counsel restriction as responsible for 'a latitude' in cross-examination which would not have been allowed 'if it were not often the only mode of suggesting an important view of the case to the minds of the jury.'"[224] Indeed, Erskine's complaint about the effect of the restriction was itself a species of abbreviated opening address, which the restriction should have prevented. In practice, however, it proved hard to stop defense counsel from making small interjections that were argumentative in character. In a theft case in 1746, for example, when evidence was adduced showing

[223] The Attorney General, Frederick Pollock, told the Criminal Law Commissioners about various cases that caused him to believe "that on more than one occasion accused persons in this country have been executed upon convictions which did not appear to be warranted by the evidence, and which evidence would not have produced a conviction if Counsel had been allowed to address the Jury . . . ." *1836 Report* 5. The veteran defense solicitor James Harmer recollected three cases in which he thought that innocent persons had been convicted and executed in circumstances in which a different result would probably have been reached had counsel been allowed to address the jury. Ibid. at 4.

[224] Cairns, *Advocacy* 48, quoting Dickenson and Talfourd, *Guide, supra* n. 163, at 382.

that the defendant did not flee, counsel remarked: "I'll only mention this, that if this Man had been conscious he had committed the Felony, 'tis certain he might have made his Escape."[225] In another theft case, after cross-examining the prosecutor about his subsequent contacts with the defendant, defense counsel observed: "Consider what the man says. On the 6th of June she was in his kitchen and he did not stop her [i.e., he did not then have her apprehended and charged] . . . ."[226] In a murder case, when evidence emerged that the defendant had expressed relief at the time of the events when he learned, mistakenly, that no fatality had occurred, defense counsel remarked on the benign light in which that evidence cast his client.[227] In the case of a man charged with a theft of household silver, when the prosecution adduced evidence that the theft occurred near the accused's bedroom, defense counsel interrupted: "You would not have the Man hanged for being fast asleep?"[228] Concluding his cross-examination of the prosecutor in that case, defense counsel said to him: "I am sorry for your Loss. I wish you may find out the Thief."[229] Cross-examining for the defense in a case of highway robbery, Garrow was quoted saying: "The Gentlemen of the Jury will observe, that one of the eyes was completely covered."[230] In view of the compressed character of the *Session Paper* reports, such asides were doubtless voiced more often than they were recorded.

In rare cases the trial judge waived the prohibition, allowing counsel to speak for an accused who was ill[231] or for a foreigner who did not speak English well.[232] More puzzling are cases in which defense counsel is recorded as making an opening statement of sorts despite the rule. In 1742, defending a gamekeeper and his helper who were being prosecuted for the shooting death of a poacher, counsel effectively made an opening speech even while saying he could not. "Mr. Hume Campbell, of Counsel for the Prisoners, said that although he knew by the Course of the Court at the Old Bailey, he was not at Liberty to observe upon the Prosecutor's Evidence, yet he apprehended, that for the Ease of the

---

[225] Robert Wilson and Barthia Whitefield, *OBSP* (Feb. 1746, #102–3), at 69, 70 (theft).

[226] Jane Leechman, *OBSP* (Dec. 1747, #69 [*sic*; misprint, should be #70]), at 39.

[227] "You will please to observe, the witness told the prisoner there was a man hurt, but nobody killed; and that was immediately before the prisoner said, he was glad of it—Glad that nobody was killed." John Stevenson, 19 *St. Tr.* 845, 859 (Chester Assizes, 1759).

[228] William Askew, *OBSP* (Apr. 1746, #167), at 118, 120.

[229] Ibid. at 120.

[230] Thomas Wood and George Brown, *OBSP* (Dec. 1784, #4), at 35, 42.

[231] "The judge said, that as the prisoner was ill, he would permit his counsel to state his defense to the jury." William Davis, *OBSP* (Dec. 1771, #40), at 16, 25 (mail robbery).

[232] The dispensation was worded cagily: "As the prisoner is a foreigner, though I cannot consistent with the practice of the court allow you to make a speech for him, yet you may state your facts to me." Charles Bairnes, *OBSP* (Feb. 1783, #197), at 292, 294 (theft).

Court, he might just open the Nature of the Defense, without making any Observations upon it."[233] He proceeded to set forth the defense contention that the weapon had discharged by accident. A few years later, in the case of William Askew, just mentioned in connection with defense counsel's interjection during the prosecution case, defense counsel also made what was in effect an opening address, commenting on the prosecution evidence just received and previewing the defense.[234] In a highway robbery case in 1783 counsel began: "This is a young man of wealthy parents, and as good a young man as ever lived. He was coming to town, he stopped to eat some oysters, and was taken up in this [matter]. He was at Grantham at the very time that the robbery was committed."[235] The problem that these cases pose is how to reconcile such evidence that the restriction was not always enforced with the defense bar's constantly voiced frustration about the rule. The easiest explanation would be to infer that instances of nonenforcement were sufficiently isolated that counsel ordinarily had to reckon with the rule being enforced.

Quite a different technique for evading the restriction on addressing the jury was for counsel to manipulate cross-examination for the purpose of making an argument. We have a good example in a murder case that arose from a stabbing among drunken sailors in a pub brawl. Defense counsel, although forbidden to argue directly that the victim died accidentally from his own weapon, made the point by framing it as a question on cross-examination: "If a Man had a sharp Knife in his Pocket, might it not run into his Body by Accident?"[236] Another example: Garrow, cross-examining a prosecutor who had brought a highway robbery case as the result of a neighborhood scuffle, asked him: "So these people that knew you so well, and knew that you knew them so well, robbed you and went home to their beds . . .?"[237] Stephen remarked of

---

[233] James Annesley and Joseph Redding, *OBSP* (July 1742), at 19 (separate pamphlet for this case, not sequentially paginated with the other trials for the sessions). The case is republished at 17 *St. Tr.* 1093.

[234] "With your Lordship's Leave I am Counsel for the Prisoner. As the Serjeant [prosecuting counsel] has candidly opened it, that there was nothing but Circumstances [that is, since there was only circumstantial evidence, the question is] whether they were such Circumstances to take away the Life of a Man . . . . [I]t amounts to this: Here is a Person indicted for being asleep. If a Person has any Character [witnesses] to support him, the Jury will never believe [the prosecution], unless there are some other Circumstances. This [prosecution would make it] . . . a Crime, that a Person shall not be awakened by a Noise, as that at best is but a doubtful case. We shall call our Witnesses to prove that he is a most sober and honest Person." William Askew, *OBSP* (Apr. 1746, #167), at 118, 120.

[235] John Valentine and Broughton Birt, *OBSP* (Feb. 1783, #169), at 256, 258. The word bracketed in text as "matter" is misrendered as "manner" in the original.

[236] Gabriel Beaugrand and Louis Brunet, *OBSP* (May 1743, ##256–7), at 167, 169 (murder, aiding and abetting murder).

[237] Robert Mitchell, *OBSP* (Dec. 1784, #190), at 196, 197.

this practice that "cross-examination tended to become a speech thrown into the form of questions . . . ."[238]

3. "Counsel Learned in the Law": The Interaction of Fact and Law

Another widely practiced evasion of the restriction against defense counsel arguing fact was for defense counsel to make arguments of fact in the guise of arguing law.

The rule against felony defense counsel, it will be recalled from Chapter 1, was a rule against "Assistance in Matters of Fact."[239] As a corollary, when "some Point of Law [arose], proper to be debated,"[240] the accused was allowed "counsel learned in the law"[241] to argue it. This branch of the rule was fully consistent with the rationale for denying counsel to the defendant on matters of fact, namely, that "every one of Common Understanding may as properly speak to a Matter of Fact, as if he were the best Lawyer."[242] Although the felony defendant had immemorially possessed the right to have counsel address the court on a point of law,[243] that right pertained "only in doubtful, not in plain cases."[244] Thus, it had seldom been exercised, apart from cases of treason and later forgery, in which affluent defendants who could routinely afford counsel were tried for offenses of intrinsic doctrinal complexity.[245] When practice changed in the 1730s, counsel combined his new license to assist the defendant in adducing fact with his older role in arguing law. Counsel's revised job description, in the words of an Old Bailey judge in 1783, was to "examine witnesses and observe upon points of law."[246]

What was not foreseen in the 1730s was the way defense counsel's engagement with the facts would invigorate his older but previously rather inconsequential role in raising points of law. Having now immersed himself in the facts of the case for purposes of examining and cross-examining witnesses, counsel was able to exploit his mastery of the facts for the further purpose of raising issues of law that emerged from the facts. This side of counsel's work produced legal precedents; dozens

---

[238] 2 Stephen, *History* 431, cited in Cairns, *Advocacy* 48.

[239] Roger North, *The Life of the Right Honourable Francis North* 66–7 (London 1742). For the passage quoted in text, see *supra* Ch. 1, text at n. 123; North was commenting on the rule as it had been applied in the trial of Stephen College, on which, see *supra* Ch. 2, text at nn. 26–35, 93–4, 138–9, 149–51.

[240] 2 Hawkins, *PC* 401

[241] Regarding the prevalence of this expression, see *supra* Ch. 1, text at nn. 120–1.

[242] 2 Hawkins, *PC* 400.

[243] Discussed *supra* Ch. 1, text at nn. 82–8.   [244] Foster, Hale MS viii.

[245] Regarding the complexity of the offense of treason, see *supra* Chapter 2, text at nn. 96–101, 172; for forgery, see *supra*, Ch. 3, n. 289.

[246] William Macnamara, *OBSP* (Sept. 1783, #641), at 857, 858 (theft of shop goods), quoted *supra*, text at n. 6.

of late eighteenth-century cases reported in Leach's *Crown Cases*,[247] as well as in the *Sessions Papers*, show defense counsel raising these fact-informed objections of law. For example, counsel commonly raised the objection that the evidence adduced at trial failed to establish some necessary element of the offense charged, hence that there was a fatal "variance" between indictment and proof. Thus, Dudley Ryder, sitting at a burglary trial at Chelmsford Assizes in August 1755, recorded in his assize diary: "Doubt was made by Cox, counsel to one of the defendants, whether as it appeared that [that defendant] was not in the house but only held the house [sic], he could be more than an accessory and then not guilty on this indictment, but I overruled it."[248] In a case at the Old Bailey in 1774, a postal worker had been indicted under a statute making it a felony to steal securities from the mail. The evidence showed that he had stolen money. "The prisoner's Counsel submitted to the Court, that this case was not within the statute, as the letter contained money and not any security relating to the payment of money mentioned in the Act."[249] The trial judge agreed and the defendant was acquitted (probably on directed verdict; the report does not say). A decade later, in a case involving a pair of women indicted for having feloniously conveyed women's clothing into Newgate prison with the intent of facilitating the jailbreak of a condemned prisoner, Garrow for the defense pointed out that the evidence showed only that the women had entered the jail, and that one of them had accompanied the disguised prisoner to the gatehouse (where he was detected). Garrow "contended that it was not proved that the prisoners *conveyed* anything into the jail"[250] as charged in the indictment. The defendants were acquitted (again, probably on directed verdict; the report does not say). A couple of months later, defending a charge of commercial theft, Garrow failed to obtain a directed verdict when he argued that the proofs established "no charge against this man . . . ." Garrow contended that his cross-examination of a particular witness established that a crucial account record could not be attributed to the defendant. The trial judge overruled the motion. "There is clearly ground enough to go to the jury."[251]

When the trial judge was less certain how to rule on such an objection, or when the judge wanted to have the point resolved authoritatively, he

---

[247] Thomas Leach, *Cases in Crown Law* (1st edn. London 1789). In this book I cite the fourth and final edition of 1815, the edition that was republished in the *English Reports*, see 1 *Leach* 1, 168 *Eng. Rep.* 103, in order to supply consistent parallel citations to the latter.

[248] Ryder, "Assize Dairy" 24.

[249] *R. v. Timothy Skutt*, 1 *Leach* 106, 107, 168 *Eng Rep.* 155, 156 (O.B. 1774).

[250] Harriot [sic] and Mary Allen, *OBSP* (Dec. 1784, #174), at 189 (emphasis original).

[251] William Price, *OBSP* (Feb. 1785, #393), 492, 494. Garrow then pressed his point on the jury. "I shall not trouble the Court with witnesses in such a case as this." Ibid. The jury called his bluff and convicted the defendant.

could refer the point to the Twelve Judges and postpone judgment until their decision. A sampling: Counsel for a defendant who was convicted at Abingdon Assizes in 1770 under a statute punishing the killing of cattle moved in arrest of judgment that the indictment was bad, because the evidence at trial showed that the animal that the defendant killed was a mare, not a cow. The trial judge referred the case to the Twelve Judges, who "unanimously agreed" that the statute reached mares.[252] By contrast, in a case of the same character, the Twelve Judges resolved for acquittal a few years later in a case in which the defendant had been convicted under an indictment charging him with stealing a cow. Defense counsel argued, and the judges agreed, "that the evidence did not support the charge in the indictment," because "a female beast of the cow kind ... if she has never had a calf is always called an Heifer," not a cow.[253]

The offense of burglary gave rise to a number of acquittals on technicalities raised by defense counsel and resolved by the Twelve Judges. In a case tried at the Old Bailey in 1778 two men were charged with the burglary of a dwelling house. Defense counsel maintained that because the evidence showed that the owner was still having repairs done on the house and had not yet moved into it, the structure was not a dwelling house. The jury convicted, "subject to the opinion of the Twelve Judges," who heard the case and "were of opinion, That a house so situated could not be considered a dwelling house, it being completely uninhabited, and therefore there could be no burglary."[254] A few years later the Old Bailey was confronted with a case involving a gang of intending burglars who had drilled a hole into the door of a house, but who had not physically entered the premises before they were stopped. Defense counsel argued, and the court agreed, that the offense of burglary required both a breaking and an entry, and that although the drilling was a breaking, no entry occurred.[255]

The apparent bias toward leniency in such rulings was surely connected to the growing aversion to capital punishment; below in this chapter I point to that sentiment as a factor that similarly inclined the judges to tolerate the truth-defeating character of adversary criminal procedure. The present point is that cases raising indictment variances and other asserted defects of law became much more common in the later eighteenth century, as defense counsel, who had been hired to probe the facts, put his knowledge of the facts to use in formulating objections on

[252] R. v. John Paty, 1 Leach 72, 168 Eng. Rep. 138, 139 (Abingdon Assizes 1770) (the trial judge who referred the case was Blackstone).
[253] R. v. Richard Cook, 1 Leach 105, 168 Eng. Rep. 155 (reference from Warwick Assizes 1774), noticed in Jerome Hall, Theft, Law and Society 89 (1935) [hereafter Hall, Theft].
[254] R. v. Lyon Lyons, 1 Leach 185, 186, 168 Eng. Rep. 195, 196 (O.B. 1778).
[255] R. v. John Hughes et al., 1 Leach 406, 168 Eng. Rep. 305 (O.B. 1785).

the law. The resulting rulings on law took a variety of forms. The examples just given instance directed verdicts and cases reserved for the Twelve Judges. Sometimes defense counsel's review of the solicitor's brief (and other preparation, if any) enabled him to raise the indictment challenge at the outset of the trial, hence in advance of any proof-taking.[256] The motion for directed verdict at the close of the prosecution case also called for a ruling of law.[257] In other cases counsel challenged the sufficiency of the indictment on a motion for new trial.[258]

Yet another technique for raising a fact-laden objection of law was for defense counsel to ask for the trial jury to return a special verdict.[259] Blackstone described such a verdict as one "setting forth all the circumstances of the case, and praying judgment of the court."[260] The special verdict left the trial judge to decide the law, commonly upon consultation with the Twelve Judges. Dudley Ryder, Chief Justice of King's Bench, described the practice in helpful detail in his assize diary for a case that arose before him at Chelmsford Assizes in 1755. The defense argued that a stabbing death in a pub brawl, prosecuted as murder, was only manslaughter, because the trial elicited sufficient evidence of provocation. Ryder's diary discloses the participation of defense counsel in drafting the language that the jury would adopt as its verdict, framing the issue that Ryder would refer to the Twelve Judges. Ryder wrote that the statement of facts ("the minutes") that became the jury's verdict "were signed by counsel for the plaintiff [sic, defendant] Mr. Harvey and Cox and by clerk of assizes, there being no counsel for the King, but not by the jury, that being thought not necessary. It was agreed I should lay this

---

[256] E.g., *R. v. John Drinkwater*, 1 *Leach* 15, 168 *Eng. Rep.* 110 (O.B. 1740) (assisting in the recovery of stolen goods before conviction of the thief, the so-called Jonathan Wild Act), in which it is reported: "Before any evidence was given, the prisoner's Counsel submitted to the Court, that this indictment could not be legally prosecuted."

[257] E.g., *R. v. John Taylor*, 1 *Leach* 214, 215, 168 *Eng. Rep.* 209, 210 (O.B. 1779) ("The Evidence for the prosecution being closed, the prisoner's counsel submitted to the court" that the evidence did not amount to forgery; the court overruled the objection, the jury convicted, but the court referred the case to the Twelve Judges, who sustained the conviction). Other examples of directed verdict at the end of the prosecution case have been mentioned above in this chapter in connection with the articulation of the production burden.

[258] For example, in a case tried in King's Bench, counsel for a defendant convicted of perjury sought a new trial on the ground that the indictment contained a spelling error (the letter "s" had been omitted from the word "understood"). Lord Mansfield refused, reasoning "[t]hat where the omission or addition of a letter does not change the word, so as to make it another word (as "air" for "heir" . . .), the variance is not material." *R. v. Beech*, 1 *Leach* 133, 134, 168 *Eng. Rep.* 168, 169 (K.B. 1774).

[259] E.g., *R. v. Joseph Sloper*, 1 *Leach* 81, 168 *Eng. Rep.* 143 (O.B. 1772) (defense counsel obtained special verdict for reference to the Twelve Judges on the question of whether embezzling letters for the purpose of defrauding the post office of the money for the postage was within a statute making it felony to steal or embezzle the contents). For the skimpy *Sessions Paper* report, see Joseph Sloper, *OBSP* (Jan. 1772, #184), at 99, 101–2.

[260] 4 Blackstone, *Commentaries* 354.

minute before the 12 judges for their opinion as in the late case of [words obscure], the consequence of which will be that when their opinion is taken it will be sent to next judge of assizes at Chelmsford, who will give judgment according to that opinion."[261]

I have emphasized above in Chapter 4, discussing the origins of the law of criminal evidence, how the rules of evidence tended to transform questions of fact into issues of law. The new law of evidence was another sphere in which fact interacted with law in the work of defense counsel. Counsel's immersion in the facts gave him the basis for formulating motions to exclude evidence—by invoking, for example, the best evidence rule,[262] the competency requirement,[263] the confession rule,[264] and the hearsay rule.[265]

Sometimes counsel's objection about a matter of law was specious, solely a pretext for commenting upon the facts. By seeking a directed verdict for insufficiency of the evidence, counsel could offer an interpretation of fact in the guise of addressing the judge, even though the intended audience was the jury. (The jury, it will be recalled, was not as yet excused from the court during the discussion of such motions.[266]) On one occasion in 1785 when Garrow engaged in this stratagem, the trial judge remarked on it. "You have had ground enough in this case, Mr. Garrow, to entitle you, in point of law, to observe upon the evidence by a side wind, which you have done very sufficiently."[267]

---

[261] Ryder, "Assize Diary" 22. The case was ultimately resolved by pardon; see Langbein, "Ryder" 125–6 n. 504. Regarding the struggle over whether a jury could be compelled to return a special verdict in seditious libel cases, see sources cited *infra*, text at n. 375. Apart from the rare political cases, juries appear for the most part to have been delighted to be able to rid themselves of difficult determinations of substantive criminal law (often about whether homicide was murder or manslaughter) by returning special verdicts, which transferred final responsibility for adjudication to the judges.

[262] *R. v. Robert Rhodes*, 1 *Leach* 24, 25, 168 *Eng. Rep.* 115 (O.B. 1742) (forgery).

[263] *R. v. William Akehurst*, 1 *Leach* 151, 168 *Eng. Rep.* 178 (Sussex Assizes 1776) (forgery) ("Lord Mansfield, after the point had been debated at the bar, received the evidence, and the prisoner was convicted"); *R. v. Priddle* [*sic*; Priddle was the witness whose testimony was challenged; the defendant was George Crossley, charged with perjury], 1 *Leach* 442, 168 *Eng. Rep.* 323 (K.B. 1787) ("The defendant's Counsel objected to [Priddle's] being examined [as a prosecution witness, because he had previously been convicted of conspiracy], and submitted to the Court that a conviction of conspiracy rendered the party infamous, and destroyed his competency as a witness"). The *Sessions Paper* reports the earlier trial and conviction: William Priddle *et al.*, *OBSP* (Apr. 1787, #448), at 580–623.

[264] John Thomas, *OBSP* (Oct. 1783, #766), at 1070, 1071 (theft of shop goods); *R. v. Jacob Thompson*, 1 *Leach* 291, 292, 168 *Eng. Rep.* 248, 249 (O.B. 1783) ("The Counsel for the prisoner submitted to the Court that [evidence concerning the pretrial investigation] amounted to a threat to take the prisoner into custody unless he would make a confession").

[265] William Jones, *OBSP* (Dec. 1783, #102), at 130, 131 (theft of iron goods), discussed *supra*, Ch. 4, text at n. 283.   [266] Discussed *supra* Ch. 4, text at nn. 307–10.

[267] William Hurt, *OBSP* (Jan. 1785, #255), at 304, 312. The judge (Adair, the recorder of London) overruled the motion and sent the case to the jury, which convicted one defendant and acquitted the other.

An objection based upon insufficiency of the evidence could be invoked not only to challenge an indictment on grounds of variance,[268] but also when counsel wished to contend that the totality of the evidence was insufficient to sustain the prosecution case. As late as 1829, when the point was discussed in a practice manual, the writers were still struggling to discern when fact became law, an inquiry that required them to distinguish between insufficiency (law) and mere "slightness" of the evidence (fact):

In cases of felony, the prisoner's counsel has never a right to address the jury on the merits of the case, but he may submit to the bench any point of law arising on the evidence, or any absolute deficiency of proof that may entitle his client to an acquittal . . . for these are matters which show that the prisoner ought not to be put on his defense.

He may sometimes submit that there is nothing for the jury to consider, as when the charge is not brought home to his client at all; and if the bench think so, they will direct an acquittal; but counsel will not be permitted to argue on the slightness of the evidence where there is any applicable to the prisoner, or to discuss questions which are properly for the jury, as questions of knowledge and intention.[269]

The line between a case "not brought home" to the defendant and one in which there was some evidence applicable to the prisoner was easy to state but hard to apply (and as the judge's wry comment on Garrow's "side wind" shows, even harder to enforce). A motion of "law" seeking a directed verdict for insufficiency of the evidence inescapably trenched on fact. Once again, the endlessly problematic distinction between law and fact turned out not to be very workable. Had defense counsel been free to state a defense based on interpretation of the facts, counsel would have been allowed to argue fact as fact. Forbidding counsel to argue fact encouraged him to argue fact as law in the ways we have seen.

Defense counsel's greater involvement in criminal cases, and the incentive that counsel had to couch his arguments as matters of law, also spurred the growth of the substantive criminal law and of the law of evidence. As questions about the application of law to fact were ever more framed as issues of law, the judges were pressed to give considered opinions (both at trial and in the Twelve Judges procedure).[270] Reporters

---

[268] For example, in a prosecution for assault with intent to rob, "[t]he prisoner's Counsel objected, that supposing the indictment to have been properly drawn, this evidence was not sufficient to support the charge, inasmuch as it did not appear that any demand either of money or of goods had been made." *R. v. William Jackson and Thomas Randall*, 1 *Leach* 267, 268, 168 *Eng. Rep.* 236, 237 (O.B. 1783).

[269] Dickenson and Talfourd, *Guide*, *supra* n. 163, at 382–3.

[270] Six MS notebooks, containing decisions rendered by the Twelve Judges' between 1757 and 1828, have survived. "Most of the cases they contain can be found in "East's *Pleas of the Crown* or in the reports of Leach, Moody and Russell and Ryan." D. R. Bentley,

began to take an interest in criminal adjudication. Leach's *Crown Cases*, the first important set of criminal law reports, was primarily devoted to cases of the 1770s and thereafter, decided either at the Old Bailey or by the Twelve Judges. As mentioned in Chapter 4, in the 1780s the *Old Bailey Sessions Papers* were also attempting to develop a market among lawyers, which helps to account for the exceptional detail of the judicial rulings and opinions reported in those years. Better reporting of assize cases began in the 1790s in the so-called *nisi prius* reports.[271] Edward Hyde East's *Pleas of the Crown* (1803)[272] was a cross between a treatise and a law report. East relied heavily on private collections of manuscripts reports of later eighteenth-century Old Bailey and assize proceedings as the sources for his account of offenses such as forgery, larceny, and rape, which underwent considerable doctrinal development in those years. As this body of literature became available, it had a cascade effect. The published precedents made it easier for counsel to identify and raise such issues, producing new precedents to feed the cycle.[273]

4. The Adversary Ethos

The growing intensity of counsel's activity bespoke a changed ethos of defensive representation, epitomized in the aggressive courtroom behavior of William Garrow. Garrow became renowned for his intimidating cross-examinations,[274] his success at evading the limits on full defense, and his creativity in devising evidentiary and other legal objections. In a trial at Essex Assizes in 1800, Garrow was defiant about his use of cross-examination to evade the ban on addressing the jury. He told the court

---

"Introduction," at 1, in *Select Cases from the Twelve Judge's Notebooks* (D. R. Bentley ed.) (1997) [hereafter Bentley, *Notebooks*] (modern edition of eighty-four of the cases not previously published). Bentley has found that the notebooks are incomplete, omitting many Twelve Judges cases that appear in the published reports. Ibid. at 22.

[271] Emphasized in John H. Wigmore, "A General Survey of the History of the Rule of Evidence," in 2 *Select Essays in Anglo-American Legal History* 691, 696 (1908) (Association of American Law Schools) (3 vols.).

[272] Edward Hyde East, *A Treatise of the Pleas of the Crown* (London 1803) [hereafter East, *PC*]. (There was a Philadelphia edition in 1806.)

[273] Making an objection in a perjury trial at Essex Assizes in 1800, Garrow reflected in passing on the growing expectation that such evidentiary points would be supported by references to published case law. "I did not consider it in the former part of my life, when I had more of this business to do, whether the objection is to be supported by authorities. Having no law library nor any law book at Chelmsford, I must state [case law] from recollection," which he proceeded to do. *The Trial of John Taylor for Forgery . . . at Chelmsford Assizes* 11 (Chelmsford 1800) [hereafter *Taylor Trial*]. (I acknowledge the kindness of Peter King, who has shared with me his copy of this pamphlet report, which he found in the Essex Record Office.)

[274] Rowlandson's cartoon, "Being Nervous and Cross-examined by Mr. Garrow," reproduced *supra* (fig. 5.2.).

with breathtaking candor: "I had a right, if I could, indirectly to convey observations to the fact; and whatever other people may say, I shall certainly take the liberty of doing it; for what the law of England will not permit me to do *directly*, I will do *indirectly*, where I can."[275] (Translation: I will do anything I can get away with.) In 1784 another prominent Old Bailey practitioner, John Silvester,[276] explained his insistence on making a tenuous legal objection in the course of defending a man accused of the capital offense of forgery: "My Lord, it is my duty standing here as a counsel for a prisoner to take every objection that lays in my power, for a man standing in his unfortunate situation."[277] From the standpoint of a prominent urban magistrate, Patrick Colquhoun, writing in 1796, defense counsel was "availing himself of every trifling inaccuracy which may screen his client from the punishment of the law . . . ."[278]

This combat ethos stood in contradiction to a view of advocacy in which fidelity to the truth should have placed bounds upon counsel's service to the client. Writing in the 1790s about how counsel should treat witnesses, Thomas Gisborne constructed a list of virtues that were mirror opposites of the behavior that brought Garrow his renown at the Old Bailey in the 1780s: "[H]e will not defame the witnesses of the adverse party; nor . . . strive to rob their testimony of the credit it deserves. He will not overawe [witnesses] . . . by brow-beating and menaces, nor impose on their simplicity by sophistry and cunning. He will not . . . insidiously labor to extract from their words a sense foreign to their intentions. He will abhor the idea of drawing those who appear against him into any seeming contradictions and perjury, when he perceives their meaning to be honest and their story in reality consistent."[279]

The sense that the tactics employed in criminal trials were unworthy was part of the reason why the Old Bailey bar was viewed as disreputable. As early as 1764 we find a pamphlet of advice for intending law students speaking of how "ignominious the name and character of a mere Old Bailey Counsel may justly appear . . . ."[280] By the nineteenth century the ill repute of the Old Bailey Bar was common discourse. The *Law Times* wrote in 1844: "The world . . . knows, and has long known, that 'An Old Bailey Practitioner' is a byword for disgrace and infamy."[281]

---

[275] *Taylor Trial, supra* n. 273, at 15 (emphasis original), quoted in King, *Crime* 229.

[276] On whom see May, Thesis 359.   [277] John Lee, *OBSP* (Jan. 1784, #203), at 241, 246.

[278] Patrick Colquhoun, *A Treatise on the Police of the Metropolis* 23 (3rd edn. London 1796) [hereafter Colquhoun, *Police*].

[279] 1 Thomas Gisborne, *An Enquiry into the Duties of Men* 377–8 (4th edn. London 1797) (1st edn. 1794).

[280] Joseph Simpson, *Reflections on the Natural and Acquired Endowments Requisite for the Study of the Law* 46 (3rd edn. London 1764) (1st edn. 1764).

[281] 3 *Law Times* 501 (28 Sept. 1844), quoted in May, Thesis 239, where, ibid. at 236 ff, there is extensive discussion of the ill repute of the Old Bailey bar.

FIG. 5.3. *"The Old Bailey Advocate Bringing off a Thief."* In a cartoon from about 1789, an Old Bailey defense counsel tramples over justice, boasting to his acquitted client, "You are not the first T[hief] that I have brought off by mere dint of Impudence."

The idea that defensive representation entailed single-minded commitment to victory received its definitive statement in Brougham's oft-quoted speech in the trial of Queen Caroline in 1820. "[A]n advocate, in the discharge of his duty, knows but one person in all the world, and that person is his client. To save that client by all means and expedients, and at all hazards and cost to other persons, and, among them, to himself, is his first and only duty; and in performing this duty he must not regard the alarm, the torments, the destruction which he may bring upon others."[282] Brougham may have been at some political risk in defending Queen Caroline, but in ordinary criminal cases counsel faced no "hazards and costs." Brougham's self-serving prattle became window dressing for a truth-be-damned standard of defensive representation that served the economic self-interest of the bar. The more latitude lawyers obtained to affect the outcome, the greater would be the demand for lawyers' services; the greater the use of lawyers for the defense, the greater would be the inducement for prosecutors to meet fire with fire by hiring lawyers of their own.

This process of strategic calculation about the need for prosecution lawyers to protect against defense lawyers began in the pretrial, in which the decision to be made was whether to engage solicitors to investigate and prepare the case. Contrast a pair of entries from 1795 in the manuscript minute book of the London Society for Prosecuting Felons. In one case a member of the society entitled to its support, Mr. Dinsdale, "reported a Burglary in his House" committed by two men, one of whom was caught in the act and bound over for trial by the Lord Mayor. The society "Resolved, that this Prosecution be carried on by the Society and that the case is too clear to need the assistance of Attorney or Counsel."[283] Accordingly, the society's help was limited to drafting and submitting the indictment. In another case a few months earlier, involving a bullock stolen from Mr. Harper and recovered from two drivers after being advertised, the minute book records that since the culprits "had employed Counsel, [Mr. Harper] submitted it to the Society of employing one of the Society's Solicitors to prevent the Offenders from escaping Justice for want of legal assistance." The society agreed and directed an officer to "take such measures as shall appear proper."[284] Evidence that the number of prosecution witnesses per case increased

---

[282] 2 *The Trial at Large of Her Majesty Caroline Amelia Elizabeth, Queen of Great Britain; in the House of Lords, on Charges of Adulterous Intercourse* 3 (London 1821) (2 vols.).

[283] Corporation of London Record Office, Society for Prosecuting Felons, Forgers, &c, Minute Book 1795 to 1800, entry for 16 Oct. 1795 (unpaginated, entries consecutive by date) [hereafter Society Minute Book]. I directed attention to these entries in Langbein, "Ryder" 127.

[284] Society Minute Book, *supra* n. 283, entry for 19 June 1795.

across the eighteenth century[285] may have a similar explanation, that criminal prosecutions had to be better substantiated in order to run the gauntlet of defense counsel.

The aggressiveness of defense counsel contrasted ever more strongly with the duty of restraint that was meant to prevent prosecution counsel from taking advantage of the restrictions on defense counsel. The legislation of 1836 eliminated the restrictions on full defense that were the predicate for the duty of prosecutorial restraint. In the debates leading to the 1836 Act the argument was recurrently made that allowing full defense would harm the defendant by allowing prosecution counsel to respond in kind to the growing aggressiveness of defense counsel. Combat would beget combat. Serjeant Spankie warned the Criminal Law Commissioners that "counsel for the prosecution would follow the bad example of the counsel for the prisoner," and that "the jury would be exposed to the corruptions of the worst arts of the forum . . . ."[286] But the argument that would carry the day in 1836, as in earlier cycles of the piecemeal expansion of adversary criminal justice, was the concern to equalize within existing practice, to even up, which in this case meant allowing defense counsel to address the jury as well as prosecution counsel.

To conclude: The judges of the 1730s admitted defense counsel for the purpose of enhancing safeguard against the danger of mistaken conviction. By admitting defense counsel but limiting him mostly to the work of cross-examination, the judges thought to confine counsel to the work of a specialist helpmate, who would merely supplement the continuing efforts of the accused to conduct his own defense. The judges expected the "accused speaks" trial to live on. But this was a miscalculation, and not simply because defense counsel evaded some of the limits placed upon him. Defense counsel worked a structural change in the criminal trial. He broke up the two roles, defending and speaking to the merits, that had previously been concentrated in the hands of the accused. By assuming the work of defending, and by insisting on the prosecutorial burdens of production and proof, counsel largely (sometimes entirely) silenced the accused. Shutting down the old "accused speaks" trial changed the very theory of the trial. The purpose of the altercation trial had been to provide the accused an opportunity to reply in person to the charges and the evidence against him. Adversary trial put in place a new conception of the trial, oriented on the lawyers. Criminal trial became an opportunity for defense counsel to test the prosecution case.

---

[285] The claim is made in Landsman, "Spirit," *supra* n. 117, at 497, 529–31, 608 (table III). Landsman tabulates the appearances of witnesses at the Old Bailey for selected years across the century, as reported in the *Sessions Papers*. Because the *Sessions Papers* were much less thorough earlier in the century, at least some of the seeming trend toward greater use of witnesses is likely to be an illusion of the sources.   [286] *1836 Report* 105.

E. Judicial Acquiescence

The transformation from altercation to adversary criminal procedure, from lawyer-free to lawyer-dominated procedure, reordered the roles not only of those who informed the court, but also of those who decided the case.

1. Above the Fray

Counsel's growing domination of the fact-adducing phase of the criminal trial came at the expense of the trial judge, who had given loose direction to the proof-taking in the age of the lawyer-free altercation trial. We recall Cockburn's account of the practice in the sixteenth and seventeenth centuries, that "[t]he admission and presentation of evidence in court was organized by the trial judge, who examined witnesses and the prisoner and commented upon their testimony as it was being given."[287] Into the eighteenth century, Beattie has written, the "common practice clearly was for the judge to take [the prosecutor and the witnesses] through their testimony line by line, acting as both examiner and cross-examiner . . . ."[288] Across the second half of the eighteenth century the trial judges began to show discomfort with this work of adducing fact, and by the early nineteenth century we have Cottu's famous observation that an English criminal trial judge "remains almost a stranger to what is going on."[289]

A revealing incident occurred in a case tried at the Old Bailey in 1790. A group of foreigners accused of murder were standing trial without counsel. At the start of the trial the presiding judge, Lord Kenyon, turned to the Old Bailey barristers who were in attendance (waiting for the call of cases in which they had been briefed) and asked: "Will any gentleman of the bar have the goodness to ask a few questions for them, as they are foreigners? Will you, Mr. Knapp?"[290] (Knapp, of course, obliged.) It is a measure of the road travelled during the eighteenth century that in place of Hawkins' confident assumption, voiced in 1721, that lawyers have "no manner of Skill"[291] in matters of fact, the Chief Justice of King's Bench,

---

[287] Cockburn, "Introduction" 109, discussed *supra*, Ch. 1, text at n. 27.

[288] Beattie, *Crime* 342. Accord King, *Crime* 312 (trial judges were "highly proactive examiners who pointedly questioned witnesses and directed the hectic flow of evidence in order to ensure that . . . the central issues at stake were rapidly brought into focus"); Landsman, "Spirit," *supra* n. 117, at 513–20. Preparing for his first tour as an Old Bailey and assize judge in 1754, Dudley Ryder recorded in his diary that he planned "to come late some days at Old Bailey on purpose to be present when a trial being on, I may hear how the judge sums up and examines witnesses." Ryder, "Assize Diary" 18, previously noticed, *supra* Ch. 3, at n. 93.

[289] Cottu, *Administration* 88.

[290] Jacintho Phararo *et al.*, *OBSP* (Apr. [*sic*, Feb.] 1790 #329), at 367, 368.

[291] 2 Hawkins, *PC* 400.

sitting in the Old Bailey seventy years later, actively recruited counsel to replace himself in the work of adducing and probing matters of fact at trial. Whereas in the early decades of the eighteenth century the judge had been expected to be counsel for the accused, by the end of the century the judges were visibly uncomfortable in the conduct of fact-adducing and anxious to cast it off on the lawyers.

What explains the judges' inclination to withdraw from the work of adducing fact? The simple answer is that the lawyers' growing mastery of the gathering and presentation of the facts put the bench at an awkward disadvantage in the conduct of proof-taking. In the lawyer-free trial of old, the judges led the fact-finding because nobody else could, but in a well-prepared adversary trial solicitors for each side had investigated the facts, prepared the witnesses, and instructed counsel. Against the new model of lawyer-conducted fact-finding, the English trial judge would always compare badly, because he came to court lacking the pretrial preparation that supported trial counsel.

Moreover, the expansion of defense counsel's role to include assisting the accused in matters of fact undercut the ancient idea that the court could be counsel for the accused. Defense counsel's job became intolerable in the hands of a judge. "Did the judge take all advantages to defeat the prosecutor and acquit the prisoner?," a debater in Parliament asked rhetorically in 1826. "Then as a judge he betrayed his oath of office. Did he decline to take those advantages? Then as counsel for the prisoner he deserted his client."[292] That same year the *Edinburgh Review* concluded: "The Judge *cannot* be counsel for the prisoner, *ought not* to be counsel for the prisoner, never *is* counsel for the prisoner."[293] The Criminal Law Commissioners in 1836 also harped on the theme that defense counsel's duties had become incompatible with the posture of the judge.[294] As the

---

[292] Remarks of Horace Twiss, 15 Parliamentary Debates 610 (1826), cited by Cairns, *Advocacy* 52 n. 1116.

[293] Anon., *Edinburgh Review* 74, 81 (1826). This essay is titled as though it were a book review, of something called "Stockton on the Practice of not allowing Counsel to Prisoners accused of Felony, 8vo. pp. 149. London 1826." The text of the essay does not discuss any such work, and I have not been able to trace it.

[294] Echoing the line from Twiss, quoted *supra*, text at n. 292, the Commissioners reported a remark made in testimony to them, that if the judge "is an efficient Counsel, he transgresses his proper power as a Judge; if he is an inefficient Counsel, the Prisoner is not properly defended." *1836 Report* 9 (quoting William Ewart MP).
    Beyond this argument that the tension between the roles of counsel and court made it impossible for the judge to serve as counsel, the Commissioners made a further argument, that counsel's shenanigans would be truth-serving. Because the judge lacked "knowledge of the real circumstances of the case," which "the accused alone is able to supply," the judge could not effectively examine or cross-examine "for the Prisoner's benefit . . . ." Ibid. at 7. The judge "would be unable to distinguish between false and true witnesses." Ibid. The Commissioners did not explain why they thought that counsel had this advantage of "knowledge of the real circumstances," but the assumption must have been that the solici-

work of gathering and presenting fact became ever more the province of counsel, hence ever more partisan, the idea that impartial judges could perform it for prosecution or defense became ever less plausible.[295]

The tendency for the judges to withdraw from the work of adducing fact was a manifestation of that structural shift in trial procedure that resulted from the identification of party production burdens and the articulation of the trial into prosecution and defense cases. By the end of the eighteenth century trial had ceased to be understood as a free-form inquiry into what happened; instead, it had become a phased proceeding oriented first to meeting and then defeating the prosecution's production burden. Each side was understood to be gathering, selecting, and presenting evidence for partisan purposes. Because the lawyers "gained such a large measure of control over the sources of available evidence [coupled with] the right to cross-examine, a right unknown to systems of trial other than the common-law system,"[296] the trial judge found himself severely handicapped in his ability to conduct the proofs. Unlike a Continental judge working from an authoritative, court-created dossier encapsulating the evidence in the case, the English trial judge came to court largely ignorant of the case he was about to try.[297]

Writing in 1806 (in what was at that time the most sophisticated account of the Anglo-American law of evidence yet produced), W. D. Evans commented that the dynamic of adversary trial made it advisable for the judge to remain passive while counsel conducted the trial. "The benefits of cross-examination are sometimes defeated by the interposition of the Court, to require an explanation of the motive and object of the questions proposed, or to pronounce a judgment on them immediately.

---

tor's brief, summarizing the solicitor's pretrial investigation, supplied it to counsel. Defense counsel had special access to the truth, the Commissioners asserted, because he "has had the opportunity of considering the Prisoner's statement before the trial, and knowing the facts, is able to present them to the Jury in the point of view most favorable to the Prisoner." Ibid. Indeed, says the Second Report at its most fantastic, "[w]hen the charge is false, [defense counsel] possesses, through his intimate knowledge of the real facts, an almost infallible key to the truth," whereas the judge, "without such means of knowledge" cannot do counsel's job. Ibid. The reasoning in this passage is that defense lawyers, having largely silenced the accused at trial and in the pretrial, were now the only people with authoritative access to his version of the events. The Commissioners conveniently assumed the defendant's version of the facts to be "the real facts, an almost infallible key to the truth." The Commissioners did not explain why it was better to entrust the gathering of that supposed truth to partisan defense lawyers, whose incentive was to win even at the price of concealing, distorting, or otherwise defeating truth.

[295] "[W]hat an absurdity it is to talk of a judge being counsel for either side, for whom if he did what a counsel should do, he would not be acting impartially, or with a strict regard to justice." "Defense of Prisoners on Trial for Felony," 1 *Legal Examiner* 601, 602 (1832).

[296] Edmund M. Morgan, *Some Problems of Proof under the Anglo-American System of Litigation* 113 (1956).

[297] Regarding earlier efforts to familiarize the judge with the indictment in advance, see *supra* Ch. 1, text at n. 29.

[The trial judge, when] acting only upon the impressions of what has already been disclosed, cannot by any possibility anticipate"[298] what counsel is attempting to show.[299] Compared to counsel, Evans was saying, the judge was simply too ignorant of the proofs and of the forensic strategies to do any good. Increasingly, therefore, the judge withdrew from the work of eliciting evidence at trial, while developing rules of evidence and of trial practice to regulate adversary-conducted proof-taking. Having never been well situated to lead the proof-taking at trial, the judges seem to have welcomed the opportunity to yield the job to counsel. The high ground above the fray was attractive territory. Withdrawing from proof-taking lightened the judges' workload and reduced their exposure to outside criticism for the conduct of those few trials that would inevitably be controversial or notorious.

2. The Unrepresented

There was one great practical limitation on the trial judge's inclination to yield his former role in adducing fact to counsel: All too often, there was no counsel. Our knowledge of the frequency of representation in felony criminal trials (previously discussed in Chapter 3[300]) is not very good. At the Old Bailey throughout the eighteenth century and long beyond, many, indeed most cases of serious crime continued to be tried without the participation of prosecution or defense counsel. The best estimate is that "[b]y the end of the [eighteenth] century, between a quarter and a third of defendants at the Old Bailey had the benefit of counsel,"[301] and that the proportion of represented prosecutors was lower. (At provincial

---

[298] W. D. Evans, "On the Law of Evidence" 148, 269 in 2 Robert J. Pothier, *A Treatise on the Law of Obligations* (W. D. Evans trans.) (London 1806) (2 vols.). On the importance of Evans, see William Twining, "The Rationalist Tradition of Evidence Scholarship," in id., *Rethinking Evidence: Exploratory Essays* 32, 42–4 (1990). Twining points to the passage from Evans that I emphasize in text; ibid. at 44.

[299] Compare Judge Frankel's account of the limitations that the mature adversary system places on judicial intervention. "[O]ur system does not allow much room for effective or just intervention by the trial judge in the adversary fight about the facts. The judge views the case from a peak of Olympian ignorance. His intrusions will in too many cases result from partial or skewed insights. He may expose the secrets that one side chooses to keep while never becoming aware of the other's. . . . The ignorance and unpreparedness of the judge are intended axioms of the system. The 'facts' are to be found and asserted by the contestants. The judge is not to have investigated or explored the evidence before trial . . . . Without an investigative file, the American trial judge is a blind and blundering intruder . . . ." Marvin Frankel, "The Search for Truth: An Umpireal View," 123 *Univ. Pennsylania L. Rev.* 1031, 1042 (1975).

[300] *Supra* Ch. 3, text and nn. 293–303.

[301] Beattie, "Scales" 228. Comparable data gathered by May for the first three decades of the nineteenth century is reviewed *supra* Ch. 3, n. 303. Both have worked from the *Sessions Papers*, which are troublesome for the purpose for the reasons discussed *supra* Ch. 4, text at nn. 24–38, 49–52.

assizes, we have seen, there is indication that the levels of representation were relatively high, at least in part because criminal work was being used as a training ground for young barristers.[302]) Although many criminal cases entailed no serious dispute (for example, offenders who were caught in the act or in pursuit or with stolen goods, or who had confessed at the pretrial examination), there was nothing in the process that matched lawyers to the cases that most needed or deserved representation. Rather, in allocating legal services, money talked, both for the prosecution and for the defense.

In some cases involving particularly affluent or determined parties, especially prosecutors, we find several counsel employed.[303] For example, when the Duke of Devonshire prosecuted a former servant for a theft, he hired the two leading Old Bailey counsel of the day, Garrow and John Silvester.[304] It is hard to think that this simple case required the legal talents of the two best lawyers then engaged in criminal practice. The more likely explanation is that the solicitor managing the case hired both to prevent the defendant from hiring either, especially Garrow.[305] The second counsel was being paid a species of hush money.

A two-tier system grew up, manifesting what I have called the wealth effect: Counsel represented the more affluent prosecutors (especially institutions) and defendants, but cases without counsel had to be processed to trial in a semblance of the old way. The unrepresented defendant was left to fall back upon the assistance of court as counsel,[306] even as the shortcomings of court as counsel were ever more understood. A defendant accused of murder reminded the trial judge at the Old Bailey in 1776: "As I am not provided with counsel, I beg, my lord, you will take

[302] *Supra*, n. 16.

[303] E.g., John Ayliffe, *OBSP* (Oct. 1759, #328), at 348 (forgery) (two counsel for prosecution, three for defense).

[304] William Mason, *OBSP* (Sept. 1788, #561), at 717.

[305] A pamphlet attack on Garrow by a solicitor whom Garrow had offended at Surrey Assizes in 1796 alleged that Garrow was shamelessly mercenary in accepting engagements. The author recounted, in the form of a letter to Garrow, that "having a brief to deliver to you [that is, instructions for counsel in a civil cause] which my clerk was finishing, I met you going into Court, and requested you not to take any brief on the other side, if offered you, as I intended you the advocate for my client, whose brief would be ready in a few minutes. 'Indeed I shall [take the other side's brief], unless you give me a retainer!,' " Garrow is supposed to have replied. Concanen, *Garrow, supra* n. 216, at 16.

[306] A pamphlet about a forgery case tried at the Old Bailey in 1779 says that the trial judge ordered the Bank of England as prosecutor to pay for defendant's lawyers. "It was the intention of the Court to have tried the prisoner on Wednesday the 17th; but as he had no money to procure solicitor or counsel, Judge Willes very humanely, and much to his honor, ordered Mr. Acton, the solicitor of the Bank, immediately to give [the defendant] ten guineas to furnish him with both . . . ." Anon., *Memoirs of the Life of John Matthieson, Executed for a Forgery on the Bank of England* 17 (London 1779) (Yale Law Libr. shelfmark RB SSP M512 c.1). I know of no other instance of such a solution to the problem of the unrepresented defendant.

my cause in hand."[307] An accused shoplifter implored the court in 1777: "As I have no counsel, will your lordship please to hear what I have to say?"[308] Cottu noticed in 1820 that cross-examination "is made by the judge, for the prisoner, when he has not the means of procuring counsel,"[309] and the *Sessions Papers* show us cases in which the trial judge did a determined job of probing the testimony of prosecution witnesses.[310] The judge was not limited to cross-examination when he distrusted a prosecution case; he could also invoke his power of judicial comment to support the accused,[311] or he could subject the indictment to special scrutiny.[312]

[307] Thomas Dempsey *et al.*, OBSP (Apr. 1776, ##367–72), at 231, 235 (request of codefendant Andrew Nihil).

[308] Sarah Armstrong, *OBSP* (May 1777, #350), at 216, 217.

[309] Cottu, *Administration* 88.

[310] E.g., Elizabeth Butson, *OBSP* (Feb. 1762, #103), at 72 (theft) (judge to prosecutor: "So, then, Madam, you form your opinion, and swear to her having taken the ring (which you did not see) merely from your having lost it, and never finding it since?").

[311] Some examples, from the middle decades of the eighteenth century:

(1) In a coining case in which the Mint relied upon accomplice testimony of the major culprit to prosecute a minor one, the judge used the summation to express his revulsion at the choice of the crown witness. "I could have wished that [the crown witness] might have been prosecuted, and this poor Woman made an Evidence." The message may have been meant for the Mint; the jury took the hint and acquitted. Anne Wilson, *OBSP* (Apr. 1746, #191), at 137, 140.

(2) Sitting at the Old Bailey in 1754 in the case of a woman charged with stealing money from a drunk, Dudley Ryder thought that "[t]he case was so plain that I told the jury I supposed they could not have any doubt; and without my summing up they found her not guilty." R. v. *Elizabeth Woodcock*, Ryder "Judge's Notes," 4, 6 (1754). At the same sessions, in a case in which one erstwhile drinking companion prosecuted the other for highway robbery, Ryder recorded in his notes: "I told the jury I thought there was no ground to find [the accused] guilty on this single evidence, and the jury found him Not Guilty." R. v. *Lloyd Davis*, Ryder "Judge's Notes," 17, 18; same case: Lloyd Davis, *OBSP* (Oct. 1754, #511), at 338.

(3) In a highway robbery case, William Moreton, the recorder of London, referred to his trial notes from an earlier prosecution brought by the same accusers against other defendants, in order to point to matters on which their testimony in the present trial "disagreed with the accounts they gave" in the former trial. Sarah Young, *OBSP* (Jan. 1759, #71), at 48, 49–50. The jury acquitted.

(4) Margaret Lovelock, charged with stealing household linen from her lodgings, was acquitted after the judge expressed the "opinion that the taking [from] the lodgings was the act of the husband, and mentioned to the jury some circumstances in favor of the prisoner." Margaret Lovelock, *OBSP* (Feb. 1762, #105), at 73, 74.

(5) William Price and two others were charged with a burglary, on the pretrial evidence of Ann Pinnock. At trial, Price contended that Pinnock accused him out of revenge, because he "was admitted an evidence against Pinnock for receiving stolen goods . . . ." After examining Pinnock, the trial judge announced his view that Pinnock and others had "scheme[d] . . . to revenge themselves on this Price, who, I verily believe has told the truth." The jury acquitted the defendants. William Price *et al.*, *OBSP* (July 1770, ##441–3), at 262, 263.

[312] In a case in which "[t]here were several Counsel for the Prosecution, but none for the Prisoner," the *Sessions Paper* explained: "It was therefore incumbent on the Court (who are of Counsel for the Prisoner) to examine the Record [from Chancery, where the alleged offense had been committed], and there was a material Variance found between that and the Indictment," hence the court directed a verdict for the accused; e.g., Joseph Ellis, *OBSP* (June–July 1743, #365), at 219 (perjury).

Contemporaries understood the wealth effect. As adversary combat came to typify the well-conducted criminal trial, resentment grew among those who could not afford counsel. "I have not a six penny piece left to pay a porter, much less [enough] to fee counsel," a woman prosecuted for forging a bond told the Old Bailey in 1757. "If I must die because I am poor, I can't help it."[313] (She was convicted and sentenced to death.) At the same sessions another defendant complained that he was having to defend himself because "I am quite disabled from having an attorney at law to act as my counsellor, having nothing to pay for his usual fees . . . ."[314] The same grievance was voiced in 1760 in colonial Maryland by a defendant sentenced to death for stealing a horse, who contended that he had been "convicted and condemned to die partly for want of money . . . to employ counsel."[315] Colquhoun, the prosecutorially minded magistrate, wrote at the end of the century that a criminal unable "to procure the aid of counsel to defend him, *is often convicted*," whereas "the hardened villain" who could use the proceeds from stolen goods to hire counsel "is acquitted and escapes justice . . . ."[316]

The Attorney General, Frederick Pollock, made light of the wealth effect when speaking to the Criminal Law Commissioners in 1835. Asked how he would "propose to supply counsel to prisoners who were too poor to obtain that assistance from their own funds," he replied that no provision was needed. "[I]t is usual now, if a prisoner professes his inability to retain counsel, for the court to assign counsel, and not unusual for the ablest and most experienced counsel cheerfully to undertake the duty of the defence."[317] Pollock may have been thinking of assizes, where young barristers cut their teeth on criminal defense work.[318] Quite a different picture of Old Bailey trials emerges from the memoir of Thomas Wontner, an attorney who had a significant criminal practice there and on assizes during this period. He depicted "rapid and indecent" Old Bailey trials for felony, whose average duration he

---

[313] Eleanor Eddacres, *OBSP* (July 1757, #285), at 263, 269.

[314] James Ashton, *OBSP* (July 1757, #253), at 243, 245 (theft).

[315] The condemned man, John Harrison was petitioning for clemency; the colonial Council advised against and the Governor was "pleased to Order Dead Warrant for his Execution . . ." *Proceedings of the Council of Maryland: Letters to Governor Horatio Sharpe 1754–1765*, 31 *Archives of Maryland* 412–23 (1911) (entry for 7 Oct. 1760). The case is cited in James D. Rice, "The Criminal Trial before and after the Lawyers: Authority, Law and Culture in Maryland Jury Trials, 1681–1837," 40 *American J. Legal History* 455, 457 (1996).

[316] Colquhoun, *Police, supra* n. 278, at 23 (emphasis original).

[317] *1836 Report* 76.

[318] Discussed *supra*, n. 16. By contrast, it is reported that "[a]t the 1841 Summer Assizes the calendar for Nottingham county contained twelve cases; in only one did the prisoner have counsel." David Bentley, *English Criminal Justice in the Nineteenth Century* 108 n. 13 (1998) [hereafter Bentley, *Nineteenth Century*], citing *The Times*, 26 July 1841.

calculated at eight and a half minutes, and in which the hand of defense counsel was typically unseen:

The rapidity with which the trials are despatched throws the prisoners into the utmost confusion. Fifty or sixty of them are kept in readiness in the dock under the court, to be brought up as they may be called for. These men, seeing their fellow prisoners return tried and found guilty in a minute or two . . ., become so alarmed and nervous . . . that . . . they lose all command over themselves, and are then, to use their own language, taken up to be knocked down like bullocks, unheard. Full two-thirds of the prisoners, on their return from their trials, cannot tell of anything which has passed in the court; not even, very frequently, whether they have been tried; and it is not, indeed, uncommon for a man to come back, after receiving his sentence on the day appointed for that purpose, saying, "It can't be me they mean; I have not been tried yet."[319]

In a system in which only the affluent had defense counsel, court as counsel appears to have degenerated into outright neglect. Withdrawal from the fray—the new model of judicial rectitude—presupposed the provision of counsel, yet the criminal justice system had not been organized or funded to supply it.[320]

The judges' ascent to the high ground above the adversary fray also caused particular discomfort in cases in which an unrepresented prosecution squared off against a represented defendant. Cairns points to indications of "increasing judicial distaste"[321] in the second quarter of the nineteenth century for the work of determining the sequence of prosecution witnesses and eliciting their testimony, work that had routinely fallen to the judge in the days of the altercation trial. "By the mid 1840s the practice was described as 'disagreeable and improper' by one judge, while another called it indecent and refused to examine the witnesses, ordering instead that the depositions be given to a barrister in court to conduct the prosecution."[322] As in the case of the unrepresented defendant, so in the case of the unrepresented prosecution, the judges were determined to escape responsibility for adducing fact in a criminal trial procedure in which adversary combat had become the presumptive norm.

F. Jury Trial

The purpose of the lawyer-free, altercation-type trial that had emerged in

---

[319] Thomas Wontner, *Old Bailey Experience: Criminal Jurisprudence and the Actual Working of our Penal Code of Laws* 59–60 (London 1833).

[320] Bentley indicates that the topic surfaced in the bills leading to the 1836 Act extending full defense of counsel. "A clause entitling poor prisoners to have counsel assigned to them was included in each of the 1833–36 Bills (counsel so assigned to act without fee)." Bentley, *Nineteenth Century, supra* n. 318, at 108.   [321] Cairns, *Advocacy* 46.

[322] Ibid., citing, *inter alia*, "Prosecuting Judges," 9 *Law Times* 256 (1847); and "Soup System—Prosecution by Magistrates," 41 *Law Magazine* 103 (1849).

the sixteenth century was to provide an opportunity for the accused to respond in person to the charges and the evidence against him. A main theme of this chapter has been that lawyerization changed the theory of criminal trial in a quite unforeseen way. Across the eighteenth century the adversary dynamic altered the very purpose of the trial, by making the trial into an opportunity for defense counsel to test the prosecution case.

This change in the function of trial was reflected in counsel's growing effectiveness in diminishing or controlling what other participants in the trial said or did. Thus, in lawyer-dominated trials the prosecutor and the other witnesses on both sides ceased to speak in their own narratives; solicitors prepared them to testify, and counsel's so-called direct examination guided them through their lawyer-prepared testimony. Witness testimony was ever more hewn to fit lawyers' scripts. The criminal accused, if he spoke at all, was subordinated to his lawyers in like fashion. This adversary dynamic also affected the role of trial jurors.

1. Muting the Jury

In the age of the altercation trial, jurors had often joined in the conversation, to ask questions or to make observations. For example, in the trial of a woman charged in 1733 with stealing money from the victim's trousers in a bawdy house, a juror is recorded asking him: "Were your Breeches up or down when you lost the Money?"[323] (answer: down). At the trial of a defendant accused of receiving stolen property, a juror questioned him about his defense: "Had not you one of the Warnings [that is, handbills] that were given out on this Occasion? For it is common to send them to Watchmakers as well as to Goldsmiths."[324] Jurors not only questioned witnesses,[325] they sometimes asked for further witnesses to be summoned,[326] and they also volunteered information about persons,[327] places,[328] and commercial practices.[329]

---

[323] Catherine Tracey, *OBSP* (Apr. 1733, #55), at 117.

[324] Edward Bodenham, *OBSP* (Dec. 1733, #6), at 35, 39–40.

[325] Juror to prosecuting witness who testified that she lived in Mutton Lane: "You said yesterday that you lived in Chick Lane?" William Price *et al.*, *OBSP* (July 1770, ##441–3), at 262, 263 (burglary).

[326] In the case of Thomas Gray, *OBSP* (July 1735), at 93 (highway robbery), "[t]he Jury withdrew and after a short stay returned into Court, and desired that for their farther Satisfaction, the People at the Stag and Hounds [a pub that figured in the trial testimony] might be sent for. A Messenger was immediately dispatched, and brought the Man of the House and his Wife back with him." The court questioned them about the details of the accused's alibi; the jury acquitted.

[327] E.g., Thomas Hardy and Henry Chapman, OBSP (Oct. 1732, ##41–2), at 242, 244 (highway robbery).

[328] E.g., Elizabeth Mark, *OBSP* (Apr. 1735, #25), at 71 (theft); Ann Dossel, *OBSP* (Sept. 1761, #280), at 355, 362 (theft).

[329] In a case involving the theft of a skein of silk, the foreman of the jury volunteered:

By the last quarter of the eighteenth century, as the initiative in adducing fact passed to counsel, it became less common for jurors at the Old Bailey to remark directly on the facts or to question witnesses. When a juror's observation entailed a statement of fact about a person or an event, it amounted to unsworn testimony, in tension with the growing emphasis upon the cross-examination of testimony. At a murder trial in 1755 one of the jurors announced: "I know something of the prisoner; may I be sworn now and tell it before my brother jurymen go out?"[330] (The judge had him sworn and he testified to an incident of drunken behavior by the defendant.[331]) Blackstone, writing in 1768, said the practice "now universally obtains, that if a juror knows any thing of the matter in issue, he may be sworn as a witness, and give his evidence publicly in court."[332]

Toward the end of the century we see counsel's attitude hardening against questioning by jurors. During a trial in 1784 Garrow was cross-examining the prosecutor about the characteristics of the allegedly stolen property. When one of the jurors asked a question of a similar sort, Garrow protested:

MR. GARROW. My Lord, if Gentlemen of the Jury, without seeing the drift of my question, are to prevent an answer by asking others, and so to decide for themselves, I despair of doing anything for the prisoner.

COURT. They may ask questions.

MR. GARROW. Certainly, my Lord, and as to the truth of this witness's evidence, that must be considered by the Jury alone; but I submit it is perfectly novel for any body except the Court to break into my examination till I have done with the witness.

COURT. Then go on.[333]

Garrow's objection, although expressed as a point of sequence (counsel examines first), had a deeper import. Questions deferred often lose

---

"Every skein of silk is knotted on account of the dyer, but where there are two knots it is a private mark." John Langford and William Annand, *OBSP* (Jan. 1788, #137), at 177, 179 (theft, receiving).

[330] John Moody, *OBSP* (Jan. 1755, #76), at 60, 66.

[331] This way of dealing with jurors who had knowledge of the events had been ordained a century earlier but was hard to enforce for incidental contributions of the sort Old Bailey jurors commonly made. In *Bennet v. Hundred of Hartford*, Style 233, 82 *Eng. Rep.* 671, 672 (Upper Bench 1650), it was held that "the Court will examine [a juror who has knowledge of the events] openly in Court upon his oath, and he ought not be examined in private by his companions." In a turn-of-the-century manual on civil jury practice, the point was stated with a qualification: "A Juror who is a Witness must be also sworn in open Court to give Evidence, *if he be called for a Witness*; for the Court and the Counsel are to hear the Evidence as well as the Jury." [Giles Duncombe], *Tryals per Pais: or the Law of England Concerning Juries by Nisi Prius* 221 (4th edn. London 1702) (emphasis supplied). (I owe this reference to S. F. C. Milsom.) I read the underscored phrase to mean that as of that time the juror who spoke had to be sworn as a witness only if called as such by one of the parties.

[332] 3 Blackstone, *Commentaries* 375.

[333] James Scott, *OBSP* (Feb. 1784, #216), at 262, 265 (theft).

their context or immediacy, become inapt, and go unasked. Garrow's deeper message in this exchange was that lawyerization had clipped the jurors' wings. Adversary criminal trial did not leave room for jurors to participate in framing the inquiry, for the same reason it pressured the judge to stand down from such work. The system of adversary presentation of the proofs was antithetical to nonadversary initiatives in adducing the facts, whether from judge or from jurors. The lawyer-conducted trial was no longer centered on the questions that, however clumsily, had been at the center of a contested altercation trial, namely, what really happened, and did the accused really do it. Adversary procedure refocused the trial on a different question—whether defense counsel had succeeded in raising sufficient doubt about the strength of the prosecution case. Defense counsel did not want other participants cluttering that inquiry with other questions, especially with questions about the truth. The age of the altercation trial—trial as an open discussion among the participants—was past.

2. The Transformation of Jury Control

Jury trial has always been fraught with danger. Jurors are untrained in the law and often inexperienced in adjudication, they decide without giving reasons, and they have no continuing responsibility for the consequences of their decisions. Because of the grave risks of error and bias that inhere in using such decision makers, the common law courts have never left juries to their own devices. Rather, the judges have undertaken to guide and oversee the work of the jury.[334]

   The practice of jury control underwent considerable change across the period during which the adversary system was recasting the conduct of the trial. The judges retreated from an older pattern of involvement in the merits of the jury's verdict. As they lost their ability to identify and correct jury error, the judges devised a new system, based on the law of evidence and the law of jury instructions, a system designed to prevent jury error. The question arises of whether these two developments, the transformation in jury control and the rise of adversary criminal procedure, may have been related.

(a) Judicial Comment

In the age of the altercation trial the trial judge could help shape the jury's verdict by exercising broad powers to comment on the merits of a case. Hale spoke of the "Excellency" of the practice by which the judge not only

---

[334] See generally Thayer, *Evidence* 137–81.

"direct[ed]" the jurors on issues of law, but was also able "in Matters of Fact, to give them a great Light and Assistance by his weighing the Evidence before them, and observing where the Question and Knot of the Business lies, and by showing them his Opinion even in Matter of Fact, which is a great Advantage and Light to Lay Men."[335] We have ample evidence of judges commenting both for[336] and against[337] the accused. In general, jurors welcomed the judge's guidance, in civil[338] as well as in criminal cases. Deep into the eighteenth century the judges were confident that juries would follow their lead. When Boswell asked Lord Mansfield in 1773 whether juries always took his direction, Mansfield answered: "Yes, except in political causes where they do not at all keep themselves to right and wrong."[339]

Sometime in the second half of the eighteenth century we find evidence of a change in attitude about the appropriateness of judicial comment on the merits. Judges continued to direct verdicts of acquittal as matters of law, but the bench became more circumspect about advising juries on the merits.[340] Little is yet known about the timing and the causes of this change of heart. Peter King has noticed that by 1788 *The Times* was editorializing that the judge should not, when summing up, make "any comment which may lead to a discovery of what his opinion on the merits may be."[341] Sir Richard Phillips, an active tract writer, insisted in 1811 that

---

[335] Matthew Hale, *The History of the Common Law of England* 164–5 (Charles M. Gray ed.) (1971 edn.) (1st edn. 1713) (posthumous publication, written before 1676) [hereafter Hale, *Common Law*].

[336] *Supra* nn. 310–11.

[337] For example, Raymond CJ, trying a woman charged with murdering her husband in 1726, advised the jury "that though it was not positively proved by any of the Evidence for the King that she was actually concerned in the Murder, yet there were very strong circumstantial Proofs of her assisting and consenting to the same, and that the other two Prisoners had confessed the same and owned that she was a Contriver thereof; upon which the Jury found her guilty . . . ." Anon., *A Narrative of the Barbarous and Unheard of Murder of Mr. John Hayes, by Catherine His Wife* 20 (2nd edn. London 1726). The offense of which she was convicted, murdering her husband, was classified as petty treason, on which see 4 Blackstone, *Commentaries* 203–4. The punishment, abolished by 30 Geo. 3, c. 48 (1790), was to be burned at the stake. The convict was typically strangled first. See 1 Radzinowicz, *History* 209–13. For other examples of judicial comment adverse to the accused, see *supra* Ch. 1, n. 97.

[338] I have elsewhere described the broad powers of comment exercised by Dudley Ryder when presiding at London-area *nisi prius* trials. Langbein, "Evidence" 1190–3.

[339] 1 Oldham, *Mansfield* 206, quoting [6] The Private Papers of James Boswell from Malahide Castle 109 (G. Scott and F. A. Pottle eds.) (1928).

[340] Already in 1754, presiding in the celebrated perjury trial of Elizabeth Canning, the recorder of London, William Moreton, said in his summation: "I shall state the evidence in the clearest manner I have been able to collect it; and if, in stating the several facts which have been laid before you in the course of this long proceeding, I should accidentally disclose my own opinion, I must desire that it may have no weight, or make the least impression on you, in determining your verdict, otherwise than as the weight of the evidence justifies it." 19 *St. Tr.* 283, 633 (O.B. 1754).

[341] King, *Crime* 249, citing *The Times* (18 Sept. 1788).

juries should resist when "[j]udges ... presume to tell a jury what their verdict must be, and that it can be nothing else . . . . Juries should be deaf to such peremptory instructions, and decide only on their own views and convictions."[342] English judges retain a power to comment, but "must make it clear to the jury ... that on the issues of fact which are left to them they are free to give his opinion what weight they choose."[343] In the United States, where the bench had been tainted by its association with imperial administration in late colonial times, there was an intensive movement to strip judges of their powers of judicial comment. From the 1780s and across the nineteenth century many states enacted statutes or constitutional provisions forbidding judges to comment on the evidence.[344]

(b) Fining or Threatening Fine

In the infrequent case in which the jury disagreed with the judge's views, if the judge cared[345] to persist in his views, he commanded a considerable array of further powers to get his way. Until 1670 judges sometimes fined jurors for returning a verdict against the weight of the evidence. The judges abandoned that power in the celebrated decision in *Bushell's Case*,[346] after it became politically controversial in the 1660s.[347]

---

[342] Richard Phillips, *On the Power and Duties of Juries* 179–80 (London 1811) [hereafter Phillips, *Juries*].

[343] *R. v. Lawrence*, 73 Crim. App. 1, 5 (Ct. Crim. Ap. 1981) (per Lord Hailsham).

[344] Kenneth A. Krasity, "The Role of the Judge in Jury Trials: The Elimination of Judicial Evaluation of Fact in American State Courts from 1795 to 1913," 62 *Univ. Detroit L. Rev.* 595 (1985). See also Renée Lettow Lerner, "The Transformation of the American Civil Trial: The Silent Judge," 43 *William and Mary L. Rev.* 195 (2000) (pointing to regional variation in the restrictions on judicial comment respecting civil jury trials). Wigmore thought that the judge's power to "comment upon the general weight of the evidence, or of particular parts of it . . . existed at common law since the beginning of jury trial, and must be regarded historically as an essential and inseparable part of jury trial." 9 Wigmore, *Evidence* § 2551, at 503. The "unfortunate" American "departure from the orthodox common law rule . . . has done more than any other one thing to impair the general efficiency of jury trial as an instrument of justice." Ibid. at 504–5, citing Thayer, *Evidence* 188 (jury trial under the American rule restricting judicial comment "is not a trial by jury in any historic sense of the words").

[345] Sometimes the judge acquiesced in a verdict with which he disagreed, e.g., Margaret Whitehead, *OBSP* (Feb.–Mar. 1759, #114), at 82, 83 (theft) ("Acquitted, contrary to the opinion of the Court"). For examples from Dudley Ryder's civil practice in the mid-1750s, see Langbein, "Evidence" 1193 and nn. 123–4. Sometimes there was a subplot when the court accepted a verdict that it thought mistaken. For example, in the case of William Sikes, charged with murder resulting from swordplay when an attempted execution on Sikes' goods went awry, Sikes claimed he thought he was being robbed. The jury acquitted "with a Check [i.e., a rebuke] from the Bench." Rather than struggle about the verdict, the court took advantage of the fact that Sikes had been charged in a second homicide arising from the same incident. The court let the first verdict stand, dismissed that jury, impanelled a new jury, and had Sikes tried to the new jury on the second indictment. The new jury convicted him of manslaughter. William Sikes *et al.*, *OBSP* (Jan. 1697), at 3–4.

[346] *Vaugh.* 135, 124 *Eng. Rep.* 1006 (K.B. 1670); also reported in *T. Jones* 13, 84 *Eng. Rep.* 1123; 1 *Freem. K.B.* 1, 89 *Eng. Rep.* 2. The case is extensively discussed in Green, *Verdict* 236–49. I

(c) Clemency

The technique of jury control that was most respectful of the jury's autonomy was for the judge to accept what he deemed an erroneous verdict of
conviction, then to overturn it by procuring the King's pardon. The script
according to Hale: "[I]f the jury will convict a man against or without
evidence, and against the direction or opinion of the court, the court hath
this salve, to reprieve the person convict before judgment, and to acquaint
the King, and certify for his pardon."[348] In eighteenth-century practice,
royal review of judicial recommendations for pardon and commutation
was a regular part of criminal procedure.[349] It was understood that the
judges exercised effective control of the outcome of royal review. When
convicting of a capital offense, juries sometimes asked the judge to recommend a defendant for clemency.[350]

---

have elsewhere explained why the rationale of Chief Justice Vaughan's opinion is dishonest
nonsense. Langbein, "CTBL" 298 and n. 105.
    Even after *Bushell's Case*, the judges retained the power to fine jurors for misbehavior. An
early *Sessions Paper* reports an instance a decade after *Bushell's Case*. A juror who had been
refused his request to avoid jury service voted against the eleven other jurors in the first two
cases tried to them. It was sworn by two of the other jurors that the dissenter had said, "If I
must be on [the jury], I'll . . . plague them . . . ." The court "laid a Fine of fifty pounds upon
him. For though Jurymen, 'tis said, are not by Law to be punished by Fines, for giving
Verdicts according to their Consciences, yet it seem both just and necessary that such misdemeanors of resolved stubbornness be restrained." *OBSP* (May 1680), at 1, 2. Dudley Ryder
recorded in 1754 that his fellow assize judge Michael Foster (later the author of Foster's
Crown Law) told him of having fined a juror £50 for departing court early. Ryder, "Assize
Diary" 12.
    [347] The near impeachment of Chief Justice John Kelyng in 1667 was the background event
that led to *Bushell's Case*. Resentment of Kelyng's behavior toward high-status grand jurors on
the Western Circuit in 1667 triggered impeachment proceedings against him in the House of
Commons. For more on Kelyng's misadventures in jury control, see Eric Stockdale, "Sir John
Kelyng, Chief Justice of King's Bench 1665–1671," in *Miscellanea* 43 (1980) (vol. 59, Publications
of the Bedfordshire Historical Record Society) (I owe this reference to Mark Kishlansky).
Among the grievances against Kelyng "was that he had spoken ill of the Great Charter, by
contemptuously using in open court, Cromwell's celebrated expostulation, 'Magna Carta,
Magna Farta.' " Ibid. at 50. Somers was bristling about Kelyng's behavior years later: [John
Somers], *The Security of English-Mens Lives* 17–18 (London 1681) (Kelyng "would have usurped
a Lordly, Dictatorian power over the Grand Jury of Somersetshire . . .").
    [348] 2 Hale, *HPC* 309–10.
    [349] Discussed *supra* Ch. 1, text at nn. 245–9; see Beattie, *Crime* 430 ff; King, *Crime* 297–333;
V. A. C. Gatrell, *The Hanging Tree: Execution and the English People: 1770–1868*, at 543 ff (1994)
[hereafter Gatrell, *Hanging Tree*]; Douglas Hay, "Property, Authority and the Criminal Law,"
in *Albion's Fatal Tree: Crime and Society in Eighteenth-Century England* 17, 40–9 (D. Hay *et. al.*,
eds.) (1975); 1 Radzinowicz, *History* 107–37.
    [350] For example, in the case of the contrite highway robber Robert Cross, who pleaded not
guilty but admitted on trial "that I am guilty of the crime that is laid to my charge," the jury
convicted but recommended him to mercy. The court asked them: "You look upon it to be
his first offense then, I suppose, Gentlemen?" The jurors are reported replying: "Yes, we do,
my Lord." Robert Cross, *OBSP* (Dec. 1783, #6), at 25, 28.
    For the 1783 mayoral year, it has been computed that Old Bailey juries recommended

The prospect of judicial manipulation of the royal pardon power constituted a significant deterrent to a jury that might otherwise have been prepared to convict against the wishes of the court. The jury was not likely to insist on its view[351] when the judge had a trump that would render the effort futile. So effective was this judicial remedy that it seems to have virtually eliminated[352] the conviction against direction as a sphere of conflict between judge and jury.

(d) Terminating a Trial Short of Verdict

The judge who sensed a looming disagreement with the jury could abort the trial before the case went to verdict, then have it tried to another jury at a later sessions. "[O]therwise," Hale explained, "many notorious murders and burglaries may pass unpunished by the acquittal of a person probably guilty, where the full evidence is not searched out or given."[353] We can understand why the judges thought it was important to have this power in a system of predominantly private prosecution, in which evidence-gathering and coordination of witnesses for trial was always a potential weak point.[354]

mercy in eighteen capital cases; pardons were granted in sixteen. Richard Makesy, "Lethal Lottery or Coherent Scheme: Pardons and Rationality in Late-18th Century London" 238 (unpub. Ph.D. thesis, City University of New York, 1993). I have pointed to notable examples from earlier decades in Langbein, "Ryder" 20–1, discussing Thomas Rolf, *OBSP* (Oct. 1754, #504), at 80 (highway robbery); and Langbein, "CTBL" 297, discussing Jane French, *OBSP* (Feb. 1732), at 89.

[351] I have noticed one instance in the *Sessions Papers* of a judge struggling to force a jury to acquit. In the trial of an accused charged with the theft of banknotes, Baron Eyre told the jury at the end of the prosecution case that there was a "chasm in the evidence" such that "I do not think it is material to call on the prisoner to make his defense, therefore, I think the prisoner must be acquitted." Uziel Barugh, *OBSP* (Sept. 1784, #785), at 1084, 1087. The jury, however, asked to withdraw, implying that they wished to deliberate over whether to follow the judge's direction to acquit. Eyre reiterated that the evidence had not proved the charge, and said icily that "if . . . you think it is a point to be debated, whether a man is to be convicted when there is no evidence against him, you may withdraw . . . ." Ibid. at 1087. The jury backed off and acquitted without withdrawing to deliberate.

[352] Peter King reports a case from Essex Assizes in 1795 in which the jury did persist in convicting against direction. The defendant was a father charged with receiving goods stolen by his daughter. The judge "stopped the evidence in favor of the prisoner and observed that it was needless to take up the time of the court as he was well satisfied of the innocence of the father and directed the jury to bring in their verdict accordingly." But "on the jury saying that there remained a doubt on that head, the evidence was continued" and a guilty verdict ultimately returned. King, *Crime* 251–2, citing a report from the *Chelmsford Chronicle*, 20 Mar. 1795. King did not investigate whether the judge arranged to have the monarch overturn the outcome by means of pardon.

[353] 2 Hale, *HPC* 295.

[354] The power was, however, used more broadly. For example, at Durham Assizes in 1790 the trial of Elizabeth Jones was stopped when one of the jurors tumbled down drunk. "Lord Loughborough C.J. discharged the jury and had a fresh jury empaneled. This provoked a protest from prisoner's counsel that she could not be tried twice. The trial proceeded

Hale maintained that the exercise of this power was quite "ordinary" at the Old Bailey.[355] In the *Sessions Papers*, which commence around the time of Hale's death, such cases were not ordinary. I have noticed only one unmistakable instance, in 1718.[356] The sources do not permit us to say whether the practice of terminating trial short of verdict was on the decline, or whether the *Sessions Papers* had a bias against relating half-told stories, or both.

(e) Rejecting Verdict and Requiring Redeliberation

When a jury returned a verdict that the judge thought was against the weight of the evidence or otherwise mistaken, the judge could refuse to accept the verdict, probe its basis with the jurors, give them further instruction, and require them to redeliberate. Hale wrote: "If the jurors by mistake or partiality give their verdict in court, yet they may rectify their verdict before it is recorded, or by advice of the court go together again and consider better of it, and alter what they have delivered."[357]

What made this technique effective was the understanding that a trial jury, civil or criminal, would on the judge's request disclose the rationale for the verdict. In *Ash v. Ash*,[358] a civil case decided in 1697, Chief Justice Holt reversed what he deemed to be a grossly excessive award of damages,[359] saying: "The jury were very shy of giving a reason for their verdict, thinking that they have an absolute, despotic power, but I did rectify that mistake, for the jury are to try cases with the assistance of the judge, and ought to give reasons when required, that, if they go upon any mistake, they may be set right . . . ."[360]

I have elsewhere[361] directed attention to an exceptionally detailed

---

nonetheless and she was convicted." D. R. Bentley, "Introduction," at 37, in Bentley, *Notebooks, supra* n. 270, discussing *R. v. Elizabeth Jones*, ibid. at 73–4. The Twelve Judges unanimously sustained the conviction, holding in effect that the ban on double jeopardy did not attach until final conviction. The power of the trial judge to terminate a case short of verdict and retry it was again endorsed in *Winsor v. R.*, 10 Cox, [1866] L.R. 1 Q.B. 289, noticed in 9 Holdsworth, *HEL* 234.

[355] 2 Hale, *HPC* 295.

[356] In the case of a man tried for bigamy in 1718, when the court saw that the evidence would be insufficient to convict, it apparently halted the trial short of verdict and "advised the Wives to provide themselves with better Evidence, till which time he was to be secured." Hugh Coleman, *OBSP* (Feb. 1718), at 5–6.

[357] 2 Hale, *HPC* 299–300 (citations omitted).

[358] *Comb.* 357, 90 *Eng. Rep.* 526 (K.B. 1697).

[359] £2,000 for an incident of false imprisonment involving the detention of a youth for a couple of hours.

[360] *Comb.* 357–8, 90 *Eng. Rep.* at 526, discussed in David Graham, *A Treatise on the Law of New Trials* 445 (1834); and in *M'Connel v. Hampton*, 12 Johns. 234 (N.Y. 1815). (I owe these references to Daniel Klarman and Renée Lettow.)

[361] The case is reproduced in full in Langbein, "CTBL" 291–3, and discussed ibid. at 294–6.

account of a criminal trial in which the trial judge vigorously employed this technique of correcting a jury verdict. Stephen Arrowsmith, accused of the rape of a young girl, was tried in 1678 at the Old Bailey with Chief Justice Scroggs presiding.[362] Exercising his power to comment, Scroggs summed up strongly for conviction. Scroggs may have left the court for the day[363] by the time the jury returned from deliberation, because the report indicates that the recorder of London, George Jeffreys, was presiding when the jury proffered its verdict of acquittal. Jeffreys refused to accept the verdict. He questioned the jurors about their thinking, explained to them why they were mistaken,[364] and sent them out to redeliberate. When a disturbance caused the jury to return to the courtroom without a verdict, the judge interrogated the jurors further. Sensing that the jury was uneasy that the child victim and another child witness had not testified on oath, the judge recalled the two children, swore them, and had them repeat their testimony on oath. After retiring for its third deliberation, the jury acquiesced in the court's view of the case and returned a verdict of guilty, contrary to the verdict it first proffered.

The sources evidence other instances of verdicts being rejected and then revised,[365] as well as cases in which juries persisted after being

---

[362] *Exact Account* 14–16. This exceptionally detailed pamphlet, discussed *supra* Ch. 1, n. 59, reports on the December 1678 trials at the Old Bailey.

[363] Dudley Ryder, new to the job of presiding at the Old Bailey, made a note in his diary in 1754 that another judge told Ryder that Ryder's immediate predecessor as Chief Justice of King's Bench, William Lee, "seldom sat [at the Old Bailey] after 4 [p.m.] and then went home to dinner." Ryder, "Assize Diary" 18.

[364] "Mr. Recorder, not conceiving [the verdict] to be according to their Evidence, would not take [it] from them without further deliberation, and labored to satisfy them of the Manifestness of the Proof. One of the Jury being an Apothecary, said it was his opinion, that a Child of those years could not be Ravished. Which the Court told him was to Elude the Statute [of 18 Eliz. 1, c. 7 (1576), making intercourse with a child under 10 to be rape, regardless of her consent], that having provided a Punishment, had done it in vain, if there were no offense, and so he did tax the Wisdom of a whole Parliament; Which ought not to be." *Exact Account* 15. Jeffreys learned that other jurors were uneasy that the two child witnesses, the victim and another, had testified unsworn, and that the jury had heard "nothing but hearsay from the other Witnesses." Ibid. at 15–16. Jeffreys defended the use of hearsay on the ground that "such Offenders never call others to be by while they commit such actions," and that the girls had not been placed on oath "because of the tenderness of their Age; but if [the jury] insisted upon it, they should be Sworn." Ibid. at 16.

[365] Anon., *The Trial of Roland Waters et al.* 4 (judge instructed that the facts admitted only of manslaughter, jury found murder, judge refused the verdict and reinstructed the jury, jury found manslaughter) (B.L. shelfmark 112.f.46(14)); 12 *St. Tr.* 113, 122 (O.B. 1688). John Baker has transcribed another such case from a manuscript of the Newgate Sessions of 1616. J. H. Baker, "Criminal Justice at Newgate 1616–1727: Some Manuscript Reports in the Harvard Law School," 1977 *Irish Jurist* 307, 313 and n. 11. Instances in the nominate reports: *Watts v. Brains*, Cro. Eliz. 779, 78 *Eng. Rep.* 1009 (K.B. 1599); *Chichester's Case*, Aleyn 12, 82 *Eng. Rep.* 888 (K.B. *c*.1641).

reinstructed,[366] but such cases were always rare. Jury courts could not have functioned if they had often been put to such internal tests of strength.

This technique of rejecting a verdict and requiring redeliberation fell out of favor, but as with other branches of the law of jury control, we do not as yet have a very clear idea about when, how, and why that happened. Already in 1721 Hawkins sounded a note of caution. "[I]f the jury acquit a Prisoner of an Indictment of Felony against manifest Evidence, the Court may, before the Verdict is recorded, but not after, order them to go out again and reconsider the Matter; but this is by many thought hard, and seems not of late Years to have been so frequently practiced as formerly."[367] We see the technique being employed by Dudley Ryder in a case of infanticide at Essex Assizes in Chelmsford in 1754.[368] In a rape case at the Old Bailey in 1788 the jury proffered a verdict of "guilty of the attempt," apparently because they were not satisfied with the evidence of penetration. The judge, the recorder James Adair, rejected the verdict, on the legal ground that the offense was not within the indictment. The foreman then reported a guilty verdict. Adair conveyed his doubt that the verdict was sound, although he was careful to concede the point of principle that the jurors alone decided questions of fact, hence that if they believed the defendant was guilty, they should convict. The jury "immediately" acquitted.[369] Peter King has directed attention to a case arising in the Old Bailey in 1789, in which the jury fought off an effort to have them redeliberate.[370] As late as 1811 Sir Richard Phillips was

[366] If the jury "stand to their verdict, the court must take their verdict and record it . . . ." 2 Hale, HPC 310. A very early Sessions Paper report discloses a case in 1675 in which a jury stood its ground after redeliberation. An ostler named Harker was indicted for horse stealing and again for stealing money fastened upon the horse. The horse and most of the money were recovered when Harker was apprehended. "[T]he Jury . . . brought him upon the first indictment for stealing the horse not guilty, upon the second they found him [guilty]; notwithstanding the Court not being satisfied with their first Verdict, sent them out again to consider of it, but they brought in the same again that he was not Guilty of Stealing the Horse, for that as they said they understood the . . . Horse was delivered to [Harker] to hold while the [prosecutor] went in, which made a Lawful possession, and therefore could be no Felonious taking him away, but the Court seemed to be of another opinion." Anon., News from Islington, or The Confession and Execution of George Allin, Butcher, Who Now Hangs in Chains near to Islington (London 1674 [1675]) 2–3 (Guildhall Libr. shelfmark A.5.4. no. 34).

[367] 2 Hawkins, PC 442. This passage was carried forward in Burn's JP manual, to which King attributes it. King, Crime 251, citing Richard Burn, 2 The Justice of the Peace and Parish Officer 487 (10th edn. London 1766).

[368] He recorded in his assize diary that the evidence showed that the accused was found kneeling over her dying child with the murder weapon, a chicken hook, at her side. On the question of whether she was sane, there was conflicting evidence. "The jury first said they were satisfied she killed the child but doubted her sanity. I explained again to them the nature of the case rather against the prisoner. They went out and in about hour and half brought her in guilty. I then told them I was very well satisfied." Ryder, "Assize Diary" 4.

[369] Joseph Fyson, OBSP (June 1788, #496), at 630, 634.

[370] The jurors are reported to have said that "they thought [the judge's effort to have them amend their verdict] not only inconsistent with equity and good conscience, but altogether

criticizing judicial probing of proffered verdicts in terms that imply that he regarded the practice as still a threat to his expansive view of jury autonomy.[371]

(f) Special Verdicts

Sometimes in a case of potential judge–jury conflict the judge would direct the jury to find a special verdict, that is, a verdict in which the jury decided the facts but left the court to determine whether those facts gave rise to criminal liability.[372] In a case reported in the *Sessions Paper* for 1710 the judge directed a jury to formulate a special verdict after he rejected the jury's proffered general verdict.[373] The power to order a special verdict became controversial later in the eighteenth century when it was caught up in the crown's effort to regulate the press by prosecuting print critics for the offense of seditious libel.[374] To overcome the reluctance of jurors to convict in such cases, some judges hit upon the device of ordering a special verdict on the question of whether or not the defendant had published the matter in question, leaving it to the bench to decide whether the publication was seditious.[375] Fox's Libel Act of 1792[376] eliminated the judges' power to compel special verdicts in such cases.

contrary to the law of Trials by Jury in as much as they had once declared the prisoner not guilty." King, *Crime* 251, citing *The Times*, 30 Oct. 1789 and 13 Nov. 1789. King does not name the defendant. The case is probably Thomas Bermingham [sic], OBSP (Oct. 1789, #779), at 936 (theft of clothing). The language that King quotes from *The Times* does not appear in the *Sessions Paper* report, which quotes the defendant as claiming that he found the items. When the jurors proffered their verdict of acquittal, Heath J instructed them that "if property is lost, and afterwards recently found in the possession of another, that is in law a presumptive evidence of the theft, unless the persons charged with the robbery can prove how they came by the property." Ibid. at 937. The jury insisted on its verdict of not guilty.

[371] "It is . . . indecorous to enquire of Juries the ground or reasoning on which they found their verdict. They have decided on their oaths and consciences, and having formally pronounced their decision, they are not bound, or required by law or by courtesy, to explain it to anyone, or to re-discuss it with the Judge." Phillips, *Juries*, supra n. 342, at 180–1.

[372] For an example showing the framing and content of a special verdict, see William Chetwynd, OBSP (Oct. 1743, #504), at 302, 312–13, 18 *St. Tr.* 290, 315–17 (O.B. 1743).

[373] John Wilder, OBSP (Sept. 1710), at 2 (tried on an indictment charging him as an accessory to the escape of a convicted felon; jury "brought him in guilty of the Fact. But the Court being of Opinion that some point of Law would arise, directed the Jury to find it Special, which they did"). Another such case: Rookewood, OBSP (Jan. 1674 [1675]), at 3–5 (robbery).

[374] Earlier press regulation had been conducted mostly through licensing measures, which had expired by the end of the seventeenth century. Philip Hamburger, "The Development of the Law of Seditious Libel and the Control of the Press," 37 *Stanford L. Rev.* 661, 661–65, 674–91 (1985).

[375] 10 Holdsworth, *HEL* 674–88; Green, *Verdicts* 318–55.

[376] 32 Geo. 3, c. 60 (1792); on the enactment, see 10 Holdsworth, *HEL* 688–92.

(g) From Correcting to Preventing Error

By the later eighteenth century, when the rise of adversary criminal justice had caused the judges to yield increasing control over the conduct of criminal trials to the lawyers, the judges' authority over the formulation of jury verdicts was weakening. The judges kept their command over the pardon power, but they surrendered the power to fine disobedient juries; they moderated their use of the power to comment upon the evidence; the power to reject verdicts became contentious, and Fox's Libel Act stripped them of the power to order special verdicts in seditious libel cases.

As the judges lost their ability to detect and correct what they perceived to be jury error, they developed a new system of jury control, whose emphasis was on preventing jury error. Damaska observes: "Since the quality of verdicts could not be checked ex post, the English system was driven to exercise great caution in admitting" suspect types of evidence.[377] Most of the nineteenth century would be needed to put the new law of jury control in place. The details have not yet been the subject of close study, but the broad outline is undoubted. Writing about the history of civil procedure in the nineteenth century, Yeazell has pointed to the elements that were equally characteristic of the history of criminal procedure: The "chief ingredients were tightened control over the proof (the law of evidence), increased stress on precision in legal guidelines (the law of jury instructions), and increased control over the relationship between evidence and verdicts (directed verdicts and new trial orders)."[378] As the judges lost much of their former authority to shape the jury's verdict and correct error in the making, they developed a substitute regime aimed at restricting the potential for the jury to err. Prophylaxis would replace cure as the guiding principle of jury control.

The question for present purposes is whether the transformation of trial procedure that was associated with lawyerization may have contributed to the transformation in jury control. The changes in the relationship of judge and jury had causes quite apart from the rise of adversary trial. The movement to restrict judicial authority over jury verdicts long predated the lawyerization of the trial. *Bushell's Case* in 1670, in which the judges resolved against fining jurors for verdicts against the weight of the evidence, was the first great landmark, and we have seen that hostility was building to other techniques of jury control before the

---

[377] Mirjan Damaska, "Of Hearsay and its Analogues," 76 *Minnesota L. Rev.* 425, at 428 (1992).

[378] Stephen C. Yeazell, "The Misunderstood Consequences of Modern Civil Process," 1994 *Wisconsin L. Rev.* 631, 642.

flowering of adversary criminal procedure in the later eighteenth and nineteenth centuries. Furthermore, the controversy over judicial influence on jury verdicts arose mostly from political cases, especially cases involving religious offenses or seditious libel. The issues and the parties in such cases differed materially from those encountered in the ordinary administration of criminal justice, although reverberations from the political cases affected thinking about the relations of judge and jury across the entirety of criminal (and civil) procedure.

There is, however, reason to think that lawyerization of the trial contributed to the weakening of the old system of judicial superintendence of jury verdicts and to the development of the new system of preventive jury control. The suggestion is that counsel's assumption of responsibility for adducing fact cost the judges some of the authority upon which the older techniques of jury control had depended. Judge and jury had worked together to discern from the spectacle of the altercation trial whether the accused was culpable. As counsel assumed responsibility for the production and presentation of the evidence, the jurors became less dependent on the judge for his "great Light and Assistance"[379] in forming their view of the case. Counsel now spoke directly to the jurors, advancing opposing interpretations[380] and suggesting outcomes. This development undercut the judge's former authority with respect to both the facts and the law, an authority that had come from his having helped elicit the facts, and from his having been the only source of professional guidance for interpreting the facts and applying the law. As the adversary system took hold, counsel for prosecution and defense came to supply the jurors with multiple and conflicting views on the facts and the law. Across time the responsibility for interpreting the evidence passed from court to counsel. By broadening the jurors' sources, the adversary system inevitably undermined the authority of the judge and increased the potential for the jury to form a view of the case different from the judge's. In this way, lawyerization of the trial contributed to the break-up of the ancient working relationship of judge and jury.

G. The Truth Deficit

1. Truth as a Byproduct

The rhetoric of English criminal procedure claimed that truth-seeking was

---

[379] Hale, *Common Law, supra* n. 335, at 165.
[380] Subject until 1836 to the limitations on full defense, to the extent defense counsel was unable to evade them. See discussion, *supra*, text at nn. 220–38.

the objective, but the institutions of criminal justice had not been organized to seek the truth effectively. In the age of the altercation trial, criminal investigation had been left to the accuser, aided by the Marian JP, who,
it will be recalled, was charged with gathering only evidence "against" the
accused.[381] The trial replicated the partisanship and amateurism of the
pretrial. In contrast to the *Aufklärungspflicht*, the duty to clarify, of the
European judge, in an English trial neither the judge nor the jury was
responsible for the evidence on which adjudication would rest. European
judges had a duty to seek the truth. English judges insisted that the jury's
"verdict does pass for truth,"[382] but this was a hollow claim, made to "cast
off"[383] on the jury the blame for error. The jurors for their part were
passive receptors of the information fed them by the partisans.

I have emphasized that lawyerization was meant to be truth-enhancing
by comparison with what had gone on before. Defense solicitors
conducted partisan evidence-gathering to counterbalance prosecution
evidence-gathering. Defense counsel was admitted to the trial primarily
in order to cross-examine for prosecution perjury. Partisanship was met
with partisanship.

Two-sided partisanship may indeed have been better than one-sided
partisanship, but it was still a poor proxy for truth-seeking. Adversary
procedure entrusts the responsibility for gathering and presenting the
evidence upon which accurate adjudication depends to partisans whose
interest is in winning, not in truth. A procedure that could make the trick-
ster William Garrow into the dominant figure in the administration of
criminal justice, which is what happened in England in the 1780s, was not
a truth-serving procedure. The adversary dynamic invited distortion and
suppression of the evidence, by permitting abusive and misleading cross-
examination, the coaching of witnesses, and the concealment of unfavorable evidence. This attribute of adversary procedure, the combat effect,
was worsened by the wealth effect inherent in privatizing for hire the
work of the adversaries who gathered and presented the evidence. We
recall the chilling lament of the woman tried and sentenced to death for
forgery at the Old Bailey in 1757, who told the court: "I have not a six
penny piece left to pay a porter, much less [enough] to fee counsel." For
her, the message of adversary justice was that "I must die because I am

---

[381] Discussed *supra*, Ch. 1, text at nn. 165–8.

[382] The words of George Treby, the recorder of London, later Chief Justice of Common
Pleas, sentencing Lord Russell to death for treason in the Rye House Plot. *R. v. William
Russell*, 9 St. Tr. 577, 666 (1683). The trial is discussed *supra* Ch. 2, text at nn. 36–7.

[383] More said of the common law judges in the sixteenth century: "They may by verdict of
the jury cast off all quarrels from themselves upon [the jury], which they account their chief
defense." William Roper, *The Lyfe of Sir Thomas More* 44–5 (E. V. Hitchcock ed.) (London
1935), cited in J. H. Baker, "Introduction," 2 *The Reports of Sir John Spelman* 42–3 (1978)
(Selden Society vol. 94).

poor . . . ."[384] The wealth effect of adversary trial procedure was a grievous shortcoming, because most criminal defendants were indigent. For
the affluent defendant, by contrast, the wealth effect bestowed potentially
outcome-altering advantages on the affluent—recall the conclusion that
two culprits "got off because a Mr. Garrow was their counsel."[385]

The lawyer-dominated system of criminal trial that emerged in eighteenth-century England was not premised on a coherent theory of truth-
seeking. Adversary procedure presupposed that truth would somehow
emerge when no one was in charge of seeking it. Truth was a byproduct.
How did a system of criminal trial that manifested this truth deficit come
to prevail? Part of the answer, which emerges from the historical materials studied in this book, is that the authorities in whose hands the system
developed did not design it. Adversary criminal trial developed piecemeal across the eighteenth century, without forethought, in a series of
measures meant to even up for advantages of the prosecution.

Furthermore, some of the failures of truth-seeking that we now associate with the adversary system trace to defects of institutional structure in
pretrial and trial procedure that were in place long before the entry of the
lawyers. We have seen (in Chapter 3) how lawyerization of the trial was
a response to the failure to develop a reliable and effective system of
pretrial criminal investigation—in the language of economics, the failure
to understand that criminal investigation should be a public good.
Similarly, the failure to develop trial courts capable of truth-seeking criminal adjudication long predated the rise of adversary procedure. The judicial office had been shaped in the Middle Ages in essentially the form that
it continued to manifest in the eighteenth century. In the trial of fact,
English common law judges were administrators rather than adjudicators. They neither investigated nor decided disputes of fact. English
judges merely processed cases for jury verdicts. The primitiveness of the
pretrial process reinforced this stunted conception of the judicial function
at trial. Unlike the Continental trial judge, who worked from a dossier
that encapsulated a thorough, official pretrial investigation, the English
trial judge was ignorant of the substance of the case. We have seen that it
was the lawyers' mastery over the facts that allowed them to wrest the
conduct of criminal trial away from the bench.

The adversary system did not have to overcome a truth-promoting
system of pretrial or trial procedure. Rather, the lawyer-dominated trial
replicated in different hands a truth deficit that had long characterized
English criminal justice. On the other hand, it is important to see that
adversary procedure represented a material worsening of the truth

---

[384] Eleanor Eddacres, *OBSP* (July 1757, #285), at 263, 269, *supra* text at n. 313.
[385] William Chatwin and John Davis, *OBSP* (June 1788, #429), at 561, 562.

deficit. The older procedure had been merely neglectful of the truth. When the adversary system allowed the lawyers to gain control over gathering and adducing the evidence, responsibility for the conduct of the proofs passed to persons who became professionally skilled at techniques of defeating the truth.

2. The Influence of Capital Punishment

By the later eighteenth and early nineteenth centuries contemporaries knew that adversary criminal procedure harbored truth-defeating tendencies. To understand how a system so flawed could gain acceptance, we need to bear in mind the growing aversion to capital punishment that characterized these years.[386] Contemporaries were peculiarly disposed to tolerate the truth-defeating consequences of adversary procedure, because in the realm of criminal trial too much truth brought too much death.

English criminal law threatened more capital punishment than the authorities thought necessary to impose. At each stage in the criminal prosecution, from charging to trial to post-verdict review, there was a continuous winnowing of the capital cohort, with the goal of leaving only the worst for execution. Especially in the later eighteenth and early nineteenth centuries, the concern became pervasive that despite this winnowing, the law both overthreatened and overused capital punishment. We find prosecutors conniving with the clerks who drafted indictments to arrange that defendants be charged with simple theft or other noncapital variants rather than burglary or theft from a dwelling house or other capital offenses.[387] It was widely known that jurors would downcharge or

---

[386] Radzinowicz's account of the growth of sentiment against capital punishment for property crimes remains fundamental. 1 Radzinowicz, *History* 399–607; see also Gatrell, *Hanging Tree, supra* n. 349, at 325–416. The contemporary reform literature is reviewed in 1 Radzinowicz, *History* 268–396. Regarding the movement to develop alternative punishments, especially transportation and imprisonment, the great work is Beattie, *Crime,* esp. 450–637. Regarding abolition, see Brian P. Block and John Hostettler, *Hanging in the Balance: A History of the Abolition of Capital Punishment in Britain* (1997).

[387] E.g., Ann Wheeler and Elizabeth Barnsley, *OBSP* (Feb. 1788, #194), at 295, 297 (prosecutor testifies he "told the clerk of the indictments that . . . I desired him not to lay it capital"). Aware of this practice, John Fielding, the court JP for Middlesex, would sometimes condition a prosecutor's recognizance under the Marian procedure on his prosecuting capitally. Thus, investigating an attempted highway robbery in 1758, in which the victim had been shot in the face, and an accomplice identified Robert Nolan as the culprit, Fielding ordered Nolan arrested, examined him, and "directed [the victim–prosecutor] to indict him on the Black Act for maliciously firing at him, as that Offense was Capital, and the attempting to rob only Transportation, esteeming the latter too slight a Punishment for so barbarous an Action. . . . [T]he said Nolan was convicted." PRO, T 1/383/75 ("Mr. Fielding's report upon the Petition of the constables of St. George's Parish," 18 Nov. 1758).

Pickpocketing (privately stealing from the person) was capital under 8 Eliz., c. 4 (1565). Because victims were commonly reluctant to invoke the death penalty for so trivial an

downvalue goods in order to defeat the death penalty (Blackstone's "pious perjury"[388]). A juror told a parliamentary committee[389] investigating capital punishment in 1819: "The majority of juries, in cases not marked with any peculiar atrocity, are desirous of discovering some circumstances in favor of the prisoners; are desirous of availing themselves of the least favorable circumstance or shadow of doubt."[390] Another juror, Richard Phillips, told the committee that jurors "are often considerably distressed" at capital cases and "are always desirous of laying hold of any circumstances in favor of the prisoner," hence jurors were "much disposed to listen to those exceptions which have been made by the counsel . . . ."[391] He recalled "a man being charged with a burglary, when I was on the jury, and a doubt existing, whether a window was quite closed, that circumstance was laid hold of by certain persons in the jury, as a ground for acquitting him of the burglary."[392]

The judges also participated in this process of mitigating the application of the capital sanction, most visibly through their command of the post-verdict clemency process,[393] but also at trial. The 1819 Committee quoted Sir Archibald Macdonald, late Lord Chief Baron of the Exchequer, "that where the punishment is very disproportionate to the offense, I would always lean to the merciful side, if I could with satisfaction to my own mind."[394] The judges construed capital statutes restrictively,[395] and

offense, caught-in-the-act offenders were sometimes punished entirely outside the processes of the law. The subject is discussed in John Fray, *OBSP* (Sept. 1785, #751), at 991 (murder). Fray was prosecuted for the murder of a pickpocket who drowned while being ducked (thrown in the water). Gould J, presiding, referred to "this common error of punishing pickpockets by ducking" as "a thing that happens, we all know, very frequently . . ." Ibid. at 996. Because Fray had not intended to drown the victim, Gould instructed the jury to "mitigate the charge and . . . reduce it from murder to manslaughter," which the jury did. Ibid. When victims did prosecute pickpockets, the juries mostly downvalued the stolen items to below the 1s. capital threshold. See Langbein, "Ryder" 53 (juries downvalued in eight of nine such cases tried at the Old Bailey in four sessions held in 1754–5; the monarch commuted the death sentence in the one capital conviction).

[388] 4 Blackstone, *Commentaries* 239, discussed in Beattie, *Crime* 419–30; Beattie, *Policing* 303–12, 339–46, 435–48; Langbein, 'Ryder' 47–55; King, *Crime* 231–7; see also 1 Radzinowicz, *History* 83–106, 138–64 (1948).

[389] *Report from the Select Committee to Consider of so much of the Criminal Law as Relates to Capital Punishment in Felonies* (London 1819) (8 Parliamentary Papers) [hereafter *1819 Report*]. On the origins and work of the Committee, see 1 Radzinowicz, *History* 526–66. The Committee also remarked on the tendency of victims to downcharge to avoid the capital sanction; *1819 Report, supra*, at 83, 84, 111.

[390] Ibid. at 99, quoting Stephen Curtis, a leather merchant.

[391] Ibid. at 93 (testimony of Sir Richard Phillips).

[392] Ibid.

[393] On which, see *supra* Ch. 1, text at nn. 245–9, and in this chapter, *supra*, text at nn. 348–52.

[394] *1819 Report, supra* n. 389, at 50.

[395] "The dominant tendency in the judicial interpretation of statutes, and particularly of

they connived with juries to downcharge or downvalue goods.[396] The judges developed the exclusionary rules of evidence, especially the corroboration and confession rules,[397] and the beyond-reasonable-doubt standard of proof,[398] rules whose breadth assured that not only some innocent defendants would be spared, but also many culpable ones.

Cottu, the French observer writing in 1820, was struck by the disdain for the truth that he found in the administration of criminal justice in England. He fixed on the mitigation of the capital sanction as the driving force: "Not thinking it . . . for the advantage of the public to punish every crime committed, lest the effect of example should be weakened by the frequency of executions, [the English] reserve the full measure of their severity for more hardened offenders, and dismiss unpunished those whose guilt is not proved by the most positive testimony. They are indifferent whether, among the really guilty, such be convicted or acquitted."[399] Cottu contrasted "that ardent desire in France to find out the truth, for which the English display so much indifference."[400]

English criminal justice threatened more capital punishment than those who administered it were willing to impose. To avoid a bloodbath, evasions of many sorts were practiced. Adversary criminal trial procedure was shaped in this milieu, absorbing what Cottu saw as indifference to truth. If we are to understand why the Anglo-American criminal procedure that emerged in this period is so truth-disserving, we must bear in mind that we settled on our procedures for criminal adjudication at a moment when we did not want all that much truth.

---

those imposing capital punishment, was to construe them strictly and in cases of doubt to the advantage of the offender." 1 Radzinowicz, *History* 83, 660–98; Hall, *Theft, supra* n. 253, at 92; Livingston Hall, "Strict or Liberal Construction of Penal Statutes," 48 *Harvard L. Rev.* 748 (1935). Lenity in the construction of penal statutes long predates the eighteenth century but was especially prominent then. Madan complained that the judges were "preferring their own *feelings as men* to the duty which they owe the public as *magistrates* . . . ." [Martin Madan], *Thoughts on Executive Justice with Respect to Our Criminal Laws, Particularly on the Circuits* 13 (1st edn. London 1785) 13–14 (1785), cited in 1 Radzinowicz, *History* 243.

[396] For example, Frederick Usop was charged with the theft of clothing valued at 28s. from a dwelling house. Theft from a dwelling above 5s. in amount was a capital offense under 10 & 11 Wil. 3, c. 23 (1699). Usop, a 43-year-old unemployed weaver, offered no reported defense. The jury found him guilty but rescued him for transportation by downvaluing the goods to 4s. 10d., having been encouraged by Baron Eyre, "the presiding judge. He told the jury that "this act of Parliament was made a century ago, [and] that which a century ago was of the value of five shillings, should rather be considered in a case like this, and in favor of life, than what we value at five shillings now; and if you are of that opinion, you may find the prisoner guilty of stealing to the value of 4s. 10d., which will acquit him of the capital part of the indictment." Frederick Usop, *OBSP* (Sept. 1784, #814), at 1130, 1131.

[397] *Supra* Ch. 4, text at nn. 116–240.   [398] *Supra*, text at nn. 35–63.

[399] Cottu, *Administration* 91–2.

[400] Ibid. at 93 n. Cottu was particularly astonished at the truth-defeating English rule excluding so much confession evidence. Ibid. at 92–3.

FIG. 5.4. *The death penalty.* Until reforms enacted in the 1830s and thereafter, the "Bloody Code" threatened the death penalty for a broad range of property crimes, including forgery, picking pockets, and shoplifting. Pressure to reduce the numbers of persons actually executed disposed the courts to be relatively unconcerned about the truth-defeating character of the developing adversary procedure. Too much truth brought too much death.

3. The Path Not Taken: English Disdain for the European Model

Once adversary criminal trial was in place, English courts were deciding life-or-death cases based on evidence gathered, presented, and tested by partisan lawyers. Adversary procedure materially worsened a longstanding defect of common law procedure, the privatization of criminal investigation. If information not before the court would help decide the case, the court had neither the mission nor the capacity to seek it out. To be sure, the trial judge would sometimes send for a missing witness, and we have seen that the judge had the authority to interrupt and postpone a trial that appeared to be deficiently prepared.[401] But such steps were taken rarely. Unlike their Continental counterparts, English judges had no prior familiarity with the evidence and no investigative resources within the court. Consider, for example, the trial of William Warner and another for a nighttime highway robbery in 1741.[402] Prosecution witnesses testified that they were certain about their identification of the two defendants, because the scene of the robbery was bright and starlit. The defendants, who were unrepresented, contended that the night was dark and rainy. Warner pitifully suggested to the trial judge, "I hope you will look into it, and see whether it did [rain] or no."[403] The court ignored this sensible suggestion for further investigation and left it to the jurors to decide, without additional evidence, between the two tales that had been presented to them. They chose the prosecutor's and hanged Warner.

English panegyrists such as Hale extolled criminal jury trial as "the best method of searching out the truth,"[404] but this was an article of faith, unresponsive to the critical failing that neither in the pretrial nor at trial did the authorities assume responsibility for investigating the events. The Marian JP was mostly the accuser's helper; and the trial court adjudicated on the basis of the evidence that the partisans selected, presented, and contested. Adversary criminal trial depends upon the deeply problematic assumption that combat promotes truth, or put differently, that truth will emerge even though the court takes no steps to seek it.

On display across the English Channel was a highly visible alternative to adversary criminal procedure. The Roman-canon procedure used in all the European states placed upon the court the responsibility to seek the truth, and gave it the investigative authority and resources to do so.[405]

---

[401] *Supra*, text at nn. 353–6.
[402] William Warner & John Newman, *OBSP* (Dec. 1741, ##5–6), at 3.   [403] Ibid. at 4.
[404] Hale, *Common Law, supra* n. 335, at 164, reasoning that the jurors had discretion to credit or discredit testimony according to whether or not they found it persuasive.
[405] The "essence" of the European procedure was that "public initiative tries from the appearance of the first signs of suspicion in the 'case' to clarify things in the sense of investigating the substantive truth. The judge appears here as the governmental organ principally

European procedure thus avoided the privatization of criminal investigation that was the central failing of English procedure. The Europeans had made criminal investigation a public function from the Middle Ages.

As best we can tell, the transformation from altercation to adversary trial that took place in England in the eighteenth century occurred without the least attention to the question of whether the truth-seeking Continental model might have offered a superior alternative, an escape from the truth-impairing partisanship of lawyer-driven pretrial and trial. Why did the English disregard the Continental model? The short answer is that even as late as the eighteenth century, European criminal procedure exhibited defects that made it appear self-evidently unworthy of emulation. The Europeans had indeed avoided the English mistake of privatizing criminal investigation and trial, but there were profound flaws in the way the Europeans had implemented their system of court-conducted investigation and adjudication.

I have written elsewhere of the great European blunder, the medieval law of torture.[406] Aware that empowering judges to seek and adjudicate the truth risked error or tyranny, medieval European law undertook to restrict judicial discretion by binding the judges to an exceptionally high standard of proof. By the thirteenth century it was settled that to convict someone of a capital offense would require the evidence of two eyewitnesses, unless the accused voluntarily confessed. This standard had the effect of preventing the court from convicting on the basis of circumstantial evidence, no matter how cogent. Because serious crimes are often committed clandestinely, the two-eyewitness rule was intolerable. Reluctant to soften it directly, the courts developed the law of judicial torture, which allowed them to examine the accused under torture when there was strong evidence that he was the culprit, but not enough to convict under the two-eyewitness rule. The precondition for torture, called half proof, was the testimony of one unobjectionable eyewitness, or else circumstantial evidence that satisfied a judicially developed scale of gravity. Further safeguards surrounded the administration of torture. Torture was not supposed to be used to extract a guilty plea, that is, an abject confession of guilt. Rather, the examiner was meant to seek details of the crime, information that only the guilty would know. Suggestive questioning (in which the examiner supplied the answer he wished to hear) was forbidden. These efforts at surrounding coercion with safeguard proved

concerned. His task is to take the whole proceeding in hand with full responsibility for justice and by his own initiative to assemble the grounds for decision in the form of a comprehensive factual investigation." Eberhard Schmidt, *Inquisitionsprozess und Rezeption* 9 (1940).

[406] John H. Langbein, *Torture and the Law of Proof: Europe and England in the Ancien Régime* 3–69 (1977) [hereafter, Langbein, *Torture*].

illusory. In case after case, the true culprit was ultimately discovered after an innocent person had confessed under torture and been convicted and executed. The safeguards were not safe enough: The ban on suggestive questioning was hard to enforce; and the innocent person examined under torture often knew enough about the circumstances of the crime to give his confession verisimilitude. By the sixteenth and seventeenth centuries courts in a number of European countries were developing techniques for escaping the two-eyewitness rule, in order to avoid the use of judicial torture,[407] but long into the eighteenth century the law of torture remained a defining feature of the Continental tradition in criminal procedure.

The law of torture disgraced Continental criminal procedure. English writers from Fortescue[408] to Sir Thomas Smith[409] to Blackstone[410] extolled the superiority of England's torture-free procedure. The English did experiment with torture for about a century, from 1540 to 1640, but confined it to Privy Council investigations, mostly in cases of treason.[411] Torture did not become a feature of ordinary criminal procedure in England because, among other reasons,[412] the two-eyewitness rule of the European law of proof did not become established in England.[413] As we have seen earlier in this chapter, English criminal procedure did not settle on its beyond-reasonable-doubt standard of proof until the end of the eighteenth century. Speaking of the Middle Ages, Maitland said: "Our criminal procedure . . . had hardly any place for a law of evidence."[414] An English jury could (and still can) convict an accused on less evidence than was required as a mere precondition for investigation under torture on the Continent. In Europe, Maitland wrote, torture "came to the relief of a law of evidence which made conviction well-nigh impossible . . . . Luckily

---

[407] Ibid. at 45–60.

[408] Fortescue, *De Laudibus, supra* n. 38, at 65 (the accused "will not be tortured" in England).

[409] "Torment . . . which is used by the order of the civil law and custom of other countries . . . is not used in England, it is taken for servile." Smith, *De Republica* 117.

[410] 4 Blackstone, *Commentaries* 138, faulting the French for "us[ing] the rack to extort a confession from the accused."

[411] Langbein, *Torture, supra* n. 406, at 81–128.

[412] See ibid. at 136–9, emphasizing in addition that "[t]he Continental jurisprudence of torture presupposed a judicial bureaucracy," and that the power to torture could not be entrusted to "[t]he country gentlemen and urban aldermen who constituted the English prosecutorial corps" under the Marian pretrial procedure. Ibid. at 138.

[413] Hale remarked that English juries "may and do often, pronounce their verdict upon one single testimony which the Civil Law admits not of." Hale, *Common Law, supra* n. 335, at 165. Regarding the two-witness requirements for treason and perjury, see L. N. Hill, "The Two-Witness Rule in English Treason Trials: Some Comments on the Emergence of Procedural Law," 12 *American J. Legal History* 95 (1968); 7 Wigmore, *Evidence* §§ 2036–44, at 263–86.

[414] 2 Maitland, *HEL* 660.

for England neither the stringent rules of legal proof nor the cruel and stupid subterfuge became endemic here."[415]

The stain of the law of torture made it easy for the English to dismiss the European model of court-conducted criminal investigation and adjudication, but there is reason to think that important elements in England would have resisted European-style procedure even if it had been torture-free. Court-conducted criminal investigation requires an investigative magistracy for the work of gathering and evaluating evidence. The problems of organizing, recruiting, training, controlling, and compensating such a corps would have been particularly unsettling to English patterns of governance, which relied upon skeletal officialdom and delegated so much authority to local gentlemen.[416] Indeed, opposition to police forces[417] and to public prosecution,[418] arising from just such concerns, remained vigorous deep into the nineteenth century.

From the time of the Reformation, disdain for Continental criminal procedure became enmeshed in English hostility to the leading Continental regimes—the papacy, the French, and the Spaniards. At least from the time of Foxe's *Book of Martyrs* (1563)[419] the Spanish Inquisition was held up for particular vilification.[420] Another source of the disdain for court-conducted criminal investigation in England was the experience with the prerogative courts, especially the courts of Star Chamber and High Commission. They became identified with enforcement of Charles I's personal rule in the 1630s[421] and were abolished in 1641 in the events that led to the Civil War and Interregnum.[422] As late as the 1870s Stephen attributed proposals for the creation of a system of public prosecutors in England to "a feeling which played a very conspicuous part in our history, excessive jealousy of the procedure founded upon the version of the Roman law which prevailed all over the Continent, and which in this country was associated with arbitrary power . . . ."[423]

---

[415] Ibid. at 659–60.

[416] The classic account remains 1 Sidney and Beatrice Webb, *English Local Government from the Revolution to the Municipal Corporations Act: The Parish and the County* (1906).

[417] Philips, "Engine" 166 ff.

[418] Philip B. Kurland and D. W. M. Waters, "Public Prosecutions in England, 1854–79: An Essay in English Legislative History," 1959 *Duke L.J.* 493 [hereafter, Kurland and Waters].

[419] John Foxe, *Actes and Monuments of these Latter and Perillous Dayes, Touching . . . the Great Persecutions . . . Wrought . . . by the Romishe Prelates* (London 1563).

[420] See William S. Maltby, *The Black Legend in England: The Development of Anti-Spanish Sentiment, 1558–1660*, at 33–43 (1971). Spain was stereotyped as a cultural inferior—cruel, deceitful, conspiratorial, treacherous. Ibid. at 6. In a similar vein, see John Miller, *Popery and Politics in England: 1660–1688* (1973).

[421] John P. Kenyon, *The Stuart Constitution* 118–20 (1966).

[422] Discussed *supra*, text at n. 124.

[423] James F. Stephen, "Suggestions as to the Reform of the Criminal Law," 2 *Nineteenth Century* 737, 750 (1877), quoted in Kurland and Waters, *supra* n. 418, 562 n. 294.

The achievement of Continental criminal procedure had been to make criminal investigation a public function, which enabled the European legal systems to make it the duty of those who conducted criminal adjudication to seek the truth. But this program went disastrously astray when it became committed to an impossible standard of proof, the two-eyewitness rule, and to the "cruel and stupid subterfuge" of judicial torture. The lesson of the centuries-long European-wide entanglement with judicial torture was that seeking truth could also be done badly. Seeking truth did not guarantee finding it. Far from seeing in European procedure a model to emulate, the English saw in the European experience a further justification for the path on which they found themselves, as they embedded a criminal procedure in which no one was responsible for seeking the truth.

In the nineteenth century a vast reform movement swept across European criminal procedure, as part of the process that led to the creation of the modern democratic states. The blunder of the Middle Ages was rectified: the two-eyewitness rule was abrogated and torture forbidden.[424] The judicial career was restructured to protect judicial independence against political intervention.[425] Further safeguards were devised, many in emulation of admired features of English criminal procedure,[426]

---

[424] Regarding the introduction of the standard of moral persuasion (*intime conviction*) in France and the influence of the French developments elsewhere in Europe, see Massimo Nobili, *Il principio del libero convincimento del giudice* 147–219 (1974). The repeal of the law of judicial torture in Prussia in 1754 under Frederick the Great had European-wide influence; see Langbein, *Torture, supra* n. 406, at 61–2, 68–9; on the acceptance in Germany of the standard of free evaluation of the evidence (*freie Beweiswürdigung*), "free" in the sense of unrestricted by the two-eyewitness rule. On the long debate about the tension between binding the judge to the law and allowing judgment based on free evaluation of the evidence, see Wilfried Küper, *Die Richteridee der Strafprozessordnung und ihre geschichtlichen Grundlagen* 219–38 (1967); on the influence of Savigny and his Prussian legislative initiatives in the 1840s in promoting acceptance of free evaluation of the evidence, see ibid. at 238 ff; Gerhard Walter, *Freie Beweiswürdigung* 73–5 (1979).

[425] Günther Plathner, *Der Kampf um die richterliche Unabhängigkeit bis zum Jahre 1848* (1935); Gustav Aubin, *Die Entwicklung der richterlichen Unabhängigkeit im neusten deutschen und österreichischen Rechte* (1906). On the range of issues implicated in the movement for judicial independence, including the determination to prevent future use of extraordinary courts, see Dieter Simon, *Die Unabhängigkeit des Richters*, esp. 2–9 (1975).

[426] English criminal procedure served "to a large extent, as a model for the legislation for the French Revolution" that began the French experiment with adapting the jury to the Continental model. Adhémar Esmein, *A History of Continental Criminal Procedure with Special Reference to France* 323, 393 ff (1913). For the later history in France, see *infra* n. 429. German scholars also paid close attention to England, e.g., Friedrich August Biener, *Das englische Geschworenengericht* (Leipzig 1852); Carl J. A. Mittermaier, *Das englische, schottische und nordamerikanische Strafverfahren* (Erlangen 1851); id., *Die Mundlichkeit, das Anklageprinzip, die Öffentlichkeit und das Geschwornengericht . . . mit Rücksicht auf die Erfahrung der verschiedenen Länder* (Stuttgart 1845).

including oral public trial,[427] defense counsel,[428] and the use of juries or mixed courts combining professional judges and juror-like lay judges.[429] European criminal procedural systems became hybrids of European and English, but they retained their defining feature, the principle that criminal courts must have the duty and the authority to seek the truth. In England, by contrast, the well-meaning reforms of the eighteenth century that resulted in adversary criminal trial had the effect of perpetuating the central blunder of the inherited system: the failure to develop institutions and procedures of criminal investigation and trial that would be responsible for and capable of seeking the truth.

[427] Marie Theres Fögen, *Der Kampf um Gerichtsöffentlichkeit* (1974).

[428] See Birgit Malsack, *Die Stellung der Verteidigung im reformierten Strafprozess: Eine Rechtshistorische Studie anhand der Schriften von C. J. A. Mittermeier* (1992).

[429] Regarding the French experiment with the jury and jury-like devices, see Antonio Padoa Schioppa, "La giura all'Assemblea Constituente francese," in Padoa Schioppa, *Trial Jury* 75; Bernard Schnapper, "Le Jury français aux XIX et XXème siecles," ibid. at 165; for the German states, see Peter Landau, "Schwurgerichte und Schöffengerichte in Deutschland im 19. Jahrhundert bis 1870," ibid. at 241; Gerhard Casper and Hans Zeisel, "Lay Judges in the German Criminal Courts," 1 *J. Legal Studies* 135, 136–41 (1972); Eberhard Schmidt, *Einführung in die Geschichte der deutschen Strafrechtspflege* §§ 284–95, at 324–42 (3rd edn. 1965); Erich Schwinge, *Der Kampf um die Schwurgericht bis zur Frankfurter Nationalversammlung* (1970 rev.) (1st edn. 1926).

Index

accomplice rule, *see* corroboration rule
accused, criminal
  conducting own defense 2, 33–5, 46–61,
    65, 253, 254
  defensive advantage, supposed 33–5,
    66
  denied counsel 11–12, 26–40
  disqualification, testimonial 51–3, 97
  informational resource, as 2, 20–1, 35–6,
    48–61, 62, 100–1, 170–1, 254, 268–73,
    277
  questioning of, ceases 281
  silencing of 5, 253, 258–61, 266–73, 276,
    281
  unpreparedness of 62–6
  unrepresented 257, 266, 314–18
  see also "accused speaks" trial; character
    rule; confession rule; corroboration
    rule; defense counsel; defense
    witnesses; evidence, criminal,
    law of; privilege against self-
    incrimination
"accused speaks" trial
  burden of proof inchoate 22–3, 56–7
  clemency and 60–1
  defense counsel, tension with 35–6, 100,
    253, 258–61
  defense witnesses, restrictions 51–6
  defensive advantage, supposed 33–5, 66
  demise of 5, 253, 258–61, 266–73, 276,
    310
  disqualification, testimonial, and 51–3,
    97
  "I leave it to my counsel" 266–73
  judges' efforts to preserve 5–6, 110,
    170–1, 254–5, 271–2, 310
  pretrial detention and 48–51
  privilege against self-incrimination,
    tension with 284
  rationale 2, 36, 48, 65, 253
  sentencing and 57–60
  see also accused, criminal; defense coun-
    sel; jury trial; privilege against self-
    incrimination; trial procedure, early
    modern
Act of Settlement (1701) 79–80, 81–2, 99
  see also judicial independence
adversary procedure
  "assigning" counsel 93–5
  burden of proof, *see* production, burden
    of; standard of proof

combat effect 1, 103–5, 265–6, 270,
  306–11, 331–4
emergence of 5–6, 254–84, 291–311
judicial role 6, 243–4, 314–18, 330–1
jury control, effect on 321–31
jury trial, effect on 319–31
latency 255–61
production burdens 258–61, 313–14, 321
theory lacking 9
Treason Trials Act (1696), origins in
  102–5
truth-disregarding 1, 6–7, 8, 35–6, 103,
  147, 265, 268–70, 287, 307–9, 312 & n.
  294, 331–4, 336
unrepresented persons 257, 266
wealth effect 1, 3, 102–3, 256–7, 315–18,
  332–3
Allen, Christopher 239
altercation, *see* "accused speaks" trial; trial
  procedure, early modern
Arnold, Edward 173–4
arraignment 26–7, 53, 83, 93–4, 159
Arrowsmith, Stephen 327
Ash v. Ash (1697) 326
assize courts 13, 15, 16–17, 24–5, 43, 49, 56,
  60, 64, 90–1, 97, 101, 150, 159, 169,
  181, 195, 237, 256, 287, 288, 303–4,
  306, 317, 324–5
attorneys, *see* solicitors; *see also* defense
  counsel; prosecution counsel
Atwood and Robbins, R.v. (1787) 212–17, 228,
  229, 232, 248, 250

Baker, John H. 23 n. 67, 216
Ballantine, William 257 n. 16, 287 & n. 159
Bank of England
  prosecuting role 109, 113, 147
  Solicitor 113
Barrow, Richard 116
Bathurst, Henry 212 n. 250
Beattie, John M. 30, 34, 45, 52 n. 204, 57, 62,
  101, 107, 114, 115 n. 34, 121, 142 n.
  174, 169–70, 183 n. 20, 273–4, 279,
  311
bench trial 20 n. 51
benefit of clergy 192, 193, 231
Bentham, Jeremy 246
Best, William 244, 251
best evidence rule 179, 248 & n. 303
beyond reasonable doubt, *see* standard of
  proof